THE 9 COMPETENCIES AND THE PRACTICE BEHAVIORS

	Competency 5: Engage in Policy Practice	6, 7, 11, 13
A.	Identify social policy at the local, state, and federal level that impacts well-being, service delivery, and access to social services	6, 11, 13
B.	Assess how social welfare and economic policies impact the delivery of and access to social services	6, 13
C.	Apply critical thinking to analyze, formulate, and advocate policies that advance human rights and social, economic, and environmental justice	6, 7, 13

	Competency 6: Engage With Individuals, Families, Groups, Organizations, and Communities	2, 4, 5, 10, 13
A.	Apply knowledge of human behavior and the social environment, person-in-environment, and other multidisciplinary theoretical frameworks to engage with clients and constituencies	2, 5, 10, 13
B.	Use empathy, reflection, and interpersonal skills to effectively engage diverse clients and constituencies	2, 4, 13

	Competency 7: Assess Individuals, Families, Groups, Organizations, and Communities	2, 6, 7, 9, 10, 11, 12, 13, 14
A.	Collect and organize data, and apply critical thinking to interpret information from clients and constituencies	6, 13
B.	Apply knowledge of human behavior and the social environment, person-in-environment, and other multidisciplinary theoretical frameworks in the analysis of assessment data from clients and constituencies	2, 6, 13
C.	Develop mutually agreed-on intervention goals and objectives based on the critical assessment of strengths, needs, and challenges within clients and constituencies	7, 13
D.	Select appropriate intervention strategies based on the assessment, research knowledge, and values and preferences of clients and constituencies	9, 10, 11, 12, 13, 14

	Competency 8: Intervene With Individuals, Families, Groups, Organizations, and Communities	2, 8, 9, 10, 11, 12, 13, 14
A.	Critically choose and implement interventions to achieve practice goals and enhance capacities of clients and constituencies	8, 10, 11, 12, 13, 14
B.	Apply knowledge of human behavior and the social environment, person-in-environment, and other multidisciplinary theoretical frameworks in interventions with clients and constituencies	2, 8, 10, 11, 12, 13, 14
C.	Use inter-professional collaboration as appropriate to achieve beneficial practice outcomes	11, 13, 14
D.	Negotiate, mediate, and advocate with and on behalf of diverse clients and constituencies	8, 11, 13, 14
E.	Facilitate effective transitions and endings that advance mutually agreed-on goals	9, 13, 14

	Competency 9: Evaluate Practice With Individuals, Families, Groups, Organizations, and Communities	2, 4, 9
A.	Select and use appropriate methods for evaluation of outcomes	4, 9
B.	Apply knowledge of human behavior and the social environment, person-in-environment, and other multidisciplinary theoretical frameworks in the evaluation of outcomes	2, 9
C.	Critically analyze, monitor, and evaluate intervention and program processes and outcomes	4, 9
D.	Apply evaluation findings to improve practice effectiveness at the micro, mezzo, and macro levels	9

Generalist Social Work Practice

Sara Miller McCune founded SAGE Publishing in 1965 to support the dissemination of usable knowledge and educate a global community. SAGE publishes more than 1000 journals and over 800 new books each year, spanning a wide range of subject areas. Our growing selection of library products includes archives, data, case studies and video. SAGE remains majority owned by our founder and after her lifetime will become owned by a charitable trust that secures the company's continued independence.

Los Angeles | London | New Delhi | Singapore | Washington DC | Melbourne

Generalist Social Work Practice

Janice Gasker

Kutztown University of Pennsylvania

Los Angeles | London | New Delhi
Singapore | Washington DC | Melbourne

FOR INFORMATION:

SAGE Publications, Inc.
2455 Teller Road
Thousand Oaks, California 91320
E-mail: order@sagepub.com

SAGE Publications Ltd.
1 Oliver's Yard
55 City Road
London EC1Y 1SP
United Kingdom

SAGE Publications India Pvt. Ltd.
B 1/I 1 Mohan Cooperative Industrial Area
Mathura Road, New Delhi 110 044
India

SAGE Publications Asia-Pacific Pte. Ltd.
18 Cross Street #10-10/11/12
China Square Central
Singapore 048423

Acquisitions Editor: Joshua Perigo
Editorial Assistant: Noelle Cumberbatch
Production Editor: Andrew Olson
Copy Editor: Megan Markanich
Typesetter: C&M Digitals (P) Ltd.
Proofreader: Annie Lubinsky
Indexer: Robie Grant
Cover Designer: Janet Kiesel
Marketing Manager: Shari Countryman

Printed in the United States of America

ISBN: 978-1-5063-7919-7

This book is printed on acid-free paper.

21 22 10 9 8 7 6 5 4 3 2

• Brief Contents •

• Detailed Contents •

• Preface •

Why another generalist text? There are three reasons this book should exist, and they all start with "new." First, there are new developments in our understanding of generalist practice. If you're old enough, you remember the days before generalist practice when we were struggling to find a way to coordinate an increasingly confusing array of practice methods: structural, functional, interactional, generic, the life model, etc. When generalist practice came along, it was an answer to many of our prayers: a common base for practice with a set of concepts like person-in-environment (PIE) and stages of change, that we could all—finally—agree on. This is why generalist practice is the glue that holds this profession together. No matter the level of education, the modality of practice, or the level of practice, everything we do flows out of the generalist implementation model (GIM). Happily, generalist practice has kept up with the times. It has been flexible enough to incorporate our growing understanding of how social work operates in its zeitgeist. Over time, we've bolstered generalist practice with the strengths perspective. We've articulated a stage of change called engagement and put it right in front of assessment. We've added considerations of spirituality and diversity. We've changed *problem-solving* to *planned change*. These past evolutions are what has allowed generalist social work practice to stay alive. But there have been more developments recently, and this book allows us to put them into context.

Some new developments that are present in this book include a focus on self-reflection that shows up as a new first stage of planned change. The evidence-based practice of mindfulness for reflection is illuminated. Also in service to self-reflection are the case studies that are presented in a unique way. We hear the thoughts of the worker as they struggle with their own impact on the helping process. Each chapter includes a validated personality survey to guide students' thinking about their own thinking and a section on the emotions of the worker in the chapter's case study. In addition, the new, more nuanced understanding of diversity is presented using the concepts cultural humility and intersectionality. Gender expression works its way in too. In that vein, the gender-neutral pronoun *they* is used throughout in its new singular form. The overall self-reflection message to students is that they should understand themselves and build a professional use of self before they begin engagement in every case.

Another development in generalist practice that underlies this book is the understanding of the stages of planned change as what the Council on Social Work Education (CSWE) now calls "ongoing, dynamic, and interactive." Here, the message to students is that you work with all of the stages all of the time. In addition, this book points out a more nuanced understanding of levels of practice. Like CSWE, we still call them micro, mezzo, and macro, but we're getting away from the idea that these levels are distinct. The message to students is that there is no hierarchy of levels of practice. We practice on all levels, all of the time. Never again should we hear students complaining that they can't do that planned change assignment because "my placement is macro—it doesn't fit in." Macro practice examples occur throughout the book specifically to assure that students come to understand this flattened hierarchy of mezzo, macro, and micro. In addition, the new term *client system representative* is employed to make macro practice feel more accessible. The idea is that we often work directly with individuals when we work with large systems, so there is no reason to be intimidated by macro practice. For context, there is a discussion of the *Grand Challenges for Social Work and Society* (Fong, Lubben, & Barth, 2018).

Finally, these days generalist practice rests on a new code of ethics. Students are introduced to the *NASW Code of Ethics* (National Association of Social Workers [NASW], 2018) in several ways: There is a feature at the end of each chapter that includes an ethical dilemma, and there is an ethical challenge question in every chapter that directs students to actually read portions of the code. For those of us who may have become used to the 1996 version, there is an appendix to the book that identifies all of the changes that appear in the 2018 version.

The second "new" that accounts for this book is that we have a new audience. While the book is friendly to the mature student, it speaks directly to the young person who lives in a dynamic culture much different from our own. One reviewer wrote that today's students' "love bite-sized information, challenges, lists, intro and summaries, outline of learning points, and presentation of content that can be dissected. I believe the author has accomplished all of these and the readability is appropriate." Readability is paramount in this text. After all, isn't the most frustrating part of teaching social work the fact that our students don't want to read? The book is full of diagrams, and concepts are also illustrated with a lot of sample "he said, she said" dialogue. Ideas are introduced in one chapter and reinforced and practiced in the next. And the next. Important concepts are infused throughout, and mastery is assessed through exercises provided in ever-increasing complexity while students' understanding of concepts develops.

The final "new" this text responds to is advancements in evidence-based pedagogy. Collaborative learning methods have been shown to be effective, particularly with women, and this text is filled with exercises that allow students to experience those modalities. In addition, concepts are introduced and revisited in increasingly complex ways. This allows reinforcement of meaning as well as integration of knowledge with other knowledge and with the self. The approach fits nicely with the types of learning CSWE has newly identified as cognitive and affective processes. In short, the book enables another concept from educational theory: transformative learning. For this reason, topics will come up in a number of chapters with each building on the previous in terms of gradations and complexity. The transformative learning that takes place as a result of this approach is essential to the beginning generalist social worker who has to synthesize theories with a developing professional self. At the end of each section, exercises are provided in ways that incorporate opportunities for students to work together with their peers to solve critical thinking challenges. Here I must stop and acknowledge the important contribution of Ed Hanna's pedagogy of critical thinking. The cognitive–affective model perfectly fits this book's focus on the use of self and our new recognition of the importance of both cognitive and affective processes in learning. Evidence-based practice is highlighted and its process is uncovered. And evidence-based methods like motivational interviewing are employed. Finally, at the end of each chapter is a detailed feature where students interact with the chapter's material in ways that address each of the CSWE 2015 educational competencies. These exercises reflect aspects of each chapter that integrate practice, research, policy, social justice, and diversity. In its new competency-based standards, CSWE has demonstrated that the curriculum doesn't have to be taught in the old silos of human behavior, policy, research, and practice. Instead, concepts can be infused throughout the curriculum, and this book does the same. The book touches on and synthesizes every area of the curriculum.

Other aspects of the book facilitate student mastery of concepts and your documentation of that mastery. For example, following each chapter, you will find a matrix noting which competencies are addressed in which sections and features that align with each of the competencies are identified. In this simple table, students will be able to recognize their progress with the competencies they must ultimately demonstrate. Faculty, please note that this matrix is in exact conformity to the sample matrix that CSWE provides in the Accreditation portion of their website.

This book should be wherever in your curriculum that you introduce, practice, or synthesize learning about generalist practice. The text is basic enough to give students that first overview in what you might call your Generalist Practice course while ultimately building a level of complexity that will make it perfect for seminar discussions. For that reason, it is appropriate for both undergraduates and foundation level graduate students. We often think foundation level MSW students have knowledge that is somehow different from that of undergraduates, but most begin their social work studies with the same tabula rasa our BSW students do. This book begins with a history of the profession that is important to new graduate students. If you want to ramp up your graduate curriculum, you could place a focus on the suggested readings at the end of each chapter. In addition, there may be room for individual chapters (available in electronic format) in your level-specific courses on individuals, families, groups, organizations, and communities on both the undergraduate and graduate levels.

References

Council on Social Work Education. (2015). *Educational policy and accreditation standards.* Alexandria, VA: Author. Retrieved from http://www.cswe.org/File.aspx?id=81660

Fong, R., Lubben, J., & Barth, R. P. (Eds.). (2018). *Grand challenges for social work and society.* New York, NY: Oxford University Press.

National Association of Social Workers. (2018). *NASW code of ethics.* Washington, DC: NASW Press.

• Acknowledgments •

This book would not have been possible without the help and inspiration of many. First, let me thank all of the social work theorists past and present who have broken the ground and shared their passion for the profession and for teaching. Thanks go to the faculty and staff of the Department of Social Work at Kutztown University of Pennsylvania for their inspiration, input, and the general dedication that allowed me to step away to write. I also would not have had the opportunity to write had not my sister, Adele, been willing to shoulder the lion's share of family responsibilities. Thanks to friends like Colin Hanna, who were willing to read early drafts, and particularly to John Vafeas, whose general support, meticulous reading, and well-thought-out input resulted in significant improvements. Thanks also go to all of the students whose seminar discussions inform a number of the case studies in the book. Finally, thanks go to my colleagues across the country who were willing to review the developing manuscript. I am humbled by your careful reading and detailed comments—nearly all of which I have addressed in one form or another. They have resulted in a much better book than would have been possible otherwise. Thanks for the love and support from Alice, Allison, Kristen, and Lisa, who help me do whatever I do, and to Arik, Chico, Alicia, and Alexis just for being their delightful selves. Finally, my deepest appreciation goes to my daughter, Alice, who is always willing to translate the evolving language of young people. She generously shared stories of her own social work practice and confirmed my suspicion that this book needed to be written.

Thank you to the reviewers:

- Janet Acker, The College of Saint Rose
- Parris J. Baker, Gannon University Social Work Program
- Sarah E. Bledsoe, University of North Carolina at Chapel Hill School of Social Work
- Kathleen Boland, PhD , LCSW, ACSW, Cedar Crest College
- Liza M. Bové, LCSWR, SUNY School of Welfare
- Andrea Cole, New York University Silver School of Social Work
- Rosalyn Barrett Deckerhoff, College of Social Work, Florida State University
- David G. Demetral, PhD & LCSW, California State University, Sacramento
- Michele Eggers, PhD, Pacific University
- Daniel Farrell, LCSW, Silberman School of Social Work at Hunter College School of Social Work
- Annalease Gibson, Albany State University
- Mark A. Giesler, Saginaw Valley State University
- Christina C. Gigler, Marywood University MSW Program
- Samuel Gioia, Portland State University

- Jo Dee Gottlieb, Marshall University
- Deanna Guthrie, University of Wisconsin–Whitewater
- Edward P. Hanna, DSW, Kutztown University of Pennsylvania
- Renie Rondon Jackson, LIU Brooklyn
- Sharon C. Lyter, PhD, Kutztown University of Pennsylvania
- Carla Mueller, Lindenwood University
- Veronika Ospina-Kammerer, Saint Leo University
- Maura McCarthy Rhodes, Sacred Heart University
- LaChelle M. Rosenbaum, Lewis–Clark State College
- Patricia Sherman, Kean University
- Dorisa A. Slaughter, MSW, CSW, Kentucky Community & Technical College System
- Rosalie Smiley, California University of Pennsylvania
- Mary Rita Weller, PhD, Kutztown University of Pennsylvania
- Kim Whorton, Jacksonville State University

• About the Author •

Janice Gasker has studied and taught social work at all levels. She has been teaching generalist social work practice for over 20 years, and is currently the bachelor of social work (BSW) program director at Kutztown University of Pennsylvania. She has coauthored a master of social work (MSW) and a doctor of social work (DSW) curriculum and has authored a number of Council on Social Work Education (CSWE) self-studies, including those required for initial accreditation and multiple reaffirmations.

Janice has also consulted with other universities on building their self-study on generalist curricula. She has published numerous articles and authored two books on childhood sexual abuse.

PART I

Conceptual Foundations

Introduction to Generalist Social Work

This introductory chapter begins with a case study, setting the stage for the format of chapters to come. It focuses on four main topics to create a foundation for the rest of the text: (1) the definition and characteristics of generalist social work practice, (2) the person-in-environment (PIE) perspective, (3) multisystem practice (MSP), and (4) the function of the generalist approach and social work education. The unique aspects of the social work profession are featured.

Learning Objectives

1.1 Explain the differences between social work and other helping professions, including the person-in-environment (PIE) perspective.

1.2 Recall the definition of generalist social work practice.

1.3 Explain the attributes of generalist social work practice.

1.4 Describe the role of generalist practice in the social work profession.

1.5 Paraphrase the competencies common to all social workers, and recall the stages of planned change.

Case Study: The Social Work Difference

Marella's footsteps sounded strangely hollow as she walked down the school hallway. The day at Thaddeus Stevens Elementary school was over for the kids. Most of the professionals had gone home too. Marella was there because it was Thursday, and she worked from noon to 8:00 p.m. on Thursday. It meant she had to have her daughter in day care until late at night, but she spent quality time with her every Thursday morning. And the change in her schedule was worth it. In the evenings, Thaddeus Stevens was transformed. Several generations of social work professionals had worked to make Thaddeus Stevens a school that was truly a part of the neighborhood. No longer was the school a place where parents came when their kid was in trouble. Now, it was a place of community support.

Thanks to Marella's social work predecessors, a number of community support activities happened in the evening throughout the week at Thaddeus Stevens. On Monday evenings, there was a family care medical and dental clinic. Both kids and family members could be seen through Medical Assistance or for a nominal fee. Tuesday was Family Library Day, where volunteers read stories to therapy dogs and kids and parents listened. Wednesday was Family Learning Day, when community members could come for English as a second language or general equivalency diploma (GED) classes while kids and volunteer teachers could explore fun things like baking soda and vinegar volcanoes. Thursday was Job Search Night. On Thursdays, employment services were available to all community members.

Social workers work with students, but their job is very different from that of a teacher or other professional.

As she turned a corner, Marella could see the job search staff arranging the chairs for job interview role plays. Marella headed down the hall to the classroom she used every Thursday for her Kids Night Out Without (KNOW) program. The "without" meant without parents, teachers or preschool siblings. Marella smiled as she remembered Alessandro, the sixth grader who named the program. He'd gone from being a kid who rarely spoke to one who had no problem raising his voice to shout out his suggestion for the name of the group. That was a year ago, and since then, the KNOW group had expanded its purpose. Originally, Marella had developed the group to provide a place for single parents to bring their school-aged children so they could participate in the Job Search Night. Now, KNOW had another purpose. It still provided care for 12 students, but the students received social work services too. The added purpose of KNOW was to allow students to share their feelings about the topic of the week and to locate community resources for families. It worked like this: Hour 1 served as behavioral therapy to allow the kids to learn appropriate socialization. To the kids, Hour 1 was actually called Horsing Around Time. Marella chose this name for the early part of the group because every day a particular teacher would stand in the hallway shouting "Stop horsing around!" Marella knew it was hard for the kids to sit still all day, so she thought she'd make horsing around okay for a while. Desks were pushed to the side of the room and playtime began. Sometimes she would have the kids play Duck, Duck, Goose or Red Light, Green Light so they'd have a chance to run around. While there was the occasional behavioral challenge, for the most part the kids ended up smiling and settled just in time for Snack. Most of the kids were hungry at the end of the day. Some of them would be getting a quick dinner and no breakfast the next morning.

At the beginning of the school year, Marella approached the principal about providing nutritious snacks on Thursday evenings. She went to the principal's office at the appointment time. That day, she dressed up a bit and made sure she wasn't late. When she entered the office, she said, "How are you, Mr. Davis?" It was in a voice only a little higher than usual. Then she sat down and glanced at a memo she had prepared. "As you know, even though we provide free breakfast and lunch, some of our kids are still hungry." She tried to stop her knee from jiggling. "So I'd like to provide a nutritious snack on Thursday evenings when I have my social work session with 12 kids." Marella had done her homework. "I've talked to the cafeteria workers about federal guidelines for nutritious foods, and I've drawn up a list of approved snacks. Alongside each I have the cost of that snack for 12 people." Marella handed her memo to the principal. He said, "You don't need the cafeteria or the cafeteria staff to do this?" No, she didn't. "Are these all allergy-free foods?" Yes, they were. Then, to her utter astonishment, he said, "See Ms. Rivera at the desk. Let her know I told you that you can be reimbursed up to $15.00 each week for snacks as long as you present a receipt." Marella was elated, knowing she had just improved the lives of 12 kids every week for the rest of the school year. And that's how Snack became a part of Thursday evenings.

After Snack was Safe Space, a group social work session in which kids talked about the theme of the week. Sometimes the theme was anger management (Count to Ten), sometimes it was family functioning (Dare to Care), and sometimes it was abuse prevention (Talking Helps). During these group social work sessions, Marella helped the students share their feelings and develop solutions to challenges they faced every day. Later, when parents and caregivers came to collect the kids, Marella snuck in some family-based social work—once she quietly provided a mom with a referral to an intimate partner violence prevention group, once she talked to a grandmother about parenting and self-care skills, and once she walked a mom to the bus stop so she could point out the location of a nearby cost-free food pantry.

If a student obviously needed individual counseling, Marella almost always referred the kid's caregiver or parent to the school counselor—Marella didn't have time to do much individual counseling. If a kid needed to be tested for intelligence to become eligible for classroom supports or if Marella wondered if a kid had a learning disability, she referred the caregiver to the school psychologist to set a time for testing. As the school social worker, she spent most of her time helping teachers modify their classroom activities to incorporate troubled kids; making visits to kids' homes to provide family counseling and prevent truancy; working with the principal to make school policies student-friendly; and interviewing kids that were identified as at risk for child abuse. It was always a hectic week, but Marella's favorite day was Thursday . . . when she could work in the program she developed herself.

Section 1.1: The Uniqueness of the Social Work Profession

In this section, we begin to look at the uniqueness of the **social work** profession.

What Makes a Social Worker Different?

Social workers often work alongside either volunteers or other human service providers without a social work background. Marella worked with a school psychologist, a school counselor, a nurse, a physical therapist, a principal, and library volunteers. People usually had an idea, or thought they had an idea, of what each of those professional roles entailed. Social work was different. When Marella said she was the school social worker, people often misunderstood social work. If she was lucky, they asked her what a social worker does. Marella wished she had a way to tell them all of the things social workers could do:

> She worked with kids *individually* and in *groups*. She worked with their *families*. She intervened on the *organizational* (school) level by working with the principal and with teachers. Most important to her personal satisfaction was that she had developed a program to serve the needs of the *community*. Marella knew that she looked at things differently than all of the people she worked with, but she didn't know how to explain it.

It's best if social workers can understand and can let people know what the profession is about. It's often misunderstood, and as a result it's often underappreciated. You will learn about five of the ways social work is a unique profession:

1. Unique social work values
2. Social work–specific and liberal arts education
3. A PIE perspective
4. The conscious use of a professional self
5. A focus on social justice

Social Work Values Support Ethical Decision-Making

One reason social work is unique is that social workers follow a code of ethics developed by social workers through the National Association of Social Workers (NASW). Social workers are rightfully proud of the *NASW Code of Ethics* (NASW, 2018). While most professions have codes of ethics, the social work code is one of a kind. It is focused on the following professional values:

- *Service*—Social workers elevate **service** to others above self-interest.
- *Social justice*—Social workers pursue social change with and on behalf of oppressed people.
- *Dignity and worth of the person*—Social workers treat each person with respect.
- *Importance of human relationships*—Social workers understand that relationships are central to change.
- *Integrity*—Social workers must maintain **integrity**. They are trustworthy and act in ways consistent with social work values.
- *Competence*—Social workers practice within their areas of **competence** and continually strive to increase professional knowledge. (NASW, 2018)

ETHICAL PERSPECTIVES

Get a copy of the *NASW Code of Ethics* (NASW, 2018). You can buy a copy from NASW or get it for free on their website. Take a look at the purpose of the *NASW Code of Ethics* (NASW, 2018) on page 2. Which values, principles, and standards seem most important to you?

Some aspects of the social work code are unique. Social justice, for example, may be seen in other professions' codes, but in ours it's up front in the core professional values. We don't just care about fairness for individuals; we care about equity for families, groups, organizations, and communities. The same thing is true with the **dignity and worth of the person**. Of course, many professionals find it important to respect the dignity of people, but social workers focus on it in every situation. Most people who choose to be social workers share these values with the social work profession. Because of the *NASW Code of Ethics* (NASW, 2018), social workers make ideal candidates for a broad range of human service jobs. The code provides for that broad range of jobs by addressing the common concerns of social workers who are child welfare workers, probation officers, educators, hospital and nursing home case managers, job coaches, program evaluators, hospice workers, family counselors, political staff members, mental health counselors and case managers, school social workers, group counselors, homeless outreach workers, youth mentors, substance abuse counselors, grant writers, crisis counselors, and more. The *NASW Code of Ethics* (NASW, 2018) is such a significant part of social work that it will be revisited throughout this text.

Specialized Career Preparation

The second reason social work is unique is our specialized higher education. We'll explore this further later on, but one main component of our educational preparation is our field or practicum education. Students in other majors may have internships, but every social work student has an internship that is particularly designed for social workers. Specifically, the internship of a social work student is one that has a set number of hours, a social work professional as a field instructor, and a structured set of skills that the intern has to demonstrate. These skills are known as competencies in social work, and every social work graduate has demonstrated the ability to carry them out in real situations. Finally, the social work internship is special in that every social work student in the field will practice ethical decision-making about real situations with vulnerable client systems. While social work educational programs all have something of an individualized stamp, we all study the same foundation subjects: human behavior in the social environment, social welfare policy, social work practice, research in social work, social work field education, and social work values and ethics. See Figure 1.1.

Person-In-Environment Perspective

The third uniqueness of social work is that every social worker views their work through the **person-in-environment (PIE)** lens. The *Encyclopedia of Social Work* calls this a "practice-guiding principle" (Mizrahi & Davis, 2008). The PIE perspective is another concept of such importance to the social worker that it will be seen throughout this text. The PIE perspective "creates uniform statements of social roles; environmental, mental, and physical health problems; and client strengths" (Karls & Wandrei, 1994, p. 3). In other words, the PIE perspective gives social workers a unique perspective and a language to describe that perspective.

FIGURE 1.1 ● Levels of Social Work Education

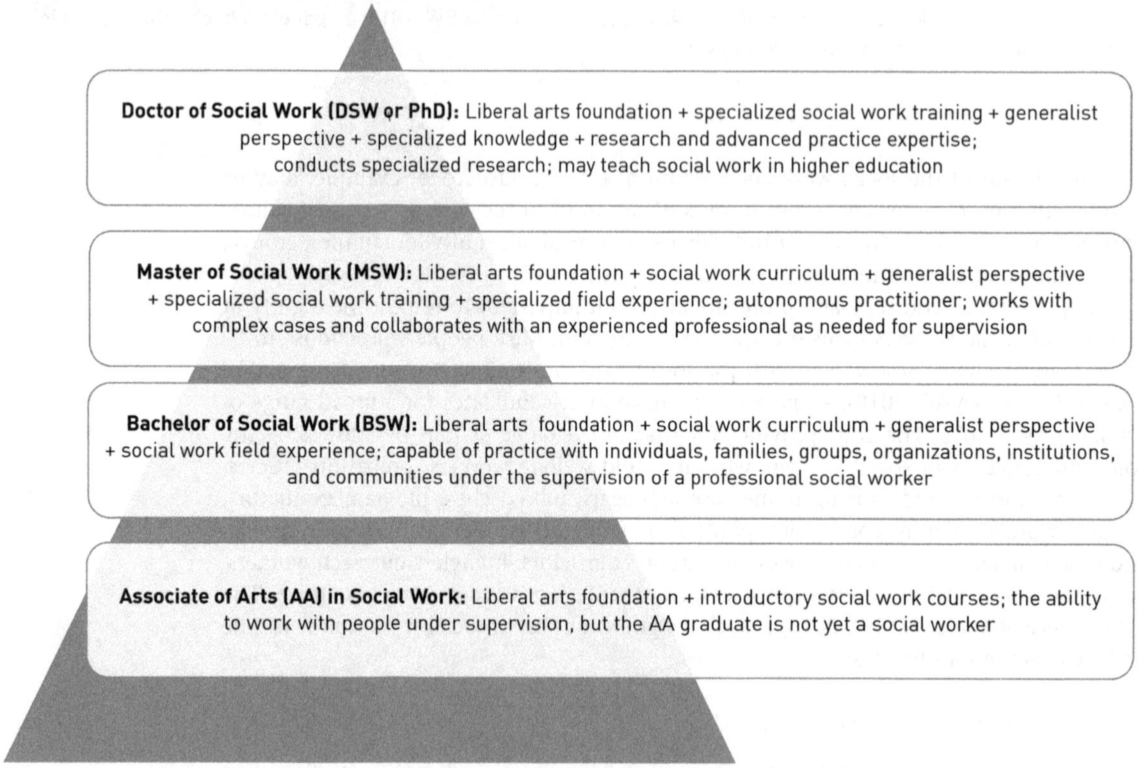

Doctor of Social Work (DSW or PhD): Liberal arts foundation + specialized social work training + generalist perspective + specialized knowledge + research and advanced practice expertise; conducts specialized research; may teach social work in higher education

Master of Social Work (MSW): Liberal arts foundation + social work curriculum + generalist perspective + specialized social work training + specialized field experience; autonomous practitioner; works with complex cases and collaborates with an experienced professional as needed for supervision

Bachelor of Social Work (BSW): Liberal arts foundation + social work curriculum + generalist perspective + social work field experience; capable of practice with individuals, families, groups, organizations, institutions, and communities under the supervision of a professional social worker

Associate of Arts (AA) in Social Work: Liberal arts foundation + introductory social work courses; the ability to work with people under supervision, but the AA graduate is not yet a social worker

Most important is the fact that PIE perspective allows all generalist social workers to perceive people as participants in

- a family,
- a culture, and
- society.

This means that individuals can be best understood by considering how they interact with all components of their environments. This allows us to seek out and identify the cause of people's challenges in that space where people interact with other people and institutions. For example, we recognize that a child's violent behavior might be influenced by a conflict-ridden household. We recognize that a teacher's classroom rules might be influenced by administration policies. A parent's behavior may be influenced by their financial concerns or unemployment. By thinking of it that way, we avoid blaming people for their situations—peoples' lives are influenced by many interacting **systems**. People may not know how to change those systems. We think of families, schools, and "big picture" things like health care as *systems* because PIE is an offshoot of general systems theory, a topic we'll cover in depth in Chapter 2. For now, know that the PIE perspective allows social workers to see peoples' problems outside of themselves and not necessarily as their fault. The PIE perspective is also important to us in that it forms part of the foundation for **multisystem practice (MSP)**, a method of understanding the situations of the people we serve and a method of carrying out social work practice.

Professional Use of Self

Fox (2013) says it well: "[In social work] specialized knowledge is necessary but not sufficient to prepare students for professional practice" (p. 7). One of the most important, unique characteristics of the social worker is their ability to be reflective. Social workers consciously identify the aspects of themselves that are affecting their work. This means that they are able to critically think about their own personal values, knowledge, and experiences to bring actions that are normally outside of awareness to consciousness. For instance, another helping professional may sit behind their desk simply because that is how the office was set up when they got there. Social workers will recognize that they may appear intimidating, will reflect on the characteristic of themselves that may derive security from that position, and will consider the best interests of the client system. The social worker is likely to think of mastering their insecurities before working with a client. They are likely to pull their chair alongside their desk to eliminate appearing to be more powerful than their clients. The social worker is taking the act of sitting in a chair, for most people an activity outside of awareness, and making it a conscious choice based on their professional values and knowledge. On a basic level, the **professional use of self** is making automatic behaviors conscious and employing them in the process of helping. We are intentional about what we do, we consider how our own feelings and beliefs influence us, and we have a purpose for each social work interaction. Our intentional work is done in the context of professional knowledge and values, so we might say this:

Professional Use of Self = conscious behaviors informed by knowledge and values

This is why the "self" is often called the most important tool in the social worker's tool kit. Of course, to make all of our behaviors conscious would be impossible. As social workers, though, to make all of our professional behaviors conscious is our goal. More details about the development of a professional use of self and the self-regulation required to develop it will be discussed in detail in later chapters.

Social Justice

Social workers seek **social justice**. Our *NASW Code of Ethics* (NASW, 2018; more on the code later) is very clear about our profession's connection to social justice. The profession's mission is to "enhance human well-being and help meet the basic human needs of all people with particular attention to the needs and empowerment of people who are vulnerable, oppressed, and living in poverty . . . Social workers promote social justice and social change" (NASW, 2018, p. 1). The definition assumes that people who are vulnerable, oppressed, and living in poverty are living with social *in*justice. Social justice can be defined in many ways (more on this in Chapter 14), but it is often associated with **human rights** (Gasker & Fischer, 2014). To the Council on Social Work Education (CSWE; 2015), human rights include freedom, safety, privacy, an adequate standard of living, health care, and education. In addition, human rights can be thought of in broad terms, as "civil, political, environmental, economic, social, and cultural" (p. 7). All of this is to say that social workers are always on the lookout for injustice in big and small ways. We work to create situations where the benefits of society are distributed to where they are needed the most.

CRITICAL THINKING AND COLLABORATIVE LEARNING EXERCISES 1.1

1. Social justice is one of the most important of the social work profession's core values. Work with a partner to discover the social justice contributions of Thaddeus Stevens, the person for whom Marella's school was named.
2. Acquire or print out a copy of the *NASW Code of Ethics* (NASW, 2018) from the NASW website.
3. In this section, we discussed how social work is unique because of our *NASW Code of Ethics* (NASW, 2018); our specialized career preparation; our PIE perspective; and our conscious, professional use of self and our focus on social justice. Form a group of four people. Each member should choose one of the five aspects of social work's uniqueness and verbally share its definition with the group.
4. Discuss with a partner what you think the phrase "with and on behalf of" means. (See the social work value of social justice.)

Section 1.2: Generalist Social Work Practice

While we've talked about how social work is a unique profession, we still haven't helped Marella to explain what social workers do in a brief and easily understandable way. In this section, we will discuss another way that social work is unique, and we will define **generalist social work practice**.

Generalist Social Work Practice

Generalist social work practice is a way of doing social work. It is a method of practice that is based on principles that are unique to social work. In short, generalist social work practice consists of the following:

> Professional efforts under the auspices of an organization guided by social welfare policies, social science theories, and an *NASW Code of Ethics* (NASW, 2018) to

> collaborate for planned change with individuals, families, groups, organizations, and communities to recognize their diverse strengths and empower them to achieve their greatest potential in a local and global environment that is socially just and sustainable . . .

This definition of generalist social work practice includes four aspects. These aspects allow social workers to assemble the knowledge, skills, and values needed for helping others. The definition's four aspects are abstract and complex. We will take them one by one.

Under the Auspices of an Organization

The word *auspice* can refer to support, backing, or authorization (see Figure 1.2). For example, we could say that generalist social workers work with the support of an organization or a program, like the support of a long-term care facility or a community partnership program. Either could hire social workers and provide them with a livelihood. We could also say that generalist social workers work with the backing of that organization or program. In other words, workers can rely on their agency or program to pay them salaries and provide such benefits as paid vacation time and matching contributions to a retirement fund. Most importantly, agencies and programs provide social workers with authorization. The organization gives the worker sanction to do their job. For instance, consider a social work service that is often resented: child protection services, particularly investigations of allegations of child abuse or maltreatment. A child's family member may rightfully demand "What gives you the right to investigate the way I parent my child?!" The social worker has a right because they are employed by an agency that is charged with doing just that. In this case, elected representatives in the federal government created a law that demands that each state will provide child protective services, including abuse investigations, to all of its citizens. When it was enacted in 1974, this law was called the Child Abuse Prevention and Treatment Act (CAPTA; U.S. Department of Health and Human Services, n.d.). States, in their turn, have elected lawmakers that decide exactly how their state will implement the federal child protective services law. The resulting state law and its regulations govern the provision of child protective services in that state, and agencies are developed to carry out those laws and regulations. To

FIGURE 1.2 • Social Workers' Authorization

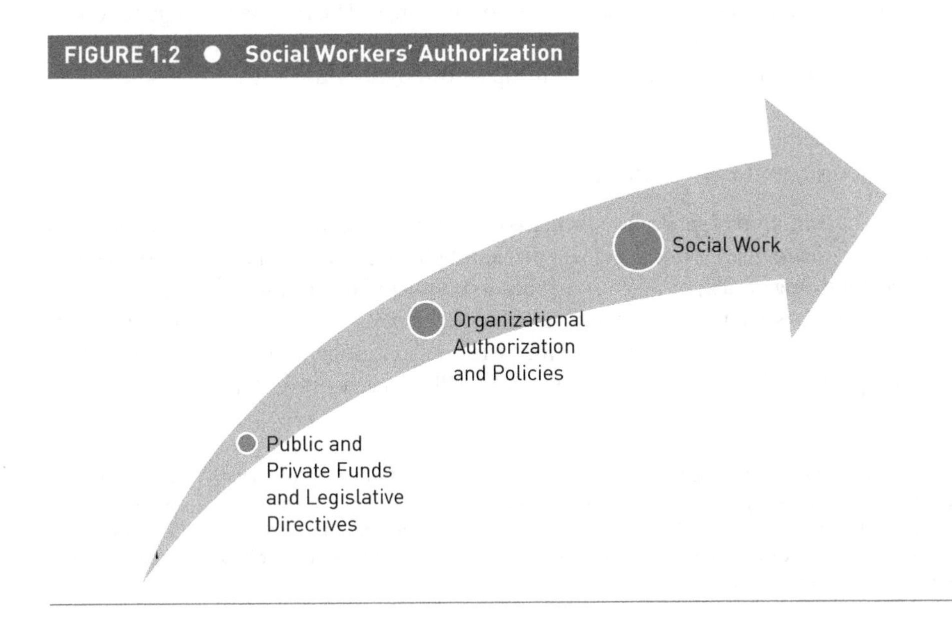

do so, agencies hire social workers. You can see that the social worker who investigates child abuse allegations is actually carrying out the will of the citizens of the country. The worker's paycheck is funded by tax dollars because elected representatives have decided that this is an important enough activity to be funded. The social worker works under the auspices of the agency that has been created or selected to carry out the child protective services law. Likewise, any social worker who is employed by an agency is given sanction to do their job because they work under the auspices of the agency.

Under the Influence of the Code of Ethics

As we've discussed, the social worker's *NASW Code of Ethics* (NASW, 2018) is a source of pride. Our code of ethics is unique, but we are not unique in having a set of ethical standards for professional behavior. In fact, most professions have codes of ethics. Any profession's code of ethics describes the behaviors related to how professionals should aspire to behave. Codes of ethics consider professionals' behaviors that occur in relationships with their consumers, their colleagues, their profession, and their community. As we'll discuss later, social work may be considered to be a profession beginning in the early part of the 1900s. Because of that, social work has had a code of ethics since 1920, when Mary Richmond developed an experimental set of ethical standards (Pumphrey, 1959, as cited in Reamer, 2013). Ethical standards in social work have been standardized by social workers and are periodically updated. Regardless of their field of practice, their agency's mission, or their job description, most every social worker's practice is guided by the *NASW Code of Ethics* (NASW, 2018).[1] Our code is unique in its focus on service and social justice. We'll say much more about the code and its use in later chapters.

With Collaboration for Planned Change

Social workers work alongside service recipients in a partnership that is formed to deliberately create change. We think about this kind of planned change as occurring in a series of stages that carry a worker and a client from their initial contact through the identification of resources and challenges to an actual change and the assurance that the change is complete and lasting. The series of stages is one way to think about planned change, but the distinction among stages is actually a false distinction. It is important to note that every social work session includes some aspect of all of the stages. The planned change process is at the center of generalist practice. Planned change is the way you are likely to think of your practice for your entire career, and it will reappear throughout this text.

Work With Individuals, Families, Groups, Organizations, and Communities

Central to the definition of generalist practice is the planned change process that crosses all levels of practice: micro, mezzo, and macro. In generalist practice, social workers think of planned change as consisting of MSP, or practice that occurs on micro, mezzo, and macro levels. **Micro practice** refers to work directly with individuals. **Mezzo practice** refers to work with groups and families. **Macro practice** refers to work with organizations, communities and institutions. Like planned change, considerations of MSP will permeate every chapter in this book.

---

[1]A similar code of ethics for social workers is the National Codes of Ethics of Social Work (provided in a variety of languages) by the International Federation of Social Workers. Other organizations such as the National Association of Black Social Workers and the Clinical Social Work Association have separate codes as well, although the *NASW Code of Ethics* (NASW, 2018) is considered to be the most comprehensive and the most widely known (Reamer, 2013).

Other professionals may see problems in one area: If they are counselors, they will see problems in individuals. Couples counselors will see problems in the interaction between the two members of an intimate relationship. Legislators will see problems as occurring among government decisions and citizens. For social workers, though, problem identification is seldom that simple. To begin with, social workers see strengths first. We look at the resources people may have in themselves and their environments. Workers see a big picture when they look at resources and challenges, with strengths and concerns happening for individuals as they interact with their social and physical environments. Social workers direct their change efforts toward individuals directly or toward individuals as they are part of families, groups, organizations, and communities. Sometimes micro, mezzo, and macro classifications are slightly different, with organizations being characterized as mezzo instead of macro level work, but the distinctions of micro, mezzo, and macro practice are used by social workers everywhere. In fact, the CSWE, the organization that oversees the accreditation of social work programs in universities, mentions multisystem practice in its documents. For example, one of the areas CSWE expects to see social workers perform is in the area of ethical and professional behavior, and the beginning of the description of that behavior reads as follows: "Social workers understand the value base of the profession and its ethical standards, as well as relevant laws and regulations that may impact practice at the micro, mezzo, and macro levels" (CSWE, 2015, p. 7).

An important way to consider these levels of practice all at the same time is to think about MSP as a method for social work practice. MSP is a way of practicing that reminds social workers that they always need to see things through a broad scope. Later on in this book, we'll be discussing this approach. It is a way of carrying out generalist social work that allows social workers to consider systems like individuals, families, groups, organizations, and communities at the same time. Each case may include work with any or all of the systems.

MSP also suggests that it is important to note the following: While the generalist social work practice definition suggests that social workers collaborate with individuals, families, groups, organizations, and communities to create change, we often work with one individual who represents that system level. For example, if you are working with a community you may be speaking with the mayor, or the representative of an organization, or a member of the borough council. It is much less intimidating to think of working with Yolanda Wilson, the borough council member, than it is to think about working with the town itself. Even though the town is the macro level of practice we're addressing, we are working directly with Ms. Wilson, and she is easy to know and to like. Similarly, even though we may be working with a family or a small group, we are frequently addressing one individual at a time. We are likely to direct our remarks to one person at a time even if family or group members are all in the room together, and we work toward change for all of the individuals in the group. Of course, if we are addressing a group, a family, or a board of directors, we may address the entire group with a single statement. In these cases, the word *client* will refer to the group. Here we don't separate individuals from groups, and we address the entire group. You might give a talk to a room of legislators, funders, or a group of staff at an agency. Consequently, we will speak about individual **clients** and we'll use the word *clients* for families as well as groups, large and small. We'll also refer to some individuals that are part of larger groups as **client system representatives**. When we speak to the mayor about community issues, we are speaking to a client system representative.

MSP also points us to the idea that the distinctions of micro, mezzo, and macro practice are actually meaningless. Like the separate stages of the planned change process, these three levels of practice are simply our way of partializing our work, or breaking complex situations into manageable parts. To understand partialization more clearly, we might think of a situation in social work with an individual where partialization is important. Imagine the following scenario between a worker and an individual client:

Worker: As you know, we agreed that this week we would start to talk about the challenges you are facing. Are you ready to do that?

Client: (*nodding her head and beginning to cry*) I'll try, but I don't know where to begin. (*crying harder now*) There's just so much. I can't take it! (*now sobbing into her hands*)

Worker: Sounds like you're feeling really overwhelmed. Suppose we take these things one at a time.

Client: (*looking up and reaching for a tissue*) Yes, I can do that.

Here, the worker uses a number of social work skills that we'll consider later in the book, but most important is partialization. The client needed to feel like her problems could be managed, and taking them one by one was essential. In a way, we social workers are doing the same kind of thing when we talk about planned change stages or MSP. We're using language that allows us to consider all angles of a case without becoming overwhelmed.

When Marella wished she could explain what made school social work different to a brief acquaintance, she could have said this: "We work to make life better for kids . . . in their families, their school, and the neighborhood." This would have reflected social work's MSP and let people know that even at face value social work is different. Later in the conversation, Marella could also have said this: "We also have a unique code of ethics, and social justice is really important to us." Figure 1.3 shows the systems operating in the environment of workers and clients.

Enabling Empowerment

The definition of generalist practice includes the term **empowerment**. This refers to the social worker's responsibility to help people help themselves. In other words, we don't create change; we help people create change in their lives. We help them to recognize their unique strengths and see that change is possible. It is tempting to say that when we empower we give people the power to change. We should be careful of the way we say that.

FIGURE 1.3 ● Multilevel Social Work Practice

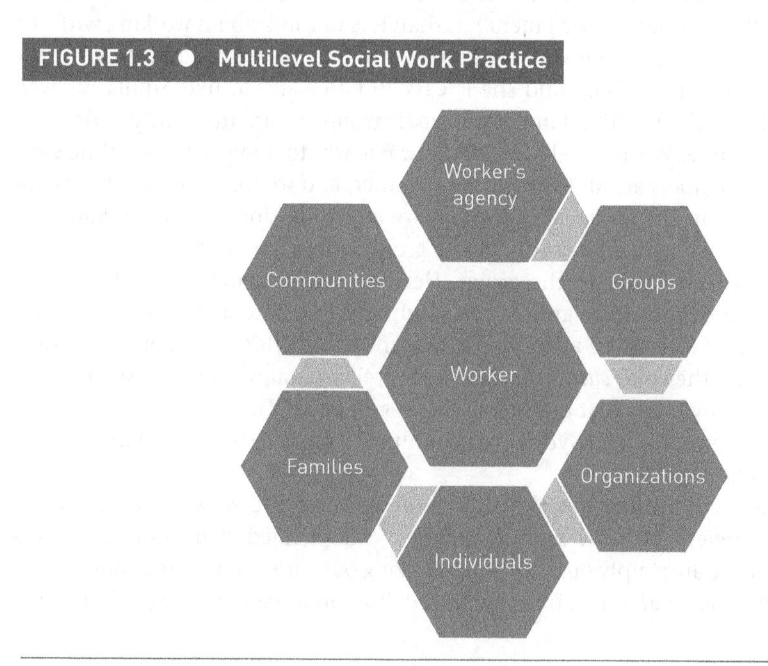

To say we give people the power to change implies that we have power that we can give to them. In fact, we are helping people to reach out to their own resources, and we are helping them to experience using their own power. This way, we can help individuals learn to empower themselves, and at some point they won't need a social worker at all. In social work, we try to work ourselves out of a job.

In a Socially Just and Sustainable Environment

Since generalist social work practice is multilevel in nature, the social worker addresses every challenge from a multilevel perspective. The PIE is one such perspective that is employed universally by social workers to understand how to locate human challenges at the intersection of environmental systems. PIE and systems will be discussed at length in Chapter 2, but for now, understand that the PIE perspective requires the social worker to work on all three levels of practice at the same time. That is, social workers often work on the micro, mezzo, and macro levels for each situation they are asked to address. Consequently, the social worker cannot ever ignore the institution and community levels of practice. In other words, we don't focus our efforts toward change solely on an individual without considering that person's environment, or the macro level systems that operate with them and around them. These systems might be available health care, the economy and personal finance, the physical environment, education, national and international policies, spirituality and religion, the justice system, government, and so forth. The social worker looks to the way these systems interact with each other and with individuals to seek out and understand **social injustice**, or situations where everyone does not have the necessary access to the benefits of the existing systems. In those situations, it is the responsibility of the social worker to address the macro systems to promote a **socially just environment** for people. This means that social workers work toward an environment where everyone has access to the benefits of existing systems needed to meet their unique needs. When an environment is **sustainable**, it includes systems whose energy levels are in balance and are likely to continue that way. The technical word for this situation is **homeostasis**, a word we'll discuss later.

Social Work Practice

To sum it up, social work practice is generalist practice, and generalist practice occurs in the following:

- Under the auspices of an organization
- Under the influence of the *NASW Code of Ethics* (NASW, 2018) and social welfare policies
- In collaboration for planned change and recognition of diverse strengths for empowerment with individuals, families, groups, organizations, and communities
- In search of a socially just, sustainable environment

CRITICAL THINKING AND COLLABORATIVE LEARNING EXERCISES 1.2

1. Work with a partner and share your ideas about being a generalist practitioner. Practice different ways to answer this question: What do social workers do?
2. Think about the terms *micro*, *mezzo*, and *macro*. Identify a mezzo level group you are involved in. Work with a partner to identify two communities that touch your lives.

Section 1.3: Characteristics of Generalist Social Work Practice

This section continues the discussion of generalist social work practice with a consideration of a number of the attributes of generalist practice.

Characteristics of Generalist Practice

The generalist social work definition has a number of components that describe its nature and inform the educational experience of social work students. We will highlight four of those characteristics, which are (1) broad knowledge base; (2) the strengths perspective on diversity; (3) social welfare and organizational content; and (4) social, economic, and environmental justice.

Broad Knowledge Base

As we've seen, there are several levels of social work education, and each builds on the others. All social workers share a foundation of knowledge that is common to people who have experienced higher education, a foundation of knowledge in liberal arts and sciences. Social workers also share a specific curriculum of liberal arts, which is necessary as a basis for the social work curriculum itself.

Liberal Arts. Most university students are engaged, at least in part, in the study of the liberal arts. And most of them do not know what liberal arts means. Think of art as in how-to-do-it—like the art of carpentry. An art is know-how about something. Liberal comes from the Latin *liberalis*, meaning "a free person." Liberal arts, then, means know-how about people and their lives. To know about people and all facets of their lives and their relationships to one another is to be educated in the liberal arts.

The first people trained in the liberal arts were students who studied around 1000 CE (as in over 1,000 years ago) who went to what was then called the *universitas*. They met their teachers in cathedrals like the one at Chartres, France, and studied liberal arts so that they could be intellectual, thinking people who might become great philosophers or teachers or government workers. It was thought that a graduate of the liberal arts (even back then the levels of qualification were called bachelor, master, and doctor) would be someone who knew all about people. Some of the topics that were studied back then will sound familiar: grammar, logic, speech, arithmetic, astronomy, and music (Barzun, 2000). As you know, today's university curriculum is quite similar, and the goal of the study of the liberal arts is also similar: to produce graduates who know about people and will be good (voting) citizens.

Liberal Arts for Social Workers. It is easy to see how study in the liberal arts is central to social work. In addition, though, social workers experience something of a specialized curriculum. There are specific areas of the liberal arts that we have all studied. For example, we don't get our bachelor of social work (BSW) degrees until we have studied political science, or government. This makes sense since the policies developed by government affect the quality of life of all people, and government policies are used to create the agencies that hire social workers. Since we work with people, we are sure to take a number of courses about human behavior, like psychology, sociology, and anthropology. We get a holistic view of people, their thoughts and behaviors, their interactions with others, and the diversity of their cultures. Since people are living organisms, we study biology. We are also concerned with social justice, so we need to know about economics. Since we are concerned with the quality of people's physical environment, we take physical science. As the profession begins to understand the importance of the physical environment, it would not be surprising to learn that all social workers would be studying environmental science as the science component of their liberal arts education. Finally, we need to critique studies in the social and behavioral sciences to engage in evidence-based practice, so we take courses about critical thinking and statistics. This broad knowledge base is one of the reasons social workers must commit to lifelong learning.

The Strengths Perspective on Diversity

Generalist social work practitioners value human dignity and worth (NASW, 2018). Consequently, we view people as individuals, and we value each one. We look to the person, their diversity, and the environment to locate resources. We'll discuss this much more in Chapter 2, but for now know a short definition of **diversity** is the difference in attributes between and among individuals and groups. Diversity can be a significant source of resources and strengths. The perspective that articulates this practice is known as the **strengths perspective** (Saleebey, 1996, 2013; Witkin & Saleebey, 2007). To take a glance at the strengths perspective, consider the following: Two case managers meet a troubled couple. They discover that much of the couple's conflict arises from the challenge of providing child care for their infant. Each feels the other does not pull their weight, but both are exhausted from their difficult jobs. One worker asks about their ethnic background and learns that they are members of a minority group. The worker recognizes that they are without many opportunities for employment, so the worker directs them to a sliding fee scale child care center. A different worker asks about their ethnic background and learns that they are members of a minority group that is known for their close family ties. This worker helps the couple to brainstorm ways of asking family members to help with child care. One of the workers here helped connect the client system to a community agency. The other recognizes diversity and attempts to deepen family ties. Both are probably equal in the opportunity to succeed, but one is based on **informal resources**, or those that already exist in the client's life. These are already present, so they are more likely to remain available. These resources could only be identified through an understanding of diversity.

Social Welfare and Organizational Context

Another unique aspect of generalist social work is its focus on the organizational context of the professional social worker. When we think of organizational context, we are thinking of the agency that employs the worker—how does that agency influence the services we provide? The generalist practitioner wonders what **social welfare** policies affect the eligibility of clients for service, the types of services provided, and the rules the workers follow. We are also concerned with the environment of the agency, how the workers get along, what type of supervision happens, what kind of pay and job benefits social workers receive, and where and what type of facility it is. All of these aspects of organizational context concern the generalist social worker because they affect the people we serve.

Social, Economic, and Environmental Justice

Social justice is one of the core values of the social work profession (NASW, 2018). Economic justice and environmental justice are aspects of social justice. Because this is such an important part of social work practice, CSWE (2015) has outlined the understanding of **social, economic, and environmental justice** required of all generalist social work practitioners:

> Social workers understand that every person regardless of position in society has fundamental human rights such as freedom, safety, privacy, an adequate standard of living, health care, and education. Social workers understand the global interconnections of oppression and human rights violations, and are knowledgeable about theories of human need and social justice and strategies to promote social and economic justice and human rights. Social workers understand strategies designed to eliminate oppressive structural barriers to ensure that social goods, rights, and responsibilities are distributed equitably and that civil, political, environmental, economic, social, and cultural human rights are protected. (pp. 7–8)

WHAT IF . . . FOCUS ON DIVERSITY

Suppose Marella was Caucasian instead of Latina. In what situations might her ethnicity prove to be a barrier in her work? In other words, what parts of her job might be harder? To identify the strengths in diversity, consider what parts of her job might be easier.

A less complicated way to think about this is that generalist social work practitioners recognize that the benefits of society are not available to all people in a fair and equitable way. A person with a physical disability may not be able to enter a historic building. A person with minimal or moderate income may not be able to attend college without crippling student loans. A person living in urban poverty may not be able to enjoy public parks. Generalist social workers work toward the equitable distribution of society's benefits, including basic human rights, economic stability, and safe and nurturing physical environments. The word *equitable* is key. Often people think that to strive for social justice is to strive for equality. The generalist social work practitioner does not work toward equality because equality means that everyone gets the same or equal amounts of available resources. This is not our goal, since we seek to have resources distributed *based on each person's needs*. For example, let's say we added up all of the social work services provided in one year and divided them up equally. Everyone would have a set number of meetings with a social worker. This is equality, and this is fine for people who need little assistance accessing society's resources, such as adequate housing. For others, though, the need is much greater. If those who need less help would share the resource, those more in need of service could receive more. In this example, a homeless person would get more meetings with a social worker because their need for housing is greater than that of most people. That is an equitable distribution of resources. Likewise, we can consider income. We have made a decision that people should have basic human rights, so government provides benefits such as cash, food stamps, low income housing, and so forth to those who cannot acquire them through an inability to work or to insufficient wages. Unfortunately, government does not always distribute enough of our society's resources to actually allow all people to have human rights: For example, we've just mentioned those who cannot find adequate housing. The social worker does not ask that wealthy people, many of whom have earned their fortunes through work, distribute their wealth equally. In that case, we would pool everyone's money and distribute it so that everyone would get the same amount. Instead, the social worker advocates for equitable distribution: We would like to pool everyone's resources and share them so that everyone in society would have enough to meet their basic human rights.

To review, the attributes of generalist social work practice include a broad, liberal arts knowledge base; the skill to carry out a strengths perspective on diversity; social welfare and organizational context; and social, economic, and environmental justice. See Figure 1.4.

FIGURE 1.4 ● Basic Differences Between Social Work and Other Professions

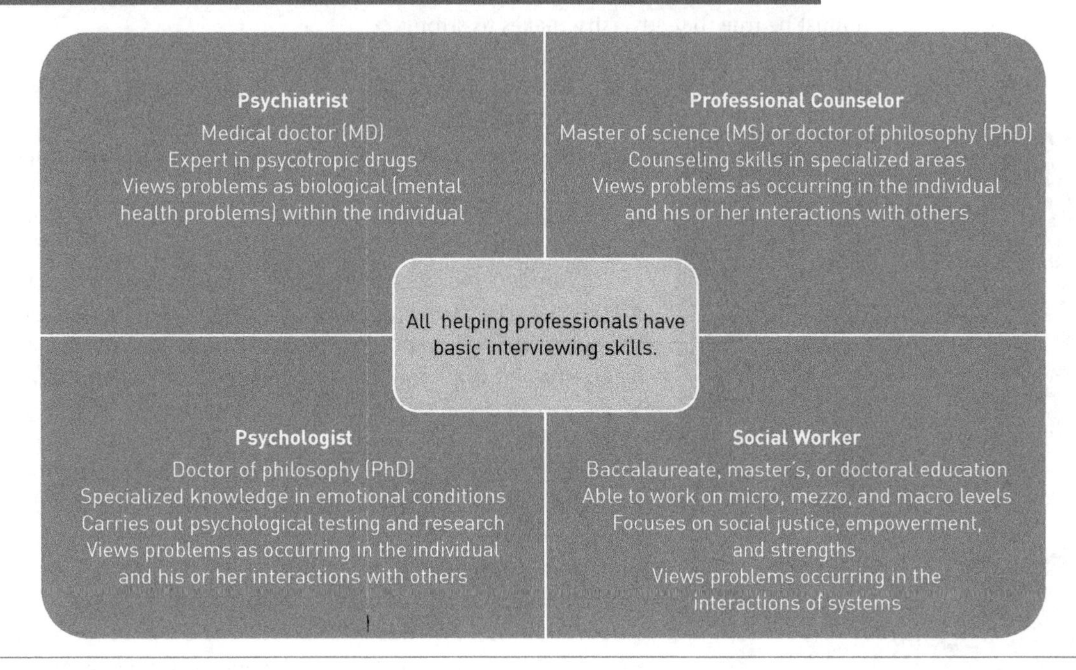

Source: Adapted from Kirst-Ashman & Hull, 2018.

CRITICAL THINKING AND COLLABORATIVE LEARNING EXERCISES 1.3

1. Consider the importance of your liberal arts courses to your social work practice. Discuss with a partner.
2. With a partner, answer the following question: How does the social work professional value of social justice make social work different from other professions? (The answer is *not* "we care about people"—others do too!)

Section 1.4: Historical Development of Social Work

This section explores some of the history of the development of generalist practice and the role that generalist practice plays in the social work profession.

The Historical Development of Social Work

If you ask social workers what people were the most influential in the development of the profession of social work, most every list would include Jane Addams and Mary Richmond. These women were very different, and they had very different methods, but they were both passionate about helping people who were economically and otherwise challenged.

How They Got That Way

It must be true that adversity makes us strong. . . .

Addams lost her mother at the age of 2. She was also gay in an era when sexual preference was not discussed. She was born with a physical challenge: She had what she called a "crooked back," or curvature of the spine, that she believed made her ugly. In fact, she defined herself as so physically unattractive that she didn't expect her father to acknowledge her on the street (Joslin, 2004). As an adult, she decided she wanted to spend her life helping people.

George Rinhart/Contributor/Getty Images

Jane Addams

Richmond's mother and her three siblings died before Mary was 4 years old. Her father, an alcoholic, abandoned her just after that. She was raised by a grandmother and a couple of aunts in a Baltimore neighborhood that would have benefited from a settlement house. Mary also decided she wanted to spend her life helping people (Agnew, 2004).

Addams lived and worked in the late 1800s to early 1900s. She was born to wealth. Many luxuries were at her fingertips, including education, and unlike most women of the day, she was able to earn a bachelor's degree.

Addams believed that she was fortunate to be able to go to school, but once she was out of school she was at loose ends. She was expected to be a part-time teacher or a wife (women had to choose one or the other), but according to her diaries, she longed for a career (Joslin, 2004). After she received her bachelor's degree, she fell into what doctors called a hysteria. (We would probably call it a depression.) This condition lasted 8 years, all through a 2-year tour of Europe. In a subsequent tour, she discovered Toynbee Hall, a settlement house in London. It was there she found her career. She came back to Chicago, and in 1989 she began Hull House, the settlement house that all social workers know.

Sewall, May Wright (1894)

Mary Richmond

The settlement house was a place where wealthy women mingled with working poor families and helped them via classes in parenting, cooking, and other skills, including art. It also provided housing for some single women. Most importantly, it provided a way for caring people to learn what economically challenged individuals and families needed, and the settlement house became a jumping-off point for policy changes like child labor laws. At the settlement house, immigrants learned about American culture and government as well as participation in civic responsibilities. Addams became a public figure and brought social work to people's attention. In this way, she helped social work to become a profession. Her prominence was something of a drawback during World War I, since she expressed her pacifist views loudly. These views drew a great deal of criticism. However, she stuck to her principles. Later, when times changed, she won the Nobel Peace Prize. Fortunately for us, she kept a diary for her whole life. Her diaries provided information for her autobiographies so we can see what it was like to bring the settlement house movement to the United States (Addams, 1930).

Richmond lived and worked in the late 1800s and wrote her most famous work, *Social Diagnosis*, in 1917 at the age of 58. She grew up in a time and place where few women became educated, and she had such a craving for books that her first foray out of the house was because she wanted to form a book club. Eventually, her passions for books and for helping came together to make her one of the most influential social workers.

Her greatest contribution to the field was to professionalize it. At the time Richmond was working and writing, there was no social work profession for her to join so she did her part by focusing on *applied philanthropy*, a term used to reflect a new focus on scientific helping (Agnew, 2004). She believed that there could be evidence-based practice (though she never would have called it that) in which standards helped human service workers to provide similar, time-tested services across populations and social class. *Social Diagnosis* is in fact a rigorous qualitative study in which Richmond looks closely at case work to determine what approaches were effective. She wrote about cases in great detail so that she could educate others. The book is impressive on its own—standards for qualitative research were not developed until about 100 years later. What is most impressive, though, is that Richmond had only a high school education. She became highly educated and took on the role of social work educator, but she did it on her own.

People generally recognize *Social Diagnosis* as a text that Richmond (1917/2012) wrote in response to the famous speech by Abraham Flexner. Flexner was asked to speak about social work, and he famously made the point that social work was not a profession since it did not have its own knowledge base, skill set, and articulated values. Richmond set out to articulate the professional nature of social work and its unique, scientific knowledge base. In her own words, she set out to

> spell out carefully the distinction between the social worker, possessing a valuable trained skill in developing human relationships, and the ordinary helpful individual or resource person, who was concerned about others but possessed no special skill or training in this area. (Richmond, 1922, cited in Murdoch, 2011, p. 92)

Richmond's career began in a charity organization society, an organization that has been identified as one that worked with individuals and families (Murdoch, 2011), viewing problems as challenges that were located in the lives of people that people themselves could fix. We might now say that this view can lead to "blaming the victim." The truth, though, is that Richmond recognized that broad social problems directly influenced individuals and families. She worked on causes for social justice; she just saw those attempts as separate from people who received home-based services.

Like Addams, Richmond felt enough passion for helping that she worked continuously on behalf of those who needed help. Just after Addams opened her policy-focused settlement house, Richmond went to work at the Baltimore Charity Organization Society. Richmond focused on what was called friendly visiting, or individual and family level casework. Her belief was that the main vehicle for helping was the one-on-one relationship that could be built between friendly visitors and the individual family members they visited.

Theories in Opposition

Social workers often see settlement houses and charity organization societies as distinctly different approaches. The first priority for the settlement house was community change, so the lion's share of resources went into efforts toward social welfare policy change. For charity organization societies, the focus was on helping one person at a time. This put Addams in theoretical opposition to Richmond. Most social workers recognize these two approaches to helping as the start of the divide—micro vs. macro—that plagued the profession in its infancy. In some ways, it continues to do so today (Agnew, 2004).

Complementary Contributions

Both Addams and Richmond lived in a time when poverty was just coming on the nation's radar. The Industrial Revolution began around the 1880s, and the process of building factories in cities created a situation where large groups of people worked in dangerous conditions, were paid poverty wages, and lived in squalor. Unlike rural poverty, where poor families were not noticeable, the Industrial Revolution brought poverty to cities where it could not be ignored (Franklin, 1986). Both Addams and Richmond responded to the crisis with a basic approach that changed the way people thought about helping others. That approach was to move from "moral certainty" to "rational inquiry" (Franklin, 1986, p. 504). In other words, prior to Addams and Richmond, people understood helping to be something that was required by religion. To many, that meant that helping was morally right, and therefore the process could be undertaken with confidence as being correct: Helping could be carried out with moral certainty in any manner the helper thought best. For Addams and Richmond, though, the idea of "scientific philanthropy" was paramount: They wanted to do good well (Agnew, 2004). Their focus was rational inquiry, or the use of scientific thinking to inform helping methods. Both Addams and Richmond placed a focus on recording and analyzing their work, creating the beginnings of a culture that connected helping with education.

Another area of similarity in the work of Richmond and Addams was that of an unstated but decidedly holistic view. In other words, to both women the environment was paramount in the change effort. Addams is known for the settlement house and is connected in most social workers' minds with change on a macro level. However, she and her workers helped individuals and small groups, conducting training sessions in everything from work skills to housekeeping to music lessons. They visited homes in the neighborhood and helped families where they lived. Addams placed a focus on providing a haven in the midst of a dark and hopeless neighborhood. She worked to help people connect with each other, and she worked to make policy change, such as labor reform, as well. So work with individuals, families, groups, institutions, and communities were all part of the practice of helping at Hull House. Likewise, Richmond's charity organization societies were focused on directly helping individuals and families in their homes. Yet Richmond recognized that social welfare policies were significant: She was instrumental in the development of child labor laws, legislation related to "wife desertion," and the reform of the Society to Protect Children from Cruelty. In 1909, she led the community change effort to organize the Pennsylvania State Conference of Social Work (Agnew, 2004, p. 113). In short, both Addams and Richmond embraced work on the micro, mezzo, and macro levels.

Development of Two Schools of Thought

Despite the basic similarity in the foundations for helping, the differences between what came to be perceived as the macro work of the settlement house and the micro work of the charity organization societies have always been highlighted. At the dawn of the profession, summer schools of philanthropy were created in New York, Boston, Chicago, St. Louis, and Philadelphia. As social work schools developed in conjunction with universities—University of Chicago, Columbia University, and University of Pennsylvania—each seemed to choose a primary method: micro or macro. Also early in the profession's history organizations were created that focused on one method to the exclusion of others. This split widened over time. For example, groups like the National Association of Schools of Social Work and Social Administration, with a macro focus, and the American Association of Schools of Social Work, with a micro focus, were developed. In that case, it wasn't long before that separation became harmful. Advances in psychiatry and Freudian thinking exacerbated the split. Both of these organizations began to accredit schools, but they proceeded in such disparate ways that both of them lost accreditation authority.

Professionalization

Professional Values. In the meantime, social work was increasingly developing all of the characteristics of a profession. We had developed a knowledge base that was rapidly expanding through the schools of social work and a skill set consistent with that knowledge base. In order to complete the process of professionalization, one component was missing: a set of professional values and ethics. Over the years, there were a number of piecemeal codes being developed that carried the profession for some time, but the most influential code of ethics was that of the NASW. The NASW delegate assembly approved the first official social work code of ethics on October 13, 1960.

AP Photo/William J. Smith

E. Franklin Frazier

Along with these developments, there were individual social workers who helped to move us toward the status of a profession. Marie Woolfolk Taylor was one of those. She is most famous for starting the first African American sorority on a college campus, but she played a great role in the development of social work through her work throughout the first half of the 1900s. She attended the Schauffler Training School for Social Services in Cleveland, Ohio, where she was the only African American student. After that, she was proud to call herself a social worker and a probation officer in Atlanta as well as showed herself to be competent in many social work settings like the NAACP (National Association for the Advancement of Colored People) and the YMCA (Young Men's Christian Association). She served on community planning commissions and boards of directors and was a financial consultant to these agencies. In 1917, she practiced directly with individuals while giving the profession great visibility as she was one of two black people to assist the Red Cross after the great Atlanta fire, and . . . the whole time she called herself a social worker (Payton-Stewart, 2017).

Keystone-France/Contributor/Getty Images

Frances Perkins

Another individual who helped to move social work toward professionalization was E. Franklin Frazier, a 1921 researcher at the Columbia School of Social Work. According to the American Sociological Association (n.d.), he studied the conditions of African Americans using scientific methods and participated in community change via the NAACP. Eventually, he was director of the Atlanta School of Social Work. He is considered to be one of the most influential African American political and social writers of his time. A research center at Howard University is named after him (Howard University, n.d.).

Like Jane Addams, Frances Perkins gave up her settled life and went to live and work at Hull House in Chicago. She worked with the people who came to Hull House, and she also specialized in social welfare policy change. Eventually, her influence reached to the federal level. She influenced groundbreaking policies like the Social Security Act (1935) during a period that saw sweeping social welfare policy development in response to the Great Depression. This set of legislation, known as Franklin Delano Roosevelt's (FDR) New Deal, was guided in part by the hand of this social worker. Frances Perkins became the first woman to be a cabinet member as she worked with FDR as his secretary of labor (Frances Perkins Center, n.d.).

Paul Popper/Popperfoto/Contributor/Getty Images

Harry Hopkins being acknowledged by President Harry S. Truman.

Another powerful influence for change in FDR's administration was Harry Hopkins. Hopkins was a unique social worker who spent time working at a settlement house in New York and later worked as a friendly visitor. Eventually, he became one of FDR's closest advisers, helping to craft

New York Daily News Archive/Contributor/Getty Images

Dorothy Height

programs like Social Security and the Works Progress Administration (WPA). Under Harry Hopkins's supervision, the WPA became America's largest employer. During WWII, Harry Hopkins, social worker, served as FDR's unofficial emissary to Winston Churchill and Joseph Stalin. As a direct influence on the social work profession, Harry Hopkins helped found the American Association of Social Workers, one of our first professional organizations (The Eleanor Roosevelt Papers Project, n.d.).

More recently, Dorothy Height brought professionalism to social work through a lifetime of activism. A graduate of the Columbia School of Social Work, she was directly involved in the many powerful social movements of the 1960s, 1970s, and 1980s. In recognition of a lifetime of public service, in 2004 she was awarded the Congressional Gold Medal along with Nelson Mandela, Mother Teresa, and Rosa Parks (NASW, n.d.). Dorothy Height was a social worker who was tireless in her change efforts for decades.

You might say that all of these individuals—Addams, Richmond, Taylor, Frazier, Perkins, Hopkins, and Height—helped to change social work from a hobby to a job to a professional career. In their own ways, they helped to develop the knowledge, skills, and values needed for social work to be a profession.

Social Work Definition

Another bit of progress toward professionalization was the first definitive description of social work by the NASW. A committee was convened, and the result was the identification of three "generic" methods as appropriate for social work practice:

- changing the individual in relation to the social environment
- changing the social environment in relation to the individual, or
- both in relation to their interaction. (Mizrahi & Davis, 2008)

Two things are important to us about this definition. One, what we think of as micro and macro practices were both included. That is a sign that social workers were looking toward professionalization and looking toward professional unity as well. Second, it is important for us to note that this first definition of social work foreshadows generalist practice in its third characteristic "both [micro and macro practice] in relation to their interaction." There is a suggestion here that both micro and macro practice could happen within the same case although that type of generalist approach was not considered necessary at the time.

Professional Social Work Education

In 1946, the CSWE, the accrediting program we know now, was developed. Eventually, CSWE was sanctioned to accredit programs—that is, to approve programs' consistency with established standards. In 1955, seven professional organizations merged to form the NASW (Mizrahi & Davis, 2008). Even within these organizations, the micro–macro separation has continued. One example of the divide is the current Association for Community Organization and Social Administration, a group within CSWE that focuses on macro work. Another current organization is the American Clinical Social Work Association. People still call themselves macro workers or micro workers. Another example is the fact that undergraduate education was not included in the CSWE Educational Policy and Accreditation Standards (EPAS) until 1982. Prior to that, the standards included only the master's level of education, which was likely to include a specialization—often either micro or macro—rather than a generalist approach. Later, CSWE articulated the common competencies that undergird generalist practice. See Figure 1.5.

FIGURE 1.5 • The Role of Generalist Practice in the Development of Modern Social Work

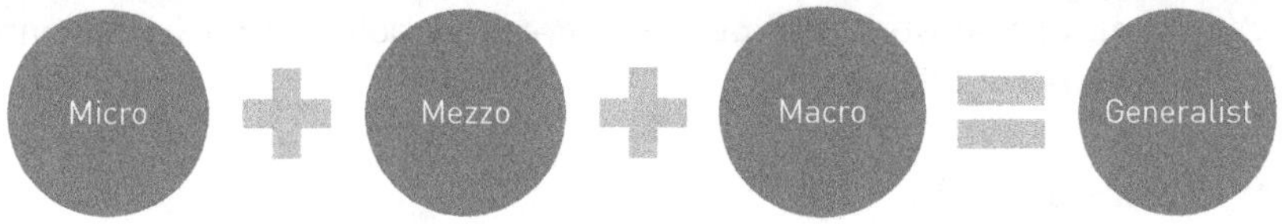

Micro + Mezzo + Macro = Generalist

The Need for Cohesion and the Role of Generalist Practice

Even as social work was becoming a full-fledged profession, disunity threatened its existence. Schools continued to follow different paths. Eventually Smith College developed a social work program that was focused, like the charity organization societies, on work with individuals. The University of Pennsylvania developed a social work program that focused on community, like settlement houses did. While this was happening, social workers saw the need for professional recognition and a need for the cohesion that could support the development of a professional identity for social work in general and social workers in particular.

Here is where generalist social work could be a significant force for change in the social work profession itself. Drawing on the commonalities that Addams shared with Richmond, generalist practice could go a few steps beyond that earlier definition of social work. Both micro and macro social work could be seen as necessary considerations in work with any social work case. Indeed, the generalist perspective could create a scenario in which micro and macro distinctions do not exist. The MSP perspective described in this book provides the foundation for such a perspective. It seems that MSP could underlie further movement toward unity in the profession. If social workers spoke with one voice, what would emerge would be a stronger profession with a clearer identity. A clear identity, that of the generalist practitioner who may or may not have an additional specialization, could evolve. In this case, the identity of the generalist practitioner, rather than the micro or the macro practitioner, would allow us to present as one profession to all of our constituents: our clients, our colleagues, and the broader community.

CRITICAL THINKING AND COLLABORATIVE LEARNING EXERCISES 1.4

1. The author Upton Sinclair often stayed with Addams at Hull House to get material for his novel *The Jungle*. Read the short Chapter 7 of that book to get an idea of the social conditions that helped Addams and Richmond see that social work had to be their careers. Note that some of today's problems are as pervasive as those depicted in the book (e.g., Chicago's homeless today still experience the cold the way Jurgis does), but today's problems are very different. Join a small group of classmates. Share your thoughts on the issues today that are pushing you to be a social worker.
2. For information about specific social work careers, visit the website of the NASW (www.socialworkers.org). Share your thoughts with a partner.

Section 1.5: Social Work Competencies

This section explores the social work competencies that should be the result of every social worker's generalist social work training. They reveal the potential for professional unity inherent in the generalist approach.

Social Work Competencies

The CSWE is the organization that oversees social work programs at colleges and universities. Your school's social work program has to get the CSWE stamp of approval every 8 years to become and remain accredited. To be accredited, programs first have to show that they operate within their university's mission statement. They should have a program mission, program goals, and program activities that are consistent with the university mission statement. For example, a university may seek to provide academic leadership in the surrounding community. If the social work program has relationships with local service providers and faculty members volunteer their expertise as advisory board representatives or program evaluators, they have gone a long way toward fulfilling that aspect of the university's mission.

Programs have to demonstrate a number of other qualifications to receive accreditation from CSWE. For example, programs have to demonstrate the ability to teach generalist social work practice. One thing they do to demonstrate that they teach generalist social work practice is to provide CSWE with a curriculum matrix. A curriculum matrix is a table, or grid, that shows each of the competencies that social workers must be able to carry out. It then connects the competencies to areas of the curriculum. In other words, the CSWE Commission on Accreditation wants to know where each competency is being taught. For example, one competency relates to ethical decision-making. The program will describe what learning objectives within courses are related to ethical decision-making. In addition, the curriculum map will show what reading assignments are about ethical decision-making as well as what assignments allow students to practice ethical decision-making. Finally, the curriculum matrix will show how students are expected to integrate their field experiences related to ethical decision-making with what they've learned in the classroom—chances are this will be managed through seminar discussions, role plays, and assignments. In short, every reading and writing assignment you complete in social work courses plays a role in the curriculum map—so don't miss any of them!

Finally, in order to be accredited, the social work program must demonstrate that its students can carry out each of the social work competencies. You will do some of those in your field experience, where you'll be working with a master of social work (MSW)–level supervisor to identify tasks that will allow you to display those competencies. For instance, you and your supervisor may determine that you will conduct intakes with clients who are new to the agency in order to demonstrate that you are able to conduct social work assessment. How will you demonstrate your knowledge of the competencies in the classroom? You'll complete assignments, participate in role play scenarios, and take exams. Ultimately, your program will show that students who are ready to graduate are capable of demonstrating that they can carry out each of the following nine competencies (CSWE, 2015):

Competency 1: Demonstrate Ethical and Professional Behavior

For this first competency, you'll be able to show that you understand social work values. You also need to know about social welfare policy—the rules and regulations that govern practice—and how it affects practice at micro, mezzo, and macro levels. You'll have to demonstrate that you can carry out ethical decision-making without being overly swayed by your own values and to show that you are familiar enough with technology to be able to use it ethically in practice. You'll have to show that you are familiar with the social work profession: its history, mission, and the roles and responsibilities involved in social work. Finally, you'll have to show that you understand the importance of lifelong learning to a social worker and be willing to promise to engage in lifelong learning yourself.

Competency 2: Engage Diversity and Difference in Practice

To achieve the second competency, you'll have to be able to explain how human experience and identity are shaped by people's difference, or diversity. CSWE describes diversity as the way a number of areas of difference come together in people. These areas of difference include but are not limited to "age, class, color, culture, disability and ability, ethnicity, gender, gender identity and expression, immigration status, marital status, political ideology, race, religion/spirituality, sex, sexual orientation, and tribal sovereign status" (CSWE, 2015, p. 7). You'll need to understand that these areas of diversity may result in a continual uphill battle against poverty, oppression, and marginalization, or the pushing aside of whole groups of people when policies are being made. On the other hand, some differences in some settings result in power and "acclaim" (p. 7).

Competency 3: Advance Human Rights and Social, Economic, and Environmental Justice

By the time you graduate, you will need to understand the fundamental rights of every person, such as freedom, safety, privacy, an adequate standard of living, health care, and education. You will need to discuss the global interconnection of oppression and human rights violations. You'll also need to understand strategies used to promote social and economic justice and to eliminate oppressive structural barriers. You'll become aware of efforts to equitably distribute social goods, rights, and responsibilities so that civil, political, environmental, economic, social, and cultural human rights are protected.

Competency 4: Engage in Practice-Informed Research and Research-Informed Practice

Social workers understand quantitative (data are numbers) and qualitative (data are words) research methods and how they are used to evaluate practice and to advance the science of social work (practice-informed research). You need to know principles of logic, scientific inquiry, and culturally informed and ethical approaches to building social work practice knowledge. Social workers understand that evidence that informs practice derives from multidisciplinary sources and multiple ways of knowing. They also understand the processes for translating research findings into effective practice (research-informed practice).

Competency 5: Engage in Policy Practice

Social workers understand that human rights and social justice, as well as social welfare and services, are mediated by policy and its implementation at the federal, state, and local levels. Social workers understand the history and current structures of social policies and services, the role of policy in service delivery, and the role of practice in policy development. Social workers understand their role in policy development and implementation within their practice settings at the micro, mezzo, and macro levels, and they actively engage in policy practice to effect change within those settings. Social workers recognize and understand the historical, social, cultural, economic, organizational, environmental, and global influences that affect social policy. They are also knowledgeable about policy formulation, analysis, implementation, and evaluation.

Competency 6: Engage With Individuals, Families, Groups, Organizations, and Communities

Social workers understand that engagement is an ongoing component of the dynamic and interactive process of social work practice with, and on behalf of, diverse individuals, families, groups, organizations, and communities. Social workers value the **importance of human relationships**. Social workers understand theories of human behavior and the social environment and critically evaluate and apply this knowledge to facilitate engagement with clients and constituencies, including individuals, families, groups, organizations, and communities. Social workers understand strategies to engage diverse clients and constituencies to advance practice effectiveness. Social workers understand how their personal experiences and affective reactions may affect their ability to effectively engage with diverse clients and constituencies. Social workers value principles of relationship-building and interprofessional collaboration to facilitate engagement with clients, constituencies, and other professionals as appropriate.

Competency 7: Assess Individuals, Families, Groups, Organizations, and Communities

Social workers understand that assessment is an ongoing component of the dynamic and interactive process of social work practice with, and on behalf of, diverse individuals, families, groups, organizations, and communities. Social workers understand theories of human behavior and the social environment, and critically evaluate and apply this knowledge in the assessment of diverse clients and constituencies, including individuals, families, groups, organizations, and communities. Social workers understand methods of assessment with diverse clients and constituencies to advance practice effectiveness. Social workers recognize the implications of the larger practice context in the assessment process and value the importance of interprofessional collaboration in this process. Social workers understand how their personal experiences and emotional reactions may affect their assessment and decision-making.

Competency 8: Intervene With Individuals, Families, Groups, Organizations, and Communities

Social workers understand that implementation is an ongoing component of the dynamic and interactive process of social work practice with, and on behalf of, diverse individuals, families, groups, organizations, and communities. Social workers are knowledgeable about evidence-informed implementations to achieve the goals of clients and constituencies, including individuals, families, groups, organizations, and communities. Social workers understand theories of human behavior and the social environment and critically evaluate and apply this knowledge to effectively intervene with clients and constituencies. Social workers understand methods of identifying, analyzing, and implementing evidence-informed implementations to achieve client and constituency goals. Social workers value the importance of interprofessional teamwork and communication in implementations, recognizing that beneficial outcomes may require interdisciplinary, interprofessional, and interorganizational collaboration.

Competency 9: Evaluate Practice With Individuals, Families, Groups, Organizations, and Communities

Social workers understand that evaluation is an ongoing component of the dynamic and interactive process of social work practice with, and on behalf of, diverse individuals, families, groups, organizations, and communities. Social workers recognize the importance of evaluating processes and outcomes to advance practice, policy, and service delivery effectiveness. Social workers understand theories of human behavior and the social environment and critically evaluate and apply this knowledge in evaluating outcomes. Social workers understand qualitative and quantitative methods for evaluating outcomes and practice effectiveness.

Planned Change Process

Competencies 6 through 9 reflect important aspects of the planned change process, a way of understanding social work that has been widely accepted (e.g., see Kirst-Ashman & Hull, 2016). All generalist social work is accomplished in a process of planned change. In brief, the process consists of a number of stages that are what CSWE calls "dynamic and interactive"—that is, they all operate all of the time and constantly interact with each other. The stages are as follows:

- *Self-reflection*—Considering a worker's own characteristics and how they may influence their work with the client system
- *Engagement*—Connecting and building the professional helping relationship with individuals that are members of families, groups, organizations, communities, or institutions
- *Assessment*—Considering the client system's strengths, resources, and challenges, as well as any imbalance among environmental systems
- *Planning*—Creating and prioritizing goals for planned change in collaboration with client system representatives
- *Implementation*—Facilitating the realization of goals through consciously selected, evidence-based practices
- *Evaluation*—Measuring the success and sustainability of the planned change effort
- *Termination and follow-up*—Determining whether the change has been successfully sustained

The stages are central to planned change and therefore to generalist social work practice. They will be explored in depth in future chapters.

Social Work Terms Used Throughout the Text

Social workers have a language of their own. To communicate effectively with each other, we all need to understand basic terms. Next we'll consider some of the social work language you'll need to understand generalist practice. Each one will be elaborated more fully throughout the text.

Client—It is difficult to label the people we work with and on behalf of. In some agencies they are called persons served. In programs they are sometimes called participants. In medical settings, they are invariably called patients. Any of these can be used, although caution should be exercised when using *patients*, since the term implies someone is sick and needs to be cured. Here we'll use client since it is most widely used and doesn't seem to have a negative connotation. In addition, note that *client* may be used to indicate a person, family, group, institution, or community. For that reason the phrase **client system** may be used where clarity is needed. Likewise, individuals that we address on behalf of a client system may be referred to as client system representatives.

Micro practice—Micro practice is social work with individuals.

Mezzo practice—Mezzo practice is social work with small groups and families.

Macro practice—Macro practice is social work with organizations and communities.

Social work interview—This is any professional social work meeting—could be with a client or an individual client system representative that is a member of a family, small group, organization, or community. The social work interview can also be called a **social work session**.

Evidence-based practice—This is the use of a combination of empirical (that is, based on observation) studies, compilations of theory-based studies and practice wisdom to facilitate conscious choices related to aspects of the planned change process. Whenever possible, the client and worker collaborate to select evidence-based practices.

Note that the first part of this book is called **conceptual foundations**. A concept is part of a theory. For example, *energy* is a concept of the relativity theory that states $E = mc^2$. Likewise, *boundary* is a concept in general systems theory. (You'll learn more about this one later, but this text will *not* cover relativity theory.) So conceptual foundations means the use of concepts from many theories to form the base for social work practice. It's a reflection of our broad knowledge base.

The New Worker: Reflective Responses

When Marella first took the job at Thaddeus Stevens, she immediately asked about supervision and was told that there was no other social worker in the building and that she was to report to the school psychologist. In a near panic, Marella said, "N-no. I need a social worker." She had spoken out of sheer fright, but looking back on it, Marella realized she'd been stressing the uniqueness of social work and had been **advocating**, or working for change, on her own behalf. At the time, she was a brand-new social worker, and she knew that if she had thought it out in advance, she would never have been so assertive. It was an enormous relief when she was told that there was a seasoned social worker at another school in the district who could provide supervision. In no time, Mary, who had an MSW degree, agreed to meet with Marella once a week to talk about Marella's work, professional use of self, and any ethical dilemmas that might crop up.

After they'd been working together for some time, Marella confessed that she had been pretty blunt when she asked for supervision from a social worker. She told Mary the story of how they had ended up working together. In response, Mary asked her what she'd learned from that experience. After a moment, Marella said she had been surprised that she got what she wanted. It had been her first day on the job, and it still felt like she had issued a demand. She was still embarrassed by it too. Her supervisor pointed out that while she might have phrased it better, it was a reasonable, in fact a responsible, request. She had to push a bit to get Marella to the important part. "Was anyone angry? Did they tell you to leave? Did they refuse the request?" Marella finally got it. The take-home lesson was that you could ask for something for yourself and you just might get it. You could turn your nervous feelings into action. And once you could do that, you could advocate for your clients too. You could work with your clients, and you could work with aspects of their social environment too. Soon after, Marella came up with the idea of asking the principal about getting money for Snack. She never would have dreamt of it before.

CRITICAL THINKING AND COLLABORATIVE LEARNING EXERCISES 1.5

1. Consider Competency 3: Advance Human Rights and Social, Economic, and Environmental Justice. In a group, divide up the following terms and provide a definition for each: *social goods, social rights*, and *social responsibilities*. Discuss a more detailed description of Competency 3 based on your definitions.
2. In a small group, discuss the meaning of "between and among" in the context of diversity.

Section 1.6: Review and Apply

CONCURRENT CONSIDERATIONS IN GENERALIST PRACTICE

Ethical Challenge

When Marella asked to have supervision with a social worker, she was asking for scarce resources to be expended on her behalf. The district had to allow her supervisor and herself a full hour each week. During that hour, both of them could have been meeting with students. Since there were always more problems than hours, it was a sacrifice on the part of the school district. Do you agree with Marella's supervisor that it was still a responsible request? See whether the *NASW Code of Ethics* (NASW, 2018) can provide any direction for your answer. Take a look at Standard 2: Social Workers' Responsibilities to Colleagues.

Human Rights

Is anyone in Marella's case being deprived of any fundamental human rights such as freedom, safety, privacy, an adequate standard of living, health care, and education?

Evidence-Based Practice

Marella used group work to allow students to identify and express emotions. Is there evidence in the scientific literature to suggest that this is an evidence-based practice? (In other words, check to see whether there are any empirical studies that demonstrate the effectiveness of group work for encouraging emotional expression.) Should Marella modify her approach?

Policies Impacting Practice

Research your state's legal policies related to mandated reporting of child abuse. If Marella believed a student was the victim of abuse, under what circumstances would she be required by law to report it? Find out how to go about reporting child or elder abuse in your state.

Managing Diversity

Like many of her students, Marella is of Latina ethnicity. This is an important element of diversity that she and the students have in common. What are some of the things that make them different?

Multisystem Practice

Identify examples of Marella's work on all levels.

Micro: ____________________
Mezzo: ____________________
Macro: ____________________

Dynamic and Interactive Planned Change Stages

Identify the aspects of Marella's generalist social work practice where she was working in the following stages:

Self-Reflection: ____________________
Engagement: ____________________
Assessment: ____________________
Planning: ____________________
Implementation: ____________________
Evaluation: ____________________
Termination and Follow-Up: ____________________

Chapter Summary

Section 1.1: The Uniqueness of the Social Work Profession

Social work is a unique helping profession in that we work on three levels of practice simultaneously. We may work with an organization to create change, but in that process we will undoubtedly convene small groups and interview individuals. As social workers, we operate under a set of core professional values, ethical principles, and practice standards otherwise known as the *NASW Code of Ethics* (NASW, 2018). We build our foundation on our liberal arts education as well as training specific to social work, and we view our work and the world around us as a series of systems that interact, a perspective known as PIE.

Section 1.2: Generalist Social Work Practice

Generalist social work practice is a form of professional helping that is conducted within an organization and with the guidance of a code of ethics. Social workers work with individuals. Individuals are part of families, groups, organizations, communities, and institutions. We work toward empowering those individuals and creating an environment where we are all granted the opportunity to reach our fullest potential.

Section 1.3: Characteristics of Generalist Social Work Practice

Generalist social work practice has four basic characteristics. Social workers have a broad knowledge base that consists of a liberal arts foundation and specialized social work education. Generalist practitioners employ a strengths perspective to view people and look to the person, their aspects of diversity, and their environment to supply the resources needed for change. Generalist practitioners also focus on the organizational context of practice, making note of the agency policies that influence them and their work. Finally, practitioners focus on social, economic, and environmental justice and work toward a society where resources are available to all people in an equitable way.

Section 1.4: Historical Development of Social Work

The social work profession is often thought of as having two methods for practice: (1) micro level, or direct work with people; and (2) macro work, or work with organizations, communities, and institutions. Since the generalist practitioner works on micro and macro levels simultaneously, generalist social work practice is well placed to provide unity for social work.

Section 1.5: Social Work Competencies

Social workers are all capable of demonstrating skills and knowledge of nine basic practice areas, or competencies: carrying out ethical and professional behavior; engaging diversity in practice; advancing human rights and social, economic, and environmental justice; engaging in practice-informed research and research-informed practice; engaging in policy practice; engaging, assessing, intervening, and evaluating with individuals, families, groups, organizations, and communities.

Recommended Websites

National Association of Social Workers (NASW): www.socialworkers.org

NASW Pioneers: www.naswfoundation.org/pioneers

National Association of Social Workers Career Choices: http://www.socialworkers.org/pubs/choices/default.asp

Council on Social Work Education (CSWE): www.cswe.org

International Federation of Social Workers: www.ifsw.org

Playworks Game Library: https://www.playworks.org/game-library

Critical Terms for Introduction to Generalist Social Work

social work 4
service 5
integrity 5
competence 5
dignity and worth of the person 5
person-in-environment (PIE) 6
systems 7
multisystem practice (MSP) 7
professional use of self 7
social justice 8
human rights 8
generalist social work practice 8
micro practice 10
mezzo practice 10
macro practice 10
clients 11
client system representatives 11
empowerment 12
social injustice 13
socially just environment 13
sustainable 13
homeostasis 13
diversity 15
strengths perspective 15
informal resources 15
social welfare 15
social, economic, and environmental justice 15
importance of human relationships 26
client system 27
social work session 28
conceptual foundations 28
advocating 28

Generalist Practice Curriculum Matrix With 2015 Educational Policy and Accreditation Standards

Chapter 1

Competency	Course	Course Content	Dimensions
Competency 1: Demonstrate Ethical and Professional Behavior		1.1. Explain the differences between social work and other helping professions, including the person-in-environment (PIE) perspective. 1.2. Recall the definition of generalist social work practice. 1.3. Explain the attributes of generalist social work practice. 1.4. Describe the role of generalist practice in the social work profession. 1.5. Paraphrase the competencies common to all social workers, and recall the stages of planned change. Feature 3: Self-Reflection Feature 4: Concurrent Considerations in Generalist Practice	Knowledge Values Knowledge Values Knowledge Values Knowledge Knowledge Skills Cognitive–affective processes Skills
Competency 2: Engage Diversity and Difference in Practice		Feature 1: Focus on Diversity Feature 4: Concurrent Considerations in Generalist Practice	Skills Cognitive–affective processes Skills Cognitive–affective processes
Competency 3: Advance Human Rights and Social, Economic, and Environmental Justice		Feature 4: Concurrent Considerations in Generalist Practice	Skills Cognitive–affective processes
Competency 4: Engage in Practice-Informed Research and Research-Informed Practice		Feature 4: Concurrent Considerations in Generalist Practice	Skills Cognitive–affective processes
Competency 5: Engage in Policy Practice		Feature 4: Concurrent Considerations in Generalist Practice	Skills Cognitive–affective processes
Competency 6: Engage With Individuals, Families, Groups, Organizations, and Communities		Feature 4: Concurrent Considerations in Generalist Practice	Skills Cognitive–affective processes
Competency 7: Assess Individuals, Families, Groups, Organizations, and Communities		Feature 4: Concurrent Considerations in Generalist Practice	Skills Cognitive–affective processes
Competency 8: Intervene With Individuals, Families, Groups, Organizations, and Communities		Feature 4: Concurrent Considerations in Generalist Practice	Skills Cognitive–affective processes
Competency 9: Evaluate Practice With Individuals, Families, Groups, Organizations, and Communities		Feature 4: Concurrent Considerations in Generalist Practice	Skills Cognitive–affective processes

References

Addams, J. (1930). *The second twenty years at Hull House*. New York, NY: Macmillan.

Agnew, E. N. (2004). *From charity to social work: Mary E. Richmond and the creation of an American profession*. Chicago: University of Illinois Press.

American Sociological Association. (n.d.). E. *Franklin Frazier*. Retrieved from http://www.asanet.org/about-asa/asa-story/asa-history/past-asa-officers/past-asa-presidents/e-franklin-frazier

Barzun, J. (2000). *From dawn to decadence: 500 years of Western cultural life*. New York, NY: HarperCollins.

Council on Social Work Education. (2015). *Educational policy and accreditation standards*. Alexandria, VA: Author. Retrieved from http://www.cswe.org/File.aspx?id=81660

Fox, R. (2013). *The call to teach: Philosophy, process, and pragmatics of social work education*. Alexandria, VA: Council on Social Work Education.

Frances Perkins Center. (n.d.). Her life: The woman behind the New Deal. Retrieved from http://francesperkinscenter.org/life-new

Franklin, D. L. (1986). Richmond and Addams: From moral certainty to rational inquiry in social work practice. *Social Service Review, 60*(4), 504–525.

Gasker, J., & Fischer, A. (2014). Toward a context-specific definition of social justice for social work: In search of overlapping consensus. *Journal of Social Work Values and Ethics, 11*(1), 42–53.

Howard University. (n.d.). E. Franklin Frazier's life & works. Retrieved from https://socialwork.howard.edu/centers/frazier-center/e-franklin-fraziers-life-works

Joslin, K. (2004). *Jane Addams: A writer's life*. Chicago: University of Illinois Press.

Karls, J. M., & Wandrei, K. E. (1994). *Person-in-environment system: The PIE classification for social functioning problems*. Washington, DC: National Association of Social Workers.

Kirst-Ashman, K., & Hull, G. (2016). *Understanding generalist practice* (8th ed.). Boston, MA: Cengage.

Mizrahi, T., & Davis, L. (2008). *The encyclopedia of social work* (20th ed.). London, England: Oxford University Press.

Murdoch, A. D. (2011). Richmond and the image of social work. *Social Work, 56*(1), 92–94.

National Association of Social Workers. (n.d.). Dorothy Height. Retrieved from http://www.naswfoundation.org/pioneers/h/height.htm

National Association of Social Workers. (2018). *NASW code of ethics*. Washington, DC: NASW Press.

Payton-Stewart, L. (2017). Marie Woolfolk Taylor (ca. 1890–1960). *New Georgia Encyclopedia*.

Pumphrey, M. W. (1959). *The teaching of values and ethics in social work education*. New York, NY: Council on Social Work Education. doi:10.1093/acrefore/9780199975839.013.829

Reamer, F. G. (2013). Ethics and values. In C. Franklin (Ed.), *Encyclopedia of social work*. Alexandria, VA: NASW Press.

Richmond, M. (2012). *Social diagnosis*. Retrieved from www.forgottenbooks.org. (Original work published 1917)

Saleebey, D. (1996). The strengths perspective in social work practice: Extensions and cautions. *Social Work*, (41)*3*, 296–305.

Saleebey, D. (2013). *The strengths perspective in social work practice* (6th ed.). Upper Saddle River, NJ: Pearson.

The Eleanor Roosevelt Papers Project. (n.d.). Harry Lloyd Hopkins. Retrieved from https://www2.gwu.edu/~erpapers/teachinger/glossary/hopkins-harry.cfm

U.S. Department of Health and Human Services. (n.d.). About CAPTA: A legislative history. In *Child welfare information gateway*. Retrieved on September 1, 2015 from https://www.childwelfare.gov/pubs/factsheets/about

Witkin, S. L., & Saleebey, D. (2007). *Social work dialogues: Transforming the canon in inquiry, practice, and education*. Alexandria, VA: Council on Social Work Education.

Recommended Readings

Addams, J. (1930). *The second twenty years at Hull House*. New York, NY: Macmillan.

Reamer, F. G. (2013). Ethics and values. In C. Franklin (Ed.), *Encyclopedia of social work*. Alexandria, VA: NASW Press.

Sinclair, U. (1906/2004). *The jungle*. Retrieved from http://www.pagebypagebooks.com/Upton_Sinclair/The_Jungle

United Nations. (1948). *Universal declaration of human rights*. New York, NY: Author. Retrieved from http://www.un.org/en/universal-declaration-human-rights

2 Multisystem Practice

This chapter continues the format of Chapter 1, beginning with a case study that is infused throughout the chapter. It highlights the simultaneous target of a number of systems and system interactions for change in every social work activity. The conceptual framework for generalist practice is explored in more depth as it directly relates to the interaction among systems. The underlying processes—beginnings, middles, and endings—in generalist practice are further developed. In addition, the potential for strength in diversity is reinforced as students begin to recognize personal characteristics as they influence work with a variety of target systems and interactions.

Learning Objectives

2.1 Describe the theoretical and conceptual framework related to multisystem practice (MSP).

2.2 Interpret the dynamic and interactive nature of the stages of planned change.

2.3 Discuss the dynamics of beginnings in the planned change process.

2.4 Explore an in-depth meaning of diversity and its impact on the worker–client interaction.

Case Study: Looking for Strengths

©iStock.com/Kritchanut

Work in inpatient behavioral health settings requires interprofessional collaboration.

Ling didn't slam the phone down exactly, but she did firmly place the receiver in its cradle, closed her eyes, and bit her lip hard. She had been trying to get an extension of insurance coverage for Ralph, but she had been unsuccessful in having additional days approved. Ralph was a 54-year-old European American client of hers at New Horizons, an inpatient facility for people with mental health concerns. Ling knew Ralph well. He had been at the facility a number of times since Ling started her job as a behavioral health social worker. Ralph was diagnosed with bipolar disorder. That meant Ralph would spend weeks, even months, able to work and share meaningful relationships with friends and relatives. Inevitably, though, Ralph would come to a point where he would lose all interest in his usual activities, would start spending increasing amounts of money, and soon after would feel as if he could not afford his medications. Without his medications, he would predictably become unable to sleep and be so irritable as to alienate his coworkers and friends. This time he nearly lost his job, only salvaging a bad situation by taking a few days off. After that, he reached out for help.

When Ralph arrived this time at New Horizons, Ling was running group that day, trying to help the program participants share their feelings and get support from their peers. She worked with each person, in turn, saying, "It's your turn . . . what would you like to share today?" She learned that Ralph was really suffering. He said he hadn't slept in 5 days, and the bright lights and the "screaming loud" voices where clients gathered in the common room were driving him up the wall. Later, Ling had time to meet with Ralph in his room. As Ralph sat on his bed talking to Ling, she watched him violently twist a corner of the sheet until it curled around on itself and then drop it, hopelessly, onto his lap.

Just 3 days after his admission, Ralph was taking four different medications, one in the morning, two at night, and the fourth only when he needed it—like when he found himself shouting "SHUT UP" at the other residents while they sat talking quietly. Even though she was used to these combinations of medications, it still struck Ling as a lot of drugs. But she couldn't deny that he suffered badly without them. On this third day, Ralph felt so much better he was able to play a constructive role in the social work group. Ling was running group again that day, and she was thrilled to hear him say he slept the whole night before. In group, he also said he was afraid he would be discharged soon. He had had an argument with his sister just before he was hospitalized, and she told him he couldn't stay with her any longer. Unfortunately, his public assistance insurance only covered the initial 3-day stay at New Horizons without a reauthorization, and that had just been denied.

On this first day of feeling better, Ralph was able to begin planning and was worried he wouldn't have a place to stay. He was also concerned about feeling stable before he returned to work. He was on a 2-week leave, and he wanted to be sure that he was feeling calm before he faced the stress of his job. Ling wished with all her heart that she could have a couple more days with Ralph. In their individual sessions, they planned to work on budgeting so that Ralph wouldn't find himself without the necessary copay for his medications at the end of the month. They also discussed the possibility of getting family members in for a family social work session to resolve family issues and hopefully get Ralph a place to stay with relatives. Ling and Ralph planned to role-play conversations with his boss so that Ralph could mend fences when he went back to work. But there wouldn't be time for any of this. Ralph would be discharged tomorrow, possibly without a place to stay. Ling hated to think that she might be working just to get him a room in a single room occupancy home knowing that he would most likely be back in the facility in a few months. She resolved to call the insurance company one more time to try to get reauthorization for a couple more days. She knew what she had to do first. She had to go around to all of the staff: the nurses, the psychiatrist, the overnight workers, and her supervisor to see whether she could find something that would provide a rationale to get Ralph a longer stay. To make it work, she had to encourage them all to describe Ralph's behavior in the worst possible light. Did he seem depressed? Was he combative? Did he describe any hallucinations? Maybe suicidal ideations? She hated that part, because she had to encourage everyone to see Ralph in the worst possible light. She would have a hard job later to help them all see Ralph's strengths. She vowed to do it.

Section 2.1: Theory in Social Work

Sometimes social work is complex. As social workers manage difficult situations like Ling's, they draw on the science of the profession to find solutions. We begin this chapter with foundation knowledge related to the influence of theory and theoretical concepts on generalist practice. Since some of the concepts are multifaceted, they'll be stated more than once in different ways to make them easier to digest. We begin with a definition of *theory*.

Definition of *Theory*

All of social work is based on theory. In general, theories have a number of basic characteristics. A theory attempts to explain some observable occurrence. It describes that occurrence by putting together ideas in logical ways. A theory can also predict future occurrences. To test a theory, people often make observations to see whether the theory's predictions are correct. Specifically, theories do as follows:

- Select and define concepts and constructs.
- Explain why the concepts were chosen.
- Put together concepts to form constructs.
- Describe the relationships between constructs.
- Predict how the constructs may be expected to relate to each other.

A theory is all about how we humans try to understand our world. In an attempt to look more carefully at theories, Kerlinger and Lee (1999) suggest that a theory should have four characteristics:

1. Select and Define Concepts and Constructs

Concepts are a way of talking about issues and everyday experiences (Langer & Lietz, 2015). They are labels for observations and ideas. We use them to express ideas that could be part of a theory. Constructs are combinations of related concepts that are the first building blocks of theory. For example, social systems theory suggests that concepts such as **system** and **energy** come together in such constructs as **system interaction**. We might say that Ralph and his family members are a system and New Horizons is a system. As these systems interact, Ralph provides energy in the form of the insurance payment for service. In return, as Ralph and his family interact with New Horizons, they receive energy in the form of social work and psychiatric and medical services. (There will be more on systems theory later.)

2. Explain Why the Principal Constructs Were Chosen

Since we can choose any concepts and constructs that can be imagined, the theory must explain why its particular concepts and constructs have been chosen. In social systems theory, constructs such as system interaction are selected in an effort to explain human behavior because they can reflect biological, psychological, and social qualities. As a single system, Ralph is an individual with biological, psychological, and social characteristics. His biological and psychological attributes are affected as they interact with the psychiatrist who prescribes medications. The psychologist at New Horizons affects his psychological attributes, and his social worker, Ling, affects his psychological and social attributes as she interacts with him and his family. Ling has resolved to learn more about the biological component of bipolar disorder. This way, she will have some more comprehensive knowledge about Ralph's **biopsychosocial** being.

3. Describe How the Constructs Relate to One Another

A theory describes the relationships among the constructs that have been identified and selected as important. This description is known as a **principle**. Flowing from constructs like system interaction are principles such as this: Systems are by their nature both part and whole (Carter, 2011). In other words, social systems theory explains that Ralph is a whole system, but he is also part of other systems such as his family and his workplace.

4. Describe How They May Be Expected to Relate in the Future

Theories make predictions. For example, social systems theory suggests human and social systems exchange energy in an effort to maintain themselves as they are (Carter, 2011). As we've seen, Ralph and New Horizons are two systems that exchange energy. When Ling does her job well, she helps Ralph create even more energy through new skills that make him more independent and able to live on his own for longer and longer periods of time. In this way, the two systems actually create more energy than they had before interacting. As these related systems came together and exchanged energy, additional energy was created . . . a process known in social systems theory as **synergy**. *The concept of energy is part of the construct of social interaction, which is part of the principle of synergy.* See Figure 2.1.

FIGURE 2.1 ● Relationships Among the Components of Theory

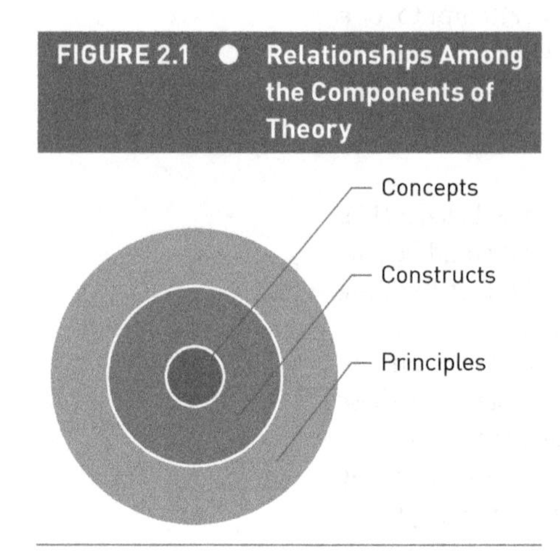

Multisystem Practice: A Model of Human Systems Interaction

A model is a way of implementing theory. Multisystem practice (MSP) is a model. It is built on a foundation of well-known theories and their concepts, constructs, and principles. The MSP model can be used to guide generalist social work practice otherwise known as the generalist implementation model (GIM).

General systems theory (von Bertalanffy, 1933/1962) along with social systems theory (Carter, 2011) serve as foundations for the MSP model. Social systems theory, as mentioned previously, builds on general systems theory. Using concepts like energy and systems, along with principles like synergy, makes the theory relate specifically to people's interactions. Once principles are developed, people may choose them to influence their viewpoint. That viewpoint is called a perspective. The GIM is built on four perspectives, or viewpoints, specific to generalist social work practice that are particularly important to the MSP model (see Figure 2.2). They are the person-in-environment (PIE) perspective (Karls & Wandrei, 1994); the family-in-environment (FIE) perspective (Gasker & Vafeas, 2010); the ecological perspective (Carter, 2011); and the strengths perspective in social work practice (Saleebey, 1996).

The GIM is implemented through social work skills informed by social work values on the micro, mezzo, and macro levels. GIM also includes the planned change process introduced earlier. Finally, the GIM includes the principle of PIE that we discussed in Chapter 1 (Kirst-Ashman & Hull, 2016; see Figure 2.3).

FIGURE 2.2 ● Perspectives Underlying the Generalist Implementation Model

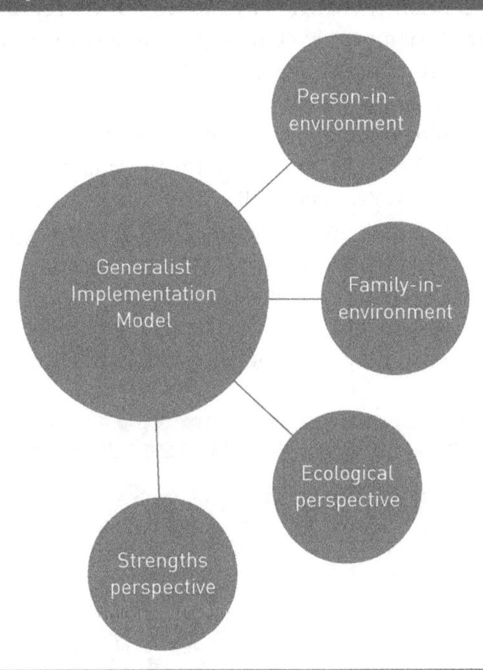

MSP builds on and enhances the GIM. The MSP model holds that humans in all sized systems are *always* affecting and being affected by multiple societal systems in their efforts to meet their needs. Most importantly, all systems affect one another with input and output all *at the same time*. Consequently, Ralph interacts with his family; he interacts with New Horizons; his family interacts with New Horizons; New Horizons interacts with the insurance company, affecting Ralph and his family; Ling interacts with New Horizons, Ralph, Ralph's family, her coworkers, her own family, and so forth. It is important to note that all of these system interactions happen *at the same time*. As a result, the social worker may target any one of those systems or interactions. For example, Ling planned to intervene in the insurance company system as it interacted with the agency. This affects Ralph, of course, but the insurance company and its interaction with the agency is the **target** for her implementations. She'll focus a part of her work there, rather than directly with Ralph.

It makes sense to say that the MSP model suggests that in order to understand a person or group of people, we might take a snapshot of all of the system interactions at one particular moment, and we might put our efforts into any of the system interactions.

Origins of the Multisystem Practice Concepts and Constructs

From General Systems Theory We've begun a discussion of general systems theory. Let's continue it. General systems theory was originally a theory developed by a natural scientist to establish a new branch of science that would connect all forms of living things (von Bertalanffy, 1933/1962). (He was successful; his work supported modern biological theory.)

General systems theory states that living organisms are systems, or functional units, often made up of two or more related elements: an atom or a molecule can be a system; your liver is a system; your class is a system. These systems are organized in hierarchical order: atom, molecule, cell, organ, organism, person, family, group, organization, community. The systems' parts relate to each other mutually so that one affects all. Systems are not static; they are constantly changing by exchanging energy. Each system is a **holon**, both a whole and a part. Systems could be thought of as looking inward to their own parts as they look outward to parts of other systems (Carter, 2011). So think of systems as holons: both part and whole. Each holon has boundaries. The **boundaries** around a system are more or less permeable, allowing more or less of an energy exchange. Even though forces in the environment may disturb systems, they try to remain in balance. This process is known as **homeostasis**. As we've seen earlier, two or more systems exchanging energy may create more energy than each one had separately: The sum is greater than its parts (von Bertalanffy, 1933/1962). This is also known as synergy. In short, general systems theory states that systems exchange energy to maintain themselves and that during that exchange of energy even more energy can be produced. That is the synergy that can be used to add energy to client systems when they work together with available resources.

FIGURE 2.3 • Features of the Generalist Implementation Model

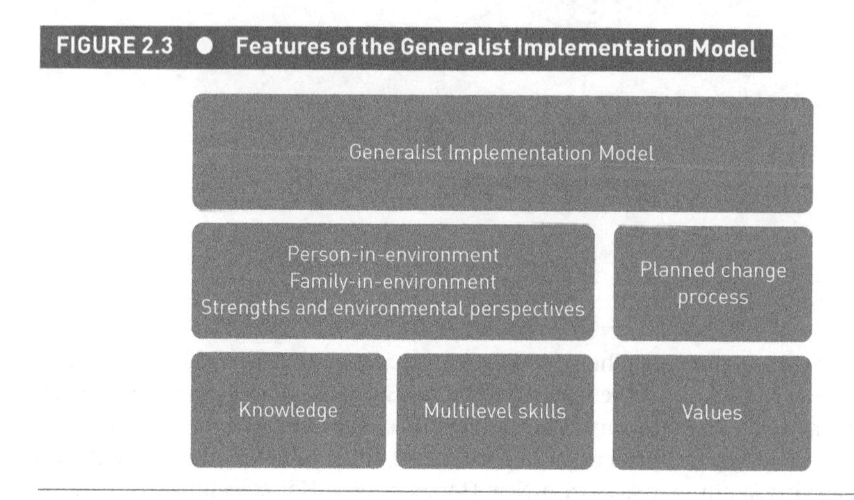

Consider a deer in the forest. The forest system provides the deer food. The deer's organs work together to create energy. The deer maintains its steady state and produces waste that ends up in the forest. The forest uses the waste to fertilize new growth, and the well-fed deer becomes pregnant . . . more energy than either had alone.

On the other hand, systems may interact and lose energy. When the interactions between systems are off balance, one system can be drained in favor of another. In this situation, new energy is not created. In fact, one system is sacrificed in favor of the other. The other system may lose energy continuously, leading eventually to a state where the system outputs more energy than it inputs. This state is called **entropy**. To use our forest example, think of a situation where a small forest surrounds a house. The homeowners meticulously rake up all of the leaves for their compost pile. They like the look of a park, so they trim new growth and kill the weeds. The ground is bare, so the deer seek greener pastures. There are few places for small animals and birds to hide, so they leave as well. Eventually, as trees get old and die they will not be replaced. If the homeowners want a forest, they'll have to institute a process called **negative entropy** (Carter, 2011). When negative entropy occurs, the disintegrating process of entropy is reversed with the infusion of new energy. In the case of our forest, the homeowners will have to go to the trouble and expense of planting more trees. In very simple human terms, you might think of a family where the main wage earner passes away. Our social safety net, in this case, Social Security benefits for survivors, will add energy to keep the system from falling into entropy.

Important concepts and constructs in the MSP model have been borrowed from general systems theory and social systems theory and bear repeating here. They are as follows:

System—A system is a functional unit often consisting of two or more elements that are related (Langer & Lietz, 2015); Any system is, by definition, part and whole.

Holon—This is a description of a system as both part and whole, facing both inward to its own parts and outward to the systems of which it is a part (Carter, 2011).

Interconnectedness—Change in any part of a system changes all of the systems and parts of systems is **interconnectedness** (Langer & Lietz, 2015).

Synergy—Exchanges of energy lead to increase in energy in living systems. Energy is not just added but compounded when systems interact (Carter, 2011).

Social Systems Theory Social systems theory is a form of general systems theory. Social systems theory applies general systems theory to social science as well as natural science (Carter, 2011). In this way, general systems theory can be expanded to be more comprehensive. At the same time, the social interactions of humans are specifically introduced and become the focus of the theory.

A boundary is an imaginary demarcation between systems. When systems interact, one does not subsume the other. Instead, they interact by exchanging energy. Boundaries are more or less permeable depending on the characteristics of the system. Some permeability is good so that energy can be exchanged. Too much permeability leaves the system vulnerable to be gobbled up by another system. On the other hand, too little permeability leads to isolation and the entropy we discussed previously. Let's consider an example. Consider a family with a very, very strong boundary. The house is isolated; the children are schooled at home. There is relatively little opportunity to exchange, and therefore create, energy. Let's say one child develops a behavior problem. This system will have a tendency to lose energy managing that problem. The system may enter entropy with the child having additional problems and the parents developing increasing stress. The stress can lead to marital conflict, affecting all of the children. All of the children begin to perform poorly academically . . . and so on. This is an example of entropy. Now, let's say the family has an ability to open its boundaries enough to accept help. Extended family members stop by to help with housework and homeschooling. A social worker begins helping the child with behavioral problems. All of the children thrive academically. The parents expand their social circle, allowing the children to have increased social contact with other children. Synergy emerges.

Important concepts and constructs from social systems theory build on those of general systems theory because they put humans and their functioning in the social environment into the general systems theory. In other words, social systems theory is a form of general systems theory that includes uniquely human elements.

Other concepts that bear repeating are as follows:

Social system—The **social system** consists of persons or groups (Carter, 2011).

Energy—Energy is an element of all systems that is shared with and exchanged between all other systems. Atoms, molecules, and social systems are composed of energy. In social systems, energy includes both information and resources shared among people; it is the system's capacity for action and its power to effect change. Energy transfers occur in exchanges, back and forth (Carter, 2011).

Boundaries—Boundaries are demarcations between two or more systems that allow us to observe relationships between systems (Langer & Lietz, 2015). Boundaries are more or less dense, or capable of exchanging energy at different rates (Carter, 2011). A boundary that is very dense and exchanges very little energy will be less inclined to create synergy.

Ecological Perspective

Again, a perspective is a way of viewing concepts, constructs, and principles. The ecological perspective grows out of social systems and general systems theory. Its main contribution to social work practice is that it focuses on action. In other words, it highlights the interactions among systems. For that reason, it is important to consider some of the concepts that are key to the ecological perspective.

Ecological concepts relevant to the MSP model include **transactions**, meaning that interactions among systems are active and dynamic, always changing; **input** and **output**, referring to the energy exchange among systems; and **coping**, or changes in systems as they adapt to changing environments (Kirst-Ashman & Hull, 2016). These are terms that help us to describe the way we use our understanding of systems in our work.

The Person-in-Environment Perspective

Given the micro, mezzo, and macro focus of social work practice, the PIE model was created as a classification system to facilitate the identification of persons' problems in living (Karls & Wandrei, 1994). The purpose of the development of PIE was to create a way to understand social work clients (individuals, families, groups, organizations, and communities) so that their needs could be identified. While the classification has some drawbacks, including a lack of focus on the strengths and resources that client systems bring to the helping process, it did have an enormous impact on the profession of social work. The result of the development of PIE was a new way of considering the interactions between persons and the social systems that surround them. In that way, PIE facilitated development of a language that unites all social workers. All social workers understand that people interact with the systems that surround them. Likewise, any professional social worker will recognize PIE; it is identified as central to the profession by the Council on Social Work Education (CSWE, 2015).

Concepts and constructs important to MSP because of their development of knowledge related to environmental systems are as follows:

Environment—This term refers to the **physical environment**, small groups, the community, and other large systems, including social environment. The social institutions in the PIE classification system include "public assistance, health . . . economic support services, religious institutions" (Karls & Wandrei, 1994, p. 15).

Interaction—According to PIE, people interact with systems and in that **interaction** problems in living can emerge. PIE identifies a number of types of interactional difficulties: power, ambivalence, responsibility, dependency, loss, isolation, and victimization. It is the work of the social worker to determine where the interactional disruption is occurring. It is important to note that PIE helps us to see problems at the site of interactions. In that way, we don't blame the person for their problems.

While some of the PIE system is less than useful, particularly its focus on pathology rather than strengths, the previously given concepts are important to the MSP model since they describe the way human systems relate to each other and focus many social work implementations outside of the person. The PIE perspective is one reason social workers are different than such professionals as psychologists, counselors, and psychiatrists. We are always looking at both the individual and the environment to locate the focus of our change efforts.

The Family-in-Environment Perspective

Since the dawn of the profession, social workers have recognized the value of the family (Richmond, 1917). Recently, though, family-centered practice has influenced generalist practice, and generalist practice has influenced family practice. So family-centered practice no longer means working with the family along with the individual. Family-centered practice literally places the family in the center of practice—not a particular family, but Family as a social institution. What that means is that policy development, research design, and program evaluation, as well as practice methods, can all have a family focus. Here is a way that family-centered research may inform practice: If a social worker evaluates the effectiveness of a substance abuse treatment facility, they are likely to measure the length of time clients remain sober. If they take the FIE perspective, they will measure how well the clients fill the roles—such as provider, mother, or father—that they occupy in their families. If that is part of the evaluation, the agency is likely to look closely at their policies related to work with clients' families. They may increase the involvement families have in individual clients' change processes. For an example of family-centered policy-making, consider that some programs only allow social workers to meet with individuals. Others are more family-centered and encourage family meetings in addition to worker–client ones.

A main component of FIE is the idea that people can define their own families. Families can be built around formal and informal adoptive relationships, same gender relationships, multigenerational relationships . . . according to the FIE perspective, even friends can create a family. This viewpoint works with PIE in that it reinforces the idea that individuals and systems interact to create energy in countless ways. Our research, policy, and practice as generalist social workers reflect this theoretical base.

Concepts and constructs important to FIE are as follows:

Family—This is one way of organizing individuals. The identification of **family** members is constructed by society and by individuals, and that identification is not always the same (Briar-Lawson, Lawson, & Hennon, 2001; Butterfield, Rocha, & Butterfield, 2010). It is best for families if they are encouraged to define their own members.

Family-centered policies and practices—With **family-centered policies and practices**, families are partners for program development, implementation, and evaluation; practices are family focused, with household management, budgeting, and relationship with other systems highlighted in a way that is consistent with the needs of individual families (Briar-Lawson et al., 2001; Butterfield et al., 2010). There will be detailed discussion on FIE in later chapters.

ETHICAL PERSPECTIVES

Take a look at the back cover of the NASW Code of Ethics *(National Association of Social Workers [NASW], 2018). You'll find a statement of the mission of the social work profession. How do these theories fit with that statement? Do you see any overlap?*

Generalist Social Work Practice

Next, we expand on the meaning of generalist social work practice since generalist social work practice is part of the foundation of the MSP perspective. Generalist practice grows logically out of general systems theory and social systems theory. As we've already discussed, practitioners work with individuals, families, groups, organizations, and communities.

The CSWE defines generalist social work practice as follows:

> Generalist practice is grounded in the liberal arts and the PIE framework. To promote human and social well-being, generalist practitioners use a range of prevention and implementation methods in their practice with diverse individuals, families, groups, organizations, and communities based on scientific inquiry and best practices. The generalist practitioner identifies with the social work profession and applies ethical principles and critical thinking in practice at the micro, mezzo, and macro levels. Generalist practitioners engage diversity in their practice and advocate for human rights and social and economic justice. They recognize, support, and build on the strengths and resiliency of all human beings. They engage in research-informed practice and are proactive in responding to the impact of context on professional practice. The baccalaureate program in social work prepares students for generalist practice. (CSWE, 2015, p. 11)

Generalist social work practice places a focus on work with systems of all sizes: individuals, families, groups, communities, and organizations. This important focus results in three concepts critical to the MSP model, which are **micro, mezzo, and macro systems**.

Micro systems are typically considered to be individuals. Mezzo systems are those in between: family and small groups. Macro systems may include large social institutions as well as community and agency organizations.

Sustainability, Globalization, and Meta Level Practice

We live in a world where people in almost every area of the globe can communicate as a global family. This enables social change in that it allows for the quick communication that can facilitate protests and even revolutions. It also enables global trade and the sharing of culture across nations that is known as **globalization** (Briar-Lawson et al., 2001). Finally, this worldwide communication allows us to see where resources, like clean water, exist and where they are needed. With that insight, we can begin to see the importance of considering the **physical environment** as a system that affects all people. As a result, it has come to the attention of social work scholars that sustainability of global resources is a significant concern of all social workers (Griese-Owens, Miller, & Owens, 2014). This insight effectively adds a level to the existing micro, mezzo, macro view: the meta level of practice. **Meta practice** is known as the consideration of "global social aspects that both overarch and interact with macro, mezzo, and micro practice" (Griese-Owens, et al., 2014, p. 47). Meta practice brings the **sustainability**, or homeostasis, of several institutions: economic, environmental, and cultural, to our worldview and affects our practice in that we don't forget to add the physical environment to our assessment of client situations to find strengths and challenges in the physical environment. In this way, we can identify **environmental racism** (Taylor, 2014) where it occurs. An example of environmental racism is where toxins in the physical environment occur more often and more seriously in areas where the most vulnerable people live. These areas can be nations or cities or apartment complexes. For example, countries that are economically developing are often subject to environmental racism, such as China's air pollution problem. Air pollution also exists in American communities near highways and in the tightly packed apartments in inner cities.

We are aware of this last case because we know that asthma is more common in children in urban settings. It is important to add this perspective to the MSP model so that the impact of the environment is considered by all social workers. The slogan "Think globally, act locally" effectively summarizes the perspective for social work practice (Briar-Lawson et al., 2001, p. 157). Generalist practitioners often begin at the local level and observe how their efforts can transform systems for social justice on the global level.

Foundations of Multisystem Practice Model

The previously given theories, perspectives, and models build on each other and come together to provide the foundation for the MSP model (see Figure 2.4).

Principles of Multisystem Practice

The principles of the MSP model are informed by concepts, constructs, principles, and perspectives from general systems theory, social systems theory, generalist social work practice models, and the strengths perspective of social work practice. Flowing from these concepts are the principles of the MSP model that describe how the concepts interact and predict the impacts that systems have on individuals:

1. *All systems interact simultaneously on the micro, mezzo, macro, and meta levels.*
2. *Systems may include individuals, families, groups, organizations, communities, and the physical environment.*
3. *Even energy exchange is positive because it results in additional energy.*
4. *As they strive to maintain their characteristics, all systems have resources and resiliency.*
5. *Cultural humility and the celebration of diversity can facilitate the identification of resources.*
6. *Uneven energy exchange among any of the systems can point to a need to increase energy in that interaction through the addition of resources.*
7. *To facilitate positive change, relevant systems, their interactions, and aspects of diversity, as well as existing resources must be identified to bring strength for change and resiliency.*

FIGURE 2.4 ● Multisystem Practice Model

Multisystem Practice Model

Person-in-environment perspective
Family-in-environment perspective
Meta-system perspective

Strengths perspective

General systems theory

Social systems theory

Ecological theory

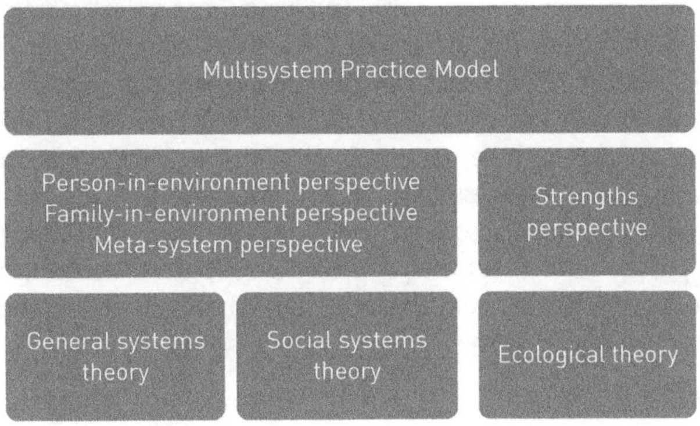

CRITICAL THINKING AND COLLABORATIVE LEARNING EXERCISES 2.1

1. Work with a partner to identify 10 examples of living systems. How does each change to adapt to its environment?
2. Identify five systems that intersect with your life. These could include school, friends, the physical environment, your family, your academic adviser, a landlord, and more. With a partner, identify 10 for each of you.

Section 2.2: The Planned Change Process

As we've said, general systems theory, social systems theory, the ecological theory, the strengths perspective, PIE, FIE, and the meta-practice perspective come together in the MSP model. We've mentioned briefly that there are eight interactive stages of a planned change process in MSP. This section further develops that idea. It is important to note that, like system interactions, each of the stages occurs all of the time.

Stage 1: Self-Reflection

This first stage of planned change begins with the social worker themselves. It is about getting ready to meet the client by taking a look at a number of characteristics about yourself. You think about your areas of diversity and how your diversity might affect the way you approach your client. In other words, you consider how you as a unique individual will respond to the person you're working with. How will your characteristics, values, and skills come together when you are face-to-face with your client, client system, or client system representative? MSP suggests that you assess the systems around you as you think about your own strengths and limitations, feelings, and thoughts. These considerations will serve to make you aware of your actions so that you can behave in an intentional, professional way. Like all of the stages, you will visit self-reflection again and again throughout the planned change process. This stage will be covered in depth in Chapter 4.

Stage 2: Engagement

Engagement has to do with two systems coming together creating a shared space that interacts with other systems in unique ways. Engagement is a meeting of hearts and minds. It requires careful planning, or **preparatory empathy**, and it requires a serious attempt to see the world the way another person sees it. It also involves a serious attempt to get in touch with the thoughts and the feelings of that client or client system representative as they reach out, often for the first time, to ask someone else for help. MSP suggests that you consider which systems you share with your client and the nature of you and your client's relationship with those shared systems. Engagement is necessary to begin to forge the **helping relationship**, a particular kind of connection that is absolutely critical to collaborating for change. You will revisit the engagement process throughout the planned change process, sometimes even again and again in the same social work interview. Engagement will be discussed thoroughly in Chapter 5.

Stage 3: Assessment

Like engagement, assessment occurs at the beginning of the helping process but continues to be revisited over time. Assessment is a process where the social worker and the client or client system representative come together and look at each of their perceptions of the way the client system interacts with many environmental systems. An important nuance of this process of assessment according to MSP is that all of these systems interact with each other all of the time, so the assessment process is about teasing out the important interactions among systems that help to identify the strengths and the resources that can be brought to bear to address the challenges faced by the client or client system. Assessment is considered in Chapter 6. See Figure 2.5.

Stage 4: Planning

Planning is the aspect of the helping process where the client system and the worker come together to identify goals and determine how they will know if the goals have been met. After the goals and measures of success are identified, the worker and the client work together to prioritize those goals and figure out how to address them. In accordance with MSP, the worker and client will look for goals that address issues at the intersection of the client and their environmental systems. In addition, MSP will direct the worker and client to look for goals between and among the environmental systems themselves. Finally, the worker and client system make an agreement (written or unwritten) that formalizes the plan. Like the others, this stage may be revisited and revised again and again throughout the helping process. It is discussed fully in Chapter 7.

FIGURE 2.5 ● The Dynamic Nature of Planned Change Stages

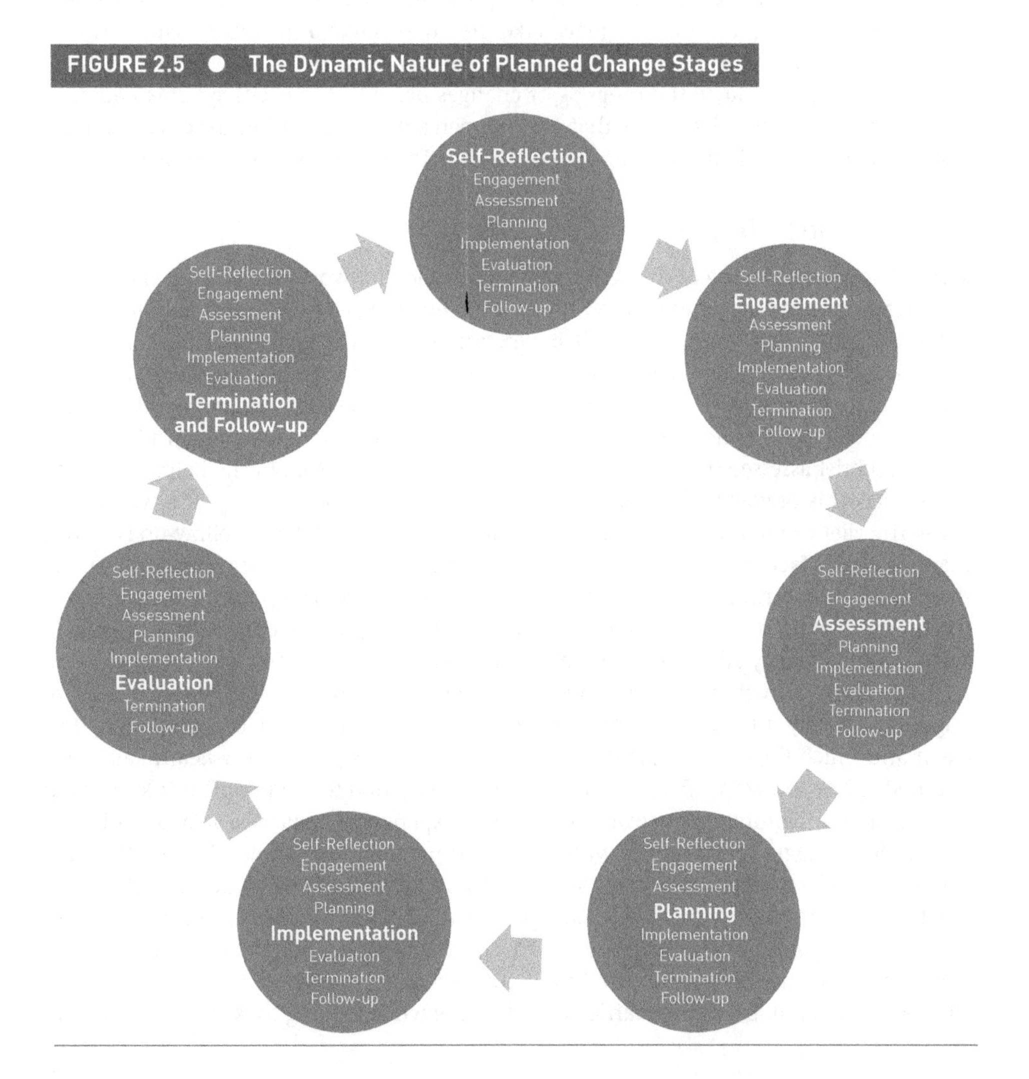

Stage 5: Implementation

In this stage of the planned change process, the worker controls the implementation of the plan that has been developed cooperatively. Worker and client or client system representative come together and carry out the plan. The worker, in consultation with the client, chooses a method of implementation that is supported by evidence. Then, the worker consults with the client to control the speed of the process and to continually monitor its completion. Actions may be required of the client, the worker, or a collaboration of both. Implementations may occur within the individual client or client system as well as where other systems overlap. This is the stage in the planned change process that Ling was attempting to carry out with Ralph. She was frustrated because she and Ralph worked together to create a plan, and they had no chance to implement it. The implementation stage will be covered in detail in Chapter 8.

Stage 6: Evaluation

The evaluation is carried out initially as the worker and client discuss evidence-informed plan implementations. The worker is responsible to evaluate the trustworthiness of the available research related to the client's situation. Evaluation also occurs as the worker and the client or client system representative monitor progress. The purpose of evaluation is primarily for the worker and client to come together to determine if progress has been made toward the implementation goals. Like the other stages of planned change, evaluation appears throughout the process as an ongoing practice activity. MSP suggests that the worker and client evaluate the progress of changes between the client systems and environmental systems as well as those that may happen among and within the environmental systems themselves. Methods of carrying out evaluation will be discussed in Chapter 9.

Stages 7 and 8: Termination and Follow-Up

Termination is the ending of the agreement, or contract, for work. Worker and client come together and determine whether the work is complete or whether the goals should be reassessed and addressed again. Ideally, it is determined that the goals have been met, and termination is initiated and carried out by worker and client together. If the worker is very fortunate, their agency will have provisions for follow up to occur. This is where the worker gets in touch with the client or client system representative sometime after termination to conduct a brief assessment related to the goals that were addressed in the helping process. If the success is ongoing, the worker can congratulate the client. If not, the worker can invite the client to return for service or can refer the client elsewhere. Follow-up is a good example of this fact: It is best if termination signals the end of the contract, not the end of the helping relationship . . . at least not until a successful follow-up occurs. Regardless of whether formal follow-up can occur, the client or client representative could request help again if agency policy allows it. Termination is covered in Chapter 9.

It's possible to say that every stage in the planned change process is the most important stage. That is why it is critical for the worker to be continually aware of which stage they are in and which stages are currently underway. For example, when Ling heard Ralph had returned to New Horizons, she needed to begin self-reflection to spend time thinking about his return and identifying her own feelings and experiences that were related to Ralph. She needed to begin to empathize with Ralph and his situation. When Ling reintroduced herself to Ralph, she needed to continue examining her feelings while beginning engagement, or reconnection with Ralph. As she spoke with Ralph trying to get information about what was going on, or assessment, she had to continually watch out for any feelings of hers that might influence her work as well as continue to reach back and find ways to remain engaged with Ralph. Later, they carried out planning while looking back at the assessment.

Meanwhile, Ling would continue to keep an eye on her feelings and pay attention to her connection with Ralph. She would make sure to consider how they would both know if the process was successful, beginning the evaluation stage. As Ling initiated the implementation she and Ralph agreed on, she was continually checking to see whether they were still on the plan and whether the assessment needed to be updated. At the same time, she continued to watch out for any changes in her feelings or her views of Ralph while maintaining their connection. Later, she needed to evaluate how close they were to achieving success. In this case, Ling was frustrated because she couldn't see as much success as she hoped. She knew Ralph needed a bit more time to realize his goals. She checked back to see whether the assessment had changed and realized that the plan had to be altered to be in keeping with the time limit she and Ralph were facing related to his termination. She had to engage in reflection about the frustration she was feeling as a result of the denial of an extension for treatment so that it did not become a barrier to the engagement that she had to form with the insurance company representative. This was true because the insurance company became another target system where Ling needed to make a connection. She had to facilitate a process of change in these two systems, not just a change in Ralph.

CRITICAL THINKING AND COLLABORATIVE LEARNING EXERCISES 2.2

1. Work with a group and come up with a statement that describes the dynamic nature of the stages of planned change.
2. Before Ling thought about using a formal evaluation of client success, she was often angry and upset when she went home in the evening. Sometimes, her feelings lasted until dinnertime. In a small group, identify other negative consequences that could occur in Ling's life because of these feelings.
3. Now have your group identify ways that Ling could have worked to relax and "leave her work at the office."

Section 2.3: Phases of Social Process

This section focuses on the use of MSP in generalist social work practice. MSP is a part of every stage of helping. Another important component in generalist practice is the social process of beginnings, middles, and endings in helping. This section kicks off the discussion on social process beginning with . . . beginnings.

Beginnings, Middles, and Endings

Gitterman and Germain (2008) have called the process of helping one which occurs in stages—beginnings, middles, and endings—but they clarify to say that the stages "ebb and flow." In other words, the phases of social process are similar to the stages of the planned change process in that they are all being considered by the social worker all the time. Beginnings, middles, and endings each have their own characteristics, but all occur over and over within the helping process.

At the beginning of a social interaction, people are often anxious. Their anxiety is based on uncertainty. What is this situation like? Is there something I should worry about? Will I behave in an appropriate way in this situation and with this person? How will they behave? On the other hand, beginnings are often characterized by hope. You hope that the situation or the person that you know nothing about will be a positive experience for you. Examples of anxieties can be found in many social interactions. You take a date to a restaurant, and you are anxious about whether they will like the restaurant. Are the prices the same as those advertised? How will the service be? You are hoping that you will share a pleasant dinner with your date, but you are just a bit concerned about whether the restaurant will turn out to be as good as you expected. What does the restaurant do first? They find you a seat to your liking, and they hand you a menu. Most of your concern evaporates when you are seated and have a chance to look at the menu. You're beginning to know what to expect.

A similar situation occurs at the start of every semester. You hope you're going to have an exciting class with lots of fulfilling experiences. Hopefully, you'll enjoy the professor's style and be challenged by the topics you'll cover. But what if the reading requirements are too much in length and too little in interest? You wonder if the course will be so difficult you won't be able to get the grade you'd like to get. So what does the instructor do first? Hand you a syllabus (or make one available electronically). There, you learn something about the course topics, assignments, and expectations. Most of your anxiety turns to hope, and you are free to begin learning.

The situation is similar for social work clients and representatives of client systems. They stand at the doorway of the helping relationship wondering if they should cross into the connection with the worker. Will the worker chuckle at their worries? Will the worker be unable to help? What if other people learn about the problem? The client or client system representative is asking for help because they hope to create change in their lives and consequently the lives of others. But they are anxious—sometimes almost paralyzed. At that point, they need to know how to allow their hope to override their anxiety. It is the worker's job to help the client or system representative make that decision in a way that is in the client system's best interest. At this moment, where the client stands at the threshold of the relationship and the worker is beckoning them to enter . . . the worker's own hope and anxiety play a role. The worker hopes to be able to help. They want to create a situation where the client will trust them and share their challenges. But as you can imagine, the worker is concerned that they will not enable the connection. What if the worker's presentation of self is not welcoming but off-putting instead? What if the worker accidentally offends the client because the worker doesn't understand the client's culture? If MSP is being used, there may be a number of systems with which the worker has to engage—what if they all feel overwhelming? Now it is the worker, not just the client, who is balancing hope and anxiety. They both need help understanding what will come next.

Many agencies have formal processes that take place in the beginning of each client relationship. These processes, like outlining what services are offered at the agency, can serve to alleviate anxiety. In addition, the steps the worker needs to take in order to allow hope to override anxiety involve the worker-centered practice you've been introduced to earlier. A specific opening statement will be discussed as we discuss engagement. In addition, Chapter 4 explains the method for carrying out the self-reflection stage to help manage the characteristics of beginnings in the planned change process. Middles and endings have their own challenges and resources. They'll be addressed as they appear in planned change.

The Relationship Between Stages of Planned Change and Phases of Social Process

Beginnings, middles, and endings correspond to the stages of planned change. Like the stages of planned change, they continue to happen over and over again within each stage. For example, let's elaborate on the situation between Ling and Ralph as it's explained previously.

When Ling met Ralph during his admission to the agency, both she and Ralph were feeling the hope and anxiety of beginnings. Later, even as they began to enter the middle phase with its own characteristics, Ling had to continually balance her own hope and anxiety as well as Ralph's feelings. She would check to make sure her hope outweighed her anxiety about Ralph's potential. Later, Ling became angry and anxious because she couldn't see as much success as she hoped. She knew Ralph needed a bit more time to realize his goals. She had to look carefully at the frustration she was feeling as a result of the denial of an extension for treatment so that it did not become a barrier to the engagement that she had to form with the insurance company representative. This was true because the insurance company became another system where Ling needed to make a connection. She knew her first step should be to carefully read the insurance company's policies.

FIGURE 2.6 • The Relationship Between Planned Change and Social Process

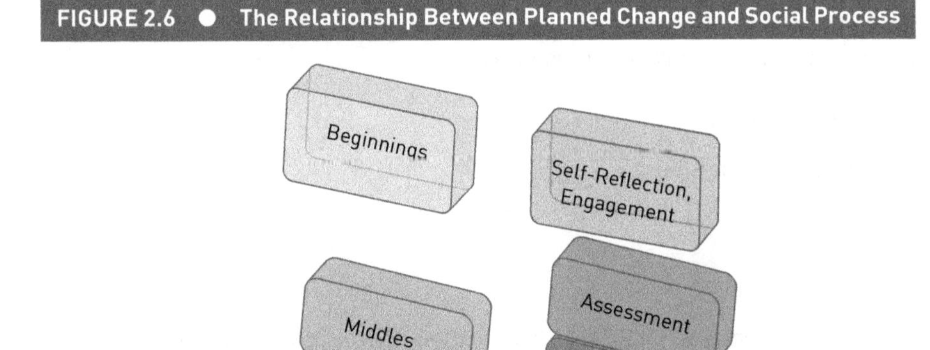

CRITICAL THINKING AND COLLABORATIVE LEARNING EXERCISES 2.3

1. Working with a partner, identify a situation where you began a new experience. Describe how your feelings played out. Did you feel hope and anxiety? What did you do—or what could you have done—to allow hope to triumph?
2. At the start of a worker–client relationship, an intake form is often used. The form is often thought of as something that may be a barrier to engagement. Given what you've learned about beginnings, can you think of any way a fill-in-the-blanks questionnaire might be used to facilitate engagement?

Section 2.4: Diversity

Part of the anxiety about beginnings happens because people are not the same. To work toward hope, the MSP model takes a careful look at diversity. This section is related to diversity and the strengths perspective. It is the foundation for the diversity discussion in Chapter 3.

Diversity and Strengths

Because of our MSP perspective, social workers believe that challenges in life occur at the intersection of systems. The intersection between Ralph, the insurance company, and New Horizons, for example, is where one of Ralph's challenges could be found. Using that perspective, we don't place the blame for individuals' situations solely on them. Because we look at the environment as well as the person, we are free to look to their strengths and unique resources as a way to help them make changes in their lives where oppression may be occurring. This focus leads us to take a careful look at difference, or diversity, among individuals and groups. To elaborate on our previous discussion in Chapter 1 on diversity, consider that diversity is critical for several reasons:

- Identity formation
- Potential for oppression
- Potential for power

Identity Formation

The first aspect of diversity refers to identity formation. "Diversity and difference characterize and shape the human experience and are critical to the formation of identity" (CSWE, 2015, p. 7). It might be said that diversity influences the way someone sees you as well as the way you see yourself. Society becomes like a mirror for us. If someone makes fun of an aspect of yourself all of your life, you will grow to identify yourself with a characteristic that you eventually despise. If an adolescent girl is continually told that her height makes her big and unattractive to boys her age, she may grow to hate that aspect of herself. Chances are, she'll spend her whole life slouching a bit. But if that girl is told her whole life that she will be a great basketball player and may grow up to be a model, she will see herself much differently. In each case, she'll present herself the way she feels and will influence others either positively or negatively. The importance of social messages is significant to her identity.

Potential for Oppression

Any kind of difference between and among groups of people can be either a resource or a potential area for oppression. For example, black Americans may face profiling in the justice system. That is, their experiences may be different, and more punitive, than those of white Americans. We might call that **oppression**, a person's experience of using energy to express their attributes only to have that energy lost. In other words, oppression means a stifling of the expression of individual and group attributes. The person's expression of themselves is effectively smothered. In this case, a black person who dresses and behaves the way a white person does is less likely to experience the punitive nature of the justice system, but their ability to express themselves is stifled. On the other hand, differences in culture, including the strong maternal family figure in the face of the relatively high imprisonment rate of black Americans, may bring resources to their lives that other groups may not enjoy. Those resources may then be recognized by the social worker and used as the means for positive change. For this reason, the generalist social worker uses the strengths perspective to identify the unique resources available where people are diverse.

SELF-REFLECTION 2: MULTIGROUP ETHNIC IDENTITY QUESTIONNAIRE

While ethnicity is only one form of diversity, knowledge of your own ethnicity is the beginning of the self-reflection that is necessary for the culturally responsive practice that will be discussed next. Consider how strongly you identify with a particular ethnic group by taking the Multigroup Ethnic Identity Questionnaire (MGEIQ) located on pages 62–63. Check your score against the scores of other people in your ethnic group. What does your score mean about your ethnic identity? Can you explain why the higher scores on the MGEIQ happen along with relatively higher scores on tests related to coping skills, feelings of mastery, self-esteem, and optimism, while lower scores on the MGEIQ go along with higher scores on tests measuring loneliness and depression? How do you think your MGEIQ score will affect your work with people of your own ethnicity? Of different ethnicities?

Diversity may be difference, plain and simple. I have gray hair; you have black. Because of our hair colors alone, we have different life experiences. Your black hair allows you to fit into social situations, such as an undergraduate classroom, composed primarily of young people of very different personal attributes. If you are shy, you may use this as a resource by complimenting someone else's hair with confidence. On the other hand, my gray hair may give me a measure of respect as an undergraduate. If I'm shy about participating in class, it may be outweighed by my comfort with my life experiences. Consequently, I may recognize that I have a lot to offer in the classroom. On the other hand, in that setting my hair marks me out as different, and that may hamper my ability to interact socially so that I may not be invited to join a study group. You can see how diversity can provide resources and at the same time can create barriers to functioning. As social workers, we are called on to remember that discrimination can be the day-to-day frustration of individuals or it can be the pervasive oppression of a group. To put it another way, diversity is difference between and among individuals or groups and difference between and among more and less powerful individuals and groups. In either case, we want to acknowledge the potential for oppression and perhaps address it in our change efforts, but we want to start by identifying the resources connected with diversity. This is the strengths perspective in social work.

The resources connected to diversity are so important that we have to be sure we recognize them. If we do, we can celebrate their strengths, attend to potential challenges, and begin to recognize our unconscious responses to them. To work toward recognizing diversity, we will begin with a definition. Diversity has been defined as having two parts: (1) individual and (2) social differences. All of these come together and intersect in ways that accentuate the power of each. Individual differences may include the following:

- Basic personality characteristics
- Health
- Learning abilities and styles
- Life experiences
- Physical presence

Social differences may include the following:

- Race or ethnicity
- Class
- Gender
- Sexual orientation
- Country of origin
- Ability
- Cultural, political, religious, or other affiliations (adapted from Milem, Chang, & Antonio, 2005, as cited in Lee & Priester, 2015)

In other words, we have both individual characteristics that make us unique and we have other characteristics that we share with others. It is these characteristics that allow people to judge us. For that reason, it is helpful to have lists of the possible attributes of diversity. Multiple factors reflect diversity, including but not limited to age, class, color, culture, disability and ability, ethnicity, gender, gender identity and expression, immigration status, marital status, political ideology, race, religion or spirituality, sex, sexual orientation, and tribal sovereign status (CSWE, 2015, p. 7). Later on, we'll discuss intersectionality in detail. For now, know that intersectionality refers to the way people's characteristics and social identities overlap and sometimes exacerbate oppression and discrimination while they sometimes enhance power in social interactions. Using these lists can help us to identify strengths and resources as well as potential areas of discrimination. Often, people consider areas of diversity alongside those of the majority or the most powerful group. So someone who is gay is often recognized as diverse because the majority of people are not. That view results in a situation where a member of the majority group is considered to be "not diverse." This view is not helpful to our work, because we may miss out on identifying the challenges that members of the majority group face.

On the other hand, let's consider a more nuanced look at diversity. If we confine ourselves to the lists of attributes, we may miss areas of difference. For example, the previously stated list does not include gender expression and it does not include age. Where a definition of diversity includes a list or a comparison to the majority, it almost always omits some group. Consider instead a definition of diversity in which we consider diversity to be *any* difference between and among individuals and groups as well as between and among more and less powerful groups.

Let's reconsider your black hair. You probably have the most common hair color in the world. Hair color is not on the list of potential areas of diversity and is not often considered as an area of diversity. Yet your black hair, if it is very straight or very curly, may be socially connected to what people define as race. It may mark you out as different in certain situations, like your classroom. If very curly black hair is an area of diversity relative to the setting, it may become an obstacle to your participation in developing friends and future study mates. You may not be able to break the ice using comments about someone's hair because no one else has hair like yours. Your hair needs special care that may not even be provided locally. You may find yourself frequently wearing a hat or a wig. What this means for us as social workers is that we need to know and use the "list" format of diversity to help recognize possible strengths and possible areas of discrimination, but we also need to recognize that there are an infinite number of possible diverse characteristics of people. Diversity can exist between your client and the majority society, or diversity can exist between you and your client, or diversity can exist between any individuals and groups. As social workers, we need to recognize all of the forms diversity can take.

WHAT IF . . . FOCUS ON DIVERSITY

Suppose Ralph were a Caucasian woman. How might his relationship with Ling be different? How do you think their difference in race or in gender would be the most challenging? Or does the combination of racial and gender differences cause the most diversity between them? Do you think this client's family relationships might be different if Ralph were a woman? Will gender be a strength or a challenge? Or both?

Strengths-Based Language

CSWE (2015) suggests that "social workers understand that, as a consequence of difference, a person's life experiences may include oppression, poverty, marginalization, and alienation as well as privilege, power, and acclaim. Social workers also understand the forms and mechanisms of oppression and discrimination and recognize the extent to which a culture's structures and values, including social, economic, political, and cultural exclusions, may oppress, marginalize, alienate, or create privilege and power" (p. 7).

In other words, recognizing strengths is important, but it is also necessary to identify areas of oppression. Sometimes areas of oppression are supported and perpetuated simply by the language we use. The importance of the society's discourse, or the words we use and the topics we discuss, is immeasurably important. Fortunately, this is an area where social workers can make an impact every day. **Strengths-based language** is important in that it helps social workers to share their strengths-based focus with others. This helps others to begin to think as we do, emphasizing people's capabilities rather than their challenges. Some examples of strengths-based language demonstrate the power of language:

Deficit-Based Language	Strengths-Based Language
This client is manipulative.	This client copes with stress by cleverly getting others to help them.
This family is poor.	This family is financially challenged at this time.
This community is run down.	This community and its residents have untapped potential.
This person is a schizophrenic.	This person has schizophrenia.
This organization has a lack of leadership.	This is an organization in transition with lots of potential.
This boy is mentally retarded.	This is a boy with intellectual challenges.
This group is unable to make a decision.	This group is in the difficult stage of role identification for its members.

What Is Culture?

As you have probably learned in some of your liberal arts courses, *culture* is a very broad term. It refers to a range of human behaviors that include the language a person speaks, the food a person eats, the entertainment a person enjoys, and the fashion a person shows off. It has to do with religion, government, how family is defined, and what it feels like to live in different countries. It also has to do with gender expectations and family responsibilities. Think about some of these aspects of your own life: What kind of government serves you? What do you believe about good government? What is your faith? Has your faith changed recently? What is your experience of gender identification? Has this been different than in the past? What do your clothes say about you? What are some of your family's traditions? What foods did you eat growing up?

Culture Evolutions

If you stopped to answer a couple of the previous questions, you may have noticed that the way you experience culture has changed. During periods of transition such as attending college or getting a divorce, you are likely to be undergoing what may be called a cultural evolution. That cultural evolution is a gradual change in yourself that can be explained through an analogy about a trampoline (Donnelly, 2016).

uccia_photography/Getty Images

New cultural experiences are often explored with peers.

The Stabilizing Frame

The trampoline analogy goes like this: A trampoline sits on a metal frame that stabilizes it. Likewise, there are aspects of your own personal culture that seldom change. They provide stability to your sense of self. For example, let's say you are an immigrant who is very proud of your heritage and you demonstrate that through joining a group that practices your country's indigenous dance. The pride in your heritage and the dance you associate with it are likely to remain a part of your personal culture. That is, you are not going to stop dancing anytime soon. Similarly, you may have pride in your ability to cook your family's ethnic foods. You are especially proud that you learned the recipes from your grandmother as a child. You are not going to stop cooking those foods anytime soon. Consider an example that is not related to ethnicity: Suppose you remember your first lessons on democracy in elementary school. The idea of representative government moved you then and continues to move you now. You think of yourself as someone who is politically active, volunteering on candidates' campaigns and even talking to people about running for a seat on your local school board. This is an aspect of you that is not likely to change.

Take a moment to identify a part of your cultural "frame." Remember that it may have to do with any of the examples just given, including your experience of spirituality and identification with a church or your identification of family members and what family means to you. To do this, you'll have to sit a few moments in silence. Set an alarm for 5 minutes, and give yourself that time to reflect on how you would describe yourself if you had to do it in a sentence or two.

The Flexible Springs and the Community Bounce

On top of the trampoline's frame is the trampoline itself, which is connected to the frame by a series of springs. These springs represent those aspects of your culture that are flexible. These are the elements of you and your experiences that can change over time, especially during times of transition. Maybe you were raised in a strict religious tradition that you and your family observed, well, religiously. When you got to college or you got married, someone took you along to an observance of an entirely different religion. You liked it. During a period of transition, even something fairly stable like religious beliefs can be called into question. So in this case, you go with your spouse or your roommate to another observance. This is like bouncing on the trampoline—it's the time where you find the springs to be flexible and you invite others to bounce with you. You get to see how others experience and express this element of your culture. Maybe you change religious practices to try them on for size. Eventually, your new religion may become part of your stable frame. On the other hand, it may remain a spring for a time, ready to be tested and possibly changed.

Identify some aspect of your culture that has begun to change recently. Consider knowledge of your heritage, fashion you use to express yourself, art, or music you enjoy. Then identify which people may have "bounced" with you, or introduced you to this new cultural element. Again, take five minutes in privacy and in silence to accomplish this. (Why should you take the time to engage in this exercise? Because it is important for you to know yourself before you can build the productive relationships that will allow you to be a good social worker. If you didn't do the first 5-minute exercise, go back and do it—it's important.)

The Safety Net

The final part of the trampoline that represents your cultural evolution is the net that surrounds the bouncy part. The net is there so you don't fly off into the air and hurt yourself. Likewise, you have cultural boundaries. Just like the boundaries in systems theory, you are surrounded by a demarcation that helps you maintain your identity. So there are cultural lines you probably will not cross. You may learn that there is a society where very young people regularly engage in sexual play with numerous partners (we'd probably call it promiscuity or even child abuse). You might also learn about a society that honors its ancestors by ingesting parts of their bodies (we'd probably call it cannibalism). You'll probably observe people who use a lot of alcohol to manage social situations (we might call it alcohol abuse). Even if you knew people who engaged in those activities, you would probably not engage in them or encourage others to do so. You'd be stopped by your cultural safety net.

Take 5 minutes, and think about some of the cultural lines you wouldn't cross. What are some things people around you might do that you would not think of doing? Would you never parade with a white supremacist group? Would you never consider moving to another country or otherwise away from your family? Identify at least one.

If you've engaged in the trampoline exercise, you've started to get some idea of your culture, or your areas of diversity. This is the beginning of developing the cultural humility you'll need to work effectively with clients.

Cultural Humility and Cultural Responsiveness

Our goal as social workers is to move toward **cultural responsiveness** as we work with client systems. Cultural responsiveness refers to being effective in work with client systems that reflect a broad array of differences: all of the types of diversity we've discussed previously. Achieving cultural responsiveness is to become adept at being able to act and even think like the members of a culture different from yours (Paine, Jankowski, & Sandage, 2016). Most important to know is that cultural responsiveness reflects a developmental process. In other words, cultural responsiveness is a constant aspiration—a goal you never entirely achieve (Bennett, 2004). Instead, you work toward cultural responsiveness in many different situations, and you will continue to do so for your entire career. If you can come near to cultural responsiveness and function in a way that is acceptable when you interact with people from cultures different from your own, you can accomplish a great deal in your work. Note that this does not mean taking on the behavior of members of a different group—like suddenly mimicking their accent. This would just make you look fake. Instead, you want to function in a way that is acceptable. For example, you would not ask an Indian woman if she would like you to hang up her "scarf." If you cannot achieve cultural responsiveness, you will experience a barrier between you and the people you work with. Note that this barrier can be present as you work with organizations (which have cultures of their own); groups, which may consist of people that represent a variety of cultures; and with individuals with their own mix of cultures including their own unique experiences. It is not sufficient to learn about a different cultural experience (Ortega & Faller, 2011). Remember that the elements of people's diversities overlap and may intensify their impact for good or for ill due to intersectionality. Intersectionality is complicated, and we'll discuss it more fully in the next chapter. For now, know that intersectionality creates a situation where attaining cultural responsiveness is always a challenge—you'll never work with someone who is exactly like you.

Attempts to reach cultural responsiveness begins with **cultural humility**. Cultural humility means that before you approach any client situation you begin by examining yourself. You think about your own culture and experiences and you critique them. This is easier said than done, of course, so you will likely choose to discuss your developing ideas about yourself with your supervisor. Take note that humility here does not mean shame. Just as you would like to move toward a place where you can respect all other cultures, you must remember to respect your own. This in itself requires work. Once you respect your own culture, you can begin to reflect other people's areas of diversity.

The fact is that we are all ethnocentric even when we don't want to be. Our worldview is so much a part of our lives that we don't even know what it is. The idea is to move away from an attitude of **ethnocentrism**, where you think that your own culture is superior to others. Be careful here—you will immediately respond with "I am not ethnocentric, I respect other cultures!" It is not that simple, though. Consider an example where a family faces the challenge of caring for an aging grandparent. For an American family of European origin, the day-to-day responses to this challenge may be draining. As time goes on, the older person's need for care increases. They may need diaper changes and an alarm on their chair so that they don't wander away and get lost. With two professional parents with demanding careers and two children with soccer games and music lessons, it becomes difficult to care for their family member. They may be able to afford live-in help and may hire a qualified person to provide that help. Or they may take the recommendation of their doctor and after long and painful soul searching may enroll their family member in a long-term care facility. This may make sense to them. A different family, immigrants from Vietnam, may also face the need to care for an aging family member. The idea of a long-term care facility may be entirely foreign to them and their work less a part of their identity. If a social worker suggests long-term care, they may be shocked and angered. Instead of choosing a long-term care facility, it would not be surprising to find that the family's female caretaker, or mother, will quit her job to care for the dependent family member. It is not sufficient for a social worker who is about to work with Vietnamese immigrants to research their culture and find that they value family highly. Instead, these are cultural differences that reflect the need for a social worker to examine their own cultural influences and to evaluate them so that they can reach a point of objectivity. What are the social worker's beliefs about family? Do they have any experience in caring for older family members? What are their opinions about long-term care? Without these questions and their answers, a worker will not speak or behave in a way that is functional in their client's culture. They won't be culturally responsive.

To further complicate a complicated topic, consider that we have been discussing managing cultural responsiveness with members of diverse groups. We recognize our own attitudes, beliefs, and experiences; then we learn about our clients' cultural groups. This means we are managing **between group differences**. In addition to this type of diversity, it is also necessary to consider **within group differences**. These differences mark the unique aspects of individuals regardless of the groups with which we might identify them. For example, we may consider that a young man who identifies as gay may have a difficult time coming out, especially to his parents. In fact, this population is at high risk of suicide. We may work with such a client, though, and find out that he has no such problem. His father suspected he was gay from a very young age and has had many years to come to terms with it.

How do we know if a client has characteristics of a group? We ask the expert. The client, the client system, or the client representative is the expert who can tell the worker about their own diverse characteristics. Once the worker is comfortable with their own beliefs, feelings, and experiences about a group, they will be more comfortable asking the client about their characteristics. For example, a researcher may assume that an older person could answer questions about their desire to age in place, that is, in their own home. If the researcher doesn't ask if this is the case, they may find their data flawed if they are asking people who are looking forward to an independent living setting. Likewise, a worker may know that many Latina women have large networks of friends and neighbors who could help with child care. If the worker assumes this with a particular client, she may agree that she does even if that is not the case. Instead, the worker may say this: "Many Latinas have a large network of friends, family, and neighbors who can help with child care. I don't want to assume that, though. Is it the case for you?"

These questions can be very uncomfortable because they often represent social taboos. It is taboo in our society to openly discuss many areas of diversity. A long history of oppression based on stereotypes is the cause. Imagine asking a black person if their ancestors are from Haiti or the Dominican Republic or Africa. The person may become defensive, waiting to hear you express a stereotype. Consequently, it is important to separate **stereotypes** and **generalizations**. If a worker recognizes that many people have beliefs about a certain group, they are recognizing stereotypes. For some individuals, stereotypes may be true. For others, though, they are not. Because of this, for culturally competent practice we need to treat stereotypes as generalizations—assumptions that need to be tested. For example, when working with an Asian American child, the worker should not assume that the child is very proficient in math. On the other hand, math may be a particular strength of this child that could be used to help them succeed. It is important to ask the expert. In this case, that would be the child or a parent or a schoolteacher. And the worker will have to be careful here because the topic is taboo for professionals too. If a worker asks a teacher if FangHsun is good in math, they may be greeted by an angry stare and the comment "You are prejudiced!" Instead, the worker may say something like "It seems like a lot of Asian kids work really hard in math. Is this the case with FangHsun?" When working with a board of directors for a new not-for-profit agency, it may be helpful for a social worker to help the organization with fund-raising or grant-writing because it is likely that they are operating on a shoestring. If the worker doesn't ask about the financial stability of the agency, they may end up doing a lot of unnecessary work due to the agency's regular fee for service funding. The worker will have to be comfortable with their own attitudes, beliefs, and experiences to objectively ask the board president how the organization is funded.

In short, culturally responsive practice is really built on social workers' understanding of their own attitudes (Ross, 2010). An attitude of cultural humility is necessary to achieve cultural responsiveness. Cultural humility is important to MSP in that it provides direction for social workers' identification of their cultures and cultural evolution, a process that is necessary prior to attempting to build relationships with others. The practice of developing cultural humility will be further explored in Chapter 4.

The Frustrated Worker: Reflective Responses

Ling had to spend some of nearly every day working with funders, insurance companies, and others to justify why her clients should have additional treatment approved. She often told herself and her coworkers that she felt offended when she had to justify her best professional judgment to a person who did not know the client and was usually not even a social worker. Many times she felt like the clients who needed an extended stay the least were those who were approved while the really critical cases, like Ralph, were denied. Often she took her frustration home. It exhausted her and sometimes kept her from enjoying dinner with her husband. Ling continued to be frustrated because she continued to tell herself the system was not fair to the clients.

Oscar Wong/Getty Images

Measuring progress helps workers and clients get past frustration.

Ling was right; it was unfair. What was worse for Ling was that it *felt* wrong. When Ling got on the phone to talk to a funder, she did it because she didn't feel right about a case. The problem for Ling was that her agency measured client success by counting the number of hours staff met with clients and by reviewing client satisfaction surveys. As a result, Ling could never be sure the client had achieved their goals. She didn't have a method of evaluating the planned change process. Once Ling looked past her anger and began specifically talking with clients about what it would look like if their goals were achieved, she began to measure clients' progress and to feel much better about her situation. When she requested extra time for a client, she could articulate clearly what the client needed to do and how they would know when it was done so she was more successful in her requests and she could more easily understand when a client she was **advocating** for was denied. It kept her from talking to all of the staff members trying to identify ways that clients were not doing well. She could measure success and keep from concentrating on problems.

CRITICAL THINKING AND COLLABORATIVE LEARNING EXERCISES 2.4

1. Working with a partner, write down 10 diverse characteristics about that person. Identify those that are similar to your characteristics and those that are different. Take turns sharing them aloud. Which ones does your partner find to be inaccurate? Which ones are really hard to say out loud?
2. Pretend you know someone with one of the diverse characteristics noted next. Identify a possible strength that may correspond with any experiences of oppression that may be present: an overweight high school student; an intellectually challenged group home resident; a smoker; a homeless person; an economically challenged single mother.

Section 2.5: Review and Apply

CONCURRENT CONSIDERATIONS IN GENERALIST PRACTICE

Ethical Decision-Making Challenge

When Ling attempted to get insurance coverage for Ralph to receive services, the insurance provider wanted a rationale for his continuation in the program. Ling had to get evidence of the severity of Ralph's problems from coworkers. How do you think Ling should handle this process? Is there a way she can avoid a clash with the social work value of respecting the dignity and worth of the person? Consider all of the core professional values when you answer.

Human Rights

If Ralph is discharged prematurely, will he be deprived of any fundamental human rights such as freedom, safety, privacy, an adequate standard of living, health care, and education?

Evidence-Based Practice

Even in the best of circumstances, Ling has a very limited amount of time to work with Ralph. She needs to use a method of practice that has been demonstrated to work in short-term helping with people who suffer from mental illness. Look in the scientific literature to see which might be the best alternative. (In other words, check to see whether there are any empirical studies that demonstrate the effectiveness of methods of short-term practice with people who suffer from mental illness.) What approach do you recommend?

Policies Impacting Practice

Research mental health treatment parity in your state. If a Medicaid recipient needs mental health services, do they face more restrictions than when they need physical health care? Is it harder to find a service provider?

Managing Diversity

Ling plans to work with Ralph on dealing with his boss. She is far younger than he is and has far less experience in the workforce. What might she do if he asks "What do you know about it, you're so young you couldn't possibly understand or know how to handle this?"

Multisystem Practice

Identify examples of Ling's work on all levels.

Micro: ____________________

Mezzo: ____________________

Macro: ____________________

Dynamic and Interactive Planned Change Stages

Identify aspects of the work between Ling and Ralph where Ling worked in the following stages:

Self-Reflection: ____________________

Engagement: ____________________

Assessment: ____________________

Planning: ____________________

Implementation: ____________________

Evaluation: ____________________

Termination and Follow-Up: ____________________

Chapter Summary

Section 2.1: Theory in Social Work

Theories describe, explain, and predict our reality. They are made up of concepts, constructs, and principles. Models for generalist social work practice may be constructed using theories such as general systems theory or social systems theory as foundations. MSP is such a model. In addition to general systems theory and social systems theory, the MSP model also builds on the strengths perspective as well as the PIE and FIE perspectives. Principles of the MSP model include the idea that environmental systems all interact simultaneously and that uneven energy exchanges between systems may be the focus for social work implementation.

Section 2.2: The Planned Change Process

Generalist social work practice is carried out in eight stages: (1) self-reflection, (2) engagement, (3) assessment, (4) planning, (5) implementation, (6) evaluation, (7) termination, and (8) follow-up. It is important to note that these stages are dynamic. This means that while one may be the focus at a particular time, all of the phases are active all of the time.

Section 2.3: Phases of Social Process

Social processes occur in phases: beginnings, middles, and endings. Beginnings are usually marked by a combination of hope and anxiety. Beginnings are associated with the planned change stages of self-reflection, engagement, and assessment.

Section 2.4: Diversity

Diversity is more nuanced than just differences among people. Diversity has three functions: (1) it affects identity development, (2) it can result in social oppression, and (3) it can result in social power. Social workers respond to the broad range of human differences through the use of the strengths perspective, especially by using language that focuses on strengths. In response to diversity, cultural responsiveness is a goal for all social workers. Cultural responsiveness is built on cultural humility, a process that begins with self-knowledge.

SELF-REFLECTION 2: MULTIGROUP ETHNIC IDENTITY QUESTIONNAIRE

Multigroup Ethnic Identity Measure

PURPOSE: To measure ethnic identity in adolescents and young adults from diverse groups

AUTHOR: Jean Phinney

DESCRIPTION: The MEIM is a 12-items measure of Ethnic Identity Exploration (EIE).

NORMS: Average score and standard deviation for 10 ethnic groups of a total sample of 5,423 are:

Ethnic Group	Mean Score	Standard Deviation
African American	2.71	.59
Central American	3.07	.56
Chinese American	3.01	.53
European American	3.03	.52
Indian American	3.04	.50
Mexican American	3.27	.58
Pakistani American	3.34	.48
Pacific Islanders	3.11	.55
Mixed Heritage	2.94	.60

SCORING: All items are summed and divided by the number of items answered. Scores range from 1 to 5.

RELIABILITY: Reliability is very good; internal consistency coefficients are typically about .84.

VALIDITY: There is excellent support for being a valid measure. From a sample of 5,423 scores are positively correlated with coping, mastery, self-esteem, and optimism, while inversely associated with loneliness and depression.

PRIMARY REFERENCE:

Phinney, J. (2013). The multigroup ethnic identity measure: A new scale for use with adolescents and young adults from diverse groups. In K. Corcoran & J. Fischer (Eds.), *Measures for clinical practice and research: A sourcebook* (5th ed.). New York, NY: Oxford University Press.

MULTIGROUP ETHNIC IDENTITY MEASURE

In this country, people come from many different countries and cultures, and there are many different words to describe the different backgrounds or ethnic groups that people come from. Some examples of ethnic groups are Latino, African American, Mexican, Asian American, Chinese, and many others. These questions are about your ethnicity or your ethnic group and how you feel about it or react to it.

Please fill in: In terms of ethnic group, I consider myself to be: ______________________

5 = Strongly agree
4 = Agree
3 = Neutral
2 = Disagree
1 = Strongly disagree

Use the numbers above to indicate how much you agree or disagree with each statement.

_____ 1. I have spent time trying to find out more about my ethnic group, such as its history, traditions, and customs.
_____ 2. I am active in organizations or social groups that include mostly members of my own ethnic group.
_____ 3. I have a clear sense of my ethnic background and what it means for me.
_____ 4. I think a lot about how my life will be affected by my ethnic group membership.
_____ 5. I am happy that I am a member of the group I belong to.
_____ 6. I have a strong sense of belonging to my own ethnic group.
_____ 7. I understand pretty well what my ethnic group membership means to me.
_____ 8. In order to learn more about my ethnic background, I have often talked to other people about my ethnic group.
_____ 9. I have a lot of pride in my ethnic group.
_____ 10. I participate in cultural practices of my own group, such as special food, music, or customs.
_____ 11. I feel a strong attachment towards my own ethnic group.
_____ 12. I feel good about my cultural or ethnic background.

My ethnicity is:

Asian or Asian American, including Chinese, Japanese, and others
Black or African American
Hispanic or Latino, including Mexican American, Central American, and others
White, Caucasian, Anglo, European American
American Indian/Native American
Mixed; Parents are from two different groups
Other: ______________________

My father's ethnicity is ____________________. My mother's ethnicity is ________________.

Critical Terms for Multisystem Practice

Generalist Practice Curriculum Matrix With 2015 Educational Policy and Accreditation Standards

Chapter 2

Competency	Course	Course Content	Dimensions
Competency 1: Demonstrate Ethical and Professional Behavior		2.1. Describe the theoretical and conceptual framework related to multisystem practice (MSP). Feature 3: Self-Reflection Feature 4: Concurrent Considerations in Generalist Practice	Knowledge Values
Competency 2: Engage Diversity and Difference in Practice		2.4. Explore an in-depth meaning of diversity and its impact on the worker–client interaction. Feature 1: Focus on Diversity Feature 4: Concurrent Considerations in Generalist Practice	Skills Cognitive–affective processes Skills Cognitive–affective processes
Competency 3: Advance Human Rights and Social, Economic, and Environmental Justice		Feature 4: Concurrent Considerations in Generalist Practice	Skills Cognitive–affective processes
Competency 4: Engage In Practice-Informed Research and Research-Informed Practice		Feature 4: Concurrent Considerations in Generalist Practice	Skills Cognitive–affective processes
Competency 5: Engage in Policy Practice		Feature 4: Concurrent Considerations in Generalist Practice	Skills Cognitive–affective processes
Competency 6: Engage With Individuals, Families, Groups, Organizations, and Communities		2.2. Interpret the dynamic and interactive nature of the stages of planned change. 2.3. Discuss the dynamics of beginnings in the planned change process. Feature 4: Concurrent Considerations in Generalist Practice	Skills Cognitive–affective processes
Competency 7: Assess Individuals, Families, Groups, Organizations, and Communities		2.3. Discuss the dynamics of beginnings in the planned change process. 2.2. Interpret the dynamic and interactive nature of the stages of planned change. Feature 4: Concurrent Considerations in Generalist Practice	Skills Cognitive–affective processes
Competency 8: Intervene With Individuals, Families, Groups, Organizations, and Communities		2.2. Interpret the dynamic and interactive nature of the stages of planned change. Feature 4: Concurrent Considerations in Generalist Practice	Skills Cognitive–affective processes
Competency 9: Evaluate Practice With Individuals, Families, Groups, Organizations, and Communities		2.2. Interpret the dynamic and interactive nature of the stages of planned change. Feature 4: Concurrent Considerations in Generalist Practice	Skills Cognitive–affective processes

References

Bennett, M. J. (2004). Becoming interculturally competent. In J. Worzel (Ed.), *Toward multiculturalism: A reader in multicultural education* (pp. 21–71). Newton, MA: Intercultural Resource Corporation.

Briar-Lawson, K., Lawson, H. A., & Hennon, C. B. (with Jones, A. R.). (2001). *Family-centered policies and practices: International implications*. New York, NY: Columbia University Press.

Butterfield, A. K., Rocha, C. J., & Butterfield, W. H. (2010). *The dynamics of family policy*. Chicago, IL: Lyceum.

Carter, I. (2011). *Human behavior in the social environment: A social systems approach* (6th ed.). New Brunswick, NJ: Aldine Transaction.

Council on Social Work Education. (2015). *Educational policy and accreditation standards*. Alexandria, VA: Author. Retrieved from http://www.cswe.org/File.aspx?id=81660

Donnelly, K. (2016). The importance of trampolines. Retrieved from http://www.abbey-research.com/portfolio_page/trampolines

Gasker, J., & Vafeas, J. (2010). The family-in-environment: A new perspective on generalist social work practice. *The International Journal of Interdisciplinary Social Sciences, 5*(2), 291–303.

Gitterman, A., & Germain, C. B. (2008). *The life model of social work practice: Advances in knowledge and practice* (3rd ed.). New York, NY: Columbia University Press.

Griese-Owens, E., Miller, J. J., & Owens, L. W. (2014). Responding to global shifts: Meta-practice as a relevant social work practice paradigm. *Journal of Teaching in Social Work, 34*, 46–59. doi:10.1080/08841233.2013.866614

Karls, J. M., & Wandrei, K. E. (Eds.) (1994). *Person-in-environment system: The PIE classification system for social functioning problems*. Washington, DC: NASW Press.

Kerlinger, F. N., & Lee, H. B. (1999). *Foundations of behavioral research* (5th ed.). Fort Worth, TX: Harcourt Brace.

Kirst-Ashman, K., & Hull, G. (2016). *Understanding generalist practice* (8th ed.). Boston, MA: Cengage.

Langer, C. L., & Lietz, C. A. (2015). *Applying theory to generalist social work practice*. Hoboken, NJ: Wiley.

Lee, O. E.-K., & Priester, M. A. (2015). Increasing awareness of diversity through community engagement and films. *Journal of Social Work Education, 51*(1), 35–46. doi:10.1080/10437797.2015.977126

Milem, J., Chang, M., & Antonio, A. (2005). *Making diversity work on campus: A research-based perspective*. Washington, DC: Association of American Colleges and Universities. Retrieved from http://www.wesleyan.edu/partnerships/mei/files/makingdiversityworkoncampus.pdf

National Association of Social Workers. (2018). *NASW code of ethics*. Washington, DC: NASW Press.

Ortega, R. M., & Faller, K. C. (2011). Training child welfare workers from an intersectional cultural humility perspective: A paradigm shift. *Child Welfare, 90*(5), 27–49.

Paine, D. R., Jankowski, P. J., & Sandage, S. J. (2016). Humility as a predictor of intercultural competence: Mediator effects for differentiation-of-self. *The Family Journal: Counseling and Therapy for Couples and Families, 24*(1), 15–22.

Phinney, J. (2013). The multigroup ethnic identity measure: A new scale for use with adolescents and young adults from diverse groups. In K. Corcoran & J. Fischer (Eds.), *Measures for clinical practice and research: A sourcebook* (5th ed.). New York, NY: Oxford University Press.

Richmond, M. (1917). *Social diagnosis*. New York, NY: RMSPell Sage Foundation.

Ross, L. (2010). Notes from the field: Learning cultural humility through critical incidents and central challenges in community-based participatory research. *Journal of Community Practice, 18*, 315–335.

Saleebey, D. (1996). The strengths perspective in social work practice: Extensions and cautions. *Social Work, 41*(3), 296 305.

Taylor, D. E. *(2014). Toxic communities: Environmental racism, industrial pollution, and residential mobility.* New York: New York University Press.

von Bertalanffy, L. (1962). *Modern theories of development: An introduction to theoretical biology* (J. H. Woodger, Trans.). New York, NY: Harper. (Original work published 1933)

Recommended Readings

Eugenides, J. (2002). *Middlesex.* New York, NY: Picador.

Paine, D. R., Jankowski, P. J., & Sandage, S. J. (2016). Humility as a predictor of intercultural competence: Mediator effects for differentiation-of-self. *The Family Journal: Counseling and Therapy for Couples and Families, 24*(1), 15–22.

Values, Ethics, and Diversity

This chapter continues the same format. It begins with a case study and focuses on three main topics to continue to build the foundation for the rest of the text: (1) the introspection and understanding of diversity required to support a professional use of self; (2) the NASW Code of Ethics (National Association of Social Workers [NASW], 2018); and (3) an ethical decision-making model for practice.

Learning Objectives

3.1 Summarize the meaning and purpose of professional use of self.

3.2 Explain the process that underlies developing a professional use of self.

3.3 Assess the generalist view of diversity.

3.4 Describe the format of the *NASW Code of Ethics* (NASW, 2018).

3.5 Interpret a method of ethical decision-making.

Case Study: Missing the Strengths in Diversity

Alfredo Ramirez had been truant from school about half of the days in September and nearly all of the days in October. As a result, his mother was in danger of being fined or even jailed. The truancy officer from the school district on the west side of town made the referral to Young People's Place (YPP), an agency for helping young people and their family members avoid entering the justice system. When he was given the case, Andy stepped out of his supervisor's office closing the door quietly behind him. With his hand still on the knob, he exhaled deeply and realized he'd been holding his breath. His face turned a little red under the freckles. In his office, Andy eagerly picked up the phone. Alfredo's grandmother answered. When Andy asked to speak to Alfredo's mother, the grandmother said, "She no good." She explained that she, the grandmother, would bring Alfredo for the appointment. Andy had trouble

Sam Diephuis/Getty Images

Workers can become distracted by administrative responsibilities.

understanding her accent—he'd avoided Spanish in college—but they got through the call, and Alfredo's grandmother said she'd get Alfredo to YPP the next Wednesday evening.

Andy had a busy week, so he didn't get a chance to think about Alfredo until Wednesday afternoon. He thought about Alfredo's age—he was 12—and he thought he might play some over-the-door basketball with Alfredo to get a relationship started. A couple of hours later, Andy stepped into the waiting room and was shocked to see it full. *Who are all these people?* He looked at the smallest person and assumed it was Alfredo.

Andy extended his hand and introduced himself. When Andy said, "Let's go back to my office," he was again shocked that the entire group got up, preparing to follow him to his office. It suddenly occurred to him that all of these people were Alfredo's family, and they intended to join him in the session. Andy had to think fast. Andy's office had been a closet only a year ago and held three people, including himself. Was the group work room available? Maybe. Andy ascended the stairs carefully, one at a time, to check. (As a result of a childhood injury, one of Andy's legs was longer than the other.) He wondered what the family was thinking about his disability. Fortunately, the group work room was open. He bumped back down the stairs, one at a time, to get the family, then back up the stairs again. He used the slow ascent to gather his thoughts. He'd been terrified that there wouldn't be a room to offer Alfredo's family. Calm after the slow trip up the stairs, he began the session with an opening statement about the fact that YPP existed to keep families out of the justice system, that he was their social worker, and that he was authorized to have 12 meetings with the family. He said they'd know they were successful if Alfredo started attending school regularly. Everyone nodded. Then Andy began introductions. He didn't take notes at first but soon realized that he couldn't remember who was who. Like a busy waiter, he took out note paper and began jotting down names and relationships. In addition to the names and relationships, Andy came to realize that the family had no idea why they were supposed to come to YPP. Was Alfredo in more trouble? Likewise, the family was not clear about the roles various workers were playing in their lives: a truancy officer came to the apartment, a child welfare worker frequently phoned, and a mentor from the local Police Athletic League came to play basketball (the outdoor kind) with Alfredo. As the rest of the family sat quietly listening while Alfredo's uncle outlined the family's confusion with all the "helpers," Andy kept trying to get Alfredo to speak. Each time he tried, the room grew abnormally silent. He instinctively turned to Alfredo's uncle . . . everyone seemed to be looking at their uncle. Suddenly Andy realized that he knew next to nothing about the family's way of communicating. While he was thinking this, Alfredo's uncle was saying something about Alfredo helping take care of his grandmother. Somehow the school bus came into the story. Time was up, so Andy got himself together and scheduled the next meeting. He knew he had a lot of information to get before then.

Section 3.1: Why a Focus on the Worker?

One of Andy's biggest problems was that he hadn't thought very much about Alfredo's case until the last minute. In this section, we begin to look at how self-reflection and the professional use of self is a way to carry out social work practice effectively. Please note that self-reflection and the professional self is a complex process that lasts a lifetime. We'll consider the basics here and explore the process in more depth in Chapter 4.

Beginning Reflections

Beginning practice with a focus on the worker is a way of approaching generalist social work. This method suggests that the social worker be their own first client. It's clear that Andy didn't spend enough time thinking about Alfredo's situation before the session. It didn't occur to him that members of Alfredo's extended family would come along and would expect to be part of the helping process, even though he remembered reading something about the importance of family in the Latino culture. In those first moments, he was so shocked he certainly couldn't think of family support as a potential resource.

Perhaps most importantly, he didn't spend enough time thinking about himself. Andy had been raised in a two-parent household in the east side of town. His current address was there too. He hadn't considered that he might have trouble relating to a young person whose father was absent and whose mother could not be relied on. Having been an only child, Andy wasn't ready to tackle a family group that filled a room without thinking about it first. He also didn't expect himself to be so nervous, even though this was his first fully independent case. To go a bit deeper, he didn't think about his feelings for his own grandmother, who was living in a long-term care facility. These were strong feelings that would affect the way he thought about Alfredo and his family. In short, Andy needed to place himself at the center of his practice.

Social workers often focus on service to clients, one of our core professional values (NASW, 2018). Our placement of service before all other values is a reflection of the meaning of our profession: We exist as professionals to help others. But each of us provides help in our own unique way, because each of us is unique. Yes, we all work within the policies, or rules, of our agencies and our programs. Yes, we all follow the *NASW Code of Ethics* (NASW, 2018) and follow an evidence-based system of planned change. But we all do these things in our own ways. The feelings we experience are our own, and they affect our practice. Sometimes, unacknowledged feelings result in inappropriate practice behaviors. In those situations, a worker needs to spend time acknowledging and responding to their feelings—that is, they have to be their own social worker before they can be anyone else's social worker. A few examples of cases where the worker needed to work with themselves before the clients are discussed later. In each of the following cases, the worker experienced a strong but unacknowledged feeling. That feeling, outside of the worker's awareness, kept each worker from recognizing the best way to work with others. Each of the workers needed to recognize their own feelings in order to respond in a way that best served the client system. The process was this: A feeling that was unknown, or outside of awareness, led to a behavior that was problematic (see Figure 3.1).

Each time, the worker needed to behave as they *thought* best . . . not in a way that *felt* the best. The feeling needed to be supplemented. In each case that follows, the worker needed to display a personal characteristic that was not present at that moment. To display a feeling or characteristic that is not present is called **displaying absent attributes**. The concept has been used in research about children as it relates to a child's ability to socialize or play by assigning absent attributes to others (Barton & Pavilania, 2012). In social work, a worker may feel one way but have to display an absent attribute: a characteristic that was missing in the worker at that moment. A worker who feels anxiety may have to demonstrate the absent attribute of confidence. In short, social workers need to think before acting. See Figure 3.2.

FIGURE 3.1 • Unknown Feelings Lead to Unprofessional Behaviors

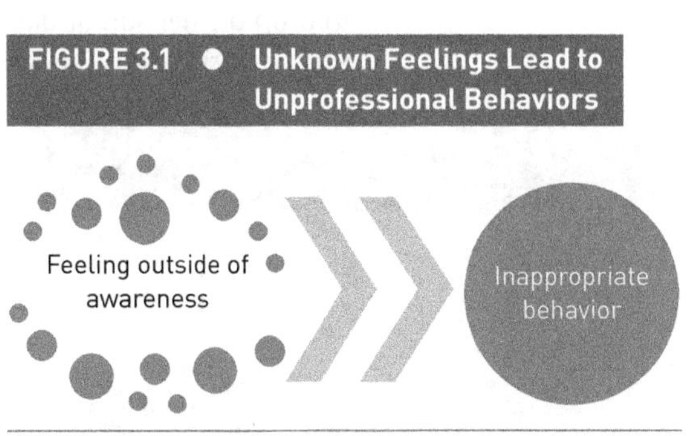

We've finally gotten to the sample cases. Here is an example of a worker who needs to identify feelings and display an attribute that is not immediately present. In this first example, the social worker was bullied as a kid. Memories of being made fun of and pushed around were central parts of the worker's childhood experiences. Since the memories were painful, the worker tried not to think about them. The memories were usually kept outside of awareness. And when the worker took a job in a residential setting for troubled

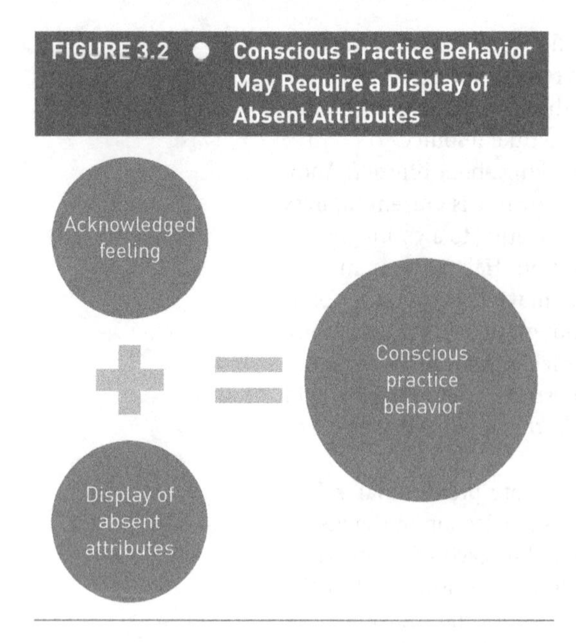

FIGURE 3.2 ● Conscious Practice Behavior May Require a Display of Absent Attributes

adolescent boys, the associated feelings were kept outside of awareness as well. Although unaware of it, the worker was actually afraid of some of the boys. As a result, the worker continually tried to make friends with the boys. Eventually, the worker found himself helping the boys to bend the rules. Because of the hidden fear, the worker had trouble **presenting as an authority figure**. The worker needed to recognize their fear and to display absent attributes. In other words, the worker needed to appear as if they had certain characteristics to best serve the client system. They had to think before they acted. Even though the worker did not feel confident or able to handle a leadership role, it was important to the clients that the worker seem as though they did. If the worker had presented as an authority figure, they would have been consciously carrying out that behavior and reflecting the social work value of service—they couldn't really help the clients while acting as their friend. See Figure 3.3.

Another example of the need to display absent attributes is the case where the social worker was functioning as an administrator and needed to work with staff members in addition to clients. Working with staff members in the role of administrator is an example of macro practice. This worker had no trouble presenting as an authority figure. The worker was employed by an agency that provided group homes for adults who were intellectually challenged, and the worker had a lot of experience appropriately presenting as an authority figure to the clients. The worker was so good at displaying authority that when they received their bachelor of social work (BSW) they were immediately given a promotion to be in charge of one of the homes. The job remained the same, but several responsibilities were added. One change was that now they were in charge of managing the staff schedules. So it was the worker's responsibility to be sure that a staff person was present in the home 24 hours a day. One staff member was experienced and good with the residents, but she was frequently late because she needed to drop off her son at day care before work. The staff member wanted to spend as much time as possible with her son, and she kept him home until the last minute. Unfortunately, every time the staff member was late, the social worker felt as if the staff member betrayed them. They felt personally injured. How could the staff member continue to be late when she knew that she kept the worker there after their shift? One day, the social worker needed to leave right on time. The staff member was late as usual, and the social worker spoke severely to her, saying that she needed to get her priorities straight and be on time or she would be reported to the main office. That staff member was never late again, but she began to do as little as possible on her shifts, developed a short temper with the residents, and soon quit. Here, the social worker had no trouble presenting as an authority figure. But the they needed to display absent attributes. In this case, they needed to be **demonstrating empathy**. Even though the social worker was dealing with a staff member, not a client, they needed to behave in accordance with the social work value of recognizing the dignity and worth of the person. The social

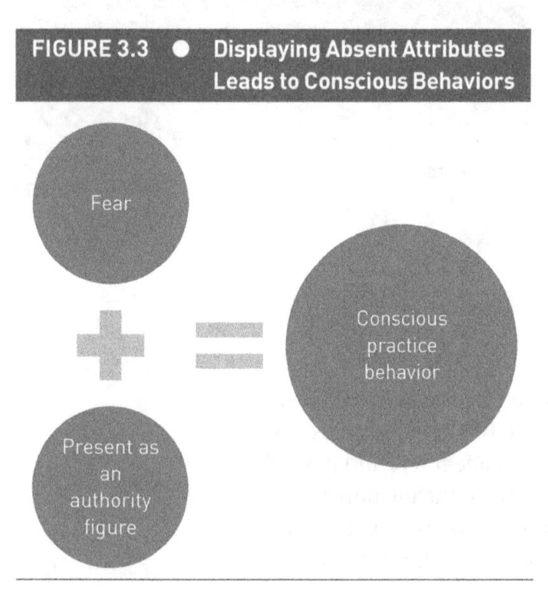

FIGURE 3.3 ● Displaying Absent Attributes Leads to Conscious Behaviors

worker really could not understand a young mother's need to spend as much time as possible with her son. But in this case, the social worker should have behaved as if they had stepped into the staff member's shoes. Of course, the social worker needed to point out the staff member's poor punctuality, but if they had displayed the absent attribute of empathy, they may have done so in a way that the staff member felt supported rather than judged. See Figure 3.4.

In each of these cases, the worker didn't **identify feelings**. Feelings of fear, injury, and anger resulted in inappropriate behavior. If the worker in the youth residential setting had recognized their fear, they could have acknowledged their fear and moved past it. The worker could have presented as an authority figure, carried out the value of service, and upheld the agency policies. Likewise, if the group home manager had recognized their feelings of betrayal, they could have displayed empathy, carried out the social work value of recognizing the dignity and worth of individuals, and kept a valued employee. Without identifying feelings, these workers behaved without thinking. Since they behaved without thinking, they literally didn't know what they were doing. We'll be discussing ways to recognize feelings in Chapter 4 as we continue exploring the importance of self-reflection in social work.

FIGURE 3.4 • Displaying Absent Attributes Leads to Conscious Behaviors

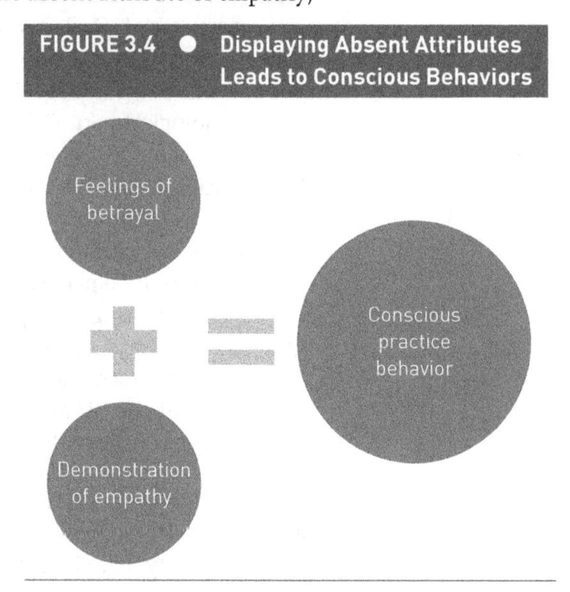

WHAT IF . . . FOCUS ON DIVERSITY

If you look carefully, you will see that Andy created strength from his diversity (disability). Can you see how he did that?

As Andy went slowly up the stairs, he wondered about what the family might think of the challenges he faced with mobility. Do you think he should bring this up during a social work interview with them? How?

Another consideration is this: Not having an elevator showed that YPP was violating the law. Can you think of a good reason for why they were doing so? How do you think Andy could bring this to the attention of the agency administration?

Suppose, like Alfredo, Andy was of Latino ethnicity. From a strengths perspective, how would that facilitate his work with Alfredo, his family, and his school? Will his real ethnicity (Irish American) create any barriers?

Professional Use of Self

In the previous cases, workers needed to engage in worker-centered practice by identifying and managing feelings so that they could behave thoughtfully and professionally. That is, they needed to develop a professional use of self. To learn the process of developing a professional use of self, first consider the meaning of the concept.

As we've mentioned earlier, professional use of self means using conscious behaviors that are informed by social work values. However, the complete definition of professional use of self is complex and abstract. Professional use of self has been said to mean a "broad range of attributes, self-knowledge, relational qualities, and self-disclosures" (Poorvu, 2015, p. 2). It is about who workers are and what they know about themselves. And the professional use of self is used primarily for the purpose of helping others. Since the definition is complex, consider the parts one at a time.

Attributes. To begin, consider the first component: a broad range of attributes. What does that mean to a social worker? Essentially, everything about ourselves. When we think about how we use ourselves in our work as tools to help others, we must include our life experiences, personal characteristics, culture, gender, and more. Our attributes, or characteristics, refer to us as biological, psychological, social, and spiritual beings. Think first of the biological part. Professional use of self includes our physical selves: Our wellness, our illness, our abilities, and our disabilities are all there whether they can be seen or not. Then there's the psychological part. Our mental selves, including our intelligence, our education, our abilities to care for others, our basic personality characteristics, and our memories are all in the social work session whether we feel it or not. Then the social part. Our culture, the traditions we grew up with, the family we knew, our values, the power we experienced, and the discrimination we faced are all with us in the session whether we know it or not. Finally, the spiritual part. Our faith in the presence of a higher being or our faith in the lack of one, the nurturing we experienced, and the alienation we may have felt as part of a faith group are all part of the session whether we believe it or not. We bring everything that we are to the session whether we want to or not. Every one of our attributes can be a barrier to our work with clients. More importantly, every one of our attributes can be a strength or resource in our work with clients and client system representatives.

Relational Qualities. Our relational qualities, or the way we interact with others, are another aspect of ourselves that we bring to the work. Maybe you are a gregarious person who is the life of the party. Put you into a board of directors meeting at a nonprofit agency and you will wow them. Your presentation of a community needs assessment may be counted on to achieve the board's approval to start a new program. But if you're that same gregarious person and you are face-to-face with a client who is quietly making peace with their own death, you might have to work a lot harder. Not that you can't be a hospice worker . . . it just won't be easy. That terminally ill person may be best served by someone who is quiet and intensely spiritual. On the other hand, that quiet social worker may be terrified at the thought of facing your board of directors or a group of landlords in a community. We all have strengths and challenges in the way we approach others. They may be a result of heredity, culture, and life experiences. Since we all need to practice with individuals as well as larger systems, we have to work with our strengths and improve areas where we feel challenged.

Self-Knowledge. To pull it together, since we're bringing all that we are to the work, it's best if we know who we are. Our self-knowledge is what allows us to take our attributes and *consciously* use them to help others. In other words, we engage in the **conscious use of self**—we try to use the attributes that we are aware of in the helping process. A social work researcher has said that the use of self should reflect self in interaction with others (Arnd-Caddigan, 2008). In other words, social workers should know themselves well enough to know that they are to some degree different in different situations. Rather than being a constant, the self can be adapted to work toward relationship building. Remember that Andy is a young man who has trained to be a social worker. That means he has a wealth of knowledge about people in his mind, such as the widely accepted knowledge that Latino people value extended family highly. Because he allowed himself to be caught off guard when he saw so many of Alfredo's family members present at the meeting, he wasn't conscious of that information and couldn't use it to help Alfredo and his family. If Andy had been aware of his knowledge at that moment, he could have pointed out the strength of that family network. This observation could have given people who felt helpless a little hope.

Also, remember that Andy has a grandmother in a long-term care facility. Andy hasn't given it much thought, but deep down, he feels that she could have achieved her dream of staying in her own home if she'd only had more help. He feels guilty that he was away at school and focused on himself when she entered the facility. If you asked Andy, he couldn't tell you about the way his grandmother's situation influenced his thoughts, feelings, and behaviors. He couldn't tell you about it because he isn't thinking about it and hasn't tried to think about it. In fact, he's tried *not* to think about it because it is painful. Not knowing about his feelings, he is likely to allow them to color his work with Alfredo's family. For example, Andy may unconsciously want Alfredo to help his grandmother. He may push him to do so, even if it contributed to his truancy and even if it was not the best thing for Alfredo or his family. For instance, it may have been best if Alfredo's mother had been called upon to carry some responsibility in the family, and it may have been best for Alfredo, who after all was only 12, to focus on his schoolwork. It has been suggested that a good worker has to heal themselves before helping others (Dewane, 2006). This line of thought says the social worker needs self-awareness and self-knowledge in order to help themselves. Andy needed self-awareness and self-knowledge. He could have gotten them through supervision as well as through work with Alfredo's family (Edwards & Bess, 1998).

To begin to gain self-knowledge, workers should ask themselves several questions:

- Why am I in this field?
- What personal need does it fulfill?
- What traits do I bring to this field? (Dewane, 2006, p. 545)

Self-Disclosure. The fourth component of the professional use of self is characterized by **self-disclosure**. Self-disclosure is the conscious sharing of personal information for the purpose of helping. This is when a worker shares some aspect of their life experiences with a representative of a client system. If you listen carefully to regular, everyday conversations, you will find that when some person relates a situation they have been struggling with, the other person often says "Oh, I've had something like that happen to me!" From there, the conversation usually goes one of two ways: Either the conversation shifts back to the first person, with that person feeling like their struggles are shared, or the conversation stays with the second person and focuses on them, leaving the first person distracted but still carrying their problem.

Self-disclosure in helping is similar in that it can be useful to the person who is struggling. It can serve to help them feel as if they are not alone. Self-disclosure can also help a person feel as if their situation is not unusual or that their feelings are to be expected under the circumstances (**normalizing** the feelings). On the other hand, self-disclosure can end up serving the worker. For that reason, self-disclosure must be used with care. It is the conscious sharing of any of the aspects of the self in order to help someone, not for the benefit of the worker. Here are two examples—one where self-disclosure is for the client and one where it is for the worker:

Group Member 1: I feel like everyone in this group is against me!

Group Member 2: That's not true.

Group Member 3: That's just like you, always thinking about yourself.

Group Member 1: *(begins to cry softly)*

Worker: (*feeling empathic for group member 1 and wanting to help her feel better*) I know how you feel. Once when I was in college, I had this class with a bunch of friends. One time we had a test, and I was the only one who did well. It was a time when the professor curved the grades, you know, when only so many people can get As. If one person gets 100%, it makes it harder for everyone else to get an A. And that was me.

> I got 100% on the first test. So the day of the next test came. I got to class just in time. My friends were all already in the room. When I walked in, they suddenly got quiet. They just stared at me, and I felt like they all resented me for doing well on the other test. It seemed like they all wanted me to do badly on this one. Suddenly I felt so alone and miserable.
>
> Group Member 2: How did you do on the test?
>
> Worker: I did very well. And I found out later that my friends really didn't resent me. It was just that they were talking about how I studied a lot for the first test when I walked in, and they were a little embarrassed to be talking about me. That was it. Once I heard that, I felt better. (*pauses*) Well, enough about me, this group is for you. Let's move on . . .

In that scenario, the worker got caught up in telling their own story. The worker probably left the meeting having a sense of **validation**, where they felt like others acknowledged that it made sense for them to feel the way they did. Unfortunately, group member 1 never got their issue resolved or even discussed. Group member 1 probably left the meeting feeling as though they shouldn't let themselves be vulnerable in the group again. What is most troubling is this: Group member 1 left a social work session feeling lonely.

Here is another example of self-disclosure. This one is between a worker and a client system representative.

Client System Representative:	I know you've been helping me and my executive team, and I hope you can help me with this problem.
Worker:	I'll sure try. Go ahead.
Client System Representative:	Well, I was giving a presentation. It was a report about how one of our social work programs performed in the last year. You know, a program evaluation report.
Worker:	(*nodding*) I do. Say more about it. (***verbal encouragement****, to keep the interview moving*)
Client System Representative:	It was an important meeting because this was a funding agency that gives us a grant to provide services to clients. If I didn't provide an impressive report, they could choose to fund a different agency. Our program could live or die based on what I said. I knew I had the responsibility to the clients we serve to keep the program going. Not to mention my colleagues . . . the staff people I'd have to lay off if I didn't get that grant continued for another year.
Worker:	What happened?
Client System Representative:	Well, I was giving my presentation, and all of a sudden it seemed like the room got quiet. I don't know how to describe it, but I knew I'd lost their attention. I don't know how it happened, but I knew I'd lost them. I can't even think about it right now because I am so upset with myself!

Worker: (*feeling empathic for the client and wanting to help them feel better; making a conscious decision to carry out self-disclosure*) I think I have an idea of what you mean. Something similar happened to me the other week when I was meeting . . . with your executive group, actually. I was talking to all of you, things got kind of quiet, and I looked up and none of you were looking at me. It felt like the floor fell out from underneath me.

Client System Representative: Exactly. Like the floor fell out from underneath me. I didn't know that kind of thing happened to you too. You always look so polished.

Worker: Yes, it did happen to me, but go on with your story.

Client System Representative: Well, I haven't heard back from the funder yet, but I need to know what went wrong so it doesn't happen again.

Worker: Sounds like you're thinking you've got to figure this out regardless of what the funder's decision is. (***paraphrasing****, or restating what the client has said in different words so the worker can be sure they understand*)

Client System Representative: That's it. I do have to figure this out regardless of what the decision is. I feel like you'll be able to help me. . . .

This scenario worked out in the client's best interest. The person felt overwhelmed by their situation, and the worker shared an experience that let the client know that they were being understood. Then the worker immediately **focused the interview** and got back to the client's situation. The client felt validated and also felt as if the worker knew something about the problem. The client felt both comfortable with the worker and comforted by the worker's empathy.

What happened that made the two situations fall out differently? In the first scenario, the worker felt for the group member and told a story about their own experiences that felt similar. The worker was making themselves vulnerable in front of the group but felt like it was worth it if they could help the group member to feel better. So far, so good. The problem occurred when the other group member asked the worker a question about their experience and the worker went off topic. The worker never went back to address the first group member's problem. The worker felt good, but the client did not. In the second scenario, the worker also was willing to make themselves vulnerable in front of the client. They told a story to show that they could be empathic about the client's situation and then went back to the client's situation and kept the focus there. The telling of the worker's story was self-disclosure, but it was really still about the client. The worker managed this by being conscious that the story was being told in the client's best interest. This indicates that the worker had a strong and growing ability to develop a professional use of self. Consciousness in the use of attributes, relational qualities, self-knowledge, and self-disclosure is the hallmark of the professional use of self. Continue reading to better understand this important concept.

CRITICAL THINKING AND COLLABORATIVE LEARNING EXERCISES 3.1

1. Working with a partner, answer the questions posed earlier in this section: Why am I in this field? What personal need does it fulfill? What traits do I bring to this field?
2. Talk to each other about what it's like to tell something personal about yourself to someone you've never confided in.
3. Work with a partner. Pretend you are presented with a complex case with an overwhelming number of problems. You feel flabbergasted just thinking about it. The client is so overwhelmed that they can't cope and desperately need to feel they are in competent hands. Identify the feeling that may affect your practice and the absent attributes you would have to display to carry out an appropriate conscious behavior. See the list of social work values in Chapter 1, and figure out what social work value you would be carrying out if you engaged in that conscious behavior.

Section 3.2: How Do We Develop a Professional Use of Self?

This section begins the discussion of how a worker goes about developing a professional use of self. It is a process that allows a social worker to identify feelings so that they can engage in conscious, value-informed behaviors. Note that *feelings* and *emotions* are technically different, but for our purposes, we'll use the terms interchangeably.

Growing a Self That Is Helpful to Others

The development of a professional use of self is a complex process that will be outlined in detail in Chapter 4. Meanwhile, consider the basics. As we've said previously, use of self involves knowing yourself. Knowing yourself allows developing awareness about your own characteristics. The goal of this knowing is ultimately to be aware of your behaviors so that they can facilitate helping and implement our professional values. Conscious behaviors can be used to build relationship and facilitate the helping process. Hanna (2013) articulates the process of consciously choosing behaviors that are informed by values: It is a four-step thinking and feeling exercise that should be one of the first parts of the planned change process. The four steps include answering the following questions:

Vasilina Popova/Getty Images

Introspection is required for developing the professional use of self

1. What do I feel?
2. What do I believe?
3. What do I know?
4. What do I do?

What I Feel

Consideration of professional behavior begins with this question: What do I feel? It seems to be a simple question, but you might find that discovering the answer is difficult. A thorough and well-considered answer will put the worker on the path toward a successful engagement and an accurate assessment of any client system. For this reason, it is important to recognize and describe our feelings. It's best to find a label for your feelings once they are recognized. To do so, use simple words like *mad, sad, happy, afraid,*

FIGURE 3.5 ● Range of Common Emotions

Emotion	Least Possible .... Most Possible
1. Surprised	______________________
2. Afraid	______________________
3. Disgusted	______________________
4. Angry	______________________
5. Guilty	______________________
6. Anxious	______________________
7. Sad	______________________
8. Happy	______________________

etc. Be specific. Answers like "I feel uncomfortable" don't work because uncomfortable can mean anxious or angry or irritated. Remember that the answer to "What do I feel?" almost never begins with "I think . . . "

Identifying your feelings takes some practice. There will be more on this in Chapter 4. For now, consider that a quick way to get a sense about how you are feeling is to look at the following list of emotions in Figure 3.5. You can place a slash on the line relative to the least possible depth of feelings on the left and most strength of possible feelings on the right. You can use the chart to point you toward your feelings in any given moment, and the more often you do it, the more quickly you can do it. Using this scale, you will be labeling your feelings in a general way based on the eight emotions that have been identified as consistent across cultures (Carlson et al., 1989).

It sounds odd, but once feelings are labeled, the worker should focus on separating from the feelings. This is because you want to observe your feelings objectively. The process requires an approach in which the worker stays in the present, feels the feelings, then pulls away. The goal is to accept the feelings, then respond—not react—to them (Hayes & Strosahl, 2004, as cited in Hanna, 2013). Often, the "What do I feel?" question is best answered in the context of supervision with a qualified supervisor in a trusting relationship. Again, we'll explore this in detail in Chapter 4.

FIGURE 3.6 ● Feelings Are Created by Beliefs

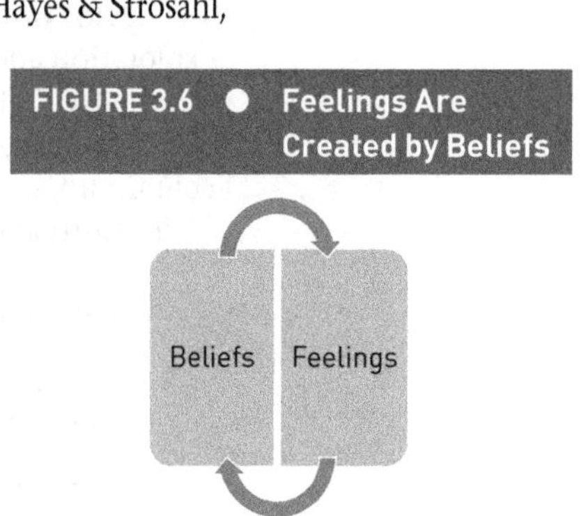

What I Believe

This part is not about feeling; it's about thinking. After labeling feelings and considering them from one step back, the worker's consideration of professional behavior includes a question about beliefs. Many writers, for example Albert Ellis (1996), the founder of rational emotive therapy, suggest that beliefs are thoughts that are influenced by (and influence) feelings (see Figure 3.6).

The Relationship Between Thoughts and Feelings

Also, beliefs both create and are created by values. Beliefs reflect cultural norms and social development. When beliefs exist outside of awareness, they are likely to be ethnocentric, or focused on the worldview of the holder of the beliefs. Most important for the social worker to know about beliefs is that they are driven by an "emotional and spiritual need for answers." This means people tend to cling to their beliefs and perceive the world through them. They are hard to give up and directly influence decision-making. For example, let's say a male social worker believes—without being aware of it—that only women are good at listening. When a troubled client shouts "You're not listening to me!" the worker may feel helpless and not be able to respond to the client's needs. If the worker were aware of his beliefs, he might be able to identify and set aside emotions of helplessness and just feel challenged to do his best work. He may say "I'm sorry you feel that way. Would you mind explaining it again?"

What I Know

Once questions about beliefs and emotions have been answered, it is the worker's task to answer "What do I know?" Often, the "knowing" process works like this: *I have emotions. Those emotions affect my beliefs. To me, my beliefs are the truth. In reality, though, I am assuming that I know something based on my emotions and the beliefs that my emotions create.* That means we think we know things that we only know because of a feeling we had about it. If someone agrees with us, then we are sure. Reality is hard to pin down! One person's truth may be another's lie, and there are as many perceptions of events as there are witnesses. The classic sociological theory of *The Social Construction of Reality* (Berger & Luckmann, 1966) explains that every person's conception of reality is influenced by the way everyone around them perceives the world.

FIGURE 3.7 ● Components of Beliefs

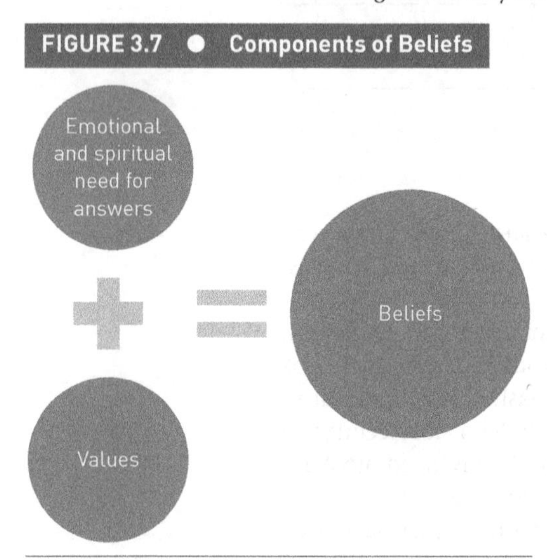

A mature answer to "What do I know?" includes a process of critical thinking, or questioning. Is what I think I know really accurate? Or do I know something based almost entirely on how I feel and what I believe? How much input into what I know has come from others who share my feelings? Critical thinking requires a worker to actively seek out knowledge (not opinion) to support or refute their knowing. For social workers, sources to explore when critically thinking about knowledge and beliefs are scientific journals, information from professional conferences and workshops, and practice wisdom, or information supervisors and others have gathered from years of social work practice.

What I Do

Critical thinking enables professional behavior. Doing is a behavior or activity—in our case a behavior or activity geared toward helping others. Ideally, this action results from the exploration and acceptance of feelings, the examination of beliefs, and the development of knowledge that has been derived from critical thinking and an examination of evidence. To understand Figure 3.8, follow the connecting lines: Read the first column down, the second column up, the third column down.

In shorthand, the process goes like this:

- Emotions happen, and thinking people can consciously identify them.
- Emotions may be driven by spiritual and emotional questions that don't allow them to be easily shifted.
- As the spiritual and emotional questions get answered, beliefs are developed.

FIGURE 3.8 ● The Process of Critical Thinking

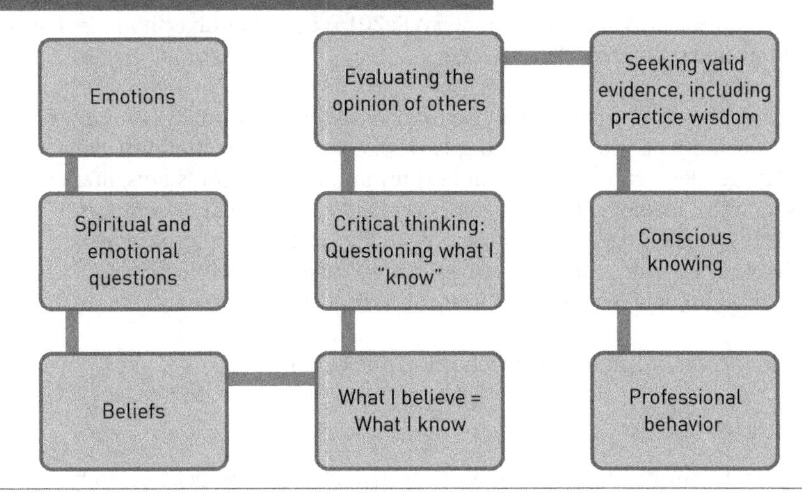

- Once beliefs are developed, people start thinking that what they only believe is actually what they know to be real.
- Mature critical thinking makes social workers wonder whether what they believe is real.
- To find out if what they believe is real, the workers wonder about others' opinions and whether they are truly believable.
- Instead of blindly following the beliefs of others, workers seek out valid evidence from scientific literature and from experts.
- They make conscious decisions about what they know and believe.
- They base their professional behavior on what they know rather than what they feel.

CRITICAL THINKING AND COLLABORATIVE LEARNING EXERCISES 3.2

1. To learn how unconscious behaviors affect your life, work with a partner and identify some behaviors that you carry out automatically, like choosing a desk in a classroom or closing the door to the bathroom. How do these affect those around you?
2. Articulate one belief you have about people in poverty. Do some research, and find out whether your belief is accurate. Share with a partner.

Section 3.3: Aspects of Diversity

One of the root causes of Andy's difficulties with Alfredo's family was that he had not considered areas of diversity. Beliefs about diversity often exist outside of awareness and therefore may become barriers to effective social work. In this section, we consider the meaning of diversity to the generalist social work practitioner. This refers to the worker's own diversity as well as the diversity of clients and client system representatives.

All Kinds of Difference

The Council on Social Work Education (CSWE; 2015) describes diversity in its Educational Policy and Accreditation Standards (EPAS):

> The dimensions of diversity are understood as the intersectionality of multiple factors including but not limited to age, class, color, culture, disability and ability, ethnicity, gender, gender identity and expression, immigration status, marital status, political ideology, race, religion/spirituality, sex, sexual orientation, and tribal sovereign status. Social workers understand that, as a consequence of difference, a person's life experiences may include oppression, poverty, marginalization, and alienation as well as privilege, power, and acclaim.

Take each aspect of this complex definition one at a time.

Intersectionality

Intersectionality can be thought of as a perspective for viewing social inequity. The idea is that diverse characteristics of people can result in oppression or power and that some groups of people may experience a number of those characteristics. When a number of characteristics come together, power can be magnified. Likewise, intersectionality can create oppression that is magnified. Specifically, intersectionality is a way of thinking about difference where gender, sexuality, class, and race are intertwined. The relationships among these areas of difference are complex, and they reinforce each other (Mattsson, 2013). People occupy social positions where areas of difference overlap (Ceaser, 2014). For this reason, it is important to identify the complexity of people and their experiences (Beyer & Woehrle, 2014). For example, in the United States oppression is often thought to be related to race. When we think of oppression exclusively this way, though, we miss important information about people's experiences. A person may experience oppression because they are African American, yes. But that person may also experience oppression as a woman, as an immigrant who is undocumented, as a practitioner of the Muslim religion. In that case, the oppression is magnified. On the other hand, intersectionality can magnify power. For example, a white person will usually experience power over others if all else is equal. If that white person is a male who is wealthy, that power is magnified. If a town council is trying to decide whether they want to allow a certain tract of land to be developed and the person making the request is a white, wealthy male, we can assume that he stands a better chance of approval even if his development plan is opposed by a group of financially challenged minority representatives.

Of Multiple Factors

There are many characteristics of people that could potentially come together and magnify power or oppression. These characteristics include but are not limited to age, class, color, culture, disability and ability, ethnicity, gender, gender identity and expression, immigration status, marital status, political ideology, race, religion or spirituality, sex, sexual orientation, and tribal sovereign status. It is important to note the phrase "include but are not limited to." This reminds people that the list of characteristics is likely to leave out some people. For example, financial capability is not on the list but is certainly an area of diversity.

Life Experiences and Intersectionality

Multiple factors of identity may be causes of oppression. These factors can multiply oppression, and people's experiences may include not just oppression but its resultant poverty, marginalization, and alienation. This suggests that a person's characteristics can come together to result in experiences that leave the person with few resources and little ability to impact their society. On the other hand, people's characteristics may come together in a positive way. Some characteristics separately and together may result in privilege, power, and acclaim. We could say that in the United States and many other Western countries to be male is to experience privilege. This may be true, but other characteristics may moderate or may boost this effect. A male who is African American with little financial capability has two characteristics that may compound experiences of oppression and economic status. He may be expected to have a much different life experience than a male who is white and wealthy. Likewise, a female may expect to experience oppression just by virtue of being female. But what about a Latina who is wealthy and a white woman who is economically disadvantaged? The two characteristics come together in different ways. Oppression will affect each person differently. Consider an economically disadvantaged white man and a wealthy black man. What else do you need to know about each before you think critically about their position in society? Andy is a white, middle-class man who has a physical disability. Alfredo is a Latino youth who is economically disadvantaged. It is Andy's job to consider all of the ways Alfredo's diversity may affect his life experiences negatively and which ways they may come together to provide power and resources. That is, it is Andy's job to consider the **intersectionality** of Alfredo's areas of diversity. The theory of social economy suggests that there is social and potentially economic value in people's characteristics (Mook, Whitman, Armstrong, & Quarter, 2015), so Andy will need to judge which of Alfredo's characteristics add to or detract from his social desirability in his current environment. It will help him to identify which characteristics are strengths.

Strengths in Diversity

While Alfredo's various diverse characteristics may contribute negatively to his life experiences, it is important for Andy to recognize that Alfredo's diversity undoubtedly contains strengths as well. It has already become apparent that Alfredo's close-knit family is a great strength. He has a number of resources in his own unique factors—his sister's unconditional love, his aunt's educational support, his teacher's empathy, his uncle's role modeling—that will moderate negative experience with positive ones. As a Latino male, Alfredo is able to display *machismo*, and he is valued in his culture for doing so. Alfredo may not realize that he is unusually handsome or bright. It is Andy's job to help Alfredo discover all of the resources that he can draw from himself, his family members, and his community.

As we've discussed in Chapter 1, the strengths perspective is a significant component of generalist social work practice that we'll be discussing throughout this book. In addition, it may be said that social workers have an ethical mandate to seek out the strengths in people's diverse characteristics. After all, one of the profession's core values is the recognition of the dignity and worth of the person.

CRITICAL THINKING AND COLLABORATIVE LEARNING EXERCISES 3.3

1. Discuss diversity with a partner. Consider how the two of you are alike and how you are different. Consider how the two of you are different from the majority of the people living in your communities. Examine what your differences bring to your life experiences. Don't forget to consider intersectionality—how do your areas of difference magnify each other?
2. Research your partner's ethnicity (even if it is your own). Discover one strength and one challenge that are common to people in that group. What is the social work value that demands you learn about clients' ethnicities?
3. For one day, make an effort to point out a strength to everyone you talk with that day. Make a note of their responses.

Section 3.4: The Code of Ethics

Here we'll explore the heart of social work: the *NASW Code of Ethics* (NASW, 2018). Our code drives our quest to behave professionally and to recognize the strengths in diversity.

Developing a Guide to Social Work Behavior

It's important for social workers to know how their *NASW Code of Ethics* (NASW, 2018) came to be. That understanding can help us to understand where the code has gotten its characteristics.

SELF-REFLECTION 3: HOPE INDEX

Hope is what lies between wishes and expectations. Andy might wish Alfredo to behave in certain ways, but if he has no hope that Alfredo can reach his goals, he is not likely to help Alfredo develop hope. In order to use the strengths perspective, to see strengths in people, you need to feel able to expect to see those characteristics you wish they had. Fill out the Hope Index located on pages 88–89. How might your score affect your social work practice?

Development

Like government's social welfare policies, the *NASW Code of Ethics* (NASW, 2018) has been developed and is updated by an elected body. In this case, members of NASW elect national representatives, or delegates. From those representatives, members are selected to be part of the Code of Ethics Review Task Force of the Delegate Assembly to create revisions. Members are approved by the NASW Board of Directors and appointed by the NASW president. The task force creates a draft of the new code, works toward approval by the Delegate Assembly, and seeks input from NASW members prior to issuing a final draft (Reamer, 2013). Since this is a long process, the code is not revised often. The edition prior to the current 2018 edition was first published in 1996.

Frederic Reamer is social work's most recognizable ethics scholar. He has been part of the most recent revisions of the *NASW Code of Ethics* (NASW, 2018) and provides a description of the document in the *Encyclopedia of Social Work* (Reamer, 2008). The first part of the code is called the Preamble, and it includes the mission of social work and its six core values:

> The primary mission of the social work profession is to enhance human well-being and help meet the basic human needs of all people, with particular attention to the needs and empowerment of people who are vulnerable, oppressed, and living in poverty. A historic and defining feature of social work is the profession's focus on individual well-being in a social context and the well-being of society. Fundamental to social work is attention to the environmental forces that create, contribute to, and address problems in living. (NASW, 2018, p. 1)

It is important to know that the mission of the profession includes two features—(1) concern for individuals' well-being and (2) concern for environmental forces. These two features mark generalist social work practice.

Values

Flowing from that mission are the six core values:

1. service
2. social justice
3. dignity and worth of the person

4. importance of human relationships
5. integrity
6. competence

(The core values will be discussed in more detail when the specific use of the code for ethical decision-making is considered later.)

Function

The second section of the *NASW Code of Ethics* (NASW, 2018) talks about its main functions. The primary function of the code is to provide values and standards to guide all social workers' professional behavior every day. Another important function is that the *NASW Code of Ethics* (NASW, 2018) serves to socialize new professionals. In other words, new social workers can learn what social work is all about by reading the *NASW Code of Ethics* (NASW, 2018). This part of the code also reminds social workers that there is help available when they try to figure out how to behave in challenging circumstances. As a result, you could use an ethical decision-making model, get supervision, and receive consultation from a social work organization like NASW.

It is important to note that this part of the code explains that there will be instances when two principles, standards, or ethical statements conflict with each other or some outside situation. This is called an **ethical dilemma**. The process of resolving this conflict is called **managing ethical dilemmas**. A part of managing ethical dilemmas is the understanding that the code is not a recipe book: It acknowledges that there are no right answers to ethical dilemmas and that two social workers may choose two very different responses to the same ethical dilemma.

Principles

Next, the *NASW Code of Ethics* (NASW, 2018) presents principles that flow from social work's mission and six core values. These principles explain exactly what is meant by the six core values. Principles are statements that implement values—in this case, the importance of human relationships. The principle associated with the value "importance of human relationships" is "social workers recognize the central importance of human relationships" (p. 6). Then, the principle is explained further. In this case, the explanation is "social workers understand that relationships between and among people are important vehicles for change. Social workers engage people as partners in the helping process. Social workers seek to strengthen relationships among people in a purposeful effort to promote, restore, maintain, and enhance the well-being of individuals, families, social groups, organizations, and communities" (p. 6).

Standards

The last section of the *NASW Code of Ethics* (NASW, 2018) includes 155 ethical statements organized into six areas of responsibility, or standards. These standards will be considered in more detail later. For now, know that social workers are responsible to the following:

- clients
- colleagues
- in practice settings
- as professionals
- to the profession
- to the broader society

An example of an ethical statement that falls under the area of Responsibility to Clients is 1.05 Cultural Competence and Social Diversity. That ethical statement reads as follows:

a. Social workers should understand culture and its function in human behavior and society, recognizing the strengths that exist in all cultures.

b. Social workers should have a knowledge base of their clients' cultures and be able to demonstrate competence in the provision of services that are sensitive to clients' cultures and to differences among people and cultural groups.

c. Social workers should obtain education about and seek to understand the nature of social diversity and oppression with respect to race, ethnicity, national origin, color, sex, sexual orientation, gender identity or expression, age, marital status, political belief, religion, immigration status, and mental or physical disability. (NASW, 2018, p. 6)

ETHICAL PERSPECTIVES

Take a look at the Ethical Principles section of the NASW Code of Ethics *(NASW, 2018) on page 5. Which of those principles do you find to be most important? Why?*

In general, the code's standards concern three kinds of issues (Reamer, 2003, 2009, 2013). (The first includes what can be described as "mistakes" social workers might make that have ethical implications. Examples include leaving confidential documents displayed in public areas in such a way that they can be read by others or forgetting to include important details in a client's informed consent document.) See Figure 3.9.

The second category of concern includes issues associated with difficult ethical decisions—for example, whether to disclose confidential information to protect a third party from harm, barter with low-income clients who want to exchange goods for social work services, or terminate services to a noncompliant client. The final category includes issues pertaining to social worker misconduct, such as exploitation of clients, boundary violations, or fraudulent billing for services rendered.

Other issues that can show up, especially for new workers, are conflicts between the worker and the values themselves. For example, as a social worker you value the dignity and worth of the person. Seems clear, right? But look at its related ethical principle. It says this: "Social workers promote clients' socially responsible self-determination." Now, suppose you have an adult client who continues to return to a relationship where their partner is controlling—doesn't allow them to get a job, doesn't allow them to go out with friends, etc. You believe the relationship to be abusive. Will you encourage self-determination and consider a broad range of options with the client, or will you place your own values about interpersonal relationships foremost and try to convince them to leave their partner? Suppose a client of yours wants to have an abortion and your religious beliefs are strongly against voluntarily terminating a pregnancy. Will you push your values, or will you help her to consider every option objectively? Social workers need to consider their own values so they don't push them on others.

FIGURE 3.9 • Format of the *NASW Code of Ethics*

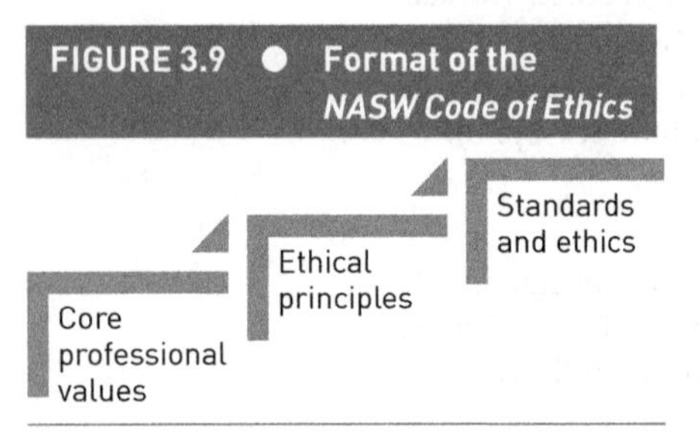

Source: NASW, 2018.

CRITICAL THINKING AND COLLABORATIVE LEARNING EXERCISES 3.4

1. Consider the core social work values. Do any of your personal values conflict with them?
2. Consider the *NASW Code of Ethics* (NASW, 2018), and choose the one ethical responsibility that seems most meaningful. Share with a partner, and discuss why this particular element of the code creates an emotional response in you.
3. Consider the one ethical responsibility that may conflict with your personal values. How can you prepare to focus on professional values in your practice?

Section 3.5: What Is an Ethical Dilemma?

In this section, we explore how to employ the *NASW Code of Ethics* (NASW, 2018) using an ethical decision-making model.

Difficult Decisions

Social workers are proud of their code of ethics. It is often at the forefront of their minds, and unlike other professionals, you will hear social workers frequently talk about their code. It is not unusual for a social worker to be heard saying this: "I can't do that. It is against my code of ethics." Another may be heard struggling not to be "unethical." The social worker's code of ethics is a part of their everyday practice, and sometimes almost every day can bring another dilemma. An ethical dilemma occurs when two or more ethical principles, standards, or ethical statements are in conflict and there doesn't seem to be a good outcome. These are the situations where a worker is torn between two or more different actions. For example, a client becomes so angry with his ex-wife's new partner that he threatens to kill him. Probably it is just angry words. But is the worker responsible to tell that person they may be in danger, violating their client's confidentiality? Or should the worker call the police? Are there any laws that address this situation? What about the worker's first responsibility—to provide service to the client?

In another situation, a young mother confesses that she has to leave her baby alone for an hour on those days when she must go in early if she wants to keep her job. The job is low-paying, but it is her only income. Should the worker try to help her solve the problem, or should the worker call Child Protective Services (CPS) immediately?

Or a client who works in human services suggests that they feel compelled to overreport the hours they spend in direct contact with clients in order to meet agency requirements. Should the staff person be reported right away or be given a chance to mend their ways? Is this the responsibility of a peer? What is at risk for the agency?

In each of these scenarios, the worker could take two or more different paths. In every case, they would not know if they have chosen the correct action. In fact, there may be no correct action. The choice may be between two evils. Two ethical social workers may encounter the same exact situation, reference the same code of ethics, and respond in entirely different ways. Neither one would be right or wrong.

Why Use a Model for Ethical Decision-Making?

Ethical dilemmas are painful. Every social worker wants to do what is best for clients and client systems. Ethical dilemmas can keep social workers awake at night, especially since none of the outcomes will be entirely good. Since two ethical social workers may choose different outcomes to an ethical dilemma, it is important for each one to be able to explain their actions. This process begins with identifying an ethical dilemma. Most often, a worker can tell if they are facing an ethical dilemma because they suddenly feel anxious about a case. A gnawing in the pit of their stomach or even a nightmare about the case can be a red flag. Frequently, the worker will take the situation to a staff meeting and put it out for others to consider. And all too often that discussion goes round and round the available options with everyone in the room becoming anxious and frustrated.

In the earlier example where the staff person was cheating on their record keeping, two different social workers may say the following:

- "This person is placing their agency at risk. Social workers have a responsibility to the broader community. It's in the code of ethics. If the funder realizes that they have been cheated, there will be an audit and funds may have to be returned.

People may be laid off, the agency may lose its good reputation, clients will suffer. Report right away!" *or*

- "Don't report right away! Social workers have a responsibility to colleagues. It's in the code of ethics. Talk to your colleague, and urge them to get help. If they don't, it is time to report them to a supervisor."

There may be no correct answer, but the worker has to be able to justify their actions and needs to feel as confident as possible in their choice. For these reasons, it is best for the worker to use an ethical decision-making model that is based on the *NASW Code of Ethics* (NASW, 2018).

Types of Decision-Making

There are many ways to think about decision-making. We'll cover them briefly here, since it is important to know that people can have very widely different perspectives on ethics. You should know that an entire book or full semester class could focus on any of these decision-making methods. We are barely scratching the surface, so you know that there is a great deal of diversity in the way people think. First, there's the **utilitarian** perspective. The balance between most good and least harm is important. From this perspective, you worry about outcomes and the balance between the good and bad. The rights perspective focuses on people making decisions based on what they think people's basic rights are. There is debate about that because not everyone agrees on exactly what basic rights are, but everyone can make their own decisions about that. The justice approach focuses on fairness, or equality. This approach has problems because people have a hard time distinguishing between equality and equity. The common good approach says that decisions should be made on compassion for everyone. The virtual approach is about behaviors. It asks this: "What kind of person will I be if I do this?" (Perry & Bratman, 2015). It's not necessary to choose one of these, but it wouldn't hurt for you to revisit them right now and see which appeals to you the most. Your own personal values will affect your ethical decision-making.

A simple mnemonic device helps us think about ethical decision-making in a broad-brush kind of way. The following table is adapted from the work of Congress (2000, p. 10):

ETHIC Model of Decision-Making

E	Examine relevant professional values and responsibilities; examine the situation from a multisystem perspective.
T	Think about what values, standards, and ethics of the *NASW Code of Ethics* (NASW, 2018) applies as well as relevant laws and agency-based policies. *Determine whether an ethical dilemma exists.*
H	Hypothesize about possible consequences of different decisions.
I	Identify who will benefit and who will be harmed in view of social work's commitment to the most vulnerable.
C	Consult with supervisor and colleagues about the most ethical choice.

Using this memorization device as our base, we'll consider a model for carrying it out in detail.

An Ethical Decision-Making Model

An ethical decision-making model (inspired by Dolgoff, Loewenberg, & Harrington, 2011; Reamer, 1995) provides direction for work when an ethical problem emerges in social work practice. A worker facing a dilemma may take the following steps to arrive at a decision on what action to take:

- CLARIFY the important values and ethical responsibilities dictated by our profession and prioritize them.
- ASSESS the situation. Think about what individuals, families, groups, organizations, and communities might be affected by your decision.
- STUDY the *NASW Code of Ethics* (NASW, 2018) for specific directions related to your issue.
- CONSIDER any legal or agency-based policies that may influence your decision.
- IDENTIFY the values or ethical standards in conflict to determine whether there is a dilemma.
- SEEK supervision with peers and a supervisor.
- IDENTIFY options.
- LIST relevant parts of the *NASW Code of Ethics* (NASW, 2018) that support each of the options.
- SEEK supervision again.
- DETERMINE a course of action. Consider professional values and responsibilities to do so.
- ACT.
- EVALUATE.

You can see that this is not a simple process. It is not meant to be. The people you serve depend on you. You will have to face ethical decisions your entire career, so you'd better become familiar with an ethical decision-making process that will serve you in the years to come. Let's think about each step one at a time.

1. Clarify the important values and ethical responsibilities dictated by our profession.

   To carry out this step, the worker should write down the six professional social work values as noted in the preamble of the social work *NASW Code of Ethics* (NASW, 2018):

   a. service
   b. social justice
   c. dignity and worth of the person
   d. importance of human relationships
   e. integrity
   f. competence

   Then the worker should carefully consider the meaning of each by considering the ethical principles outlined in the *NASW Code of Ethics* (NASW, 2018). Of course, you don't need to write these down, but reading them will help you get into the mind-set you need for ethical decision-making in social work.

   i. Value: *Service*

      Ethical Principle: *Social workers' primary goal is to help people in need and to address social problems.* Social workers elevate service to others above self-interest. Social workers draw on their knowledge, values, and skills to help people in need and to address social problems. Social workers are encouraged to volunteer some portion of their professional skills with no expectation of significant financial return (pro bono service).

ii. Value: *Social justice*

Ethical Principle: *Social workers challenge social injustice.* Social workers pursue social change, particularly with and on behalf of vulnerable and oppressed individuals and groups of people. Social workers' social change efforts are focused primarily on issues of poverty, unemployment, discrimination, and other forms of social injustice. These activities seek to promote sensitivity to and knowledge about oppression and cultural and ethnic diversity. Social workers strive to ensure access to needed information, services, and resources; equality of opportunity; and meaningful participation in decision making for all people.

iii. Value: *Dignity and worth of the person*

Ethical Principle: *Social workers respect the inherent dignity and worth of the person.* Social workers treat each person in a caring and respectful fashion, mindful of individual differences and cultural and ethnic diversity. Social workers promote clients' socially responsible self-determination. Social workers seek to enhance clients' capacity and opportunity to change and to address their own needs. Social workers are cognizant of their dual responsibility to clients and to the broader society. They seek to resolve conflicts between clients' interests and the broader society's interests in a socially responsible manner consistent with the values, ethical principles, and ethical standards of the profession.

iv. Value: *Importance of human relationships*

Ethical Principle: *Social workers recognize the central importance of human relationships.* Social workers understand that relationships between and among people are an important vehicle for change. Social workers engage people as partners in the helping process. Social workers seek to strengthen relationships among people in a purposeful effort to promote, restore, maintain, and enhance the well-being of individuals, families, social groups, organizations, and communities.

v. Value: *Integrity*

Ethical Principle: *Social workers behave in a trustworthy manner.* Social workers are continually aware of the profession's mission, values, ethical principles, and ethical standards and practice in a manner consistent with them. Social workers act honestly and responsibly and promote ethical practices on the part of the organizations with which they are affiliated.

vi. Value: *Competence*

Ethical Principle: *Social workers practice within their areas of competence and develop and enhance their professional expertise.* Social workers continually strive to increase their professional knowledge and skills and to apply them in practice. Social workers should aspire to contribute to the knowledge base of the profession.

Next, the worker should write down the six areas of a professional social worker's responsibilities:

a. clients

b. colleagues

c. in practice settings

d. as professionals

e. to the profession

f. to the broader society

These, too, should get careful consideration. The *NASW Code of Ethics* (NASW, 2018) suggests the following:

i. **Standard: Responsibility to Clients**
Meaning: Service to clients is paramount. However, obligations to society or on occasion to legal requirements may supersede the responsibility to clients. Clients should be informed of this possibility.

ii. **Standard: Responsibility to Colleagues**
Meaning: Professional peers, supervisors, supervisees, and trainees are all considered to be colleagues.

iii. **Standard: Responsibility in Practice Settings**
Meaning: This standard refers to the social worker's employing or hosting agency and reflects any responsibility such as record keeping, seeking supervision, and generally following established policies.

iv. **Standard: Responsibility as a Professional**
Meaning: Social workers are responsible to display competence and to avoid allowing their personal lives to interfere with their ethical duties.

v. **Standard: Responsibility to the Social Work Profession**
Meaning: Social workers should strive to uphold the high standards of the profession and should participate in the research process to help develop the profession's knowledge base.

vi. **Standard: Responsibility to the Broader Society**
Meaning: Social workers should feel a responsibility for all society from local communities to global considerations. Social workers should not fail to advocate for living conditions where obligations to human rights are met through both social and political action.

2. **Assess the situation.**
The second step in the ethical decision-making process is for the worker to consider the situation from multiple levels in terms of individuals, families, groups, organizations, and communities. The perspectives of all of the key people should be considered.

3. **Think about the *NASW Code of Ethics* (NASW, 2018) for any statements that directly address your situation.**
Consider the values, the standards, and individual ethical responsibilities as well.

4. **Consider any legal or agency-based policies that may influence your decision.**
Sometimes an illegal act may become apparent in ethical decision-making. Other times, an action may seem desirable that is against agency policy. The *NASW Code of Ethics* (NASW, 2018) states that social workers have obligations to the community as well as the agency, but it does not specifically say that a worker cannot break the law or agency policy. The worker will have to weigh the importance of this factor. Maybe they risk losing their job. Maybe they risk criminal charges. These scenarios require careful consideration.

5. **Determine whether an ethical dilemma exists. Identify values and standards in conflict.**
   The next step in the ethical decision-making process is the application of the values, principles, standards, and ethical statements to the case. This step involves identifying those that are in conflict. Note that sometimes a situation feels uncomfortable and taking action is difficult, but there is truly only one option that is ethically correct. In these situations, there is no ethical dilemma.

6. **Seek supervision from peers and a supervisor to hypothesize about possible consequences of different decisions.**
   Sometimes peers will have faced dilemmas similar to the one you are facing. The more options you can create, the better.

7. **Identify options associated with the values and standards in conflict.**
   Sometimes, there are many options for actions. Often, though, the conflicting values and standards point to one action or a corresponding, opposite one. Often these can be expressed as a question with a yes or no answer. If possible, simplify your dilemma by distilling it down to two options. For example, the ethical statement referring to client confidentiality alongside the ethical statement that says our primary responsibility is to promote the well-being of clients forces the worker to think carefully before answering this question: Should I call CPS?

8. **List parts of the code that support each of the options.**
   As values and standards are considered, ideas supporting each ethical option will emerge. It is best to write them down.

9. **Seek supervision again.**
   At this stage, two or more concrete options have been identified and a rationale for each can be articulated. This information should be shared with a supervisor or a group for peer supervision. Others will provide additional perspectives and help to determine which action outweighs the other. The worker will consider specific duties as outlined in the code as well as scientific literature that may demonstrate options for workers in these situations.

10. **Determine a course of action.**
    Here, the worker considers the pros and cons of taking each of the options. They are guided by the professional values and responsibilities they carefully considered at the beginning of the process. Consultation with the supervisor will help determine the ultimate choice.

11. **Act.**
    The worker takes action. Note that sometimes taking action means not doing anything at all.

12. **Evaluate.**
    The worker thinks carefully of all of the outcomes that have occurred based on their actions and returns to the supervisor and peers so that all can learn from the experience.

The process may be written down using the following table:

1. Write down social work values. a. b. c. d. e. f. Order these by your perception of importance.	Write down ethical standards. a. b. c. d. e. f. Order these by your perception of importance.
2. Assess the situation. Identify relevant people. Identify relevant social systems.	
3. Identity values or standards in conflict. Does an ethical dilemma exist? Y/N	Identify relevant ethical requirements from the *NASW Code of Ethics* (NASW, 2018).
4. Seek supervision. What are the important questions?	
5. Identify a question ("Should I . . .") and at least two possible responses. a.	b.
6. List relevant systems, laws, agency policies, and specific ethical duties that support each option.	
7. Seek supervision. Seek information from the *NASW Code of Ethics* (NASW, 2018) list of duties, from scientific literature, experts, and peers. Consider your own prioritization of the values and areas of responsibilities.	
8. Determine a course of action. Consider pros and cons of various actions. Take action.	
9. Evaluate and share results.	

A Sample Ethical Dilemma

To try out the ethical decision-making model, consider a dilemma on a macro level that is similar to the one mentioned earlier where a worker was fudging their records of client services. Let's say Sandy works at a not-for-profit social work agency that relies on grants and private donations for its survival. She knows that raising money is always a challenge for the executive director. She's assigned the task of developing a creative format for the agency's annual report. The idea is to make the report attractive and easy to read so that donors will feel good about the work the agency is doing and give more money. One day, the executive director comes into Sandy's office and closes the door. The director tells her to falsify the report so that the agency looks better. When Sandy hesitates, the director tells her that they are working with a big donor who has strict performance benchmarks. This donor's contributions will help the agency exist for the next year. The director points out that they are just asking her to stretch a couple of numbers by a few percentage points. They let her know that without this large donation one of her coworkers may be laid off.

She might follow the decision-making model like this:

1. Write down social work values. a. service b. social justice c. dignity and worth of the person d. importance of human relationships e. integrity f. competence Order these by your perception of importance.	Write down ethical standards. a. clients b. colleagues c. in practice settings d. as professionals e. to the profession f. to the broader society Order these by your perception of importance.
2. Assess the situation. Identify relevant people. The executive director The board of directors My supervisor	Identify relevant social systems. Individuals (feelings of integrity as a professional may be compromised; coworker could be laid off) Community (some services could be eliminated if a staff person is laid off)
3. Identity values or standards in conflict. Does an ethical dilemma exist? Y/N Yes, an ethical dilemma exists: Social Justice: "Social workers strive to ensure access to needed information, service, and resources." Integrity: "Social workers honestly and responsibly and promote ethical practices on the part of the organization with which they are affiliated." Seek supervision. What are the important questions? Questions are about reporting or complying without question.	Identify relevant ethical requirements from the *NASW Code of Ethics* (NASW, 2018). Social Workers' Ethical Responsibility to Clients 1.01 Commitment to clients: "primary responsibility is to promote the well-being of clients . . . clients' interests are primary" Social Workers' Ethical Responsibility to Colleagues 2.05 Consultation: "Social workers should seek the advice and counsel of colleagues whenever such consultation is in the best interests of clients." Social Workers' Ethical Responsibilities as Professionals 4.04: Social workers should not permit their private conduct to interfere with their ability to fulfill their professional responsibilities.

4. Identify a question ("Should I . . .") and at least two possible responses. **Should I falsify the report?** **Yes. Follow the director's request.** **Yes, but report to supervisor for consultation.**	Should I falsify the report? **No. I should stand on my integrity.** **No. I should refuse and should get help from my supervisor to report the executive director to the board of directors**
5. List relevant systems, laws, agency policies, and specific ethical duties that support each option. Agency policy demands workers follow supervisors' directions Community: clients' interests will be primary; they will receive services.	Agency policy: If funding does not come in, agency's budgetary policy will require board to instruct director to lay off a staff person
6. Seek supervision. Seek information from the *NASW Code of Ethics* (NASW, 2018) list of duties, from scientific literature, experts, and peers. Consider your own prioritization of the values and areas of responsibilities. Supervisor is likely to support a decision to refuse to falsify the report, but they are not able to protect the worker from possible consequences.	
7. Determine a course of action. Consider pros and cons of various actions. Take action. See possible outcomes, which follow this table.	
8. Evaluate and share results.	

Outcome Option A

Sandy believes that a false report is unethical. However, she tells herself that the community benefit is of greatest importance. She falsifies the report. The agency gets the grant. Sandy is offered a promotion, but she never feels quite comfortable. When an opportunity arises, she quits and moves to another agency.

Outcome Option B

Sandy falsifies the report but seeks consultation from her supervisor. Her supervisor disapproves but understands Sandy's struggle and will support her emotionally either way. Her supervisor cannot protect Sandy from any consequences her actions might take. Sandy is offered a promotion but instead makes a lateral move to another program within the agency. She continues to feel uncomfortable about her decision.

Outcome Option C

Sandy writes the report accurately and submits it to the director. She is not fired, but she is passed over for her next promotion. When an opportunity arises, she makes a lateral move to another program within the agency. She maintains a friendly relationship with her supervisor, who respects her decision.

Outcome Option D

Sandy writes the report accurately. She seeks consultation from her supervisor about reporting the director's actions to the board of directors. Her supervisor will support her but will not participate as she fears her job is at risk. Sandy writes a report to the chair of the board of directors and testifies at a private meeting of the board. The director is fired. Sandy becomes known among social workers across the agency as a kind of hero, but administrators are wary of her and she will not be offered a promotion.

Consider the following ethical dilemma yourself:

A Dilemma in Andy's Case

Andy met again with Alfredo and his family. At the end of that meeting, he felt like he was establishing relationships with the family members and that he had gotten a lot of information. The person he learned very little about was Alfredo, so he scheduled a time for him to meet with Alfredo alone. At that meeting, Andy learned that Alfredo idolized his older brother, Manfred. Manfred spent time with Alfredo, keeping him off the streets, and Manfred often told Alfredo that he needed to go to school if he wanted to make anything of himself. Manfred was potentially a great resource for Alfredo. But Alfredo also told Andy that Manfred often smoked marijuana in the evenings in his bedroom. Alfredo often sat with his brother in his room since Manfred had a big TV so he was regularly being exposed to the smoking and to the smoke. Andy did some research and found that marijuana is considered to be a gateway drug, or one that leads young people to use more dangerous drugs. Andy also learned that Alfredo was at high risk for developing an addiction based on his mother's history. The situation became complicated when Alfredo made it clear that he didn't want Andy to tell anyone, especially not the child welfare social worker, who was in the process of determining whether Alfredo's grandmother was an adequate caregiver. Andy knew that if Manfred became angry he could undermine Andy's relationship with Alfredo. Manfred might also cut off his mostly positive relationship with Alfredo. He wondered what to do.

The more Andy thought about it, the more confused and concerned he became. He knew he didn't want to file any reports until he spoke with Manfred or another family member, but he just didn't know what to do. At last, he brought the situation to supervision, telling his supervisor he needed help. Andy's supervisor suggested he complete the ethical decision-making process before the next supervisory meeting. He completed the ethical decision-making table the following way:

1. Write down social work values.	Write down ethical standards.
a. importance of human relationships	a. clients
b. service	b. colleagues
c. social justice	c. to the broader society
d. dignity and worth of the person	d. in practice settings
e. integrity	e. as professionals
f. competence	f. to the profession
Order these by your perception of importance.	Order these by your perception of importance.

2. Assess the situation. Identify relevant people. Alfredo Manfred Alfredo's grandmother Alfredo's uncle Child welfare worker Mentor Probation officer	Identify relevant social systems. Justice system (marijuana use and truancy) Public child welfare (current investigation) Family School Mentor agency
3. Identity values or standards in conflict. Does an ethical dilemma exist? Y/N Yes: Service (client well-being conflicts with confidentiality) Responsibility to the broader community (community danger related to drug abuse and the social worker's responsibility to the welfare of the community conflicts with confidentiality) Seek supervision. Consider what questions are important. Questions are about confidentiality and the worker's relationship with the client. Other questions concern the value of Alfredo's family to his development.	Identify relevant ethical requirements from the *NASW Code of Ethics* (NASW, 2018). 1.01 Commitment to clients: primary responsibility is to clients . . . clients' interest are primary . . . social workers' responsibility to the larger society or specific legal obligations may on limited occasions supersede the loyalty owed clients . . .
4. Identify a question ("Should I . . . ") and two possible responses. Should I confront Manfred? Yes. Speak directly to Manfred, or speak to another family member.	No. Don't confront Manfred or suggest that Alfredo do so. Don't make a report to the probation officer or the child welfare worker.
5. List relevant systems, laws, agency policies, and specific ethical duties that support each option. Alfredo is at risk of future substance abuse. Confront Manfred or help Alfredo to confront him. Discuss potential implications of actions on child welfare investigation.	The worker–client relationship would be harmed, perhaps irrevocably, and if so, no further service could be provided. Manfred may become angry and refuse to spend time with Alfredo while undermining the worker–client relationship. The child welfare investigation could lead to a foster care placement for Alfredo.
6. Seek supervision. The supervisor finds dilemma compelling, states that Andy will be supported for the time being regardless of his decision, and agrees to brainstorm specific courses of action. Future developments may require immediate confrontation and reports.	
7. Determine a course of action. Take action.	
8. Evaluate and share results.	

The Complacent Worker: Reflective Responses

When Andy took Alfredo's case, he was almost smug, behaving like he could just jump in without any planning. He waited until the afternoon of the day he expected to have the social work interview with Alfredo to even think about it. Perhaps he was swamped with other work and didn't feel like he had time to attend to Alfredo's situation. Regardless of that, though, Andy didn't give the case the time and energy it deserved. Alfredo was a client in need, and Andy was not considerate of his needs.

Image Source/Getty Images

Workers may experience painful emotions as part of self-reflection

There were a lot of things Andy could do when beginning a case to avoid the pitfalls of being complacent. For one, he could identify areas of diversity. In this case, Alfredo is Latino, an ethnicity that is not the dominant one in this country. In addition, Alfredo's ethnicity is different from Andy's. For both of those reasons, it was important for Andy to absorb any information he could get about Latino boys of Alfredo's age in economically challenged urban areas. His job was to recognize characteristics of many Latinos so that he could check with Alfredo to see whether they were accurate for him. In other words he has to explore the diversity of Latinos (**diversity between groups**), and he also has to explore how Alfredo may be different from other Latinos (**diversity within groups**). At that point, he would need to **evaluate the scientific literature** to learn all he could. Next, it would be wise of Andy to talk to experienced social workers at his agency. That way, he could gain their **practice wisdom**, or ideas that those social workers have gotten after many years of work with the population. As we've said, he would have to begin to identify strengths and resources that Alfredo's areas of diversity included. He'd also need to recognize any types of **discrimination** (perhaps teachers didn't expect their Latino students to do well, so they spent little time with them) or **institutional oppression** (perhaps Alfredo's family could not afford the school dress code) that Alfredo might face. These steps are the beginnings of the development of preparatory empathy, a process that will be elaborated in Chapter 4.

CRITICAL THINKING AND COLLABORATIVE LEARNING EXERCISES 3.5

1. Work in a small group. Consider Andy's ethical dilemma and determine a course of action. What do you think might be the consequences of your action?
2. Discuss with a partner the way you have changed your idea of your own diversity since reading this chapter.
3. Take the following test (adapted from Dolgoff, Loewenberg, & Harrington, 2011), and share your answers with your classmates. Discuss any differences in your responses.
   a. True or False The *NASW Code of Ethics* (NASW, 2018) was created by federal legislation.
   b. True or False An ethical dilemma is a question a client asks you that you can't answer.
   c. True or False The *NASW Code of Ethics* (NASW, 2018) is directed at organizations, not individuals.
   d. True or False Workers decide between good and bad options, not two bad options.
   e. True or False I know the mission of the social work profession.
   f. True or False The code explains how to handle any conflicts among the standards.
   g. True or False A person of good morals will not have trouble making ethical decisions.
   h. True or False The code does not apply to community organizers or researchers.

i. True or False Ethical decisions are scientific and should be the same among workers.
j. True or False Diversity is an important consideration in ethical decision-making.
k. True or False Workers' personal values play no role in ethical decision-making.
l. True or False An excellent social worker won't have trouble making ethical decisions.

Section 3.6: Review and Apply

CONCURRENT CONSIDERATIONS IN GENERALIST PRACTICE

Ethical Decision-Making Challenge

When Andy met with Alfredo alone, they began to develop a professional relationship, and Alfredo confided a lot of details about his family life. The next day, Alfredo's grandmother called to say that she wanted to know what Alfredo talked about. How do you think Andy should handle her request? Take a look at 1.06(d) of your *NASW Code of Ethics* (NASW, 2018) to inform your answer. Consider whether your suggestion might damage Andy's relationship with Alfredo or his relationship with Alfredo's grandmother.

Human Rights

Is anyone in this case being deprived of any fundamental human rights such as freedom, safety, privacy, an adequate standard of living, health care, and education?

Evidence-Based Practice

Andy had to decide whether to request that Alfredo meet with him alone or whether he should continue to meet with the family. Look in the scientific literature to see which might be the best alternative. (In other words, check to see whether there are any empirical studies that demonstrate the effectiveness of individual and family work with adolescent boys who are Latino.) What approach should he take?

Policies Impacting Practice

Research the penalties for truancy in your school district. Find out how these policies are developed and enforced. Figure out whether Andy would have to report any future incidences of truancy, where he would have to register the report, and what the consequences might be for Alfredo and his family if they lived in your area.

Managing Diversity

Andy and Alfredo are different in many ways: age, appearance, ethnicity, financial capability, etc. What are some ways they are alike?

Multisystem Practice

Identify examples of Andy's work on all levels.

Micro: ____________________

Mezzo: ____________________

Macro: ____________________

Dynamic and Interactive Planned Change Stages

Identify aspects of the interview between Andy and Alfredo's family where Andy worked in the following stages:

Self-Reflection: ____________________

Engagement: ____________________

Assessment: ____________________

Planning: ____________________

Implementation: ____________________

Evaluation: ____________________

Termination and Follow-Up: ____________________

Chapter Summary

Section 3.1: Why a Focus on the Worker?

Worker-centered practice is a way of carrying out generalist social work practice. It stresses the need for the social worker to develop self-knowledge. Self-knowledge related to emotions allows the development of the professional use of self so that professional behaviors can be conscious behaviors.

Section 3.2: How Do We Develop a Professional Use of Self?

The foundation for the development of the professional use of self is a critical thinking model in which social workers ask themselves the following questions: What do I feel? What do I believe? What do I know? What do I do? It involves social workers' efforts to identify their emotions and check whether they are based on accurate thoughts.

Section 3.3: Aspects of Diversity

Diversity refers to the intersectionality, or overlap, of individuals' characteristics such as age, class, color, culture, disability and ability, ethnicity, gender, gender identity and expression, immigration status, marital status, political ideology, race, religion or spirituality, sex, sexual orientation, and tribal sovereign status. Areas of diversity may create situations of oppression and/or of power.

Section 3.4: The Code of Ethics

The *NASW Code of Ethics* (NASW, 2018) is a guide for social workers to manage such situations as mistakes, difficult ethical decisions, and misconduct. It is based on six core professional values and six areas of social workers' responsibility. The *NASW Code of Ethics* (NASW, 2018) does not provide concrete answers to dilemmas, so an ethical decision-making model is important for practice.

Section 3.5: What Is an Ethical Dilemma?

A process for ethical decision-making involves considering the professional values and standards before conducting multilevel assessment and an analysis of those professional values and standards that are in conflict. Seeking supervision, taking action, and evaluating results are important components of the process.

SELF-REFLECTION 3: HOPE INDEX

PURPOSE: To measure hope

AUTHORS: Sara Staats and Christie Partlo

DESCRIPTION: The Hope Index (HI) is a 16-item instrument designed to measure hope, defined as the interactions of wishes and expectations. The HI has been shown to be sensitive to cultural events or threats such as war or economic prosperity.

SCORING: The HI is scored in the following way: The score for Wish (0–5) is multiplied by the score for Expect (0–5) for each item and then summed for a total HI score of 0–400. There are two subscales: the HopeSelf scale (items 1, 3–8, 15) and the HopeOther scale (items 2, 9–14, 16). These subscales are scored by multiplying the eight wish items in each subscale and multiplying them by the eight expect items. These scores are then summed for a range of 0–200.

NORMS: The mean totals for college students were approximately 217, 240, and 237. College women tend to have higher scores than college men, and older respondents tend to have higher HopeOther than HopeSelf scores.

RELIABILITY: The HI has fair to good internal consistency with alphas for the subscales that range from the upper .70s to the mid .80s across several samples. Data on stability were not available.

VALIDITY: The HI establishes some construct and discriminative validity with several of the subscales showing significant differences across time depending on external conditions.

PRIMARY REFERENCE:

Staats, S., & Partlo, C. (2013). A brief report on hope in peace and war; and in good times and bad. In K. Corcoran & J. Fischer (Eds.), *Measures for clinical practice and research* (5th ed., pp. 378–379). New York, NY: Oxford University Press.

THE HOPE INDEX

Instructions: Read the items below and circle 0, 1, 2, 3, 4, or 5 on the left hand side to indicate the extent that you would wish for the item mentioned. Then circle 0, 1, 2, 3, 4, or 5 on the right hand side to indicate the extent to which you expect the thing mentioned to occur.

To what extent would you *wish* for this? 0 = not at all 5 = very much		To what extent do you *expect* this? 0 = not at all 5 = very much
Item		
0 1 2 3 4 5	To do well in school, in job, or in daily tasks.	0 1 2 3 4 5
0 1 2 3 4 5	To have more friends.	0 1 2 3 4 5
0 1 2 3 4 5	To have good health.	0 1 2 3 4 5
0 1 2 3 4 5	To be competent.	0 1 2 3 4 5
0 1 2 3 4 5	To achieve long range goals.	0 1 2 3 4 5
0 1 2 3 4 5	To be happy.	0 1 2 3 4 5
0 1 2 3 4 5	To have money.	0 1 2 3 4 5
0 1 2 3 4 5	To have leisure time.	0 1 2 3 4 5
0 1 2 3 4 5	Other people to be helpful.	0 1 2 3 4 5
0 1 2 3 4 5	The crime rate to go down.	0 1 2 3 4 5
0 1 2 3 4 5	The country to be more productive.	0 1 2 3 4 5
0 1 2 3 4 5	Understanding by my family.	0 1 2 3 4 5
0 1 2 3 4 5	Justice in the world.	0 1 2 3 4 5
0 1 2 3 4 5	Peace in the world.	0 1 2 3 4 5
0 1 2 3 4 5	Personal freedom.	0 1 2 3 4 5
0 1 2 3 4 5	Resources for all.	0 1 2 3 4 5

Recommended Websites

Council on Social Work Education (CSWE): www.cswe.org

National Association of Social Workers (NASW): www.socialworkers.org

Critical Terms for Values, Ethics, and Diversity

displaying absent attributes 69
presenting as an authority figure 70
demonstrating empathy 70
identify feelings 71
conscious use of self 72
self-disclosure 73
normalizing 73
validation 74
verbal encouragement 75
paraphrasing 75
focused the interview 75
intersectionality 81
ethical dilemma 83
managing ethical dilemmas 83
utilitarian 86
diversity between groups 96
diversity within groups 96
evaluate the scientific literature 96
practice wisdom 96
discrimination 96
institutional oppression 96

Generalist Practice Curriculum Matrix With 2015 Educational Policy and Accreditation Standards

Chapter 3

Competency	Course	Course Content	Dimensions
Competency 1: Demonstrate Ethical and Professional Behavior		3.1. Summarize the meaning and purpose of professional use of self.	Knowledge Values
		3.2. Explain the process that underlies developing a professional use of self.	Knowledge Values
		3.4. Describe the format of the *NASW Code of Ethics* (NASW, 2018).	Knowledge Values
		3.5. Interpret a method of ethical decision-making. Feature 3: Self-Reflection	Knowledge
		Feature 4: Concurrent Considerations in Generalist Practice	Cognitive–affective processes
Competency 2: Engage Diversity and Difference in Practice		3.3. Assess the generalist view of diversity. Feature 1: Focus on Diversity	Skills Cognitive–affective processes
		Feature 4: Concurrent Considerations in Generalist Practice	Skills Cognitive–affective processes
Competency 3: Advance Human Rights and Social, Economic, and Environmental Justice		Feature 4: Concurrent Considerations in Generalist Practice	Skills Cognitive–affective processes

Competency	Course	Course Content	Dimensions
Competency 4: Engage In Practice-Informed Research and Research-Informed Practice		Feature 4: Concurrent Considerations in Generalist Practice	Skills Cognitive–affective processes
Competency 5: Engage in Policy Practice		Feature 4: Concurrent Considerations in Generalist Practice	Skills Cognitive–affective processes
Competency 6: Engage With Individuals, Families, Groups, Organizations, and Communities		Feature 4: Concurrent Considerations in Generalist Practice	Skills Cognitive–affective processes
Competency 7: Assess Individuals, Families, Groups, Organizations, and Communities		Feature 4: Concurrent Considerations in Generalist Practice	Skills Cognitive–affective processes
Competency 8: Intervene With Individuals, Families, Groups, Organizations, and Communities		Feature 4: Concurrent Considerations in Generalist Practice	Skills Cognitive–affective processes
Competency 9: Evaluate Practice With Individuals, Families, Groups, Organizations, and Communities		Feature 4: Concurrent Considerations in Generalist Practice	Skills Cognitive–affective processes

References

Arnd-Caddigan, M. (2008). Use of self in relational clinical social work. *Clinical Social Work Journal, 36*(3), 235–243.

Barton, E. E., & Pavilania, R. (2012). Teaching pretend play to children with autism. *Young Exceptional Children, 15*(1), 5–17.

Berger, P. L., & Luckmann, T. (1966). *The social construction of reality: A treatise in the sociology of knowledge*. New York, NY: Penguin.

Beyer, J., & Woehrle, L. M. (2014). *Research in social movements, conflicts, and change*. Bingley, England: Emerald Group Publishing.

Carlson, C. R., Collins, F. L., Stewart, J. F., Porzelius, J., Nitz, A. A., & Lind, C. O. (1989). The assessment of emotional reactivity: A scale development and validation study, *Journal of Psychopathology and Behavioral Assessment, 11*, 313–325.

Ceaser, D. (2014). Significant life experiences and environmental justice: Positionality and the significance of negative social/environmental experiences. *Environmental Education Research, 21*(2), 205–220. doi:10.1080.13504622.2014.910496

Congress, E. P. (2000). What social workers should know about ethics: Understanding and resolving practice dilemmas. *Advances in Social Work, 1*(1), 1–25.

Council on Social Work Education. (2015). *Educational policy and accreditation standards*. Alexandria, VA: Author. Retrieved from http://www.cswe.org/File.aspx?id=81660

Dewane, C. J. (2006). Use of self: A primer revisited. *Clinical Social Work Journal, 34*(4), 543–558.

Dolgoff, R., Loewenberg, F. M., & Harrington, D. (2011). *Ethical decisions for social work practice* (8th ed.). Belmont, CA: Brooks/Cole.

Edwards, J. K., & Bess, J. M. (1998). Developing reflectiveness in the therapeutic use of self. *Clinical Social Work Journal, 26*(1), 89–105.

Ellis, A. (1996). *Better, deeper, and more enduring brief therapy: The rational emotive behavior therapy approach*. New York, NY: Brunner/Mazel.

Hanna, E. P. (2013). A cognitive emotional methodology for critical thinking. *Advances in Applied Sociology, 3*(1), 20–25.

Mattsson, T. (2013). Intersectionality as a useful tool: Anti-oppressive social work and critical reflection. *Affilia: Journal of Women and Social Work*, 8–17. doi:10.1177/0886109913510659

Mook, L., Whitman, J. R., Armstrong, A., & Quarter, J. (2015). *Understanding the social economy of the United States*. Toronto, Canada: University of Toronto Press.

National Association of Social Workers. (2018). *NASW code of ethics*. Washington, DC: NASW Press.

Perry, J., & Bratman, M. (2015). *Introduction to philosophy: Classical and contemporary readings*. New York, NY: Oxford University Press.

Poorvu, N. L. (2015). When social workers have serious physical illnesses: Changes in use of self and ethical dilemmas. *Health and Social Work, 40*(2), 1–9. doi:10.1093/hsw/hlv009

Reamer, F. G. (1995). *Social work values and ethics*. New York, NY: Columbia University Press.

Reamer, F. G. (2003). *Social work malpractice and liability: Strategies for prevention* (2nd ed.). New York, NY: Columbia University Press.

Reamer, F. G. (2006). *Ethical standards in social work: A review of the NASW code of ethics* (2nd ed.). Washington, DC: NASW Press.

Reamer, F. G. (2008). In T. Mizrahi & L. E. Davis (Eds.), *Encyclopedia of social work* (20th ed.). New York, NY: Oxford University Press. doi:10.1093/acref/9780195306613.001.0001

Reamer, F. G. (2009). *The social work ethics casebook: Cases and commentary*. Washington, DC: NASW Press.

Reamer, F. G. (2013). *Series: Foundations of social work knowledge* (4th ed.). New York, NY: Columbia University Press.

Staats, S., & Partlo, C. (2013). A brief report on hope in peace and war; and in good times and bad. In K. Corcoran & J. Fischer (Eds.), *Measures for clinical practice and research* (5th ed., pp. 378–379). New York, NY: Oxford University Press.

Recommended Readings

National Association of Social Workers. (2018). *NASW code of ethics*. Washington, DC: NASW Press.

Grobman, L. M. (2011). *Days in the lives of social workers: 58 Professionals tell real life stories from social work*. Harrisburg, PA: White Hat Communications.

The Planned Change Process

PART II

4 Self-Reflection

A unique first stage of the planned change process is self-reflection. Self-reflection builds on the topics presented in Chapter 3, including diversity and professional use of self. Self-reflection as a stage in the planned change process allows students to become more intentional about the need to work with themselves before they work with clients. Students begin to understand how they can develop empathy and cultural humility through a concrete introspective process. They expand on their understanding of how their thoughts, feelings, and experiences may affect practice. In addition, they will discover the importance of self-care for the prevention of compassion fatigue.

Learning Objectives

4.1 Articulate the meaning of self-reflection in work with systems of all sizes.

4.2 Practice the development of cultural humility through self-reflection.

4.3 Appraise the scientific support for the practice of mindfulness for self-reflection.

4.4 Practice the process of developing empathy.

4.5 Identify aspects of supervision that facilitate self-reflection and professional use of self.

4.6 Explore potential barriers to productive supervision.

4.7 Practice using self-reflection for self-care.

Blend Images - Jade/Getty Images

Work with organizations can impact many people.

Case Study: Fund-Raising for Organizations

Amy was ecstatic to be offered a position at an adoption agency. She was adopted herself, so she could relate to the adopted children. And she was considering adopting a child herself, so she was experiencing the issues that families face from both sides. She was excited to help the children and families and sat right down to work. But Amy's fingers were very cold as they rested on the keyboard. Her supervisor had suggested that she rely on the Microsoft Office program Excel to help make her event planning easy. She knew she should know how to use Excel, but she had never used it before. It seemed to her to be a computer thing about numbers, and Amy avoided numbers whenever possible. So when her supervisor asked her to create an Excel file of all of the donations she accepted for Chinese New Year, she felt her head begin to pound. How could she make all of the phone calls she had to make to get gift donations and plan the event for adoptive families while learning a new computer program as well? She wouldn't do it, she decided. She'd keep careful records on paper and then when her supervisor asked about her progress, she'd just get the answers from her notes. Amy could have spent time exploring her feelings about the new software, and she could have identified the beliefs that kept her from learning. But that took time, it was hard, and Amy wanted to get right to the task. She didn't want to get in touch with any negative feelings like anxiety. A successful program was the purpose of her work, after all. So Amy set to work and spent the whole week phoning potential donors and planning the event. She was good at her job. When she contacted a corporation, she thought carefully about the corporation and about her feelings asking for donations. She discovered she was nervous asking for donations, but she knew to display confidence, and she was careful to begin to build a relationship with the person on the other end of the phone by taking time to describe her agency. Eventually, she was able to collect gifts that conveyed a connection to Chinese culture. She was able to do this over and over. There were nearly 100 potential donors on her list, and she succeeded more often than not. She had done well at her task and couldn't wait for her next supervisory meeting so she could announce her triumph. Her bubble was burst, though, when her supervisor reminded her that she would need to send thank-you notes out to all of the donors. "Don't worry," her supervisor said. "You have all of their addresses in Excel and can easily do to a mail merge to get a letter printed for every donor. It will only take you a few minutes."

Section 4.1: Self-Reflection

This section begins the discussion of the first stage of the planned change process: self-reflection.

Self-Reflection

As we've discussed in Chapter 3, **self-reflection** is necessary to develop a professional use of self. Since self-reflection reveals different aspects of you for every different case, it begins every planned change process. Every case touches us in unique ways, so we have to do self-reflection over and over again. Workers consider themselves first. In self-reflection, workers practice thinking about their feelings, thoughts, and behaviors. During planned change, the social worker begins an intersection between themselves and another—be it an individual client, a client system representative or a client system itself. In systems terms, the worker's system begins to exchange energy with the client system. Information will be exchanged. Feelings will be shared. Secrets may be shared. Vulnerability will happen on both sides. When a social worker thinks about a new client, the sense of intersection or energy exchange can sometimes feel overwhelming. This is appropriate, as the connection is one of great intimacy. Amy felt that intimacy as she worked with the donors. She was fund-raising for an agency, but she had to develop relationships with each of the potential donors.

Achieving Awareness

Because of the intimacy of the connection between social worker and client system, it is important that the worker be available emotionally and intellectually for the client or client system representative. It is also important for the worker to be resilient in the face of the client's distressing life circumstances. In addition, self-reflection is necessary to generate awareness on the part of the social worker. The awareness of behavior is at the core of the social work professional use of self.

As we've seen, self-reflection is a process of bringing feelings, thoughts, and behaviors into awareness, and it is central to developing helping relationships with others. You might say that self-reflection is a worker's process of becoming intentional. The social worker strives to be intentional in all of their professional actions. Self-reflection is a way to get there (see Figure 4.1).

ETHICAL PERSPECTIVES

Did Amy have an ethical responsibility to learn about new technologies that might benefit her clients? Read the Preamble of the NASW Code of Ethics *(National Association of Social Workers [NASW], 2018) to find out.*

Most important to the self-reflection stage in planned change is the worker's recognition of his or her own feelings. The intentional social worker must be aware of their own emotional reactions to each case. Remember that the critical thinking process related to self-reflection—"What do I feel/believe/know/do?" (Hanna, 2013)—begins with an identification of the worker's feelings. It is important to begin the critical thinking process by identifying emotions as they appear during each case. Self-reflection is the first stage in the planned change process, but it is also an action word. Self-reflection facilitates the worker's identification of feelings, thoughts, and behaviors through self-awareness. In other words, self-reflection serves to develop the awareness of thoughts, beliefs, and behavior and ultimately the conscious, or professional, use of self. Remember that when we start something new we often have feelings that are associated with beginnings. Since self-reflection is stressed at the beginning of the planned change process, it carries with it the characteristics of beginnings: anxiety and hope. Self-reflection, then, should begin with a search for those feelings.

Amy's situation is a good example of a need for self-reflection about feelings, because she was facing challenges on the **macro** level of practice. She was reaching out to large systems through client system representatives to get donations, and she was planning a program for

FIGURE 4.1 • Elements of Self-Reflection

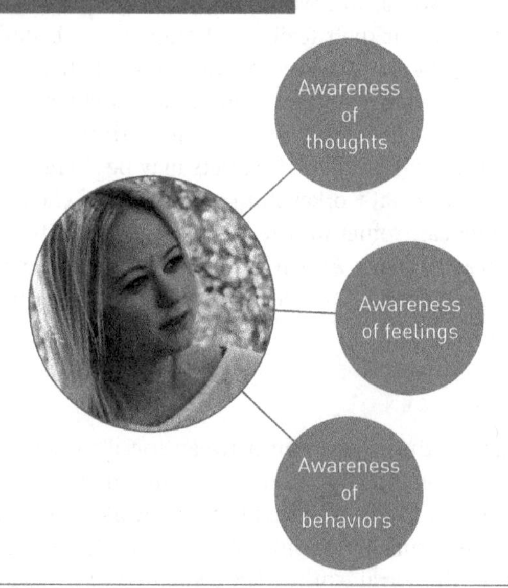

Source: Photo by Kelsey Vere.

a large number of individuals and families. Fund-raising and program planning are usually considered macro practice. Social workers don't always think about identifying feelings and beliefs as a necessary part of practice with large systems. In this case, though, Amy was challenged by her feelings and her thoughts about the Excel software. At this point, Amy should have identified her strong feelings and physical reactions to the case. For Amy, a red flag was her anxiety. The moment her supervisor mentioned Excel, Amy began to feel anxious. Then she got a headache, and her fingers were ice cold. That was her second red flag. At that point, Amy could have engaged in self-reflection and identified her feelings. She could have stopped what she was doing and start the "What do I feel/believe/know/do?" process we've begun to consider in Chapter 3. More details on this process appear later on in this chapter. In the meantime, consider that Amy probably had another level of anxiety to deal with. Remember that she was adopted herself and had brought a Chinese culture into a middle-class American culture. She was the only Asian at her school, and many people found it easier to ignore that she was "different." While Amy was proud of her heritage, she learned that it was more comfortable around schoolmates and their parents if she pretended to be the same as everyone else. As a result, she wasn't used to recognizing difference and she wasn't comfortable bringing the topic into the conversations. In the next section, we'll consider managing culture in the planned change process.

CRITICAL THINKING AND COLLABORATIVE LEARNING EXERCISES 4.1

1. Talk with a partner about your feelings of anxiety and hope related to beginning any new experience. Consider your feelings before the process began and what they are now. If your feelings changed, talk about how that happened.
2. Here is an example of general systems theory in action. Working with a partner, answer the following simple question: How did your studying go last night? After you have had the discussion, consider the types of energy that were exchanged between you and your partner. Information? Empathy? Others? How would you describe the boundary that existed between your two systems?

Section 4.2: Developing Cultural Humility

This section expands on the discussion of self-reflection: the development of cultural humility and sensitivity.

Developing Cultural Humility

In addition to bringing feelings, thoughts, and behaviors to awareness, another benefit of self-reflection is the development of **cultural humility**. Remember that social workers place a focus on the strengths inherent in **diversity**. Cultural humility includes self-reflection aimed at recognizing unintentional and intentional racism and other aspects of harmful prejudice (Ross, 2010). Cultural humility is working hard to recognize that others have values, behaviors, beliefs, and experiences that may be very different from yours but not less valuable or important. When you identify your feelings, thoughts, and behaviors you are likely to recognize that you think of your own culture as being the center of the world while other cultures are different. In other words, self-reflection leads to a process toward cultural humility, and cultural humility leads to an appreciation of the strengths and challenges of diversity. Here's an example of how self-reflection can lead to an understanding that others see the world differently than you: Most people who own German shepherd dogs have animals (and furniture) covered with black-and-tan hair. Some German shepherds, though, are white. If you own a white German shepherd, white is the center of your perception of your dog. You may get so used to your white German shepherd that you think of it as "normal" and you start telling people you have a German shepherd without saying white. In that case, you might look at other dogs and think of them as "shepherds of color." In the same way, the owner of a black-and-tan shepherd is likely to always call your shepherd white and think of their black-and-tan shepherd as normal. It takes work to think about other perceptions as people's experiences that are very different from yours and no less valuable. The way you see the world is the way you see it. Most people don't have to bother thinking of the world in any different way, but social workers do.

Social workers require cultural humility. Cultural humility is a prerequisite to cultural sensitivity and responsiveness. Cultural humility is dynamic in that it requires constant self-reflection (Tervalon & Murray-Garcia, 1998). Remember that being **culturally responsive** means that a social worker is working toward being able to act and maybe even think like a member of a different culture (see Figure 4.2). This competency requires knowledge of the different cultures, but it is not limited to knowledge. It also requires self-reflection: the self-reflection needed to identify the feelings, thoughts, and behaviors about a culture that exist outside of the worker's awareness. These feelings, thoughts, and behaviors include bias and stereotyping that are outside of awareness as well as a worker's recognition of their own possible areas of privilege or oppression. It includes an understanding about community mistrust, where diverse people may mistrust the majority culture due to historical practices (Ross, 2010). Again, to be culturally responsive is to engage in a process where you exercise cultural humility, or the recognition of how your own values and behaviors differ from, but are not superior to, the values and behaviors of other cultures. Cultural humility is needed to become culturally responsive. It is important to note that the practice of becoming culturally responsive by recognizing values of self and others means that the work of individuals can assure that organizations and communities can become culturally responsive.

Tasks for Developing Cultural Humility for Cultural Responsiveness

The foundation for cultural humility is knowledge. The worker has to be fully aware of aspects of their own culture. Even though yours is the culture you live in, you may need to do some research to be better informed. For example, let's say your grandparents emigrated here from Greece. You consider yourself to be American. You seldom stop and think that not everyone knows how to make baklava just the way they like it without a recipe. It's

FIGURE 4.2 • Moving Toward Cultural Responsiveness

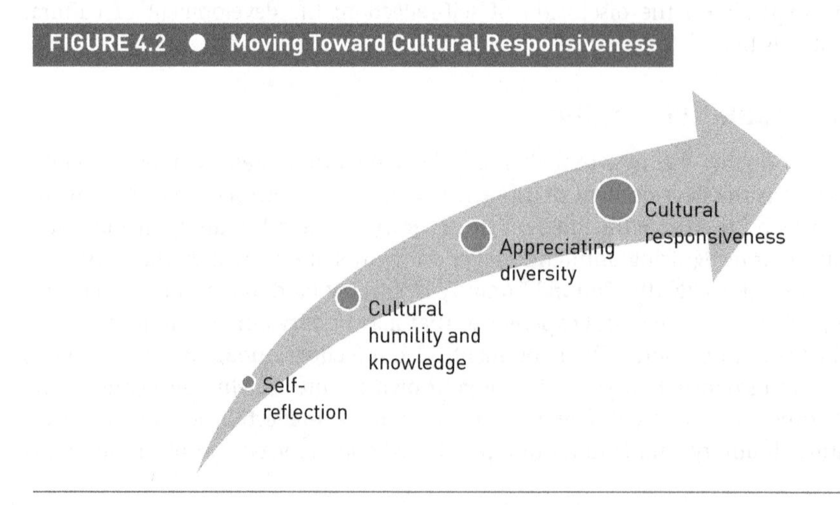

something to be proud of. You also seldom stop and think about how friendly almost all of your family members are and how they frequently welcome others into their family gatherings. The friendly, gregarious culture that you live in is also something to be proud of. It's possible to have **ethnic identity**, or the recognition of membership in a particular group, for more than one group. You may think of yourself as Greek American and American at the same time. In that case, your **total identity** includes more than one component of ethnicity (Tajfel, 1981). It is essential that you recognize your own identity so that you can recognize difference in others. Once you recognize difference, you can learn about it. It is essential for you to gain knowledge about the way other cultures experience their ethnicity. In your case, you need to know how others reach out to those who are not part of their group. Every culture is not gregarious, and a quieter, more passive approach to life and family is neither better nor worse than what you're used to. Constantly seeking knowledge about the lives of others as well as your own is the first step toward cultural humility.

Paine, Jankowski, and Sandage (2016) have outlined the dimensions of cultural humility:

- *Self-awareness:* The understanding of the worker's own limitations related to cultural understanding
- *Low self-focus:* The focus is on the other
- *Interpersonal receptivity*: Openness to difference
- *The ability to regulate emotions*
- *The appreciation of value in others*

In other words, the social worker who hopes to develop cultural humility needs to know themselves and their limitations about diversity and cultural understanding. When faced with the client, the worker has to let go of their own cultural beliefs and allow the client to be the expert of their own culture. The culturally humble worker is curious and thinks about feelings before expressing them. Overall, cultural humility requires the social work value in which we respect the dignity and worth of the person. Cultural humility is the beginning of developing cultural responsiveness (see Figure 4.3).

FIGURE 4.3 • Elements of Cultural Humility

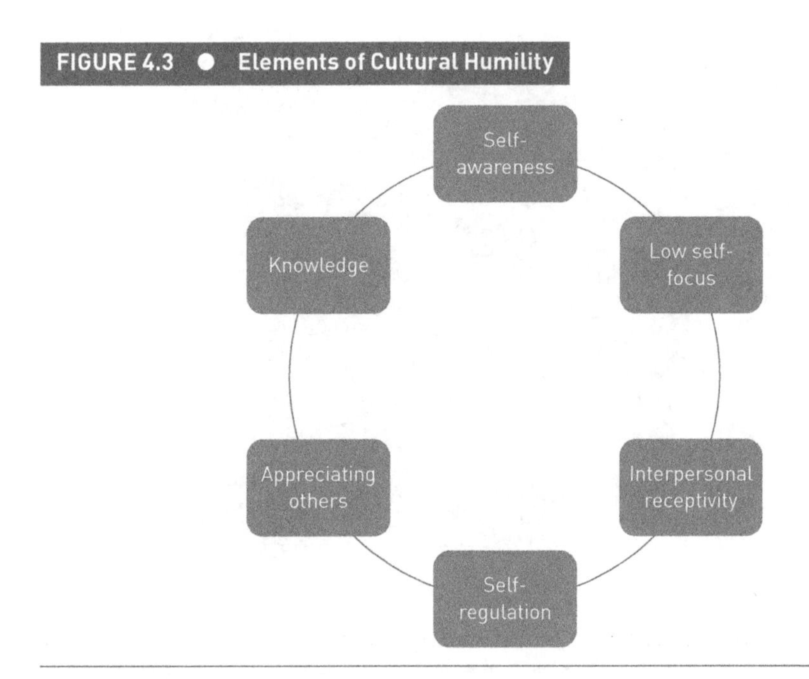

When Amy began to work at her agency, she had experience in fund-raising, but she hadn't worked at an adoption agency. At first, she thought she could contact businesses to ask for donations without a problem. Then she learned that the gifts were supposed to have a Chinese cultural relevance. Next, she found out that most of the businesses she would be contacting were Chinese-owned. She immediately became uncomfortable, since her own experience of adoption was through assimilation, where the adopted child succeeds by fitting into the culture of their adoptive parents. When Amy thought about her Chinese identity, she almost felt as if she were keeping a secret. What she didn't know is that in some families, adoption does not lead to the loss of the child's cultural heritage. Sometimes the adoptive parents assimilate into practices of the child's native culture while the child is assimilating into the parents' culture (Berry & Sabatier, 2010). If Amy had thought about her feelings, she might have recognized that they were getting in the way of explaining to donors that she wanted donations that were connected to Chinese culture. She needed to become aware of her own anxiety so that she could think about her relationship with the donors in a different way. She needed to develop empathy for them and their views on their ethnic heritage, so she needed to accept her own. As she made the phone calls, she eventually became comfortable talking about the Chinese theme to the donors, but it took a while. It would have happened more quickly if she had engaged in self-reflection and become culturally sensitive to her own experiences as well as the donors' point of view.

The outcome of self-reflection should be a worker who might be called **culturally sensitive** (Kadushin & Kadushin, 2013). The culturally sensitive worker has cultural humility as well as the following characteristics:

1. Approaches clients with respect, warmth, acceptance, and empathy
2. Understands that groups have their own characteristics (**intergroup differences**) but all individuals are different as well (**intragroup differences**)

In addition, the culturally sensitive worker recognizes that organizations and communities have their own cultures (see Figure 4.4). For example, they are able to identify

FIGURE 4.4 • Marks of the Culturally Sensitive Worker

Source: ©iStock.com/jhorrocks; ©iStock.com/Kritchanut; ©iStock.com/FG Trade; ©iStock.com/ivanastar; ©iStock.com/MStudioImages; ©iStock.com/warrengoldswain; ©iStock.com/Mlenny; ©iStock.com/Juanmonino; ©iStock.com/AleksandarNakic; ©iStock.com/Weekend Images Inc.

unequal distribution of power within communities and facilitate fair decision-making processes among community partners (Ross, 2010). Other elements of diversity that you may not have considered include differences for people who live in rural, urban, and suburban neighborhoods. Cultural responsiveness is never achieved—it is always sought. For this reason, it is easy to see that self-reflection not only begins the planned change process but is a dynamic part of every stage of planned change.

Cultural Responsiveness in Practice

Further direction on how social workers can work toward cultural responsiveness comes from NASW in its "Standards and Indicators for Cultural Competence in Social Work Practice" (2015). A series of standards points to ways all of us can practice and reflect our respect for difference. Some of the standards reflect topics we've already discussed and are worth repeating:

Standard 1: Ethics and Values. Workers who are culturally responsive respect the *NASW Code of Ethics* (NASW, 2018) and work to achieve self-awareness; cultural humility; and, most importantly, a lifelong commitment to understanding and valuing cultural difference.

Standard 2: Self-Awareness. Culturally responsive workers appreciate their own culture. They recognize that as professionals their own culture may include power over their clients and client system representatives. They work to understand the way power dynamics affect the helping relationship.

Standard 3: Cross-Cultural Knowledge. The specialized knowledge that social workers need to continually develop includes understanding cultures relative to their history, tradition, values, family systems, artistic expressions, immigration and refugee status, tribal groups, religion and spirituality, sexual orientation, gender identity and expression, social class, and mental and physical abilities.

Standard 4: Cross-Cultural Skills. Social workers must consider the ways culture affects and is affected by micro, mezzo, and macro practice, including policy practice and research.

Standard 5: Service Delivery. Social workers should be aware of the culturally appropriate services that exist in their communities so that they can connect clients to those services appropriately. They should also recognize gaps in existing culturally appropriate services so that they can advocate for their development.

Standard 6: Empowerment and Advocacy. Advocacy should be carried out with, and on behalf of, multicultural groups.

Standard 7: Diverse Workforce. Another area for advocacy is for social workers to strive to have a diverse staff of social work providers. A comment that you make to your supervisor may ultimately affect the hiring process at your agency.

Standard 8: Professional Education. Social workers are responsible to share their cultural knowledge and awareness with other workers. It is also important for social workers to share this information with other professionals, like doctors, nurses, psychologists, teachers, and counselors. When sharing your cross-cultural knowledge, consider the culture of the professionals you're addressing. You don't want to come off as a self-righteous person who is lecturing others.

Standard 9: Language and Communication. Effective communication should be foremost as workers consider that clients may not be proficient in English, may not be literate, and may communicate through technology or sign language. A diverse staff or professional training may be necessary for workers.

Standard 10: Leadership to Advance Cultural Competence in the Community. Social workers should take their understanding and celebration of diversity into their community as well as into their agencies.

CRITICAL THINKING AND COLLABORATIVE LEARNING EXERCISES 4.2

1. Find a reading about the people of your own ethnic heritage. See whether you can find characteristics of your own culture: foods, ceremonies, music, etc. Are these expressions of culture part of your life experiences? Share what you find with a group.
2. Make a note of your feelings as you shared the information about your ethnicity with the group and heard about the ethnicities of others. What do you think your feelings mean?
3. Join a group, and research another culture including their history, traditions, values, family systems, artistic expressions, foods, immigration and refugee status, tribal groups, religion and spirituality, sexual orientation, gender identity or expression, social class, and mental and physical abilities. Note that a culture may be the expression of an ethnic group, like Colombian Americans or another type of group, like people who identify as LGBTQ.

Section 4.3: The Method of Self-Reflection

This section begins the discussion of a process for carrying out self-reflection. The practice of mindfulness is useful.

The Method of Self-Reflection

We have seen that bringing thoughts, feelings, and behaviors into awareness is a critical part of a worker's professional use of self. It is not always simple to do this. Remember that beginnings often include feelings of anxiety because they are not known. For that reason, self-reflection as the first stage of planned change can be particularly anxiety-producing. This is especially true when the reflection includes feelings that may be painful. No one likes to experience painful emotions, so most people try to put them out of their minds. Social workers need to reach out to them instead. Social workers constantly search for their feelings to figure out how they influence their beliefs and behavior. To do this, they need a process to identify feelings that they know about and those that are out of awareness.

The Science of Mindfulness

One method of identifying feelings is the practice of **mindfulness**. Overall, mindfulness is an idea that is often received with skepticism. Since mindfulness is similar to meditation and is often misunderstood, it is sometimes seen as a spiritual practice that has little or no basis in science. In social work, it may be considered to be "mystical" or "New Age" (Garland, 2013). Since we are most concerned with evidence-based social work practice, it is important to explore and critique the available scientific literature on the topic.

Operationalization

In any kind of scientific inquiry, we recognize attributes that things have in common and think about the ways that they are different. In this way, we conceptualize what we are looking at. Next, we define terms precisely, or **operationalize** them, so that research can be conducted consistently over time (Rubin & Babbie, 2015). Unfortunately, mindfulness has suffered from a lack of clarity in the scientific literature. This lack of clarity can undermine even the best scientific inquiry and has been stressed as a need in social work research on mindfulness (Garland, 2013). Probably the simplest definition of mindfulness is a "moment-to-moment awareness or paying attention to the moment without judgment" (Lynn, 2010, p. 290). In a review of current literature, Turner (2008) found a definition of mindfulness that included three building blocks:

- *Attention*—In mindfulness practice, attention refers to a clear focus on your own experience in the present. This means paying attention to your breathing, your body as it is still or as it moves through space, any aches or pains you may have, and so forth. Here is where you begin to identify feelings that you may have outside of your awareness.
- *Intention*—Intention refers to the fact that mindfulness is achieved through practice.
- *Attitude*—Attitude reflects an acceptance and non-judgmental approach to the practice of mindfulness. In other words, you don't evaluate your thoughts and feelings as you experience them, you simply note that you are experiencing them (Shapiro, Carlson, Astin, & Freedman, 2006).

For the purpose of scientific research in social work, consideration should be given to Garland's (2013) broad definition of mindfulness. This definition was derived from an in-depth review of scientific literature and is part of a discussion about how mindfulness can be researched. This composite, measurable definition of mindfulness as it has been published by the journal *Social Work Research* (Garland, 2013) states that mindfulness is the following:

- *State*—A condition where a person "monitors the content of consciousness" (Garland, 2013, p. 440). In other words, mindfulness is what you are doing when you think about what you are thinking and feeling.
- *Practice*—A repeated attention on one thing, such as breathing, while letting go any distracting thoughts as they come.
- *Trait*—A characteristic that can be developed over time. The trait of mindfulness includes "exhibiting nonjudgmental, nonreactive awareness of one's thoughts, emotions, experiences, and actions in everyday life" (Baer, Smith, Hopkins, Krietemeyer, & Toney, 2006/2013, p. 440). It refers to the development of the characteristic states of mindfulness that may lead to durable, or lasting, changes in traits (Garland, 2013; Garland, Farb, Goldin, & Fredrickson, 2015). Researchers (Hölzel et al., 2011) have said that the development of traits related to mindfulness practices increases brain tissue density in parts of the brain that are related to emotion regulation, learning, memory, and the ability to shift perspective. Emotional regulation or self-regulation means to be in a state of nonreactivity. This term describes the lack of a strong, usually negative, emotional response. It's a letting go of the tension that is associated with strong feelings and it is a significant part of the professional use of self.

Empirical Support

Using this definition of mindfulness, a review of literature suggested that mindfulness is useful for relaxation but also for much more. Randomized controlled research studies have shown that mindfulness practice helps workers to develop a kind of regulation of the self, or the ability to control emotions, to enhance coping, and to promote workers' resiliency (Garland, 2013). It is well demonstrated that the practice of mindfulness can ease stress as it is measured by physical responses like heart rate and neurological changes (Gotink et al., 2016). Previous research found mindfulness significantly increased positive affect; self-compassion (Shapiro, Brown, & Biegel, 2007); overall well-being (Christopher & Maris, 2010; Grepmair et al., 2007); and decreased anxiety, depression, and stress (Christopher & Maris, 2010; Grepmair et al., 2007; Shapiro et al., 2007). All of these could be good at strengthening workers against the stress that is part of social work. Finally, it has been shown that changes in brain activity that result in higher self-compassion occur with the practice of mindfulness (Lutz et al., 2016). In fact, the practice of mindfulness has been shown to facilitate healthy coping specifically in social workers (Decker, Brown, Ong, & Stiney-Ziskind, 2015), and a study that reviewed research on mindfulness and stress concluded that mindfulness helps combat compassion fatigue among health care workers (Westphal et al., 2015). (There will be more on compassion fatigue later.) In addition, mindfulness has been shown to help people focus more and be more satisfied at work (Good et al., 2016). In other words, high-quality research studies show that mindfulness increases the worker's ability to control their feelings and to manage the sometimes overwhelming feelings associated with sharing other people's problems (Garland, 2013; Shapiro et al., 2006).

To review, mindfulness is . . .

- *a state, or way of being;*
- *a practice, or way of behaving; and*
- *a trait, or a fixed characteristic of a person (Garland, 2013).*

That is, you can be in a state of mindfulness when you focus on sensations that are within you. Mindfulness is a way of creating silence by becoming aware of things that we usually ignore, like breathing. In fact, the practice of mindfulness can begin with a simple focus on your breathing. It is a peaceful way of getting in tune with yourself and your feelings. For this reason, it is an effective way to begin the process of self-reflection that is needed for the planned change stage of self-reflection.

The exercise below helps to understand the practice of mindfulness:

> Bring your attention to the places where your body makes contact with the chair in which you are sitting . . . Notice your legs . . . Notice your back . . . Notice the borders between where your body makes contact and stops making contact . . . Hold that awareness for a few moments . . . Now, have some thoughts about chairs . . . Think about your favorite chair. What is it like? . . . Remember some of the worst chairs you have had the displeasure of sitting in . . . What were they like? . . . How would you describe the chair you are sitting in right now? What do you think of it? (Boone, 2014, p. 11)

If you didn't carry out the previously given exercise while you were reading, go back and do it. Spend a few moments on each ellipsis (. . .), and focus on the exercise. It is inevitable that you will have distracting thoughts. In that case, "the distraction may be visualized as a fluffy cloud, floating into and out of the practitioner's awareness" (Turner, 2008, p. 97). You won't understand mindfulness until you try it.

Mindfulness can become a trait in that you can practice it, develop it as a way of being, and enhance your ability to achieve the state again and again. It has been said that with practice mindfulness is an "orientation we can return to in any given moment" (Boone, 2014, p. x).

Usefulness in Planned Change

Recall that culturally responsive practice requires cultural humility and critical thinking. Managing emotional reactivity, or self-regulation, as well as identifying your own thoughts and feelings are essential to critically evaluating your own thinking. In the critical thinking exercise "What do I feel/believe/know/do?" it is essential to begin with a recognition of feelings that are specific to a specific case. When contemplating your feelings about a case, you may have to confront your own biases related to the diverse characteristics of your clients. In this case, to achieve the cultural humility necessary for culturally competent practice, you will be facing uncomfortable emotions that you'd rather ignore. To reach for these feelings and identify them, consider the following exercise:

Mindfulness of Painful Emotions

1. Feel the emotion (when considering a case). Take a moment to get in touch with the emotion. Don't choose an emotion that is too overwhelming when you first do this exercise. Now, imagine the emotion as a wave in the ocean. It comes toward you, like a wave coming toward the shore, and then recedes. Follow the flow of the waves as they rise to a peak and then recede and finally break.

2. Next, imagine that you are on a warm beach, the sun warming your face and a cool breeze blowing on your face. Imagine that the emotion is a wave on the ocean and the cool breeze blowing on your face makes the emotion a little lighter and less intense.

3. Imagine yourself at the beach, where the water is so blue that you can see the crystal-white water as the waves come toward the shore—flowing, rising, and then receding and breaking.

4. Imagine that the emotion is intense but only when you look at it from a distance—as you would look at the ocean from a distance. As you get closer, just as the waves become less intense as they reach the shore, so, too, do your emotions. Imagine that the sun warms your body and the cool breeze cools your face; observe the emotion as small and less intense.

5. Go back and forth between the image of the ocean, which allows you to feel comfortable and steady, and the emotion, which makes you feel tense and afraid. As you go back and forth, notice the breath as you inhale and exhale. Feel the rhythmic flow of the breath.

6. Notice the flow of the breath in and out and the waves flowing toward and away from the shore. Paying close attention to the emotion, notice how you can increase and decrease its intensity—how it can flow in and out like the waves of the ocean.

7. Notice how you can influence your feelings as you pay attention to them in this way. Notice how going back and forth between the comforting experience of being on the beach and the mindfulness of an emotion changes your experience of the emotion (adapted from Marra, 2004, cited in Hick, 2009).

CRITICAL THINKING AND COLLABORATIVE LEARNING EXERCISES 4.3

1. Working with a partner, explain how mindfulness is practiced to each other. Discuss how you feel about practicing mindfulness.
2. Conduct the mindfulness exercise about painful emotions with a partner. Take turns reading the exercise for each other. Once you have identified an emotion, carry out the "What do I feel/believe/know/do?" exercise.

Section 4.4: Developing Empathy

This section considers how mindfulness practice can facilitate the development of empathy.

The Meaning of Empathy

Empathy is the bedrock of social work practice. Empathy allows connection. It is the ability to take on the worldview of another person, to understand their perspective. If you are to stand inside another person and look out with their eyes, you would need to know something about their culture, something about their experiences, something about the things that bring them joy and the things that give them pain. You will begin to understand their thoughts, their feelings, and their actions (Grant, 2014). If you can do that, you can develop the ability to show it. You'll do this through the things you say that seem to fit the situation. Your client or client system representative will feel a connection. Once you display empathy, you can begin to build a relationship. Developing and showing empathy is probably the most important skill you will use as a social worker. In fact, workers' empathy has been found to have strong effects on clients' physical, mental, and social well-being (Gerdes, Lietz, & Segal, 2011).

Developing Empathy

Many social work students can develop empathy pretty well naturally. Probably you are the kind of person that others often reach out to for some kind of assistance. It may seem like everywhere you go, you are being asked for help. People are likely to connect with you because you are talented at developing empathy for a broad range of people. For this reason, many talented people feel that they don't need formal education. After all, they don't find it difficult to build helping relationships. The assumption that you don't need education because you find it easy to help others is a big mistake for several reasons. First, if you rely on instinct someday you will find yourself against a wall when it comes to developing empathy. For example, you may have to work with a parent who has abused their child. Just try to understand that person's thoughts, feelings, and actions without training. It is really hard. Second, someone who develops empathy without training is likely to go too far. When you create empathy, you can easily become overinvolved, resulting in a terrible toll on your own well-being. You are likely to burn out and go become an accountant when you really want to be a social worker! Thomas and Otis (2010) found that burnout is not necessarily caused by seeing distressful events or hearing people talk about distressful events. It is not even caused by showing empathy or care to suffering people. Instead, it is caused by an inadequate boundary that the worker maintains around their professional self. For this reason, it is important to develop what Gerdes et al. (2011) has called **accurate empathy**.

Accurate empathy has several features (Grant, 2014, p. 341):

- *Affective sharing*—Being mindful of the client's experience; being self-reflective about the worker's barriers to understanding
- *Self–other awareness*—A worker's sense of self separate from the client
- *Self-emotion*—The conscious effort to control personal emotional reactions

SELF-REFLECTION 4: FIVE FACET MINDFULNESS QUESTIONNAIRE

The practice of mindfulness has five aspects:

1. *Observing*—Attending to inner and outer experiences
2. *Describing*—Labeling those experiences
3. *Awareness*—Attending to the here and now
4. *Nonjudgmentalness*—Accepting inner experiences
5. *Nonreactivity*—Allowing thoughts, emotions, and experiences to come and go; not getting carried away by experience

Test your own mindfulness state with the Five Facet Mindfulness Questionnaire (FFMQ) from the academic journal *Assessment*. In which states of mindfulness are you most proficient? Think about what area of mindfulness you could practice to improve your ability to engage in cultural humility and empathy for client systems. What are some activities you can engage in to improve your mindfulness traits?

FIGURE 4.5 ● Elements of Empathy

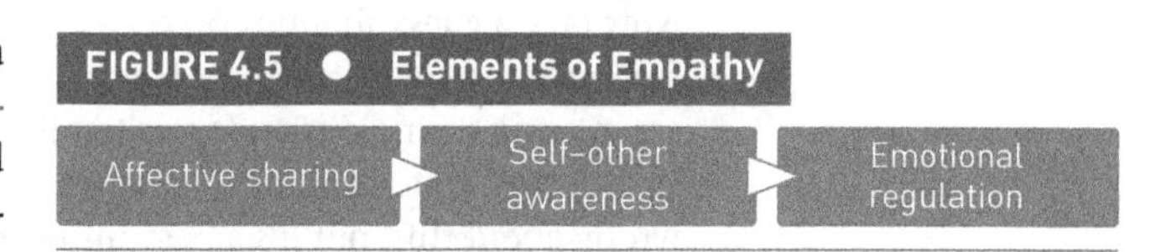

In other words, as you think about meeting a new client, you engage in **preparatory empathy** (Shulman, 1992). You think about them, and you reflect on how much you can't possibly understand due to your own experiences (more on preparatory empathy below). You keep a clear identity separate from the client and from the client's distress. Finally, for your own sake as well as the client's, you identify your feelings and determine which of those should be expressed in the client's best interest. You also use your identification of feelings to engage in the "What do I feel/believe/know/do?" exercise to help you manage diversity (Hanna, 2013). In this process, you'll determine whether you need to display absent attributes. (See Chapter 3 for a discussion of absent attributes.)

Preparatory Empathy: How to Make It Happen

Gaining Information

Consciously planning to empathize with a person before meeting that person is preparatory empathy. To practice preparatory empathy, you begin by considering everything you know about a client or client system. Gain this information any way you can. For example, if the client used your agency's services in the past, get ahold of the previous worker and get their impressions. (Be careful. Your colleague may have become too involved to be objective and may make negative comments: You'll have to interpret them from a strengths perspective.) Say you ask a worker about a couple you're going to work with dealing with marital issues.

A coworker may say "No wonder he wants to go out drinking with his friends all the time. She is so controlling." This gives you information. Now frame it from a strengths perspective. In this case, it is likely that both husband and wife are lonely. They have both found ways to cope, but those ways are damaging their relationship. Another way of getting information is by reading a file if your client has received service from your agency in the past. You can also research anything you know about the client from the information you have. Maybe you need to research a mental or physical health problem or understand the side effects of medications. Use mindfulness practice to identify your feelings about the case. If you have strong feelings, you should engage in the "What do I feel/believe/know/do?" exercise.

Interpreting Diversity

Once you've gained information and reflected on your feelings about the case, you need to think about interpreting diversity. This kind of interpretation is sort of educated guessing. You will go back to what you know about diversity—how there are many types of diversity, how difference can result in oppression or power, how different experiences will affect the way difference plays out in people's lives. You won't have all of the information you need to fully develop empathy, but you'll have some. Use the information you have to fill in as many blanks as you can. Once you make some guesses about the client's elements of diversity, you have to again explore your own feelings. You will need to engage in mindfulness, identify your feelings, and engage your cultural humility. Try to understand what may be the person's experiences of their different types of diversity.

Intelligent Guessing Example

Take a guess like this: You are going to work with an undergraduate freshman who needs help managing college. You think about their elements of diversity: You guess they will be in their late teens, and you'll guess that they have just graduated from public high school. Here you are imagining **concrete elements of diversity**. Think about what you know about the client's culture. What about their race and ethnicity? What about their gender expression? The type of neighborhood they come from? How about their family's income? Now take a guess about **affective elements of diversity**. How is this person likely to be feeling about their struggles? How may they be feeling about asking for help? Perhaps they are missing their old friends and family. Perhaps they are moving from a rural environment to an urban one. Perhaps they worry they will fail and be expelled. Of course, you can be wrong about this, but it's a beginning. You're beginning to take the other's perspective.

Preparing to Feel

Now consider any experience you have had that is similar to your client's. Chances are, you've had a similar experience beginning college or going to summer camp or even an extensive visit to relatives when you were young. You will use mindfulness and sit in silence to remember how you felt back then. This will take a few moments of time and silence. You should really try to reexperience your feelings. Go ahead and feel the discomfort. This practice marks the difference between a good and a great social worker: the willingness to feel the discomfort.

WHAT IF . . . FOCUS ON DIVERSITY

To what ethnic group did you assume Amy to belong? Think about why you made that assumption. Suppose Amy was African American with a particular accent that made her ethnicity obvious to people on the phone? Do you think her ethnicity may have an impact on her success in getting donations?

Find out what kind of Chinese New Year gifts would be appropriate and culturally sensitive for adoptive families.

Experiences That Are Harder to Reach

It is often the case that your client is not of an age (either younger or older) that you can easily relate to. Suppose you are going to work with an aging woman who has just found herself in a long-term care facility against her will. You have not had that experience. But you might know someone who has had that experience—perhaps a parent or grandparent. It's also very possible that you have had a similar experience in a different context. Here, for example, you may again touch base with your college experience. Remember your first night in the dorm with a stranger for a roommate and your parents heading back home. If you never stayed in a dorm, think about the first time you went to sleep in an empty house or apartment with no one else at home. It's not the same experience the older woman is having, for sure, but it's an emotional hook to grab hold of. Again, feel that feeling. Sit with it a bit. Be willing to experience the discomfort.

Experiencing and Releasing Distress

If you are true to the preparatory empathy process, you will spend some time feeling uncomfortable. Of course, you don't want that to continue. You will store away that experience to be drawn out when you meet with your client. Again, it is possible that your educated guesses about diversity are not accurate. The client may have feelings much different than you imagined. Still, you have built a strong emotional connection with the client that is ready immediately.

Now it is time to get back to your everyday emotions. You have to let go of your old feelings. This is important so that your empathy can be accurate, or safe. Once you let go of the past feelings and experiences, you can get to the present and be more objective about your client's concerns. You will need this separation to keep a boundary around yourself and to be nonreactive, or to practice self-regulation, about how you express your feelings. Practicing the mindfulness exercise above can help with this process. You may need to discuss your thoughts and feelings about your experience, so having a trusted supervisor is important. The point is to get in touch with your past, painful feelings and then let them go. At this point, you are ready to meet with your client.

CRITICAL THINKING AND COLLABORATIVE LEARNING EXERCISES 4.4

1. Identify a client situation that may seem foreign to you—for example, someone experiencing stress within their church council, someone experiencing substance abuse, someone considering an abortion, someone whose home improvement plans are stymied by a town ordinance, someone whose child has just died. Work with a partner to identify your feelings about that situation.
2. Once you have identified your feelings, try to identify some situation in your life that has some similarity to that hypothetical client's situation.
3. Practice the mindfulness exercise about letting go of painful emotions.

Section 4.5: Supervision

Planned change is built on relationships between workers and their clients. In the same way, supervision between a social worker and their supervisor is built on a relationship of trust. Once that trust is established, the supervisory relationship serves to enhance a worker's competency. No worker is so experienced that they don't need supervision. This section continues the process of self-reflection through the use of supervision. It begins with a discussion about the development of the supervisory relationship and moves to the various purposes of supervision. You will need to know and build on the information in this section later: Supervision will be discussed in more depth in Chapter 13.

Engaging in the Supervisory Relationship

The supervisor–worker relationship is similar to the worker–client representative relationship. Supervisors and workers collaborate to engage in a process similar to the planned change process. In fact, the supervisory relationship is widely known to be a **parallel process** to that of the worker–client relationship (McMillin, 2012). To begin that process, supervisor and worker practice self-reflection to develop empathy for the other. Then, both the supervisor and the worker spend time engaging in relationship building. Each must trust the other for the planned supervisory change process to occur. In particular, trust between the two of them is needed for the worker to engage in the self-reflection needed to continuously improve their ability to facilitate planned change with their clients. On the other hand, both worker and supervisor must maintain boundaries, a concept that will be discussed later. First, consider the purposes of supervision.

Purposes of Supervision

Social work supervision has three purposes. The three purposes of supervision are administration, education, and support (Kadushin & Harkness, 2014).

Administration

The supervisor is first and foremost responsible to the agency. For that reason, supervisors must ask difficult questions about whether you're getting your work done and what your relationship is with your colleagues. We'll go into the details of the administrative aspects of supervision in Chapter 13, but for now know that it is critical. Unfortunately, sometimes supervision begins and ends with administration even though other purposes of supervision are just as important (Chapman, Oppenheim, Shibusawa, & Jackson, 2003).

Education

The second purpose of social work supervision is education. Often, supervisors educate workers based on their own experience, or **practice wisdom** (Council on Social Work Education [CSWE], 2015). Workers need to collaborate with supervisors to identify areas of growth that are required. The supervisor can recommend informed colleagues, readings, and workshops for the worker if the worker is able to allow the supervisor to see their challenges.

Workers and supervisors are friendly, not friends.

Support

The third component of supervision is support. Workers face troubling situations, and they need to be able to tell their stories and express their feelings. To get to the bottom of the situation, the worker will have to **self-disclose** information to their supervisor. This can become problematic if both worker and supervisor forget the purpose of the self-disclosure and make the connection deeper and beyond the purpose of support in supervision. At that point, a **boundary** violation may happen.

Boundaries in Supervision

Many times as a worker begins to trust their supervisor, they begin to share information about their domestic partner or intimate friend. This may begin in a very legitimate way. For example, the worker may have a very happy home life and have trouble understanding why an unhappy spouse does not leave a painful situation. If the worker does share some information about their relationship with their partner, a complicated situation occurs. The idea is that enough information should be shared but not too much. In this situation, both worker and supervisor should be aware (here is the importance of awareness again) that the personal information is being shared for a particular reason. It should be understood that the purpose of sharing information is always about intentionally improving service. For someone with a happy home life who is trying to develop empathy for an unhappy or abused person, it would be appropriate to share this situation with a supervisor to help get perspective.

While the supervisor–worker relationship is built on trust and is therefore similar to the worker–client relationship, it's not identical. Once the trusting relationship is built, the worker and supervisor must together concentrate on maintaining boundaries around each other's lives and experiences. Remember that a boundary may be thought of as the limit of a system (Carter, 2011). In other words, both supervisor and worker collaborate to share the aspects of themselves that are necessary for supervisory planned change to occur . . . and no more. In this way, supervisors can help workers to effectively use introspection in the self-reflection stage. If the worker shares too much information, they can easily get a helping relationship created with their supervisor. The result is that further administration and education in supervision is likely to fall by the wayside. It will grow increasingly difficult for the supervisor to ask the worker whether their paperwork is complete when they know that the worker has been up all night arguing with their partner about their partner's controlling behavior. Ideally, the worker will share only what information is needed for the supervisor to help them identify barriers to their work.

CRITICAL THINKING AND COLLABORATIVE LEARNING EXERCISES 4.5

Work in a large group. Discuss people's experiences with supervision in their past jobs or volunteer experiences. Were the experiences limited to administration? Which kinds of experiences were helpful?

Section 4.6: Barriers to Supervision

This section will further explore the barriers that can occur in the supervisory relationship that make it harder for the worker to engage in meaningful self-reflection.

Why Barriers Develop in Supervision

Some time ago, Kadushin (1999) wrote about barriers that come between supervisors and workers. A major reason that barriers develop in supervision is **role acceptance**. For effective supervision to happen, the supervisor has to accept a role where they are the authority figure. They have to consistently stay in that role even when it becomes difficult to feel like they always have the answers. Likewise, the worker has to accept the role of learner. As an employee, that role is by its nature compliant. The worker has to accept direction and advice from a supervisor even when they think the supervisor is wrong or when the worker is considerably older than the supervisor. There are a number of problems that can happen when either person is uncomfortable in their role. Kadushin (1999) has identified a number of specific relationship problems that can get in the way of good supervision and competent social work. Note that the following situations should be understood as interactions that happen outside of people's awareness. It is assumed that workers and supervisors do not try to avoid difficult situations just because they want their work to be easier. Instead, the interactions below occur outside of consciousness. Knowing about them can bring these barriers to awareness where they can be managed by both worker and supervisor. (Here is yet another time awareness is important.) As adapted from Kadushin (1999), four of these interactions consist of the following:

- *Flattering the supervisor excessively*
- *Developing a friendship with the supervisor*
- *Sneakily pointing out a supervisor's lack of knowledge*
- *Continually asking simple questions to avoid uncomfortable situations*

"You're the Greatest"

This barrier often occurs when a worker has not been able to complete their work on time. They don't want to get to the part of supervision where administration takes place and the worker has to account for their incomplete work. Basically, the worker is unconsciously avoiding taking the compliant role of a supervisee. To avoid the administrative questions, the worker begins to flatter the supervisor. They tell their supervisor that they've never learned so much from a supervisor before, that the supervisor's practice wisdom is so great, that they look up to the supervisor as a mentor. Taken separately, these statements may be perfectly appropriate, but taken all at once they may result in a problem: After the worker has spent a significant amount of time flattering the supervisor, it is only human that the supervisor will find it difficult to make demands on the worker even if those demands are reasonable and based on agency policy. In this way, a barrier is placed in the supervisory relationship. Workers and supervisors alike should know to take a close look at themselves if they find themselves overly flattering the other person.

"Friends Don't Let Friends Fail"

In this barrier to supervision, the supervisor is not comfortable maintaining distance in the authority role, and the worker is uncomfortable accepting direction and advice. Specifically, the worker is unconsciously trying to avoid being evaluated. A good performance evaluation is conducted collaboratively, with both parties stating their opinions and coming to agreement on what the evaluation says. Most importantly, a good evaluation will result in suggestions for further professional growth. Still, most people become anxious about their performance being assessed (think of your last exam), and they try to avoid it. In this barrier, good evaluation is hindered by a crossing of supervisor–worker boundaries. As workers share personal information and go too far, supervisors step into the role of helper: This is very comfortable for them. In and of itself, that is a serious problem. Next, it can get even worse. Both worker and supervisor can end up sharing personal stories and situations. They become more like peers or even friends, and it becomes more and more difficult for the supervisor to evaluate the worker's performance as anything but "wonderful." Be cautious when you hear the word *wonderful*.

"I Just Have One Question"

Like most of the behaviors that cause barriers in supervision, "I just have one question" would be perfectly appropriate, even desirable, if it just happened once. But when a question turns into a long list of inquiries that occur at the beginning of the supervisory session, it can become a barrier by taking up all of the time. When a worker has trouble being compliant, they may ask question after question in each supervisory session. The questions serve the purpose of taking up time so that there is no chance for the supervisor to bring up administrative issues. In this way, the worker guarantees that there isn't a chance for the supervisor to check on the worker's late paperwork.

"What Was It Freud Said About That?"

This barrier to productive supervision occurs when a worker is not comfortable being compliant and a supervisor is not confident in the supervisory role. If the supervisor is not good at portraying the absent attribute of confidence, both worker and supervisor are vulnerable to this barrier. Here, the worker asks a question about a little known fact that is relevant to the agency. For example, the worker may ask the supervisor this: "What was that stage in Erikson's developmental stages where adolescents are rebellious? You know, the fifth one? What's it called?" Chances are, the new worker only knows this relatively trivial piece of information because they recently read about it in one of their college courses. Naturally, the supervisor cannot come up with *identity vs. identity diffusion* off the top of their head. The supervisor, not able to display confidence, mumbles some response. The worker knows very well that the supervisor does not know the answer, and the supervisor knows that the worker knows. Of course it will be difficult for the supervisor to then provide a critical evaluation or make a demand for work from the worker. An appropriate response for the supervisor to make is "I have no idea. Why don't you look it up?"

Responses to Unconscious Barriers

Using mindfulness, workers and supervisors can recognize when they have anxiety about a supervisory session. This process will help them to identify what coping mechanisms they are using to avoid their anxiety. Once they are aware of the barrier, it can be removed. Most often, the best way to respond to these barriers is to remember to say "I don't know" when you're not sure of something. When workers and supervisors are comfortable admitting that they don't know something, they have little need for unconscious coping mechanisms.

Removing Barriers With Theory

To remove the barriers that occur in the supervisory process is to identify feelings and critically examine the thoughts that lie behind them, as in the "What do I feel/believe/know/do?" exercise. Another way to remove barriers is to be aware of the planned change process as it occurs in supervision. As mentioned above, the planned change process is a parallel process to supervision in that each stage occurs in a similar way in supervision and in work with clients and client system representatives. Since the process is similar to work with clients, the worker is empowered to play a role in the mutual change process. In this way, the worker can make suggestions about the process of supervision. The worker should keep the following stages in mind:

- *Self-reflection*—The worker identifies feelings related to supervision and thinks critically about them to engage in conscious, professional behavior. It is helpful for the worker to spend some time engaging in mindfulness practice so they can begin to identify their feelings about supervision.

- *Engagement*—The worker and supervisor build a professional relationship before beginning tasks; agency mission is clarified; job description is reviewed.
- *Assessment*—The worker and supervisor examine the worker's strengths and challenges related to the job description, including their knowledge and skills, the worker's relationship with the supervisor, and the agency atmosphere and policies.
- *Planning*—The worker and supervisor construct goals for the worker to achieve during supervision. Tasks related to worker's lifelong learning may be identified.
- *Implementation*—Worker and supervisor meet weekly for a full supervisory session in which the goals and their achievement form part of the focus in addition to administration, education, and support.
- *Evaluation*—Worker's performance evaluation is conducted by both worker and supervisor individually, and then they compare their thoughts. The worker's evaluation is a combination of the thoughts and opinions of both the worker and the supervisor. At this time, the supervisor may be willing to think about the worker's evaluation of the supervisory process itself.
- *Termination*—When the worker or supervisor is ready to leave, they share their thoughts and feelings about the supervisory process.
- *Follow-up*—The worker may ask the supervisor for an employment reference in the future.

CRITICAL THINKING AND COLLABORATIVE LEARNING EXERCISES 4.6

Work with a partner. You and your partner should both evaluate your performance in the classroom. Share your impressions. How do you feel having a peer evaluate your performance?

Section 4.7: Self-Care

Self-reflection has been explored for the purpose of bringing feelings, thoughts, and behaviors into awareness. It was noted that while this process can be extremely fulfilling, it can also be a painful experience. This section explores the potential of self-reflection for self-care.

Compassion Fatigue

It is well known that social workers engage in empathy for clients in terribly upsetting situations. On a positive note, developing empathy can help workers to better understand themselves and even build on their own coping skills. On the other hand, developing empathy, especially as it is described above, can be painful and can even drain a worker's ability to continue in the job. Workers can easily experience troubling feelings as they try to stand in the shoes of people who are suffering. It is easy for them to get stress-related symptoms. The process of developing stress-related symptoms in the face of repeatedly developing empathy for people in painful situations is called **compassion fatigue** (Bush, 2009). Scientific research has shown that compassion fatigue can result in more than just discomfort. Compassion fatigue can result in ongoing levels of stress, where people feel stressed about their jobs even when they are not working. It can cause physical and emotional exhaustion when people are at work, leaving them no energy to engage in recreation or relationships. At home, people may withdraw from significant relationships and experience irritability or depression. At work, they may even find that they are less able to do their jobs. They find it harder and harder to develop empathy (Bush 2009; Decker, Bailey, & Westergaard, 2002; Gough, 2007).

Indicators of Compassion Fatigue

- *Inability to continue to develop empathy*
- *Sadness*
- *Hopelessness*
- *Physical exhaustion*
- *Emotional exhaustion*
- *Feelings of stress*
- *Withdrawal*
- *Irritability*

Prevention

Obviously it is essential to guard against compassion fatigue. Remember that mindfulness practice can help prevent compassion fatigue (Westphal et al., 2015). Another method of prevention is developing close relationships with your coworkers (Kanno, Kim, & Constance-Huggins, 2016). Next, it is important to develop the accurate empathy we've just discussed. Keep appropriate emotional boundaries between yourself and your clients. Maintain your general wellness too. Traditionally, strategies to maintain wellness have included socialization, recreation and leisure time, good nutrition, and exercise. That means don't isolate yourself entirely even if you have a lot of schoolwork, remember to have fun even if you're employed outside of school, take time to plan meals and eat right, and make sure you don't sit more than you need to. Currently, most research focuses on mindfulness practice for stress reduction such as the exercise provided earlier. Keep in mind that the practice of self-reflection, the first stage in the helping process, is in and of itself potentially dangerous to workers in situations of inappropriate empathy and poor boundaries. Be sure to focus on the present, not on negative thoughts. We must take action to guard against compassion fatigue, perhaps using mindfulness techniques and certainly using the general wellness practices noted above. Also, it is important for workers to recognize that indicators of stress, including headaches, sleeping too much or too little, eating too much or too little, snapping at your friends, and having an inability to continue to develop empathy for clients are all red flags for compassion fatigue. Workers must respond immediately when it happens. Take care of yourself. As we've seen, mindfulness practice is a well-known method of relieving stress. Here is an example of the use of mindfulness for stress relief:

Do the exercise sitting or lying down. Follow the directions, taking time between each sentence. The exercise should last about 15 minutes:

> Take a few moments to be still. Congratulate yourself for taking some time for meditation practice. Bring your awareness to your breath wherever you feel it most prominently in your body. It may be at the nose, neck, chest, belly, or somewhere

else. As you breathe in normally and naturally, be aware of breathing in, and as you breathe out, be aware of breathing out. Simply maintain this awareness of the breath, breathing in and breathing out. Be aware of breathing out. There is no need to visualize, count, or figure out the breath; just be mindful of breathing in and out. Without judgment, just watch the breath ebb and flow like waves in the sea. There's no place to go and nothing else to do, just be in the here and now, noticing the breath—just living life one inhalation and one exhalation at a time. As you breathe in and out, be mindful of the breath rising on the inhalation and falling on the exhalation. Just riding the waves of the breath, moment by moment, breathing in and breathing out. From time to time, attention may wander from the breath. When you notice this, simply acknowledge where you went and then gently bring your attention back to the breath. Breathing normally and naturally, without manipulating the breath in any way, just be aware of the breath as it comes and goes. As you come to the end of this meditation, congratulate yourself for taking this time to be present, realizing that this is an act of love. (Stahl & Goldstein, 2010, p. 57)

JPM/Getty Images

Self-reflection can mean facing incompetency

Along with all of these methods of stress relief and self-care, be sure to seek appropriate supervision. In the context of healthy boundaries, your supervisor is an important resource for stress relief (Kapoulitsas & Corcoran, 2015). Overall, workers should prioritize meeting their own needs. It's like what they tell you in an airplane: Put the oxygen mask on yourself first; then you can help others.

Self-Reflection: The Fearful Worker

Amy could do Internet searches, make PowerPoint presentations, and use social media. She didn't know how to use Excel, though, and she found out the hard way that she shouldn't have pretended she did. What Amy was using was a display of confidence, but supervision is not a place for a worker to display confidence; it is a place to ask questions. In Amy's case, she didn't want to appear stupid in front of her supervisor. She needed to identify her feelings of anxiety and shame and think about her belief that every person in her school and in the agency was proficient with Excel. If she had done some asking around, she could have used critical thinking and identified the fact that not everyone in the agency knew Excel. In fact, Amy's supervisor was making the incorrect assumption that because Amy was a young adult she must know "everything" about computers. Once Amy recognized that she wasn't alone, she could allow herself to be unsure. She could allow herself to say "I don't know."

CRITICAL THINKING AND COLLABORATIVE LEARNING EXERCISES 4.7

1. Work with a partner. Identify six activities that each of you do to take care of yourselves. How often do you do them? What are the times you are least likely to do them?
2. Make a plan for attending more to your needs. Share it with a friend.

Section 4.8: Review and Apply

CONCURRENT CONSIDERATIONS IN GENERALIST PRACTICE

Ethical Decision-Making Challenge

When Amy was first confronted with Excel, she thought she might get by without learning it. If she had paid attention to Standard 3 in the *NASW Code of Ethics* (NASW, 2018), she might have behaved differently. If you substitute the word *school* for *employer* in that section of the code, are you behaving ethically as a student?

Human Rights

Is anyone in this case being deprived of any fundamental human rights such as freedom, safety, privacy, an adequate standard of living, health care, and education? Think about the adoptive parents as well as those who would like to be adoptive parents.

Evidence-Based Practice

Amy's agency was attempting to create support among the adoptive families by creating an event they would be happy to attend. Are there any activities that Amy should carry out during the event that would help the families connect with each other? Look in the scientific literature to see what activities might foster engagement among members of a support group. Can she just organize a party, or is there something specific that should happen at the party?

Policies Impacting Practice

Research the policies related to adoption in your state. What is the difference between public adoption and private adoption related to eligibility, cost, and family outcomes?

Managing Diversity

Find out whether it is better for adopted children to be connected to their ethnicity of origin or whether it is better for them if their adoptive parents expect them to embrace their adoptive family's ethnic group and family traditions.

Multisystem Practice

Identify examples of Amy's work on all levels.

Micro: ______________________

Mezzo: ______________________

Macro: ______________________

Dynamic and Interactive Planned Change Stages

Identify aspects of Amy's work where she worked in the following stages:

Self-Reflection: ______________________

Engagement: ______________________

Assessment: ______________________

Planning: ______________________

Implementation: ______________________

Evaluation: ______________________

Termination and Follow-Up: ______________________

Chapter Summary

Section 4.1: Self-Reflection

The first stage in the planned change process is self-reflection. Self-reflection is where the worker uses introspection to become aware of their thoughts, feelings, and behaviors. The goal of self-reflection is for the worker to become intentional in what they do.

Section 4.2: Developing Cultural Humility

Another benefit of self-reflection is the development of cultural humility. Cultural humility is the worker's self-awareness about their own prejudices so that they can fully understand the values of other cultures. Cultural humility is required for workers to become culturally sensitive.

Section 4.3: The Method of Self-Reflection

The process of developing cultural sensitivity can be carried out using mindfulness techniques. In mindfulness practice, a person becomes aware of their physical sensations. They also pay attention to their thoughts and accept them without judgment. Using mindfulness exercises can help workers to identify the negative feelings. This process helps workers to develop cultural responsiveness.

Section 4.4: Developing Empathy

Cultural sensitivity is necessary to develop empathy. Empathy is a way of getting in touch with another's thoughts and feelings. Accurate empathy is developing empathy that is safe and not too painful for the worker. A process of the development of empathy can allow a worker to begin to develop empathy before meeting a client.

Section 4.5: Supervision

Developing empathy can be emotionally draining, so supportive supervision is an important aid to self-reflection. Social work supervision has three elements: (1) administration, (2) education, and (3) support. Appropriate boundaries are important to developing a trusting supervisory experience.

Section 4.6: Barriers to Supervision

Barriers can come between a worker and supervisor, often because one or the other is not comfortable in their role. These barriers can often be overcome with the recognition of feelings related to the supervisory process. Barriers can also be overcome by becoming aware of how supervision can be a planned change process.

Section 4.7: Self-Care

Self-reflection can also be useful to prevent and respond to compassion fatigue. It is important for workers to engage in self-care to provide the best service to clients and client systems.

SELF-REFLECTION 4: FIVE FACET MINDFULNESS QUESTIONNAIRE

AUTHORS: Ruth A. Baer, Gregory T. Smith, Emily Lykins, Daniel Button, Jennifer Krietemeyer; Sharon Sauer, Erin Walsh, Danielle Duggan, L. Toney, and J. Mark G. Williams

PURPOSE: To measure five aspects of mindfulness

DESCRIPTION: The 39-item instrument assesses five interrelated dimensions of mindfulness: observing; describing; acting with awareness; nonjudgmentalness; and nonreactivity. It is useful when evaluating a wellness and health promotion program. Since mindfulness is so highly associated with psychological well-being and the absence of mental health symptoms, it is a useful goal to monitor most implementations.

NORMS: The Five Facet Mindfulness Questionnaire (FFMQ) has been tested with a number of groups including college students. Average scores of the five facets among college students were as follows:

Observe Score (OS): 24

Describe Score (DS): 26

Act Aware Score (AAS): 25

Nonjudgmental Score (NJS): 28

Nonreactive Score (NRS): 21

SCORING: Sum the following items to score each facet of mindfulness:

OS: 1, 6, 11, 15, 20, 26, 31, 36

DS: 2, 7, 12, 16, 22, 27, 32, 37 (reverse score 16 and 22—meaning a score of 5 = 1 and a score of 2 = 4, etc.)

AAS: 5, 8, 13, 18, 23, 28, 34, 38 (reverse score all)

NJS: 3, 10, 14, 17, 25, 30, 35, 39 (reverse score all)

NRS: 4, 9, 19, 21, 24, 29, 33

RELIABILITY: The FFMQ has adequate to good reliability with alpha coefficients ranging from .72 to .91.

VALIDITY: The FFMQ has excellent evidence of validity. The five-facet structure was supported by factor analysis, with the scale scores having moderate correlations to suggest they are independent but are interrelated constructs. Meditation experiences are associated with each scale, except for AAs in a sample of 1,107.

PRIMARY REFERENCES:

Baer, R. A., Smith, G. T., Hopkins, J., Krietemeyer, J., & Toney, L. (2013). Using self-report assessment methods to explore facets of mindfulness. Assessment, 13, 27–45. In K. Corcoran & J. Fischer (Eds.), *Measures for clinical practice and research: A sourcebook* (5th ed.). New York, NY: Oxford University Press.

Baer, R. A., Smith, G. T., Lykins, E., Button, D., Krietemeyer, J., Sauer, S., Williams, J. M. G. (2013). Construct validity of the Five Facet Mindfulness Questionnaire in meditating and nonmeditating samples. In K. Corcoran & J. Fischer (Eds.), *Measures for clinical practice and research: A sourcebook* (5th ed.). New York, NY: Oxford University Press.

FIVE FACET MINDFULNESS QUESTIONNAIRE

Please rate each of the following statements using the scale provided. Write the number in the blank that best describes your own opinion of what is generally true for you.

1 = never or very rarely true
2 = rarely true
3 = sometimes true
4 = often true
5 = very often or always true

_____ 1. When I'm walking, I deliberately notice the sensations of my body moving.
_____ 2. I'm good at finding words to describe my feelings.
_____ 3. I criticize myself for having irrational or inappropriate emotions.
_____ 4. I perceive my feelings and emotions without having to react to them.
_____ 5. When I do things, my mind wanders off and I'm easily distracted.
_____ 6. When I take a shower or bath, I stay alert to the sensations of water on my body.
_____ 7. I can easily put my beliefs, opinions, and expectations into words.
_____ 8. I don't pay attention to what I'm doing because I'm daydreaming, worrying, or otherwise distracted.
_____ 9. I watch my feelings without getting lost in them.

_____ 10. I tell myself I shouldn't be feeling the way I'm feeling.
_____ 11. I notice how foods and drinks affect my thoughts, bodily sensations, and emotions.
_____ 12. It's hard for me to find the words to describe what I'm thinking.
_____ 13. I am easily distracted.
_____ 14. I believe some of my thoughts are abnormal or bad and I shouldn't think that way.
_____ 15. I pay attention to sensations, such as the wind in my hair or the sun on my face.
_____ 16. I have trouble thinking of the right words to express how I feel about things.
_____ 17. I make judgments about whether my thoughts are good or bad.
_____ 18. I find it difficult to stay focused on what's happening in the present.
_____ 19. When I have distressing thoughts or images, I "step back" and am aware of the thought or image without getting taken over by it.
_____ 20. I pay attention to sounds, such as clocks ticking, birds chirping, or cars passing.
_____ 21. In difficult situations, I can pause without immediately acting.
_____ 22. When I have a sensation in my body, it's difficult for me to describe it because I can't find the right words.
_____ 23. It seems I am "running on automatic" without much awareness of what I'm doing.
_____ 24. When I have distressing thoughts or images, I feel calm soon after.
_____ 25. I tell myself that I shouldn't be thinking the way I'm thinking.
_____ 26. I notice the smells and aromas of things.
_____ 27. Even when I'm feeling terribly upset, I can find a way to put it into words.
_____ 28. I rush through activities without being really attentive to them.
_____ 29. When I have distressing thoughts or images I am able just to notice them without reacting.
_____ 30. I think some of my emotions are bad or inappropriate and I shouldn't feel them.
_____ 31. I notice visual elements in art or nature, such as colors, shapes, textures, or patterns of light and shadow.
_____ 32. My natural tendency is to put my experiences into words.
_____ 33. When I have distressing thoughts or images, I just notice them and let them go.
_____ 34. I do jobs or tasks automatically without being aware of what I'm doing.
_____ 35. When I have distressing thoughts or images, I judge myself as good or bad, depending on what the thought/image is about.
_____ 36. I pay attention to how my emotions affect my thoughts and behavior.
_____ 37. I can usually describe how I feel at the moment in considerable detail.
_____ 38. I find myself doing things without paying attention.
_____ 39. I disapprove of myself when I have irrational ideas.

Recommended Websites

"Self-Care Exercises and Activities" from University of Buffalo School of Social Work: https://socialwork.buffalo.edu/resources/self-care-starter-kit/self-care-assessments-exercises/exercises-and-activities.html#title_6

"Microsoft Tech Support" from 24/7 Techies: www.247techies.com/ppc/microsoft-tech-support.php?gclid=CNGswu31h9ACFQhkhgod2AEE6g

Critical Terms for Self-Reflection

self-reflection 105
macro 106
cultural humility 107
diversity 107
culturally responsive 108
ethnic identity 109
total identity 109
culturally sensitive 110
intergroup differences 110
intragroup differences 110
mindfulness 112
operationalize 113
accurate empathy 116
preparatory empathy 117
concrete elements of diversity 118
affective elements of diversity 118
parallel process 120
practice wisdom 120
self-disclose 120
boundary 120
role acceptance 121
compassion fatigue 124

Generalist Practice Curriculum Matrix With 2015 Educational Policy and Accreditation Standards

Chapter 4

Competency	Course	Course Content	Dimensions
Competency 1: Demonstrate Ethical and Professional Behavior		4.1. Articulate the meaning of self-reflection in work with systems of all sizes. 4.5. Identify aspects of supervision that facilitate self-reflection and professional use of self. 4.6. Explore potential barriers to productive supervision. 4.7. Practice using self-reflection for self-care. Feature 3: Self-Reflection Feature 4: Concurrent Considerations in Generalist Practice	Cognitive–affective processes Knowledge Skills Knowledge Skills Cognitive–affective processes Skills Cognitive–affective processes Skills Cognitive–affective processes
Competency 2: Engage Diversity and Difference in Practice		4.2. Practice the development of cultural humility through self-reflection. Feature 1: Focus on Diversity Feature 4: Concurrent Considerations in Generalist Practice	Values Skills Cognitive–affective processes Skills Cognitive–affective processes Skills Cognitive–affective processes

(Continued)

(Continued)

Competency	Course	Course Content	Dimensions
Competency 3: Advance Human Rights and Social, Economic, and Environmental Justice		Feature 4: Concurrent Considerations in Generalist Practice	Skills Cognitive–affective processes
Competency 4: Engage In Practice-Informed Research and Research-Informed Practice		4.3. Appraise the scientific support for the practice of mindfulness for self-reflection.	Knowledge
		Feature 4: Concurrent Considerations in Generalist Practice	Skills Cognitive–affective processes
Competency 5: Engage in Policy Practice		Feature 4: Concurrent Considerations in Generalist Practice	Knowledge
Competency 6: Engage With Individuals, Families, Groups, Organizations, and Communities		4.4. Practice the process of developing empathy.	Cognitive–affective processes
		Feature 4: Concurrent Considerations in Generalist Practice	Skills Cognitive–affective processes
Competency 7: Assess Individuals, Families, Groups, Organizations, and Communities		Feature 4: Concurrent Considerations in Generalist Practice	Skills Cognitive–affective processes
Competency 8: Intervene With Individuals, Families, Groups, Organizations, and Communities		Feature 4: Concurrent Considerations in Generalist Practice	Skills Cognitive–affective processes
Competency 9: Evaluate Practice With Individuals, Families, Groups, Organizations, and Communities		Feature 4: Concurrent Considerations in Generalist Practice	Skills Cognitive–affective processes

References

Baer, R. A., Smith, G. T., Hopkins, J., Krietemeyer, J., & Toney, L. (2013). Using self-report assessment methods to explore facets of mindfulness. *Assessment, 13*, 27–45. In K. Corcoran & J. Fischer (Eds.), *Measures for clinical practice and research: A sourcebook* (5th ed.). New York, NY: Oxford University Press.

Baer, R. A., Smith, G. T., Lykins, E., Button, D., Krietemeyer, J., Sauer, S., . . . Williams, J. M. G. (2013). Construct validity of the Five Facet Mindfulness Questionnaire in meditating and nonmeditating samples. In K. Corcoran & J. Fischer (Eds.), *Measures for clinical practice and research: A sourcebook* (5th ed.). New York, NY: Oxford University Press.

Berry, J. W., & Sabatier, C. (2010). Acculturation, discrimination, and adaptation among second generation immigrant youth in Montreal and Paris. *International Journal of Intercultural Relations, 34*(3), 191–207. doi:10.1016/j.ijintrel.2009.11.007

Boone, M. S. (Ed.). (2014). *Mindfulness and acceptance in social work*. Oakland, CA: New Harbinger.

Bush, N. (2009). Compassion fatigue: Are you at risk? *Oncology Nursing Forum: Clinical Challenges, 36*(1), 24–28.

Carter, I. (2011). *Human behavior in the social environment* (6th ed.). New Brunswick, NJ: Aldine Transaction.

Chapman, M. V., Oppenheim, S., Shibusawa, T., & Jackson, H. M. (2003). What we bring to practice: Teaching students about professional use of self. *Journal of Teaching in Social Work, 23*(2/3), 3–14. doi:10.1300/J067v23n03_02

Christopher, J. C., & Maris, J. (2010). Integrating mindfulness as self-care into counseling and psychotherapy training. *Counseling and Psychology Research, 10*(2), 114–125.

Council on Social Work Education. (2015). *Educational policy and accreditation standards*. Alexandria, VA: Author.

Decker, J. T., Brown, J. L. C., Ong, J., & Stiney-Ziskind, C. (2015). Mindfulness, compassion fatigue, and compassion satisfaction among social work interns. *Social Work & Christianity, 42*(1), 28–42.

Decker, J. T., Bailey, T. L., & Westergaard, N. (2002). Burnout among childcare workers. *Residential Treatment for Children and Youth, 19*(4), 61–77.

Garland, E. L. (2013). Mindfulness research in social work: Conceptual and methodological recommendations. *Social Work Research, 37*(4), 439–448. doi:10.1093/swr/svt038

Garland, E. L., Farb, N. A., Goldin, P. R., & Fredrickson, B. L. (2015). Mindfulness broadens awareness and builds eudaimonic meaning: A process model of mindful positive emotion regulation. *Psychological Inquiry, 26*(4), 293–314.

Gerdes, K. E., Lietz, C. A., & Segal, E. A. (2011). Measuring empathy in the 21st century: Development of an empathy index rooted in social cognitive neuroscience and social justice. *Social Work Research, 35*(2), 83–93.

Grant, L. (2014). Hearts and minds: Aspects of empathy and wellbeing in social work students. *Social Work Education, 33*(3), 338–352. doi:10.1080/02615479.2013.805191

Grepmair, L., Mitterlehner, F., Loew, T., Bachler, E., Rother, W., & Nickel, M. (2007). Promoting mindfulness in psychotherapists in training influences the treatment results of their patients: A randomized, double-blind, controlled study. *Psychotherapy and Psychosomatics, 76*, 332–338.

Good, D. J., Lyddy, C. J., Glomb, T. M., Bono, J. E., Brown, K. W., Duffy, M. K., . . . Lazar, S. W. (2016). Contemplating mindfulness at work. *Journal of Management, 42*(1), 114–142.

Gotink, R. A., Meijboom, R., Vernooij, M. W., Smits, M., & Hunink, M. G. (2016). 8-week mindfulness based stress reduction induces brain changes similar to traditional long-term meditation practice: A systematic review. *Brain and Cognition, 108*, 32–41. doi:10.1016/j.bandc.2016.07.001

Gough, D. (2007). Empathizing or falling in the river? Avoiding and addressing compassion fatigue among service providers. *JADARA*: The *Journal for Professionals Networking for Excellence in Service Delivery with Individuals who are Deaf and Hard of Hearing, 40*(3), 13.

Hanna, E. P. (2013). A cognitive emotional methodology for critical thinking. *Advances in Applied Sociology, 3*(1), 20–25.

Hick, S. F. (2009). *Mindfulness and social work*. Chicago, IL: Lyceum.

Hölzel, B. K., Carmody, J., Vangel, M., Congleton, C., Yerramsetti, S. M., Gard, T., & Lazar, S. W. (2011). Mindfulness practice leads to increases in regional brain gray matter density. *Psychiatry Research, 191*(1), 36–43.

Kadushin, A. (1999). Games people play in supervision. *Reflections: Narratives of Professional Helping, 5*(3) 53–64.

Kadushin, A., & Harkness, D. (2014). *Supervision in social work*. New York, NY: Columbia University Press.

Kadushin, A., & Kadushin, G. (2013). *The social work interview* (5th ed.). New York, NY: Columbia University Press.

Kanno, H., Kim, Y. M., & Constance-Huggins, M. (2016). Risk and protective factors of secondary traumatic stress in social workers responding to the great East Japan earthquake, *Social Development Issues, 38*(3), 64–78.

Kapoulitsas, M., & Corcoran, T. (2015). Compassion fatigue and resilience: A qualitative analysis of social work practice. *Qualitative Social Work, 14*(1), 86–101.

Lutz, J., Bruhl, A. B., Doerig, N., Scheerer, H., Achermann, R., Weibel, A., . . . Herwid, U. (2016). Altered processing of self-related emotional stimuli in mindfulness meditators. *NeuroImage, 124*, 958–967.

Lynn, R. (2010). Mindfulness in social work education. *Social Work Education, 29*, 289–304. doi:10.1080/02615470902930351

Marra, T. (2004). *The dialectical behavior therapy workbook for overcoming depression and anxiety*. Oakland, CA: New Harbinger.

McMillin, S. E. (2012). Mentoring as parallel process. *Reflections: Narratives of Professional Helping, 18*(3), 4–7.

National Association of Social Workers. (2015). *Standards and indicators for cultural competence in social work practice*. Washington, DC: Author. Retrieved from https://www.socialworkers.org/LinkClick.aspx?fileticket=WmWvxnhEnmI%3d&portalid=0

National Association of Social Workers. (2018). *NASW code of ethics*. Washington, DC: NASW Press.

Paine, D. R., Jankowski, P. J., & Sandage, S. J. (2016). Humility as a predictor of intercultural competence: Mediator effects for differentiation of self. *The Family Journal, 24*(1), 15–22.

Ross, L. (2010). Notes from the field: Learning cultural humility through critical incidents and central challenges in community-based participatory research. *Journal of Community Practice, 18*, 315–335. doi:10.1080/107

Rubin, A., & Babbie, E. R. (2015). *Research methods for social work* (9th ed.). Boston, MA: Cengage.

Shapiro, S. L., Carlson, L., Astin, J., & Freedman, B. (2006). Mechanisms of mindfulness. *Journal of Clinical Psychology, 62*(3), 373–386. doi:10.1002/jclp.20237

Shapiro, S., Brown, K., & Biegel, G. (2007). Teaching self-care to caregivers: Effects of mindfulness-based stress reduction on the mental health of therapists in training. *Training and Education in Professional Psychology, 1*(2), 105–115.

Shulman, L. (1992). *The skills of helping: Individuals, families, and groups*. Itasca, IL: F. E. Peacock Publishers.

Stahl, B., & Goldstein, E. (2010). *A mindfulness-based stress reduction workbook*. Oakland, CA: New Harbinger Publications.

Tajfel, H. (1981). *Human groups and social categories: Studies in social psychology*. New York, NY: Cambridge University Press.

Tervalon, M., & Murray-Garcia, J. (1998). Cultural humility versus cultural competence: A critical distinction in defining physician training outcomes in multi-cultural education. *Journal of Healthcare for the Poor and Underserved, 9*(2), 117–125.

Thomas, J. T., & Otis, M. D. (2010). Intrapsychic correlates of professional quality of life: Mindfulness, empathy, and emotional separation. *Journal of the Society for Social Work and Research, 1*(2), 83–98.

Turner, K. (2008). Mindfulness: The present moment in clinical social work. *Clinical Social Work Journal, 37*, 95–103. doi:10.1007/s10615-008-0182-0

Westphal, M., Bingisser, M., Feng, T., Wall, M., Blakley, E., Bingisser, R., & Kleim, B. (2015). Protective benefits of mindfulness in emergency room personnel. *Journal of Affective Disorders, 1*, 79–85.

Recommended Readings

Bollinger, R. A., & Hill, P. C. (2012). Humility. In T. Plante (Ed.), *Religion, spirituality, and positive psychology: Understanding the psychological fruits of faith* (pp. 31–48). Santa Barbara, CA: Praeger.

Grant, L. (2014). Hearts and minds: Aspects of empathy and wellbeing in social work students. *Social Work Education, 33*(3), 338–352. doi:10.1080/02615479.2013.805191

Grepmair, L., Mitterlehner, F., Loew, T., Bachler, E., Rother, W., & Nickel, M. (2007). Promoting mindfulness in psychotherapists in training influences the treatment results of their patients: A randomized, double-blind, controlled study. *Psychotherapy and Psychosomatics, 76*, 332–338.

Jastrowski-Mano, K. E., Salamon, K. S., Hainsworth, K. R., Anderson-Khan, K. J., Ladwig, R. J., Davies, W. H., & Weisman, S. J. (2013). A randomized, controlled pilot study of mindfulness-based stress reduction for pediatric chronic pain. *MD Alternative Therapies, 19*(6).

Stahl, B., & Goldstein, E. (2010). A mindfulness-based stress reduction workbook. Oakland, CA: New Harbinger Publications. (An electronic version is available along with hard copy that has a companion CD.)

Engagement

This chapter begins exploration of the aspects of planned change that include direct worker–client system interaction. The second phase of planned change, engagement, is explored on multiple levels. Students continue to consider how they can recognize the impact of their own thoughts, feelings, and experiences. The case study here relates to substance use since work with people who misuse substances is often done outside the context of family work . . . with deleterious results. This aspect of work in the substance use field highlights the importance of multisystem practice (MSP). As discussed in previous chapters, MSP facilitates recognition of the importance of systems like families, small groups, and organizations. Another system that emerges as significant is the agency and its policies. This chapter continues the demonstration of the use of MSP in the context of beginnings.

Learning Objectives

5.1 Describe the role of the worker in facilitating the planned change process during engagement.

5.2 Practice skills related to engagement.

5.3 Review the aspects of beginnings in social work interactions.

5.4 Articulate an opening statement that reflects the difference between a social work interview and a conversation.

5.5 Review self-care through a cognitive process.

Case Study: Making a Connection

Jaime left her supervisor's office and straightened her jacket as she moved through the outpatient substance abuse facility. She stopped in the hallway and took a deep breath, slowly exhaling. *Focus.* She found Bob sitting alone in the waiting room. Her preparatory empathy told her he was likely to be uncomfortable sitting in a professional waiting room, so she put on her most engaging smile and thrust her hand out toward him for a handshake. "You must be Bob." Bob, a 35-year-old Caucasian man, rose tentatively to greet her and accept her offer of a firm handshake with his own wilted, chilly hand. Jaime noticed how incongruous the weak handshake was in the face of his heavy work boots and jeans. "I'm Jaime. Would you like to come into my office where we can speak privately?"

Rob Melnychuk/Getty Images

A cluttered office can get in the way of relationships with clients.

Jaime purposefully made direct eye contact for a fleeting second, still smiling, and motioned toward the hall. With a tilt of her head, she said, "Let's go." In the office, she grabbed a stack of files off the only chair and placed them on her desk, where they joined any number of other piles. Moving her chair around to the side of the desk, she sat down and leaned a bit toward Bob, making sure that her arms weren't crossed. She made indirect eye contact, looking at his face but not directly into his eyes, and she leaned her chin on the back of her hand just as he was doing. "As I said, I'm Jaime. I'm a social worker here at New Hope, where we work to help people achieve and maintain sobriety." Jaime knew that she was quoting from the agency's mission statement, and it made her feel comfortable and secure. "It's my job to help you on that path." Jaime let a few seconds of silence go by. Then she said, "Bob, if any client is committed to change, I'm committed to them. So, if you are committed to change, then I am committed to you." She already liked Bob, and she wanted to help him. In that moment, she allowed those feelings to show. And it worked. Bob nodded, made eye contact with her, and displayed a small, hopeful smile. A connection was made. Jaime knew it. She was sure enough that she moved things along. "You and I have just six 1-hour meetings, so do you feel okay about us starting right away?" Again, she left a couple of seconds go by. She felt relief. *He knows what we're here for. If he stays sitting, he's willing to at least think about working on change.* And she was glad she mentioned 1 hour. *I don't have any more time than that with all of this paperwork.*

As they talked, Jaime nodded frequently and often said "um hmm." She and Bob established that he believed group work would be important to his ongoing recovery but that he just couldn't get himself to fully participate in group. They also established that Bob's wife often complained that he was always at New Hope for group meetings. She had told him that her life hadn't improved since he stopped drinking—he still wasn't available to spend time with her. Bob said that at that point in his argument with his wife, their teenaged daughter, Sam, could be counted on to sulk and drag off to her bedroom.

Jaime wanted to move on with the meeting, but she knew that engagement was just beginning. When Bob went back to discussing his relationship with his wife, Jaime decided to tell him a bit about herself to help the two of them connect. "Bob," she said, "I'm not married so I don't know what it's like to live with a person when the two of you are in disagreement a lot of the time. Help me to understand what that's like." Bob seemed relieved to be able to share his experiences. Later, when he talked about Sam, she said, "I often have to deal with my sister's sulky teenager, but I don't know what it's like day to day. Could you tell me more about that?"

Jaime was on her way to establishing engagement with Bob. She was beginning assessment—MSP—and she already suspected she would have to see whether Bob would agree to a family session. Clearly the stress he perceived in his home must be considered as a possible barrier to his recovery. At New Hope, the agency's unwritten policy was that family work be done in the family home if at all possible. Jaime knew that would help her assessment of family dynamics immensely. But inside, her stomach fell. *That means travel time, documentation time lost. And that means doing paperwork on Saturday. Again.*

She inwardly shook herself and went back to her assessment. *This is a social work session; it's* for *the client. Focus.* Bob had already begun sharing information that would prove to be significant to his recovery. It seemed like she wouldn't have much trouble getting the intake form completed, but she thought she'd better help Bob recognize his strengths right away. "Bob," she said, "thanks for sharing those important things about your family life. That tells me you're a really strong person. We're going to have to be talking about a lot of personal stuff in the coming weeks, so I'm glad you're strong enough to share and are off to such a good start."

Section 5.1: Engagement

In this section, we begin to look at a definition of the second of the interactive stages of the planned change process: engagement.

Engagement

Engagement is the second step in the planned change process, continuing beginnings. Think of engagement as the building of a working relationship. This is a relationship that is necessary for any planned change to take place (Goldingay & Land, 2014). It is a relationship with a working agenda as well as a feeling component. As it is an exchange between two systems, engagement is an opening up of boundaries on both sides. It is acceptance, and it is vulnerability. It is giving great thought to a person's current feelings as they are influenced by the intersectionality of their history of discrimination and of power, of their ethnic and racial identity, of their sense of their own life story. For that one moment when engagement begins, it is an unconditional acceptance of the other. It is an emotional connection and a working partnership. And sometimes, it is very difficult to achieve. See Figure 5.1.

Acceptance and Vulnerability

Engagement is the connection between a worker and a client or client system representative. It is a personal connection that incorporates feelings. Workers display **genuineness** (Kadushin & Kadushin, 1997) to convey that they truly care about clients. For example, Jaime said, "If you are committed to change, then I am committed to you." When she said this, she wasn't just mouthing a trite phrase. She meant it, and she showed that she meant it in several ways including a tone of voice that signaled compassion. We'll say more

FIGURE 5.1 ● Aspects of Engagement

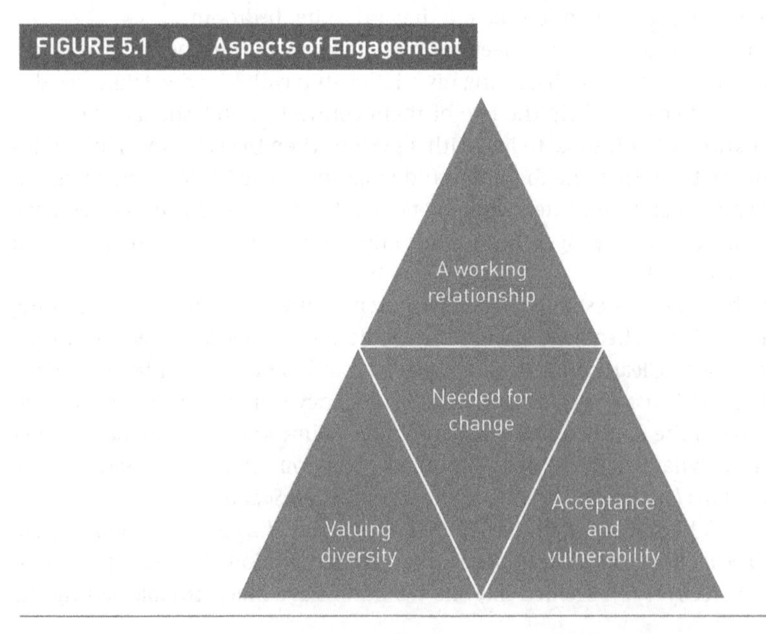

about the other skills she used in a moment, but for now you should realize that engagement is facilitated when workers really show they care. When workers show they care, they become vulnerable. As we've mentioned before, it is important to have **accurate empathy** (Gerdes, Lietz, & Segal, 2011). In other words, you should feel *with* a client but not *for* a client. We'll discuss some ways that you can think about engagement to help you to keep that boundary, or invisible limit to your interaction. This way, you'll be able to be compassionate without making yourself too vulnerable.

Valuing Diversity

The value a worker places on diversity is built into engagement. In order to truly accept a client or client system, workers have to consider how clients and client systems are different from themselves. As we've discussed, understanding diversity includes a consideration of the intersectionality of culture, ethnicity, gender expression, experiences of power and oppression, family constellation, and more. A worker who is engaged with a client has recognized and found strengths in the system's areas of difference.

A Working Relationship

Although engagement is partly about feelings, it is a professional relationship. In other words, it's a working relationship that exists for a purpose. We've discussed how social work sessions are different from conversations, and it's important to remember that one aspect of that difference is purpose. It's tempting to take feelings of engagement and move them into a friendly conversation, but the social work interview has a purpose and a working agenda.

Needed for Change

Another aspect of engagement is that it is absolutely necessary for real change to occur (Goldingay & Land, 2014). Many times a worker begins a relationship with a client or client system representative with a long list of things to do. There is likely to be an intake form, or a way for the agency to get a record of the client and their situation. There is likely to be a pressing concern, or even a crisis, that has brought the client to the worker. An agenda for future work has to be created. Given all of these, it may be tempting to take a professional attitude, jump in, and get some problems solved. This is okay if you work in a bank. Social work is different. You might think of it this way: A client or a system faces a problem. There is a barrier between them and the solution. The client or client system representative can probably see the solution, but they can't see how to get there. They need the worker to bridge that gap. Crossing a bridge requires trust in the bridge itself. That's why social work does not happen without engagement. Wait as long as you need to before you move on in planned change. In some practice settings like crisis intervention, it is important to move quickly through the stages of planned change, so the worker may really feel pressed to move on quickly. Remember that without engagement there won't be any change. You have to connect with a client first, and then you have to keep on connecting all through the process. Consider this example: A social worker is chairing a staff committee to beautify their building so workers and clients will be more comfortable. The group decides that a new use of the space will work well, but it requires a worker to change offices. It's easy for the group to see the solution, but the individual whose office is to change has to trust the chair of the committee for them to be able to reach that solution and commit to using a different space.

System Interactions

Remember that when systems interact, there is an energy exchange and a balanced energy exchange can create synergy (Carter, 2011). Jaime was hoping for this in her working relationship with Bob. She was hoping that she and Bob could be mutual partners. The worker's view in engagement is that all representatives of client systems are assumed to be capable partners. The social worker is not the expert who will tell the representative of a client system how to solve their problems. Instead, the social worker is more like the lead partner: responsible to manage the planned change process and the partnership itself through the use of the expertise they've developed in their education. Since the worker has the responsibility to manage the progression through the stages of planned change, there is an immediate power differential between worker and client system. The worker needs to consider their power as they work with clients toward self-determination.

As we discussed in the last chapter, when a social worker meets a client or client system representative, it's not a friendship, but it's not entirely business, either. It is the worker's responsibility to set the boundary. To create a friendship with a client is mostly to make the worker feel good—to believe "I am likable." We always have to be careful that we're not meeting our own needs for affirmation when we're working with a client. This is a challenge in work with individuals and families, but it's even more challenging in macro social work practice. When we're working with the representative of a client system—a teacher in a school or a council member in a town, for example—we are likely to be working with someone who feels like a peer. When we're developing engagement and acting in a friendly way, it's easy to begin to feel like a friend. Most importantly, a friendship with a client is not in the client's best interest. A whole host of problems can occur when the client feels the worker is a friend, including a tendency to "perform" to impress their "friend" rather than developing self-motivation. If Bob maintains his sobriety primarily because he wants to come and tell Jaime that he is successful, his change is not likely to continue when their work is done. Another problem when clients feel like their worker is a friend is that the client is being set up to be hurt. The moment the worker has to enforce a professional boundary like "I can't come to dinner at your house," the client is bound to feel injured. Then engagement is set back and has to be begun all over again.

It's important for a client not to feel like their worker's friend, but the alternative to a relationship that feels like a friendship should not be "all business." To make the social work session no different from a meeting with a bank loan officer will help avoid a friend-to-friend relationship, but it is taking it too far. Often, the "all business" approach is simply a way for the worker to hide from the emotional connection that goes along with real client engagement.

In social work engagement, it is the worker's role to control the process. The worker must carefully guide relationship building: feel and reveal the genuine feelings of empathy and connection while maintaining a professional distance. Remember that all stages of planned change are dynamic and interactive. Engagement occurs at the beginning of the work and throughout every single worker–client interaction. It's so important that we'll be discussing engagement throughout this book.

Involuntary Clients

Sometimes individuals and groups come to us when they don't want to. Some may be court-ordered, such as a parent seeking child custody in a divorce settlement or a person facing the consequences of an illegal addiction. Sometimes it will be a young person whose parents have forced them to talk to a social worker.

In these situations and others like them, the social worker has an extra challenge. Most of the time, these individuals and group members will offer one-word answers as often as possible. Other times, they may be entirely silent. The previously given aspects of engagement offer us clues as to what is going on. First, we know that we need engagement to facilitate change, and we know that we need a balanced partnership for the work to take place, so we've got to keep working at it. It's best if we immediately acknowledge that the client or client system does not want to be part of the change process. Next, we know that the process requires acceptance and vulnerability. We can begin our process of developing empathy by imagining the situation that has resulted in the client's unwillingness to accept us or their unwillingness to experience vulnerability, or both. Then we can consider that the individual or group member we are working with is exercising their only choice: the choice that has to do with participating in the planned change process. They have no other choices except to take or reject help, so they often exercise their freedom to say no. Our first response in this situation should be to work hard to experience empathy—particularly by exploring the intersectionality of their areas of diversity. It may be the case that they are experiencing oppression in several areas of their lives. The meeting with you is put on them and may be experienced as just another type of oppression. It is possible that inside a gruff exterior is a person who is frightened of change.

Skills for Working With Involuntary Clients

One of the main skills for work with clients has to do with your control of the **pace of the interview**. The pace of the interview relates to the speed between comments (Kadushin & Kadushin, 1997). In this case, your client may be answering your questions minimally or not at all. When that happens, we have to exercise a great deal of patience and pace the interview to match the responses. As they take time with their responses, you take time with your questions. This means you will find the experience of being silent quite a bit of the time. Your **purposeful use of silence** will give the opportunity for the client to respond to their fullest potential (Kadushin & Kadushin, 1997). This is an example of a situation where the professional social work interview requires you to behave in a socially unacceptable way just as if you were bringing up a taboo topic. We don't easily tolerate silence in our everyday conversations, so leaving a silence in the social work interview is uncomfortable. Your discomfort can be really worthwhile, though. Think about it this way: Since we don't allow silence in conversations, your use of silence in the social work interview can be a great gift to your client. You show that you respect their need to think before they speak.

In addition to using silence and pacing the interview slowly, you might also use open-ended questions, or questions that cannot be answered in one or two words (Miller & Rollnick, 2013). For example, you might say "I imagine you don't want to be here today. What is that like for you?" Finally, it is often helpful to label feelings. You might break through their unwillingness to participate by asking this: "Are you angry that they're making you come today?"

CRITICAL THINKING AND COLLABORATIVE LEARNING EXERCISES 5.1

1. Think of your relationships with different service providers: doctor, dentist, mail carrier, hairdresser. Talk with a partner about how big a role emotion plays in your relationship to those people.
2. Work with a partner. Pretend that they're trying to ask you about the answers to next week's test. Imagine that you don't want to talk today. Give one-word answers and at some point stop speaking entirely. See what it feels like to experience extended silence in a conversation. Exchange roles.

Section 5.2: The Relationship

This section considers the role of the social worker in engagement as well as some more of the skills a social worker needs to begin to engage with a client system. It considers how MSP requires engagement in several systems for every case.

The Relationship

Engagement is about sharing responsibility for planned change among many systems. For example, Jaime is trying to share responsibility for Bob's sobriety with herself, her agency, Bob, his insurance company, and his family members. She would like to establish engagement with all parties and to partner with the aim of an open-minded exploration about who all of these people are and what this particular helping process will look like. When responsibilities for planned change are shared, all partners take responsibility for success and for challenges. This kind of **mutual partnership** results in the understanding that if Bob or a family member does not show up for an appointment, opting out of service is not necessarily a rejection of service. Instead, it is an event that is a *shared responsibility* and requires exploration, not judgment. In fact, to create shared responsibility, Jaime may have to offer services repeatedly. To be successful, she'll need to be clear about her expectations and explore the reasons for no-shows with Bob and his family in a way that is nonjudgmental. She'll need to respond to the system's needs and, as we have seen in our discussion on the self-reflection phase, she'll need to continue to offer services in a responsive, not emotionally reactive, way. As we've said earlier, she'll even have to be willing to accept some of the responsibility herself. As she develops relationships with representatives of the various systems, she'll have to explore her emotions so that she can use her professional self. Having prepared herself to manage her own emotions and life experiences in the self-reflection phase, Jaime must allow her own emotions and the **self-disclosure** of life experiences to enter the interaction only in a conscious way, purposefully and carefully putting her emotional reactions into the developing intersection with the client (Kadushin & Kadushin, 1997). Ultimately, she is the facilitator of the planned change process, so she needs to continue to develop the relationship for as long as the partnership lasts, even when it may feel painful to her because it is hard for her to isolate her own feelings from the process. She may need to continue to engage with the family even though they may miss appointments and throw off her entire work day.

The Skills

Jaime and Bob began to engage in the planned change process due in large part to Jaime's ability to carry out engagement skills. Jaime did a number of things right in her initial session with Bob: her professional dress, her smile, her handshake, direct and indirect eye contact, the placement of her chair, the establishment of boundaries, her use of silence, and her opening statement. A total of ten skills will be discussed next.

1. *Appropriate attire*—A social worker's **professional presentation** is an important part of the client's first impression. In a survey of social work educators, Scholar (2013) discovered that educators agreed on several issues related to clothes. Since there is little research on the way clients expect or prefer social workers to dress, the educators could not use evidence-based suggestions for their students. Instead, they depended on practice wisdom: personal experiences, anecdotes, and the logical extension of theory. For those educators, the overarching belief was that social work students should dress like social workers when they are in the field. Social workers must blend into their environments. For example, Jaime straightened her jacket carefully on her way to meet Bob. She chose to

wear a conservative suit of slacks and jacket because she was a new worker and she knew she looked younger than her chronological age. In that instance, her outfit represented a way for her to both feel and project self-confidence. In other words, her outfit helped her to adopt the **professional identity** of a social worker. In addition, she helped her client to relax in the knowledge that he was dealing with a professional. Similarly, a young man may project confidence with a navy blazer over his khaki slacks and light blue oxford shirt. Other times, a suit or blazer would not be appropriate. For example, a worker in an emergency housing shelter for women would not want to wear expensive clothing and jewelry that would create a barrier between them and the clients. The worker might be able to develop empathy for clients but wouldn't be able to clearly express it if the clients perceive a socioeconomic barrier. Instead, the worker would want to wear an outfit that might be described as business casual: dress slacks and flats for a woman and khaki pants with loafers for a man. In some cases, neither the suit nor the casual business dress would be appropriate. For example, a female or male worker in a long-term residential facility for youth might appear standoffish in a suit or casual business wear. In that case, a worker may even wear clean, new-looking jeans.

It appears that there are few universal rules for social work dress, but some things go well in any setting: First, good personal hygiene goes without saying. Second, tight clothes are almost always bad. Third, jewelry should be kept to a minimum. Finally, any emphasis on the worker's sexuality should be avoided.

Here is a word on tattoos, piercings, and other body modifications: Researchers reviewed literature related to body modifications (Williams, Thomas, & Christensen, 2014). They discovered that 1 in 5 American adults has tattoos and 1 in 11 has piercings other than in the ears. A relevant perspective for social workers is that nearly every tattoo or other body modification is a self-expression, making it an example of empowerment. On the other hand, body modifications can lead to stigma or prejudice. So, is it okay for social workers to display body modifications? One answer is simple: agency policy. If agency policy states that tattoos must be covered up and evidence of piercings removed, then employees must abide by the policy or work to have the policy changed. Where there is no formal agency policy, workers should proceed with caution. There may be an informal, or unwritten, policy that forbids the exhibition of body modification.

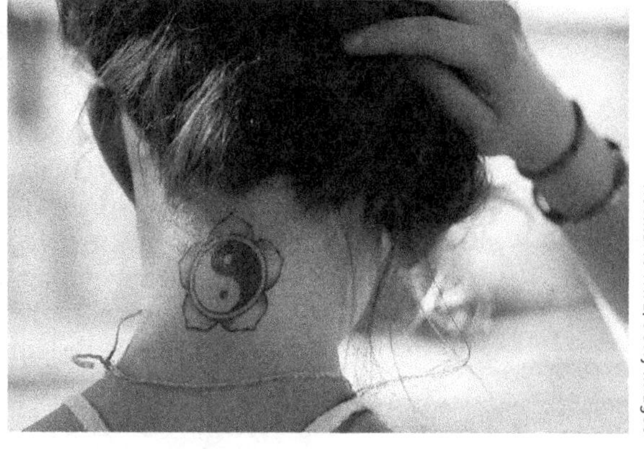

Rosmarie Wirz/Getty Images

Body modifications should be displayed only after careful consideration.

In the absence of any agency policy, the question for the worker to consider in all aspects of body modification is its function or purpose in the context of the work. A body modification may aid in the engagement process if the client is displaying body modification themselves. However, it may not be appropriate for a worker to indulge in the self-expression of a body modification if it is potentially off-putting to a client or if it is modeling behavior that may be fine for the worker but not for the client. What could be okay for "us" and not okay for "them"? Consider a young professional social worker with a university degree and an ideal job. If this worker gets a small, visible tattoo, it will have entirely different social consequences than if her young, undereducated, economically challenged client gets one. The latter is potentially facing racism, sexism, classism, and many other prejudices that a body modification could exacerbate. If that's the case, it may not be helpful for the worker to model body modification to the client. Therefore, the worker needs to consider how their body modification will impact clients—like self-disclosure, body modifications should be exhibited only if they are in the client's best interest. When in doubt, cover it up.

You should have seen by now that professional presentation is very important in social work. Do you know of any other professions where professional presentation is important? Think about it a moment. Social workers should take their places among all of these professional groups.

2. *Her smile*—Jaime's **engaging smile** was Bob's first impression of her, and it was a good one. The ordinary smile is a universally recognized indicator of happiness and hospitality (Park, Han, & Hyun, 2015). So long as no more than a moderate amount of teeth is revealed in a smile, it is a connector of people. Study participants experienced smiles that appeared to them to be genuine as an indicator of trustworthiness, and those smiles were predictors of cooperation (Centorrino, Djemai, Hopfensitz, Milinski, & Seabright, 2015). What does a genuine smile look like? Here, the social worker may engage in evidence-based practice. An extensive body of literature indicates that the smile perceived to be genuine is one in which the eyes crinkle and the lips turn up symmetrically (Krumhuber et al., 2007). If you need more reason to smile in social work engagement, know that studies of nonhuman primates suggest that turning up the lips and baring teeth indicate that the smiling primate will not abuse his or her power (Preuschoft & van Hooff, 1997). In short, smiles are powerful social lubricants that can be used consciously to facilitate engagement. This, like other engagement skills, is important in social work with individuals, families, groups, organizations, and communities.

3. *Eye contact*—Uono and Hietanen (2015) conducted a review of the literature on eye contact and found many studies on the topic. Interestingly, it has been suggested that the human eye has evolved to include the white sclera because it enables us to quickly see the direction of a person's gaze. That gaze is apparently a critical part of human bonding. Many changes in the brain have been observed to occur in periods of direct gaze, including those that "motivate approach" (p. 1). Unfortunately, we can't simply expect to look into our clients' eyes and make a connection. There are cultural differences in the way people perceive eye contact. People whose families who have lived for a few generations in America are said to be very assertive in their eye contact. They make eye contact directly, hold it long, and attempt to do it relatively frequently. It is expected, and it is interpreted as friendly interest and honesty. If eye contact is made indirectly in America, it may be assumed to be shyness, nervousness, or even dishonesty. On the other hand, members of Hispanic, Middle Eastern, Native American, and Asian cultures are widely expected to make very little **direct eye contact** and become uncomfortable when another is looking directly into their faces. Often, they make **indirect eye contact**. They may look at a person's face to get a sense of where and how the person is looking. In fact, Uono and Hietanen (2015) learned that Japanese children are taught to look at a person's neck . . . it is possible to see where a person is gazing without looking into their face, a behavior that is likely to be perceived as rude. Of course, a social worker meeting a member of an unfamiliar culture should conduct research and attempt to learn about that culture's eye contact expectations since it is such a significant part of engagement. On the other hand, it may be impossible to tell at first whether the person has been fully acculturated to American society. In addition, some mental health issues play a role in eye contact. For example, a person on the autism spectrum is likely to find direct eye contact extremely uncomfortable. If a person attempts to force direct eye contact where it is unwanted, they may create a great deal of anxiety. So how do you know what to do? A good way to manage this problem is to look briefly at another person and test if they make direct eye contact, whether they make direct eye contact but only fleetingly, or whether they make only indirect eye contact. Don't force it, and experiment gently and periodically until you feel you have it right for that individual.

4. *Embodied mirroring*—Another type of nonverbal communication is **embodied mirroring**. It seems simple to say that doing what a client or client system representative does will facilitate engagement, such as when Jaime put her chin on her hand as Bob did. However, embodied mirroring is actually a powerful, evidence-based practice. Essentially, doing what another does with their nonverbal expressions can be a great connector of people. Blum (2015) did a review of the available research on embodied mirroring and found it well established that mirroring has its own neurons in the brain and that imitating others activates those neurons. Conscious mirroring creates empathy and positive interactions with people. It allows a physical sense of another person that unconsciously promotes understanding. While it usually happens outside of awareness, mirroring can be done on purpose to great effect.

Westend61/Getty Images

Embodied mirroring helps establish relationships.

You've just read that a smile, eye contact, and mirroring are important skills that social workers use to engage clients. Do you find that you do these things automatically all the time? Maybe you need to practice a few.

5. *Pointing out strengths*—**Pointing out strengths** is the direct application of the strengths perspective as discussed in Chapter 2. Jaime said, "Thanks for sharing those important things about your family life. That tells me you're a really strong person." She was pointing out a strength of Bob's that he probably didn't recognize. In some cases, it is difficult to identify a strength in clients and client system representatives, but it is always a strength if someone is willing to accept help.

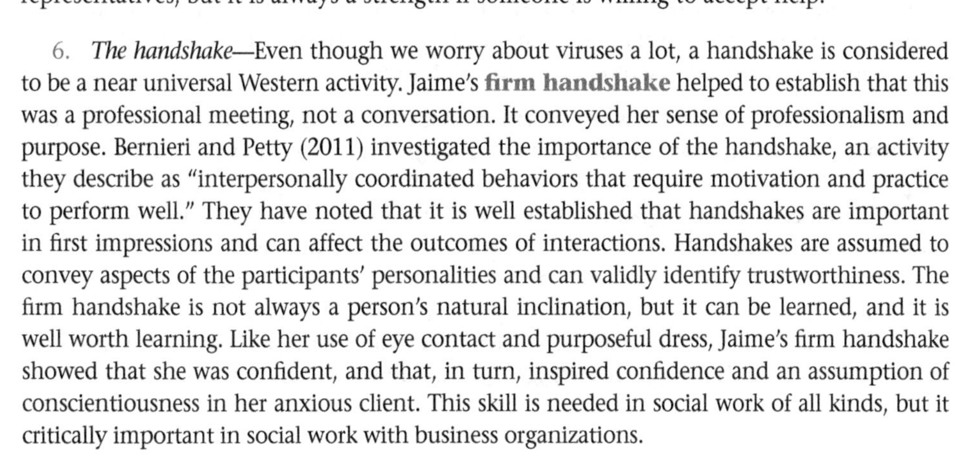

6. *The handshake*—Even though we worry about viruses a lot, a handshake is considered to be a near universal Western activity. Jaime's **firm handshake** helped to establish that this was a professional meeting, not a conversation. It conveyed her sense of professionalism and purpose. Bernieri and Petty (2011) investigated the importance of the handshake, an activity they describe as "interpersonally coordinated behaviors that require motivation and practice to perform well." They have noted that it is well established that handshakes are important in first impressions and can affect the outcomes of interactions. Handshakes are assumed to convey aspects of the participants' personalities and can validly identify trustworthiness. The firm handshake is not always a person's natural inclination, but it can be learned, and it is well worth learning. Like her use of eye contact and purposeful dress, Jaime's firm handshake showed that she was confident, and that, in turn, inspired confidence and an assumption of conscientiousness in her anxious client. This skill is needed in social work of all kinds, but it critically important in social work with business organizations.

7. *Boundary setting*—As we've discussed, **boundaries** set limits on systems and social work sessions (Carter, 2011). One important boundary is related to the length of the session. In this scenario, Jaime mentioned to Bob that they had a limit of six, 1-hour sessions. Six sessions is sometimes the limit of work that a funder, like an insurance company or in this case an employer, will support. One hour is a very traditional time. Many social work sessions, including staff meetings and such, are expected to last 1 hour. A social worker does themselves a favor, though, if a meeting with a representative of a client system is actually ended just before the hour is up. The "50-minute hour" is a good way to draw a boundary around a session as it allows the worker to show the client out, sit down behind the desk, and complete the paperwork necessary to document the session. If the session includes an intake such as this one did, a more extensive report may be required. In that case, it's best to leave the next hour open on the schedule. Time to complete paperwork is an essential

part of a social worker's job. In fact, Jaime's full 60-minute sessions may have contributed to her feeling overwhelmed with paperwork. If an agency's policy is that face-to-face contacts must last 1 hour, time must be set aside in the day (not lunchtime!) to complete paperwork. If that isn't possible, agency policy should be addressed as a potential area for macro level assessment and planned change.

Hero Images/Getty Images

Simple seating arrangements impact relationships

What do you think of the picture to the left? Does the physical placement of both parties invite engagement?

8. *Active listening*—Jaime demonstrated nonverbal communication by nodding a lot in her session with Bob. It is traditional practice wisdom in social work that nodding helps another person continue dialogue; it is often accompanied by "umm hmm" as another method of demonstrating **active listening**. This and many other listening skills were originally developed by the psychologist Carl Rogers. His work is read and researched extensively (Elkins, 2009).

9. *Physical placement*—Jaime made sure to sit at the side of her desk rather than behind it. Another bit of practice wisdom is that a person sitting behind a desk is portraying power. In general, a social worker wants to demonstrate to the representative of a client system that they are engaged in a mutual planned change process where they are partners. For this reason, they often achieve appropriate **physical placement** by rearranging their offices or pulling their chairs alongside of their desks. In work with families and groups, this consideration may lead the worker to establish an arrangement of chairs where everyone can see everyone else. In work with groups and organizations, beware of the rectangular conference table—people cannot see those who sit next to them.

10. *Clarification*—In everyday conversations, we often assume we know what someone else means. Your friend may say she stayed up all night studying, and you may assume that she got no sleep at all. What she may mean, though, is that she stayed up until 3:00 and then went to bed until noon. Jaime wanted to know Bob as much as she could, so she used questions that began with the phrases "help me to understand" and "could you tell me more about that?" Other phrases you can use for **clarification** include "what exactly do you mean by the word ____?" and "I heard you say ________. Is that right?" Clarification can also be used with phrases that help identify the way clients are feeling. For example, you might say "Sounds like you're feeling ______. Can you tell me more about that?"

CRITICAL THINKING AND COLLABORATIVE LEARNING EXERCISES 5.2

1. With a partner, practice a firm, professional handshake. Why do you think the handshake has been identified as a nearly universal interaction in Western society? Do you think it is common in Eastern cultures? How will you find out?
2. See whether you and a partner can create a genuine-looking smile (even if you are not happy).
3. Practice eye contact with a partner, and try to determine how long it takes for direct eye contact to appear confrontational. Practice indirect eye contact. Choose one ethnic group, and locate a juried article or book that describes their eye contact practices and preferences. (This group can be your own!)

Consider whether you own professional-looking attire and where you might acquire reasonably priced pieces.

Section 5.3: Process Awareness

Since engagement is the second stage in the planned change process, in this section we'll continue to look at the beginning of the social worker–client system interaction. We'll consider the ways beginnings of social processes are experienced by clients and workers.

WHAT IF . . . FOCUS ON DIVERSITY

Suppose Jaime were an African American male instead of an African American female. Suppose she identified as transgender.

How would you expect Jaime and Bob's interactions to be? (Make sure your answer is informed by research about the way diverse groups perceive each other.)

Process Awareness: Knowledge and Reflection

Like self-reflection, engagement continues the beginning phase of social interaction (Shulman, 2015). It sounds weird: to continue beginnings. Remember that interactions between people have different characteristics at the beginning, the middle, and the end. The beginning can last longer than one meeting, so engagement continues the beginning phase that started with self-reflection. In engagement, the worker's thoughts and feelings are similar to those during the self-reflection phase. As we have discovered in the previous chapter, some important reflections on the part of the worker include cultural identity and bias as well as experiences of power and privilege alongside those of discrimination. To briefly restate, the worker must examine their desire to help and remove it from themselves, enabling them to accept rejection without feeling rejected and to celebrate successes without owning them entirely. Both client system rejection of the helping relationship and successes in the planned change process are best understood to be shared experiences with clients. We all play a role in the rejection of service, and we all play a role in success. This process will be further discussed later in this chapter.

In this second phase, engagement, the client's thoughts and feelings need to be examined. It's likely that the first time the client system representative reaches the door of the agency, they feel anxious. We know Bob did, because his hand was cold and his handshake weak. In her classic work, Perlman (1957) suggested that clients begin to anxiously evaluate the agency the moment they step through the door, examining the furniture and the state of the waiting room looking for cues to the way they will be treated. Likewise, the client evaluates the home visitor from their first step across the threshold. Clients are usually anxious about the problem that brings them to the social worker. That anxiety is magnified by the anxiety of placing trust in the unknown agency and unknown worker. This anxiety on the part of the client can manifest in a number of ways. For example, the client may begin a gushing expression of feelings or the client may be entirely silent. The obvious pain the client is experiencing can push the worker toward having a goal of helping the client express themselves, to comfort, and to allow the client to ventilate their feelings with many sympathetic nods and assurances. There is a place for **ventilation**, where the worker helps the client express feelings. There is also a place for **containment**, where workers help to stop the expression of feelings that has turned into a flood of words.

The beginning of the planned change process is also a place for the worker to express **empathy** and perhaps even **sympathy.** Empathy, as discussed in the previous chapter ("I imagine you were very angry then . . ."), is a kind of standing in the other's shoes. As we've seen, empathy begins before the worker even meets the client and continues throughout the helping process. On the other hand, sympathy is much less often appropriate. Sympathy is nearly pity and can disempower a client. For example, saying "I'm so sorry you are in this terrible, terrible situation" is not likely to motivate a client to take their problem into their own hands. On the other hand, there are situations when sympathy is appropriate, such as "I'm sorry your child is so sick."

There is more to beginnings than managing anxiety, though. An important component of early meetings is to set the stage for future work. If the first helping session is only sharing painful experiences, the client or client system representative will likely expect that experience to continue in every session thereafter. Too much ventilation can keep the client from experiencing mutuality and self-determination in the planned change process. We might say "Well begun is half done." Balance responses to troubling feelings with a purposeful working through of the planned change process. The opening statement is an important way to get the work started as a partnership rather than "I'll hand my problem over to you, and you fix it." Done well, the opening statement can help the client feel powerful and move from anxiety to excitement at the prospect of moving forward.

CRITICAL THINKING AND COLLABORATIVE LEARNING EXERCISES 5.3

Discuss with a partner the way you felt on the first day of school this semester. Were you feeling mostly hopeful or mostly anxious? When did those feelings change?

Section 5.4: The Opening Statement

In this section, we'll discuss and practice the all-important **opening statement**. Part of the discussion of the opening statement is a consideration of something your friends are likely to ask you one day: What makes a social work interview different from a conversation?

The Opening Statement

The opening statement sets the stage for *every* interaction with *every* client system. A recurring part of the engagement phase of the planned change process, the opening statement draws a boundary around the interaction, marking it as a purposeful, professional meeting that is held in the context of the policies of an agency or institution. Before considering the elements of the opening statement, consider its context. The opening statement is used in a social work interview, not in a conversation. If a worker crosses paths with an agency representative with whom she has been consulting on employee relationships, is that brief interaction a conversation or a social work interview? On the other hand, if a friend, not a client, seeks advice on a serious and intimate life challenge, is that a conversation or a social work interview? Classic social work theory identifies five aspects of an interaction that mark it as a professional interview as opposed to an informal conversation.

Interviews Are for Clients, Not Workers

A social work interview is *for* the client. Regardless of the target system size, the social worker must remember that their own needs are not the focus of the meeting. The worker may feel a sense of gratification from a positive interaction, but that should flow from the client system's success in some aspect of planned change. Any statement that the worker makes on his or her own behalf does not belong in the social work interview. Here are two examples—one obvious and the other not so much.

A worker who is teaching life skills takes a family to a drugstore to observe their spending habits and takes a few moments to pick up some shampoo that she has not had time to purchase. *This is not good*; she's taken the focus off the family, perhaps missing important information, and has conveyed the message that the family is not her priority.

One more example, more subtle, is provided in the following interaction.

Worker:	You have worked together as a group successfully!
Group Member:	I think we began to really work together when you suggested we develop rules for the group.
Another Group Member:	Yes, that was rough, but once we came through it we had smooth sailing.
Third Group Member:	And now we have met all of our goals. I, for one, am very proud of myself.
Worker:	I'm proud of all of you!

SELF-REFLECTION 5: ALCOHOL OUTCOME EXPECTANCIES SCALE

Take the Alcohol Outcome Expectancies Scale, and score as noted with the scale on pages 160–161.

How can this self-reflection help you to develop empathy for someone like Bob who has a history of alcohol misuse?

Here, the worker seems to be pointing out strengths and identifying successes with the group. But consider carefully what a worker says when they say "I'm proud of you." To be proud is to credit oneself for a successful accomplishment, such as a teacher who is proud of an honor student. The teacher is recognizing that she played an essential role in the student's development. Likewise, a parent who is proud of a successful athlete is stressing that promising genes and effective parenting are essential to the athlete's performance. The teacher and the parent are both emphasizing their own role and inadvertently underlining their relative power in the interaction. Their power is apparent when you consider that someone who can say "I'm proud of you" can also say "I'm *not* proud of you." The implication is "I could be proud of an achievement of my own, but you wouldn't be here without me." This may actually be true in a professional social work relationship, but it is not the aspect we want to highlight. In an interaction that is *for* the client, a better phrase might be "I think we can all be proud of ourselves." Note that the flip side of this interaction ("I didn't do anything, you did it all!") rings false, because, of course, the social worker did have a hand in the success.

Think about how you feel when you help a friend. If you offered advice and they took it successfully, would you say that you were proud of them? Why or why not?

Professional Relationship

Relationship is the second aspect of the professional interview as engagement continues in an ongoing way. Meaningful change is not likely to occur outside of the professional relationship. In other words, the relationship between the worker and the client system is actually the catalyst of change. In systems theory language, the client system is aided in change by the new intersection of the relationship between itself and the worker. For this reason, it is incumbent on the worker to facilitate a meaningful relationship beginning in the initial phases of planned change and continually going forward in the process. This is another reminder of the importance of first impressions and the skills of engagement. A conversation can occur outside of a relationship—between you and a neighbor, a dental hygienist, or grocery clerk, for instance—but planned change requires relationship.

Partners in Professional Relationships

Another way conversations and social work interviews differ is in the choice of partner. In conversations, it is possible to select one partner and reject another. One hair stylist may be selected over another based on their skill or friendliness. A friend may be selected for a conversation over an acquaintance. However, the social worker must build a relationship and conduct interviews with client systems served by the agency. Areas of diversity must be recognized and addressed, but workers seldom have choice about whom they will serve.

Hill Street Studios/Getty Images

Specific considerations are needed when an individual is forced to see a social worker.

An Agency's Umbrella

The social work interview occurs under the auspices of a program or agency. This means that the interview is bound by policies, or rules. First and foremost is the agency mission, a formal statement that outlines the scope of services and places a boundary around what may be discussed. A social worker can converse on any topic, but social work interviews are specific to the agency. When a worker is unsure about whether a particular service might be offered, the answer requires only a look at the agency mission. An agency may require that sessions be 50 minutes long when a conversation's length is based on the preference of the partners. A social worker may be mandated by federal and state laws to report suspected child or elder abuse where a private conversation has no such demands. An agency may charge a fee for service, but informal talk is cheap!

Taboo Topics

Finally, the interview and the conversation differ on the discussion of **taboo topics**. Discussion of taboo topics, those that are usually without social sanction, are demanded of the worker. For example, a person's budget is not usually discussed among friends, business associates, or acquaintances. Can you imagine a businessperson turning to another in the elevator and asking this: "How can you afford that suit when you send your kids to private school?" Can you image one chief executive officer asking another this: "We share the same funding source . . . how did you manage to hire away my staff with higher salaries?" In contrast, a social worker may need to ask about the individual, household, or organizational financial plan to determine whether a challenge exists there for the client system. Something like "We've been talking about your personal finances. How did you work that manicure into your budget?" may need to be said. Or the worker may need to say "How high is the rent you charge in this community compared with what you charge elsewhere?" Social sanctions are very effective. So to discuss money, sex, politics, religion, or any of a number of taboo topics can make the speaker extremely uncomfortable. Clients and representatives of client systems are likely to feel that discomfort and avoid the taboo topics. The social worker must bring them up.

What are some topics you would never bring up in a conversation with your mother, an older person, or a young child? Think about how you might bring those topics up in a social work interview.

Now the importance of the opening statement becomes clear. Neither partner in an interaction should be confused about whether it is an informal conversation or a professional social work interview.

The Opening Statement Further Developed

Components of the opening statement are as follows:

- Agency mission
- Worker's role
- Purpose of the interview
- Time allotted

Each segment of the opening statement plays a role in the very beginning of every interview whether it is with an individual or the representative of a larger client system. The first segment—the **agency mission**—refers to the social function, or purpose of the interview, of the agency or program. It is likely to be reflected in the agency or program's mission statement. This part of the opening statement serves to draw a boundary around the work by setting the context in a deliberate fashion. In the case study at the beginning of the chapter, Jaime mentioned the agency's mission to help people "achieve and maintain sobriety." This may be useful in future meetings as the skill of **gentle confrontation** may be necessary (Kadushin & Kadushin, 1997). For example, Bob may someday ask Jaime to overlook what he describes as a brief relapse and claim there is no need to discuss it. In that case, Jaime can gently remind Bob of the agency mission and quietly insist that the discussion take place.

Addressing the **worker's role** in the opening statement reminds both the worker and the client system of the limits that agency policy and other rules and regulations place on the worker–client relationship. The worker's role is reflected in their job description.

Most importantly, the **purpose of the interview** is clearly stated in the opening statement in order to clarify what topics might be discussed. Similar to an agenda in a formal meeting, the purpose statement is best put as a question or in some form that allows that client to suggest revisions to the direction of the interview.

Finally, stating the **time allotted** for the interview is significant in that it prepares the client for the end of the session. This allows the worker to place clear limits on time spent without feeling as if they are imposing on the client. More significantly, a client may have an issue they would like to address but find it to be a difficult topic to introduce. In that case, it is easier to raise the topic at the very end of the session . . . the classic **doorknob comment**. When a client's meeting about substance abuse recovery ends at 10:00 a.m. and at 9:55 a.m. the client states that they are considering an extramarital affair, they are making a doorknob comment. In this instance, it is important for the worker to enforce the ending time that was agreed on at the outset of the session. If the worker allows the session to run over, the client will never again have the opportunity to introduce a difficult topic as a doorknob comment . . . they will never know when they'll be reaching for the door. A useful response to a doorknob comment is "This is important, let's start with it next time."

The Opening Statement in Practice

Here is how the opening statement between Jaime and Bob sounded:

Jaime: As I said, I'm Jaime. I'm a social worker here at New Hope, where we work to help people achieve and maintain sobriety. *(Here she combines her introduction with a statement of the agency function. This may prove to be important later. As* *we considered previously, if Bob reports that he has relapsed, Jaime will not have to confront him with the mission of the agency as she has stated it at the beginning of the interview.)*

Jaime: It's my job to help you on that path. As the social worker, I'll be meeting with you for your individual work. You and I will set goals and create a plan for achieving them. Does this sound all right to you? *(Here she provides space—her conscious use of silence—for Bob to point out any concerns he has about the helping process.)*

Bob: *(hesitantly)* I guess it seems okay.

Jaime: I hear you hesitating, and I'm wondering if you're anxious about this process. Do you have any questions or concerns you'd like to share? *(She is labeling feelings—by using her empathy to imagine how he may feel and helping him recognize it. She is also gently* ***probing****—or asking questions in a forthright way that may not be socially acceptable—for Bob to answer so that he can play an active role in the helping process.)*

Bob: No. I guess I'm just a little nervous. *(Jaime's guess at his feelings is based on her understanding of the dynamics of beginnings in the social process and it has proven to be correct. Bob responds by acknowledging the feeling, allowing the session to move forward.)*

Jaime: I bet this all seems to be happening so fast. *(She's expressing empathy.)*

Bob: *(He nods, taking a deep breath and seeming to relax a bit.)*

Jaime: You and I have just six, 1-hour meetings, so do you feel okay about us starting right away? *(She is probably moving too fast here. She is used to multitasking and doing her work effectively and quickly. In addition, she's been taking paperwork home, and it is affecting her personal relationships. It's hard for her to match her pace to Bob's . . . the pace he needs to engage with her and begin to trust the helping process. Instead, if she had realized she was moving too quickly, she could have stopped to jot down a note to force herself to slow down and give Bob a chance to think about his answers.)*

Consider an example of an opening statement on the mezzo level of practice with Bob's family:

Jaime: I'm glad the three of us were able to get together today. As you know, I'm Jaime and I work at New Hope to support Bob's recovery. He and I have worked out a plan for him to maintain sobriety and a crisis plan in case he is in danger of relapsing. As his wife and daughter, you have a huge impact on his life. And he has a huge impact on yours. So we're all in this together. Today I'm hoping we can take an hour to talk about how all of you can support each other. Should we have anything else on the agenda? *(Jaime used silence to give everyone a chance to think. She didn't rush forward, because engagement was just beginning, and she wanted to make sure that all of the family members felt like they were partners in the planned change process.)*

Finally, here is an example of the opening statement in macro level work.

Jaime: Hello? *(At Bob's request, Jaime is calling his employer. Her target system is his employment, and her client system representative is his boss. Bob has had difficulty in the past with absences from work due to drinking in excess the night before. He's also been sent home for appearing intoxicated on the job. For these reasons, he's used up all of his paid time off. Bob's not sure his boss really believes he is seeking help for his addiction, so he'd like Jaime to help him request* *flexibility in using the Family and Medical Leave Act to take some unpaid time off here and there so he could attend meetings. He gives her written, informed consent to do so.)*

Boss: *(shouting into the phone at a construction site)* Johnson here!

Jaime: Hi, this is Jaime Adams. (*She raises her voice and talks slowly.*) I'm working with Bob Jones, and I hope we could talk about his recovery and how it affects his work for just 3 minutes. Is there a better time for us to talk?

Boss: (*sighs*) Now's as good a time as any. I can give you 3 minutes.

Jaime: I appreciate it! I'm working at New Hope helping Bob through his recovery. I know you're aware that he is working on staying sober, and one of his goals is to do well at work.

Boss: Oh, when Bob is sober, he is great. I just wish he could stay that way.

Jaime: That's what I called to talk about. Sometimes Bob has meetings that cut into the workday. I know he's used up all of his paid time off for this year, and I expect he's going to be asking to use some unpaid time off soon. I was hoping I could answer any questions you might have about the reasons he'll need to be off the job every once in a while during the next 6 weeks.

Boss: Okay, I have a few questions . . .

Informed Consent

When Bob asked Jaime to advocate for him with his boss, he provided an important component of beginning the work with a client: **informed consent**. This is the process where a client or client system representative is given the opportunity to accept or reject the worker's offer of help. In order to do so, they need to understand what they're getting into. Because this aspect is so critical to developing true partnerships with clients, the *NASW Code of Ethics* (National Association of Social Workers [NASW], 2018) goes into great detail about informed consent. The content is summarized next:

1.03 Informed Consent

a. Social workers should only work with clients when they have informed consent. To be informed, clients need to hear clear, understandable language about:
    - The purpose of services
    - Risks related to the services
    - Limits to the services due to insurance or agency policy
    - Costs
    - Other ways to get help
    - The right to refuse help at any time
    - How long the consent is in effect
b. Social workers should make sure all clients understand informed consent to the best of their ability. This may mean using written and verbal explanations as well as interpreters.
c. If the client can't understand informed consent, the social worker should try to get it from a third party, like a parent, when the worker is sure the third party is acting according to the client's wishes.

d. Where clients receive services involuntarily, the worker should explain what the services are and at what point the client can refuse them.

e. Social workers who provide services through electronic media should be sure the client understands the risks, including risks to confidentiality. [More on the use of technology in social work in Chapter 15.]

f. Any kind of technology used to provide services should only be done with informed consent that is obtained prior to any use. Social workers should make sure that technology allows ways for the worker to verify the identity and location of clients (NASW, 2018).

g. Social workers who use technology to provide social work services should make sure the technology makes sense for the client and that they are able to use and access it. Social workers should consider the client's "intellectual, emotional, and physical ability to use technology to receive services and ability to understand the potential benefits, risks, and limitations of such services" (p. 8). If client doesn't want to use services provided through technology, social workers should help them to find alternatives.

Confidentiality and the **limits of confidentiality** are closely related to informed consent. If a person agrees to accept help, they must be helped to understand that the worker will not discuss their situation except under very particular situations. The foundation statement here is "What a client discloses is confidential, and not to be repeated outside the session." That's confidentiality. Our *NASW Code of Ethics* (NASW, 2018) says this: "Social workers should respect clients' right to privacy" (p. 11). The code goes on to help us understand exactly what privacy means:

A worker shouldn't ask what they don't need to know. Only ask a client about personal information if it is required by your agency (as on an intake form) or if it is central to the work you're doing with your client. This is what is meant by privacy. For example, if a client needs help to quit smoking, it's not likely that you need to ask about their sex life. Maybe you need to ask, but it is not likely. On the other hand, a client may volunteer very personal information even if you don't ask. Once it's out there, it becomes part of your confidential interaction with a client and should not be shared with others. This is what is meant by confidentiality. Confidentiality should be discussed early in the worker–client relationship so that trust can be formed.

Part of the discussion about confidentiality is usually an agreement called a release of information. This form is signed by the client when they understand that the worker will need to share information about them with others as a matter of course. These typical transactions may include letting an insurance company know whether they have shown up for their sessions or whether they are progressing toward their goals. Another typical release of information relates to other professionals. A social worker may need to discuss a client's situation with a worker who is working for a different agency providing different services. For example, a social worker may need to let a probation officer know that the client is working toward their goals as planned. Likewise, a social worker will need to discuss the client's situation with their supervisor. A release of information form should include this topic, especially if part of supervision includes reviewing tapes of client sessions.

Once confidentiality is discussed between worker and client, it is important to immediately help the client understand the **limits of confidentiality**, or where confidentiality ends with or without a client's consent. Sometimes workers talk about this as "breaking" confidentiality, a phrase that indicates just how important these actions are to workers. Our trust with a client is sacred, but it is limited. The *NASW Code of Ethics* is very specific about the limits to confidentiality and how to help clients understand them (NASW, 2018). The basic rule is this: "The general expectation that social workers will keep information confidential does not apply when disclosure is necessary to prevent serious, foreseeable, and imminent harm to the client or others" (p. 12). Serious, foreseeable, and imminent harm could include a client who states that they have harmed or neglected a child or an older adult, a client who states that they may harm themselves, or a client who states that they may harm another person.

Look at these categories carefully. When we consider breaking confidentiality, or sharing a client's private statements with others, we think about the welfare of:

- Children
- Age-dependent adults
- Any other person who may be at risk
- The client themselves

ETHICAL PERSPECTIVES

According to the NASW Code of Ethics *(NASW, 2018), what should a social worker do when they are not clear about a confidentiality related issue? See Section 2.05(a).*

We'll talk more specifically about self-harm and thoughts of suicide later, but all of these categories have one thing in common: They are taboo topics. Remember that one of the ways a social work interview is different from a conversation is that the worker is sometimes responsible to bring up topics that are not usually part of everyday conversations. These taboos are very difficult to discuss but are required of the worker as they consider whether confidentiality needs to be broken to protect someone.

If you suspect, even for a moment, that your client is facing any of these situations, you must ask whatever questions you need to ask to determine whether there is danger. The following questions might be included in these:

- "Have you ever had to leave your child alone to manage your other responsibilities?"
- "Have you ever been so frustrated with your parent that you are afraid you may hurt them?"
- "You said you felt like killing your girlfriend's new partner. Can you say more about those feelings?"
- "You sound like you're feeling hopeless and you've hinted that you may have lost the will to live. Do you think about hurting yourself?"

In general, you share all of these situations with your supervisor as soon as possible. For the purposes of supervision, you don't need to be sure that any of these situations are occurring. It is not breaking confidentiality to ask your supervisor their opinion or to ask what questions you should be considering. If your supervisor is available and you face any of these concerns during a session, it would not be out of place for you to explain that you need to get consultation from a supervisor due to your concerns. Excuse yourself and go ask a supervisor about the situation. They'll help you to come up with the appropriate questions. Keep in mind, though, that you should only ask for help on these sensitive topics if you can assure privacy. You might ask for supervision in a secure electronic way or in person where there is a private space, but you never ask in a hallway, waiting room, or elevator. Your supervisor will help you understand your ethical responsibilities. In most of these previously given situations, you have legal obligations to report potential harm as well as ethical ones. Find out what your legal obligations are in your state when you suspect child or elder abuse or neglect, suicidal ideation, and potential for attempted assault.

CRITICAL THINKING AND COLLABORATIVE LEARNING EXERCISES 5.4

1. Consider how to tell a friend with a personal problem that you are having a conversation, not a social work interview and explain the difference. Role-play with a partner. What are the skills that you might use in both a conversation and a social work interview?
2. Role-play Jaime's opening statement for the next time she and Bob meet. How might she discuss agency function and worker's role in a way that does not sound repetitive? Do you think she needs to say these things for every interview? Why?
3. Pretend that Bob tells Jaime that he feels angry and betrayed when Sam sides with her mother during family arguments. Bob doesn't seem the type to harm anyone, but how can Jaime be sure that Sam is not in danger?

Section 5.5. Vulnerability in Engagement

PeopleImages/Getty Images

Workers experience emotional responses to engagement.

This section focuses on the worker's vulnerability in engagement. It suggests following the critical thinking process for self-care.

The Vulnerable Worker: Reflective Responses

We've said that engagement requires vulnerability on the part of the client and the worker. For the client, the characteristics of beginnings—hope and anxiety—play an important role. The client doesn't know what to expect. But the worker feels the same way. Workers hope to engage with the client or client system representative and we fear that it won't happen. Then there is **compassion**, where we feel the client's pain and we really want to help. We have to develop feelings of compassion in order to develop empathy, and we have to express them in a genuine way so that the client believes that we feel them. The feeling (or affective) part of this equation is part of what makes us vulnerable, but think about the critical thinking exercise we explored previously. Feelings are influenced by beliefs that may or may not be accurate. We need to identify these feelings and thoughts to critically think about the way we behave so that we can be emotionally nonreactive and intentional in our work. That same critical thinking can help us protect ourselves from the painful feelings that can go along with engagement. Remember that one of the best ways to avoid compassion fatigue is to recognize the contribution you're making. Critical thinking will help you feel better and help you be an intentional—and more effective—worker.

Here's an example of how critical thinking can make a worker more resilient as well as more effective:

Bob missed his second appointment with Jaime. He didn't show up, and he didn't call. Jaime started to have a stomachache. This was her red flag. She knew she needed to engage in self-reflection. She used a mindfulness exercise to recognize that she was feeling both anxious and angry. She decided to identify her beliefs in the "What do I feel/believe/know/do?" exercise. She came up with two ideas that contradicted each other.

I've Really Screwed Up!

The belief Jaime had that was connected to her anxiety was that she was at fault for Bob's absence. She believed that she hadn't allowed a strong enough engagement to occur. Maybe he didn't trust her enough to return. If she had clung to that belief, a couple of bad things could have happened. First, she could have lacked the ability to engage in an evaluation process that would help her improve her own practice. Second, she may have reacted to Bob in a reactive way the next time they spoke. By behaving without intention, she could miss an opportunity to say something that would help Bob to meet his goals. For example, if she focused on her feelings of anxiety, her confidence would be undermined. She might excuse Bob's behavior too quickly by saying "It's okay" immediately when he called to make an excuse.

Once she drew on her knowledge, she could see that her belief was probably not entirely true. Instead of blaming herself entirely, she needed to draw on her knowledge about engagement and recognize that she and Bob were partners. Odd as it sounds, both Jaime and Bob were responsible for his absence. Once she recognized that, she knew that nothing was her fault entirely. Certainly, Bob made the choice not to attend his scheduled meeting, but Jaime knew that she should critically evaluate her own practice. She sought supervision and asked what she could have done differently. As her supervisor helped her talk through the process of her initial meeting with Bob, she recognized that she may have moved too quickly early on in the session and may have done better to focus a bit longer on engagement. She promised herself that she would spend more time just getting to know Bob at the beginning of their next meeting. At the same time, she recognized that Bob shared responsibility with her. This helped her to behave intentionally. When she spoke to Bob next, she said, "Sorry you couldn't get here. I was concerned that you had relapsed. Are you going through a rough period right now?" Overall, her anxiety lessened. She could go home that day and not worry about her ability to do her job.

PeopleImages/Getty Images

Our compassion for clients makes us emotionally vulnerable.

My Client Is Irresponsible!

Jaime also identified feelings of anger about Bob's missed appointment. Once she identified the anger she felt, she realized that she believed Bob to be irresponsible. She was very angry, assuming that he just didn't care enough to show up. She did the critical thinking exercise again. She realized that she didn't know if Bob was acting in an irresponsible way. There could have been any number of real reasons for his absence. He had an old car. It could have broken down. Maybe he got a minor injury at work. Finally, he could be struggling with his addiction. After all, if he could become and stay sober on his own, he wouldn't need her help in the first place. Once she replaced her immediate beliefs with those thoughts, she was able to speak with Bob in a practical but compassionate way. Imagine if Bob had called to explain his absence while Jaime was still angry. She may have said, "I see you are not serious about your recovery." And Bob may have answered, "I have a wife who judges me all the time, I don't need you to do the same." If she'd stayed angry, she could have lost Bob as a client. Instead, she was able to express compassion while not letting him off the hook for the missed session. Her anger dissipated. Instead of clinging to angry feelings, she went home feeling like she had done a good job that day.

CRITICAL THINKING AND COLLABORATIVE LEARNING EXERCISES 5.5

1. Think about something you have strong feelings about right now. Are you thinking that someone or something has caused those feelings? Share with a partner, and ask them to help you identify the beliefs you hold about the situation that are making you feel even more angry or anxious.
2. Answer the following questions on a scale from the Interpersonal Reactivity Index (Davis, 1980), and consider how your answers might affect your social work practice: Use the following answer scale: A = Does not describe me to E = Describes me very well.

I often have tender, concerned feelings for people less fortunate than me.

Sometimes I don't feel very sorry for other people when they are having problems. (reverse score)

When I see someone being taken advantage of, I feel kind of protective toward them.

Other people's misfortunes do not usually disturb me a great deal. (reverse score)

When I see someone being treated unfairly, I sometimes don't feel very much pity for them. (reverse score)

I am often quite touched by things that I see happen.

I would describe myself as a pretty soft-hearted person.

Section 5.6: Review and Apply

CONCURRENT CONSIDERATIONS IN GENERALIST PRACTICE

Ethical Decision-Making Challenge

Jaime completed a home visit for the purpose of assessing family strengths, areas of diversity, and challenges. The next afternoon, she got a call from Sam, Bob's daughter. Sam said she wanted to talk with Jaime about her own addiction issues but she didn't want Jaime to tell her mom or dad. Using the ethical decision-making model, determine whether this was an ethical dilemma. Be sure to focus on the legal and agency policies that are related to the situation.

Human Rights

Is anyone in this case being deprived of any fundamental human rights such as freedom, safety, privacy, an adequate standard of living, health care, and education? Think about all of the family members.

Evidence-Based Practice

Jaime believed that she should work with Bob's family as well as Bob. See whether there is any support for that approach in the scientific literature.

Policies Impacting Practice

Research the Family and Medical Leave Act. What provisions does it make for workers with addictions?

Managing Diversity

Bob is a middle-aged, Caucasian skilled craftsman. What privileges does society bestow on him because of those characteristics? What areas of oppression might he face because of the same characteristics? What are potential areas of diversity that Jaime still doesn't know about Bob?

Multisystem Practice

Identify examples of Jaime's work on all levels.

Micro: ______________________

Mezzo: ______________________

Macro: ______________________

Dynamic and Interactive Planned Change Stages

Identify aspects of Jaime's work where she worked in the following stages:

Self-Reflection: ______________________

Engagement: ______________________

Assessment: ______________________

Planning: ______________________

Implementation: ______________________

Evaluation: ______________________

Termination and Follow-Up: ______________________

Chapter Summary

Section 5.1: Engagement

Engagement, where a worker and client form a working relationship, is the second stage of the planned change process. Several marks of engagement include a working agenda, acceptance and vulnerability on the part of the worker and the client, and a strengths-based view of diversity. Most importantly, engagement must be understood as a requirement for lasting change.

Section 5.2: The Relationship

A number of social work skills facilitate engagement. They include a professional presentation, an engaging smile, appropriate eye contact, embodied mirroring, pointing out strengths, a firm handshake, setting appropriate boundaries, active listening, physical placement, and clarification. Appropriate practice behaviors can be identified using available evidence, including the use of scientific literature and practice wisdom.

Section 5.3: Process Awareness

Beginnings in social processes include both anxiety and hope for the worker and for the client. Clients' anxieties can be managed through the use of several skills: containment, ventilation, and expressions of empathy and (much less often) sympathy. Workers should balance the response to anxiety and a purposeful beginning to the planned change process.

Section 5.4: The Opening Statement

The opening statement is an integral part of every social work interaction. It includes a worker's statement of their agency's mission, their role in the agency, the expected length of the session, and an explicitly stated purpose of the meeting.

Section 5.5: Vulnerability in Engagement

Workers become vulnerable in engagement. If they get caught up in their emotions, they can fail to evaluate their own practice and can behave in less-than-effective ways. Using the critical thinking method of identifying feelings, beliefs, and knowledge can support the worker through vulnerability.

SELF-REFLECTION 5: ALCOHOL OUTCOME EXPECTANCIES SCALE

PURPOSE: To measure alcohol outcome expectancies

AUTHORS: Barbara C. Leigh and Alan W. Stacy

DESCRIPTION: The AOES is a 34-item scale designed to measure alcohol outcome expectancies—that is, the beliefs that people hold about the effects of alcohol on their behavior, moods, and emotions. Previous research has shown these expectancies are correlated with drinking behaviour in adolescents and in adults and may play a role in the initiation and maintenance of dysfunctional drinking of alcohol. Several subfactors exist. The subfactors for positive expectancies were: social facilitation (items 1, 20, 23, 26, 28, 32); fun (items 5, 7, 10, 14, 17, 24); sex (items 16, 22, 25, 29); and tension reduction (items 21, 31, 34). The subfactors for negative expectancies were: social (items 2, 8, 18); emotional (items 4, 12, 27); physical (items 13, 15, 30, 33); and cognitive performance (items 3, 6, 9, 11, 19).

NORMS: The AOES was studied with 588 introductory psychology students. No mean scores were provided.

SCORING: Items are on a 6-point likelihood scale. Scores are a simple sum of the scores within each subscale.

RELIABILITY: The AOES has excellent internal consistency and test-retest reliability.

VALIDITY: Positive and negative expectancy were equally related to actual alcohol use.

PRIMARY REFERENCE:

Leigh, B. C., & Stacy, A. W. (2013). Alcohol outcome expectancies: Scale construction and predictive utility in higher order confirmatory models. In K. Corcoran & J. Fischer (Eds.), *Measures for clinical practice and research: A sourcebook* (5th ed.). New York, NY: Oxford University Press.

ALCOHOL OUTCOME EXPECTANCIES SCALE

Here is a list of some effects or consequences that some people experience after drinking alcohol. How likely is it that these things happen to you when you drink alcohol? Please record the number that best describes how drinking alcohol would affect you, using the following scale:

1 = No chance

2 = Very unlikely

3 = Unlikely

4 = Likely

5 = Very likely

6 = Certain to happen

(If you do not drink at all, you can still fill this out: Just answer it according to what you think would happen to you if you did drink.)

_____ 1. I am more accepted socially

_____ 2. I become aggressive

_____ 3. I am less alert

_____ 4. I feel ashamed of myself

_____ 5. I enjoy the buzz

_____ 6. I become clumsy or uncoordinated

_____ 7. I feel happy

_____ 8. I get into fights

9. I have problems driving

_____ 10. I have a good time

_____ 11. I can't concentrate

_____ 12. I feel guilty

_____ 13. I feel sick

_____ 14. It is fun

_____ 15. I get a hangover

_____ 16. I have more desire for sex

_____ 17. I feel pleasant physical effects

_____ 18. I get mean

_____ 19. I have problems with memory and concentration

_____ 20. I am more outgoing

_____ 21. It takes away my negative moods and feelings

_____ 22. I become more sexually active

_____ 23. It is easier for me to socialize

_____ 24. I feel good

_____ 25. I am more sexually responsive

_____ 26. I am able to talk more freely

_____ 27. I feel sad or depressed

_____ 28. I am friendlier

_____ 29. I am more sexually assertive

_____ 30. I feel more social

_____ 31. I get a headache

_____ 32. I feel less stressed

_____ 33. I experience unpleasant physical effects

_____ 34. I am able to take my mind off my problems

Critical Terms for Engagement

engagement 138
genuineness 138
accurate empathy 139
pace of the interview 141
purposeful use of silence 141
mutual partnership 142
self-disclosure 142
professional presentation 142
professional identity 143
engaging smile 144
direct eye contact 144
indirect eye contact 144
embodied mirroring 145
pointing out strengths 145
firm handshake 145
boundaries 145
active listening 146
physical placement 146
clarification 146
ventilation 147
containment 147
empathy 147
sympathy 147
opening statement 148
relationship 149
taboo topics 150
agency mission 151
gentle confrontation 151
worker's role 151
purpose of the interview 151
time alloted 151
doorknob comment 151
probing 152
informed consent 153
confidentiality 154
limits of confidentiality 154
compassion 156

Generalist Practice Curriculum Matrix With 2015 Educational Policy and Accreditation Standards

Chapter 5

Competency	Course	Course Content	Dimensions
Competency 1: Demonstrate Ethical and Professional Behavior		5.1. Describe the role of the worker in facilitating the planned change process during engagement. 5.5. Review self-care through a cognitive process. Feature 3: Self-Reflection Feature 4: Concurrent Considerations in Generalist Practice	Cognitive–affective processes Knowledge Skills Knowledge Cognitive–affective processes Knowledge
Competency 2: Engage Diversity and Difference in Practice		Feature 1: Focus on Diversity Feature 4: Concurrent Considerations in Generalist Practice	Values Skills Cognitive–affective processes Skills Cognitive–affective processes
Competency 3: Advance Human Rights and Social, Economic, and Environmental Justice		Feature 4: Concurrent Considerations in Generalist Practice	Skills Cognitive–affective processes

Competency	Course	Course Content	Dimensions
Competency 4: Engage in Practice-Informed Research and Research-Informed Practice		Feature 4: Concurrent Considerations in Generalist Practice	Knowledge Skills Cognitive–affective processes
Competency 5: Engage in Policy Practice			
Competency 6: Engage With Individuals, Families, Groups, Organizations, and Communities		5.2. Practice skills related to engagement. 5.3. Review the aspects of beginnings in social work interactions. Feature 4: Concurrent Considerations in Generalist Practice	Cognitive–affective processes Skills Cognitive–affective processes
Competency 7: Assess Individuals, Families, Groups, Organizations, and Communities		Feature 4: Concurrent Considerations in Generalist Practice	Skills Cognitive–affective processes
Competency 8: Intervene With Individuals, Families, Groups, Organizations, and Communities		5.4. Articulate an opening statement that reflects the difference between a social work interview and a conversation. Feature 4: Concurrent Considerations in Generalist Practice	Skills Cognitive–affective processes Knowledge
Competency 9: Evaluate Practice With Individuals, Families, Groups, Organizations, and Communities		Feature 4: Concurrent Considerations in Generalist Practice	Skills Cognitive–affective processes

References

Bernieri, F. J., & Petty, K. N. (2011). The influence of handshakes on first impression accuracy. *Social Influence, 6*(2), 78–87.

Blum, M. C. (2015). Embodied mirroring: A relational, body-to-body technique promoting movement in therapy. *Journal of Psychotherapy Integration, 25*(2), 115–127.

Carter, I. (2011). *Human behavior in the social environment: A social systems approach* (6th ed.). New Brunswick, NJ: Aldine Transaction.

Centorrino, S., Djemai, D., Hopfensitz, A., Milinski, M., & Seabright, P. (2015). Honest signaling in trust interactions: Smiles rated as genuine induce trust and signal higher earning opportunities. *Evolution and Human Behavior, 36*(1), 8–16.

Davis, M. H. (1980). A multidimensional approach to individual differences in empathy. *JSAS Catalog of Selected Documents in Psychology, 10,* 85.

Elkins, D. N. (2009). *Humanistic psychology: A clinical manifesto.* Colorado Springs, CO: University of the Rockies Press.

Gerdes, K. E., Lietz, C. A., Segal, E. A. (2011). Measuring empathy in the 21st century: Development of an empathy index rooted in social cognitive neuroscience and social justice. *Social Work Research, 35*(2), 83–93.

Goldingay, S., & Land, C. (2014). Emotion: The "E" in engagement in online distance education in social work. *Journal of Open, Flexible and Distance Learning, 18*(1), 58–72.

Kadushin, A., & Kadushin, G. (1997). *The social work interview: A guide for human service professionals* (4th ed.). New York, NY: Columbia University Press.

Krumhuber, E., Manstead, A. S., Cosker, D., Marshall, D., Rosin, P. L., & Kappas, A. (2007). Facial dynamics as indicators of trustworthiness and cooperative behavior. *Emotion, 7*(4), 730–735.

Leigh, B. C., & Stacy, A. W. (2013). Alcohol outcome expectancies: Scale construction and predictive utility in higher order confirmatory models. In K. Corcoran & J. Fischer (Eds.), *Measures for clinical practice and research: A sourcebook* (5th ed.). New York, NY: Oxford University Press.

Miller, W. R., & Rollnick, S. (2013). *Motivational interviewing: Helping people change* (3rd ed.). New York, NY: Guilford Press.

National Association of Social Workers. (2018). *NASW code of ethics*. Washington, DC: NASW Press.

Park, H., Han, J., & Hyun, J. (2015). You may look unhappy unless you smile: The distinctiveness of a smiling face against faces without an explicit smile. *Acta Psychologica, 157*, 185–194.

Perlman, H. H. (1957). *Social casework: A problem-solving process*. Chicago, IL: University of Chicago Press.

Preuschoft, S., & van Hooff, J. (1997). The social function of "smile" and "laughter"; variations across primate species and societies. In U. Segerstrale & P. Molnar (Eds.), *Nonverbal communication: Where nature meets culture* (pp. 171–189). Mahwah, NJ: Lawrence Erlbaum.

Scholar, H. (2013). Dressing the part? The significance of dress in social work. *Social Work Education, 32*(3), 365–379.

Shulman, L. (2015). *The skills of helping individuals, families, groups, and communities* (8th ed.). Belmont, CA: Brooks/Cole.

Uono S., & Hietanen, J. K. (2015). Eye contact perception in the West and East: A cross-cultural study. *PLoS ONE, 10*(2): e0118094. doi:10.1371/journal.pone.0118094

Williams, D. J., Thomas, J., & Christensen, C. (2014). "You need to cover your tattoos!": Reconsidering standards of professional appearance in social work. *Social Work, 59*(4), 373–375.

Recommended Readings

Centorrino, S., Djemai, D., Hopfensitz, A., Milinski, M., & Seabright, P. (2015). Honest signaling in trust interactions: Smiles rated as genuine induce trust and signal higher earning opportunities. *Evolution and Human Behavior, 36*(1), 8–16.

6 Assessment

This chapter continues the exploration of the aspects of planned change that include worker–client system interactions. It covers the third stage in planned change: assessment. The case study addresses some of the challenges of work with families, particularly in the complexity of assessment as well as the experiences of home visits. The consideration of a wide variety of systems of all sizes is necessary for assessment. This chapter identifies and describes these systems.

Learning Objectives

6.1 Describe the role of the worker in facilitating the planned change process during assessment and compare assessment and diagnosis.

6.2 Explain home visits and safety issues related to them.

6.3 Summarize the assessment process with multisystem practice (MSP).

6.4 Demonstrate the role of the worker and the agency in the assessment phase.

6.5 Recall multisystem practice (MSP) in assessment, and prepare to identify situation-specific target systems.

6.6 Practice the use of a genogram in the assessment process.

6.7 Practice the use of an ecomap in the assessment process.

Case Study: Social Work With Families

©iStock.com/Highwaystarz-Photography

Family members can be an important part of work with individuals.

Jaime had determined from her first meeting with Bob that she would need to meet with his family to help support him in his recovery from alcohol abuse. She planned to continue the assessment she began when she met with Bob initially. Agency policy directed that she conduct family sessions at family homes whenever possible, so she drove up to Bob's ranch house at 3 minutes before the hour on a sunny day during the week after their initial meeting. She double-checked that she had Bob's address right and went up to the door. The house looked fine from the curb, one of a set of middle-class homes in a neat, clean, uniform development. Once she got past the gate in the picket fence, though, she got a different picture. The grass was cut, but there were high tufts around each of the fence posts. She nearly tripped on a loose paving stone on the way to the door, and when she got there she found the screen in the screen door repaired with broad silver duct tape. She tried the bell. When she didn't hear a ring, she knocked. A tired-looking blonde woman answered the door. She said, "You must be the girl from New Hope."

Jaime put on a bright smile and said, "That's right. I'm Jaime. You must be Patricia. May I come in?" Patricia welcomed Jaime and asked her to come inside. Jaime walked into the dimly lit living room, and Patricia pointed to a couch for her to take a seat. Jaime sat on the couch, nearly gasping as she sank further and faster than she expected. She reset her smile and asked Patricia if her husband, Bob, and her daughter, Sam, were at home. Patricia said that Bob hadn't gotten in from work yet, then turned her head toward the stairs and yelled, "Samantha, get down here!" Jaime took in quite a bit of information before she asked a single question. First, there were some repairs overdue on the house. She wondered if Patricia was self-conscious about them. Second, Jaime knew that the repairs were often delegated to men in Caucasian families like Bob's. Did that mean they were a source of contention between Bob and Patricia? Was it due to the attention Bob paid first to his addiction and then later to his recovery? Or was it a financial problem? Jaime also noticed that Patricia's hair was not clean, and she wore it pulled back in a tight ponytail, revealing a fraction of an inch of gray at the roots. Jaime wasn't judging; she was observing. She wondered if Patricia had the time or ability to nurture herself. Jaime considered that Patricia might even be depressed. Jaime would keep that possibility in the back of her mind. Finally, Jaime noticed that the living room was not well lit and that the television was on at a high volume. Coming into the room from a sunny day felt oppressive. All of these observations were part of Jaime's assessment of Bob and his family. It was important information that Jaime would include as she formed the most complete picture of them she could.

Patricia's yell to Samantha seemed overly loud, but there was no response at all. In the awkward silence that followed, Jaime searched for something to say to begin engagement with Patricia. She didn't want to start the session before Bob and Sam arrived, so she needed to find some small talk to use to connect with Patricia. Jaime reached down to get her notebook from her briefcase and stole a look at Patricia. She saw Patricia glance toward the television and quickly said, "That's a favorite show of mine too. Hopefully we can catch the end of it before the others arrive."

Section 6.1: Assessment and Multisystem Practice

In this section, we'll discuss the third of the interactive stages in the planned change process: assessment. We'll also consider how assessment differs from diagnosis.

A Broad Look at Systems

Assessment is the third step in the planned change process, but like engagement and self-reflection, it continues throughout the work. Each session requires some exploration of the current situation. That exploration takes place on multiple levels. In this chapter's case study, Jaime considers all three levels of practice all the time. She needs to determine the status of Bob's recovery during each meeting as well as the changing dynamics of the family system. Even when she meets with Bob alone, she'll be asking about the mezzo level: his family relationships and his progress in his group meetings too. Working on the macro level, she'll continue to consider the impact of larger systems, like agency policies and health care. Even the front desk will ask this: "Are there any changes to your insurance since you were last here?" Multisystem practice (MSP) facilitates initial assessment on all levels of practice and provides a concrete baseline for future interactions. See Figure 6.1.

FIGURE 6.1 ● Dynamic Nature of Planned Change

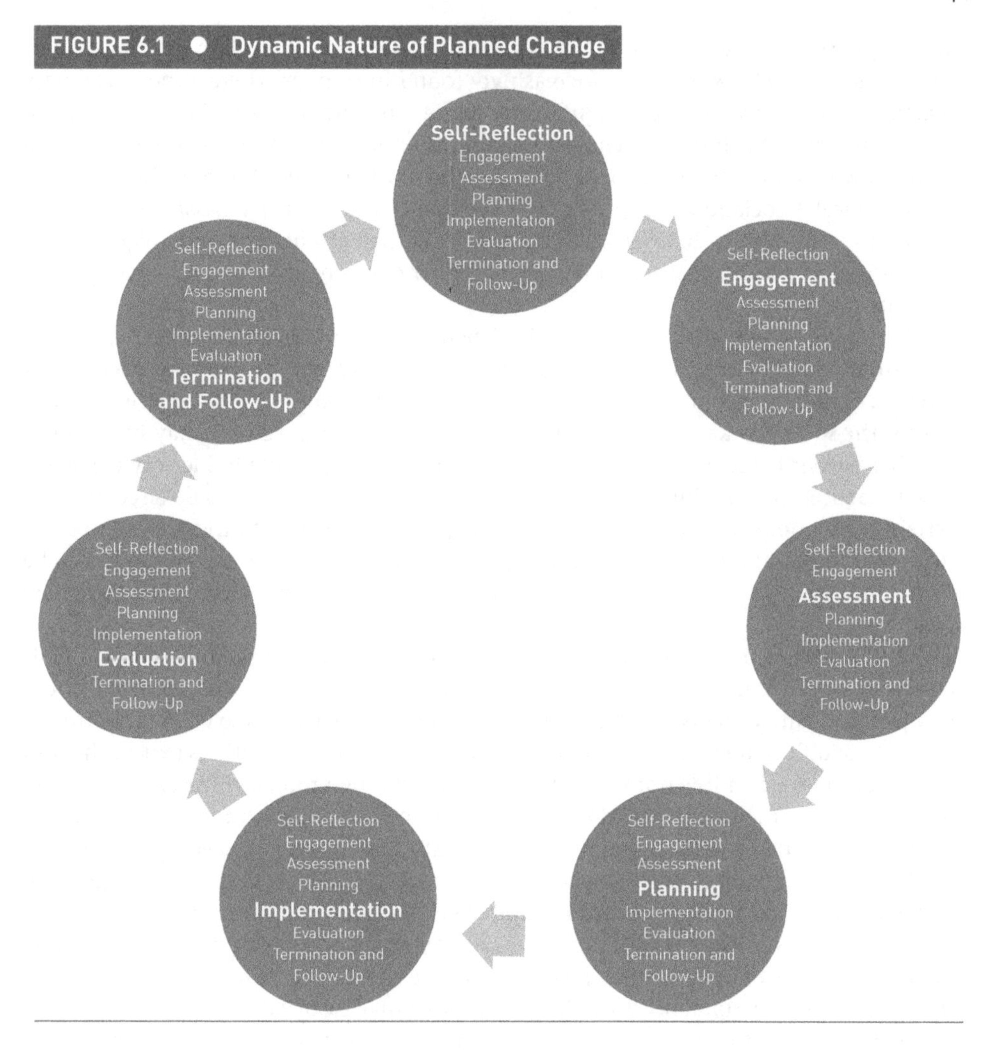

Assessment is a conversation that describes the client system in a way that is useful (Miley, O'Melia, & DuBois, 2013). It is the component of planned change in which the worker and the client collaborate to identify the strengths, the areas of diversity, and the challenges related to each environmental system that is relevant to the client system (Kirst-Ashman & Hull, 2018). While each environmental system is assessed separately, it is important to remember as previously discussed that all systems influence *all* other systems *all* of the time. The assessment process considers the interactions among the relevant systems, seeking to find uneven relationships, where the energy exchanged between systems is not in balance. Once those uneven interactions can be identified, implementations can be considered at those points. Overall, the purpose of assessment is to provide direction for the planning phase of planned change. It is important to note that a worker conducting initial assessment might sound mechanical if they are not careful. Be sure to let the client direct the conversation when possible. Rather than "Are you married? Do you have any children? What are their ages?" you might just say "Tell me about your family."

Assessment vs. Diagnosis

Before continuing with our discussion of assessment in practice, it is essential to consider the difference between assessment and diagnosis. This is because both assessment and diagnosis are often important to our client systems on the micro and mezzo levels of practice. Social workers are increasingly found in settings where either customary practice or insurance reimbursement requirements include the need for each client to be "diagnosed." This process includes the identification of symptoms and pairing them with known conditions that may be found in the most current edition of the American Psychological Association's *Diagnostic and Statistical Manual of Mental Disorders* (American Psychiatric Association, 2013). For example, to be labeled as suffering from major depressive disorder, a person must report feeling a number of symptoms that have been present for at least 2 weeks.

There are pros and cons to **diagnosis**. A benefit is that a diagnosis is often required by insurance companies and other funders to receive financial support for social work services. So a diagnosis sometimes helps meet the requirements of those who are paying for the social work services, and if services aren't paid for, we can't stay in business. Another benefit is that once a diagnosis is established it is possible to identify evidence-based practices or those implementation techniques that are known to be effective with certain populations. Finally, sometimes it is helpful to a person and those close to them to understand what problem they are facing. One of their most pressing questions may be "Why am I feeling this way?" and that question can often be answered with an accurate diagnosis.

If we consider learning theory, though, we can identify an important negative that is associated with diagnosis. A diagnosis is by its nature a label. That label can impact the way people identify themselves and the way they expect themselves to behave (Goffman, 1959). In addition, they may find themselves behaving in the way others expect them to behave at times when it is not necessary: the self-fulfilling prophecy. For example, most of us experience times when we don't feel like getting out of bed in the morning. We're a little tired or perhaps catching a cold and would like to stay bundled up in the covers. Still, we get up; responsibilities call to us. A person who feels that way one morning and who carries a diagnosis of depression may just stay in bed. No one will be surprised, and the person will feel like it is acceptable and expected. That person may very well be capable of getting out of bed; they just don't believe they are capable. If they stay in bed, their condition may spiral downward. Likewise, that diagnostic label may travel with the client from service to service and affect the way others view the client. It is important, then, to use diagnostic labels carefully and to discuss their use with clients. Social workers tend to favor the assessment process over the diagnostic one because it avoids labels and reflects the person-in-environment (PIE) perspective. We'll discuss the assessment process further in a bit. For now, consider the importance of the home visit in family-based assessment.

CRITICAL THINKING AND COLLABORATIVE LEARNING EXERCISES 6.1

1. Work with a partner. One of you should think about your GPA (an assessment of your success as a student). The other should ask the following questions:
   - Is the GPA an accurate or fair assessment of your school performance?
   - What things have influenced your GPA so far?
   - How do you feel about sharing this information with someone else?
2. Switch roles.

Section 6.2: Evidence-Based Practice

This section covers home visits: their benefits in assessment and their challenges. Safety is a particular concern.

Social Workers Outside of the Office

The Home Visit

The home visit has been a part of social work since the profession's inception. In Chapter 1, we discussed the importance of Mary Richmond's (1917/2012) *Social Diagnosis* to the profession's development. In that work, Mary Richmond discusses home visits, which hearken back to the "friendly visitors" of days gone by, and she demonstrates how **home visits** can be an excellent setting for assessment. Bob's reason for seeing Jaime was to develop an ability to participate fully in group work related to his problem with substance abuse. But when Bob began the session by reporting challenges he faces in his relationships with his wife and daughter, it became clear that the mezzo level of practice would be important for considerations of family as well as small groups. While Jaime struggled with the time commitment it entailed, she knew her agency policy . . . family work is done in the home whenever possible.

Safety considerations are paramount in home visits.

Home Visit Benefits

The agency policy about home visits was purposeful. There are many benefits to home visits (Allen & Tracy, 2004; Ryan & Yang, 2005). The worker literally meets the clients where they are, sharing the experience of getting to the neighborhood and walking up to the house. They begin to develop empathy as they take in the feel of the neighborhood. Reaching Bob's neighborhood, Jaime entered a fairly new, middle-class development consisting of a square area with about 15 houses. Each had four front windows framed by shutters, a front door with a knocker, vinyl siding, and a small front yard. Each had a small deck around back that sported an elaborate cooking grill. Jaime tried to imagine what it would be like to be Bob, coming home after a day at work. She wondered if he would feel pressure to look and act like all of the other residents. She wondered if Patricia felt the same pressure. Visiting the neighborhood gave Jaime an insight she could not have gained in the office.

Inside the home, Jaime experienced a small glimpse of family life. The first thing she noticed was that all of the window shades were down and all the drapes drawn. Apart from a couple of dim table lamps and the television screen, it was quite dark. Jaime wondered if anyone in the home was feeling depressed. The closed drapes might signify a withdrawal from others, a characteristic of depression. She told herself she'd be sure to keep her eyes open to the possibility. Her hypothesis might be entirely unsupported—the drapes might be closed because a family member gets migraines and needs to rest in semidarkness. But this is another observation that Jaime gleaned from the home visit that she would not have gotten in the office. Despite the obvious benefits of home visits, social workers should not conduct them without careful forethought. Sometimes safety issues arise when workers go out into the field to meet with clients.

Safety and Home Visits

Larkin (2018) has suggested that there are three kinds of safety in social work: physical, psychological, and professional. Each can make the job hazardous in its own way.

Physical Safety

Physical safety refers to avoiding bodily harm. It suggests some kind of attempted or actual assault, either a direct blow, a knife or a gunshot wound, a dog attack, or an object that has been thrown. These are occurrences that social workers often do not expect to experience. After all, they care for their clients and want what is best for them. Why would a client attack them?

Unfortunately, attacks do happen, and they happen too frequently. Social workers have been hurt, permanently injured, and even killed while practicing. The attitude that our clients won't hurt us is dangerous, because it makes us vulnerable. The fact is that many times we are the bearer of bad tidings: Young children may need to be removed from the home, adolescents or adults with mental health issues may face involuntary inpatient treatment, a social worker may get caught in the middle of a situation of intimate partner abuse, or a social worker may be visiting a client in a neighborhood that is generally unsafe. There are reasons social workers may get into these situations: Since the profession's inception, it has been accepted that social **justice** is best served by working directly in challenged neighborhoods and in the homes of clients. It is, after all, why we all say that social workers "meet the client where the client is." In addition, the profession's first core value is service (National Association of Social Workers [NASW], 2018), and many social workers feel an obligation to provide service even in the face of potential physical harm.

Fortunately, some precautions can and should be taken. Lyter and Abbott (2007) have identified a number of actions agencies and individual social workers can take to remain safe. First, it is the agency's responsibility to provide a safety plan and post the plan prominently. On the macro level, agencies should conduct training specifically related to safety on an ongoing basis. This training should be conducted for all agency staff members and should include "non-violent crisis implementation training, personal safety techniques, de-escalation techniques, and risk assessment" (Lyter & Abbott, 2007, p. 25). Agencies should also be open to feedback from all workers.

Agencies do not bear all of the responsibility, though. It is the worker's job to carry out safe practices as well. Lyter and Abbott (2007) have made recommendations for safe practices on the part of workers:

- Visit preparation
    - Conduct as thorough an assessment as possible before interacting with the client system. The self-reflection phase discussed in the previous chapter will be best carried out in the context of safety considerations.
    - Let the client know the purpose of the meeting when you set the appointment. Use the opening statement discussed later in this chapter even during phone contacts.
    - Become familiar with the neighborhoods of potential visits. Visit the place, and ask questions like "Where is the nearest gas station?" to get a sense of whether the neighborhood is isolated.
    - Wear comfortable clothing that will blend in the neighborhood. Safe shoes are most important.
    - Work with a partner. If you must go without a fellow worker on a visit that holds any potential for violence, you can always ask for a police escort.
    - Make sure your car is reliable or you have public transportation that is accessible.
    - Know exactly where you are going, even if this requires visiting the community on a day before your appointment.
    - Leave the office with plenty of time. Don't rush.

- Visit management
  - Show confidence and be assertive. Be polite, but don't hesitate to put yourself forward. When conducting a home visit, you take your office with you. For example, it is appropriate to ask that the television be turned off when you are ready to begin your session with your opening statement.
  - On the other hand, it is important that you respect your client's ownership of the home. A simple "Where would you like me to sit?" can convey that respect.
  - Stay alert to your environment even as you focus on the meeting.
- Crisis management
  - If you have any sensation that you may be in danger, say something like "Please excuse me" or something like it and get out.
  - If an incident does occur in which you are hurt or threatened, take care of yourself first. Then be sure to document it before you forget details. The agency should have an incident report form. Fill it out honestly; do not play down any incident.
  - Talk about it with your supervisor. Take any benefit the agency offers, such as a paid day off or a meeting with an employee assistance program (EAP) professional.

Be sure you have your phone with you, and be sure it is charged. Let someone at your agency know where you are going and when you will be back. If you do not arrive back on time and you do not call to notify them, they will call you. If you do not answer your phone, they should call the police without hesitation.

Psychological Safety

The **psychological safety** of workers is important. As much as social workers pride themselves on being able to manage difficult situations and to avoid feeling betrayed or angry or sad about clients' behaviors due to our understanding of human behavior, real, lasting harm can be done without actual violence. Some psychological dangers come from threats of violence, vandalism of personal property such as cars, or demeaning language. Because we want to trust our clients and our relationships with them, any hateful behavior from one of them can be shattering. As has been discussed in the self-reflection phase, allow yourself to have your feelings without judgment. It is possible to work with them and ease your pain, but it is important to acknowledge them first.

Vicarious Trauma

Vicarious trauma could be the result of the ongoing compassion fatigue we've discussed earlier or from one extremely troubling interaction with a client. Cox and Steiner (2013) express vicarious trauma as a change in a worker's worldview that results from an empathic connection with the trauma of others. Getting close to people who are traumatized can result in feeling traumatized yourself, and that trauma is connected with coming to feel cynical and pessimistic as well as feeling unsure of the way you have thought about yourself and others in the past. It is decidedly uncomfortable and damaging, and successful "cures" for vicarious trauma have not been identified. Consequently, the best treatment is prevention. It is commonly suggested that resiliency is built by good general self-care including time spent in cultivating spiritual, creative and recreational activities (Cox & Steiner, 2013). In addition, Baird & Kracen (2006) suggest that workers who have experienced trauma themselves are more likely to experience vicarious trauma, and it has been suggested that workers who see and hear about human-caused trauma, like sexual abuse, are more likely to experience vicarious trauma than those who see and hear about trauma that may happen to anyone, such as cancer (Cunningham, 2003).

As a result, it makes sense that a worker who has experienced childhood abuse would be best off avoiding the field of child welfare, and people in general who are very sensitive to trauma should avoid fields where human-caused trauma is prevalent. It is, of course, impossible to avoid listening to or seeing troubling events as a social worker, so self-care should be a requisite part of practice. Pay attention to your physical wellness and consider using the mindfulness exercises described in Chapter 4 for stress reduction. When you have experienced too many painful client experiences, seek support. Cox and Steiner (2013) learned from licensed clinical social workers that the most effective coping was reported to be changing the way you think about your client's painful experiences: One way is to think about how your practice in the future will be improved from your experience, another is to think about how you have helped someone by being a good listener, and the third is to focus on how much of an honor it is to be told something so intensely personal. Again, prevention is best . . . focus on self-care early. See Figure 6.2.

Agency Culture

To some agencies, worker safety of all kinds is a priority. These agencies don't send workers to dangerous areas without a partner or police protection. They pay attention to where workers are and when they might return, provide days off in cases of physical harm, and offer counseling for psychological effects of helping in difficult situations. On the other hand, please be aware that some agencies develop a culture in which reports of physical or psychological harm are downplayed or even made the butt of jokes. The relatively new worker who reports incidents of minor injury or threats to physical well-being may be viewed as a beginner who is not competent. The worker who accepts employee assistance benefits, or counseling, following an attack may be seen as weak. Generally, this attitude is a kind of institutional coping mechanism in cases where workers are frequently in danger. The agency identity becomes "we have the most difficult clients and we can handle them." This sort of grandiosity may keep fear at bay, but it can be a barrier to self-care. Besides, some fear may very well be appropriate.

FIGURE 6.2 ● Response to the Psychological Pain of Helping: Change Your Thinking

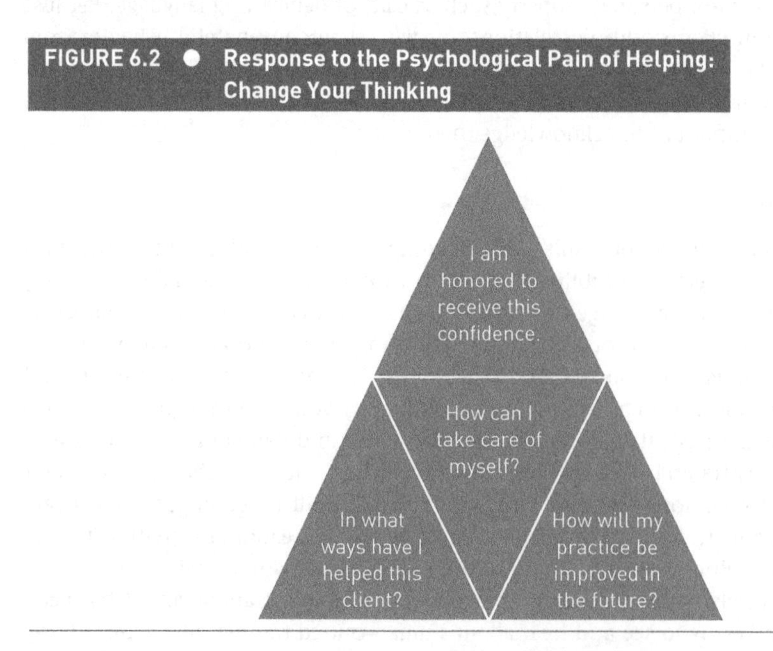

Professional Safety

Finally, **professional safety** is a challenge workers face in that there may be legal ramifications of our work. Purchasing **malpractice insurance** is a personal decision, but it should be considered seriously. It is likely that an agency will have insurance for workers, interns, and volunteers, but if you unintentionally violate agency policy you may disqualify yourself from agency support in the face of legal action. In addition, there is a professional threat that is more personal. If you have experienced violence, been threatened, or even witnessed violence, you may feel betrayed or angry toward the profession. The result may be the loss of emotional support from colleagues or even a change of careers.

It is unfortunate that social workers have to give such serious consideration to their own safety in the course of their jobs. However, it is a reality that is best accepted. Cautious behavior and agency support can create safe working conditions in most situations. If carried out safely, the home visit has enormous potential for engagement, assessment, and implementation of planned change. Jaime was particularly interested in carrying out a home visit to continue her initial assessment. She was using MSP as applied to social work assessment.

CRITICAL THINKING AND COLLABORATIVE LEARNING EXERCISES 6.2

1. Discuss the previously discussed safety considerations with a partner. Are there any suggestions that you might find particularly difficult to implement? Focus specifically on self-care. How might you begin practicing self-care now? Share strategies with your partner.
2. Identify a friend who has never been to your home and invite them over. Use the experience to develop empathy for a client who is having a social worker conduct a home visit: Discuss with a partner what your experience was like having a new person come into your home. (Please use safety precautions: Invite a friend you've known for a while to visit during daylight hours when someone else is also at home.)
3. Discuss with a partner why you think engagement is such an important part of assessment.

Section 6.3: The Practice of Multisystem Practice

In this section, we'll begin to look at a scientific form of assessment that provides specific directions for conducting assessment with a client system. Assessment is based on MSP as described in Chapter 2. To use MSP in assessment, we'll first consider the relevant environmental systems.

Assessment

Conducting assessment in the context of MSP facilitates collaboration between a worker and a number of client system representatives. The purpose of this collaboration is to identify the character of the interaction between and among systems. Once systems and interactions are identified, uneven energy exchange can be identified and those uneven interactions may be targeted for change efforts.

Identifying Relevant Systems: The Principles of Multisystem Practice

The MSP method describes, explains, and predicts human behavior based on the simultaneous interaction among multiple systems, including individuals, families, groups, organizations, and communities. A logical extension of the components of the MSP method as described in Chapter 2 is a series of principles that describe and predict system interaction.

1. There are a number of large and small systems that interact with each other and with every client system.
2. These systems may include individuals, families, groups, organizations, communities, and characteristics of the physical environment.
3. Systems exchange energy to survive. A balanced energy exchange may lead to synergy, where an unbalanced exchange may lead to entropy.
4. In any particular case, systems large and small interact with the client system; they all interact with each other as well.
5. Systems of particular importance to the client system must be identified by collaboration between the worker and the representative of the client system during the ongoing assessment process.
6. Uneven energy exchange between systems allows one or more systems to maintain their characteristics at the expense of a system that is being drained of energy.
7. Even those systems that may be contributing to others at their own expense have resiliency, or the ability to maintain functioning even in the face of difficulty, as well as other resources.
8. The worker and the client system representative work to identify uneven energy exchanges, as they are likely to negatively impact the client system. The interaction between the systems where there is an uneven energy exchange holds potential for the implementation of planned change. Resources to support planned change may be identified through an examination of the client systems' areas of diversity as it has been previously defined. The worker may facilitate the discovery of those strengths through the practice of cultural humility as it is described in Chapter 4.

A series of systems may be identified to guide the worker as they hunt out areas of strength and systems with uneven energy exchange. In other words, each client system will interact with each of the systems, and each of the systems will interact with each other. All of these interactions may result in energy exchange that is balanced and creates synergy or energy exchange that is unbalanced and negatively impacts at least one of the systems. Relevant systems include the following:

- Health care
- Economy or personal finance
- Physical environment
- Education
- National and international policies
- Spirituality and religion
- Justice

- Individuals, family, community, and peers
- Government
- Social welfare policies

There may be other systems that are relevant, primarily due to individual areas of diversity among client systems, and they should be added to the assessment as needed.

As you can see, there are many systems we have to juggle in our heads in order to complete an MSP assessment. Here is a riddle to help you remember most important environmental systems:

What do you say about a man who writes music for fast dances?

Answer:

He pens jigs.

Use this mnemonic device to help you remember the environmental systems that impact clients on all levels of practice:

- **H**ealth care
- **E**conomy or personal finance
- **P**hysical environment
- **E**ducation
- **N**ational and international policies
- **S**pirituality and religion
- **J**ustice
- **I**ndividual, family, community, and peers
- **G**overnment
- **S**ocial welfare policies

Bonita Cooke/Getty Images

An Irish jig.

CRITICAL THINKING AND COLLABORATIVE LEARNING EXERCISES 6.3

Memorize the systems involved in comprehensive assessment. Can you think of any systems in your life that are not listed?

Section 6.4: First Steps in Assessment

In this section, the first elements of assessment are discussed: assessment of the worker and assessment of the agency.

The Worker's Strengths, Diversity, and Challenges

The first system to assess in determining the client system's strengths, diversity, and challenges is that of the worker. The worker and the agency are systems that interact with the client from the moment of the decision to seek help. Considering the worker involves addressing any aspect of the interaction with client systems. It is significant that the worker practice ongoing professional use of self as it is employed first during the self-reflection phase. Remember that the worker's goal is to choose behaviors consciously in the context of professional values and ethical standards.

To work toward professional use of self as discussed in Chapter 4, Jaime followed the fourfold path to critical thinking and value-driven choices (Hanna, 2013). Here, Jaime was able to discover that she had preconceptions of her client based on diversity. Using the critical thinking "What do I feel/believe/know/do?" process described earlier, she could identify her preconceptions and discuss how to manage them through the supervisory process. For example, when Jaime was given Bob's case file, she was surprised to see herself slam it down on her desk. Since that type of behavior was very unusual for her, Jaime discussed it with her supervisor. Through the discussion, Jaime remembered that a high school acquaintance had been involved in a drunk driving accident and had been killed. A middle-aged Caucasian man had been driving the car that caused the accident. Jaime remembered that initially she was more angry than sad. It seemed such a waste of a promising life and so unfair that the man who had caused the accident walked away with minor injuries. Once Jaime recognized that she connected white males and alcoholism with wanton destruction, she was able to think about Bob's case differently.

ETHICAL PERSPECTIVES

What does the NASW Code of Ethics *(NASW, 2018) say that is related to self-reflection and the professional use of self? See Section 4.05(a) to find out.*

What Do I Feel?

Jaime knew she would have to stop periodically and make sure she was not expressing her anger in her meetings with Bob. For example, when Jaime stayed at the office late one evening to meet with Bob, he cancelled their appointment at the last minute. Jaime told herself she could use that time to file some of the folders on her desk, but she was strangely agitated. When she knocked over a vase and nearly threw it against a wall, she knew she could ignore her anger no longer. She had to accept it. She allowed herself to feel the anger and to express her true thoughts: "This client is not motivated to change!" And she knew she needed to talk with her supervisor before she returned Bob's call. If she had continued to hide her anger, it could have remained with her, affecting her personal life and influencing what she believed about the client and herself.

What Do I Believe?

Since Jaime had recognized her anger and reconciled herself to it, she was able to drop a potentially harmful belief: She didn't know it at first, but she believed that all white men were powerful and wealthy, with resources that could buy them out of consequences for their behavior. And if they weren't powerful and wealthy, they must be very lazy, because all white men have social opportunities that members of minority groups like herself were denied. When Bob told Jaime that he had missed his last appointment because his patched up car broke down, her first thought was a sarcastic "oh, right." But since she had accepted and acknowledged her anger she was able to at least consider that she might have inaccurate beliefs about Caucasian men. She was able to refrain from expressing any sarcasm toward Bob for the moment. See Figure 6.3.

What Do I Know?

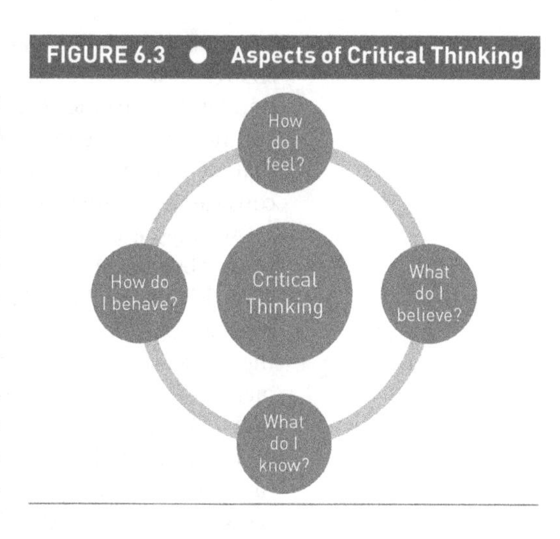

FIGURE 6.3 • Aspects of Critical Thinking

Acknowledging her anger (What do I feel?) allowed Jaime to recognize her beliefs about white men (What do I believe?). She needed to critically examine those beliefs (What do I know?). And that meant she needed to seek out evidence. Jaime started by doing an online search of "Are all white men rich?" and she found a plethora of sites that helped young women find rich, white men who would date (and hopefully bankroll) needy women. It was not exactly what she'd been looking for. So she decided to get serious—she had not gone to college for nothing—and looked up the U.S. Census Bureau. She learned that the poverty rate for families of two adults and two children was $24,036 in 2014. *Wow, who could live on that?* She also learned that in the United States, 15% of people lived in poverty in 2014. She was interested in African American poverty, since that was her ethnicity, that of her family, and many of her friends. She learned that 37% of families that identified as black or multiracial lived on a household income under $24,999. Almost 4 in 10 of all the black and multiracial families in the United States lived under the poverty level in 2014. Jaime sat back in her chair. She knew it was bad, but she didn't know it was that bad. Again, she began to feel anger toward the white men who had all the advantages of good schools, good houses, good food, high expectations, and hope. But then she looked at the same chart for white families. And found that 22%, or 2 in 10 white families, lived on less than $24,999 per year. The rate was better than black families, yes, but not good. Not every white man had advantages.

How Do I Behave?

Once she had used critical thinking, instead of being angry and sarcastic to Bob, Jaime was able to begin to develop empathy (How do I behave?). When he told her his car broke down, she said, "I'm so sorry to hear that, it must be so frustrating."

Her supervisor pointed out to her that being willing to follow the fourfold process showed her openness and willingness to be reflective so that she could act, not emotionally react, to client situations.

When she considered her challenges as part of the assessment process, though, Jaime was also forced to confront the fact that she was overwhelmed with paperwork and that the situation was affecting her work with her clients. See Figure 6.4.

FIGURE 6.4 • Elements of Assessment

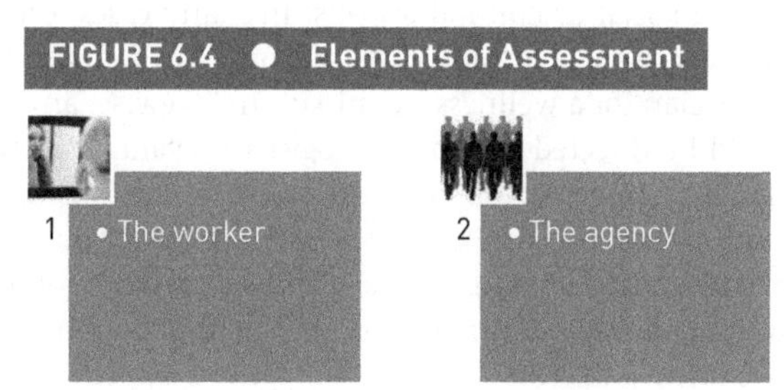

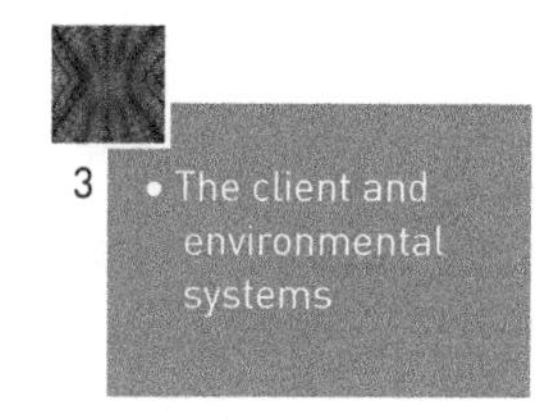

Beginning Steps in Assessment: The Agency

The second component in MSP assessment is the agency, its internal policies and staff qualifications, physical facility, and location. We've already discussed one agency policy: the one stating that family sessions are to be conducted in the home if at all possible. We've touched on another policy: eligibility requirements and limitations to treatment. The agency's location is also important, since Jaime learned that Bob could not take public (like a bus) or private (like Uber) transportation to get to his appointment because he didn't have funds. All three of these should be recognized as rules governing practice that flow from laws, regulations, and funding sources. As such, they may or may not be subject to change. It is the worker's responsibility to recognize agency policy and to seek to understand it. Understanding a policy means finding out how it became a policy in the first place and how many people it effects. It means considering how people are impacted in ways that are intended and ways that are unintended. It means evaluating whether the policy is consistent with social work values (Karger & Stoesz, 2014).

At times, a worker may evaluate a policy and find it wanting. For example, the agency policy about eligibility for service stated that absences could result in dismissal from the program. In this case, Jaime knew that Bob would have attended sessions using public or privately provided transportation if he had the funds. She considered that the small emergency fund in the office was often used for such items as medications for children or clothing for employment interviews. It seemed to her that it could be used for minimal transportation costs as well. Jaime used the planned change steps to address the policy issue. Jaime *reflected on* the agency's standpoint. There was never a lot of money available for anything like new office furniture, for example. She knew she'd have to tread lightly. Using her solid relationship with her supervisor, she *engaged* her in a discussion about the need for some clients to have bus passes. Part of that *assessment* process included Jaime discovering that the emergency fund was small but it often had money left over at the end of the month. She also assessed the problem by discussing it with her coworkers. She found that only a handful of their clients would benefit from an occasional free bus pass or Uber fee. The interaction between the client systems and the agency was out of balance, but the emergency fund was a resource that was untapped. Jaime *planned* possible implementations with the help of her supervisor, and they decided to put a formal request to the director. Jaime actively *implemented* this advocacy effort by writing a formal memorandum for her supervisor to review and pass along to the director. Later, Jaime was elated to find that her request was approved. She *implemented* the policy immediately by explaining the new policy to Bob so that he could use it if he found himself without transportation again. Later on, she knew she'd have to *evaluate* the new policy—she wasn't sure the clients would not use bus passes for other purposes and then find themselves unable to attend their sessions anyway. She decided to *follow up* with coworkers after three months to see how the transportation support policy was working.

Beginning Steps in Assessment: The Client System

The next part of the assessment is to consider the client and their biological, psychological, and social or cultural aspects. In many cases, other interdisciplinary collaboration is necessary. If there are any physical concerns, for example, the client should be brokered to a physician for a wellness examination. Likewise, any suspicion of mental health concerns should be directed to a psychologist for evaluation. Family-related issues should be considered by carefully assessing the types of relationships individuals have formed. In terms of cultural aspects, the client's areas of diversity must be examined by the worker and the client together, looking for the client's perception of identity, strengths, and challenges of diversity considering power and privilege as well as potential areas of discrimination. On the macro level, the same considerations apply: Organizations include individuals with biological and psychological strengths and challenges while they have their own unique cultural environment. Jaime's experience in carrying out this process will be discussed next.

Next Steps in Assessment: Environmental Systems

To continue assessment, the worker next discusses a series of environmental systems with the representative of the client system. To elaborate on what we previously discussed, these systems include the following:

- *Health care*—This is adequacy of insurance coverage and availability of services to the family and in the community. **Health care** is a significant part of the quality of life for individuals, families, groups, and communities. Assessment should consider the accessibility of quality health care as well as its cost.

- *Economy or personal finance*—This is employment and unemployment rates, adequacy of wages, and the ability to create and maintain a household budget. Unemployment and underemployment—working fewer hours or with less responsibility than qualified for—are some of individuals' greatest discontents. Childless men who are unemployed long term are particularly vulnerable as there is no federal cash benefit for them.
- *Physical environment*—This refers to home or apartment maintenance, the quality of housing, and neighborhood safety. Unsafe neighborhoods are a problem for many urban dwellers. Areas of low-quality housing sagging under poverty and substance addiction make it difficult even to develop goals. Residents may not be having their basic needs met.
- *Education*—This is level of **education**, quality of the area's public schools, or any further education needed. Assessment should consider current education level as well as aspirations of individuals. Communities should be assessed for quality of education available to residents.
- *National and international policies*—These are federal policies that relate to states as well as foreign countries. Assessment should consider any policies that have direct impact on practice as well as those that impact quality of living. Federal policies can impact grants for social work services and research into social problems.
- *Spirituality and religion*—They are two very different things. Religion is an organized activity and social institution whose policies may be repressive to some populations but whose organized activities can provide strength and support. Spirituality is an individual concept of a higher power, also potentially a great source of strength and resiliency. To determine a client's strengths, it is important to assess their spirituality as well as the impact of the institution of religion on the client system.
- *Justice*—Like religion, the justice system is a two-edged sword. Community policing and crime prevention activities can make neighborhoods safer. On the other hand, profiling and racially correlated police violence and arrests result in proportionally more male minorities imprisoned, injured, and killed in interactions with the justice system.
- *Individual, family, community, and peers*—Assessment should consider all levels of practice directly related to the client system. The client system is usually determined by agency policy. Where the client system is a community, the situation faced by groups of individuals should be considered. Where family is the client system, individual members' strengths and challenges should be assessed. Peers may be friends, colleagues, or fellow treatment group members.
- *Government*—Assessment should examine the impact of **government** on other systems. For example, government may directly impact systems through grants for service and research. Other resources may be relevant, such as relocation funds for those affected by climate change.
- *Social welfare policies*—**Social welfare policies** that directly impact practice may be located on the federal or the state level. State policies are created within the context of federal policies but may be quite different, such as the eligibility for SNAP, the Supplemental Nutrition Assistance Program, formerly known as food stamps.

Systems	Strengths and Diversity	Challenges
Social worker	What I feel, believe, know, do	Barriers to self-reflection
Agency	Qualification of staff, internal policies, physical facility and location	Barriers to staff input into policies, funding limits
Client system representative: (name)	Biological, psychological, cultural aspects: power, privilege, identity	Biological, psychological, cultural aspects: discrimination
Health care		
Economy or personal finance		
Physical environment		
Education		
National and international policies		
Spirituality and religion		
Justice		
Individual, family, community, peers		
Government		
Social welfare policies		

CRITICAL THINKING AND COLLABORATIVE LEARNING EXERCISES 6.4

Consider the statement "There are hardly any men in social work." Carry out the "What do I feel/believe/know/do?" critical thinking exercise. Have you changed your mind? Is there any action you should take?

Section 6.5: Multisystem Assessment in Practice

Identifying Strengths, Diversity, and Challenges

In this chapter's case study, Jaime began the assessment process early in the engagement phase. The two stages of planned change overlapped because Jaime was already juggling systems in her mind as she worked to build a relationship with Bob. Once she felt they had a working relationship, she formally moved to the assessment stage using a chart to aid her understanding.

To a degree, the assessment process at New Hope is established by policy. Like many programs and agencies, it has a standardized **intake form**. The intake form facilitates assessment as well as the documentation of data needed to meet funding and program evaluation requirements. For example, the intake form may require information like date of birth, allowing the worker to establish the client's age. This information may be part of the information necessary for getting insurance payments to support the client's service. This information also reminds the worker to consider what she knows about human development as she works with this client. For example, if the client is 60 years old, she will guess that the person is interested in generativity, or passing on life's lessons to the next generation and "giving back" to individuals and the community (Erikson, 1968). She'll want to ask about this to determine where the client is developmentally.

Note that the intake form facilitates two stages of planned change: (1) assessment and (2) evaluation. The assessment phase serves to identify potential areas for the implementation of planned change, and it is necessary to begin thinking about possible goals and how to measure success.

Because assessment is so closely tied to engagement, Jaime did not want to place a clipboard between herself and the client. So she only took notes on a tablet that she placed on her desk under her elbow. She avoided using the intake questionnaire form as well; after the first few intake sessions, she knew the questions by heart and could work them into the interview seamlessly as the topics arose. This way, she could complete the intake form after the session and avoid creating a barrier between her and her client.

- *Health care*—When Bob mentioned the effects of a hangover on his work, Jaime used that reference to his health to bring up the topic of health care.
- *Economy or personal finance*—When Bob mentioned the potential cost of sending Sam to college, Jaime grabbed the opportunity to talk about his job and his wages.
- *Physical environment*—In Bob's case, Jaime found the best way to understand his **physical environment** was to do a home visit and experience it herself.
- *Education*—When she got Bob talking about his work, Jaime was able to lead the session into a discussion of the level of educational preparation he needed for his job. Once he mentioned Sam and her upcoming college expenses, Jaime was able to segue into a discussion of the quality of schools in their area.
- *National and international policies*—Jaime considered Bob to be an expert of his own situation, and he ended up teaching her about the connection between imports and exports of construction materials to his employment and the occasional threats of unemployment that he faced.
- *Spirituality and religion*—Jaime took the opportunity to discuss spirituality with Bob when they talked about group treatment for substance abuse. He stated that he was aware that the self-help groups that met at New Hope placed a large focus on spirituality and that while his spirituality was a comfort to him his discomfort in speaking about it in public was one reason he had a hard time speaking during group meetings.
- *Justice*—Bob was an inadvertent beneficiary of the institutional oppression that exists in the justice system. Once he was on his way home to his suburban neighborhood when he was pulled over for running a stop sign, and the police officer, who must surely have smelled the alcohol on his breath, told him to go directly home without any charges. That may not have been the case had he been a member of a minority group.
- *Individual, family, community, and peers*—Because Bob identified his wife and daughter as sources of stress, Jaime asked him for details about his perception of them. She knew she would be able to make her own observations when she conducted the home visit. Bob's friends tended to use alcohol heavily. She

looked forward to getting him into a treatment group where he might develop connections with other peers.

- *Government*—Jaime knew that thanks to grants through the federal U.S. Department of Health and Human Services that there were several evidence-based options for working with clients who experienced substance abuse. She knew she had to do some critical reading of research and learn about them.
- *Social welfare policies*—Jaime learned that Bob worried about unemployment but wasn't sure what his benefits would be if he were to become unemployed.

After Jaime and Bob talked through all of the items on the assessment chart, it was Jaime's job to document the interview.

Multisystem Practice Chart in Practice

Systems	Strengths and Diversity	Challenges
Social worker: *Jaime Adams*	Openness, self-awareness, reflection Committed to work; good educational foundation; trusting relationship with supervisor; carried out I feel, I think, I believe, I do process with open mind	Tends to be overwhelmed with workload, particularly paperwork
Agency	Good safety practices; family session home visits; open to employee suggestions for change; low staff turnover; experienced and qualified supervision; sound financial base	Tied to treatment limitations based on insurance requirements; location not ideal for center-city dwellers
Client System Representative: *Bob Jones* (based on employee assistance program [EAP] eligibility; evidence base of substance abuse suggests importance of family as well as individual and small group work)	Biological, psychological, cultural aspects: power, privilege, identity Recent medical exam reveals basic good health Has excellent self-awareness Able to care about wife, daughter	Biological, psychological, cultural aspects: discriminations Recent and extensive history of alcohol abuse; limited social connections beyond coworkers who typically drink together off hours
Health care	Employer provides EAP that pays for six social work interviews	Regular health insurance is costly and does not cover substance abuse treatment
Economy or personal finance	Employed in construction despite drinking	Has called in sick numerous times due to late night drinking If relapse, there is constant danger of injury Construction business in general slowing due to slowing in housing market
Physical environment	Home in a desirable suburban area	Cannot get to appointments without extended public transportation ride when car is broken down Home in need of minor repairs

Systems	Strengths and Diversity	Challenges
Education	High school, vocational technical training, graduated with honors showing intelligence and diligence in academic work; has sophisticated knowledge of current events	Frustrated with few social interactions related to educated analysis of current events
National and international policies	Tariffs remain low on imported steel, keeping prices down and supporting the construction industry	Tariffs may change and affect the construction industry negatively; fatalist about government's response to terrorism and immigration; experiencing anomie
Spirituality and religion	Believes in the Judeo-Christian God that will be congruent with the Alcoholics Anonymous philosophy	Has difficulty expressing personal beliefs May benefit from family church attendance Feels anger and confusion about radical Islam and terrorism
Justice	Has avoided driving under the influence of alcohol arrest by luck, use of friends for transportation, and drinking at home	If relapse, there is danger of driving under the influence of alcohol
Individual, family, community, and peers	Intact nuclear and extended family with positive relationships; cares intensely for wife and daughter Willingness to address substance abuse in both individual and small group settings	Wife feels neglected; Sam is unhappy and uncommunicative
Government	State "no fault" divorce policies may make it a routine process for Bob and his wife to give up on their relationship—a decision they may regret later	
Social welfare policies	Private, not-for-profit agency contracts with employer to provide EAP	Limited public funds for substance abuse treatment and limited to convicted offenders

CRITICAL THINKING AND COLLABORATIVE LEARNING EXERCISES 6.5

1. Memorize the systems involved in comprehensive assessment. Be sure to have a solid understanding of each one.
2. Work with a partner to identify your strengths, diversities, and challenges as a student.

Section 6.6: The Genogram

The assessment process concludes with two visual aids to assessment: the genogram and the ecomap. This section will cover the genogram. This last component of assessment will inform the Planning phase of the planned change process.

What Is a Genogram?

Think genealogy, like studying a family tree. That's the "geno" part. "Gram" is short for diagram. So a **genogram** is a diagram of a family. It is also a map of family patterns and relationships. The format of a genogram is pretty standard as it appears next. It was developed by a committee of theorists including Murray Bowen, who is widely considered to be the father of family therapy (McGoldrick, Gerson, & Shellenberger, 1999). A formal genogram includes many symbols to indicate various individual characteristics. Most social workers know how to create some form of a genogram. We'll consider the basic method.

A genogram consists of a series of circles that represent women and squares that represent men. These are connected on the genogram in a way that reflects their relationships with each other. Most often, these are biological relationships, but the genogram can also indicate other relationships such as children who enter a family through adoption or friends who are considered to be family. Couple relationships, whether they are married or not, can be indicated. Finally, the genogram includes a series of lines that connect the people and their relationships to each other. The genogram in social work is typically used in micro and mezzo practice, but don't write it off as a method in macro practice. For example, a worker may use a genogram in micro practice, helping the client to recognize family members who may be resources for the client. On the mezzo level, a worker may have a family collaborate on completing a genogram so they can develop insights into their relationships. On the macro level, a social worker who is consulting with a board of directors may have each member complete a genogram as a way to engage the members and get them to recognize their family resources and get ready for tasks that they need to complete collaboratively. The genogram is even used to represent complex families in juvenile and criminal courts. The court may also use the genogram in child welfare cases to consider emergency placement with family members, or **kinship care**.

On any level, the genogram has several purposes. One is to help the worker and client recognize members of the client's family. Another is to plot relationships to make them visible and understandable to a client system. Finally, the genogram serves to point out individual characteristics or events that repeat themselves across the generations. For example, diabetes may repeat itself in grandparents and parents. This would point out the need for children to be tested for the disease. Since information is most valuable over time, the genogram should cover at least three generations.

SELF-REFLECTION 6: THE FAMILY CELEBRATIONS INDEX

One way to measure how content family members are is to consider how often they celebrate special occasions. Take the Family Celebrations Index (FCEL; McCubbin, McCuban, & Sievers, 2013) on pages 160–161 to see how much your family celebrates.

What does this exercise tell you about the diverse nature of your family? How can you use it to recognize the diversity of other families?

The Genogram in Practice

To complete a genogram, the worker starts with a system, usually an individual. This individual is represented by a square for a man or a circle for a woman. Where one person is identified as the person being served by the agency, the outline of the square or circle is double. The worker then collaborates with the individual to add family members and to identify important relationships.

For example, when Jaime worked with Bob about his family, she began with Bob since Bob was the client identified by Jaime's agency. Jaime was going to work with the whole family, but Bob was formally the client of New Hope. Jaime included important characteristics about Bob like what's in Figure 6.5.

FIGURE 6.5 ● Individual

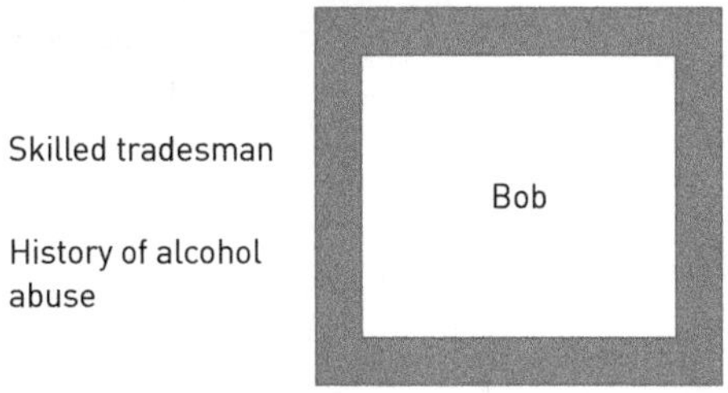

Skilled tradesman

History of alcohol abuse

Bob

This is the information Jaime has about Bob. She'll continue to look out for strengths and challenges so that she can add them later.

Next, Jaime will add Patricia (see Figure 6.6).

FIGURE 6.6 ● Couple

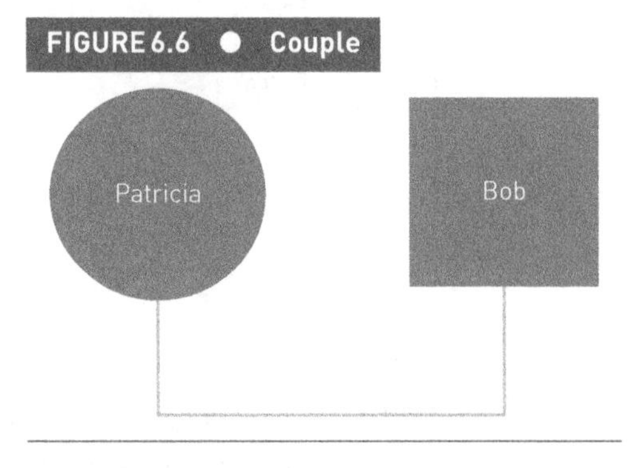

These symbols would also include material such as important information about Patricia. The information is likely to include challenges facing Patricia, like her concern for her relationships with both Bob and Sam. It also could include strengths, like her ongoing support to Bob despite her experience of him as a person abusing alcohol. All of these individual characteristics may cross generations and may help to identify family resources. For example, Patricia's mother may be an accomplished cook, which is something Patricia excels at as well. Cooking might be identified as something they both could share with Sam.

Next, Jaime will add another generation to the genogram (see Figure 6.7).

FIGURE 6.7 ● Expanding the Genogram

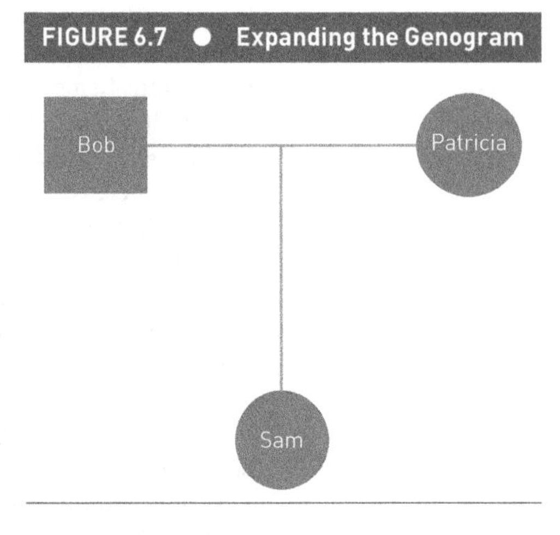

Next, another generation will be added so that Bob and Patricia's parents can be identified.

Finally, Jaime will use lines to indicate relationships among the family members. Where she doesn't know much about the relationship, she just leaves the genogram as it is. Where she does know about the types and importance of relationships, she'll use different types of lines to describe significant relationships. For example, she'll use two parallel lines to indicate a very close relationship, a dotted line to show a distant relationship, and a saw-toothed line to show a relationship filled with tension. Deaths are indicated by an X over the person's symbol. When a client or family and worker collaborate to identify the types of relationships that exist among family members, the family may develop important insights. It is powerful to see relationships in a diagram. Next is the genogram Jaime created with Bob, Patricia, and Sam (see Figure 6.8).

WHAT IF . . . FOCUS ON DIVERSITY

Jaime is considerably younger than Bob. How do you think this will help or hinder her ability to get Bob and his family to share assessment information? How do you think the assessment would go if Jaime were Bob's age?

FIGURE 6.8 • The Multiple Generation Genogram

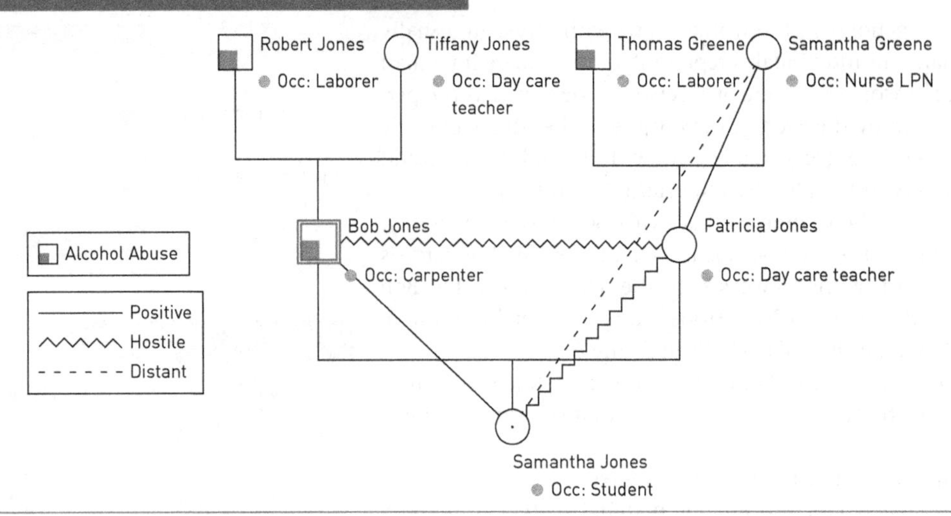

You read the genogram just as you would read a chart or a table. Start with the big picture (usually the title), and then gradually zoom in. We see here that the genogram is about the Roberts family and that it consists of three generations. Bob and Patricia both have two parents living, and they have one daughter, Sam. Information about three generations helps to identify future relationships and important characteristics that may be inherited. Both Bob's father and Patricia's father have histories of alcohol abuse. With this information, Jaime would be concerned about the potential for Sam to be at risk for addiction-related behaviors and mental health issues (Tootle, Ziegler, & Singer, 2015). Jaime will make sure there is information and prevention services in place before she closes this case.

Take a look at relationships as they appear on the genogram. Patricia has a tense relationship with both Bob and Sam. That makes her the most vulnerable person in the family. While Bob is sometimes worried about what he perceives to be her moodiness, he has an enduring relationship with her. Like Patricia, he recognizes that their marriage is filled with tension. It's important to note that Patricia's mother, Samantha, may be a resource for the family. The two women are close and could potentially find ways to include Sam in their relationship. Jaime will explore whether Samantha can help to connect Patricia and Sam and, if so, whether she needs some supports to do that. For example, Patricia and Samantha, may need help finding transportation to visit at each other's homes rather than maintaining their relationship mostly by telephone and text messaging.

Given these considerations, it's clear that the genogram helps both the worker and the client to identify strengths, challenges, and possible resources. Jaime may leave a copy with the family.

Diversity in Genograms

The genogram can be used with diverse family forms (Genopro, 2016; McGoldrick et al., 1999). It serves the same function as any other genogram, but it can also serve to help family members recognize that their family structure is just as legitimate as any other (see Figure 6.9). Seeing the genogram in writing and sharing it with others helps to make it seem real (Berger & Luckmann, 1967).

FIGURE 6.9 • Diverse Genogram Elements

For example, you could indicate a same-sex couple simply like this:

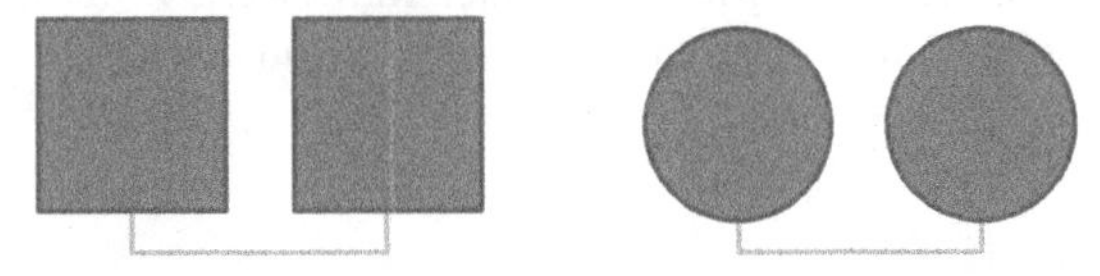

You would show adoption and foster care like this:

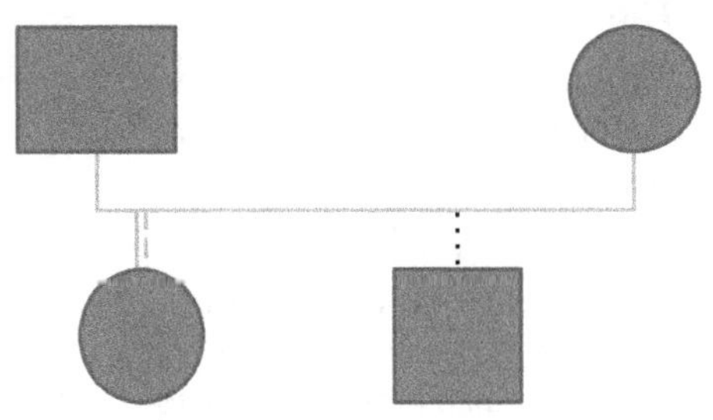

Gay individuals can be charted like this:

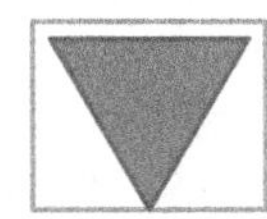

And you might consider depicting transgender people like this:

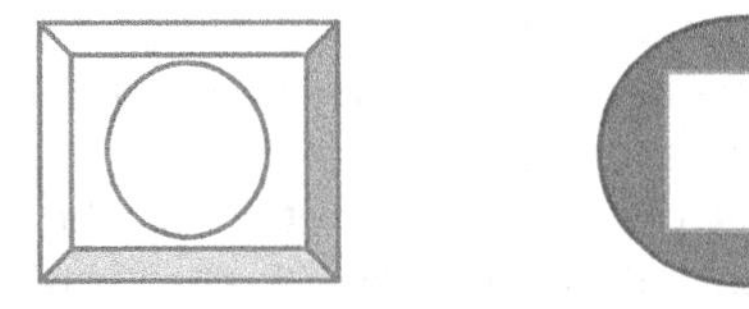

Finally, to show marriage, divorce, and cohabitation, here is a graph of a woman who is divorced and living with a person in a new relationship:

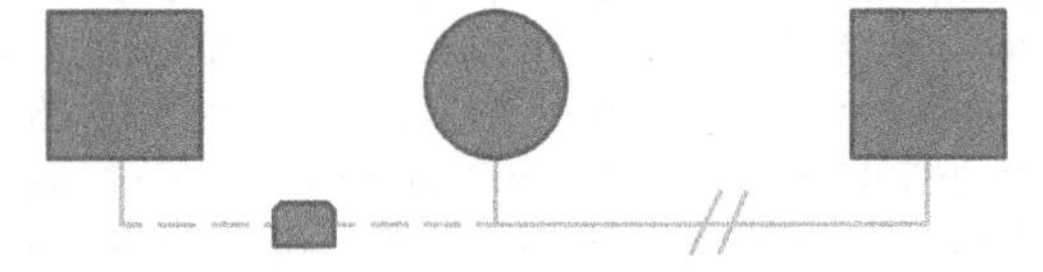

Finally, in her new relationship she may have a pet:

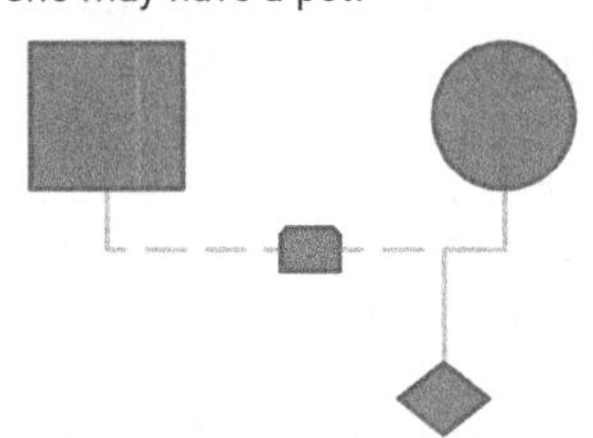

CRITICAL THINKING AND COLLABORATIVE LEARNING EXERCISES 6.6

Create your own genogram of at least three generations. Interview family members to get as much information as you can. Carefully consider why you didn't have all of the information as well as any information that people were reluctant to share. Use these thoughts to develop empathy for a client who is sharing genogram information with a worker they just met. How can the worker facilitate the interview?

Section 6.7: Ecomaps

A Snapshot of Systems

Like the genogram, an **ecomap** provides a diagram for both worker and clients to gain insights into a case. This section covers the ecomap in practice.

FIGURE 6.10 • Diagramming a Societal Institution

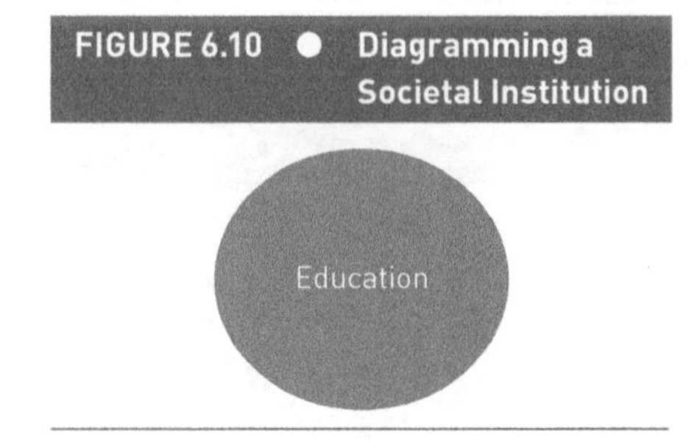

What Is an Ecomap?

Like a genogram, an ecomap is a visual aid to the planned change process. In a way, it is a picture of the PIE perspective. Instead of showing a family, though, the ecomap provides a way to visualize the social environment. The idea is to create a picture that reflects the systems as they interact with and around the client. What might the systems be? Remember that we discussed systems as made up of two or more related elements. They can be people, families, or broader social institutions like government or religion. Multilevel assessment suggests a number of those systems.

Again, the diagram includes circles. This time, though, the circles represent systems rather than individuals. For example, to diagram education as an environmental system, we would simply write what we see in Figure 6.10.

The ecomap then simply grows by adding a series of circles. Each represents one of the systems included in the assessment process (see Figure 6.11).

Like the genogram, the ecomap can also be completed with the client or client representative as a way to help both client and worker to see the systems within their environment. Jaime and the Roberts family collaborated to develop an ecomap that reflected the relevant systems. Jaime referenced her assessment of the systems to create the ecomap. She used lines to indicate the relationships among the systems. Remember that all systems have boundaries that may be more or less permeable. The system boundaries allow energy exchange that—if it is an even exchange—may enhance both systems through synergy. Systems may be out of balance and deplete energy. Remember that this process is called entropy.

Jaime began the ecomap by the creating a circle for Bob. She decided to work with all of the family members, but her agency's purpose in this case was to respond to Bob's concerns related to alcohol abuse. As a result, the agency recognized Bob as the **identified client.** The family-in-environment (FIE) perspective we discussed earlier taught Jaime to focus on the family as a whole, though, so she created a circle for family members that could be called the **target system** (Pincus & Minahan, 1973) since she'd be working Patricia and Sam as well. Note that Samantha is listed as a family member on the ecomap since Jaime suspected she might have an important role to play in the planned change process.

In the ecomap, lines show relationships just like in the genogram. Solid lines indicate connection, so they are generally representative of relationships that are strengths. Jagged lines indicate challenges, so they generally reflect systems out of balance or potential implementation sites. Dotted lines indicate tenuous relationships. These are often potential resources so they can be sites for implementation as well.

FIGURE 6.11 ● Ecomap Elements

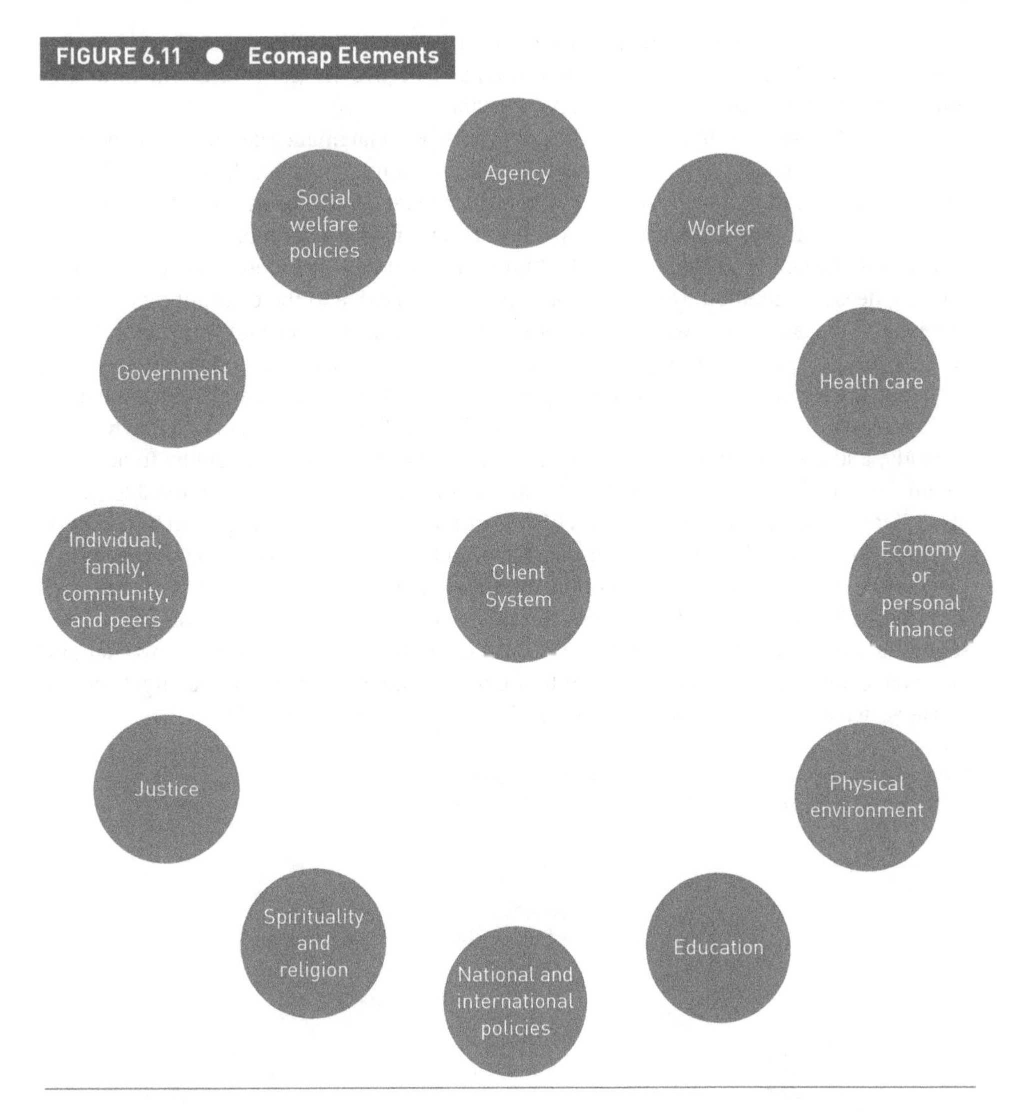

Jaime used a jagged line to reflect the tension between Sam and school since Sam was having some behavioral challenges there. She used a straight line to indicate the mutual relationship she was building between herself and the family as well as with Bob as an individual. Because her relationship with her agency was a mutually positive one, she indicated that with a solid line showing an arrow going in both directions.

At the same time Jaime experienced a positive relationship with the agency, the family was experiencing tension due to the extensive amount of time Bob was spending attending support groups there—time that was resented by both Patricia and Sam. On the other hand, Bob and the family were getting help through the services Jaime was providing. For this reason, there is a line of tension as well as a solid line between the agency and the family.

The employment and social policy circles are also connected to the family, because of the policy that facilitates Bob's paid leave when he needed it in the past for alcohol-related time off and when he needs it in the present for his appointments with Jaime. It is important to note that line of tension because it may turn out that it is the aid leave policy itself that is the problem. In that case, the policy could become the target system.

The positive experience the family experienced with health care resulted from Bob's health care insurance that he received through his job, allowing all of the family members to access health care. For this reason, health care is connected to the family. A solid line reflected this relationship.

The physical environment represents a challenge for the family, since all family members, especially Patricia, worried about the repairs needed in the house and how they affected both long-term maintenance and appearance.

An area of tension existed between the family and personal finance because the family had a number of challenges related to finances. Patricia was unhappy about the household maintenance that went undone due to a lack of funds for materials as well as Bob's preoccupation in the past with his addiction and in the present with his recovery. Materials needed to be purchased, and the family needed to consider hiring a handyman to respond to some of the most pressing needs. In addition, transportation was a challenge due to the constant maintenance required on the family car. Neither Bob nor Patricia was careful with a budget and didn't consciously set budgeting priorities, so they ended up using their adequate income in ways that didn't make them happy. These represent potential areas for goal setting and implementation.

For **spirituality and religion**, Jaime drew a solid line. The family attended church together regularly, and this represented the one activity that they carried out as a family. In addition, spirituality was closely tied to the group Bob attended. Although he wasn't comfortable talking about it much, he reported that he found his sense of spirituality to be a support in his recovery.

Finally, note that there is a relationship between the school and national policies. While local school boards make many school-related decisions, they are guided by state and federal law. In this case, federal law does not require that a social worker be present in every school. If Jaime has a lot of clients like Sam that would benefit from a social worker and don't have one at school, she may want to use the federal or local policy as a target system.

Here's what the Roberts family's ecomap looked like. See Figure 6.12.

FIGURE 6.12 ● Bob, Patricia, and Samantha

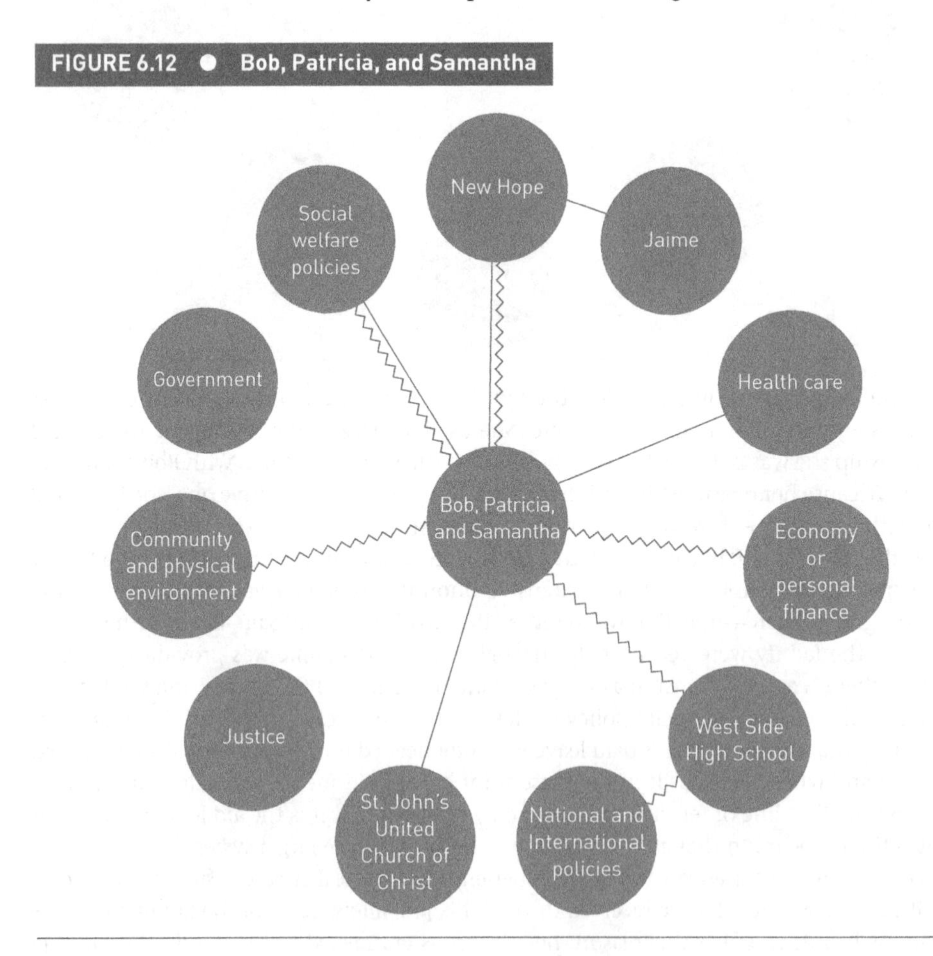

Once Jaime documented the findings from her assessment, she gave thought to which systems interact in relation to Bob's situation of concern. She scheduled a meeting with Bob to identify system interactions that might be unbalanced, or marked by uneven energy exchanges, and to prioritize areas for planned change in those system interactions. Prior to the meeting, she gathered her thoughts about which system interactions she might point out to Bob. Otherwise, she kept her mind open to his ideas of areas of strengths and those of challenges. She planned to develop hypotheses about where successful, multisystem change efforts might be made and looked forward to the planning phase, which would be composed of that activity.

An organized office can be facilitated by self-reflection.

The Overwhelmed Worker—Reflective Responses

Jaime was honest in her self-reflection. She practiced the form of mindfulness that has been discussed in depth in Chapter 4. She acknowledged that her office was full of files. She admitted that there were Saturdays when she came back to the office to catch up on paperwork, and she was dismayed to face the reality that there were times when she rushed Bob because she was used to moving from task to task at a high speed. Her worries about paperwork even broke into her thoughts as she was meeting with Bob. Bob could easily have sensed her urgency and stopped answering rapid-fire questions.

Jaime carried out the "What do I feel/believe/know/do?" exercise and found that she felt anxious and overwhelmed and that she believed the agency's policies were to blame for her feelings. That's what she'd been thinking for weeks. When she attempted to answer the "What do I know?" component, though, she had to engage in critical thinking. She realized that she assumed the workload was to blame, but she needed to investigate that assumption.

Jaime's response to her reflection was to ask her supervisor to tell her whether all of the other workers were feeling as overwhelmed as she was. When she found out some were and some weren't, she asked to have a discussion at a staff meeting where people could share their coping mechanisms.

CRITICAL THINKING AND COLLABORATIVE LEARNING EXERCISES 6.7

Work with a partner. Give your partner enough information so they can draw an ecomap with you of you and your environment. Reverse. Discuss how you feel about sharing the information with someone else.

Section 6.8: Review and Apply

CONCURRENT CONSIDERATIONS IN GENERALIST PRACTICE

Ethical Decision-Making Challenge

A few days after the family meeting, Sam called Jaime to say that she was worried about her own addictive behaviors. Jaime is used to working with adults that have problems with substance abuse. See Section 1.04 to help Jaime determine whether she can help Sam.

Evidence-Based Practice

Find out whether there is any evidence that substance abuse support groups based on spirituality are successful for clients like Bob and Sam.

Policies Impacting Practice

Find out the age at which a young person may seek substance abuse treatment without their parents' permission.

Managing Diversity

Sam's areas of diversity are not necessarily those of her family. In what ways might she be different?

Multisystem Practice

Identify examples of Jaime's work on all levels.

Micro: ______________________

Mezzo: ______________________

Macro: ______________________

Dynamic and Interactive Planned Change Stages

Identify the aspects of Jaime's work with the family that were addressing the following stages:

Self-Reflection: ______________________

Engagement: ______________________

Assessment: ______________________

Planning: ______________________

Implementation: ______________________

Evaluation: ______________________

Termination and Follow-Up: ______________________

Summary

Section 6.1: Assessment and Multisystem Practice

During assessment, the worker continues the engagement process and works with the client to identify the systems that form the environment of the client system. Assessment may be greatly facilitated by meeting with the client in their home.

Section 6.2: Evidence-Based Practice

Home visits offer unique opportunities for workers to meet clients in their physical environment and conduct thorough assessments. A concern with family visits is risks to the worker's safety. Many of these risks can be avoided using some evidence-based precautions.

Section 6.3: The Practice of Multisystem Practice

To formulate a comprehensive assessment, the worker and the client system representative work together to identify systems whose energy exchange may not be in balance. Those systems include the worker; the agency; health care; economy or personal finance; physical environment; education; **national and international policies**; spirituality and religion; justice; individual, families, community, and peers; government; and social welfare policies.

Section 6.4: First Steps in Assessment

The worker is the first consideration in assessment, as the worker is in charge of facilitating the planned change process. Self-reflection is the beginning of work with any client system. Likewise, every social work interview takes place in the context of the agency, so assessment of the agency policies as they relate to a particular client system is also one of the first parts of assessment.

Section 6.5: Multisystem Assessment in Practice

The worker works with the client using verbal and nonverbal skills to continue the relationship established during engagement to identify the relevant strengths of the system as well as the challenges it faces. The worker approaches assessment with the idea that diversity may reflect areas of strength and resources.

Section 6.6: The Genogram

The genogram is a graphic that depicts family members and their relationships through at least three generations. It is a visual aid that helps the worker to collaborate with clients and client system representatives to better understand their family members and their relationships with them.

Section 6.7: Ecomaps

The ecomap is a visual aid that helps the worker to collaborate with clients and client system representatives to better understand their relationships to the systems around them. It depicts the PIE perspective.

SELF-REFLECTION 6: FAMILY CELEBRATIONS INDEX

PURPOSE: To measure a family's special events

AUTHORS: Hamilton I. McCubbin and Anne I. Thompson

DESCRIPTION: The Family Celebrations Index (FCEL) is a nine-item instrument designed to measure family celebrations, or the extent to which a family celebrates special events. The basis for this measure is that celebrations can be viewed as facilitators of family functioning and perhaps as indicators of family strengths.

RELIABILITY: The FCEL has fair internal consistency with an alpha of .69.

VALIDITY: The FCEL has good concurrent validity with significant correlations with several family scales.

PRIMARY REFERENCE:

McCubbin, L. D., McCubbin, H. I., & Sievers, J. A. (Eds.). (2013). *Family well-being: Stress, coping, resilience—Assessment measurements for research and practice*. In K. Corcoran & J. Fischer (Eds.), *Measures for clinical practice and research: A sourcebook* (5th ed.). New York, NY: Oxford University Press.

Please read each special event or occasion, and decide how often your family celebrates (i.e., takes time and effort to appreciate the event or special situation) on these occasions. Please circle the appropriate answer: Never (0), Seldom (1), Often (2), and Always (3). Please respond to all items.

We celebrate these special moments:

(Continued)

(Continued)

We Celebrate These Special Moments:	Never	Seldom	Often	Always	Not Applicable
Friend's special events	0	1	2	3	No friends
Children's birthday(s)	0	1	2	3	No children
Relatives' birthdays or anniversaries	0	1	2	3	No relatives
Spouses' birthdays	0	1	2	3	No spouse
Religious occasions (holy days, etc.)	0	1	2	3	
Yearly major holidays (i.e., 4th of July, New Year)	0	1	2	3	
Occasions (i.e., Valentine's Day, Mother's Day)	0	1	2	3	
Special changes and events (i.e., graduation, promotion)	0	1	2	3	None to celebrate
Special surprises and successes (i.e., passed a test, good report card)	0	1	2	3	None to celebrate

Note: Please do not distribute without permission from the author Jason Sievers jasievers@gmail.com.

Recommended Websites

Alcoholics Anonymous: www.aa.org

Critical Terms for Assessment

diagnosis 168
home visits 169
physical safety 170
justice 170
psychological safety 171
vicarious trauma 171
professional safety 173
malpractice insurance 173
health care 178
education 179
government 179
social welfare policies 179
intake form 180
physical environment 181
genogram 184
kinship care 184
ecomap 188
identified client 188
target system 188
spirituality and religion 190
national and international policies 192

Generalist Practice Curriculum Matrix With 2015 Educational Policy and Accreditation Standards

Chapter 6

Competency	Course	Course Content	Dimensions
Competency 1: Demonstrate Ethical and Professional Behavior		Feature 3: Self-Reflection Feature 4: Concurrent Considerations in Generalist Practice	Cognitive-affective processes Knowledge Skills Skills Cognitive-affective processes
Competency 2: Engage Diversity and Difference in Practice		Feature 1: Focus on Diversity Feature 4: Concurrent Considerations in Generalist Practice	Values Skills Cognitive-affective processes Skills Cognitive-affective processes Skills Cognitive-affective processes
Competency 3: Advance Human Rights and Social, Economic, and Environmental Justice		Feature 4: Concurrent Considerations in Generalist Practice	Skills Cognitive-affective processes
Competency 4: Engage in Practice-Informed Research and Research-Informed Practice		Feature 4: Concurrent Considerations in Generalist Practice	Knowledge Skills Cognitive-affective processes
Competency 5: Engage in Policy Practice			
Competency 6: Engage With Individuals, Families, Groups, Organizations, and Communities		Feature 4: Concurrent Considerations in Generalist Practice	Cognitive-affective processes Skills Cognitive-affective processes
Competency 7: Assess Individuals, Families, Groups, Organizations, and Communities		6.1. Describe the role of the worker in facilitating the planned change process during assessment and compare assessment and diagnosis. 6.3. Summarize the assessment process with multisystem practice (MSP). 6.4. Demonstrate the role of the worker and the agency in the assessment phase. 6.5. Recall multisystem practice (MSP) in assessment, and prepare to identify situation-specific target systems. 6.6. Practice the use of a genogram in the assessment process.	Skills Cognitive-affective processes

(Continued)

(Continued)

Competency	Course	Course Content	Dimensions
		6.7. Practice the use of an ecomap in the assessment process. Feature 4: Concurrent Considerations in Generalist Practice	
Competency 8: Intervene With Individuals, Families, Groups, Organizations, and Communities		6.2. Explain home visits and safety issues related to them. Feature 4: Concurrent Considerations in Generalist Practice	Skills Cognitive-affective processes
Competency 9: Evaluate Practice With Individuals, Families, Groups, Organizations, and Communities		Feature 4: Concurrent Considerations in Generalist Practice	Skills Cognitive-affective processes

References

Allen, S. F., & Tracy, E. M. (2004). Revitalizing the role of home visiting by school social workers. *Children & Schools, 26*(4), 197–208.

American Psychiatric Association. (2013). *The diagnostic and statistical manual of mental disorders* (5th ed.). Washington, DC: Author.

Baird, K., & Kracen, A. C. (2006). Vicarious traumatization and traumatic secondary stress: A research synthesis. *Counseling Psychology Quarterly, 19*(2), 181–188.

Berger, P. L., & Luckmann, T. (1967). *The social construction of reality: A treatise on the sociology of knowledge*. Garden City, NY: Anchor Books.

Cox, K., & Steiner, S. (2013). Preserving commitment to social work service through the prevention of vicarious trauma. *Journal of Social Work Values and Ethics, 10*(1), 52–59.

Cunningham, M. (2003). Impact of trauma work on social work clinicians: Empirical findings. *Social Work, 48*(4), 451–459.

Erikson, E. H. (1968). *Identity, youth and crisis*. New York, NY: Norton.

Genopro. (2016). Family relationships in genograms. Retrieved from https://www.genopro.com/genogram/family-relationships

Goffman, E. (1959). *The presentation of self in everyday life*. Garden City, NY: Doubleday.

Hanna, E. P. (2013). A cognitive emotional methodology for critical thinking. *Advances in Applied Sociology, 3*(1), 20–25.

Karger, H. J., & Stoesz, D. (2014). *American social welfare policy: A pluralist approach* (7th ed.). Boston: Pearson.

Kirst-Ashman, K. K., & Hull, G. (2018). *Generalist social work practice*. Stamford, CT: Cengage.

Larkin, S. (2018). *A field guide for social workers: Applying your generalist training*. Thousand Oaks, CA: Sage.

Lyter, S., & Abbott, A. A. (2007). Home visits in a violent world. *The Clinical Supervisor, 26*(1/2), 17–33.

McCubbin, L. D., McCubbin, H. I., & Sievers, J. A. (Eds.). (2013). Family well-being: Stress, coping, resilience—Assessment measurements for research and practice. In K. Corcoran & J. Fischer (Eds.), *Measures for clinical practice and research: A sourcebook* (5th ed.). New York, NY: Oxford University Press.

McGoldrick, M., Gerson, R., & Shellenberger, S. (1999). *Genograms: Assessment and intervention.* New York, NY: W.W. Norton.

Miley, K. K., O'Melia, M. W., & DuBois, B. L. (2013). *Generalist social work practice: An empowering approach.* Boston, MA: Pearson.

National Association of Social Workers. (2018). *NASW code of ethics.* Washington, DC: NASW Press.

Pincus, A., & Minahan, A. (1973). *Social work practice: Model and method.* Itasca, IL: F. E. Peacock.

Richmond, M. (2012). *Social diagnosis.* Retrieved from www.forgottenbooks.org. (Original work published 1917)

Ryan, J. P., & Yang, H. (2005). Family contact and recidivism: A longitudinal study of adjudicated delinquents in residential care. *Social Work Research, 29*(1), 31–39.

Tootle, W., Ziegler, J., & Singer, M. (2015). Individuals are continents; or, Why it's time to retire the island approach to addiction. *Substance Use and Misuse, 50*(8), 1037–1043. doi:10.3109/10826084.2015.1007684

Recommended Readings

Goffman, E. (1959). *The presentation of self in everyday life.* Garden City, NY: Doubleday.

7 Planning

This chapter covers the planning portion of planned change. It also continues the discussion of the phases of social process. Beginnings have been discussed; this chapter carries on with the middle phase. Motivational interviewing (MI) is presented as a possible approach to goal setting.

Learning Objectives

7.1 Learn the planning process in the context of self-reflection and assessment.

7.2 Review the use of visual support via genograms in planning.

7.3 Review the use of visual support via ecomaps in planning.

7.4 Articulate a method for planning using motivational interviewing (MI).

7.5 Demonstrate understanding of the process of goal development for future evaluation.

7.6 Paraphrase a method of budgeting that can be shared with clients.

CASE STUDY: CHILD WELFARE INVESTIGATION

Susan hung her coat in her cubicle. Just as she sat down at her desk she dashed off a quick text to her daughter to wish her good luck on her first college exams. Susan's day began like any other. The light on her desk phone was blinking, letting her know there was a message, undoubtedly a case that needed immediate action. Susan held back a sigh. The law required that Susan begin an investigation today to determine whether neglect allegations were substantiated, or demonstrated to be true, so she knew she should begin as soon as possible. In this case, a neighbor reported three children under the age of 10 left unattended in the afternoons. Apparently, the kids made a ruckus, alternatively arguing, laughing, and crying as they played ball in the apartment building hallway. Using the information she had, Susan identified the truancy officer from the children's elementary school to find out whether they had been attending school regularly. Emily, William, and Jayden Smith were unfamiliar names to the truancy officer,

SpeedKingz/Shutterstock.com

Potentially harmful conflict can arise when children are unattended.

meaning they'd been regularly attending school. So far, so good. When Susan called the school nurse, though, she learned a different story. The nurse was in a long process of requesting that the Smith children get their annual checkups. That meant there was a possibility of one of the children needing medical care that they weren't getting. That afternoon, Susan took a moment to think about the Smith family. She sat quietly and identified the feeling she often felt at the beginning of cases . . . anger. *How could a parent leave their kids unattended? Who knew what might happen? And how could a parent choose not to take their kids to the doctor for a checkup and the shots they needed?* Then Susan spent some time connecting with how it felt when her own kids were small. She had been a single mom, and she immediately got anxious just thinking about how she rushed to get to the day care on time each evening, how she struggled with guilt when the kids didn't feel well but had to go to daycare anyway. After considering those thoughts, she was able to think critically about her angry feelings. She believed a mom who was neglectful was uncaring, but that wasn't necessarily the case. She knew many parents worked hard to be sure they gave their kids the best care possible. At that point, she started to feel empathy for a parent who wasn't able to mind their kids. Whatever the circumstances, there was likely to be a lot of anxiety involved. With that preparation, she looked forward to helping the mom in this case. She arrived at the Smith apartment at 5:00 in the evening and found the expected unruly play in the hallway. Emily was trying to get William to give Jayden the ball while Jayden sobbed loudly. Susan grabbed a tissue from her purse and bent to wipe Jayden's nose. Instantly all of the kids became silent at the presence of this strange grownup. Just then, Brittany Smith walked in from work and looked suspiciously at Susan. Susan reached out to shake hands with Brittany, who hesitated before returning the gesture. Susan briefly explained who she was and where she worked. She said right away that her job was to see whether the kids were okay and that she was not interested in taking them from their home. She could see Brittany become angry and had to ask if they could all go into the apartment. Once inside, Susan smiled brightly as Brittany quickly removed toys from the sofa so Brittany could sit down. Susan explained that she needed to get some information and apologized that she'd have to take notes. It didn't take long for her to discover that Brittany worked at a restaurant from 9:00 to 5:00 and that the bus didn't get her home until 5:30. The kids got home from school at 4:30, so there was an hour each day when Brittany was not there. Emily had a key to the apartment and let all of them in. Shortly after that, the problems began.

Section 7.1: Assessment and Multisystem Practice

This section provides the context for the planning stage of the planned change process. Susan efficiently managed her feelings so that she could develop empathy for the clients in this case. She quickly developed a tenuous relationship with Brittany, so this section begins with a discussion about the assessment information she gathered.

Assessment and Multisystem Practice

As Susan asked Brittany the questions on her intake form, she kept in mind the categories of multisystem practice (MSP) assessment. She completed some of the categories before the interview, based on what she knew about the case. Then she was able to jot down items in the assessment table as she completed her agency's intake process. Here is the chart she completed using her own form of shorthand as she spoke with Brittany and the three children:

Multisystem Practice in Action

System	Strengths and Diversity	Challenge
Social worker: *Susan*	Openness, self-awareness, reflection Many years' experience; committed to work; good educational foundation; carried out "I feel, I believe, I know, I do" process with open mind	Must work to maintain empathy
Agency	Activities based on federal and state law	Staff can be overworked; substantial documentation requirements
Client system representative: Brittany (24), Emily (8), William (6), and Jayden (3)	Biological, psychological, cultural aspects: Power, privilege, identity Cares about kids, single moms common in area Doesn't face discrimination at work where some members of minority groups have a difficult time being hired Kids have friends and like teachers	Biological, psychological, cultural aspects: Discriminations Consistent child care is needed; single mom status can have negative connotations such as during job search Mom: Needs emotional and physical respite Needs opportunity to get kids for physicals History of good relationship with mother and peers = potential for development; relationship with landlord could be improved (past late payments = slow to complete repairs)
Health care	Medical assistance for family	Finding the co-pay could be hard Need for kids' checkups and shots
Economy or personal finance	Has full-time job that is expected to last	Needs to develop financial capacity
Physical environment	Neighborhood considered safe	Broken window unsafe
Education	All children attend school regularly. Brittany has a high school diploma.	Emily is experiencing some behavioral problems in school. After-school program?
National and international policies	State policy allows medical assistance; federal and state policies offer service in alleged neglect situations for safety and risk assessments	
Spirituality and religion	Brittany has fond memories of church attendance and community	Church may help support family
Justice	Family visitation available for father who is incarcerated	Need to consider whether child–father relationship would be positive for kids
Individual, family, community, and peers	History of positive relationship with mother but broke off due to disapproval of Brittany and William (kids' dad)	Relationship with children's father cut off Possible for Brittany to improve relationship with mother?
Government		Little knowledge of local government—how to report negligent landlord if needed
Social welfare policies	Federal policy allows possible follow-up service to help stabilize family if neglect can be corrected.	Very extreme cases: Courts can be petitioned to remove children from the home

CRITICAL THINKING AND COLLABORATIVE LEARNING EXERCISES 7.1

1. Work with a partner. Identify some time when you normally do two things at once. Maybe you play a computer game while watching your favorite show with friends. Maybe you study your Spanish vocabulary when you are at a stoplight.
2. Why do you think you're able to do these things at the same time?
3. What's the risk of something going wrong?
4. In what situation could you complete a questionnaire such as an intake form while considering the categories of the assessment chart?

Section 7.2: Smith Family Genogram

In this section, we'll review the use of the genogram.

As Susan and Brittany collaborated on identifying the makeup of Brittany's family, a lot of information became available. The **genogram** reflected the individuals as well as their relationships to each other (see Figure 7.1).

Reading the Genogram

We can see that the genogram is about the Smith family and that it consists of three generations. This is a strength in and of itself. Some families don't know much about their family members. Emily has information about her grandparents that allows Susan to enter them on the genogram, helping to identify future relationships and important characteristics that may be inherited. Three of the grandparents have passed away—one related to an addiction and another to a possible suicide. With this information,

FIGURE 7.1

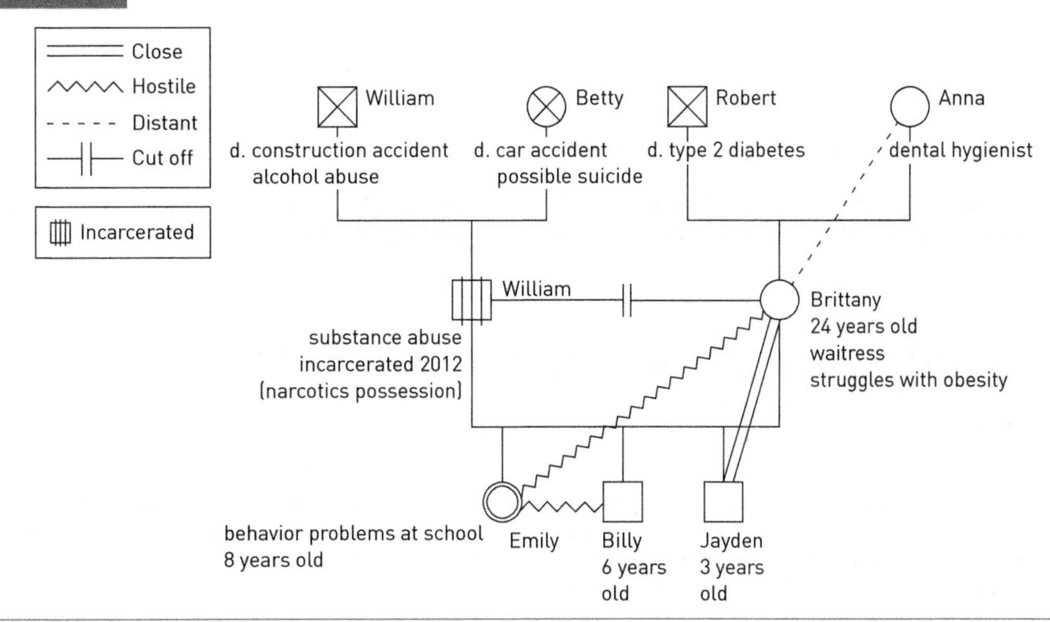

Susan would be concerned about the potential for other family members to be at risk for addiction-related behaviors and mental health issues (Tootle, Ziegler, & Singer, 2015). Susan will make sure there is information and prevention service in place before she closes this case. She may suggest a psychological evaluation to family members who seem to be at risk. It's also important to note the presence of diabetes in the grandparents' generation. Although it's not directly inheritable, type 2 diabetes in one family member puts others at higher risk (Collins, Ryan, & Truby, 2014). Next, it's possible to see that Emily's mother copes as a single mother and is successful in holding down a job. She struggles with obesity, which means she is at serious risk for diabetes. This highlights a physical health concern for Brittany and the need for medical assessment and either medical treatment or prevention services. In a case like Brittany's, where there is concern about a physical problem, the worker immediately makes a referral to a medical professional to have the situation evaluated. Emily's father is incarcerated and, like his father, he suffers from addiction. Susan will attempt to get more information about him as her work with Brittany and Emily continues. Moving to the next generation, note that Emily is 8 and she has two brothers, Billy and Jayden, who are ages 6 and 3.

Finally, take a look at relationships as they appear on the genogram. Emily has a tense relationship with both Billy and her mother. That makes her the most vulnerable person in the family. Brittany has a strong relationship with Jayden but not the other children. It's important to note that Brittany's mother, Anna, may be a resource for the family. Brittany is not close to her mother right now, but there is not a tense relationship. Susan will explore whether Anna can be a resource to Brittany and, if so, whether she needs some supports to do that. For example, Anna may be willing to babysit, but she may need help in getting beds and age-appropriate toys at her house. William may also be a resource. Although Brittany is cut off from him and he is currently incarcerated, he could still have a relationship with Emily and her brothers. Susan will explore the possibility.

In addition to facilitating assessment, completing the genogram helped reinforce the engagement that was developing between Susan and the family. It helped everyone visualize the family with its strengths, challenges, and possible resources. To continue to set up the possibility for concrete planning, Susan needed to complete an **ecomap**.

WHAT IF . . . FOCUS ON DIVERSITY

Susan is considerably older than Brittany. How do you think this will help or hinder her ability to get Brittany to share assessment information? How do you think the assessment would go if Susan were Brittany's age?

CRITICAL THINKING AND COLLABORATIVE LEARNING EXERCISES 7.2

Find a willing friend, and complete their genogram for as many generations as possible. Leave a copy with them so they can interview family members and fill in the blanks. Then exchange roles. Each of you should interview family members and check back in with your partner to share information and discuss how it felt to conduct the interviews.

Section 7.3: Smith Family Ecomap

Ecomaps

This section covers the ecomap in Emily's case.

The Ecomap in Practice

Susan and Brittany collaborated to develop an ecomap that reflected the relevant systems. Susan referenced her assessment of the systems to create the ecomap. She used lines to indicate the relationships among the systems. Remember that all systems have boundaries that may be more or less permeable. The system boundaries allow energy exchange that—if it is an even exchange—may enhance both systems through synergy. Systems may be out of balance and deplete energy. Remember that this process is called entropy.

Susan began the ecomap by creating a circle for Emily. She decided to work with all of the family members, but her agency's purpose in this case was to respond to a possible child neglect situation with Emily. As a result, the agency recognized Emily as the **identified client.** The family-in-environment (FIE) perspective taught Susan to focus on the family as a whole, though, so she created a circle for family members that could be called the **target system** (Pincus & Minahan, 1973) since she'd be working with Brittany and assessing the needs of all three children. Note that both William and Anna are listed as family members just as they appear on the genogram. Susan used a jagged line to reflect the tension between Emily and Brittany as well as Emily and Billy.

On the ecomap, she used a straight line to indicate the mutual relationship she was building between herself and the family as well as with Emily as an individual. Because her relationship with her agency was a mutually positive one, she indicated that with a solid line.

At the same time, Susan experienced a positive relationship with the agency, the family was experiencing tension due to the neglect investigation. If all goes as well as possible, the investigation will be closed and the Smith family will have received services. At that point, the jagged line would become solid to indicate a positive relationship. The social welfare policy circle is also connected to the family because of the policy that requires the investigation of possible child neglect. It is important to note that line of tension because it may turn out that it is the policy itself that is the problem. In that case, the policy could become the target system.

Because of the support Brittany received from some neighbors who were also single mothers, another solid line went between the physical environment and the family. This line represents the neighborhood and represents a potential resource for the family.

The positive experience the family had with health care resulted from medical assistance, a social welfare policy, so both of those systems were shown as connected to the family. A solid line reflected the positive relationship between social welfare policies and health care. This is another resource; Susan would make sure that the family received all of the health care benefits available to them.

The institution of government interacted positively with the family due to laws that regulated landlords. This relationship among systems reveals that the family gets positive energy from that system in that they have some legal protections related to their apartment. Government was tied tenuously to justice, though, since the landlord was not following laws related to the upkeep of rental properties.

An area of tension existed between the family and personal finance because Brittany had challenges with a number of related systems: She had insufficient income for her needs and she had limited budgeting skills. These represent potential areas for goal setting and intervention. Note that the line between education and personal finance shows a tenuous connection. In this way, you can see that the systems of education and personal finance could have a more positive relationship: Personal finance could be taught in public schools. This represents a potential area for intervention that is outside direct work with the family. At some point in the future, Susan could work through her school board to get some level of personal finance education put into the regular curriculum.

The tension Emily felt in school where she was having trouble with behavioral issues was reflected with another jagged line. Still, another jagged line reflected the tensions due to the investigation: National policy regulated child welfare services and the justice system enforced any violations. For now, the family experienced tension from both reflecting the most important challenges faced by the family.

For spirituality and religion, Susan drew a dotted line. This was an area where there was a tenuous relationship. Remember that Brittany had good memories of her past experiences with church, but she did not currently practice any spiritual rituals or experience any religious community.

Finally, note here is another situation where the school would benefit from a social worker. Susan may target that system for policy level change.

Figure 7.2 shows what the Smith family's ecomap looked like.

FIGURE 7.2 ●

CRITICAL THINKING AND COLLABORATIVE LEARNING EXERCISES 7.3

You made an ecomap of your own during your work in the last chapter. Revisit it, and note whether any system relationships have changed. Are there any you would like to see changed?

Section 7.4: Establishing Goals

Susan will need to work with Brittany to establish goals next. This section describes an evidence-based method for carrying out the planning stage of planned change: motivational interviewing (MI).

Filling in the Boxes of Planned Change

Remember that a method of practice like the planned change process is a social worker's way of **partializing practice**, or taking a situation that is complex and making it manageable. As we've said, all of the planned change stages occur at the same time, but overall they are followed as a process from beginning to end.

Think of the planned change process as a series of boxes. The boxes, taken one by one, are guides to practice. Within each box, the social worker occupies several roles and implements a number of skills based on evidence-based theories of change and methods of practice. Each case provides an opportunity to consider the relevant theories and their implementation. Social work roles, skills, and a number of theories and methods of practice will be discussed later in this book. One method of practice, though, works especially well in the planning stage: motivational interviewing (or MI).

Foundations of Motivational Interviewing

Motivational interviewing (MI) has been described as a conversation about change. Founded by research practitioners around 1982, it is a method of planned change that has been demonstrated to meet help meet planned change goals in over 200 randomized clinical trials (Miller & Rollnick, 2013). Keep in mind that a randomized clinical trial is the gold standard of research. Researchers—in this case social science researchers including social workers—randomly assign clients to receive the intervention while other clients receive an alternate type of help. In this case, MI has not only been demonstrated to be successful but it has been demonstrated to outshine other methods in a lot of different settings with a lot of different client populations across levels of practice. Here are some recent examples of demonstrated client system success. MI has been found to be successful as a treatment or educational method in the following:

- Treatment of mental disorders (Dean, Britt, Bell, & Stanley, 2016; Keeley et al., 2016; Westra, Constantino, & Antony, 2016)
- Work with families (Simmons, Howell, Duke, & Beck, 2016)
- Work with individuals (Whitaker et al., 2016)
- Training of health care providers (Maloney & Ehrlich-Jones, 2017; Mullin, Saver, Savageau, Forsberg, & Forsberg, 2016)
- Community-based services (Simmons, Howell, Duke, & Beck, 2016)

Here is a note on research: Even though there are hundreds of thousands of articles about MI (Miller & Rollnick, 2013), we still can't say that the method has been proven to be effective. In fact, we never say "proof" in social science. This is because unlike physical science that takes place in a lab, our kind of science is about different types of people in different environments. They are never the same twice, so we can never really repeat a study. A situation that was demonstrated one time may not happen again. Also for this reason we can't say that a method "caused" a change. All we know is that in one situation with one group of people the practice method seemed to be successful. We never know what actually caused change because it was many things at once. We might be able to figure out the most important factor in a change process, but we still don't know exactly what happened for each individual. So even though there is a lot of evidence that MI is successful, we still need to keep an open mind in every situation. Practice methods are not one size fits all.

ETHICAL PERSPECTIVES

Why is it important to work alongside the client to establish goals? See Standard 1: Social Workers' Ethical Responsibilities to Clients in the NASW Code of Ethics *(National Association of Social Workers [NASW], 2018) to find out.*

Klaus Mellenthin/Getty Images

Clients can be motivated when workers affirm even the smallest success.

What Motivational Interviewing Does

When social workers use MI, they are helping clients to visualize their ideal lives. Many times people are caught up in their problems, and they can't picture what it would be to be happy and content. The idea is to help clients to know what they want and to recognize how they might get it. MI methods also help clients get past their ambivalence, or uncertainty, about change. It helps them to make conscious choices about whether or not they want to change themselves and their lives. The purposes of MI fit very well with the social work strengths perspective in that they look to the clients to identify challenges and solutions.

MI identifies and develops the following:

- How people see the problem
- What really matters to them
- What they wish for
- What things are frustrating or stressful
- What they wish were different in their lives
- What they feel hopeful or confident about
- What they see as their strengths
- What they would change (*if* they decide to; Orr & Stein, 2016)

How to Do Motivational Interviewing

In order to help people find out what they want, decide if they want to change, and figure out what they might have to do to make changes, MI uses four basic skills. We'll take them one at a time.

Open-Ended Questions

As we've discussed, **open-ended questions** are questions that can't be answered with a word or two. For example, if you don't feel like talking and I ask if you are married, you might answer yes or no. There are other ways you might answer this question that might facilitate conversation, like "I'm planning to soon" or "Yes, but I can't wait to get out of it," but if you don't want to talk you'll say yes or no. If I want to make you a full partner in the conversation, I would ask a question like "Could you tell me about the important people in your life?" That would be an open-ended question.

Here's an example of the use of an open-ended question that you might use as a part of MI:

Client:	I don't want to talk to you.
Worker:	Sounds like you're not feeling talkative today. More like keeping to yourself?
Client:	Yes.
Worker:	What is that like for you?

Here's another example:

Parent:	I'm so mad I'm not talking to that kid.
Worker:	(*to the adolescent who is present*) How does it feel to hear that?

And in a macro setting:

Agency volunteer spokesperson:	We're all tired of not being appreciated. In fact, we're ready to quit.
Worker:	Sounds like you got together and found out you're all unhappy.
Spokesperson:	Yes.
Worker:	What was that meeting like?

Notice that in each of these examples the worker helped a client identify his or her feelings first and then moved to thinking about ideas second. It's kind of like the way you practice self-reflection or the "What do I feel/believe/know/do?" exercise. The open-ended question can help get to the feelings before asking a client to begin the work of change. It shows that you recognize that the client should be a partner in the interview, not just someone who answers questions.

SELF-REFLECTION 7: GENERALIZED EXPECTANCY FOR SUCCESS SCALE

Optimism is partly a personality trait, or an attribute of yours that is not likely to change. It is also partly a learned way of looking at the world. Look at the Generalized Expectancy for Success Scale (GESS) on pages 221–222, and see what you think about your own level of optimism. Share with a partner ways you think your level of optimism may influence you as a social worker.

Affirmations

This second skill in MI is the **affirmation**. This is a way of recognizing a client's successes. You may even recognize a client's efforts when there doesn't seem to be any success. It's best to stay with facts and to be specific. For example, you might say "You worked really hard on staying focused on your tasks this week," but you would probably not say "That was great!" Also, remember that "I'm proud of you" is a statement that probably does not reflect 100% of a client's efforts.

Here's an example of the use of affirmations in MI with an individual:

Client: I was able to exercise three times this week, but I didn't get to walk on the other two days like we planned.

Worker: You really stayed focused on the exercise!

In a small group:

Client system representative: Finally during this session we completed our ground rules.

Worker: You really worked hard on putting those together. Now that your ground rules are complete, you're really going to go far.

In a board of director's meeting:

Committee chairperson: I'm hoping I can present this report at the meeting.

Worker: Your group finished that report right on time!

Remember to be sincere whenever possible with your affirmations. There may be times when you have to display an absent attribute and act like you're appreciative even when you're not, but most of the time you'll be using affirmations when you really mean it. With affirmations, you'll see your clients flourish.

Reflective Statements

Making a **reflective statement** is a way to find out if you understand what a person means. There is a process that occurs in meaning making that is outlined by Miller and Rollnick (2013). The process begins with a speaker's meaning. The speaker "encodes" the meaning into a statement. The listener hears the words then "decodes" them to identify their meaning. At that point, the listener should reflect on the statement to find out for sure what the speaker meant. Sometimes, this simply means repeating the speaker's exact words in the form of a question.

Here is an example in work with an individual:

Client: I want to get out more.

Worker: Meaning you want to get out of the house to be with friends?

In a family session:

Client: This week he let me cool down a bit after work before asking about my day.

Worker: You really appreciated the chance to cool down a bit after work?

In a macro setting:

Staff person: Today I was able to enter all of your data.

Worker: You were able to get all of the information into the computer?

You might want to try this exercise to get good at making reflective statements: Spend the day reflecting on whatever anybody says to you out loud. To do this, make sure you ask a question after at least one of every person's statements.

Summarization

To **summarize** is to gather everything that has been discussed and hold it up to the client to help them understand the "take-home" messages from the session. It allows the client and worker to collaborate and consider whether there is anything that has been missed. Summarizing can be very important in the planning phase, since it allows all of the partners in an agreement to come to a clear understanding.

Here is an example in work with an individual: "I think we said today that I'd be responsible for gathering a list of community resources this week and you'd be making the telephone calls we discussed. Is that right?"

An example in work with a small group at a staff meeting: "It seems like we've all learned today that it's a great idea to bring ethical dilemmas to our staff meetings."

An example in a macro setting: "So we said that in the upcoming community needs assessment I'm going to put together the numbers and you're going to do the interviews. And we're going to make sure to keep each other updated on our progress, right?"

See Figure 7.3.

FIGURE 7.3 ● Motivational Interviewing Skills

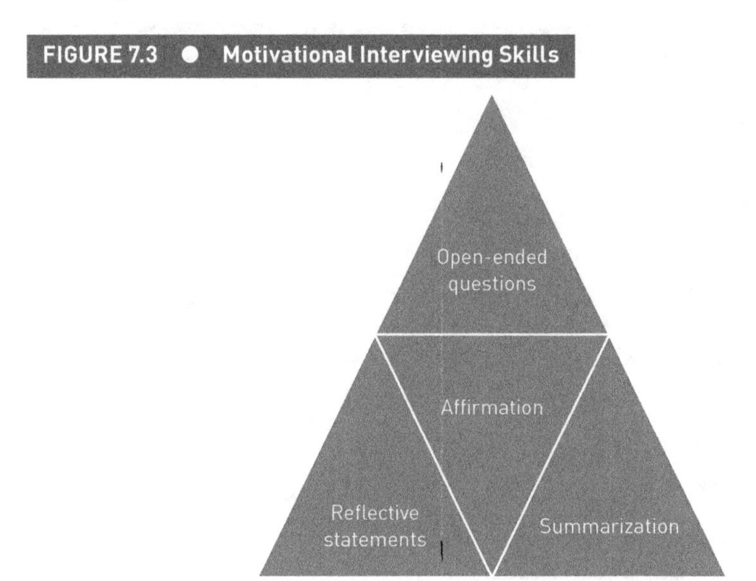

CRITICAL THINKING AND COLLABORATIVE LEARNING EXERCISES 7.4

1. Role-play this scenario: One of you is the social worker, and one is a client who wants to give up smoking. Ask questions to help the client state the following:

   What they see as the problem with smoking

   What really matters to them about smoking

   What they wish for themselves

   What things are stressful about quitting

   What they wish were different in their lives

   What they feel hopeful or confident about

   What they see as their strengths

   Whether they really want to quit

2. Now switch roles, and do the exercise again. Make sure the person playing the client has spent some time in preparatory empathy so they play the role well!

Section 7.5: Developing Goals

This section carries on the planning process with the development of goals for planned change.

Creating Goals: Identifying System Interactions

The ecomap made the areas for intervention easy to see. Susan looked for positive connections as well as systems in tension and systems with tenuous connections. Remember that solid lines represented strengths, while tension and tenuous connections indicated challenges or possible targets for change. Susan and Brittany looked at the genogram and the ecomap to identify the connections between systems.

Identifying system interactions is the foundation for the planning stage. Once the strengths and challenges of system interactions are identified, workers and clients can collaborate to create goals. Next, they establish objectives, or the observable and measurable components of goals. Finally, they make an agreement, or contract, about "who will do what by when." Finally, they develop a plan to measure goal achievement. We'll take these steps one at a time (see Figure 7.4).

Systems Interacting

System Group	System 1	System 2	System 3	System 4
1	Emily	Brittany		
2	Emily	Billy		
3	Brittany	Anna		
4	Education	Emily		
5	Personal finance	Brittany	Education	
6	Individual, family, community, and peers	National policy	Justice	Family
7	Health care	Social welfare policies	Family	
8	Spirituality and religion	Family		
9	Government	Justice		
10	Community	Family		

FIGURE 7.4 ● Steps in the Planning Stage

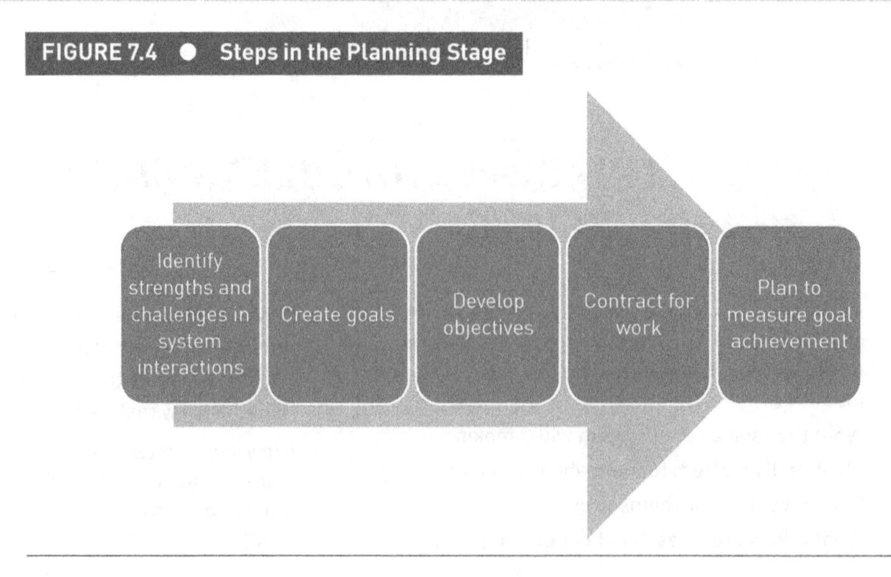

Taken together, there were 10 groupings of systems interacting in some way that was off balance. Susan and Brittany worked to identify the way those systems were interacting.

Creating Goals: Recognizing Strengths and Challenges

To begin to establish goals, Susan and Brittany considered the types of interactions and relevant resources and challenges. Susan used open-ended questions, affirmations, reflective statements, and summarization to help Brittany recognize the strengths in her situation. They found there were strengths and challenges within each system group:

Tension Between Individuals in the Family System

Susan: How do you see the problems you are facing? *(open-ended question)*

Brittany: I hate it that Emily and I don't get along.

Brittany, Emily, Billy, and Jayden were residing together, but there were many arguments between Emily and Brittany as well as Emily and Billy. Brittany identified this as the most important of her concerns.

Potential Resource in the Extended Family

Susan: What do you wish for? *(open-ended question)*

Brittany: I wish we wouldn't argue so much at home, and I wish that I got along better with my own mom.

Brittany and Anna had a prior relationship that could be reconnected.

Conflict Between the Education System and the Family

Susan: Emily, I understand you get good grades in school. You must work very hard. *(affirmation)* Can you tell me what you wish were different about school? *(open-ended question)*

Emily: I hate it that I'm always getting into trouble.

Emily was capable of succeeding at school, but she was demonstrating behavioral problems.

Uneven Balance Between Family and Economy or Personal Finance System

Susan: What things are stressful in your life? *(open-ended question)*

Brittany: I never seem to have enough money.

Susan: So you wish your monthly budget looked different? *(reflective statement)*

Brittany: I wish I *had* a budget.

Susan: Your daughter must get her intelligence from you. I'm sure you could learn about budgeting. *(affirmation)* Would you be willing to learn some budgeting tips?

Brittany: I would.

Brittany didn't have the skills to create a household budget, but she was willing to learn.

Tension Between Child Welfare Policies and Family; Potential Resource

Susan: I want you to know that I'm here to help, and I want every success for you. You should also know, though, that there has been an allegation of child neglect. The best possible outcome would be that we clear up any problems right now, and I can close the case soon. The worst possible outcome is that the kids stay with foster parents until you get organized.

Brittany: I don't want that!

Susan: I see that you're a single mom who holds down a full-time job. I know you have many talents. *(affirmation)* How would you like your child care arrangements to look? *(open-ended question)*

Following federal child welfare policies, the children and family care agency was conducting an investigation into possible child neglect. This investigation could have positive outcomes or could ultimately result in placing the children into foster care, an outcome that was not desirable to any of the family members.

Tension Between Health Care System and Family

Susan: It's great that you were able to arrange for you and the kids to have health care insurance. *(affirmation)* Do you feel confident that you can continue to do the necessary paperwork to show that you are eligible? *(open-ended question)*

Social welfare policies and available health care providers allowed the family to experience high-quality care as long as Brittany continued to complete the necessary paperwork to demonstrate the family's eligibility for service.

Potential Resource in System of Religion

Susan: I see a lot of strengths in your family, and I want to keep looking for more. *(affirmation)* For some people, spirituality or religion is important. How would you describe your spiritual beliefs? *(open-ended question)*

Brittany: I used to go to church every Sunday when I was a kid. Youth group, too.

Brittany had a former relationship with a spiritual community and could reconnect with the group.

Government and the Justice System Have a Tenuous Relationship

Susan: What's another thing you could change if you want? *(open-ended question)*

Brittany: I'd like to have this broken window fixed! The cardboard over it doesn't keep out the cold.

Laws protected renters from landlords who did not maintain safe living spaces, but these laws were not enforced related to Brittany's landlord.

Community as a Potential Resource

Susan: What do you feel hopeful about? *(open-ended question)*

Brittany: I just met a new neighbor, and I hope we'll get to be friends.

The family lived in a community of supportive single moms, but Brittany hadn't recognized them as resources.

System Strengths and Challenges

In our scenario so far, the worker has conducted an assessment, collaborating with the client to identify strengths and challenges in all of the environmental systems. The worker tied planning to assessment by referencing the genogram and ecomap. These visuals helped to develop a picture of the relationships between and among the systems in the client's life. Using MI, the worker helped the client to see where systems interacted in balance and where they were out of balance. Finally, the worker and client will work to create goals.

As a result of the interview, Susan and Brittany created the following table:

System Group	System	Strength	Challenge
1	Emily, Brittany	Family is intact	Frequent arguments Need for supervision of children
2	Emily, Billy	Family is intact	Frequent arguments
3	Brittany, Anna	Relationship could be strengthened	Need to reconnect
4	Education, Emily	Intelligent	Behavior problems Need to explore availability of after-school care
5	Personal finance, Brittany	Willing to learn about finances	Need a monthly budget
6	Children and families agency National and international policies Individual, family, community, and peers	Intervention beginning Potential improved family functioning Willing to arrange physicals and child care	Co-pay needed for physicals Child care needs to be identified Investigation could result in foster care placement
7	Health care Social welfare policies Individual, family, community, and peers	Systems in positive interaction	Continue eligibility; use resources to get kids physical exams and necessary shots
8	Religion and spirituality Individual, family, community, and peers	Could strengthen connection	Reconnect
9	Government, justice, community, or physical environment	Laws that protect renters	Landlord unresponsive
10	Individual, family, community, and peers	Supportive single moms	Evaluate support available

Creating Goals: Building on Strengths

Taken together, the strengths of the system interactions could be used to respond to the challenges. With input from Emily, Susan and Brittany created the following responses to the challenges that were facing the family:

Goals

First, it is necessary to identify **goals**. Goals are specific statements that describe ideal circumstances. They represent the intentions of the client and the worker and guide intervention efforts. Goals can be measured. Ultimately, a goal is a statement about how the worker and client will know whether the intervention has been successful.

Developing goals is a mutual process. That is, the client and worker collaborate to identify them. Generally, the worker strives to empower the client and allow them to identify and create goals. For that reason, most goals are **client-driven goals**. On the other hand, the worker may have goals of their own. These **worker-driven goals** usually reflect the mission of the worker's agency. For example, Brittany identified a series of challenges that faced her family, but she did not place child care as a priority. She didn't want to think about the idea that she might be neglecting her children, so she put it out of her mind and focused on related challenges. It was left to Susan to make sure that she would be able to close the case with the children safe and the family intact. She would consider whether goals were met and whether there was **sustainable change**—likely to last over time.

Using the table they created, Brittany and Susan created the following goals:

1. Have supervision for Emily, Billy, and Jayden at all times.
2. Keep the family healthy.
3. Have fewer family arguments.
4. Reduce Emily's outbursts at school.
5. Develop a monthly budget.
6. Reconnect with a spiritual community.
7. Get the window fixed.

Objectives

Once goals are established, **objectives** can be developed. Objectives are tasks that need to be carried out to accomplish a goal. Susan and Emily identified the following tasks that were necessary to carry out the goals.

Goal	Objective
Have supervision for Emily, Billy, and Jayden at all times.	Connect with neighbors for possible sharing of child care. Connect with Anna for possible child care.
Keep the family healthy.	Arrange for checkups and necessary shots for kids. Advocate for immediate appointments at the local clinic. Budget for co-pays.
Have fewer family arguments.	Connect with a family counselor.
Reduce Emily's outbursts at school.	Connect with a school social worker.
Develop a monthly budget.	Immediately work with Susan. Later, consider online personal finance classes at local community college.
Reconnect with a spiritual community.	Connect with neighbors for possible community churches to explore.
Get the window fixed.	Advocate by working with the landlord to meet apartment safety requirements.

Note that Susan helped Brittany to use the ecomap to identify potential resources that she already had: neighbors and her mother. Susan knew that if those efforts failed, Brittany would have to get paid day care. It was important to get supervision for the children immediately.

Next, it is important to be sure that worker and clients understand their expectations of each other. One way to achieve this is to identify "who will do what by when."

Goal	Objective	Who	What	When
Have supervision for Emily, Billy, and Jayden at all times.	Connect with neighbors for possible sharing of child care. Connect with Anna for possible child care.	Brittany	Talk with a neighbor. Call Anna.	Immediately
Get physical exams for kids.	Get checkups and necessary shots for the kids.	Brittany	Make an immediate appointment for kids at a health care clinic.	Immediately
Reduce Emily's outbursts at school.	Connect with the school social worker or teacher.	Susan	Get information. Arrange an appointment for Emily.	In one week
Have fewer family arguments.	Connect with a family counselor.	Susan Brittany	Identify a social work family counselor. Make an appointment for family counseling and parenting skills training.	In one week
Develop a monthly budget.	Participate in online personal finance classes at the local community college.	Susan	Provide information about budgeting. Identify budget training programs.	In one week
Reconnect with a spiritual community.	Connect with neighbors to identify possible groups to explore.	Brittany	Talk with a neighbor about their spiritual practices.	In one month
Get the window fixed.	Work with the landlord to meet apartment safety requirements.	Susan	Advocate with the landlord.	In one week

Contracting for Work

In order to plan the intervention stage, it is best to develop a **contract** for the work to be done. A contract is an agreement between a worker and a client. It can be discussed or written down (Kirst-Ashman & Hull, 2017), but its secret is specificity.

Since Susan and Brittany completed the chart about who will do what by when, it was easy to create a contract. The objectives, or tasks, that had to be completed in order for Emily to reach her goals were complicated, so Susan developed a written contract. (One benefit of the written contract was also for **record keeping**: The contract allowed Susan to keep a record of her agreement with Brittany. This was important—particularly because Susan knew that many cases like Brittany's ended up in court. A judge could ask Brittany to show her case file.) We'll discuss record keeping further later on. For now, just know that a written contract can be a good way of keeping track of a client's progress.

Susan and Brittany developed the following written contract:

CONTRACT FOR REACHING GOALS

Brittany will do the following:

Talk with a neighbor and Anna today to see whether there are child care resources available.

Set appointments for physical exams for all three children by next week.

Make an appointment with a social worker for family counseling by next week.

Talk with a neighbor about their spiritual practices.

Susan will do the following:

Identify a social work family counselor immediately.

Get information on social work services for Emily at school, and make an appointment for Emily in one week.

Identify a financial literacy class in one week.

Contact the landlord about broken window.

____________	____________
Brittany Smith	Susan Richards
Date	Supervisor

Goal Attainment Scaling

We've said that all of the planned change stages are addressed by workers all of the time. The contract is a plan for work in the implementation stage of the planned change process. In addition, the worker must plan for the evaluation stage. This planning is done by identifying what success will look like for a particular client. **Goal attainment scaling (GAS)** is one of many methods for measuring goal achievement (Rubin & Babbie, 2017). Focusing on tasks and their level of completion, GAS can be used to measure outcomes on all levels of practices, including work with individuals and program-wide assessment. GAS will be covered in detail in Chapter 9, but for now know that a method like GAS for measuring the success of the social work process is begun in the planning stage.

CRITICAL THINKING AND COLLABORATIVE LEARNING EXERCISES 7.5

1. Use the ecomap you already created with your partner. You should both identify two systems that are out of balance and create one goal. Try to use MI techniques to help each other vision your success.
2. Work together to identify objectives you need to carry out to achieve your goal. See whether you can go so far as to create a timeline for yourself.

Section 7.6: Planning Process Example

This section reviews the process of planning—this time in work with two children.

Addressing the Children's Arguing

Susan recognized that Emily and Billy frequently argued. She suspected the problem stemmed from the fact that Emily was in charge of the other two children when Brittany was away. When Brittany came home, Emily was expected to step out of that role, and she no longer had permission to reprimand Billy. When Brittany was gone and it was time for her to step in and reprimand Billy, he was understandably angry. Emily became angry, too, and the result was a loud argument that had become violent on occasion.

Susan and Brittany had planned for family counseling so Brittany could find out how to manage the situation. But when she called for an appointment, she learned that she would have to wait 6 weeks for an appointment. She asked Susan to help right away, and Susan decided to manage the problem two ways. First, she would spend time teaching Brittany parenting skills so that her own agitation didn't make the children's arguments worse. Then, Susan planned to work with Emily and Billy alone. Brittany was thrilled to have some time to take Jayden out, just the two of them, and Susan was free to work with Emily and Billy.

Susan remembered that one of the family's system groups that was out of balance was that of Emily and Billy. The strength for the two of them as a system was that the family was intact, while arguing was the challenge they faced.

System Group	Systems	Strength	Challenge
2	Emily, Billy	Family is intact	Frequent arguments

When the systems out of balance were identified, Susan worked with Emily and Billy to establish a goal. Both children agreed that it would be good if they didn't fight so much.

Establishing Objectives

Once Susan, Emily, and Billy agreed to their goal it was time to develop at least one objective. Again, Susan worked with both children. She was trying to identify a way that everyone would know if the goal was on its way to being achieved.

Susan accomplished the identification of objectives by using MI techniques. She asked the following questions:

Susan: Emily and Billy, what really matters to you about fighting?

Emily: Mom gets mad at us.

Billy: Mom yells a lot.

Susan: When you think about fighting, what do you wish for?

Emily: I wish he would listen to me.

Billy: I wish Emily would stop trying to boss me.

Susan: Emily, let's try to do this as if it were not your job to boss Billy. Billy, let's try to do this in a way that you play with Emily as if she were your friend.

Emily and Billy: Okay.

Susan: When you think about stopping your fighting and playing together in a friendly way, what gives you stress?

Emily: It won't be fair! He will cheat.

Susan: Billy, if Emily doesn't boss you, can you try to play without cheating?

Billy: *(hesitates)* Okay.

Susan: I'm glad you stopped to think about it. You should both know that you won't be perfect every time. You can be on the road to "no more fights" but you will probably fight once in a while.

Susan: What do you feel hopeful about? Do you think you can play just one time without fighting?

Emily:	Maybe if Mom played too.
Billy:	Maybe.
Susan:	What are you good at when it comes to playing?
Billy:	She's good at knowing the rules.
Emily:	He's good at cheering.
Susan:	Are you ready to quit fighting?
Emily and Billy:	*(excited)* Yes!
Susan:	What would it look like if you started to quit fighting?
Emily:	When we throw the ball back and forth, he wouldn't bounce it real hard so it flies over my head and I have to run really far to get it.
Billy:	And she wouldn't boss me!

Then Susan began to get specific so that the kids would know when they were successful.

Susan:	How often do you think you throw the ball back and forth before a fight starts?
Emily:	Only about five times.
Susan:	Okay, so anytime you throw the ball more than five times without fighting you are on your way to quitting . . .

In this way, Susan established an objective for Emily and Billy.

Goal	Objectives
Stop arguing	Throw the ball back and forth more than five times in a row.

Next, Susan helped Emily and Billy figure out an exact plan for achieving their goal.

Goal	Objective	Who	What	When
Stop arguing.	Throw the ball back and forth more than five times in a row.	Emily	Ask Brittany to play ball with her and Billy.	This evening after dinner
		Billy	Join in the game and play fairly.	When mom is able to play

Susan wrote down the objective and the plan in a contract that both kids could understand. She included Brittany so the game could be supervised:

CONTRACT FOR REACHING GOALS

Emily will do the following:

- Ask Mom to play ball with her and Billy.
- Try not to argue when things go wrong.

Billy will do the following:

- Try to play fairly.
- Try not to argue when things go wrong.
- Count the times the ball has gone back and forth.

Emily and Billy:

- Stop playing after the ball has gone back and forth six times.

Brittany:

- Play with the kids one time after dinner.

____________	____________
Emily Smith	Billy Smith
____________	____________
Date	Susan Richards

Reflective Responses: The Artistic Worker

©iStock.com/RossHelen

Social work can include creative expression.

Susan prided herself on being artistic. She surrounded herself with beautiful things and had painting and pottery as hobbies. A quick decision to go to an art museum on her day off was a real treat. One thing Susan was not, though, was organized. She felt cramped by forms and procedures, recognizing the value of spontaneity and creativity. A datebook was nothing more than a necessary evil. Susan's desk was like her home—a comfortable jumble of things. It was not surprising that Susan hated the planning aspect of planned change. She hated tables, and she hated details. She found out early in her career, though, that it was not as easy for everyone as it was for her to visualize a group of activities. Many times clients became confused about the goals she was suggesting. As a result, they were not empowered to carefully develop their own goals. Susan began to realize that the little details were important and that some people needed those details to be written down. As a compromise with herself, she began to write down genograms and ecomaps as well as goals and objectives . . . but she drew creative little doodles on them. Often, her doodles were an additional way to engage with clients, especially children.

CRITICAL THINKING AND COLLABORATIVE LEARNING EXERCISES 7.6

Work with a partner. Identify a goal you would like to achieve, and help your partner to identify objectives using the MI questions Susan used with Emily and Billy.

Section 7.7: Review and Apply

CONCURRENT CONSIDERATIONS IN GENERALIST PRACTICE

Ethical Decision-Making Challenge

Susan was authorized to petition the courts asking for protective custody, or removing children from homes, when they were in imminent danger. Brittany had admitted that the children were not supervised in the afternoons and that they were not receiving their required shots at regular physical exams. Should Susan work to place the children in foster care while Brittany made child care arrangements, or should she develop a safety plan for child care? Using the ethical decision-making model, determine whether this was an ethical dilemma and how Susan might proceed in a manner consistent with the *NASW Code of Ethics* (NASW, 2018), particularly related to Sections 1.01 and 1.02.

Evidence-Based Practice

Susan decided to help Brittany develop a personal budget. Is that a practice that is shown to be effective in improving family functioning? See whether you can find any evidence in the scientific literature. Do you think there might be practice wisdom that supports the development of a budget?

Policies Impacting Practice

Social workers are mandated reporters. They are required by law to report certain situations such as suspected child abuse and elder abuse. Find out the specific requirements for mandated reporting in your state.

(Continued)

(Continued)

Managing Diversity

When she first got the case, Susan had to work at not feeling angry toward Brittany for potentially neglecting her children in favor of her job. What areas of Brittany's diversity can help explain her behavior?

Multilevel Practice

Identify examples of Susan's work on all levels.

Micro: ____________________

Mezzo: ____________________

Macro: ____________________

Dynamic and Interactive Planned Change Stages

Identify the aspect of the interview between Susan and Brittany where Susan was working in the following stages:

Self-Reflection: ____________________

Engagement: ____________________

Assessment: ____________________

Planning: ____________________

Implementation: ____________________

Evaluation: ____________________

Termination and Follow-Up: ____________________

Summary

Section 7.1: Assessment and Multisystem Practice

Planning is the fourth in the phases of planned change. After the worker has practiced self-reflection, they work to engage with the client and form an assessment. Once assessment is complete, the worker facilitates a process of identifying goals, how the goals might be achieved, and how both worker and client will know when the goals are successfully met.

Section 7.2: Smith Family Genogram

To review, the genogram is a diagram used in the beginning of the planning phase that represents family members, ideally for at least three generations. The diagram shows the individuals as well as their characteristics such as age, health, physical or medical concerns, and any other strengths or resources related to their situation. The genogram also shows the important relationships between family members and graphs their characteristics: Perhaps there is a strong, mutual relationship; perhaps there is a tension-filled relationship; perhaps two people are only tenuously connected. These relationships highlight systems that are resources to each other and systems that are out of balance that may benefit from goal planning and intervention.

Section 7.3: Smith Family Ecomap

Again, the ecomap is a diagram of a person, family, organization, or community in its social and physical environment. It consists of a series of circles set around an individual system. Each of these circles represents an environmental system, and the ecomap shows the relationships between the environmental systems and the client system. The ecomap is used in the beginning of the planning stage to help the worker and client recognize the interactions among systems that may reflect resources and those that may reflect potential areas of planning and intervention.

Section 7.4: Establishing Goals

MI is an evidence-based practice. It helps social workers to know what to say in a social work interview. Using MI, workers use open-ended questions, affirmations, reflective statements, and summarization to find out how clients see problems, how they dream about the future, and what they would change about their situations. This process is key to identifying goals that clients feel motivated to achieve.

Section 7.5: Developing Goals

The process of goal development is one that occurs out of the collaboration of worker and client system. They begin by creating statements about what the client and worker perceive to be desirable outcomes. Then they identify the tasks necessary to achieve the goals and create a clear plan for how those tasks might be carried out. During this process, client and worker are clear about what situations will reflect success, providing an example of the stages of planned change overlapping: Evaluation is always a part of planning.

SELF-REFLECTION 7: GENERALIZED EXPECTANCY FOR SUCCESS SCALE–REVISED

PURPOSE: To measure optimism

AUTHORS: W. Daniel Hale, Lydia R. Fiedler, and C. D. Cochran

DESCRIPTION: The GESS–R [or Generalized Expectancy for Success Scale–Revised] is a 25-item measure designed to assess dispositional optimism. Working within the framework of Rotter's social learning theory, the generalized expectancy for success (of dispositional optimism) is conceptualized as the belief held by a person that he or she is likely to attain his or her valued goals or outcomes in most situations encountered. People with a high generalized expectancy for success not only report higher level of self-esteem and general well-being but also are more likely to risk engaging in behaviors that may lead to desired outcomes.

NORMS: Normative data have been collected on samples including 400 college students, 100 middle-class individuals employed full-time (ages 18–60), and 100 retired elderly individuals (ages 55–85). Means are relatively stable across these three groups. For one sample of college students, the mean was 99.16 (SD = 13.06); for employed individuals and an elderly sample, the means were 103.33 (SD = 9.08) and 97.97 (SD = 12.75), respectively.

SCORING: The GESS–R is easily scored by reverse scoring (1 = 5, 2 = 4, 3 = 3, 4 = 2, 5 = 1) items 9, 13, 17, 20, and 23 and then summing the individual item scores. Higher scores reflect greater optimism.

RELIABILITY: A test–retest study showed stability over six weeks to be good with a coefficient of .69.

VALIDITY: Research findings include significant correlations with the Life Orientation Test (a measure of dispositional optimism), Rosenberg Self-Esteem Scale, self-ratings of health, and other related measures. With regard to predictive validity, the GESS–R seems to be a good predictor of the kinds of behavioral outcomes expected of optimists.

PRIMARY REFERENCE:

Hale, W. D., Fiedler, L. R., & Cochran, C. D. (2013). The revised Generalized Expectancy for Success Scale: A validity and reliability study. In K. Corcoran & J. Fischer (Eds.), *Measures for clinical practice and research: A sourcebook* (5th ed.). New York, NY: Oxford University Press.

GESS–R

Please indicate the degree to which you believe each statement would apply to you personally by circling the appropriate number, according to the following key:

1 = highly improbable

2 = improbable

(Continued)

(Continued)

3 = equally improbable and probable, not sure

4 = probable

5 = highly probable

In the future, I expect that I will

1.	succeed at most things I try	1	2	3	4	5
2.	be listened to when I speak	1	2	3	4	5
3.	carry through my responsibilities successfully	1	2	3	4	5
4.	get the promotions I deserve	1	2	3	4	5
5.	have successful personal relationships	1	2	3	4	5
6.	handle unexpected problems successfully	1	2	3	4	5
7.	make a good impression on people I meet the first time	1	2	3	4	5
8.	attain the career goals I set for myself	1	2	3	4	5
9.	experience many failures in my life	1	2	3	4	5
10.	have a positive influence on most of the people with whom I interact	1	2	3	4	5
11.	be able to solve my own problems	1	2	3	4	5
12.	acquire most of the things that are important to me	1	2	3	4	5
13.	find that no matter how hard I try, things just don't turn out the way I would like	1	2	3	4	5
14.	be a good judge of what it takes to get ahead	1	2	3	4	5
15.	handle myself well in whatever situation I'm in	1	2	3	4	5
16.	reach my financial goals	1	2	3	4	5
17.	have problems working with others	1	2	3	4	5
18.	discover that the good in life outweighs the bad	1	2	3	4	5
19.	be successful in my endeavors in the long run	1	2	3	4	5
20.	be unable to accomplish my goals	1	2	3	4	5
21.	be very successful in working out my personal life	1	2	3	4	5
22.	succeed in the projects I undertake	1	2	3	4	5
23.	discover that my plans don't work out too well	1	2	3	4	5
24.	achieve recognition in my profession	1	2	3	4	5
25.	have rewarding intimate relationships	1	2	3	4	5

Recommended Websites

"How to Create a Gantt Chart in Excel" from Smartsheet: https://www.smartsheet.com/blog/gantt-chart-excel

Critical Terms for Planning

genogram 201
ecomap 202
identified client 203
target system 203
partializing practice 205
motivational interviewing (MI) 205
open-ended questions 207
affirmation 208
reflective statement 208
summarize 209
goals 213
client-driven goals 213
worker-driven goals 214
sustainable change 214
objectives 214
contract 215
record keeping 215
goal attainment scaling (GAS) 216

Generalist Practice Curriculum Matrix With 2015 Educational Policy and Accreditation Standards

Chapter 7

Competency	Course	Course Content	Dimensions
Competency 1: Demonstrate Ethical and Professional Behavior		Feature 3: Self-Reflection Feature 4: Concurrent Considerations in Generalist Practice	Knowledge Values
Competency 2: Engage Diversity and Difference in Practice		Feature 1: Focus on Diversity Feature 4: Concurrent Considerations in Generalist Practice	Skills Cognitive–affective processes Skills Cognitive–affective processes
Competency 3: Advance Human Rights and Social, Economic, and Environmental Justice		Feature 4: Concurrent Considerations in Generalist Practice	Skills Cognitive–affective processes
Competency 4: Engage In Practice-Informed Research and Research-Informed Practice		Feature 4: Concurrent Considerations in Generalist Practice	Skills Cognitive–affective processes
Competency 5: Engage in Policy Practice		Feature 4: Concurrent Considerations in Generalist Practice	Skills Cognitive–affective processes
Competency 6: Engage With Individuals, Families, Groups, Organizations, and Communities		Feature 4: Concurrent Considerations in Generalist Practice	Skills Cognitive–affective processes

(Continued)

(Continued)

Competency	Course	Course Content	Dimensions
Competency 7: Assess Individuals, Families, Groups, Organizations, and Communities		7.1. Learn the planning process in the context of self-reflection and assessment. 7.2. Review the use of visual support via genograms in planning. 7.3. Review the use of visual support via ecomaps in planning. Feature 4: Concurrent Considerations in Generalist Practice	Skills Cognitive–affective processes
Competency 8: Intervene With Individuals, Families, Groups, Organizations, and Communities		7.4. Articulate a method for planning using motivational interviewing (MI). Feature 4: Concurrent Considerations in Generalist Practice	Skills Cognitive–affective processes
Competency 9: Evaluate Practice With Individuals, Families, Groups, Organizations, and Communities		7.5. Demonstrate understanding of the process of goal development for future evaluation.	Knowledge Skills
		7.6. Paraphrase a method of budgeting that can be shared with clients. Feature 4: Concurrent Considerations in Generalist Practice	Skills Cognitive–affective processes

References

Collins J., Ryan, L., & Truby, H. (2014). A systematic review of the factors associated with interest in predictive genetic testing for obesity, type II diabetes and heart disease. *Journal of Human Nutrition and Diet, 27*, 479–488. doi:10.1111/jhn.12179

Dean, S., Britt, E., Bell, E., & Stanley, J. (2016). Motivational interviewing to enhance adolescent mental health treatment engagement: A randomized clinical trial. *Psychological Medicine, 46*(9), 1961–1969. doi:10.1017/S0033291716000568

Hale, W. D., Fiedler, L. R., & Cochran, C. D. (2013). The revised Generalized Expectancy for Success Scale: A validity and reliability study. In K. Corcoran & J. Fischer (Eds.), *Measures for clinical practice and research: A sourcebook* (5th ed.). New York, NY: Oxford University Press.

Keeley, R. D., Brody, D. S., Engel, M., Burke, B. L., Nordstrom, K., Moraliz, E., . . . Emsermann, C. (2016). Motivational interviewing improves depression outcome in primary care: A cluster randomized trial. *Journal of Counseling Psychology, 84*(11), 993–1007.

Kirst-Ashman, K. K., & Hull, G. H. (2017). *Understanding generalist practice* (7th ed.). Stamford, CT: Cengage.

Maloney, A. R., & Ehrlich-Jones, L. (2017). Implementing motivational interviewing training: Strengthening the role of the registered nurse. *Journal of Nursing Education and Practice, 7*(8), 51–56.

Miller, W. R., & Rollnick, S. (2013). *Motivational interviewing* (3rd ed.). New York, NY: Guilford Press.

Mullin, D. J., Saver, B., Savageau, J. A., Forsberg, L., & Forsberg, L. (2016). Evaluation of online and in-person motivational interviewing training for healthcare providers. *Family Systems Health, 34*(4), 357–366. doi:10.1037/fsh0000214

National Association of Social Workers. (2018). *NASW code of ethics*. Washington, DC: NASW Press.

Orr, B., & Stein, M. (2016). *Motivational interviewing workbook for change agents*. Lancaster, PA: eVision.

Pincus, A., & Minahan, A. (1973). *Social work practice: Model and method*. New York, NY: F. E. Peacock.

Rubin, A., & Babbie, E. R. (2017). *Research methods for social work* (9th ed.). Boston, MA: Cengage.

Simmons, C. A., Howell, K. H., Duke, M. R., & Beck, J. G. (2016). Enhancing the impact of family justice centers via motivational interviewing: An integrated review. *Trauma, Violence, Abuse, 17*(5), 532–541. doi:10.1177/1524838015585312

Tootle, W., Ziegler, J., & Singer, M. (2015). Individuals are continents; or, why it's time to retire the island approach to addiction. *Substance Abuse and Misuse, 50*(8/9), 1037–1043.

Westra, H. A., Constantino, M. J., & Antony, M. M. (2016). Integrating motivational interviewing with cognitive-behavioral therapy for severe generalized anxiety disorder: An allegiance-controlled randomized clinical trial. *Journal of Consulting Clinical Psychology, 84(9)*, 768–782.

Whitaker, A. K., Quinn, M. T., Munroe, E., Martins, S. L., Mistretta, S. Q., & Gilliam, M. L. (2016). A motivational interviewing based-counseling intervention to increase postabortion uptake of contraception: A pilot randomized controlled trial. *Patient Educational Counseling, 99*(10), 1663–1669. doi:10.1016/j.pec.2016.05.011

Recommended Readings

McGoldrick, M., Gerson, R., & Shellenberger, S. (1999). *Genograms: Assessment and intervention* (2nd ed.). New York, NY: W. W. Norton.

Orr, B., & Stein, M. (2016). *Motivational interviewing workbook for change agents*. Lancaster, PA: eVision.

Implementation

This chapter continues the series of chapters that cover stages in planned change. This stage is that of implementation. This chapter's case study focuses on the process of local policy change to show an accessible change on the macro level. It demonstrates how the planned change process can be useful across levels of practice and demonstrates how planned change stages are dynamic and interactive, particularly in long change processes. Also, the middle phase is considered in the context of the implementation process. This long-term change process of the case study demonstrates the potential for challenges faced in the middle of the process along with approaches to meet and resolve them.

Learning Objectives

8.1 Describe the implementation process in the context of planned change.

8.2 Understand the characteristics of middles in social process.

8.3 Consider a flowchart of the implementation process.

8.4 Reflect on the use of education as implementation in various social work roles.

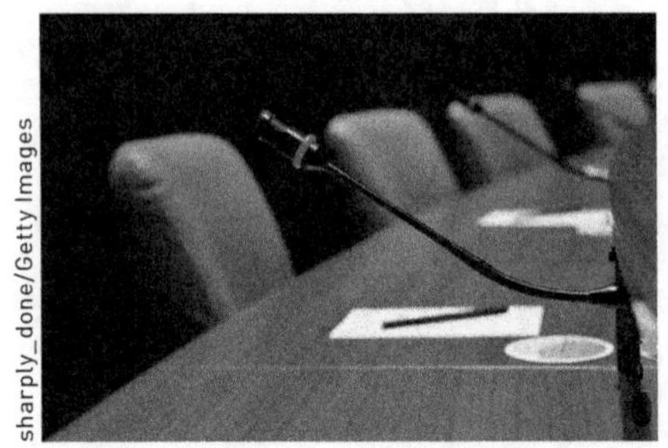

sharply_done/Getty Images

Planned change can be implemented on a community level.

Case Study: Macro Practice on a Local Level

Jeannine opened the door to the transitional living home and bent to pick up the mail. One envelope was postmarked from the municipal building and concerned the town pool. Admission policies were changing. For one thing, the membership cost had gone up. Worse than that, though, was the change in membership categories. Suddenly unrelated members of the same household were not able to use a family swimming pass. Jeannine felt her heart sink. The three men in the group home where she worked always shared the cost of a family pool pass. Going to the pool was one of their favorite summer activities. It allowed them a chance to get out, and it was quality time they shared with staff as well. Jeannine knew the clients' budgets, and she immediately knew that they could not afford individual pool passes. A family pass (defined as "immediate family: two adults and up to three children") was $396 while the individual fee was $275. Before, when the family pass was "members residing in the same household," the residents divided $396 by three and each paid $132. If they would have to pay the individual membership fee, they would have to pay $275. The clients could budget for $132 over the winter, but $275 was out of the question. Jeannine blew out a breath and made herself calm down. It was easy to recognize that she was feeling angry, but it took a while to figure out why. It wasn't fair. Her clients were working to get back into community life since they'd been in inpatient behavioral health facilities. They needed all the help they could get. It seemed to Jeannine that the membership for her clients should be free! Then she engaged in the critical thinking exercise that is part of self-reflection. She looked up the pool's website and found that it was funded almost entirely by memberships—the town couldn't just be handing out free passes to anyone who seemed to need them. Once she realized that, she recognized that instead of being angry she needed to advocate. It took one click of the mouse to find the town's website. They had a list of town council members and their contact information as well as the location of town council meetings.

Section 8.1: Implementation

This section discusses implementation in the context of the planned change process.

Implementation puts the work in social work. This stage is where the carefully crafted plan is carried out. Worker and client collaborate to complete the tasks that they identified in the planning stage. Don't forget that during implementation change happens. Change is hard, and maintaining change is harder. When a worker helps a client make a plan, they are acting like an architect creating a blueprint. During implementation, the worker is managing the construction site. The client is doing most of the actual work, but the worker is necessary to give direction, help read the blueprint, and cheer on the progress.

The goal of implementation is sustainable change. This idea shows the importance of social work. Here's an example of sustaining change on the micro level of practice: Let's say a person goes to see their doctor, and they find out they have many health problems that seem to be caused by their weight. The doctor tells them they need to take in fewer, healthier calories, so the doctor gives the person the name of a good nutritionist. The nutritionist creates a meal plan, provides recipes, and even develops a grocery shopping list. The person leaves the nutritionist's office full of hope and good intentions, goes to the grocery store, and begins to implement the new plan. The person has begun to make a change. They carried out the doctor's recommendation, and they are beginning to follow the direction of the nutritionist. This all sounds perfect, but we know from innumerable empirical studies that over the long term this plan hardly ever works.

Enter the social worker. The social worker can intervene through the planned change process and facilitate the change and its continuation. As you know, the social worker does nothing until they examine their own thoughts and feelings about the case to create empathy for the client in their complete environment. Then, the social worker works with the client to build a relationship. Next, the worker spends time talking to the person for assessment. Then, and only then, can a plan be made. Once a plan is made, implementation begins. In systems terms, the worker creates an exchange of energy that will hopefully be balanced and will hopefully create synergy. In that synergy, change will be created. Self-reflection, engagement, assessment, and planning all have to happen to create the synergy that will make change. Once change happens in the implementation stage, the worker is in a good place to help the client maintain the change. Maintaining change is considered to be part of implementation. In other words, if some type of maintenance is not achieved, the implementation is not successful even if change happened initially.

Go back to the last paragraph. It reads "The worker creates an exchange of energy that will hopefully be balanced and will hopefully create synergy. In that synergy, change will be created." Change comes of implementation, but what, exactly, does implementation look like?

Consider Jeannine's real-life situation. When she heard about the pool membership cost, she engaged in self-reflection and developed empathy for the people in charge of the pool. She knew the next thing she needed was an assessment, so she looked again at the website. She read some town council meeting minutes and learned that it was the council members that were in charge of the maintenance of the pool. Jeannine pictured an ecomap with her group home residents in the middle. She imagined a line of tension between the residents and the system of government—in this case the town. Since her clients could do nothing to change their fixed incomes in the next few months, Jeannine knew that her **target system** was the town government. It was there she would direct her change efforts.

Peathegee Inc/Getty Images

Political decision-makers can be very approachable.

Jeannine began her implementation by identifying her client. In this case, she would work with **client representatives**, or people who represented the governance of the pool. She found a list of town council members and noticed that one of the members, Cordor Ghandi, lived just down the street from the group home. Cordor would be Jeannine's client representative. Immediately Jeannine felt nervous about contacting the woman, but she remembered seeing Cordor doing yard work—in shorts, wearing a silly sunhat, pushing a wheelbarrow. It made her seem like a regular person, and it made her easier to approach.

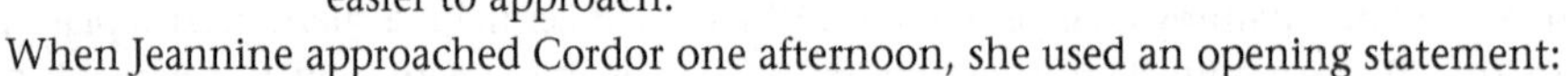

When Jeannine approached Cordor one afternoon, she used an opening statement:

Jeannine: Hi. I'm Jeannine Anderson and I work at Safe Haven, an agency that helps transition people from inpatient care back to the community. (*Note that she said "inpatient care" instead of "behavioral health institutions" or "residential behavioral health care." Everyone in the neighborhood knew that the men lived in a group home, but she could give them some confidentiality by not letting anyone know why.*)

Cordor: Hi. Nice to meet you.

Jeannine: (*smiling and looking at Cordor directly, but not directly in her eyes*) I'm working at the home up the street right now, and it's my job to be sure everything runs smoothly. I wonder if I could talk with you for a few minutes about the town council.

In this way, Jeannine included all of the elements of the opening statement: the mission of her agency, her job within the agency, the purpose of the meeting, and how long she expected it to take.

As soon as Jeannine mentioned her agency and the location of the group home, she and Cordor had common ground in that they shared the neighborhood. This helped to build a relationship so Jeannine could continue her assessment. (At this time, she was carrying out additional assessment during the planning phase.) Jeannine learned from Cordor that the council members were easygoing and the meetings informal. She also learned that they had not spent much time discussing the pool fees for this year. Cordor said she was pretty sure some members didn't even know why the phrase "immediate family" became part of the pool policy. Jeannine worked with Cordor to create a plan where Jeannine would come to a council meeting prepared with some mathematical calculations. Jeannine learned that there was a procedure to get on the council agenda. She could either get 35 signatures on a petition, or she could get sponsored by a council member. At this, Cordor smiled. She was happy to sponsor Jeannine to address the council. Later, Jeannine talked to her supervisor to make sure she was on the right track and that her planned implementation fit into the agency's mission. Then the hard part came: Jeannine had to wait 2 months for the next council meeting. In the meantime, she thought about what she would wear and how she could present herself professionally. But 2 months was a long time to wait. There seemed to be a crisis every other day with the group home residents, and she ended up working long hours. She had a performance evaluation at work and focused on that for a while. Her personal life and that of her family was also important. In all, she was so occupied she almost forgot about the upcoming town council meeting. She'd made a good beginning on the pool membership project through self-reflection, engagement, assessment, and planning—but now she was stuck in a long middle phase. The rest of her planned implementation seemed far away. In this case, the beginning of the implementation consisted of nothing more than waiting.

WHAT IF . . . FOCUS ON DIVERSITY

Cordor is Asian American (Indian); Jeannine is European American. How might the interview gone differently if their ethnicities were reversed? Suppose Cordor had been a man. Do you think the interaction would have been different?

CRITICAL THINKING AND COLLABORATIVE LEARNING EXERCISES 8.1

1. Why do you think government officials like town council members, mayors, and legislators are sometimes intimidating? Imagine yourself taking an issue to a person like this. Are you anxious? What are you telling yourself about them? Is there a level of anxiety that is appropriate? Discuss in a small group.
2. If you have experience talking to someone in a government position, share your experience with your group.

Section 8.2: The Middle Stage of Social Process

This section is about the middle phase of social process. This is the phase that usually occurs during the Implementation stage of planned change, and it is the place where Jeannine got momentarily stuck.

Remember that a process of change occurs in phases (Gitterman & Germain, 2008). As we've said before, the beginning phase of the change process is usually marked by anxiety. This anxiety comes from worry, hope, and not knowing what to expect. Many agencies have set procedures, like completing intake forms, which help move clients and workers into a hopeful beginning of the helping relationship.

Middles, though, are different. Middles happen during the implementation stage, after the structured beginnings of assessment and planning. At that point, both worker and client often ask this: *What next?*

Since the middle phase consists of implementation, it is a working phase for both clients and workers as they attempt to carry out their plan and achieve their goals. Middles can go one of two ways: (1) Either the middle of a social process is a time of energy and powerful change, or (2) it is a time of doldrums when everyone feels like quitting. For this reason, the middle phase is a time of commitment or retreat. Both client and worker reaffirm their focus on change, or they begin to lose interest or feel hopeless.

The middle of the social process is a vulnerable time for the client and the process itself. Remember that all of the stages of planned change happen all the time, so while the implementation is taking place the worker must do the following (see Figure 8.1):

- Continue self-reflection to maintain their empathy.
- Continue assessment to check whether there are any changes in the client's situation.
- Maintain engagement.
- Take note of whether the plan is being followed.

Certain situations can influence the experience of middles. For example, where the worker and client have built a trusting relationship, the client may experience the middle phase as one where they have a partner in the difficult change process. A client who feels supported; who sets small, doable goals; and who achieves some goals is likely to feel

FIGURE 8.1 ● Interactive Stages of Planned Change Over Time

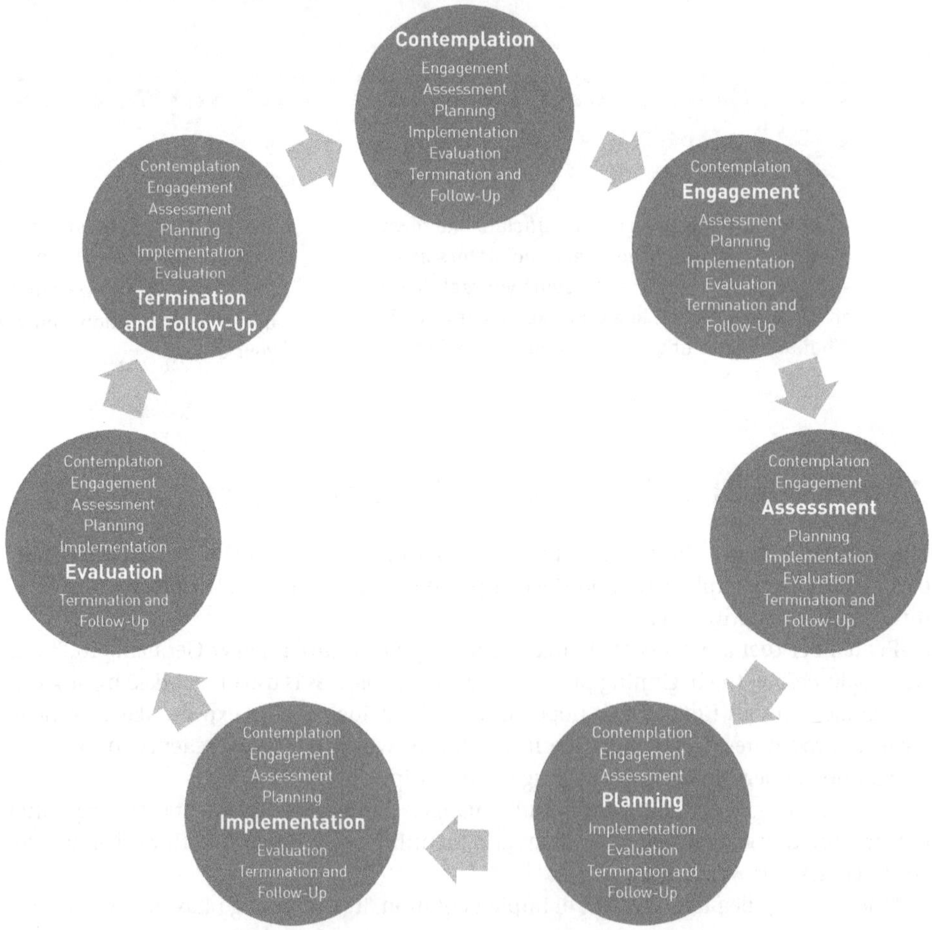

confident and look forward to fulfilling others. On the other hand, if a client experiences failure in the social work process, they may feel like giving up. They may feel like their goals are impossibly difficult, and they might experience a break in the process. For example, work responsibilities may cause a client to skip a social work interview. In fact, this is a time when both clients and workers experience the feeling that they may as well skip this next meeting. Suddenly, other things seem more important and take priority. For that reason and others, there may be a long time between social work interviews, and both client and worker may feel hopeless. It is the worker's responsibility to help the middle move from sluggish and unproductive to energetic and goal-oriented.

Different Middle Phases of Planned Change

To help clients in sluggish middles get to the productive, energetic form of middles, it is helpful to consider why they started the social work process in the first place. Simply **revisiting goals** can really motivate people. Here is an example of moving to productivity in a small group:

Worker: A lot of you seemed to come in late today. Can you tell me what's going on? *(open-ended question)*

Group Member 1: For some reason, I just didn't feel like coming today.

Group Member 2: I didn't either. My main thought was "Why bother?"

Worker: I'm glad you decided to come! *(affirmation)* But I don't think any of us want to spend time doing something that doesn't accomplish anything. *(normalization)* Can any of you remember why we were here in the first place? *(open-ended question)*

Energetic, Productive Middles	Sluggish Middles
Successful engagement	An unplanned break in the helping process or a long waiting period
The development of confidence	Feeling unsure of themselves
Experience of success	Success delayed
Incremental goals	No "light at the end of the tunnel"

Here is an example of moving to productivity in work with an individual:

Worker: I'm sorry you weren't able to be here last week. What was going on? *(open-ended question)*

Client: I think I had the beginning of a headache.

Worker: I'm sorry to hear that. *(displaying empathy)* I know this is a time in the process where we all feel like there's really no point to continuing. *(normalization)*

Client: *(relieved)* You're right. It does feel kind of pointless right now.

Worker: Let's go back and think about why we got started working together.

Here is an example of middles in macro work on the agency level:

Worker:	Seems like we lost some traction there for a bit. We weren't able to arrange a time to meet for the past 2 weeks. Everyone seems to have been busy.
Staff Committee Member:	It's that time of year. We're all busy.
Worker:	You're right. We're all busy now.
Staff Committee Member:	Well, we may as well get going on our project.
Worker:	Hang on a minute. I think we'd better talk about why it has been hard for us to get together. I don't think it's just because we're busy. We're always busy. I think it has to do with the fact that we've been working awhile on this project and it feels like we haven't been getting anywhere. Make sense?

During this last statement, the worker is carrying out an essential social work skill: exploring taboo topics. Remember that we've talked about how the exploration of taboo topics is one of the elements of the social work interview that distinguishes it from a conversation. In this last scenario, neither the worker nor the group members wanted to be held accountable for their recent absences. In a normal conversation, the excuse "we were all very busy" would probably be accepted and the group would go on. The problem with that approach in a social work interview is that the group is likely to stay in this stagnant state. The next time the group is scheduled to meet, several people will be absent. After that it will be hard to reschedule. The worker will have lost control of the process and will likely to be willing to quit themselves. When the worker simply said to "hang on a minute," they were effectively stopping that downward spiral.

CRITICAL THINKING AND COLLABORATIVE LEARNING EXERCISES 8.2

Look up the word *doldrums*. Work with a partner, and discuss how you have experienced the seventh week of a 15-week semester in the past. Did you have any absences at that time? Did you complete papers at record speed? Did you experience doldrums? Imagine how feelings like those might influence the way you practice social work.

Section 8.3: Implementation Interviews

This section explains the process that occurs during each interview within the implementation phase.

Remember that we have been trying to identify exactly what implementation looks like. Nestled within the planned change stage of implementation is an interview process that moves the worker and the client from the plan to the achievement of goals. There is a series of steps that occur in the implementation interviews. The purpose of the first step is to find out if the client is ready to get to work. Before anything else happens, the worker reengages with the client. This may just involve a quick statement: "It's nice to see you again!" This gets the interview started.

The Task-Centered System

The process of implementation we'll be using here is built on a long-standing method of change called **task-centered** change. The task-centered system has evolved over many years and has been shown to be effective, or evidence based, in use with many client populations and systems (Hepworth, Rooney, Rooney, Strom-Gottfried, & Larsen, 2017).

Task-centered work is geared toward time-limited helping. Most social work settings focus on time-limited helping for two reasons. First, the organizations that fund social work practice (government, foundations, insurance companies, private individuals) expect social workers to complete their work in an efficient and effective way. Secondly, it is important to use a time-limited method since the *NASW Code of Ethics* requires that clients be encouraged to be empowered and to engage in self-determination (National Association of Social Workers [NASW], 2018). One important way to empower people is to be sure that clients do not come to rely on us entirely for long periods of time. With the exception of some residential programs, our goal is always to efficiently help people to help themselves, so we want to use a time-limited helping process like task-centered helping.

Most important for us, the task-centered approach can be used to support many different types of implementations (Hepworth et al., 2017). We'll be using the task-centered approach as a way to frame implementation. You'll notice that our implementation process is built on the client and worker's ability to plan tasks to respond to challenges and to carry out those tasks to reach goals. The implementation stage is based on the completion of tasks.

SOCIAL WORK IN THE NEWS

Patricia Olsen of the *New York Times* reported the story of a social worker who had a compelling interest in animals. Due to his contacts in the world of animal shelters, he learned that a shelter was interested in affecting the community. They wanted to prevent animal cruelty through education, and they decided to aim their efforts at children. The worker was recruited to build the educational program for local kids. Once the program was developed, he became its administrator. A new community resource was born.

Identify the levels of practice this worker carried out. Reference the news media and *NASW News* as well as professional newsletters to locate some unusual settings for social work. With an open mind, you may someday create a new community resource yourself.

Check If There's a Crisis

In the initial part of the interview stage, the worker makes a quick assessment to determine whether there is a crisis. (Crisis implementation is a method of practice that we'll discuss later. For now, just know that the first step in an implementation interview is to determine whether there is a crisis.) A crisis is an event that feels threatening or damaging in a really crushing way. People either experience so much emotional distress that they can't use their normal coping mechanisms or they find that their old coping mechanisms are not effective in the new, immensely troubling situation (Kanel, 2015). In systems terms, a system has been whacked out of homeostasis and will struggle to regain it before any normal functioning can occur. You can see that your carefully designed plan for change is not going to be helpful here at all.

The beginning of the implementation interview is the time to assess for crisis, to ask how things are going for the client with an open-ended question, and to listen carefully to the answer. If the answer is negative or if the client dismisses your question, stay there and examine it. It is possible that a crisis has occurred but the client is afraid to begin to talk about it. They may feel that a dam is about to break and that their emotions will come bursting out in an uncontrollable way. It is not unusual for people in crisis to say "I'm not going to start crying because I'm afraid I won't stop." For that reason, it is important to stay with your attempt to assess crisis until you are sure your client is really ready to work.

FIGURE 8.2 ●

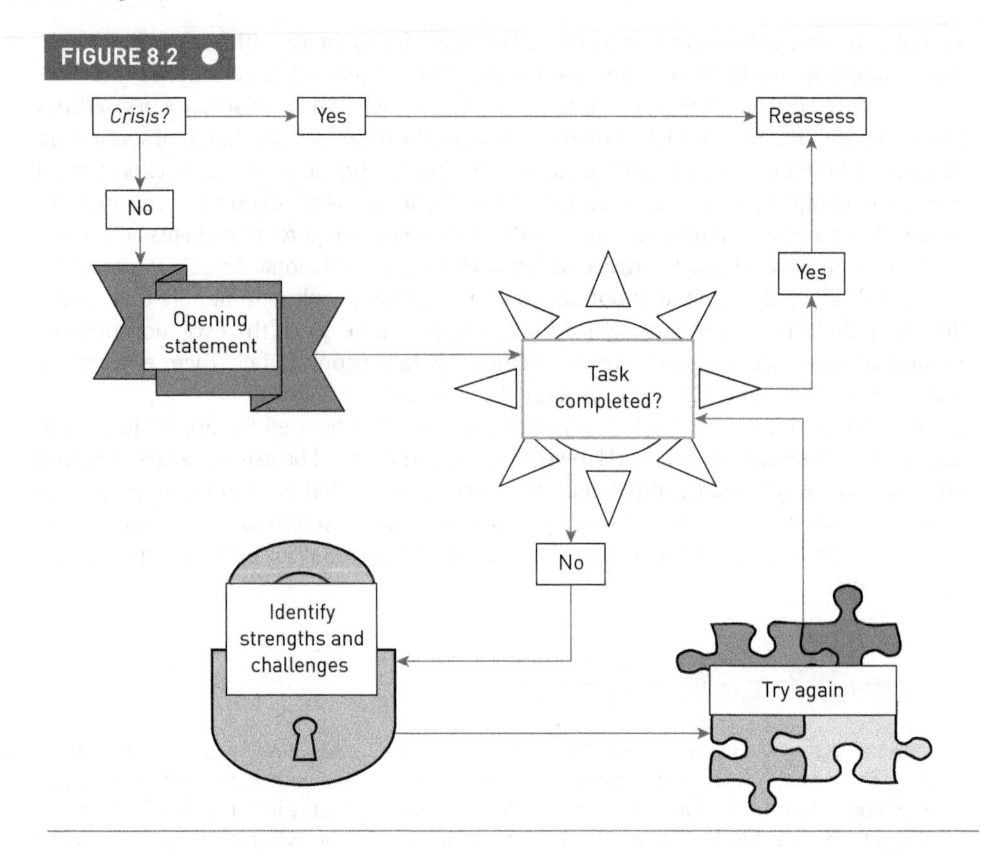

The beginning of your implementation with an individual interview may look like this:

Worker: How was this week for you? *(assessing for crisis; open-ended question)*

Client: (*slowly*) Oh, okay I guess.

Worker: You don't sound really sure about that. *(stating the obvious, taboo topic)* Can you tell me more about your week? (*open-ended question*)

The beginning of an implementation with a small group might look like this.

Worker: Anything we need to be sure to talk about today? Everything fine to go on with our plan? *(assessing for crisis; open-ended question)*

Group Member 1: Sure, go ahead.

Group Member 2: I guess. Go ahead.

Worker: I see some people nodding their head yes, but most of you are not nodding. Let's find out what's going on for all of you.

Here's how the beginning of an interview with a community coalition might look.

Worker: I'm glad to see you all here today. *(affirmation)* Are there any additions to the agenda?

Group: (*silence*)

Worker: Everyone is awfully quiet today. Are you sure there's nothing we should have at the top of the agenda?

In each of these scenarios, the worker finds out if the client is ready to work in the implementation process. If there is a crisis, it needs to be dealt with first through crisis implementation as it will be discussed later. If there is no crisis, though, the implementation interview moves forward.

If There's Not a Crisis . . .

If you've checked carefully and discovered that the client is ready to work, you know that you can move forward as planned. Of course, the next step is the opening statement. You know this by now: You remind the client of your agency's purpose and your job, and you explain what you expect to be the purpose of the meeting along with the amount of time the meeting will last. At this point in the work, you may have met with the client a couple of times. It may seem odd to talk again about your agency's purpose and your role within it. It's worth finding a relaxed way of doing that, though, because in the future you may need to remind yourself or your client what your goals have been all along.

Revisiting the Opening Statement

It may look like this:

Adolescent Client: (*talking fast*) I have to tell you what happened this week. I went to get my car washed, and I decided to do it by hand rather than drive through the sponge thing. It was a great thing I did! (*talking still faster*) I was in the little box, spraying away on my car, and the most gorgeous person walked in. I almost sprayed them! It turned out that the change machine was broken, and they needed a couple of quarters and I happened to have them. So I told them they'd owe me the money and they'd better pay it back sometime. Ha! So after I washed my car, I decided to vacuum it too. Then there was another happy coincidence. They wanted to vacuum their car too! And you know I was embarrassed about my car because I have all of that stuff in there. You know how it gets when you work from your car: You always end up eating in your car, which is really unhealthy, but anyway . . .

Worker: I'd love to hear the rest of that story if we have time at the end of the session, but I think we'd better get started on our plan for today. As I keep saying like a broken record, Alternatives is an addiction treatment center for all kinds of addictions, and it's my job to help people meet their goals for their recovery. Our plan for this meeting was to talk about how your safety plan is working, and we have only 45 minutes left. That's why I had to interrupt you, but I really hope we'll have time at the end for me to hear your story.

Check on Progress

At this point in the implementation interview, you've done the quick assessment and you know there is no crisis. You've completed the opening statement, and you have the client there, ready to work. Now you check how they've been doing on the tasks you discussed during the planning stage—you make a **task assessment**. You're checking here to see whether they are carrying out their contract. A number of things can happen at this stage. Your client may tell you the following:

- Yes, they have carried out their task successfully.
- Yes, they've carried out part of their task.
- No, they didn't feel like it (or didn't have time, or forgot, or almost any other reason).
- No, they tried but it didn't work.
- No, there was a very real reason that was out of their control.

A worker responds to a "yes" report in one of two ways: (1) If the task has been only partially completed, the worker helps the client to **identify strengths and challenges** on the way to trying again, and (2) a "yes, the task is entirely completed" calls for a reassessment—the worker reassesses by either looking to the contract for the next task or planning for the maintenance of change.

"Yes, a little" *Identify strengths and challenges.*

"Yes, it's done!" *Check for other tasks; plan to maintain change.*

Should the client's report be any kind of "no," the worker needs to explore further. Sometimes the client will report a reason for the task being incomplete that sounds like an excuse. The client may be managing their anxiety by providing what seems like a rational reason for the incomplete task. The worker then reassesses by revisiting the contract to see whether the goals still apply. Like anyone, a client is not likely to complete a task if they are not working toward goals they would like to see accomplished. On the other hand, the no may be for a legitimate reason that was out of the client's control, in which case the worker can take this opportunity to reassess and be sure the task is feasible.

Finally, the "no, I didn't complete the task" may be because the client tried but was unsuccessful. In that case, it is the worker's job to help the client to see the barriers to goal completion and help the client address them.

Reports on Task Completion and Worker Responses

Client Report	Explanation	Worker Response
Yes	Task completed	Reassess: Revisit the contract for (1) the next task or (2) plan for maintenance.
Yes	Nearly complete	Identify strengths and challenges: Try again.
No	Tried but not successful	Identify strengths and challenges: Try again.
No	Some excuse	Reassess: Revisit the contract to see whether goals still apply.
No	Legitimate reason	Reassess: Is the task feasible?

A simple flowchart illustrates this process:

- Every implementation interview begins with a quick assessment to figure out whether there is a crisis.
- Next, the worker determines whether the goal has been met.

- If the goal has been met, the worker reassesses to see whether there are other goals or whether the client needs to consider methods for goal maintenance.
- If the goal has not been met, the worker checks to see whether the goals reflect the client's goals. Is the client truly interested in achieving them?
- The worker also checks to see whether each task is one that the client can manage. This might be another chance for the worker to help the client identify challenges and reach for the resources that are available.

Here are some examples of responses the worker may make to these different scenarios. When the worker asks if a task is completed and the answer to the task assessment questions is yes, the task social work interview may look like this:

Worker: Were you able to make the phone call we discussed? (***close-ended question****; needs a yes or no answer*)

Client: I did.

Worker: Great! (*affirmation*) Tell me about it. (*open-ended question*)

When the answer to the task assessment question is "yes, almost," the social work interview may look like this:

Worker: Were you able to make the phone call we discussed?

Client: Yes. I mean, almost. I got the number and made the call. They didn't answer, but I was able to leave a message.

Worker: Great! Let's look at how we can be sure that this call is a success. I know you are really good at making plans, (*recognizing strengths*) so do you think you should make a plan to call again if you don't get a return call in a couple of days? (*The worker provides advice but empowers the client to decide for themselves.*)

When the answer to the task assessment question is "no, with an excuse," the social work interview may look like this:

Worker: Were you able to make that call we discussed?

Client: No, I wasn't. I just didn't have time this week.

Worker: Let's take a look at this. (**focusing the interview**) I wonder whether the phone call will still meet your goals or whether your goals may have changed.

When the answer to the task assessment question is "no, I tried but it didn't work," the social work interview may look like this:

Worker: Were you able to make that call we discussed?

Client: No. I tried to make the call, but I seem to have written the number down wrong, and I couldn't find it in a web search.

Worker: I'm sorry that happened to you. (*expression of empathy*) I know you're good with phones. (*recognizing strengths*) Do you think it makes sense to just enter it into your phone contacts for the time being?

When the answer to the task assessment question is "no, I couldn't" for a legitimate reason, the social work interview may look like this:

Worker: Were you able to make the call we discussed?

Client: No. I couldn't. I can only afford limited minutes on my phone, and I ran out for the month.

Worker: Okay, seems like you tried. (*displaying empathy, recognizing strengths*) Let's take a look at whether this is possible for you at all. (*focusing the interview*) We may need to come up with a different plan.

The Process of the Implementation Meeting

Note that in a case where the goal is not complete, the worker moves to identifying the client's strengths and challenges. That process results in an opportunity to identify the best method for helping the client use their strengths to create change.

CRITICAL THINKING AND COLLABORATIVE LEARNING EXERCISES 8.3

Work with a partner. Take turns discussing a task of yours that went undone this week. Explain it to your partner, and practice appropriate responses.

Section 8.4: Implementation Methods

This section begins to put the meat on the bones of the implementation process. We begin to explore different ways to help clients on all system levels move from identifying their strengths and challenges to making sustainable change. We begin the discussion of the different roles that social workers play in the course of their jobs.

Methods of Implementation

When a worker and client face an uncompleted task, strengths and challenges need to be identified so they can determine a method for moving on through the change process.

In Jeannine's situation, the town council was the target system, and Cordor, the council member, was her client representative. In their first interview, Cordor gave Jeannine information about the strengths and challenges of the council. For example, she pointed out that the council members were accessible, or "laid-back." She also pointed out that at least some of the members weren't aware that the "immediate family" phrase had found its way into the pool membership policy. As a result, Cordor was saying that the council members needed information. Jeannine talked with her about how the dollars and cents information might be helpful if a policy change were to happen.

SELF-REFLECTION 8: THE RATHUS ASSERTIVENESS SCHEDULE

It takes assertiveness, or what has been called social boldness to approach people in authority positions and to carry out many other macro level social work tasks. On the other hand, too much assertiveness can be thought of as aggressiveness, certainly an undesirable trait. Take the Rathus Assertiveness Schedule (RAS) on pages 246–247 and test your own level of assertiveness. Discuss how your level of assertiveness matches the average for college students. How might this affect your practice? Is there something you would like to change? If so, how might you educate yourself about assertiveness?

Social Workers' Roles

A **role** in social work may mean many things. It may mean a role model. Often, social workers—especially those who work with young people—serve as role models. They do this through careful self-disclosure so that their clients can get a glimpse of their personal lives. For example, a person taking a university course or a series of continuing education workshops may disclose that they have turned down a chance to hang out with friends to stay home and study. Social workers may also serve as role models for each other as they share their professional identities and aspects of their personal lives that show their commitment to social work values.

Another meaning for *role* in social work is the role of social work in the **multidisciplinary agency**. Multidisciplinary agencies are those where social workers join other professionals to collaborate in work with clients. For example, medical social workers work with nurses, physicians, physical therapists, occupational therapists, chaplains, and more. In that kind of setting, a social worker carves out particular responsibilities and reliably carries them out as part of the interdisciplinary team, an idea we'll discuss further in Chapter 15.

Finally, a role in social work can be a description of a group of related responsibilities. For example, in the **case manager** role, a social worker may discover community resources; refer, or **broker**, clients to those resources; coordinate team meetings; and follow up on referrals. We'll discuss the role of case manager further in Chapter 15. What is important for now is that the social worker may play the role of case manager while playing the role of advocate, counselor, mediator, and more. There are a wide variety of roles that social workers can play in the context of a single job description. These roles are carried out as workers engage in implementation with clients to help them move from planning to goal achievement.

Social Worker as Educator

Educator is one of the many roles that social workers can play (Kirst-Ashman & Hull, 2017). One way to step in when a client doesn't complete a task is to recognize that the client has the ability to learn and to share information with them. We'll discuss additional social work roles in Chapter 10. For now, know that in the course of their jobs social workers can wear a lot of hats, and one of them is that of an educator.

The social worker in the role of educator tries to share information for a specific purpose. What this means is that **education** is a method of implementation. Education is a common implementation method and an important one (Cagle & Kovacs, 2009). Information is valuable to clients and client systems. It can provide more than one boost to the helping process: People can gain new insights and can learn new skills. Since a social worker is expected to share information with people, they have to know how to do that effectively. Many people think that to educate someone simply means to share information with them in any way at all. They may find creative ways to do so, like to use a whiteboard or support a discussion with a video, but the professional social worker cannot just do what "feels right." Remember that the social worker uses **evidence-informed practice**, or techniques that have been shown to be successful based on systematic research. Evidence-informed practice is based on a worker's lifelong learning that includes asking questions about the effectiveness of various methods of practice with a range of client systems (Gibbs, 2003). We'll be discussing evidence-based practice in more detail in the next chapter. For now, know that education as a method of implementation has long been accepted by social workers as an effective way to help clients reach their goals. In addition to selecting a method of practice like education, it is also important for a social worker to carry out that method consistent with techniques that have been shown to work. When a social worker plays the role of educator, they base their work on theory and best practices in education.

One of the most influential educational theorists has been Paulo Freire (1996). Freire's philosophy of education begins with the idea that people interact with and transform their environments. Sound familiar? It should, since this idea is consistent with the general systems theory and the person-in-environment (PIE) perspective that guides so much of what we social workers do. Freire's idea is that when people experience education, they can look at their environment and their place in it at arm's length. They can think critically about the way they interact with other people. That way, they can be aware of the ways what they say and do affect the community. As they learn, they notice how all of the members of the community come together to set the tone of the group. As a result, education can have a powerful impact on individuals, the environment, and the community. For individuals, education causes a new awareness; a new sense of their own dignity and worth; and most importantly, a hope that they can create change.

Freire suggests an approach to education that is useful for social workers since it fits with social work values. Self-determination is a key component. Education should be about talking *with*, not talking *at*. The person who is serving as a teacher should find out the worldview and the goals of the people who are students, a process that's developed through dialogue. This is the opposite approach from the "banking" approach of education that we often experience in school. In the banking approach, the student serves as the bank where teachers deposit their own knowledge. The teacher talks about a topic, students are expected to hold onto that knowledge, and later students are expected to spit it out again in the form of answers on some kind of test. This approach assumes that the teacher has all of the knowledge and the student has none. On the other hand, an approach based on dialogue allows the teacher to learn with the student. The student ends up feeling like a "master of their own thinking" (Freire, 1996, p. 105).

To carry out the dialogue-based approach, social workers can use the motivational interviewing (MI) techniques we've previously discussed to find out what is important to clients. Open-ended questions are especially helpful, as are reflections. The idea is to share your worldview and ask the other person to share theirs. Then you find out what the person wants to learn and figure out how they think about it and what they already know. At that point, knowledge can be exchanged. Don't be surprised to find out you have learned something yourself. An example of beginning a dialogue approach to education might go like this:

Worker: Sam, tell me what you think about how you got into trouble just now. *(open-ended question)*

Sam: I hate Joey. He makes fun of me and I just want to hit him with my desk.

Worker: So you threw your desk at him. *(confrontation)*

Sam: I did. And I'm not sorry, either!

Worker: Sounds like you were really mad. *(labeling feelings)* I see that you lost your recess privilege, and I guess that makes sense to me. ***(explaining own worldview)*** Someone could have been hurt, so the teacher's trying to make sure you don't do that again. Does it make sense to you to try to figure out how to stop throwing your desk? ***(identifying educational goals)***

Sam: Yeah, I'm gonna try real hard. I really need recess to keep me calmed down. ***(sharing client's worldview)***

Worker: I didn't know you really needed recess to keep calmed down. *(The worker learns new information that may be useful for future clients.)* It makes sense, though. *(affirmation)* Do you want to learn some other ways to calm down? *(identifying educational goals)*

At that point, the worker would talk with Sam some more and share what she knows about methods for anger management. She would not teach those methods right away. Instead, she'd help Sam talk about how his experiences of successfully coping with anger might overlap with research-informed methods. At that point, she'd be using Freire's method of "problem-posing" (Smith-Maddox & Solorzano, 2002, p. 69). In the problem-posing method, education doesn't happen until the client recognizes exactly what the problem is and how information can help solve the problem. By helping Sam come to the realization that he needed to learn about anger management if he wanted to reach his goal of having recess, the worker helped Sam get invested in the educational process. Eventually, Sam could learn new skills as well as come to his own insights about how to manage anger in the classroom. If the worker had started out trying to teach Sam anger management skills, she probably would have had little success. As we say in social work, she had to "meet the client where the client is."

Education to Gain New Insights

In this chapter's case study, Jeannine hoped to get the council members to **gain new insights**. She hoped their new insights would inspire them to make the policy changes she wanted to see happen.

When Jeannine and her residential clients spoke to the town council, she let a dialogue happen between the council and the clients. Council members asked questions, and the clients talked about how important the swimming pool was to them. They talked about getting out, being around other people, and doing the same thing in the same place as their neighbors. They talked about getting to know their staff members better. Finally, they told the council members that they had lived together for a long time and considered themselves to be family.

Then it was Jeannine's task to provide the concrete information that Cordor had suggested would help Jeannine's cause. Her macro level implementation looked like this:

Jeannine: I guess you had an important reason for changing your pool admission policy. *(displaying empathy)*

Council Member: I'm afraid the pool doesn't get financial support from the town. Its upkeep depends on memberships, and the costs keep rising.

(Jeannine nodded, using nonverbal communication skills to let the council member know that she was paying attention.)

Council Member: That's why we occasionally have to raise the membership fee. When we found that places like daycares were getting passes for every child in their care on a family membership, we felt we had to do something.

Cordor: I guess that must be why the decision was made to include the "immediate family" clause into the membership policy.

Council Member: Sorry, but we felt we had to do what we did when we changed the membership policy.

At that point, the room became quiet. Jeannine had raised an issue, and the council member responded. It seemed like Jeannine's time for implementation was at an end. But no change had occurred. She needed to get the council members to gain new insights or they would just keep thinking about the pool in the same old way. But they seemed to think the interaction was over. They didn't see a need to change the way they were thinking.

Then Jeannine decided to do two things: (1) She would use humor to lessen the tension in the room, and (2) she would try educating the council on the real financial impact of their decision.

Jeannine did it like this: "I see that you are struggling to keep pool afloat, as it were." She stopped, smiled, and was gratified to see the council members smile too. "I've learned something new here. I didn't know you are responsible for the pool financially. I bet you've been looking to learn how to assure it stays in the black."

Again, the council members nodded and smiled. There was a sense of relief in the room.

Jeannine had acknowledged that she learned something new and affirmed that the council members were diligent about trying to fund the pool. Then she worked to get them to commit to the educational process and to share ideas to gain new insights:

"Would you like to consider an idea I have that will help support the pool?" Again nods from the council members. "The thing is," Jeannine continued, "our agency has four group homes in town. Every one of them gets a family pass each year. At $396 for each family pass, they pay a total of $1,584. Since none of the clients has the resources to buy an individual pass, under the new policy they won't buy any passes at all. The town isn't gaining the price of more individual passes, the town is losing $1,584. I'm hoping you would consider making a family pass good for any people who are full time residents in a house."

When Jeannine shared the information that way, the town council members who were most concerned about the finances of the pool gained new insights and were convinced that they should respond to the situation. Ultimately, the council decided to consider "family" to be all of the people who resided in a house full time, up to a maximum of six people.

ETHICAL PERSPECTIVES

Jeannine wasn't just working on behalf of her clients. Other people in the community would benefit by her work as well. Is there anything in the NASW Code of Ethics *(NASW, 2018) that suggests she should care about helping the community?*

Use of Humor

Stop here for a moment. Take notice what Jeannine did to make her efforts successful. First, she carried out the stages of planned change in the flexible way that works best. In this case, she used engagement skills during the implementation phase as she would in any phase. Her **use of humor** was perfectly timed. The council members had said their piece, and the room had gone silent. Her time was up, but she rescued the situation by ending the silence with humor. Being funny actually allowed the implementation to move forward.

Providing Evidence

Jeannine finally made her case successfully when she **provided evidence**. She helped the council members to see that they would benefit by changing their policy. Essentially, her arithmetic helped them to gain insight into their own best interests. Note that Jeannine had done her homework. She followed Cordor's advice that was part of their planning process, and she knew the numbers beforehand. Note that while math may not be your favorite class, it is sometimes necessary. Jeannine's calculations included simple addition and multiplication. As a result of her work with the numbers, she was impressive in the meeting. She **displayed confidence** easily because she knew her stuff, and the council members respected that.

Jeannine was able to make change on a community level through education. Her clients benefited immediately, and it looked like the change would continue for the foreseeable future. To recap, Jeannine took her imaginary ecomap where government had a tension-filled relationship with her clients and selected the government as the target system. She identified a client representative who was a council member representing town government. She assessed the situation through her client representative and made a collaborative plan of action. She reflected on her feelings of indifference in the supervisory process, and she turned a sluggish middle into a productive one by revisiting her goals in her supervisory process. Finally, she took on the role of educator to intervene in the target system. Ultimately, she knew she was successful because her clients were able to use the pool. Later on, she'd check with Cordor to see whether the change would likely be a permanent one. She would need to do this follow-up to be sure there would be **sustainable changes**.

Education to Learn New Skills

The previously given examples show how education as implementation can be successfully used in the planned change process by helping people gain new insights. Education can also be used to teach new skills.

Here's how the role of educator used to teach new skills might look in work with a family:

Client: I just don't know what to do when Jimmy throws these tantrums. If he doesn't get his way, he screams until his face turns red.

Worker: I hear you're working hard to be a good parent. *(affirmation)* What's your usual response to Jimmy? *(open-ended question)*

Client: I usually give him what he wants. This feels wrong, but I don't know what else to do. *(sharing her worldview)*

Worker: It may not be wrong, but I believe getting what he wants after a tantrum will teach him to scream more often. *(sharing her worldview)*

Client: Do you have any ideas on what to do?

Worker: What does Jimmy like to do? *(open-ended question)*

Client: He loves for me to read to him and gets very quiet when I do.

Worker: That's a good observation on your part. *(affirmation)* Maybe we can use that. I know a technique that we know works for many families. When a tantrum happens, you place the child in some isolated place—like sitting on the stairs, for example. They stay for 1 minute for every year they are old. For Jimmy, he'd only be on the stairs for 3 minutes. But I think we can modify that technique for Jimmy since we know about how much he likes you to read to him.

Client: I can tell him that if he remains quiet for 3 minutes I'll read part of his favorite book to him.

Worker: Good idea!

Worker and client shared worldviews. Based on that, the worker asked questions to find out what they could learn from the client. After that, the worker was able to work with the client to come to a solution using information they both had. Since the client made a contribution, they left the interview truly feeling like a "master of their own thinking."

The Indifferent Worker: Reflective Responses

When Jeannine had to wait 2 months for the next council meeting, she was frustrated. Later, though, she started to be indifferent—she found that she didn't really care either way. When she began to feel like that, she went to her supervisor to get some direction. She wondered out loud whether the pool membership situation was really a big deal. Did she make a fuss over nothing? Her supervisor asked her why the situation had bothered her to begin with. She said she felt like it wasn't fair, but when she realized that the pool needed the memberships to be maintained, she wasn't sure. Her supervisor asked her to imagine the consequences of carrying out her implementation. What would change for the clients? Jeannine was ashamed to admit that she had forgotten all about her clients wanting to go to the pool and how it seemed to help them in many ways. She had gotten tangled up in the process of talking with the councilwoman and thinking about how she would address the council. Then all that time went by, and she went into the doldrums. Once her supervisor pointed out her original goal, Jeannine regained her energy. And a surprising thing happened. Jeannine realized that her clients could be part of the solution: She didn't have to advocate *for* them; she needed to advocate *with* them. If she were to help them prepare to address the council themselves with her help, they had a lot of work to do before the meeting.

CRITICAL THINKING AND COLLABORATIVE LEARNING EXERCISES 8.4

Work with a partner. Imagine your least favorite class—particularly one where the instructor uses the "bucket" method. Ask your partner to role-play with you and "teach" you one concept from the class. (You have to make sure they understand the concept first.) Try to find ways for both of you to share your views about the subject and to participate in the learning.

Section 8.5: Review and Apply

CONCURRENT CONSIDERATIONS IN GENERALIST PRACTICE

Ethical Decision-Making Challenge

When Jeannine originally thought about advocating for her clients by attending a town council meeting, she assumed she'd go on her own. Is there anything in the *NASW Code of Ethics* (NASW, 2018) that points out the benefit of supporting the clients to attend themselves? See Standard 1.02.

Human Rights

Is anyone in this case being deprived of any fundamental human rights such as freedom, safety, privacy, an adequate standard of living, health care, or education? At first, Jeannine thought her clients' membership in the pool should be free. Was she right? Think about whether the use of a public swimming pool qualifies as a fundamental human right.

Evidence-Based Practice

Find out whether it is better for people exiting inpatient behavioral health care to live in transitional housing programs, with family, or with friends. Identify how the researchers defined *residence*.

Policies Impacting Practice

Look up the current cash benefit for people who receive Supplemental Security Income (SSI). Is the annual income above or below the U.S. government's poverty level? By how much?

Managing Diversity

Imagine that Jeannine managed a transitional living program for six adolescent boys of various ethnicities. Do you think she would find it harder or easier to get the town council to change pool admission policy?

Multilevel Practice

Identify examples of Jeannine's work on all levels.

Micro: ______________________

Mezzo: ______________________

Macro: ______________________

Dynamic and Interactive Planned Change Stages

Identify aspects of Jeannine's work where she worked in the following stages:

Self-Reflection: ______________________

Engagement: ______________________

Assessment: ______________________

Planning: ______________________

Implementation: ______________________

Evaluation: ______________________

Termination and Follow-Up: ______________________

Chapter Summary

Section 8.1: Implementation

Implementation is the stage in planned change where goals are carried out. The goal of implementation is not just change but sustainable change. The worker helps guide the client or client system representative through the process of completing tasks as described in the planning stage.

Section 8.2: The Middle Stage of Social Process

The planned change process usually faces the characteristics of middles in social process. The middle of a process can be marked by sluggishness and a sense of futility or it can be marked by dynamic, productive change. It is the worker's job to help clients move from sluggishness to energetic change. This often involves helping clients to remember their original goals and recognize manageable tasks.

Section 8.3: Implementation Interviews

There is a process that occurs in every interview in the implementation stage. During that process, the worker assesses whether there is an immediate crisis and either focuses on that or begins to assess whether tasks have been completed. If the tasks have been completed, the worker reassesses to determine whether there are additional tasks or whether sustainability of change should be the next focus. If the tasks have not been completed, the worker assures they are appropriate then helps clients identify their strengths and needs so that barriers to task completion can be overcome.

Section 8.4: Implementation Methods

During the implementation stage, social workers carry out a number of roles to help clients meet their goals. One of the most important roles social workers play is that of educator. In the role of educator, social workers share information for a particular purpose, usually to help client systems gain new insights or learn new skills. The social worker carries out the role of educator in different ways to respond to different situations but always to help the client or client representative to reach their goals.

SELF-REFLECTION 8: RATHUS ASSERTIVENESS SCHEDULE

PURPOSE: To measure assertiveness.

AUTHOR: Spencer A. Rathus

DESCRIPTION: This 30-item instrument was designed to measure assertiveness, or what the author called social boldness. Respondents are asked to rate 30 social situations according to how characteristic each is of their own experience. The Rathus Assertiveness Schedule (RAS) does not seem to be affected by social desirability.

NORMS: Data are reported for undergraduates aged 17–27. The mean RAS score was .294.

SCORING: Items are rated in terms of how descriptive the item is of the respondent. Ratings are from +3 to -3. Seventeen items, indicated by an asterisk (*) on the scale, are reverse-scored. (For these items, a score of +3 becomes a score of -3, etc.).

RELIABILITY: The RAS has evidence of good internal consistency and stability. Split-half reliability was .77. Test-retest reliability over an eight week period was .78.

VALIDITY: The RAS has good concurrent validity. Scores on the instrument have been shown to correlate with measures of boldness, outspokenness, assertiveness, aggressiveness, and confidence.

PRIMARY REFERENCE:

Rathus, S. A. (2013). A 30-item schedule for assessing assertive behavior. In K. Corcoran & J. Fischer (Eds.), *Measures for clinical practice and research: A sourcebook* (5th ed.). New York, NY: Oxford University Press.

RAS

Indicate how characteristic or descriptive each of the following statements is of you by using the code given below.

+3 = Very characteristic of me, extremely descriptive

+2 = Rather characteristic of me, quite descriptive

+1 = Somewhat characteristic of me, slightly descriptive

-1 = Somewhat uncharacteristic of me, slightly nondescriptive

-2 = Rather uncharacteristic of me, quite nondescriptive

-3 = Very uncharacteristic of me, extremely nondescriptive

_____ 1. Most people seem to be more aggressive and assertive than I am.*

_____ 2. I have hesitated to make or accept dates because of "shyness."*

_____ 3. When the food served at a restaurant is not done to my satisfaction, I complain about it to the waiter or waitress.

_____ 4. I am careful to avoid hurting other people's feelings, even when I feel that I have been injured.*

_____ 5. If a salesman has gone to considerable trouble to show me merchandise that is not quite suitable, I have a difficult time saying no.*

_____ 6. When I am asked to do something, I insist upon knowing why.

_____ 7. There are times when I look for a good, vigorous argument.

_____ 8. I strive to get ahead as well as most people in my position.

_____ 9. To be honest, people often take advantage of me.*

_____ 10. I enjoy starting conversations with new acquaintances and strangers.

_____ 11. I often don't know what to say to attractive persons of the opposite sex.*

_____ 12. I will hesitate to make phone calls to business establishments and institutions.*

_____ 13. I would rather apply for a job or for admission to a college by writing letters than by going through with personal interviews.*

_____ 14. I find it embarrassing to return merchandise.*

_____ 15. If a close and respected relative were annoying me, I would smother my feelings rather than express my annoyance.*

_____ 16. I have avoided asking questions for fear of sounding stupid.*

_____ 17. During an argument I am sometimes afraid that I will get so upset that I will shake all over.*

_____ 18. If a famed and respected lecturer makes a statement which I think is incorrect, I will have the audience hear my point of view as well.

_____ 19. I avoid arguing over prices with clerks and salesmen.*

_____ 20. When I have done something important or worthwhile, I manage to let others know about it.

_____ 21. I am open and frank about my feelings.

_____ 22. If someone has been spreading false and bad stories about me, I see him/her as soon as possible to "have a talk" about it.

_____ 23. I often have a hard time saying no.*

_____ 24. I tend to bottle up my emotions rather than make a scene.*

_____ 25. I complain about poor service in a restaurant and elsewhere.

_____ 26. When I am given a compliment, I sometimes just don't know what to say.*

_____ 27. If a couple near me in a theatre were conversing rather loudly, I would ask them to be quiet or take their conversation elsewhere.

_____ 28. Anyone attempting to push ahead of me in line is in for a good battle.

_____ 29. I am quick to express my opinion.

_____ 30. There are times when I just can't say anything.*

Recommended Websites

"Community Social Workers" from SocialWorkLicensure.org: http://www.socialworklicensure.org/types-of-social-workers/community-social-workers.html

Critical Terms for Implementation

target system 228
client representatives 228
middles 229
revisiting goals 231
task-centered 232
task assessment 235
identify strengths and challenges 236
close-ended question 237
focusing the interview 237
role 239
multidisciplinary agency 239
case manager 239
broker 239
educator 239
education 239
evidence-informed practice 239
explaining own worldview 240
identifying educational goals 240
sharing client's worldview 240
gain new insights 241
use of humor 242
provided evidence 242
displayed confidence 242
sustainable changes 243

Generalist Practice Curriculum Matrix With 2015 Educational Policy and Accreditation Standards

Chapter 8

Competency	Course	Course Content	Dimensions
Competency 1: Demonstrate Ethical and Professional Behavior		Feature 3: Self-Reflection Feature 4: Concurrent Considerations in Generalist Practice	Knowledge Values Knowledge Values Knowledge Values
Competency 2: Engage Diversity and Difference in Practice		Feature 1: Focus on Diversity Feature 4: Concurrent Considerations in Generalist Practice	Skills Cognitive-affective processes Skills Cognitive-affective processes
Competency 3: Advance Human Rights and Social, Economic, and Environmental Justice		Feature 4: Concurrent Considerations in Generalist Practice	Skills Cognitive-affective processes
Competency 4: Engage in Practice-Informed Research and Research-Informed Practice		Feature 4: Concurrent Considerations in Generalist Practice	Skills Cognitive-affective processes
Competency 5: Engage in Policy Practice		Feature 4: Concurrent Considerations in Generalist Practice	Skills Cognitive-affective processes
Competency 6: Engage With Individuals, Families, Groups, Organizations, and Communities		Feature 4: Concurrent Considerations in Generalist Practice	Skills Cognitive-affective processes

Competency	Course	Course Content	Dimensions
Competency 7: Assess Individuals, Families, Groups, Organizations, and Communities		Feature 4: Concurrent Considerations in Generalist Practice	Skills Cognitive–affective processes
Competency 8: Intervene With Individuals, Families, Groups, Organizations, and Communities		8.1. Describe the implementation process in the context of planned change.	Knowledge
		8.2. Understand the characteristics of middles in social process.	Knowledge Cognitive–affective processes
		8.3. Consider a flowchart of the implementation process.	Knowledge
		8.4. Reflect on the use of education as implementation in various social work roles.	Knowledge Skills
		Feature 4: Concurrent Considerations in Generalist Practice	Skills Cognitive–affective processes
Competency 9: Evaluate Practice With Individuals, Families, Groups, Organizations, and Communities		Feature 4: Concurrent Considerations in Generalist Practice	Skills Cognitive–affective processes

References

Cagle, J. G., & Kovacs, P. J. (2009). Education: A complex and empowering social work implementation at the end of life. *Health & Social Work, 34*(1), 17–27.

Freire, P. (1996). *Pedagogy of the oppressed.* New York, NY: Penguin Education.

Gitterman, A., & Germain, C. B. (2008). *The life model of social work practice: Advanced in theory and practice* (3rd ed.). New York, NY: Columbia University Press.

Gibbs, L. E. (2003). *Evidence-based practice for the helping professions.* Pacific Grove, CA: Brooks/Cole-Thomson Learning.

Hepworth, D. H., Rooney, R. H., Rooney, G. D., Strom-Gottfried, K., & Larsen, J. (2017). *Direct social work practice: Theory and skills* (10th ed.). Boston, MA: Cengage.

Kanel, K. (2015). *A guide to crisis implementation* (5th ed.). Stamford, CT: Cengage.

Kirst-Ashman, K. K., & Hull, G. H. (2017). *Understanding generalist practice* (7th ed.). Stamford, CT: Cengage.

National Association of Social Workers. (2018). *NASW code of ethics.* Washington, DC: NASW Press.

Rathus, S. A. (2013). A 30-item schedule for assessing assertive behavior. In K. Corcoran & J. Fischer (Eds.), *Measures for clinical practice and research: A sourcebook* (5th ed.). New York, NY: Oxford University Press.

Smith-Maddox, R., & Solorzano, D. G. (2002). Using critical race theory, Paulo Freire's problem-posing method, and case study research to confront race and racism in education. *Qualitative Inquiry, 8*(1), 66–84.

Recommended Readings

Delgado, M. (1999). Community social work practice in an urban context: The potential of a capacity-enhancement perspective. New York, NY: Oxford University Press.

Evaluation, Termination, and Follow-Up

This chapter rounds out the ongoing discussion of the planned change process as well as the characteristics of the beginnings, middles, and endings of social process. Students explore the thoughts, feelings, and behaviors that occur in various situations in the evaluation and termination stages of planned change. Evaluation is discussed in full here, particularly as it occurs throughout the dynamic, interactive planned change process. The case study is related to foster care. When it comes to termination, foster care is a particularly challenging field of practice. The worker is likely to have formed a working relationship with a child or children who have experienced real or perceived abandonment and the associated guilt can be crippling. This chapter allows the student to consider the value of planned termination as well as the importance of drawing boundaries around termination when the temptation to remain connected with clients is strong. Vignettes explore termination and the use of evaluation throughout the planned change process and follow-up at its conclusion.

Learning Objectives

9.1 Explore the process of evaluation.

9.2 Identify types and purposes of evaluation.

9.3 Learn about the use of goal attainment scaling (GAS) for work with systems of all sizes, including individual and program effectiveness measurement.

9.4 Learn about terminating the planned change process.

9.5 Consider the importance of follow-up as a stage in the planned change process.

Case Study: Adoption in a Rural Setting

Carmen's knuckles were white as she gripped the steering wheel. She drove carefully, only 5 miles per hour. Not because the speed limit was 5 miles per hour—it was 10 in the mobile home park—but because she did not want to get where she was going. Carmen had been working with Andrea for 18 months, and today was their last meeting. When she arrived at the trailer, Carmen wasn't out of the car before Andrea was throwing herself into her arms. At a tall 14, Andrea was leaning down to hug Carmen, her blond hair mixing with Carmen's jet black ponytail. They both knew it was their last meeting. Tears were streaming down over Andrea's flushed cheeks, and Carmen had to admit that tears were filling her eyes as well. As Carmen got out of the car, she put her arm around Andrea's waist, and they walked toward the trailer where Andrea's new parents waited.

Endings can bring up powerful emotions for workers and clients.

They went inside and slid around the table to find seats. Carmen saw that Andrea's parents were beaming. They had been Andrea's foster parents for 6 months and then completed a successful request to adopt her. Carmen was right there the whole time. She had been handed the Snyder application to be foster parents and had built relationships, done an in-home assessment of the safety of the place, and assessed the appropriateness of the family. This part had been hard. The Snyders, a Caucasian family, were not comfortable working with Carmen at first. She was Latina, and they weren't used to having relationships with Latinas. In fact, they lived in a rural area that was mainly made up of white people, and they both grew up surrounded by the stereotypes people develop when they have few interactions with others. More than once, Carmen had to self-reflect on the strong feelings she had when the family rejected her help. But when the Snyders saw Carmen working hard to help them, appearing at the trailer week after week, month after month, they began to trust her entirely.

Carmen had prepared both Andrea and the Snyders for the transition from Andrea's residential placement to a home and watched all three of them manage that transition with her help. She helped the Snyder family to understand their extended family with a genogram and helped Andrea find her place in it. An ecomap showed Open Door Adoption as a positive resource for the family, and they all came to see the agency as a reliable source of support. This idea was cemented when Carmen stepped in and advocated for Andrea to start at her new school in the middle of the academic year when the building administration was dragging its feet.

Carmen, in fact, was the face of Open Door's consistent support. She was there when David, Jackie, and Andrea decided to create a forever family, and she helped them set goals and make plans for that to happen. Sometimes she helped them get over conflicts, and other times she listened while they shared their joys. Carmen grinned a little through her tears as she remembered the time Andrea bounded out of the trailer to tell her about their first parent–teacher conference. It was the first time in her life that she had parents attending. And now the paperwork was complete, the celebrations ended, and it was time for Open Door Adoption to close the case. To Andrea's parents, this marked a new beginning for their family. They wouldn't be reporting to the agency how Andrea was doing in school, how she made out at the dentist's office, how they were all getting along . . . nothing. They'd be left on their own, and they couldn't wait. "Now, we're going to be normal," said Jackie, with a broad smile. Carmen quickly wiped her eyes and got out the Snyder file. She bent over the most recent case recording page to hide her sad face and wrote the date more slowly and carefully than was needed. When she was composed, she put on a bright smile and said, "It looks like we're all having strong feelings today. Let's take turns talking about them."

Section 9.1: Evaluation in Planned Change

This section covers evaluation in planned change: what it is and how it gets carried out.

The Meaning of Evaluation

Evaluation is the process of checking to see whether clients benefit from social work. We plan evaluation early in the planned change process, we carry it out throughout the process, and we measure again at the end of the process. The details go like this:

- *The planning stage is where evaluations begin*—At that time, the worker and client develop goals that reflect concrete activities and expected outcomes. In other words, they are **measurable goals and objectives**, or tangible ideas of what is expected to happen. For example, "becoming happy" is not a useful goal, but "spending time with friends at least once a week" will be a better way for the client and the worker to figure out if the planned change process is working. Another form of evaluation also occurs in the planning stage when the worker reviews the available information about how to proceed with this particular client in this particular situation. The purpose of this evaluation is for the worker to find evidence-based ways to provide the implementation of the planned change process. The evaluation process used to find evidence-based practice methods is described in detail below.
- *The implementation stage is also a place for evaluation*—Implementation provides an opportunity to check in with the client system to see whether goals are on the way to being met. Using the type of implementation identified during the evidence-based information review, the worker constantly thinks about whether the implementation is working. To evaluate work on all system levels during the process of helping is called **process evaluation** (Rubin & Babbie, 2017). In that stage, the client and the worker collaborate to find out if the process is going as planned. This might happen using an **informal evaluation**, a simple conversation about the client's and worker's ideas about whether goals are being met. On the other hand, process evaluation can be a **formal process evaluation** where some specific measuring tool is used, like a test of knowledge, a measure of emotions or beliefs, or goal attainment scaling (GAS). We'll talk about these types of evaluations later. During the process evaluation, workers and clients also evaluate the appropriateness of the current goals.
- *The next important stage is evaluation itself*—During the evaluation stage of planned change, workers along with clients and client system representatives collaborate to complete **outcome evaluation.** Outcome evaluation is a necessary part of the planned stage process since it helps the clients and client system representatives to recognize their successes. Outcome evaluation also allows the worker to determine two things: (1) whether the implementation has been successful with this client system and (2) whether it could be expected to be successful with other client systems in the future. In addition, this evaluation of an individual client system can be combined with other individual client system evaluations to help determine if whole programs or agencies are providing effective service. Outcome evaluation is likely to be a formal evaluation.
- *Evaluation is again important during termination*—During the termination stage of planned change, evaluation can be used to help clients plan for the future. If the outcome evaluation shows where the clients' efforts were most successful, the client can plan to do the same things in the same way to be sure they continue to be successful after social work services are over. In the same way, evaluation can show situations where clients were not successful. Studying these situations can highlight what tasks were tried and found to be challenging. Workers and clients can work together in the termination process to **anticipate the future.**

- *Follow-up* is all about evaluation as well. During this stage, when the worker checks back with the client or client system representative sometime after termination, the goal is to determine whether the successful changes continued. This evaluation supports a plan for the client to return to service, to be referred elsewhere, or to celebrate ongoing success. This is also an opportunity for a generalist social worker to see the long-term effects of the social work intervention and begin to establish the base for evidence-based practice.

Why Evaluate?

Evaluation is important to social workers for lots of reasons. These reasons include our commitment to our *NASW Code of Ethics* (National Association of Social Workers [NASW], 2018), our wish to help clients see their successes, our need to show others that our planned change implementations work, and to learn from our mistakes.

Developing Competence

First, our *NASW Code of Ethics* (NASW, 2018) requires evaluation. The ethical standard related to social workers' ethical responsibilities to the social work profession addresses evaluation specifically. Section 5.02 states that social workers should "monitor and evaluate policies, the implementation of programs, and practice implementations" (p. 27). This ethical requirement is based on the core social work value of **competence** and flows out of the related social work principle that social workers should "develop and enhance their professional expertise" (p. 5). One way to develop and enhance expertise is to measure the success of your work and another is to evaluate existing knowledge to see what might apply to your work. To meet this ethical requirement, you need to constantly review the scientific literature in social work and other disciplines to be sure you are giving your clients the best service possible. In short, you need to do evaluation to continuously improve your work.

Recognizing Progress

Another reason for evaluation is to help clients see their progress. This is one more aspect of our ethical responsibilities. We're required to help clients carry out self-determination. The first standard in the *NASW Code of Ethics* is that of Social Workers' Ethical Responsibilities to Clients, and the second ethical requirement in that standard is for workers to "assist clients in their efforts to identify and clarify their goals" (NASW, 2018, p. 7). As evaluation helps clients see their development, it makes them full partners in the change process. A family may decide that its goals include keeping the kids in school every day. When they see their progress in this area, they may decide to add the goal of reducing arguments. That additional goal was only possible when they recognized their success with the first. This provided an opportunity for self-determination because the clients chose whether to continue with the work or not once the first goal was met. In an organization, the administration may work to improve staff morale through team-building exercises. If they recognize success in that area, they are free to move on to encouraging staff to work together on implementing policy changes. Evaluation will help give them the confidence to move forward.

Clients, client system representatives, and workers should all know what's going on in evaluation. Process evaluation that is **transparent evaluation** allows the clients to be aware of their active participation in the ongoing measure of success. This helps clients to see where they have been and where they are going. For example, a worker may work with an individual who is having doldrums in the middle of their planned change process. Perhaps a person who is trying to quit smoking has had a cigarette and wants to give up their process of change. A worker who can show client progress will keep the process moving. They could show that the client started with 15 cigarettes a day and went to 10, then

FIGURE 9.1 •

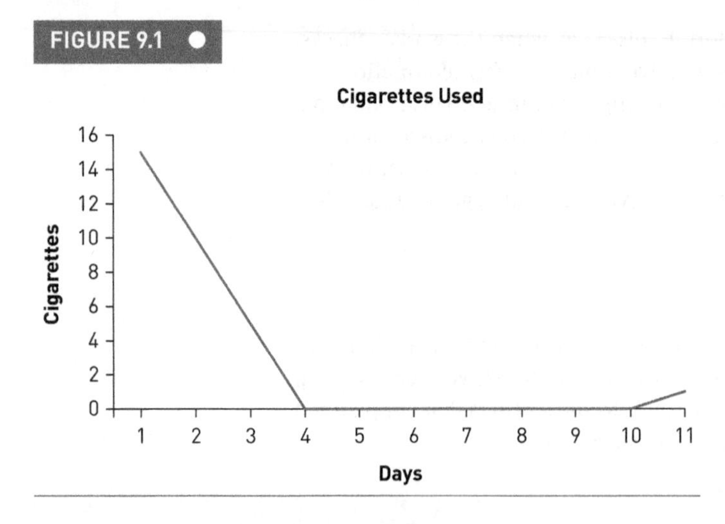

went to 5, and finally went to none for 1 week. This will help the client to see that a relapse is just part of a process that is on a mostly upward swing.

Figure 9.1 shows how a worker might graph that progress for the client.

For another example of the importance of transparent process evaluation, consider this macro practice situation: Administrators want to help agency workers do home visits with five clients each week. They may begin with one and move to two and then three as the weeks progress. For the next 2 weeks, the workers may feel as if they are failing, but if they have participated in marking their success on a whiteboard in the office, they may see very clearly that one of the weeks had a long weekend and another was marked by a snowstorm. They were making slow but steady progress. Regardless of the level of practice, evaluation can help workers as well as clients to have the energy to move forward.

FIGURE 9.2 • Purposes of Evaluation

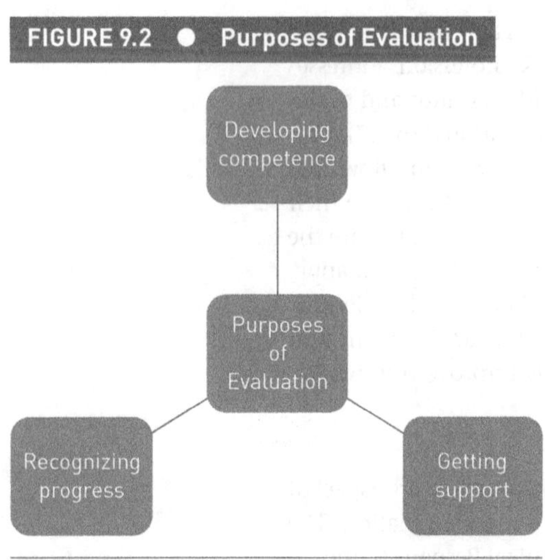

Getting Support

Finally, evaluation helps us to stand up for ourselves. Many people are skeptical about the value of social work, so research can help them to understand what social work practice is worth (Rubin & Babbie, 2017). We need others to understand the value of social work because we need to get financial support. We may need support from people who are not entirely convinced that what we do has value. Just about every time an agency gets money to provide its services, the person or organization that is making the donation or payment wants to be sure that their money is being well spent. Each time an agency asks for financial support, it has to show a plan for answering this question: What did you accomplish with this money? Evaluation gives us the answer (see Figure 9.2).

ETHICAL PERSPECTIVES

Agency financial support helps clients have options and choice in the services available to them. See where this issue is addressed in the NASW Code of Ethics *(NASW, 2018). Start with Section 6.04.*

CRITICAL THINKING AND COLLABORATIVE LEARNING EXERCISES 9.1

1. Play with Excel. Make a column marked "Days" and add 1, 2, 3, . . . 7. Then make a column marked "Minutes of Studying," and fill it out with your best estimate of how much time you've spent studying each day over the past week. Highlight both columns, click on Insert. Choose a line graph, and see what you come up with. Would you like to change what that scale looks like next week?

Section 9.2: Three Types of Evaluation

This section discusses three different types of evaluation that are used by all social workers.

Types of Evaluation

Just as there are different purposes for evaluation, there are different kinds of evaluation. These include evaluations

- to develop and support evidence-based, or research-informed, practice;
- to measure goal attainment for individuals and programs; and
- to see whether clients are satisfied with the services they've received.

Evaluation for Research-Informed Practice

As we've said, competent social workers need to know what practice approaches are best suited to the clients they're serving. To accomplish this, they need to explore the research that is available, and they have to evaluate that research. In this way, our practice is based on the best scientific knowledge, or evidence, that we can find to inform our practice. For that reason, practice that is **research-informed practice** is often called **evidence-based practice** (Langer & Leitz, 2015; see Figure 9.3).

FIGURE 9.3 • Practice Informs Research and Research Informs Practice

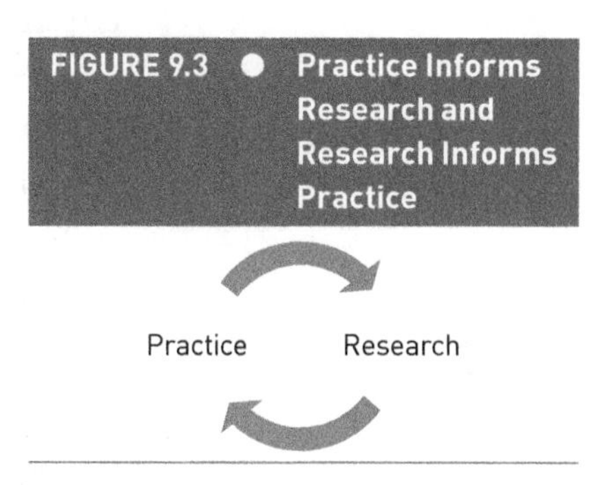

Evidence-Based Practice

Evidence-based practice has its supporters and its skeptics (Gibbs & Gambrill, 2002; Langer & Leitz, 2015; Thyer & Myers, 2011). Supporters believe that evidence-based practice encourages workers to ask questions, look for answers, and find evidence (Langer & Leitz, 2015). Supporters of evidence-based practice also note that when workers use evidence-based practice their own experiences can help others decide what research questions to ask. The idea of using practice examples to inform future research is what the Council on Social Work Education (CSWE; 2015) calls **practice-informed research**. In this way, there is a feedback loop where evidence informs practice and practice informs future research. For example, a worker uses the motivational interviewing (MI) techniques we've discussed to help a couple get through marital conflict. They carefully measure what they did and how successful their efforts were. Then that worker or a researcher knows what to research to see whether those techniques might be a good idea for use with other clients in similar situations. Keep in mind that one social worker can be the person finding the evidence for their own practice, practicing and gaining more evidence, and then developing more research based on those findings. Of course, many people are often involved: Practicing workers can look up studies to get direction for their practice alongside researchers who are designing their studies based on what practitioners have found. Supporters believe the process of evidence-based practice keeps people from relying too much on knowledge that people think they have about their own practice rather than information that they know about their own practice (Engel & Schutt, 2017). This all sounds very good: Practice relies on science, and the development of knowledge relies on practice experience. Remember that there are skeptics of evidence-based practice as well as supporters. The skeptics have some good points. Skeptics worry that people may apply a practice method that really doesn't fit the client just because the research says it will work. They also worry that they may not even know how to carry out the method anyhow, a problem called a lack of **fidelity** (Langer & Leitz, 2015). They figure it's kind of like making a cake for a pie contest with a recipe in grams when you think in ounces. You may want to rethink your choice of recipe, and while you can learn how to measure in grams, you had better do that before you start cooking. Another concern about evidence-based practice is that it is possible that some payment sources like insurance companies may demand the use of a practice that has been identified as evidence-based whether or not it is best for your clients (Rubin & Babbie, 2017). Still another concern is that the process of evidence-based practice disregards the knowledge that workers have gained over many years of practice in a similar setting with similar clients. This is knowledge called practice wisdom, and it has been recognized as legitimate (CSWE, 2015). Finally, skeptics may feel that client self-determination is taken away when the worker is deciding implementation strategies without input from the client or client system representative.

The answer seems to be a definition of evidence-based practice that relies on the supporters and acknowledges the skeptics. Let's try this one:

- Evidence-based practice is social work practice that is
  - part of lifelong learning that supports decision-making (Gibbs & Gambrill, 2002) and
  - encourages workers to integrate evidence with their
    - professional values (Thyer & Myers, 2011),
    - clients' circumstances (Gibbs & Gambrill, 2002),
    - practice wisdom (Rubin & Babbie, 2017), and
    - client choice (O'Neill, 2015).

In other words, social workers should always be learning about their clients from scientific sources. That's a given, and you should remember that statement. Here it is again: Social workers should always be learning about their clients from scientific sources. However, workers should not stop there. They should tailor their work toward what they have learned as long as they also consider their professional values, who their clients are, what they and others already know, and what their clients want.

Process of Evaluating Research for Evidence-Based Practice

The first step in making decisions about evidence-based practice is the development of a question. This question asks this: "What implementation has the best effects?" Keep in mind that multisystem practice (MSP) reminds us that by "implementation" we mean considering work with individuals, families, groups, organizations, and communities *all at the same time*. For this reason, when we ask about what implementation is best, we are asking about direct implementation with individuals, families, or groups, but we also mean "What program has the best effects?" or "What policy has the best effects?" (Rubin & Babbie, 2017).

When Carmen began her work with Andrea and her new parents, she had two basic questions. First, she wondered what types of implementation would be best to help all of the family members call themselves a family. She wanted to know the best method for helping the family to develop a sense of unity. She suspected that she would have achieved that goal when Andrea would start to call David and Jackie Mom and Dad since that goal had all of the qualities of good practice wisdom: It was a tradition in the agency that a child who called their adoptive parents Mom and Dad was on their way to a pretty smooth transition to a forever home. This idea had the authority of her supervisor, who had worked in the field of adoption for many years, and it made common sense. All together, these elements indicated legitimate practice wisdom (Rubin & Babbie, 2017; see Figure 9.4).

FIGURE 9.4 • Elements of Practice Wisdom

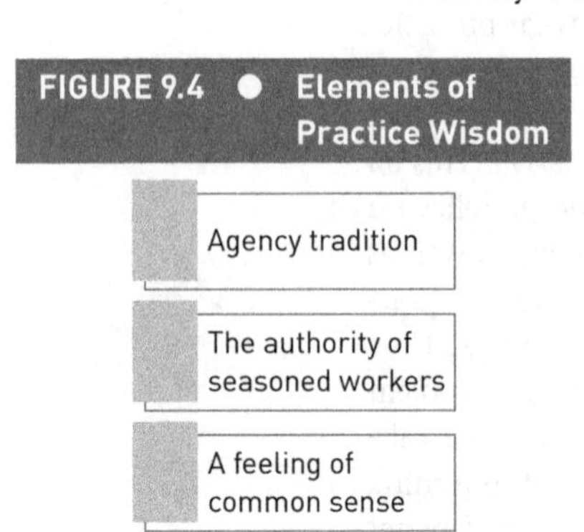

Second, Carmen had another question as she approached the scientific literature: She wanted to know what types of agency policy and programming would best help the family feel united.

So Carmen began the second step of the evidence-based practice process. She conducted a literature review. First, she went to the website of the NASW and signed in as a member. She used the journal *Social Work* published by NASW because as an NASW member she could get full articles for free, but mainly she used the journal because she knew that it was **peer reviewed**. In other words, reputable social work researchers had read each article, asked for revisions, and approved the final product.

In the NASW website, Carmen clicked on Resources and Information and the journal *Social Work*. She went to the advanced search bar and searched "foster care" and "adoption." She saw that some of the results that she got were very old, so she sorted the search by "newest to oldest." Eventually she found an article that contained both foster care and adoption called "In-Home Implementation with Families in Distress" (Waisbrod, Buchbiner, & Possick, 2012). That article was qualitative—where the data studied were words. In this study, the words analyzed were case studies. Carmen felt that an article with four in-depth case studies might teach her something about her work with this family. She learned that in-home implementations seemed to be successful and that families can be helped by encouraging them to make stories, or narratives, about their lives. The situations in the case studies were not exactly like Andrea's, but Carmen felt like she got some good ideas that could be **transferable** to her case. In other words, the situation that concerned her seemed similar enough to the case studies to transfer the findings of the study to her thinking about Andrea and her parents. Carmen knew from her research class that she could not **generalize** the article's findings to other cases because the **sample** (four cases) was so small. In other words, she shouldn't feel confident that she could repeat exactly what the workers did in the case studies, but she could use the case studies to get some good ideas. In addition to developing some support for the idea that home visits were helpful as agency policies in adoption agencies, she learned that a useful implementation method with families of foster care and adoption is the use of a photo album to help families tell stories about unity. The article noted that the use of a photo album is based in narrative theory. Carmen wondered whether the use of narrative in the planned change process was evidence-based, so she looked up narrative theory. She didn't find much about that in *Social Work*, so she knew she had to go further.

Using Google Scholar, she searched "narrative" and "adoption" and found a peer-reviewed article called "Adoption Narratives, Trauma, and Origins" (Homans, 2006). She quickly saw that this article reviewed the importance for adoptive families to create their own stories about their family origins. Next, she checked the photo album idea with her supervisor. Her supervisor's practice wisdom supported the idea of using the photo album to help the family tell their past story and move forward. She told Carmen that this was a technique used by some of the workers at her agency as a regular practice. Carmen thought it made sense.

WHAT IF . . . FOCUS ON DIVERSITY

Carmen is practicing in a rural community. Sometimes there is a shortage of social workers in rural areas. Suppose Jackie tells Carmen that her aging mother is healthy but needs help to stay in her home. If she doesn't get help soon, Jackie will feel obligated to bring her mother home to the trailer, where it will be so very crowded that everyone agrees conflict is certain to happen. Carmen looks and finds that there is no community-based in-home care or independent living assistance agencies. Carmen knows that there is a countywide Area Agency on Aging, but she also knows that they are so backed up that a worker will not be able to see Jackie's mom for weeks or even months. She makes the referral, but what should she do next?

Carmen's process included the following steps in evaluating for evidence-based practice (also see Figure 9.5):

- Developed a research question
- Searched for evidence in peer-reviewed journals
- Evaluated the articles she found to see if they were up to date and whether the research methods seemed to fit the research question
- Considered how the article sampled participants and whether the article might be appropriate for her client system
- Checked her conclusions using her supervisor's practice wisdom, her values, and her clients' preferences.

When she saw that the Snyders' trailer included a small shelf for photo albums, Carmen asked if they would be willing to look at them as a way of thinking about their family. She told them that there were other things they could do, like develop a journal or a scrapbook. David and Jackie liked the picture idea. Andrea was excited to see David and Jackie in their younger days. Andrea saw a side of her parents that she hadn't seen before. As they told stories about their families and their activities in the past, Andrea was spellbound. Finally, Carmen suggested that they begin to print out some of the current photos they had on their phones. There were many that included all three of them, and as they began to choose some photos to print, they began to tell their story as a family waiting for a special child and carrying the story forward to include the new photos of the special child herself. During this time, they were creating a family narrative that helped to cement their relationships. It was during this meeting that Carmen asked Andrea to consider calling David and Jackie Mom and Dad. She asked Andrea what she thought of that. Andrea smiled shyly and nodded her head. David and Jackie looked at each other and smiled broadly, and both of them wiped tears from their eyes. Carmen pointed out that calling David and Jackie Mom and Dad could become an objective of theirs to help carry out their overall goal to become a permanent family. All three were enthusiastic. Carmen was happy to know that she and the family had created a measurable goal that they could work on right away and in the

FIGURE 9.5 ● The Elements of Developing Evidence-Based Practice

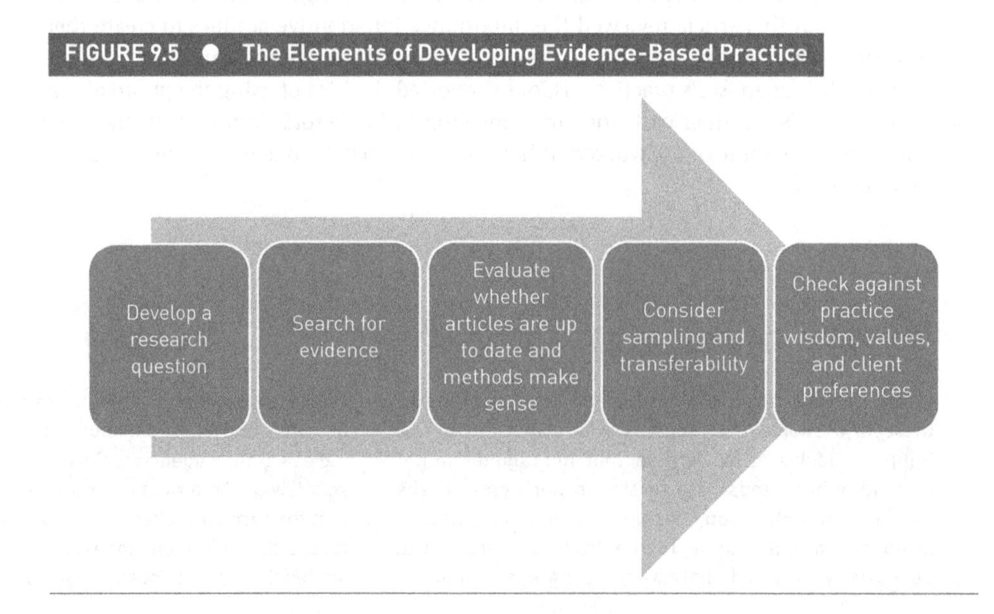

future. By the end of the meeting, everyone had laughed and cried. Carmen asked them to go over her own entrance into the family system and how she had played a role in getting the family together. That way, she became part of the narrative as well. Andrea took a picture of Carmen to put into the album. Carmen felt good about the implementation process and the way they had developed a new objective even though she was carrying out termination. Her goal was measurable, so she could use a measurement instrument called goal attainment scaling (GAS), which we'll talk about in a minute. Not only did she have a measurable goal for now and the future, but she knew that if she ever needed to help her agency understand the importance of home visits as a standard policy in adoption permanency planning, she could easily provide empirical support as well as practice wisdom.

Evaluation for Client Progress and Goal Attainment

Now we know that using evaluation during the planning stage of planned change helps develop evidence-based practice. That is, evaluation carried out during planning assesses the value of research for decision-making. The traditional use of evaluation, however, is evaluation to see how well clients are doing in the middle and at the end of planned change.

Checking for progress is an evaluation that happens over and over again throughout implementation. For that reason, progress evaluation is often informal evaluation. As we've said, it can involve a simple interaction within the social work interview that has the clear purpose of checking on clients' progress of reaching their goals. Use an opening statement when you are conducting informal evaluation. For Carmen, the process looked like this during a meeting in her office at the agency:

Carmen: Good morning. Thanks for being here. I know you've been having some car trouble, so I really appreciate your finding a way to get here. *(engagement, display of empathy, affirmation)*

David: We borrowed a car from neighbors.

Carmen: As you know, here at Open Door we work to help kids find forever homes. *(agency function)* My job is to support the adoption process. *(worker role)* I'd like to spend the next few minutes finding out how well we're doing. *(length of time, meeting purpose)* Does that make sense to all of you? Is there any immediate problem that we should address before we get into this? *(assess for crisis)*

Jackie: No problems here. I want to talk about Andrea's grades, but that can wait until later.

Carmen: David?

David: All good.

Carmen: Andrea?

Andrea: Everything's okay.

Carmen: Okay, let's get started then. Would you please talk about your experience of Open Door so far?

When an opening statement is used, both the worker and the client system are very clear about the fact that evaluation is going on. That will make everyone stop and think about their opinions on their goal achievement.

In addition to conversations about goal attainment, it is possible to have formal process evaluations. These take the form of established measures of success. They could take the form of scales, like the Hope Index you completed in Chapter 3. Formal process evaluations may also take the form of tests about knowledge. For example, if you were helping a bunch of girls learn about intimate partner violence, you might give them a multiple-choice test about the behaviors that are considered to be abusive before you begin work with them. Then you'd repeat the test afterward to see what they learned. If you imagine those girls taking that test, you can see that the test itself will help them to learn. In work with families, groups, organizations, and communities, you might give the same scale or test to every participant or you might just test the client representative. For example, if you were helping an organization to be more responsive to staff needs you might give a Job Satisfaction Scale to all of the employees. If you were working with a town, you might ask the borough council to participate in an evaluation, or you might just give it to the council manager.

Client Satisfaction Measures

One way to measure the success of your work is to ask your clients and client system representatives if they are satisfied with the service they received. There are many client satisfaction measures available (Corcoran & Fischer, 2013). The measures can be used online, over the telephone, or given to clients for pen and paper use. This is a very convenient way of finding out how many of the clients are experiencing the agency's work, and they can reveal things the worker or the agency could do differently to better serve them. There are several things that require extra thought when you are trying to measure client satisfaction. **Social desirability bias** is a concern. In other words, clients may want to answer the survey in a way that the worker and the agency expects it to be completed. You don't get meaningful responses because the client is trying to please. There has to be a way for clients to feel that their responses won't be judged harshly. One way is to assure them that no one will find out what they said.

For that reason, **confidentiality in research** is paramount for client satisfaction measures. Many times, clients don't wish to offend their social worker or they would be embarrassed to learn that their social worker knew their responses to the survey. So clients must have assurances that their survey responses will be confidential. If a client is not convinced of their confidentiality, they will not answer honestly, and the outcomes will be meaningless. There are some practices to avoid and some to embrace to get honest, meaningful outcomes on a client satisfaction measure. First, what you *don't* do is to have the worker hand a written survey to a client. Even though the client may be taking the survey home to complete, they will feel as if their worker will know who completed the survey. Likewise, there should not be an open area for storage of completed surveys. For example, no client should see a pile of surveys on the desk of an administrative assistant. The results may be entirely confidential, but the client will not believe it. One way to get around this problem in perception is to offer the survey through the post office. If the survey comes on paper in the mail, there may be a greater feeling of confidentiality for the client. On the other hand, you will undoubtedly have a hard time getting responses. The same is true for computer-generated surveys. Many people simply won't bother to complete them. If they do, you may find that **selection bias** is at work. In that case, the only people who complete the survey are either very pleased with the service or very dissatisfied. To respond to that bias, you might try having a computer available so that clients can complete the survey without leaving the office. You will again run into confidentiality concerns, but perhaps computer-generated results will feel more confidential to the client. If clients are directed to a computer as a matter of course they are likely to complete the survey. Of course, this brings up the question of **research ethics**. We want to be sure that clients don't feel that their service is influenced by their willingness or unwillingness to complete a survey. This assurance might be most effective if it is stressed verbally.

To take advantage of this opportunity, the agency can offer the survey over the phone. In this way, the survey is given by an agency representative who is unknown to the client, lending a feeling of confidentiality and an assurance that they are free to answer the questions or not. For these reasons, telephone interviews may be an effective way of completing client satisfaction surveys. Not every client will be available, phone numbers will be outdated, and extremely vulnerable populations may not have phones at all—not only that but this method is costly in terms of time: The agency has to pay someone to administer the surveys. It is important to know that while all of these methods for measuring client satisfaction have drawbacks, they are all valuable in some way even if they serve only to let clients know that the agency cares what they think. If the agency wants to know clients' opinion of services, then client satisfaction measures should be attempted. In any kind of outcome measure, it is easy to say that there are research biases, and we might as well not bother. If that's the attitude, we will never have any research in social work at all. At that point, the worker will do well to hire an expert so that the research gets completed.

SELF-REFLECTION 9: PATIENT SATISFACTION SURVEY

Think about some service you've received recently. Maybe you've gone to the dentist or had your car serviced. While you are thinking about that, complete the Patient Satisfaction Survey on pages 270–271. How would your service provider have to administer this questionnaire to get you to believe your responses were confidential? To get you to complete it at all? The brevity of the survey may be helpful to get you to complete it, but was there anything you would have liked to say that was not mentioned on the survey?

Program Evaluation

Program evaluations are often required by funding sources. In these cases, evaluations are conducted to determine the success of the program overall. This type of evaluation is an outcome, or **summative evaluation**, or one that helps determine whether the program should be continued or abandoned in favor of an alternative (Engel & Schutt, 2017). To **measure program effectiveness**, it is always tempting to measure how many clients were served or how many hours of service were provided. This is not a sufficient measure of effectiveness. Instead, numbers of clients served may be an important component of **measuring agency efficiency**. Measuring how many resources (such as how many hours the agency has to pay staff to complete a task) is a good way of assuring funders that their money has been well spent. However, the funder also wants to know if the program is a success. Counting clients served is not sufficient because the agency may have served a lot of people but only made their problems worse. To supplement measures of how many and what types of clients are served, program goals must be made central to program evaluation. If the evaluation centers on the program goals, funders can easily see whether goals are completed. A good way to measure goal completion for programs is GAS as discussed in the next section.

CRITICAL THINKING AND COLLABORATIVE LEARNING EXERCISES 9.2

In a large group interview, ask your social work program director how they measure program outcomes. Ask if measures are formal or informal; summative or formative; measures of effectiveness or efficiency.

Section 9.3: Goal Attainment

This section covers a particular method for measuring success on the micro, mezzo, and macro levels for both process and outcome evaluation. This method is called **goal attainment scaling (GAS)**.

GAS can be used with systems of all sizes to measure the effectiveness of services (Rubin & Babbie, 2017). To use the GAS, you identify a small number of goals and make sure that their objectives are measurable. Remember that in work with individuals, families, or groups, the goals are developed between the client or client system representative and the worker, and each goal is accomplished through a series of objectives. In work with organizations and communities, the goals are based on the mission of the agency, and they, too, have specific objectives that are used to carry them out. Because the GAS forces you and the client or client system representative to be specific about outcomes for each objective, both of you are clear about what you are working toward. If you are clear about what you are working toward, you will know when you have achieved success. Success may be related to knowledge gained (like individual information on parenting skills or community literacy levels), status changes (like going from homelessness to sheltered or from a community's high unemployment to low unemployment), or improvement of a condition (like from a mental illness to wellness or from an organization's inaccessible building to an accessible one). The GAS measures various levels of success, so it can be used as motivation or a call for work. Consider the possible outcomes for each objective, and rank them from +2 to –2. Zero is the expected outcome.

Consider this example: Carmen and Andrea's family were working toward successful adoption. The most fundamental objective Carmen's agency used to move toward that goal was the completion of a large packet of complicated forms. The family needed to complete the forms before the adoption was finalized. Since some of the forms required a specific activity, like getting a physical, the enormous task was easy to put off. Carmen knew that most families had trouble with the paperwork, so she wanted to know the status of the objective in an ongoing way. She also wanted to provide some motivation. The GAS seemed perfect. Here's how it looked:

GOAL ATTAINMENT MEASURE

Client(s): Jackie, David, Andrea Worker: Carmen Diaz

Theme of Goal/Problem Area: Adoption Success

Behavior to Be Measured: Paperwork Completion

Date of Goal Attainment Scaling Implementation: August 21, 2017

Projected Final Scoring Date: February 21, 2018

Level of Outcome	Objective
Best possible success (+2)	All forms complete and submitted
More than expected success (+1)	All forms for the family to fill out complete and all necessary forms distributed to others (doctor, dentist, references)
Expected level of success (0)	Forms completed but no distribution to others
Less than expected success (–1)	Simple forms completed
Most unfavorable outcome (–2)	No form completed

Initial Rating (baseline)/Date: ______/______

Ongoing Rating/Date: ______/______

Ongoing Rating/Date: ______/______

Final Rating/Date: ______/______

Follow-Up Rating/Date: ______/______

FIGURE 9.6 • Chart of the Adoption Paperwork Completion

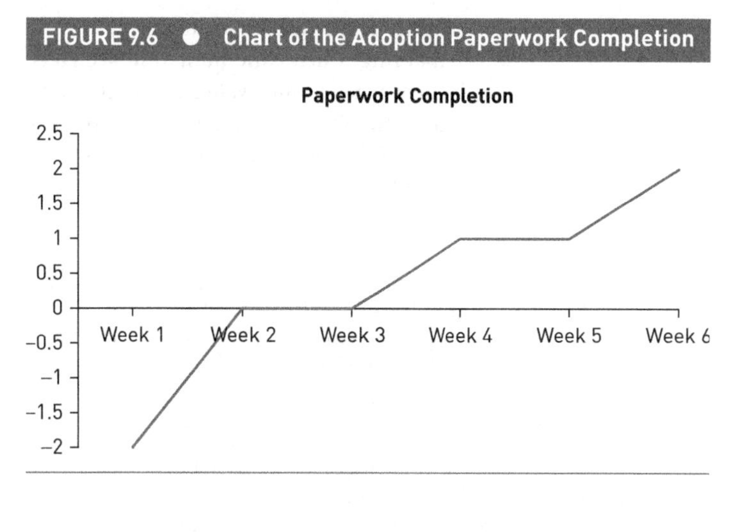

Once Carmen began to get scores on the GAS, she was able to record them and place them on a chart that made it easy for Andrea's family to see their success. The first score is called the **baseline**, or the measure of the client system's situation before planned change begins. In this case, Carmen determined the baseline to be –2, because the family didn't have the tasks before planned change began. In other situations, the baseline may be measured several times to get a clearer picture of where the client system is in the process of change. For example, a worker may get a baseline of a behavior from the client's file as it was collected during the initial meeting. Later, one or more baseline measures may take place before intervention on that particular goal is addressed. See Figure 9.6.

Each time Carmen met with the family, they used the GAS to reflect on their progress. It was particularly challenging to get the forms to professionals and references. Using the GAS, Carmen was able to help them identify barriers and complete the objective.

Back at the agency, Carmen's supervisor was creating a GAS form for her staff. The agency mission was to facilitate permanent outcomes for children. Sometimes, families were reunited after a child spent a while in foster care and the goal was family permanency. Other times, family reunification wasn't possible, and adoption became the goal for individual children. Either way, the agency was responsible to have a team of foster parents available at all times. That is, in order to respond to the goal of having foster families ready, the agency had the objective of recruiting new foster families. Carmen's supervisor was continually

GOAL ATTAINMENT MEASURE

Staff member(s): Betty, Joan, Sally Supervisor: Kim

Theme of Goal/Problem Area: Have foster families ready

Behavior to be Measured: Recruitment

Date of Goal Attainment Scaling Implementation: June 1, 2017

Projected Final Scoring Date: May 31, 2018

Level of Outcome	Objective
Best possible success (+2)	More than 10 families recruited and trained this month
More than expected success (+1)	Ten or more families recruited and trained this month
Expected level of success (0)	Ten or more foster families recruited this month
Less than expected success (–1)	Three or more foster families recruited but not trained this month
Most unfavorable outcome (–2)	Fewer than 3 new families recruited this month

Initial Rating (baseline)/Date: ______/______

Ongoing Rating/Date: ______/______

Ongoing Rating/Date: ______/______

Final Rating/Date: ______/______

Follow-Up Rating/Date: ______/______

facing a shortage of foster families, so she implemented some efforts for staff to carry out that might help. She wanted to keep a constant watch on their success in recruitment, and she wanted to motivate staff, so she decided to use the GAS and measure their success each month. We've talked about how the supervisory process and the planned change process are parallel. It was obvious in the GAS—the line for "client" became "staff" and the line for "worker" became "supervisor." Her program level GAS is shown on page 263.

CRITICAL THINKING AND COLLABORATIVE LEARNING EXERCISES 9.3

Work with a partner. Discuss a goal you have, and identify a measurable objective. Help your partner to create a GAS for you. Discuss how the process felt as you were interviewed and your partner helped you identify levels of success. How might that process feel if you were receiving social work services about a private and emotional problem?

Section 9.4: Termination

This section introduces you to the idea of ending the planned change process in an intentional way.

Termination

Termination means to close the planned change process. It doesn't necessarily mean that the client or client representative will never see each other again, but it might. For that reason, it's important that we carry out termination in a thoughtful way. Termination is full of emotion for all of us—workers, clients, and client system representatives.

First, let's think about what a "good" termination might look like. When the worker and a client end the planned change process, what would we hope for? Well, we'd hope for everyone to walk away from the table feeling like they could go on and be successful. For the client, it means that they feel like they have a reasonable chance to continue with the progress they've made. For the worker, it means they are confident in the client's ability to maintain their changes. It also means the worker leaves the table feeling like they've done their best, and they leave the client ready to reach their full potential.

As we saw in Carmen's case, there may be really strong emotions regardless of whether the best possible outcome has been reached. As we've been saying, strong feelings on the part of the worker need to be examined and managed through self-reflection on behalf of the client and the planned change process. The client is probably going to have strong feelings, too, around termination. In this case, the client's emotions about the same event have to be looked at right along with the worker's. Another task of termination is to make plans for the future. Follow-up should be discussed as well as the option for restarting the planned change process. We'll discuss why all of these things may not be possible shortly, but for now know that there are three tasks in the process of termination (see Figure 9.7):

1. Discuss ending emotions of client and worker.
2. Plan for follow-up.
3. Plan for future return or referral.

Feelings About Endings

FIGURE 9.7 ● Termination Tasks

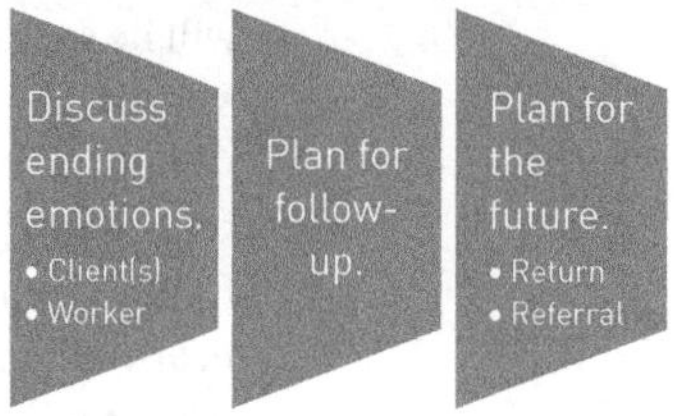

Like beginnings and middles, endings have characteristics that we can identify and use in our clients' best interests. Let's go back to the restaurant analogy we considered when we talked about beginnings in Chapter 2. Remember that when you go out to eat with a new person at a new place, you have the same kind of feelings that you have at the beginning of any social process. You are excited and hopeful, but you are anxious. You don't know what to expect from the place or the person. Let's carry the analogy forward and say that it is during the meal you have the experience. It may be great! You may love the food and the sparkling conversation. You hate for the night to end, so you go out for dessert later. Or, the food may be okay, the service lousy, and in the middle you may feel like going home. When it comes to the end of the meal, it's time for you to evaluate. You check with your partner, saying "All in all, what do you think?" And there could be a number of answers: "Everything was wonderful, and I loved spending time with you!" Or "The food was okay, but I have to get home . . . early class tomorrow." So there could be more excitement and a wish for everything to go on, or there could be disappointment and a sadness about hopes that weren't fulfilled. Sometimes endings are celebrations in themselves. Sometimes, endings are bittersweet. Sometimes, they're just sad.

All endings will not feel the same, and it would be best if we could be prepared so that we can help ourselves and our clients get through that stage. It has been suggested that worker and client emotions may vary in part because of the circumstances of the ending (Kirst-Ashman & Hull, 2018).

Here are some of the variables that affect termination feelings:

- Outcome
- Length of time
- Type of ending

Outcome

To some degree, termination feelings are, of course, dependent on outcome. When goals are met, there is more satisfaction than if goals are not met, and the more goals, the more satisfaction. Chances are, satisfaction will grow with the number of goals the client achieves. But there is more to termination than that.

Length of Time

Some types of planned change happen over long periods of time. In a residential setting like a group home, for example, people may work together day in and day out for years. On the other hand, the entire planned change process may happen in the space of a 15-minute crisis helpline call. The longer the time spent working together, the stronger the feelings are likely to be.

Type of Ending

"Type" is another variable that affects the strength of termination feelings. Types may be planned, time-limited, or unplanned. Sometimes the ending happens because all goals are met and there is a feeling of celebration. These are **planned endings**, and this was Carmen's situation. Andrea went from foster care to forever home. There is likely to be some sadness at this type of ending, but overall there is a feeling of satisfaction. There may be a bit of anxiety too. Both the worker and the client are going to be wondering if the changes will be sustainable. Again, the feelings will probably be strongest if the work has gone on for a while, but some degree of these feelings will be present even if the helping was short-term.

Sometimes, whether we're ready or not, termination happens because it has to: the service is **time-limited**, and the time is up. Many times this has to do with how much funding is available for the social work service. This type of termination can be particularly heartbreaking. You may find that you have been working successfully with a client who is near to reaching their goals only to have the time limit force you to stop the work. The goals were within reach, but now it feels doubtful that they will happen. Again, the longer the work has been going on, the stronger the feelings are going to be.

Finally, termination may happen because a client decides to end it. This is called an **unplanned termination**. The client may have decided to quit, but we have not been part of that decision. Sometimes, this means the client announces that they don't think they're getting what they need, and they're quitting the process. Sometimes, it means that the client just stops showing up. This can even happen when you are doing home visits. Sometimes, the family is suddenly never home, and they don't answer their phone. This can leave you feeling like you have failed in some way, like you are responsible for the loss of the hopes. You are likely to feel sad, even if the sudden termination had nothing to do with you. See Figure 9.8.

How to Make a Good Ending Happen

The way to make termination positive is to treat termination like any other stage of the planned change process: Make it interactive with the other stages. Termination may be discussed during the first opening statement, where the worker may say something like "and the agency will be with you as long as you need us." (Don't promise that *you'll* be with them as long as it takes—you may end up taking another job or getting a promotion.) On the other hand, you may have to say something like "We have the next 6 weeks to work on this, so let's get started."

FIGURE 9.8 ● Influences on Termination Feelings

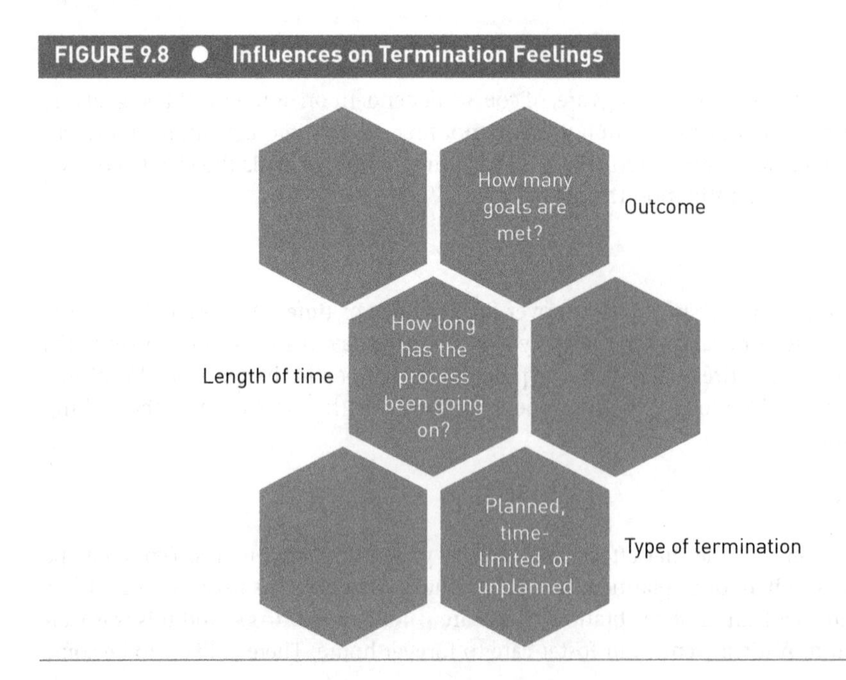

You really should begin with your initial self-reflection. As you work to master your feelings and develop empathy for your client system, it's best to think about how you might feel if the process is a success and how you might feel if it doesn't work out as planned. This will help you to do the "What do I feel/believe/know/do?" process when you get to the termination stage.

You'll have another opportunity to talk about termination during the planning stage. You may say something like "We could be working a long time on that goal, let's have some short term goals as well." Or you may say "Let's make sure we make every goal doable pretty quickly, we'll talk about how to keep them up at the end of our short time together."

You have the same opportunity at implementation: "It's great that you're getting so far since our time together is limited" or "Before we move on let's make sure the changes are going to stick. After all, we have a lot of time to be careful."

Finally, it's natural to talk about endings during evaluation. Unfortunately, it's often the case that if you mention some kind of limitation on services at engagement and leave it at that, you'll find that when you get to the evaluation part your client "forgot" that there was a limit. This can happen with systems of all sizes: the entire family, group, or executive team can "forget" that you had to end service at a particular time. So remember to treat termination like any other phase of planned change and make it interact with all of the other stages.

CRITICAL THINKING AND COLLABORATIVE LEARNING EXERCISES 9.4

Work with a partner, and reflect on a relationship that you've had with a particularly poor ending. Identify exactly what made the ending feel negative, and think about what would have made it a functional ending.

Section 9.5: Follow-Up

This section is about the final stage of the planned change process: follow-up.

Follow-up is the most neglected of the stages of planned change. This is primarily because funding sources seldom allocate resources for funding follow-up efforts. However, agencies and individual workers can commit to the practice of briefly touching base with clients and client systems after the service is complete. Follow-up provides a couple of opportunities. First, it is the opportunity for the worker and the agency to find out if goals are met. Secondly, it is an opportunity for the worker and the agency to learn about the services that they use as referrals. In other words, if the workers at an inpatient mental health facility are all sending clients to a particular counseling service at discharge, it would be best if they knew the clients were receiving the services effectively and as expected. We'll talk more about this when we talk about case management in Chapter 15.

Ideally, the worker should contact the client or client system representative at a predetermined time after services were terminated. Just as with any stage of planned change, follow-up can be discussed throughout the process. If that happens, the client will expect to hear from the worker at an established time and will have a chance to think about what their responses will be and whether they want to ask for further assistance.

At the time of follow-up, the worker follows up on the assessment they conducted at the beginning of the planned change process. It is important to know whether the success they experienced is maintained, but it is also best to find out whether the client's situation has changed at all. Workers should reference their notes about cases when they do follow-up, and they should document the follow-up as well, since there may need to be additional follow-ups.

Three outcomes can be the result of follow-ups. First, the gains may be maintained in relatively unchanged circumstances. In this case, the success was sustainable. For situations like this, the worker helps the client plan for the future, identifying what worked in the planned change process in case it needs to happen again. The worker also lets the client know whether their agency is available for future services or whether they would be able to provide referral services in the future. A second outcome of follow-up might be that the success of the planned change process is ongoing, but the client's situation has changed and different services are necessary. If the worker's agency can help, the client can be assisted in signing up for services again. If the worker's agency cannot help, they can refer the client for service elsewhere. Finally, it can be the case that the success was not sustained. In those situations, the worker helps the client to understand what was helpful about the process and what went wrong. The worker helps the client make a decision about future services. They will have to decide whether they want services and whether they want to go back to the agency or try to find an alternative. The worker will help either way. Since client successes don't always last, follow-up is essential to the planned change process. When an agency does not encourage follow-up, that practice can become part of a worker's efforts to develop and improve agency policy in the best interest of clients.

Reflective Responses: The Sad Worker

Carmen felt devastated when she went into supervision the day she had terminated services with Andrea. When she had left the meeting with the family, Andrea got upset again and was still crying when Carmen pulled away. Carmen explained to her supervisor that her mind kept going to the idea that Andrea had been abandoned many times before. Her mother gave her up to her grandmother; then her grandmother gave her up to foster care. She had been given up by two foster families after that. Carmen felt like she was creating another situation of abandonment. Carmen's supervisor reminded her about good endings. She reminded her that she had been talking to Andrea all along about the termination of services, so this ending didn't come as a surprise. In that way, the supervisor said, Carmen had provided an ending that Andrea could trust. Because of that, Andrea would be comfortable seeking help in the future. She would also probably be more likely to establish close relationships with others without expecting them to suddenly abandon her. Carmen recognized that she could think critically about her sadness. When she stopped blaming herself for abandoning Andrea, she was able to recognize that her supervisor was right. Carmen resolved to test this idea of Andrea developing new relationships and being comfortable to ask for help in the future when she conducted follow-up in 6 months.

Yuri Nunes/EyeEm/Getty Images

Critical thinking aspects of self-reflection can combat the painful emotions related to endings.

CRITICAL THINKING AND COLLABORATIVE LEARNING EXERCISES 9.5

Discuss in a small group why you think many services like auto dealers and online businesses work so hard at gaining follow-up once you've had an interaction with them. How do they benefit?

Section 9.6: Review and Apply

CONCURRENT CONSIDERATIONS IN GENERALIST PRACTICE

Ethical Decision-Making Challenge

Read Sections 1.15 and 1.16 in the *NASW Code of Ethics* (NASW, 2018). Do you think Carmen was behaving in an unethical way when she terminated services with Andrea? What might she have done differently?

Human Rights

Is anyone in this case being deprived of any fundamental human rights such as freedom, safety, privacy, an adequate standard of living, health care, and education? Based on the Universal Declaration of Human Rights, does a foster child have their human rights met?

Evidence-Based Practice

Find out whether there is any evidence that follow-up results in a return to service.

Policies Impacting Practice

Find out what happens when a student drops out of your college or university. Is there any follow-up? If not, do you think there should be?

Managing Diversity

Imagine Carmen's clients lived in a city. Do you think they would have had an easier time accepting Carmen, a Hispanic woman, if they did? Why?

Multilevel Practice

Identify examples of Carmen's work on all levels.

Micro: ____________________

Mezzo: ____________________

Macro: ____________________

Dynamic and Interactive Planned Change Stages

Identify aspects of Carmen's work where she worked in the following stages:

Self-Reflection: ____________________

Engagement: ____________________

Assessment: ____________________

Planning: ____________________

Implementation: ____________________

Evaluation: ____________________

Termination and Follow-Up: ____________________

Chapter Summary

Section 9.1: Evaluation in Planned Change

Evaluation is the process of checking to see whether clients benefit from social work. There are three purposes of evaluation. First, evaluation helps develop competence. Whether a worker is evaluating current literature to find best practices or evaluating their own work, evaluation helps the worker to improve their practice. Another purpose of evaluation is recognizing progress. This is good for the worker and the client or client system representative. Finally, evaluation of programs allows social workers to get the funding they need to continue their work.

Section 9.2: Three Types of Evaluation

Three categories of evaluation include research informed practice, where evaluation helps workers to choose appropriate ways of working with clients; goal attainment, where client system representatives and workers determine whether individual or program goals have been met; and client satisfaction, where the worker and the agency find out how clients would rate the services they've received.

Section 9.3: Goal Attainment

The GAS can be used with systems of all sizes to measure the effectiveness of services. It forces workers and clients to be clear about goals and objectives and breaks down tasks into manageable bits. The GAS allows ongoing measures of how the client system is progressing toward meeting their goals.

Section 9.4: Termination

Termination is the planned change stage where worker and client close the process. There are three tasks that need to be completed during termination. First, the worker must initiate discussions about the feelings that happen for both themselves and their clients. Next, the worker needs to help the client plan for a follow-up contact. Finally, they need to plan for the aftermath of follow-up—either continue with successful coping mechanisms, future return to the agency, or referral elsewhere for services. Discuss ending emotions of client and worker.

Section 9.5: Follow-Up

Follow-up is the final change phase. It is often neglected due to a lack of funding but should be carried out if at all possible, since it is the opportunity for workers to learn about the success and ongoing challenges of the services they've provided as well as the usefulness of any of the services they've introduced to their clients from other programs or agencies.

SELF-REFLECTION 9: PATIENT SATISFACTION SURVEY

PURPOSE: To measure client satisfaction with behavioral health treatment

AUTHOR: National Healthcare for the Homeless Council

DESCRIPTION: The patient satisfaction survey consists of open- and close-ended questions that can be completed by individuals and compiled by an agency to assess the quality of services provided.

NORMS: No data available.

SCORING: Higher scores indicate greater satisfaction.

RELIABILITY: No data are available. Test–retest correlations were not provided.

PRIMARY REFERENCE:

Patient Satisfaction Survey. (2015). National Healthcare for the Homeless Council. Retrieved from http://www.nhchc.org/wp-content/uploads/2015/10/sample-survey-behavioral-health.pdf

PATIENT SATISFACTION SURVEY: BEHAVIORAL HEALTH SERVICES

We would like to know how you feel about the services we provide so we can make sure we are meeting your needs. Your responses are directly responsible for improving these services. All responses will be kept confidential and anonymous. Thank you for your time.

Your Age: _____

Your Race/Ethnicity: ___ Asian ___ Pacific Islander ___ Black/African American ___ American Indian/Alaska Native ___ White (Not Hispanic or Latino) ___ Hispanic or Latino (All Races) ___ Unknown

Your Sex: Male ____Female ____

Please circle how well you think we are doing in the following areas:

	GREAT 5	GOOD 4	OKAY 3	FAIR 2	POOR 1
Ease of getting care:					
Ability to get in to be seen	5	4	3	2	1
Hours the center is open	5	4	3	2	1
Convenience of center's location	5	4	3	2	1
Prompt return on calls	5	4	3	2	1
Waiting: Time in waiting room	5	4	3	2	1
Staff:					
Provider Listens to you	5	4	3	2	1
Takes enough time with you	5	4	3	2	1
Explains what you want to know	5	4	3	2	1
Gives you good advice and treatment	5	4	3	2	1
Administrative assistant:					
Friendly and helpful to you	5	4	3	2	1
Answers your questions	5	4	3	2	1
Facility:					
Neat and clean building	5	4	3	2	1
Ease of finding where to go	5	4	3	2	1
Comfort	5	4	3	2	1
Do you feel safe?	5	4	3	2	1
Privacy	5	4	3	2	1
Confidentiality: Keeping my personal information private	5	4	3	2	1
The likelihood of referring your friends and relatives to us:	5	4	3	2	1

What do you like best about our center? ____
____
____

What do you like least about our center? ____
____
____

Suggestions for improvement? ____
____
____

Thank you for completing our survey!

Critical Terms for Evaluation, Termination, and Follow-Up

measurable goals and objectives 252
process evaluation 252
informal evaluation 252
formal process evaluation 252
outcome evaluation 252
anticipate the future 252
competence 253
transparent evaluation 253
research-informed practice 255
evidence-based practice 255
practice-informed research 255
fidelity 255
peer reviewed 257
transferable 257
generalize 257
sample 257
social desirability bias 260
confidentiality in research 260
selection bias 260
research ethics 260
summative evaluation 261
measure program effectiveness 261
measuring agency deficiency 261
goal attainment scaling (GAS) 262
baseline 263
planned endings 265
time-limited 266
unplanned termination 266

Generalist Practice Curriculum Matrix With 2015 Educational Policy and Accreditation Standards

Chapter 9

Competency	Course	Course Content	Dimensions
Competency 1: Demonstrate Ethical and Professional Behavior		Feature 3: Self-Reflection	Knowledge Values
		Feature 4: Concurrent Considerations in Generalist Practice	Knowledge Values
		9.4. Learn about terminating the planned change process.	Cognitive–affective processes
		9.5. Consider the importance of follow-up as a stage in the planned change process.	Cognitive–affective processes
Competency 2: Engage Diversity and Difference in Practice		Feature 1: Focus on Diversity Feature 4: Concurrent Considerations in Generalist Practice	Skills Cognitive–Affective Processes Skills Cognitive–affective processes
Competency 3: Advance Human Rights and Social, Economic, and Environmental Justice		Feature 4: Concurrent Considerations in Generalist Practice	Skills Cognitive–affective processes

Competency	Course	Course Content	Dimensions
Competency 4: Engage in Practice-Informed Research and Research-Informed Practice		Feature 4: Concurrent Considerations in Generalist Practice	Skills Cognitive–affective processes
		9.2. Identify types and purposes of evaluation.	Skills
Competency 5: Engage in Policy Practice		Feature 4: Concurrent Considerations in Generalist Practice	Skills Cognitive–affective processes
Competency 6: Engage With Individuals, Families, Groups, Organizations, and Communities		Feature 4: Concurrent Considerations in Generalist Practice	Skills Cognitive–affective processes
Competency 7: Assess Individuals, Families, Groups, Organizations, and Communities		Feature 4: Concurrent Considerations in Generalist Practice	Skills Cognitive–affective processes
Competency 8: Intervene With Individuals, Families, Groups, Organizations, and Communities		Feature 4: Concurrent Considerations in Generalist Practice	Skills Cognitive–affective processes
Competency 9: Evaluate Practice With Individuals, Families, Groups, Organizations, and Communities		Feature 4: Concurrent Considerations in Generalist Practice	Knowledge
		9.1. Explore the process of evaluation.	Knowledge
		9.2. Identify types and purposes of evaluation.	Knowledge
		9.3. Learn about the use of goal attainment scaling (GAS) for work with systems of all sizes, including individual and program effectiveness measurement.	Knowledge Skills

References

Corcoran, K., & Fischer, J. (2013). *Measures for clinical practice and research: A sourcebook* (5th ed.). New York, NY: Oxford University Press.

Council on Social Work Education. (2015). *Educational policy and accreditation standards*. Alexandria, VA: Author.

Engel, R. J., & Schutt, R. K. (2017). *Fundamentals of social work research* (4th ed.). Thousand Oaks, CA: Sage.

Gibbs, L., & Gambrill, E. (2002). Evidence-based practice: Counterarguments to objections. *Research on Social Work Practice, 12*(3), 452–476.

Homans, M. (2006). Adoption narratives, trauma, and origins. *Narrative, 14*(1), 4–26. doi:10.1353/nar.2005.0026

Kirst-Ashman, K. K., & Hull, G. (2018). *Generalist social work practice*. Stamford, CT: Cengage.

Langer, C. L., & Leitz, C. A. (2015). *Applying theory to generalist social work practice: A case study approach*. Hoboken, NJ: Wiley.

National Association of Social Workers. (2018). *NASW code of ethics*. Washington, DC: NASW Press.

O'Neill, M. (2015). Applying critical consciousness and evidence-based practice decision-making: A framework for clinical social work practice. *Journal of Social Work Education, 51*(4), 624–637. doi:10.1080/10437797.2015.1076285

Patient Satisfaction Survey. (2015). National Healthcare for the Homeless Council. Retrieved from http://www.nhchc.org/wp-content/uploads/2015/10/sample-survey-behavioral-health.pdf

Rubin, A., & Babbie, E. R. (2017). *Research methods for social work* (9th ed.). Boston, MA: Cengage.

Thyer, B. A., & Myers, L. L. (2011). The quest for evidence-based practice: A view from the United States. *Journal of Social Work, 11*(1), 8–25.

Waisbrod, N., Buchbiner, E., & Possick, C. (2012). In-home implementation with families in distress: Changing places to promote change. *Social Work, 57*(2), 121–132. doi:10.1093/sw/sws020

Recommended Readings

Pooler, D. K., Wolfer, T., & Freeman, M. (2014). Finding joy in social work II: Intrapersonal sources. *Social Work, 59*(3), 213–221. doi:10.1093/sw/swu020

PART III

Practice Across Systems

Roles and Skills in Work With Individuals

This chapter begins the section related to evidence-informed practice in systems of all sizes, starting on work with individuals. It looks at the way work with individuals crosses fields of practice and levels of practice. In addition, it examines the roles social workers play in work with individuals and the skills necessary for work in each role.

Learning Objectives

10.1 Examine the way work with individuals crosses fields and levels of practice.

10.2 Discuss the social work role of educator and the skills associated with it.

10.3 Explain the social work role of counselor and the skills associated with it.

10.4 Discuss the social work role of supporter and the skills associated with it.

10.5 Describe the social work role of advocate and the skills associated with it.

10.6 Learn about the role of student learner in social work.

Case Study: Aging Out of Place

Andrea felt her heart begin to race as she neared Room 327. She hesitated before knocking on the hospital room door. *I'm bringing nothing but bad news.* Knocking softly on the open door, she stepped just inside the room and said, "This is Andrea. May I come in?" If the older woman resting in the bed said yes, Andrea couldn't hear it over the loud television. She took another step and asked in a louder voice, "Pearl, okay for me to come in?" Pearl, an 85-year-old African American woman, looked up and said, "Well I guess you're in already. What do I have to say about it?" Andrea sighed inwardly but put on a bright smile. "Hello, Pearl," she said in a voice louder than the television. "I'm here to talk about your discharge." Pearl immediately grabbed the television's remote control and struggled with it until she was able to turn the volume down and looked at Andrea expectantly. "I have good news. Your doctor said you can be discharged tomorrow. The fluids surrounding your heart are lower, and you can get by with a pill rather than the IV in your arm." The older woman brightened visibly. "I'll be glad to get out of here." Andrea knew why Pearl wanted to get out. She wanted to get back to her daughter Dorothy's house because she felt she was useful there. Her two grandsons were old enough to be on their own after school, but Pearl knew she was company for them and helped to remind them to do their homework until Dorothy got back from her job. Andrea was so happy to know that Pearl felt useful and that the arrangement was reciprocal. When the boys came in after school, they shared a snack with Pearl and told her about their day. It was an arrangement that suited everyone. Andrea knew she had to be firm with the next part of the interview, so she began with an opening statement. "Pearl, as you know, I'm the hospital social worker, and I am supposed to work with you on getting you safe at home again. If it's okay, I'd like to talk with you for a few minutes about that." Pearl propped herself up on her elbows. "Is Dorothy here?" she asked. Andrea knew that Pearl had been living with Dorothy since Pearl's husband died the previous year. "I imagine she'll be in after work like she usually does," Andrea said. And then she knew she had to get on with it. "Pearl, your doctor wants you to go to a rehab center before you go home to Dorothy's place. Dr. Andrews spoke to the physical therapist, and they believe you need to get stronger before you go home. You know you've fallen a few times already, and we don't want to risk that happening again." Pearl closed her eyes, and Andrea saw the tears start to leak out. This was the part she'd been dreading. She knew that Pearl wanted to go home, and she knew that patients often felt like a rehabilitation center was just a nursing home by another name. Andrea soon had to terminate her relationship with Pearl, and she wished she could do it on a happy note. She also knew that next week was Pearl's 92nd birthday and that she'd have to spend it in rehab. On top of that, she knew that if she saw Pearl again, it would be because she was deteriorating rapidly. She felt like crying herself. But she knew she didn't have that luxury. She needed to help Pearl learn about rehab centers. And that meant she had to give her a chance to express her feelings. Andrea felt the pull of a thousand tasks. She had six patients to visit that morning, and she had team meetings to attend. There were a lot of good excuses for her to escape her own feelings by excusing herself and getting out of Pearl's room. No, she really didn't have that luxury either. She was here to serve Pearl, and she knew she would have to spare a few minutes. "Pearl, why the tears?" she asked. "Tell me what you're feeling."

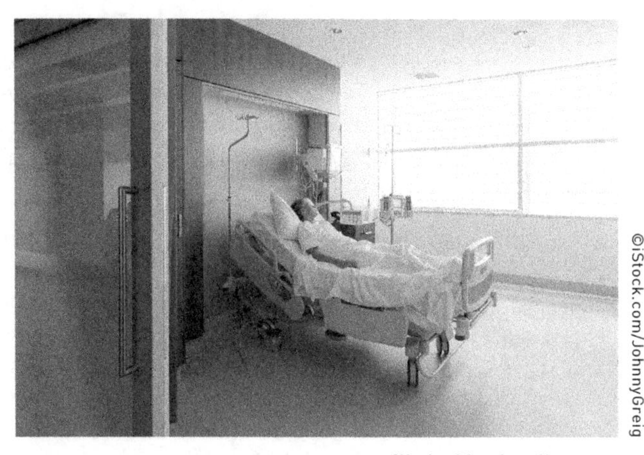

Work with aging clients may involve referrals to inpatient rehabilitation centers.

Section 10.1: Generalist Social Work With Individuals

This section is about the importance of the roles and skills used in work with individuals. They are used on all levels of practice with every population that social workers serve.

Multisystem Practice With Individuals

We've spent a lot of time discussing the nature of generalist social work practice. Remember back to chapter one, where we explained that generalist social work practice consists of

> professional efforts, under the auspices of an organization; guided by social welfare policies, social science theory, and a Code of Ethics to collaborate for planned change with individuals, families, groups, organizations, and communities to empower them to achieve their greatest potential in a local and global environment that is socially just and sustainable.

To review, this means that generalist social work practitioners are professionals that work for an agency (which may include an independent agency, or "private practice"). Generalist social workers are guided by a code of ethics and theories for practice. They look to the social and physical environment as areas that will benefit from change efforts. As a result, generalist practitioners work with individual, family, group, organization, and community-sized systems.

Also, remember that social workers use a planned change process to partialize their work so that it doesn't become too overwhelming to manage. Within that planned change process, the work can be further partialized into roles and skills. Social workers occupy various roles and use identifiable skills to carry them out.

Social work roles and skills are practices that can be used on every level: micro, mezzo, or macro. Often, we divide up roles among the levels for simplicity's sake. Keep in mind the idea that most roles and skills are used when working on all levels of practice. This is particularly true for roles and skills that we often identify as those used with individuals. The roles we play and the basic skills we use for work with individuals are always used: across system sizes and across fields of practice. We have discussed the way social workers often address one individual at a time. Even if we talk with a group, a family, or a community meeting as a group on the mezzo level of practice, we use individual skills, partly because we still often talk with one person at a time in those settings. In addition, social workers in any field of practice will use individual skills. Whether the worker is working in child welfare, organizational settings, aging services, family counseling, medical settings, group work, crisis implementation, and more, they continually draw on their skills for work with individuals.

Finally, skills with individuals are important across all phases of social process. Think once again about the characteristics of beginnings: anxiety and hope. Individual skills are used to engage people and help them feel that positive change is possible. In middles, when we are searching for the motivation to go on, we draw on individual skills to revisit goals, focus change efforts, and identify client strengths as well as barriers to success. When it comes to endings, we need our individual skills to manage feelings of termination, evaluate progress, and plan for the future.

WHAT IF . . . FOCUS ON DIVERSITY

What age did you envision Andrea and the doctor to be? What ethnicity did you imagine?

Think about why you chose those aspects of diversity. How might your "out of awareness" choice influence your social work practice?

CRITICAL THINKING AND COLLABORATIVE LEARNING EXERCISES 10.1

1. Review the definition of generalist practice. Do you understand it differently from the way you did back in Chapter 1? Discuss with a partner how you think you have changed in your experience of social work education since then.
2. Discuss the practice theories, models, and perspectives that provide the foundation for generalist social work practice. Don't forget to include multisystem practice (MSP).

Section 10.2: The Social Work Role of Educator

This section is about the social work role of **educator**. We consider the role and the skills that allow us to carry it out.

The Social Work Role of Educator

Here we are building on the discussion about the use of education in social work practice that we began in Chapter 8. When a social worker prepares for an interview, conducts an assessment, and creates a plan, it often becomes clear that the client system needs education. Very often there is no appropriate service available or accessible in the community, so the education falls to the social worker. For that reason, a role that social workers often carry out is that of educator.

Please note that engagement is necessary in the education process, and that means the development of empathy has to happen along with a worker's self-reflection. Also note that learning is not likely to happen if people cannot express their feelings first. Skills like labeling feelings and expressing warmth, empathy, and genuineness (WEG) are skills that the social worker needs before education begins. We'll discuss education as an interactive practice in the next section. For now, know that you don't approach an individual as if you were going to give a presentation to your classmates. You need to work within the context of relationship, and you need to be competent.

Comstock/Getty Images

In social work, education is collaborative.

It should go without saying that the social worker must become competent in the content that the client needs. As we discussed in Chapter 9, information should be sought from reputable sources: preferably juried journal articles or books that contain citations to journal articles. Many times, there is very good information available online, but that has to be used with extreme caution. As we've said, sites that end in .edu or .gov are generally valid. Sometimes a site is developed by an individual researcher, in which case you should be able to look that person up to make sure they are legitimate. Some sites will be put up by an individual clinician or even by a person who is suffering from the problem you are researching. These sites can sometimes be legitimate. Find out by seeing if some of their ideas are also reflected in the traditional, peer reviewed journal or legitimate book. Caution: You should *NOT* attempt to teach anyone a topic that is taught regularly by a medical professional who is particularly trained in the topic. This includes physical problems (which you refer to a physician) and medication interactions (which you refer to a pharmacist). In general, you must be competent in the subject area, and your supervisor must affirm that you are.

In addition to being competent with the knowledge base, social workers must be competent in evidence-based educational practices. In other words, the social worker must know something about the way the best teachers teach. To begin, know that simply telling someone something is not the best way to teach. Remember that this is called the "banking system" because someone is handing another person something and expecting them to hold on to it. This is similar to taking a class where the professor does nothing but lecture and a little while later you take an exam to show that you have held onto the information. Probably you have already discovered that the banking method is not sufficient. For this reason, you undoubtedly take notes, read the textbook, and study the notes and the textbook. If you know something about how you learn best, you might also write important concepts on index cards, or take practice quizzes, or discuss the concepts in a study group. These last activities are more in keeping with a practice that is called active learning. Put simply, active learning has to do with students taking some kind of action and then thinking about it. Activities can be reading, writing, or discussion, or the completion of projects (Riley & Ward, 2017). People can be asked to read something before or even during your discussion. You might give an "assignment" to a client and have the person write answers during or after your session. Finally, you may give information and then discuss how it relates to the person's life. In short, you are engaging the learner in the learning process. We'll revisit Freire (1998) and note that someone in an educator's role should be "open to new ideas, open to questions, and open to the curiosities of the students as well as their inhibitions" (p. 49). A social worker in the role of educator is teaching within an interaction, not transferring knowledge. For example, Pearl needed information about rehabilitation centers, but she was not going to listen until her feelings were heard and she could share her apprehensions as well as the knowledge she already had.

Education Skills

In order to carry out the role of educator in the context of a teaching interaction, the social worker will use many social work skills. Keep in mind that each skill requires a particular attribute. As we've discussed before, the worker may have to engage in mindfulness exercises and may have to display absent attributes to carry out a particular skill. Notice that the use of mindful, critical thinking about emotions and identifying the need to display absent attributes are the same skills that workers use in the engagement phase and throughout the planned change process. These skills are foundational and are used in most social work roles, including the social work role of educator. Some critical skills are discussed next.

Preparatory Empathy

As we've discussed before, in the self-reflection stage of the planned change process, it is important to remember the client's characteristics and challenges prior to working with them in any social work role. The worker must be willing to take the time to learn and think about the client before they meet for the first session and every one after. It is most important for workers to critically think about their own feelings and thoughts.

Displaying Warmth, Empathy, and Genuineness

The clinical work of the psychologist Carl Rogers is some of the most widely read and widely researched in the world (Elkins, 2009). For this reason, the work of Carl Rogers is at the foundation of nearly all of the skills we will discuss in this and other chapters. Rogers focused on **reflective listening**, or reflecting back to clients what they are saying so that they can connect their words to their feelings. One critical component of this work is to demonstrate empathy and a willingness to appreciate a client with **unconditional positive regard** (Arnold, 2014). Unconditional positive regard is a phrase Rogers coined. He meant that the client should always be met with a feeling of warm acceptance (Goldfried, 2007). Because of this idea of unconditional positive regard, or caring about a client as they are in the present moment, many of the skills social workers use are grounded in Rogers' work. Not least is the skill of **displaying warmth, empathy, and genuineness (WEG)**. This skill, probably the most recognized in social work, is part of the foundation of many forms of helping because Carl Rogers, like others, has struggled to practice reflective listening without sounding fake. To display WEG, the worker actually combines a lot of other skills. One component skill is the **engaging smile**. As we've discussed earlier, people instinctively engage with someone who smiles. Another skill we've discussed is appropriate **eye contact**. You have to carefully assess what type of eye contact is appropriate for a client, based on cultural and individual factors.

Another component of WEG is **tone of voice**. This skill is hard to describe. Suffice it to say that your tone of voice can convey caring. Try saying something like "You are a genuinely caring person." Now say that same phrase sarcastically, as if it were the exact opposite of what you really mean. There you have an idea of what a genuine tone of voice does not sound like, which should give you an idea of what one actually does sound like. It is important to note that Rogers often referred to mirroring the client's phrases in reflective listening, but he also focused on the *tain*, or the back of the mirror (Elkins, 2009). He was pointing out that the back side of the mirror (the black part you see if you hold a mirror facing away from you) does not necessarily reflect what is in front of the mirror. This means that the worker doesn't necessarily share or agree with the client's thoughts and the feelings that flow out of them. In other words, to display WEG the worker may have to display the absent attributes we've previously discussed. Again, every social work skill requires some attributes, and the worker may have to use them even if they aren't immediately available. Attributes that are particularly associated with WEG include **empathy**, **receptivity**, and **patience**. We know from previous chapters that empathy is the ability to feel with a client, not for them. When you think of receptivity, think of our discussion about diversity and cultural humility. To be truly receptive, you must be culturally humble. You take in difference with an open mind and a sense of curiosity. Finally, patience refers to the ability to pace the interview with the client's need and use silence as needed.

Use of Silence

The **use of silence** is another way of engaging in reflective listening. Carl Rogers found the use of silence to be so important that he often uttered very few words in a session. As we touched on earlier, the use of silence can be extremely important to clients who have not had a chance to share their story and their feelings with anyone. Even when the social worker plays the role of educator, there may be much more silence than in an everyday conversation. Think about the times your professors ask a question to gauge student interest. A lot of silence often follows, right? Social workers need to practice allowing silence even though it may feel very uncomfortable. Research has revealed that counselors think about the session, observe the client, and convey interest while they are giving the client space to speak at their own pace (Hill, Thompson, & Ladany, 2003). The use of silence requires patience and self-confidence. You must be self-confident to avoid worrying about looking as if you don't know what to say.

Paraphrasing or Making Reflective Statements

Another way of reflective listening is **paraphrasing** or making **reflective statements**. As we've discussed in the section of Chapter 7 related to motivational interviewing (MI), to make a reflective statement is to repeat what the client just said using different words. This helps the client feel that you are paying attention. It also helps you to make sure you understand what the client means to say. In work with a flabbergasted parent, a social worker may say "So did I hear you say that Sally's soccer practice is scheduled at the same time as Benny's gymnastic sessions?" Specific attributes needed for this skill include patience and the ability to focus intently on what the client is saying.

Labeling Feelings

Many times clients don't recognize that they have a strong feeling, and they don't know exactly how they feel. They may only know that they are uncomfortable. Since feelings can get in the way of the learning process, **labeling feelings** may be important in the social work role of educator. It also may be important for a client to recognize exactly what feeling they have. A learner may become frustrated when they don't understand a concept, but anger can seem like frustration. If a learner is angry, a more immediate response is necessary. Try statements like "You seem excited," "Looks like you're frightened," and "I hear you say you are mad about it." Use feeling words like *mad, sad, glad, afraid,* not words like *think* or *believe* as in "So you're thinking this is a frustrating situation?" Other feeling words are *satisfaction, disgust, apprehensiveness, nervousness,* and *hopefulness*. To carry out this skill, you need focus and empathy.

Open-Ended Questions

We've discussed **open-ended questions**, particularly as they are used in the planning stage of the helping process. These are questions that cannot be answered in a word or two. For example, when playing the role of the social work educator, you might say "What was the most important thing we discussed today?" rather than "Did you understand me?" Patience, focus, and receptivity are necessary to carry out this skill. You need to be willing to take the time to listen carefully to answers that may be less than efficient.

Offering Service

Social workers often discover—during the assessment stage of planned change or at some time throughout the process—that clients have challenges other than those that brought them in for service originally. At that time, it is important that the worker **offer service** in response to those needs. The service may be provided by the social worker and/or their agency, or the service may be provided elsewhere in the community. In situations where the service is provided in the community by another provider, the social worker takes on another role: that of broker. This is another complex role that will be covered in Chapter 15 on case management. Self-confidence and empathy are required on the part of the worker. You must be sure of available services in your agency and elsewhere. If you're not sure, you need enough self-confidence to say "I don't know, but I'll find out."

Giving Information

Of course social workers in the role of educator use the skill of **giving information**. The social worker attempting this skill must be competent in the knowledge area and must be able to show self-confidence. This competence should be affirmed by the supervisor. Remember that this skill is an interactive one. Keep in mind that the educational process is not a "banking" of information but an interaction where both clients and workers share information and ask questions. As always, the education skills above serve as the foundation for this one.

Skills for Interactive Education

Skill	Description	Example	Required Worker Characteristic(s)
Preparatory empathy	Considering client situations prior to meeting the client as is done in the self-reflection stage of the planned change process	"I've been thinking about that and I wonder . . ."	Self-reflection
Displaying warmth, empathy, and genuineness (WEG)	Conveying that the worker truly cares about the client and is willing to try to understand them	(*in a soft voice with a slow tempo*) "That must have been hard for you."	Empathy Patience Receptivity
Use of silence	Asking a question, then allowing the client time to consider	"What do you think of that?" (*up to 20 seconds of silence*)	Self-confidence Patience
Paraphrasing/reflective statements	Restating the client's last statement in different words	"I understand you to say . . ."	Patience Focus
Labeling feelings	Naming the feeling the client is expected to have; providing validation or giving the client an opportunity to disagree and label their own feelings	"Seems like you're feeling _______." "I wonder whether you're feeling _______." "Sounds to me like you're feeling ______."	Focus Empathy
Open-ended questions	Asking a question that requires elaboration rather than a one-word answer	"What was that experience like for you?"	Patience Focus Receptivity
Offering service	Recommending social work services, especially when client has not requested them	"I think you might benefit from talking to someone about that. What do you think?"	Self-confidence Empathy
Giving information	Teaching, with active interaction with worker and client	"I've recently learned how to make a budget. I can help you make one if you like."	Display of self-confidence Competence

A Sample Social Work Interview in the Role of Educator

Andrea: I'd like to share some things with you about rehab centers, or short-term care, and long-term care, like what you might call nursing homes.

Pearl: I don't see a difference.

Andrea: *(use of silence; maintains eye contact; nods head; nonverbal encouragement)*

Pearl: My friend Mabel went to a rehab, and she never came home.

Andrea: I'm sorry to hear about Mabel. *(expression of sympathy)* I wonder if that made you scared of rehab centers. *(labeling feelings)*

Pearl: I know what they are. These places are where you go to die. I want to go home. At least I could die there.

Andrea: Thanks for sharing your thoughts. *(verbal encouragement)* It helps me get to know you better. I heard you say you'd like to get home. Can you tell me more about your life at home? *(open-ended question)*

Pearl: My daughter takes good care of me. I hate to be a burden, but I don't want to be in a hospital for the rest of my days.

Andrea: I'm sorry you even have to think about that. *(uses a slower pace, gentle tone, reaches over to touch Pearl's forearm: displaying WEG)* I wonder if it would help if you learned more about rehab centers. Would you mind if I tell you about some things I've seen when I've visited them? *(offering service; close-ended question)*

Pearl: *(silence but maintains eye contact)*

Andrea: I have had a lot of patients go to rehabs, so I went to see one. *(display of competence)* I saw people sitting in regular chairs and wheel chairs watching TV. I also saw them playing bingo, singing in a choir, and setting up a special dinner. They had special exercises to do and worked with physical therapists. Then they went to occupational therapy and cooked meals using a stove, microwave, and refrigerator. The idea is to get people as independent as possible and then send them home again. *(giving information)*

Pearl: *silence*

Andrea: I hear you being silent. Does that mean you are angry about this? *(labeling feelings)*

Pearl: N-no. I don't know what I am.

Andrea: *(use of silence giving Pearl a chance to respond)*

Pearl: I don't know what I am feeling.

Andrea: If I were you, I think I'd be scared. *(display of empathy; labeling feelings)*

Pearl: *(nods)*

Andrea: I'd worry that if I went to some kind of facility I wouldn't come back home again. *(self-disclosure)*

Pearl: That is what I'm afraid of.

Andrea: I see that you haven't lost any of the use of your good brain. *(pointing out strengths)* Suppose we make a list of the pros and cons of going to a rehab center? *(engaging in active learning)*

CRITICAL THINKING AND COLLABORATIVE LEARNING EXERCISES 10.2

1. Consider the Freire quote given earlier about the qualities of a good educator: They should be "open to new ideas, open to questions, and open to the curiosities of the students as well as their inhibitions." Discuss in a group how you might carry this out in a class presentation.
2. Work with a partner to identify as many words as you can that describe different feelings. Practice demonstrating them with facial expressions, and see whether your partner can label your feelings correctly.

Section 10.3: The Social Work Role of Counselor

This section covers the social work role of counselor.

Social Worker as Counselor

It's a bit tricky for a social worker to think of themselves as a counselor. This is because there is such a thing as a licensed professional counselor, and that person may not be a social worker. In addition, social workers sometimes refer clients to other types of counselors. However, social work is among several types of helping professions that help people by playing the role of counselor. A social work counselor can be a temporary role or a job description. Let's take a look at the differences among types of counselors.

Social Work Counseling

As you already know, social workers use MSP to locate challenges in a variety of systems in individuals' lives. That means we need skills for work with individuals, families, groups, organizations, and communities. As you've also seen, when we're not working with individuals we are often working with client systems representatives. As you're beginning to understand, that means we use a wide variety of skills and we're always on the lookout for client situations and situations outside of the client that we can target for change. Think of our social work ecomap where we map systems out of balance. We need a broad knowledge base and the flexibility to work with people in many different ways. Sometimes the help we offer comes in the form of education, and sometimes the help comes in the form of **social work counseling**. In that role, we use many skills that have evolved from a variety of social and psychological theories that we'll talk about in a minute. *We usually use counseling skills to facilitate clients' abilities to carry out the plans they have created in the planning stage.* This is particularly true of BSW level generalist practitioners. BSW graduates are likely to use counseling skills in the context of their generalist practice, but specialized counseling training is likely to be the purview of the MSW level practitioner. Overall, social workers in the role of counselor may have bachelor's (baccalaureate), master's, or doctoral level training.

Social workers use a variety of skills in work with individuals.

SELF-REFLECTION 10: THE LIKING PEOPLE SCALE

How much do you like people? Interpersonal orientation plays an important role in the way people develop socially and interact with others.

Take the Liking People Scale on pages 304–305, and compare your score to the mean score for college students. This applies to you even if you are more mature than the typical college student. Which questions seemed to affect your score the most? Did those questions seem to be valid? Do you think it is possible to care about humanity if you don't generally like to associate with a lot of people? Did you learn anything about yourself that may affect your career as a social worker? Discuss your score with a group of fellow students.

Peopleimages/Getty Images

The support of all family members is so important it is a social work role in and of itself.

If you recall from the first chapter, a number of professions help people primarily by talking with them, and along with social workers, they have basic interviewing skills.

Licensed Professional Counselors

Another profession that helps people primarily by talking to them is the **licensed professional counselor**. Counselors are most often prepared with master's or doctoral level training, and they use many of the same skills social workers use in working with individuals. In addition, they may be qualified to work with some specific problems. For example, a licensed professional counselor may be certified to work with people who suffer from specific mental illnesses. For this reason, the social work counselor who has a different set of competencies may refer clients to licensed professional counselors for service specifically related to those particular clients' concerns. On the other hand, the licensed professional counselor is more likely than the social worker to focus on the individual and not consider other systems. Here is an example: A school counselor may work with a student on behavior problems by meeting with the student each week. In another situation, a school social worker may meet with the student and provide counseling. They may be specially trained to offer social work counseling to the population they serve. But here is the main difference: The social worker is also sure to meet with the teacher, the nurse, and family members. The social worker may do a home visit. If there is a school policy that needs to be changed, the social worker will meet with school administration to advocate for the student. We see a bigger picture.

Marriage and Family Counselors

Like the licensed professional counselor, the **licensed marriage and family counselor** is usually a master's or doctoral graduate who provides office-based counseling. They are likely to perceive problems between the adult partners in a family or in the family itself, and their training is specialized in that work. Again, their specialized training may make them candidates for referrals from social workers who may or may not have the necessary competence to provide that service. Their counseling sessions include couples, families, and sometimes individuals. As you might expect, social workers also use similar skills and may have similar training, they just view additional systems for possible change.

Certified Substance Abuse Counselors

Unlike any of the counselors we have discussed, the certified substance abuse counselor may have a limited number of college courses and may be a peer support counselor. In other words, the **certified substance abuse counselor** may be recovering from a substance abuse problem. Their personal expertise is respected in the substance abuse treatment field. Other substance abuse counselors may have bachelor's, master's, and doctoral degrees. They are likely to perceive problems within individuals, although they are sometimes willing to spend some time working with families. Their specialized training and the specialized agency settings for their practice may make them candidates for referrals from social workers. As with other helping professionals, social workers also use similar skills. They just view other systems for possible change.

Psychologists

Psychologists are also professionals who use talking to help clients. They are sometimes prepared as master's level clinicians, but they most often have doctoral degrees. They share the use of counseling skills with social workers and counselors, but their area of expertise is that of psychological testing. For example, the social worker in a school may refer a student they suspect to have attention deficit hyperactivity disorder to a psychologist for testing that will potentially confirm that diagnosis. The psychologist may not function as a counselor at all.

Psychiatrists

The **psychiatrist** is a medical doctor who works primarily with individuals. While they must talk with clients to discover their symptoms and diagnose their mental health concerns, their primary function is to prescribe and monitor the medications that are necessary to help clients cope with mental illness. The psychiatrist's services are sometimes denigrated by counseling professionals because their appointments are often brief and because the medications they prescribe often take weeks or even months to reveal any changes. For those reasons, it is often the role of the social worker to recognize the need to refer clients to psychiatrists, to help clients explain their symptoms concisely, and to facilitate their use of medications as prescribed. Because many professionals identify themselves as counselors, it is critical that social workers carrying out that role identify themselves as social workers and work as always with MSP. Like all helping professionals, psychiatrists ought to be respected. Since they are not functioning as counselors, it is no surprise that their meetings with patients are brief.

Put simply, the social worker looks for opportunities to work with the both the individual and the environment. That is the basic difference between us and other helping professionals (see Figure 10.1).

Social workers acting in the role of counselor use all of the skills used in interactive education. To review, they include nonverbal encouragement; verbal encouragement; paraphrasing; labeling feelings; displaying WEG; use of silence; open-ended questions; offering service; and giving information. In social work counseling, additional skills are used. See the chart later in the chapter about explaining the skills used in the social work role of counselor. Keep in mind that carrying out each skill requires certain worker characteristics. You may need to display absent characteristics to carry out that skill. A number of skills are described next.

Ventilation

Working with receptivity and patience, **ventilation** is the skill in which workers allow clients the space to share their feelings. They both allow and encourage clients their own type of expression. Those may include talking, yelling, crying, artwork, journaling,

FIGURE 10.1 ● Skills and Attributes of Various Helping Professions

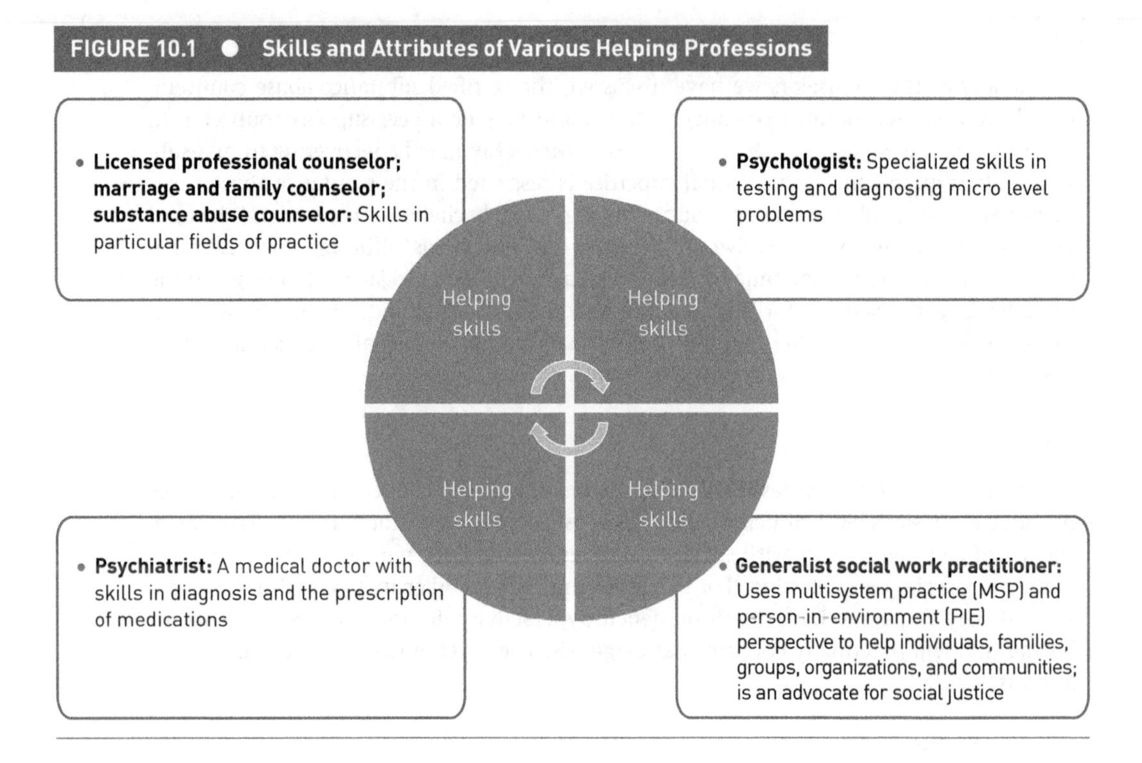

the creation of music, play, or dramatic expression. Often the worker shares in that expression—especially if it is one of joyfulness. Or a worker may silently hand a tissue to a client who is tearing up. Note that when a client is crying, it is often hard for the worker not to cry along with them. A little bit connotes empathy. Too much can express hopelessness. Remember that all of your actions, expressions, and words should be based on conscious decisions about what is in the best interest of the client.

Containment

Since expressions of feelings, especially sadness, anger, and frustration, can become overwhelming, social workers sometimes use the skill of **containment** to help clients move forward toward responding to the challenge that makes them upset. This means allowing ventilation but then putting the brakes on it. A good rule to follow is that containment should follow closely on the heels of ventilation if the situation is one where the client has some control and can act to make changes. Workers need to be receptive to the expression of feelings, but they need to focus the interview to provide containment.

Stating the Obvious

Sometimes a client is not aware of a situation that they have been talking about for a while. In this case, it is often helpful for the worker to **state the obvious**, or make a statement describing the situation. Know that the obvious is, well, obvious. A person may complain about their friends being unavailable, their spouse working too much, and their teenager staying out too late. The worker's response may be this: "Sounds like you're feeling lonely." For this reason, as soon as the client realizes that you have just succinctly described what is going on, they may have a sudden breakthrough in their understanding of their situation but may respond by saying "No kidding!" This is why the worker needs self-confidence as well as empathy to use this skill.

Probing

Probing is a questioning skill where the worker continues asking open-ended questions to help clients to express the whole story (Kadushin & Kadushin, 1997). Sometimes clients are not open to the thoughts themselves, and other times they fear expressing them. Workers need empathy to recognize that the client isn't sharing the whole story as well as the patience to slow down the pace of the interview in response to the client's needs. "Can you tell me more about that?" is always a good probing question.

Displaying Cultural Responsiveness

Remember that in order to **display cultural responsiveness**, the worker needs to strive to behave the way a member of the client's culture would behave. As we've said in Chapter 2, the worker must **exercise cultural humility** and be willing to accept information about the client's culture from the client. If you are not sure how to behave, you might consider asking the client how they would respond to a friend in the situation you are examining in the session (Murphy & Dillon, 2015). To carry out this skill, workers need to be comfortable with their own culture and have to have the self-confidence to say "I don't know exactly how to do this. Can you help?"

Role Play

A **role play** may be a response to a situation where the client is unsure of how to address another person in an emotionally charged situation (Knapp, 2010). The worker plays one person's part, and the client plays another. Then they switch. Often the worker plays the part of the client so that the client can see how they are presenting themselves. In this way, the client can also experience empathy for the person they need to confront. The worker needs to be confident enough to make mistakes in a role play. The client is likely to say "No, it wouldn't be like that," and this will be a moment of learning for both worker and client.

Identifying Irrational Beliefs

Using the skill of **identifying irrational (or automatic) beliefs**, the worker shares the critical thinking skills they've learned in their own self-reflection (Murphy & Dillon, 2015). Keep in mind that feelings flow from beliefs, and those beliefs may be false. The worker may ask this: "What are you telling yourself when you feel that way?" This skill requires focus and the willingness to slow down to let the client examine their own thoughts.

Normalizing

Normalizing is a skill used to help a client understand that others in the same situation would likely feel the same way or do the same things that the client is currently feeling or doing (Hansen, 2008). The worker may say that "many of the people I work with react the same way to that situation." The client feels relief knowing that their problems are being faced and managed by others. The worker needs to experience empathy for the client to know when normalization is needed, and they also need to be able to focus the interview. It is often necessary to interject normalization after ventilation.

Partializing Challenges

Often clients are overwhelmed by the life challenges they face. Once they are allowed to ventilate, they may need to hear that they can take problems one at a time. The worker helps by teaching the client how to **partialize challenges**, or organize the challenges into manageable parts (Shulman, 2016). The worker might ask this: "Why don't we talk about your wellness challenges first and then move on the work issues?" This skill also requires both empathy and patience.

Setting Considerations

Using **preparatory empathy** to determine what kind of setting will make the client comfortable, the worker tries to create an atmosphere conducive to sharing. As we've said before, **setting considerations** may include rearranging the office so that there is not a desk between the worker and client (Kadushin & Kadushin, 1997). Other setting considerations include the client's opportunity to experience privacy and confidentiality as well as the room decorations, background music, etc.

Taboo Topics

Remember that one of the things that separates a social work interview from a regular conversation is the worker's ability to discuss **taboo topics**, or ideas that our culture tells us not to speak about (Shulman, 2016). The worker needs a lot of confidence about their relationship with the client as well as a lot of self-confidence to bring up a taboo topic. Sex, money, spirituality, and political affiliation are some of the topics that are often considered to be taboo.

Focusing the Interview

As we've seen, the worker's ability to **focus the interview** is a prerequisite to many other skills. To carry out the skill of focusing the interview, the worker needs to have a relationship with the client and a careful plan about the purpose of the interview. Using self-confidence in their ability to stick with the session plan, the worker gently brings the client back to the issue at hand. The opening statement at the beginning of the interview facilitates the use of this skill. The exception to this situation is when a crisis has occurred. In that case, the session plan changes.

Calling for Work

Like focusing the interview, the skill of **calling for work** is predicated on the ability of the worker to help the client set clear goals for the interview. In that way, the worker can reference the purpose of the meeting to help the client take on difficult topics. Again, the worker needs self-confidence, or at least a display of it, to carry out the skill.

Managing Doorknob Comments

As we've said earlier, the **doorknob comment** is a statement tossed out over their shoulder by the client as they leave the session. Often that comment is a difficult issue for the client, and they only build up the courage to say it as they are leaving the meeting. The worker will be tempted to ask the client to sit down and further explore the important comment. If they do so, though, they will be establishing a potentially damaging precedent. If the client was only able to build up the courage to make the statement just as they were leaving, they must be confident that the session was going to end on time. If you allow the client to stay past the end of the session to discuss the doorknob comment, they will never again know when the end of the session will come. Doorknob comments are important, and by letting the session run over, you may destroy any future opportunities for the client to bring up sensitive issues at the end of the interview. The client has to be confident that the session will end on time to make a doorknob comment. Rather than letting the session run over, it is best to say "That sounds important. We'd better start with that the next time we meet."

Cautious Advising

As we've been saying all along, the planned change process is a collaborative one. For that reason, it is seldom appropriate for the worker to hand out advice to the client. It is better for the client to come to their own insights with our assistance rather than for us to tell them what to do. Still, occasionally it is permissible for the worker to engage in **cautious advising** or to make a suggestion to the client (Kadushin & Kadushin, 1997). This will be based on the worker's empathy for the client and their competence in the area that is being discussed. Don't make suggestions unless you know what you are talking about. It is better to seek supervision and make your suggestion the next time you meet.

Expression of Sympathy

Like cautious advising, **expressions of sympathy** should be used relatively seldom and with special care. Expressions of sympathy should be used in situations where the client has little to no control over events that are overtaking them. The worker needs the accurate empathy we've previously discussed for the ability to step back from the client's negative feelings so as not to let the client feel hopeless.

Reflecting on Spirituality

Spiritual beliefs are highly personal, so spirituality is potentially a taboo topic. For that reason, **reflecting on spirituality**, or asking about a client's beliefs in a higher power, is most often done in the context of the client's solid engagement with the worker and in the planned change process. Workers need self-confidence. However, spirituality may be an important part of a session because it is potentially an important aspect of a person's life that can provide strength and a sense of meaning (Murphy & Dillon, 2015). As in other areas of client diversity, the worker needs to be comfortable with their own diverse characteristics. In this case, the worker has to be willing and able to discuss their own sense of spirituality if needed in the session.

Behavioral Rehearsal

Sometimes it is helpful for a client to engage in **behavioral rehearsal**, or practicing a behavior right in the session with the worker available to give feedback. The worker needs competence and empathy to direct the client in a useful way. Behavior rehearsal may be necessary for a client to complete a planned task.

Use of Humor

When a difficult situation seems hopeless, the **use of humor** can be a great way of making the issue seem manageable. After all, if it were truly hopeless, you wouldn't laugh about it, right? You just have to be very careful using this skill, or the client may feel that you have invalidated their concerns. If you are someone who makes jokes frequently, you will have to carefully examine when and how you use humor in the professional social work interview.

Validation

Validation is particularly important when something painful has happened (Murphy & Dillon, 2015). If a client is mugged, for example, a police officer may lecture them on being in a questionable neighborhood at night. In response, they feel even worse, because their feelings about the crisis have been invalidated. The first thing they do is to find someone who will listen to their story. It is not most important for them to feel like the person believes them. Instead, it is important that they feel heard and get the message that it is understandable to feel the way they do. They don't need to hear "Oh, that is awful!" and they definitely don't need to hear "Are you sure that's exactly what happened?" The worker might instead label their feelings and facilitate ventilation. Self-disclosure may be important.

Self-Disclosure

Self-disclosure is a skill that the worker uses to display empathy (Miller & Rollnick, 2013). As we've discussed in Chapter 5, self-disclosure must be used with caution. The worker needs to use the skill consciously and in a way that is beneficial for the client, not for themselves.

Getting Informed Consent

Social workers often have to ask clients to complete and sign forms. Sometimes those forms have consequences. In other words, the client is making a choice when they sign the form. Rather than simply placing a form in front of a client and asking them to sign it (which they will likely do, often without reading it), the social worker has to use the skill of **getting informed consent**. They use their accurate empathy to help them understand how to present the information about the consequences of signing the form and make sure the client understands them before signing.

What to Say When You Don't Know What to Say

There will be times when your knowledge of skills fails you. The client or client system representative will simply overwhelm you with problems. You may find yourself simply not knowing what to say next. In those situations, all you have to say is something like "Let me think about that a moment." Your client will feel like you are listening very carefully. They may also ask you a question that you don't know how to answer. In that situation, you can say something like "Let me get back to you on that," or "I don't know, but I can find out." Saying "I don't know" is the mark of a confident person.

Relevant Skills in the Social Work Role of Counselor

Skill	Description	Example	Required Worker Characteristic(s)
Ventilation	Allowing and encouraging the expression of emotion	"It's okay to cry."	Receptivity Patience
Containment	Facilitating the control of ongoing emotional expression	"I see that you're really distressed. Let's talk about it more."	Receptivity Focus
Stating the obvious	Putting what has not been stated into words	"Is it the case that you're really angry at your boss?"	Self-confidence Empathy
Probing	Reaching for unstated emotions or thoughts	"I hear you saying you're sad, but what do you think is behind that feeling?"	Patience Empathy
Displaying cultural responsiveness	Being able to think like persons of another culture	"I've heard that Latinas are emotionally expressive. Do you feel like shouting about that?"	Self-confidence Comfort with own culture

Skill	Description	Example	Required Worker Characteristic(s)
Role play	Acting out an interaction the client is planning to have	"Okay, let's practice. You pretend to be your girlfriend, and I'll play you. Then we'll switch roles."	Self-confidence Empathy
Identifying irrational beliefs	Identifying the thoughts that underlie strong emotions	"Can you tell me what you're thinking when you feel that way?"	Focus
Normalizing	Teaching a client that their feelings and thoughts are not unusual for someone in their position	"Many organizations experience what you're describing."	Empathy Competence
Partializing challenges	Breaking problems into manageable pieces	"I'm hearing you say that you have two sets of problems: one that relates to work and one that relates to your son. Is that right?"	Empathy Focus
Setting considerations	Taking care that the setting for the interview meets the client's needs and is safe for worker and client	"Please sit anywhere you'd like. I'm going to close the door for privacy if that's okay with you."	Empathy
Taboo topics	Stating what is not acceptable in everyday conversation	"So right now you hate your mother?"	Empathy Self-confidence
Focusing the interview	Keeping the interview consistent with goals	"That is fascinating, I'm glad you shared it. But let's get back to what we said we'd talk about today."	Self-confidence
Call for work	Specifically requesting that the client address goals	"That's all very important, but I was wondering if you were able to complete your tasks this week."	Self-confidence
Managing doorknob comments	Keeping to the time limit of sessions even when the client introduces an important topic right at the end of the meeting	"You have really surprised me with that. I'll make a note so that we can begin with it when we meet again."	Self-confidence Focus
Cautious advising	Telling the client what you think they should do (use very seldom)	"I'd like you to think about what would happen if you told her exactly how you feel."	Self-confidence Competence Empathy
Expressing sympathy	Saying you are sorry for something in the client's life (seldom used, only when the situation is out of the client's control—e.g., the death of someone close)	"I'm so very sorry this happened."	Accurate empathy
Reflecting on spirituality	Allowing the client space to get in touch with and express their beliefs in a higher power	"Do you believe in a higher power?"	Self-confidence Empathy
Use of humor	Easing tension with some humorous statement	"So right about then you took out your handy water gun and sprayed her, right?"	Self-confidence Empathy

Skill	Description	Example	Required Worker Characteristic(s)
Behavioral rehearsal	Allowing the client to practice a desired behavior	"That will be challenging to do the first time. Why not try it here first?"	Empathy Competence
Validation	Acknowledging feelings without judgment	"I can see why you would feel that way."	Empathy Self-confidence
Self-disclosure	Sharing the worker's own experiences	"I had something similar happen to me . . ."	Accurate empathy
Getting informed consent	Making sure that clients fully understand their options and possible consequences	"I need to ask you to sign this paper, but I want to make sure you understand . . ."	Accurate empathy

A Sample Social Work Interview in the Role of Counselor

Andrea: Good afternoon, Pearl. How are you feeling today?

Pearl: *(tears beginning to flow)* They just told me my cat died while I was in here.

Andrea: Pearl, I'm so very sorry that happened. Was your cat sick? *(expression of sympathy)*

Pearl: Yes, she was. I'm not really surprised. *(wiping tears, turning away)*

Andrea: It's okay to cry. Anyone would cry in your situation. *(validation, normalization)* Our pets are like our family members. *(ventilation)*

Pearl: *(now crying again)* I had Tabby for 20 years. She was a good friend and my only companion.

Andrea: You must be feeling very sad. *(labeling feelings)*

Pearl: Yes, and lonely.

Andrea: You're feeling alone? *(paraphrasing)*

Pearl: Yes, I was always thinking about her while I was in here. Now there's no one to think about.

Andrea: Pearl, do you believe in a higher power? *(reflecting on spirituality)*

Pearl: Yes. I wonder if Tabby will be in heaven when I get there.

Andrea: What do you think? *(probing)*

Pearl: I think she deserves to be. Yes, I think she will.

Andrea: So maybe you could still be thinking about her? *(cautious advising)*

Pearl: I guess I can. Thank you.

CRITICAL THINKING AND COLLABORATIVE LEARNING EXERCISES 10.5

Work with a partner. You will role-play using the social work counseling skills listed previously. Remember setting considerations, and begin with this statement: "Social work counseling is complicated!" Let your partner respond, and work to use each one of the skills.

Section 10.4: The Social Work Role of Supporter

The Social Work Role of Supporter

Once a social worker has collaborated with a client to create a plan for achieving change, it is often the case that the client needs education or counseling to achieve their goals. On the other hand, the social work implementation that is needed may simply be cheerleading. The social worker may need to encourage and support people as they begin and carry out their planned change process. For that reason, we identify one role that the social worker plays as that of supporter. Supporting clients is an important role that is likely to be needed in addition to every other role a social worker plays.

Westend61/Getty Images

Social workers may advocate for families in a variety of settings.

As is the case in the social work role of educator and counselor, note that engagement is absolutely necessary for a social worker to play the role of supporter. It is always important for the worker to develop empathy during their self-reflection. Another thing all of the social work roles have in common is that people must express their feelings first.

While providing support, the social worker will use many social work skills that are used in other roles as well as some that are most important in the support role. Remember that each skill requires a particular attribute that may be present in the worker. On the other hand, the worker may have to display the absent attribute as we've discussed previously by engaging in mindfulness exercises. On page 296 is a chart of social work skills that are most important to the supporter role along with the attributes workers need to carry them out.

Nonverbal Encouragement

Using **nonverbal encouragement**, the worker silently helps the client tell their story and express their feelings (Shulman, 2016). To carry out this task, the worker nods, makes appropriate facial expressions, uses eye contact appropriately, and makes small sounds like "mm-hmm." The worker needs empathy as well as patience to allow the client space to think and to speak.

Verbal Encouragement

Using **verbal encouragement** is the skill of making short statements that let the client know the worker is interested and wants them to continue (Shulman, 2016). The worker may say "go on," or "I see," or "I'm listening." This skill usually accompanies the use of nonverbal encouragement. The worker needs patience as well as the ability to allow the client to set the direction of the interview.

Affirmation

Like verbal encouragement, this skill helps the client to continue sharing their thoughts and feelings. **Affirmation** acknowledges that the client is saying something important (Miller & Rollnick, 2013). The worker must have empathy as well as objectivity. Using these characteristics, the worker affirms behaviors and ideas with statements like "You are working hard" or "You're on your way to meeting your goal." Self-defeating behaviors are not supported as they might be if the worker used only verbal and nonverbal encouragement.

Empowerment

Social workers **empower** people when they help them to see the choices available to them (Murphy & Dillon, 2015). Note that this is not the same as "giving" a client a choice. Choices are not the social worker's to give. They belong to the client, and the social worker is there to point them out. Using empathy and the patience to take the time to help clients identify their choices, social workers help clients identify choices and explore the pros and cons of those choices.

Pointing Out Strengths

Like affirmation, the skill of **pointing out strengths** is about letting the client know that you expect them to succeed (Saleebey, 2012). By pointing out strengths inherent in the client ("You're very intelligent/positive/hopeful"), the worker acknowledges aspects of the client that will bolster their self-confidence. The worker needs to be objective, as the client will know if you are going overboard with praise, and the worker needs to be focused so that real strengths can be identified.

Exploring Task Completion

When **exploring task completion**, the worker gently reminds the client what the plan was and asks whether the client's agreed-upon tasks were completed. If the tasks were not completed, the next step is for the worker to examine what went wrong. Perhaps there was a lack of self-confidence, a fear of what would happen when the task was completed, or a need for new skills. At the same time, the worker has to be open to the idea that the client has no interest in completing the task. If so, it is back to the planning stage. The worker must have self-confidence to recognize that the plan they facilitated is somehow flawed.

Summarization

With **summarization**, the worker sums up an area of content, a session, or the entire planned change process (Kadushin & Kadushin, 1997). Using a clear focus on the task, the worker ticks off items that have been achieved or discussed. Another way to complete this task is to ask the client to provide the summary with a statement like "I think we've discussed a lot today, help me make a list."

Skills for the Supporter Role

Skill	Description	Example	Required Worker Characteristic(s)
Nonverbal encouragement	Making eye contact, nodding, having an open body position	The worker nods while making eye contact to encourage the client to continue.	Empathy Patience
Verbal encouragement	Making brief statements or sounds that encourage a client to continue	"Mmm. Please go on. Aha. Tell me more about that."	Patience Focus

Skill	Description	Example	Required Worker Characteristic(s)
Affirmation	Recognizing a client's successes or efforts	"I see that you didn't entirely reach your goal, but you worked really hard!"	Empathy Objectivity
Empowerment	Allowing the client choice throughout the planned change process	"What do you want to work on next?"	Empathy Patience
Pointing out strengths	Recognizing and verbalizing observed client characteristics that may become resources	"From what you tell me, I see you are a very determined person. I think you'll be able to figure this situation out."	Objectivity Focus
Exploring task completion	Asking clients directly whether they completed planned tasks	"Did you have a chance to work on our plan?"	Self-confidence Focus
Summarization	Holding up the important elements of the interview	"We've covered a lot today, including . . ."	Focus

A Sample Social Work Interview in the Role of Supporter

Andrea: Pearl, last time we met we planned for you to read over the brochures from two different rehabilitation centers. Did you have a chance to do that? *(exploring task completion)*

Pearl: No. I can't read that fine print.

Andrea: I can help you with that. *(offering service)* Would you like me to read them to you? *(empowerment by enabling choice)*

Pearl: Please tell me how these places are different.

Andrea: I hear that you are willing to consider these places! *(affirmation)* You are an open-minded person. *(pointing out strengths)*

Pearl: I try to be.

Andrea: What are your thoughts about rehab centers now? *(leans forward, maintains eye contact—nonverbal encouragement; use of silence)*

CRITICAL THINKING AND COLLABORATIVE LEARNING EXERCISES 10.6

Work with a partner. Identify some task you need to do but detest. Have your partner use the skills related to the supporter role to help you become more likely to do it.

Section 10.5: The Social Work Role of Advocate

Remember that one of the core values of the social work profession is social justice. In practice, that means social workers reach toward social change when individuals or groups are vulnerable or oppressed. To be vulnerable is to be lacking in necessities, such as services, information, or anything that leaves a person susceptible to losing their human rights. To be oppressed is to be blocked from participating in decision-making processes. For example, someone who is homeless is vulnerable, and someone who is unable to vote because their voting location is not accessible is oppressed. Pearl was in danger of being both vulnerable and oppressed: She needed access to rehabilitation centers and education so that she could make an informed choice. Andrea needed to advocate.

Where clients are at risk of being vulnerable or oppressed, social workers work to create change. In systems language, social workers intervene in the social environment where tension exists between their clients and some system that interacts with them. Social workers address situations when there is an unequal energy exchange where the client's energy is being drained by some system's lack of a response to the client's needs. In short, we get people what they need. Sometimes this includes access to information, the provision of any kind of service and resources, and the ability to play a role in decision-making. Social workers are constantly on the lookout for situations of social injustice. To do so, we have to continually remind ourselves that the status quo may not meet the needs of our clients. Most importantly, we have to be able to imagine a different world where clients' needs are met.

There is one caveat: Social workers only play the role of advocate when clients cannot do so themselves. If a client has direct control over a situation and there is time for them to address that situation themselves, the social worker should play the role of educator and counselor to facilitate the client taking action on their own behalf. For example, Pearl was angry about taking medications. When Andrea took the time to ask her why, she said she didn't know why she was taking them. Andrea could have asked a nurse, but instead she worked with Pearl until she had the necessary skills to ask for herself. In that case, advocacy was not needed.

To play the role of advocate, the social worker will need to draw on skills from every social work role, since advocacy may address a variety of system characteristics. Some skills that specifically relate to the role of advocate appear next.

ETHICAL PERSPECTIVES

See Section 6.01 of the NASW Code of Ethics *(National Association of Social Workers [NASW], 2018) to reflect on the social worker's responsibility related to advocacy.*

Displaying Confidence

As we've said before, there are times when social workers need to display the absent attribute of confidence. Remember to begin with a powerful, level tone of voice. Try not to sound robotic, but don't be too soft-spoken, either. Next, consider your nonverbal communication: Are you dressed appropriately? Are you standing up straight? Are you able to make direct eye contact? Don't forget your genuine smile and firm handshake. Finally, like any other skill, **displaying confidence** requires the practice of self-reflection. By using self-reflection, workers avoid getting too anxious to approach an individual as a target for change. They also avoid becoming too angry about an unfair situation to be effective. We'll talk more about the skill of persuasion in Chapter 14.

Displaying Competence

Don't try to **display competence** if you are incompetent. It sounds simple, but the reality is that when you take on the role of advocate, you need to be informed. If at all possible, work with your supervisor or an experienced colleague so that you have the knowledge you need to make a logical argument. Use self-reflection so that your argument doesn't have anger or anxiety in it—just facts. In the role of advocate, you shouldn't be modest or humble. Don't be afraid to let your competence show. A social worker needs to be informed, focused, and determined to display competence (Shulman, 2012).

Networking

Networking is the social work skill where workers develop and maintain relationships with other professionals. This practice helps the social worker to gain access to resources for their client and get valuable information that is needed for the role of advocate. Social workers need self-confidence to develop relationships with other professionals, and they need empathy. The skill of empathy is part of networking because the worker must understand their colleague in order to approach them successfully. If the worker wants information from a school social worker, for example, they don't ask at 3:00 p.m. when the worker is fulfilling their school bus monitoring requirement.

Skills for the Advocate Role in Work With Individuals

Skill	Description	Example	Required Worker Characteristic(s)
Displaying confidence	Showing self-confidence using verbal and nonverbal communication	Andrea excused herself to get a busy nurse's attention, then asked about the purposes of Pearl's medication.	Self-reflection
Displaying competence	Letting another know that you are informed	Andrea had basic knowledge of the purpose of the medication Pearl was taking	Knowledge Focus
Networking	Keeping in contact with other professionals who can help or provide information	Andrea stayed in contact with nurses when a client is hospitalized.	Empathy Self-confidence

A Sample Social Work Interview in the Role of Advocate

PeopleImages/Getty Images

It can feel hopeless when clients have few options for care.

Andrea: How are you feeling today? *(engaging smile; approachable tone of voice; eye contact)*

Pearl: I'd like to sit up.

Andrea: I see that you've slid down in the bed. *(reflective listening)* Have you asked your nurse to adjust the bed and get your head on the pillow? *(call for work)*

Pearl: I said I wanted to sit up, and they adjusted the bed. But I'd like to sit in a chair. I sat in a chair yesterday.

Andrea: Sounds like you did a good job asking for what you need, but I think they may have misunderstood you. *(affirmation)* Maybe you should ask specifically to sit in a chair. *(cautious advising)*

The nurse's aide enters the room to remove the lunch tray.

Pearl: I'd like to sit in a chair.

Nurse's aide: I'll be sure to let them know.

Andrea stops to check in 1 hour later. Pearl is still in bed. Andrea phones her contact in the physical therapy department *(networking)* and learns that there is an order in the chart for Pearl to sit in a chair for a part of each day. Andrea takes on the role of advocate.

Andrea approaches the nurses' station stand and locates the nurse in charge of Pearl. *(engaging smile; approachable tone of voice; eye contact; networking)*

Andrea: Excuse me, Clara. *(engaging smile)* Pearl would like to sit in a chair, and I hear from PT that she needs to sit in a chair each day. *(displaying competence and confidence)*

Clara: I'll get someone in there to help her into her chair.

Andrea: Thanks!

Andrea stops by 30 minutes later and finds Pearl sitting in her chair.

CRITICAL THINKING AND COLLABORATIVE LEARNING EXERCISES 10.5

Work in a small group. Brainstorm something that you all recognize to be a need for students (e.g., a training on sexual assault or intimate partner violence; a new policy about alcohol on campus). You won't necessarily carry out the advocacy, but work together to identify two people on campus who may be able to provide information about campus policy on the issue.

Section 10.6: The Social Work Role of Learner

Many times throughout a social worker's career they are faced with a situation that is completely unfamiliar. Of course this happens to students, but you should know that the most seasoned professional has to accept the role of learner at times.

Attentiveness

The skill of **attentiveness** is important so that the learner can gain knowledge, but in addition to gaining knowledge, the worker has to let others know that they are paying attention. What does attentiveness look like? As you might imagine, attentiveness includes the basic verbal and nonverbal skills that are at the foundation of nearly every other skill. On the other hand, there is more to social work attentiveness than what you do in class so that your professor does not call you out for daydreaming. In social work, the learner often has to observe another worker as they work with a client. They must balance attentive looking at the client with an engaging smile with attentive looking at their colleague. The worker should be sure to look at all participants in the conversation with equal attentiveness.

Willingness to Learn

A social worker must demonstrate a **willingness to learn** at all times. We learn from supervisors, from colleagues, from scientific literature, and from our clients. Self-confidence is needed to freely admit that you need to learn about something, and the best way of demonstrating self-confidence is to say "I don't know, but I'll find out."

Skills for the Learner Role

Skill	Description	Example	Required Worker Characteristic(s)
Attentiveness	Showing concentration	Looking back and forth between client and a colleague	Focus
Willingness to learn	Allowing others to see that you don't know something	"I don't know the answer to that question."	Self-confidence

A Sample Social Work Interview in the Role of Learner

Andrea: Hello, Pearl. I have my supervisor, Bonnie, with me. Bonnie, this is Pearl. Pearl, this is Bonnie. *(Andrea play bows, faking formality—use of humor.)* I'd like her to talk with you about your insurance coverage because I'm not very sure of that myself. *(self-disclosure)* Bonnie often helps me out when I don't know what I'm doing. Is it okay if she joins us? *(getting informed consent)*

Pearl: Sure. Any friend of Andrea's is a friend of mine. *(She said it lightly with a big smile. Pearl is getting comfortable and following up on Andrea's humor with a little joke of her own.)*

Andrea: *(looking back and forth between Bonnie and Pearl to show attentiveness)* I hope it's okay with both of you if I take some notes. *(showing willingness to learn)*

The Hopeless Worker: Reflective Responses

When Andrea first began work at the hospital, she was overwhelmed with the many responsibilities of discharge planning. The variety of follow-up services that people needed was mind-boggling. She struggled to manage them all, and she thought that referral to a rehabilitation center was just another referral. Then she had to make her first referral to an aging adult. She learned that from the perspective of many adults, a rehab center was the worst possible outcome. When faced with the patients who had no hope of returning home from the hospital because of their need for continuing care that was not provided by the hospital, her mind often drifted to her own mother and how she would feel in that situation. She felt hopeless. There seemed to be no alternative, and the patients were so frightened and opposed to the idea.

A firm knowledge base can help workers feel hopeful.

Andrea took her concerns to her supervisor; she found out that it was possible to tour rehabilitation centers. She called one of the social workers at a local facility to set up a time to visit. That visit changed her view entirely: She found out that most people stayed temporarily in rehabilitation centers as well as received physical and occupational therapy, basic medical care, and social work services. The goal of the rehabilitation center was to get people back to the functioning level they enjoyed before they got sick. Most of them returned home. Seeing her referral source firsthand allowed her to feel much more confident about brokering clients to those facilities. She had resolved her own feelings of hopelessness through self-reflection and critical thinking. Afterward, she was able to convey a sense of hope to her clients.

CRITICAL THINKING AND COLLABORATIVE LEARNING EXERCISES 10.6

Think of something you feel that you "ought" to know and ask about it (something like "Professor, when is that paper due?" Try not to begin with "This is a dumb question but . . .").

Section 10.7: Review and Apply

CONCURRENT CONSIDERATIONS IN GENERALIST PRACTICE

Ethical Decision-Making Challenge

Use the ethical decision-making model to explore whether Andrea should point out to Pearl that it is possible for her to leave the hospital against medical advice as long as she signs a form saying she wants to do so. Consider Sections 1.01 and 1.02 of the *NASW Code of Ethics* (NASW, 2018).

Human Rights

Which of Pearl's human rights, including freedom, safety, privacy, an adequate standard of living, health care, and education, are at risk of being violated?

Evidence-Based Practice

Find out the typical outcome when an older person enters a rehabilitation center. Is it more likely to be a discharge to their home or a discharge to a long-term care facility?

Policies Impacting Practice

What are the policies related to power of attorney related to older people who have been hospitalized. At what point does the designated person take on the role of decision maker? Find out how Medicare recipients pay for rehabilitation centers. How many days does Medicare reimburse?

Managing Diversity

Imagine Andrea was nearing retirement age. Will she have an easier change engaging with Pearl?

Multilevel Practice

Identify examples of Andrea's work on all levels.

Micro: ______

Mezzo: ______

Macro: ______

Dynamic and Interactive Planned Change Stages

Identify aspects of Andrea's work where she worked in the following stages:

Self-Reflection: ______

Engagement: ______

Assessment: ______

Planning: ______

Implementation: ______

Evaluation: ______

Termination and Follow-Up: ______

Chapter Summary

Section 10.1: Generalist Social Work With Individuals

Work with individuals is the basis for all social work. The roles social workers occupy and the skills they use as they work with individuals cross all fields and levels of practice as generalist practitioners work with individual clients and client system representatives.

Section 10.2: The Social Work Role of Educator

Social workers may play the role of educator as they work with individuals. When doing so, they focus on the idea that education is an interactive process. To carry out this process, they use some foundational skills that are often used in MSP. These skills include displaying preparatory empathy, displaying WEG, using silence purposefully, paraphrasing or making reflective statements, labeling feelings, asking open-ended questions, offering service, and giving information.

Section 10.3: The Social Work Role of Counselor

Social workers often play the role of social work counselor when they work with individuals. It is important that they identify themselves as social workers and use MSP to distinguish their work as being that of the generalist social work practitioner. In the role of counselor, some of the skills social workers use include allowing ventilation, carrying out containment, stating the obvious, probing, displaying cultural responsiveness, role-playing, identifying irrational beliefs, normalizing, partializing challenges, making setting considerations, bringing up taboo topics, focusing the interview, calling for work, managing doorknob comments, providing cautious advising, expressing sympathy, reflecting on spirituality, using humor, engaging in behavioral rehearsal, expressing validation, cautiously using self-disclosure, and getting informed consent.

Section 10.4: The Social Work Role of Supporter

In order to help clients get through the planned change process and reach their goals, social workers almost always play the role of supporter. The skills associated with this role include nonverbal encouragement, verbal encouragement, affirmation, empowerment, pointing out strengths, exploring task completion, and summarization.

Section 10.5: The Social Work Role of Advocate

Social workers work on behalf of clients to create social change when people are vulnerable and oppressed and cannot advocate for themselves. Skills used to carry out the role of advocate are displaying confidence, displaying competence, and networking.

Section 10.6: The Social Work Role of Learner

Social workers are lifelong learners. In the role of learner, the social worker's most important task is to be willing to learn or to be willing to show that they don't know something. In addition to willingness to learn, social workers in the role of learner exhibit attentiveness purposefully.

SELF-REFLECTION 10: LIKING PEOPLE SCALE

PURPOSE: To measure interpersonal orientation.

AUTHOR: Erik E. Filsinger

DESCRIPTION: This 15-item instrument measures one aspect of interpersonal orientation, the general liking of other people. Interpersonal orientation plays a significant role in one's social development and adjustment. The theoretical point of departure of the LPS is that the degree of liking people influences whether one approaches or avoids social interaction.

NORMS: One hundred forty college students (57 males and 83 females) from diverse demographic backgrounds had a mean of 59.4 with a standard deviation of 8.14.

SCORING: Respondents rate each item in terms of their agreement or disagreement. Ratings are quantified from 1 to 5 as follows: a = 1, b = 2, . . . e = 5. Items 4, 6, 8, 9, 10, and 15 are reverse scored; total scores are the sum of all the items, with a range of 15 to 75. Higher scores indicate greater liking of people.

RELIABILITY: The reliability of the LPS was estimated using Cronback's alpha to test internal consistency. The LPS had good to very good internal consistency from two samples of college students (.85 and .75, respectively).

VALIDITY: The instrument generally has good validity evidence. In three separate samples, the LPS was shown to have good concurrent validity, correlating with the amount of time spent alone, the number of close friends, scores on a misanthropy measure, and social anxiety. The instrument has also been shown to correlate with four measures of affiliation motivation, with social self-esteem, and with the ability to judge others.

PRIMARY REFERENCE:

Filsinger, E. E. (2013). A measure of interpersonal orientation: The Liking People Scale. In K. Corcoran & J. Fischer (Eds.), *Measures for clinical practice and research: A sourcebook* (5th ed.). New York, NY: Oxford University Press.

LPS

The following questions ask your feelings about a number of things. Since we are all different, some people may think and feel one way; other people think and feel another way. There is no such thing as a "right" or "wrong" answer. The idea is to read each question and then fill out your answer. Try to respond to every question, even if it does not apply to you very well. The possible answers for each question are:

A = strongly agree

B = moderately agree

C = neutral

D = moderately disagree

E = strongly disagree

_____ 1. Sometimes when people are talking to me, I find myself wishing that they would leave.

_____ 2. My need for people is quite low.

_____ 3. One of the things wrong with people today is that they are too dependent upon other people.

_____ 4. My happiest experiences involve other people.

_____ 5. People are not important for my personal happiness.

_____ 6. Personal character is developed in the stream of life.

_____ 7. I could be happy living away from people.

_____ 8. It is important to me to be able to get along with other people.

_____ 9. No matter what I am doing, I would rather do it in the company of other people.

_____ 10. There is no question about it—I like people.

_____ 11. Personal character is developed in solitude.

_____ 12. In general, I don't like people.

_____ 13. Except for my close friends, I don't like people.

_____ 14. A person only has a limited amount of time and people tend to cut into it.

_____ 15. People are the most important thing in my life.

Recommended Websites

American Clinical Social Work Association: https://acswa.org

Critical Terms for Roles and Skills in Work With Individuals

educator 279
reflective listening 281
unconditional positive regard 281
displaying warmth, empathy, and genuineness (WEG) 281
engaging smile 281
eye contact 281
tone of voice 281
empathy 281
receptivity 281
patience 281
use of silence 281
paraphrasing 282
reflective statements 282
labeling feelings 282
open-ended questions 282
offer service 282
giving information 283
social work counseling 285
licensed professional counselor 286
licensed marriage and family counselor 286
certified substance abuse counselor 287
psychologists 287
psychiatrist 287
ventilation 287
containment 288
state the obvious 288
probing 289
display cultural responsiveness 289
exercise cultural humility 289
role play 289
identifying irrational (or automatic) beliefs 289
normalizing 289
partialize challenges 289
preparatory empathy 290
setting considerations 290
taboo topics 290
focus the interview 290
calling for work 290
doorknob comment 290
cautious advising 291
expressions of sympathy 291
reflecting on spirituality 291
behavioral rehearsal 291
use of humor 291
validation 291
getting informed consent 292
nonverbal encouragement 295
verbal encouragement 295
affirmation 296
empower 296
pointing out strengths 296
exploring task completion 296
summarization 296
displaying confidence 298
display competence 299
networking 299
attentiveness 300
willingness to learn 301

Generalist Practice Curriculum Matrix With 2015 Educational Policy and Accreditation Standards

Chapter 10

Competency	Course	Course Content	Dimensions
Competency 1: Demonstrate Ethical and Professional Behavior		Feature 3: Self-Reflection Feature 4: Concurrent Considerations in Generalist Practice	Cognitive–affective processes Skills Cognitive–affective processes
Competency 2: Engage Diversity and Difference in Practice		Feature 1: Focus on Diversity Feature 4: Concurrent Considerations in Generalist Practice	Skills Cognitive–affective processes Skills Cognitive–affective processes
Competency 3: Advance Human Rights and Social, Economic, and Environmental Justice		Feature 4: Concurrent Considerations in Generalist Practice	Skills Cognitive–affective processes
Competency 4: Engage In Practice-Informed Research and Research-Informed Practice		Feature 4: Concurrent Considerations in Generalist Practice	Skills Cognitive–affective processes
Competency 5: Engage in Policy Practice		Feature 4: Concurrent Considerations in Generalist Practice	Skills Cognitive–affective processes
Competency 6: Engage With Individuals, Families, Groups, Organizations, and Communities		Feature 4: Concurrent Considerations in Generalist Practice	Skills Cognitive–affective processes
Competency 7: Assess Individuals, Families, Groups, Organizations, and Communities		Feature 4: Concurrent Considerations in Generalist Practice	Skills Cognitive–affective processes

Competency	Course	Course Content	Dimensions
Competency 8: Intervene With Individuals, Families, Groups, Organizations, and Communities		10.1. Examine the way work with individuals crosses fields and levels of practice.	Skills
		10.2. Discuss the social work role of educator and the skills associated with it.	Skills
		10.3. Explain the social work role of counselor and the skills associated with it.	Skills
		10.4. Discuss the social work role of supporter and the skills associated it.	Skills
		Feature 4: Concurrent Considerations in Generalist Practice	Cognitive-affective processes
Competency 9: Evaluate Practice With Individuals, Families, Groups, Organizations, and Communities		Feature 4: Concurrent Considerations in Generalist Practice	Skills Cognitive-affective processes

References

Arnold, K. (2014). Behind the mirror: Reflective listening and its tain in the work of Carl Rogers. *The Humanistic Psychologist, 42*, 354–369. doi:10.1080/08873267.2014.913247

Elkins, D. N. (2009). *Humanistic psychology: A clinical manifesto*. Colorado Springs, CO: University of the Rockies Press.

Filsinger, E. E. (2013). A measure of interpersonal orientation: The Liking People Scale. In K. Corcoran & J. Fischer (Eds.), *Measures for clinical practice and research: A sourcebook* (5th ed.). New York, NY: Oxford University Press.

Freire, P. (1998). *Pedagogy of freedom: Ethics, democracy, and civic courage*. New York, NY: Rowman & Littlefield.

Goldfried, M. R. (2007). What has psychotherapy inherited from Carl Rogers? *Psychotherapy: Theory, Research, Practice, Training, 44*(3), 249–252. doi:10.1037/0033-3204.44.3.249

Hansen, J. C. (2008). Community and in-home models. *Journal of Social Work Education, 44*(3), 83–87.

Hill, C. E., Thompson, B. J., & Ladany, N. (2003). Therapist use of silence in therapy: A survey. *Journal of Clinical Psychology, 59*, 513–524.

Kadushin, A., & Kadushin, G. (1997). *The social work interview: A guide for human service professionals* (4th ed.). New York, NY: Columbia University Press.

Knapp, H. (2010). *Introduction to social work practice: A practical workbook.* Thousand Oaks, CA: Sage.

Miller, W. R., & Rollnick, S. (2013). *Motivational interviewing: Helping people change.* New York, NY: Guilford Press.

Murphy, B. C., & Dillon, C. (2015). *Interviewing in action in a multicultural world* (5th ed.). Stamford, CT: Cengage.

National Association of Social Workers. (2018). *NASW code of ethics.* Washington, DC: NASW Press.

Riley, J., & Ward, K. (2017). Active learning, cooperative active learning, and passive learning methods in an accounting information systems course. *Issues in Accounting Education, 32*(2), 1–16.

Saleebey, D. (2012). *The strengths perspective in social work practice* (6th ed.). Upper Saddle River, NJ: Pearson.

Shulman, L. (2012). *The skills of helping individuals, families, groups, and communities* (7th ed.). Belmont, CA: Brooks/Cole.

Shulman, L. (2016). *The skills of helping individuals, groups, and families* (8th ed.). Itasca, IL: F. E. Peacock.

Recommended Readings

Goldfried, M. R. (2007). What has psychotherapy inherited from Carl Rogers? *Psychotherapy: Theory, Research, Practice, Training, 44*(3), 249–252. doi:10.1037/0033-3204.44.3.249

Hill, C. E., Thompson, B. J., & Ladany, N. (2003). Therapist use of silence in therapy: A survey. *Journal of Clinical Psychology, 59*, 513–524.

Roles and Skills in Work With Families

This chapter continues the series of chapters on work with various system levels. It explores the family-in-environment (FIE) perspective as well as social work roles and skills in work with families. Along the way, we discuss the importance of allowing self-determination in the identification of family members. The chapter rounds out with discussions of financial capacity building and crisis intervention, including suicidal ideation, with families.

Learning Objectives

11.1 Learn about work with families from the family-in-environment (FIE) perspective.

11.2 Explore the characteristics of interactions within families.

11.3 Articulate the social work role of family mediator and related skills.

11.4 Articulate the social work role of family facilitator and related skills.

11.5 Consider financial capacity building with families.

11.6 Describe crisis intervention, including suicidal ideation, with families

Case Study: Developmental Disabilities

Sahara decided to wear her suit on Monday since she had team meetings all day. When she reflected on the meetings to come, she realized that she felt strongly that family members should be involved in the team meeting with the caseworker, a community-based agency leader, the residential program director, and the client. Sahara represented the direct staff of the residential program. She knew all of the clients personally, and she felt for them as the professionals talked over their heads about their goals and challenges. It was too often the case that the interdisciplinary team was working on behalf of a client who wasn't invited to speak a word at the meeting. Even though the meetings were called family

©iStock.com/Imagesbybarbara

People often forget that individuals with developmental disabilities can form and enjoy romantic relationships.

meetings, family members had the same experience as the clients. Some family members of the developmentally disabled adults Sahara worked with were very involved in their adult child's lives, yet they too often left an interdisciplinary meeting without speaking. She found that she had to manage feelings of anger that she felt toward her colleagues at the table, none of whom were social workers. When she examined the beliefs behind her anger, she recognized that the other professionals weren't taught a generalist perspective or the social work *NASW Code of Ethics* (National Association of Social Workers [NASW], 2018), so they couldn't be expected to act like social workers and recognize the importance of all of the systems in a client's environment. That thought helped her to channel her anger into empathy. She decided she would be responsible to advocate and make sure to invite clients and families to speak. She faced an even greater challenge when Missy came up on the agenda. Missy was a developmentally disabled adult who had recently moved from a group home to an independent living arrangement. She came alone, since she didn't have any family members who were involved in her life. When the team asked Missy how her new apartment was working out, she said she was lonely. Sahara wondered out loud whether Missy was seeing Sam, her boyfriend. Missy explained that Sam and she no longer lived close to each other and that there was no way that they could get together in the evenings or on weekends. She had to be content with Sam's daily phone call. She said it made her happy to hear the phone ring while she was getting ready for work even if she didn't have time to pick it up. She seemed resigned to the fact that she could seldom see Sam, and the professionals around the table nodded sympathetically. To Sahara, there seemed to be no reason why Sam and Missy couldn't get together, except that neither one was very comfortable using public transportation. Sahara knew that another challenge faced by the couple was the fact that Sam's residential programming was provided by a different agency. If Sam and Missy were to get together, visits would have to be coordinated among staff members of two agencies. She wished that Sam, and maybe someone from his agency, could have been at the meeting so that they could set a goal about Missy and Sam socializing. That way, the staff would be reminded to respond by helping Missy make plans to see Sam. Then Sahara had an idea for advocacy. She knew she had to speak up. "Missy, I know you've said that Sam is your fiancé. Do you think he is your family member? Would you like to ask him to attend a family meeting like this one?"

Section 11.1: The Family-in-Environment Perspective

This section reintroduces the family-in-environment (FIE) perspective and further develops its relationship to generalist practice.

Work With Families From a Family-in-Environment Perspective

As we've said, families have always been a central concern to social workers (Richmond, 1917/2012). We have always recognized that families play an important role in individuals' quality of life. On the other hand, we haven't always agreed what a family is, so our first task is to define the elements of the family. Our mainstream society's definition of family is usually considered to be the **nuclear family**: biological mom, dad, and kids. This means that government and agency policies are often made to respond to the needs of that group. For that reason, policies such as Temporary Assistance for Needy Families

(TANF) work to help the parents or guardians care for children but not neighbors who may carry sole responsibility for a child. Families with dependent grandparents and adult couples without children are not necessarily eligible for this **cash assistance** benefit either. Here is another example. An insurance policy is available for a mom, dad, and dependent children. While that insurance policy covers married couples, federal policies do not require that it cover couples who live together outside of marriage. Fortunately, this definition has been expanded somewhat. For example, increasing numbers of government and agency policies recognize a domestic partner to be a family member. These ideas are beginning to take hold in the broader community. For example, a grandparent is usually considered to be a family member who is often entitled to family services, especially if they live in the same household as the nuclear family. Most people also understand that families may be blended: mom, stepdad, and siblings; dad, stepmom, and siblings. In blended families, though, we still often refer to the children as either siblings or half siblings. If we do that, we consider the people as making up two families when they may define themselves as a one large family group: two moms, two dads, and kids. When the family is experiencing an important transitional event like a high school graduation, all members of "both sides" may be present. If you ever observe a situation like that, watch how the photos are taken. Is there a group photo that includes everyone, or are there photos of different components such as graduate, dad, and stepmom, or graduate, mom, and stepdad? Is there a photo of graduate, biological mom, and biological dad? A social worker may intuit which people family members consider to be family, or we may think we know and actually be wrong. FIE helps social workers sort all that out.

ETHICAL PERSPECTIVES

Where does the NASW Code of Ethics *(NASW, 2018) ask workers to consider clients' own definitions of family? Consider Section 1.05(b).*

FIE is part of the foundation of generalist practice. Building on the person-in-environment (PIE) perspective, FIE suggests that generalist social workers consider the family system to be a pivotal part of any client's social system (Gasker & Vafeas, 2010). You might think of it like this: FIE reminds you that it may be important to put a genogram right into the ecomap. All systems that affect individuals also affect the family system. FIE considers the experience of each individual to include some experience of being a member of a family, whether it is a traditional family or not. For that reason, we need to consider families when we practice, including when we develop policies, or guidelines, for our agencies and other systems.

What is a family? We know from Missy's case that a family is often considered to be people related biologically ("by blood") or by marriage. That's why the professionals running the team meeting all believed that Missy didn't have a family. Sahara's multisystem practice (MSP) viewpoint showed otherwise. She recognized that Missy identified Sam as a family member. For that reason, Sahara was able to recognize that Sam would be a legitimate part of a professional meeting for families.

Think about the people that you are close to. Are you close to your traditional family members? Are there any people that would traditionally be called family members that you don't feel close to? Are there any people in your life that you consider to be family even though they aren't considered to be family by the U.S. Census Bureau or the Internal Revenue Service? Think about them as you consider the family characteristics that are described next. Like many people, you may not define your family as the traditional nuclear family. Instead, you may define it as a **relational family**, or **family system**, a group based on your own choices (Briar-Lawson, Lawson, & Hennon, 2001). Using the terms *relational family* and *family system* to refer to couples or groups of people who define themselves as family members is one way to experience cultural humility—to broaden our expectations of what a family is—and consequently to engage in culturally sensitive practice. As with all elements of diversity, we need to allow clients to be the experts, to teach us their worldview. We shouldn't assume we know who family members are, even if we have a form we have to fill out that is related only to biological family. On the other hand, we may need to help relational family members to recognize each other as family. Because they have so often filled out forms that asked for family members related biologically or by marriage, they may have adopted that outlook themselves. These simple questions—"What people around you act like family members? Do you feel like some people are members of your family even if you're not related?"—may allow a client to recognize their own diversity. Once they're given the opportunity to think about it, they may identify neighbors, friends, coworkers, ex- (divorced) relatives, and even pets as family members. Those people may bring invaluable resources to the individuals in the family.

On the other side of the coin, any random group of people is not a family. For example, a group of teenagers on a study abroad trip may feel like siblings by the time they get back, but they are not likely to consider themselves to be one family for long. Overall, there are traditionally four elements that all family members share (Briar-Lawson et al., 2001):

- A history
- Emotional bonding
- Mutual support
- Identity

A History

Family members share a mutual history. Over time, they stock up experiences that they have shared. Often these experiences become a part of the stories the family tells over and over. The day Susie won the public speaking award or the day Johnny got lost at the mall may be tales that are revisited every Thanksgiving. The history may be long—over decades—or it may be relatively short. History is about shared experiences and the stories that are told about them. It is important that stories about people's shared experiences be told and retold. These stories become part of the glue that holds families together. That's why short-term stories are important too. A new adoptive family may have to begin developing collaborative stories when a child is already an adolescent. Other family relationships are short because children are young. Families separated by miles may have the challenge of creating shared experiences and stories electronically. A grandfather reading a bedtime story to a child over the phone is an experience that can become a story later. From a different angle, some experiences may create stories that are too painful to tell. Family secrets can be held about painful memories like childhood abuse. In those

Sofie Delauw/Getty Images

Family members bond emotionally.

cases, members cannot share closeness in the way they would if all of the stories were shared among all family members. To complicate matters further, family members may have very different perspectives on painful experiences, and those perspectives can be the cause of a great deal of family friction among family members. For example, a sibling may have a story about being emotionally abused by a parent while other siblings did not experience the incidents in a similar way. Conflict can follow when family members don't agree on the history of the family. This often leaves some stories spoken among some family members but not others. Family closeness happens when everyone's perception of events can be valued. The upshot of all this is that family stories don't just hold people together; they actually shape who we are, who we believe we are, and how others see us. As our stories involve other family members, they shape how we view them as well (Witkin, 2014). We'll talk about the way individual family members relate to each other in the next section.

Emotional Bonding

Another characteristic of family members is that they experience emotional bonding. Social bonding theory suggests that family bonds are the most important bonds that people experience (Gottfredson & Hirschi, 1990). Adolescents' relationships to their mothers have even been shown to help them avoid harmful behaviors like smoking (Mahabee-Gittens, Khoury, Huang, Dorn, & Ammerman, 2011). Put the family members in a theme park where some get physically separated from the others, and you will see the anxiety that can come from physical separation. It works emotionally as well. Family members share a connection that may feel positive, negative, or both. Over time, some individual family members will be more bonded to others, and over time, the bonding can change among different people. For example, a family member who is doing an internship at one family member's place of work is likely to spend at least some time bonded very closely to that family member. Or two adult family members may find themselves living close to each other. In that circumstance, a close bond may form that is strong for life. So the degree of bonding differs among family members and can change over time. Like a shared history, bonding is another way of keeping family members together and keeping them apart. We'll discuss shortly the way that some types of bonding can be positive and others can be painful to individuals and harmful to the family system.

Mutual Support

Individually and together family members support each other to a greater or a lesser degree. It is important to note that a well-functioning family is a kind of social welfare agency that looks out for its members. Members find ways to meet the needs and wants of individual family members and the family itself. For example, family members may pull together to care for an aging family member. It is important for social workers to realize that the family is its own best support. **Natural supports**, or those that occur in the community without professional influence, are the best kind of supports for individuals—either on their own or as a supplement to professional services (Tsai, Desai, & Rosenheck, 2012). Family is the most common natural support. In fact, family members may have successfully supported each other and the family system for years before finding themselves in a meeting with a social worker. Before providing professional resources, the social worker will look to the strengths in the family. It has been the practice for some time to develop programs to support families as the best way to support clients, even when there is a history of child abuse (Devaney & Dolan, 2017). Unfortunately, some families lack the necessary skills to support each other over long periods of time. Emotional distance or conflict can undermine people's ability and willingness to provide support.

Family Identity

Finally, family members think of themselves as belonging to each other. Sometimes this identification is represented by names: surnames all family members hold in common, or first names that are reused over generations. Other times, everyone's name is different, but the family's shared identity may be shown in special events like birthday parties. Family identity reveals the boundary the family shares with its environment. As we've said, a boundary is an imaginary line around a system that can be flexible or inflexible. Boundaries may allow a great deal of exchange of energy in the form of relationships and resources, or they may exist on a broad spectrum of flexibility: Where the boundary is too permeable, family members move in and out of their family identity and may not participate in the mutual support that is needed. In other situations, the family boundary is too inflexible. Family members may avoid using resources from other systems as their family identity is so solid that it keeps outsiders out when their entrance into the family system may be beneficial for all. Healthy boundaries will be a middle ground where family members feel a sense of belongingness without keeping all others at bay (Hart & Luckock, 2006).

CRITICAL THINKING AND COLLABORATIVE LEARNING EXERCISES 11.1

1. Work with a partner, and share some family stories that get told over and over in your family. Try to identify a story that is about more than one family member, and share it at a family gathering. Share with your partner your observations about how the story holds most or all of the family members together.

Section 11.2: Interactions Within Families

Working from the FIE perspective, this section discusses the way families operate in the social environment and within their own family systems. It points out that family interactions may be positive or may be harmful.

fstop123/Getty Images

Some family members serve as caregivers.

FIE recognizes that families impact our lives every day. Put simply, your family members have as much or more power to improve your life than anyone else. On the other hand, there are few people who can be so good at making your life miserable. Think about that. People often feel connected to family members even though they may have hurtful experiences with some family members. Others know that their family is their home, with support being guaranteed. They may believe "home is where the heart is, and home is wherever they have to take you in." What makes the difference between the experiences of family members who feel supported and who do not?

FIE and systems theory give us some clues. We can think of the family as a system made up of elements that exchange energy with other systems. Those elements are individuals. As families and family members interact with other systems, they may share energy and consequently create it (synergy). Two systems may be out of balance and drain one of the systems (entropy), or they may engage in even energy exchange and maintain a balance of energy (homeostasis).

Individual Tasks

Individual family members help maintain homeostasis by exchanging energy. This energy often takes the form of shared tasks. Some family members may supply financial support. Others may provide tasks related to children and child-rearing. You might think of the child-rearing tasks as related to procreation, socialization, and social control. Other **family tasks** include emotional support for family members: morale and motivation. At times, these tasks coalesce into roles. In other words, when a family member consistently carries out a series of tasks, they may develop an identity where they are the person who can be counted on to carry out those particular tasks. **Family roles** are made up of expectations (White & Klein, 2002). For example, a grandmother may be expected to provide emotional support, or morale, for the family while a father may be expected to provide financial support.

Parts of the Family Are Interdependent

FIE also reminds us that family members are all elements of the family system. As tasks coalesce into roles, it becomes clear that roles fit together to help the family function. Family members' expectations for each other are predictable and comfortable for some, if not all, family members. Sometimes an individual occupies a single role all the time, and other times roles are exchanged as family needs change. We'll discuss different family roles later.

Boundaries Encircle Families

Another element of families that is highlighted by FIE is that boundaries are important to families. As we've said, a boundary is permeable. Ideally, it allows necessary resources into the family. Often, though, it is either too permeable to maintain family identity or too inflexible to allow people and resources to enter. The **family boundary** is often shaped by shared family experiences. For example, the oldest child plans a birthday party with friends and, for whatever reason, at the time of the party no friends arrive. After that, every child's birthday celebration is restricted to family members. The experience has resulted in a boundary that is inflexible in this particular situation. It is important to note that family boundaries may change over time based on changes in family experiences, in the family membership, or in the members themselves. A new person, such as a social worker, may be added temporarily to the family system, and a change in any individual will impact the entire family (Titleman, 1998). When a family honors a social worker by allowing them to enter their space, the family is immediately changed in some way.

Families Work Toward Homeostasis

FIE and systems theory also point us to the idea that families, like other systems, work toward homeostasis. The family system works to keep the balance of energy through the roles they occupy. Members exchange energy by carrying out their individual roles. Like all systems, families strive to maintain balance within the system. The family strives for this balance, or homeostasis, whether it is functional or not. For example, one partner may feel role strain through their conflicting roles of both provider and caregiver, but everyone else in the system feels comfortable. What may be needed is **role flexibility** so that others can share in the responsibilities (Winkel & Clayton, 2010). Still, all elements of the system may work to maintain the current homeostasis. The result may be entropy in one of the elements. The partner experiencing role strain may become ill, for example. In this case, a social worker could help to facilitate role flexibility and family stability through a planned change process that includes the entire family.

In our case study of Missy and Sam, we have seen that Sam is taking on the role of caregiver by calling Missy every day. In return, Missy used to help pay for their entertainment. When the occasions for entertainment disappeared, Sam began to feel role strain. He was serving as caretaker while Missy was only carrying out the role of the consumer of care and doing it inconsistently. It turned out that while Missy could have been a caring consumer and even sharing the caretaker task, she often was not able to answer the phone. The two of them needed the skills and opportunity to carry out other family tasks. We'll elaborate on family roles in the next section.

Families as a Social System

Properties of Systems Theory	Families as Social Systems
Individuals' tasks help maintain homeostasis.	Tasks include care of family members, procreation, socialization, social control, morale and motivation, and production and consumption.
All parts of the family system are interdependent.	Relationships are based on shared values and expectations that vary by culture and social class.
Boundaries separate systems from one another and their environment; boundaries are flexible to a degree; boundaries separate single elements within systems.	Boundaries, or demarcation lines, separate the family system from its environment, including school, work, etc.; boundaries also exist between the individuals in the family.
Adaptive tendencies ensure homeostasis.	Families interact with resources, culture, economy, social welfare policies, health care, the physical environment, the education system, the justice system, etc.

Source: Adapted from Butterfield, Rocha, and Butterfield (2009).

Hero Images/Getty Images

Alliances in families can help achieve common goals.

Family Roles

We've established that basic family tasks are completed by individuals carrying out various roles. The roles are sets of expectations that can become predictable when they are carried out by one individual consistently.

Provider

Since families work as mini social welfare agencies, an important role is that of the **provider**, or the person or persons who bring financial resources to the family. In the traditional family, the father figure is the provider, although now more than half of American families share the provider role among both partners (Lee, Lee, & Chang, 2014). Children, especially adolescents, can be providers as well. Someone who is eligible for cash benefits can also be a provider in the family. In a highly functioning family, roles can be flexible when needed. For example, if one partner loses their job, the other partner can work additional hours to help make ends meet. In addition, keep in mind that a family member who receives public cash assistance benefits can also function as provider.

Caregiver

Another traditional role in the family is that of **caregiver,** or a person who shares in the support of other family members. The caregiver often applies to the socialization and care of children. In the same way, it may apply to other family members such as an aging parent or a partner. Like all family roles, the more flexible, the better. If one member can stand in for another as needed in the role of caregiver, **role strain** is less likely to occur. **Role enhancement** suggests that the more roles a person can exchange, the more skills, experience, and coping strategies can be developed. As people become more competent in a variety of roles, they are less likely to feel overloaded by their family responsibilities (White & Klein, 2002). Role overload, or role strain, is likely to be felt when a number of roles have to be managed simultaneously. For example, women often feel role strain when they are expected to supply financial resources as well as caregiving of children and an aging parent. Fathers can feel the same role strain as well. For the most part, the strain of role overload can be alleviated when family members share tasks, but sometimes the amount of caregiving and breadwinning is overwhelming for all. It has been shown that roles are best managed when people are satisfied with the division of household labor (White, 1999).

Less Functional Roles

Other roles that family members carry out can become ingrained in each person and can ultimately become and reflect problems in the family. Wegscheider-Cruse's role theory has been shown to be trustworthy, especially in situations where substance abuse or some other addiction is present (Veriano, Peterson, & Hicks, 1990). Some of Wegscheider-Cruse's roles that have been supported by Veriano and colleagues (1990) as well as other scientific studies follow:

- *Dependent*—The dependent is a person who acts irresponsibly. They are likely to be dependent on some additive substance or addictive behavior such as alcohol, drugs, gambling, or video games. Sometimes the dependent person's role diverts attention from more serious family issues. Resources such as finances and companionship are drained due to the focus on the addiction. The drain in resources results in conflict where family members look to the dependent member to supply support and don't get functional responses. Instead, they get something like this: "Stop nagging me! I can quit whenever I want to. Your nagging makes me do it!"
- *Enabler*—This is one who is dependent on the other's addiction to support their own way of being. An enabler may be called codependent when their family member's addiction is used to rationalize their own addictive behaviors. "Of course I'm gaining weight. My partner is out all the time, and I eat when I'm lonely." The system seeks balance, but homeostasis can accommodate both dependent and independent behavior to the detriment of the family. Frequently codependent, an enabler—usually an adult—unknowingly facilitates the addiction: "I hate it when you drink. Now I have to call in sick for you again."
- *Hero*—The hero, often a child, helps the family to feel normal. The hero feels pressure to excel to keep some positive balance in the system. While pressure to succeed drains energy, the hero receives cheers wherever they go.

"Hey, everyone"—in the midst of a family argument—"I got a 4.0!" As adults the hero children may cut themselves off from the family.

- *The scapegoat*—The scapegoat serves as someone to blame. The entire family, including the dependent person, may look at the scapegoat whenever there is a problem. The scapegoat often expresses the family's anger and has behavioral problems, removing tension from the family system. "Everything's my fault. So what if I threw a desk at school?" The scapegoat is often the brunt of the mascot's jokes.
- *The mascot*—The mascot's task is to bring fun into the home. They bring jokes and laughter, but they also serve as someone that others need to take care of. This role helps to add energy to the rest of the system but loses energy in that the mascot must not express anger.
- *The lost child*—The lost child tries at all costs to avoid conflict. For this reason, they can often be found in the background at family gatherings. This is the family member who doesn't cause the family trouble but feels neglected themselves. They may produce little energy, but they are not big consumers either: "Someday, we're going to go somewhere, and they'll forget to bring me home."

Of course some families do not resemble Wegscheider-Cruse's idea of family roles at all, but those roles are worth considering during assessment when a social worker is dealing with a family with multiple problems. When Wegscheider-Cruse's roles are considered, we should take direction from the strengths-based focus of FIE. Like other roles, these serve a purpose in the functioning of the family. It is best to bear in mind that the role is meeting a need, so it is allowing the family to function as well as it does. It's best to identify the strength of the coping mechanism—the need as well as the role.

Overall, what is most important to remember about any family roles, including the common roles of provider and caregiver, is that roles are built on expectations about tasks that are necessary to the family in some way. When roles are flexible, people's expectations change and they learn new skills to carry out roles. Synergy is created in this process called role enhancement. When role enhancement occurs, one person can take on the expectations of another seamlessly. Remember also that when that exchange of role expectations does not happen efficiently because individuals are stuck in their roles with fixed expectations, role strain can develop, draining both the individual and the system of energy.

Micro Level Interactions Within the Family

Individual interactions play an important role in family functioning. As we've seen, individuals themselves are systems within the family system. As such, they exchange energy among themselves in predictable ways (Titleman, 1998). Several ways of interacting include forming alliances, experiencing fusion, triangulation, and experiencing cutoff. These can be observed in the Smith family genogram (see Figure 11.1).

When an **alliance** is formed, two or more people in the family join together to achieve common goals. They may be working toward individual goals for each of them or goals for the welfare of the family. These may be positive goals and be marked by good feeling. An alliance, for example, could consist of two siblings who work together to convince their parents to let them have computer time. On the other hand, alliances can be formed as a coping mechanism in the face of stress or crisis. For example, those two siblings may work together to get away with incomplete homework by blaming a third sibling for spilling juice on their papers.

FIGURE 11.1 ●

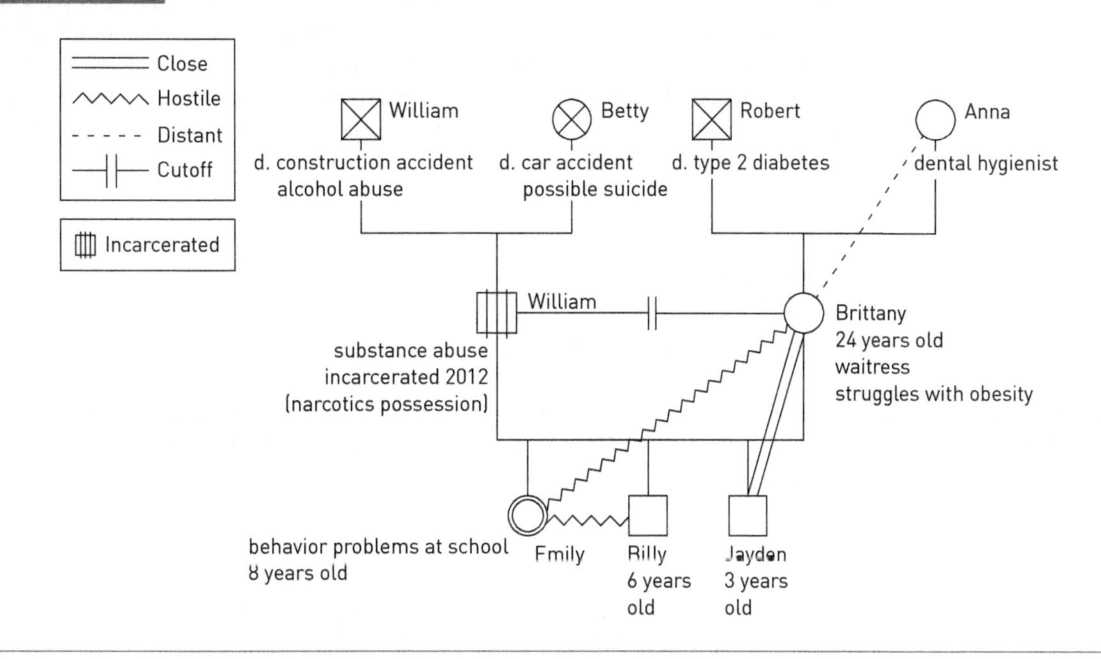

When an alliance is formed to cope with stress, that connection can become a **fusion** between two people. These people work together to manage stress in unhealthy ways. They maintain their connection so closely that others are not included. For example, a mother and a son can be fused while a father and a daughter are fused. Each parent feels "their" child is not to blame for conflict but is quick to reprimand the other child. Each child sees the other as a favorite, and sibling conflict ensues. In addition, it is inevitable that the parents will argue about parenting skills. In Figure 11.1, Brittany has an alliance with Jayden. She may have difficulty disciplining him, and she is not likely to support Emily when she has responsibility for Jayden, causing more tension between her and Emily.

Fusion may expand to include three people, causing **triangulation** (Titleman, 1998). Like alliances, triangulation can be positive or negative. A triangle can be stable, with three people who are individuals with healthy boundaries who work together to help each other and the family function. For example, two children can become a triangle with a mother during the crisis of their father's serious illness. On the other hand, triangulation can be a set of three people who experience fusion. That is, they relate to each other intimately and exclude others. The people involved tend to lose a sense of individuality—their personalities become fused and they cope with crisis by keeping others out and developing stressful relationships with others. As in two-person fusion, the three people can begin to react to crisis in predictable ways that may not serve the purpose of the family. A father and two siblings can respond to a mother's substance abuse by forming a triangle where they take care of each other in her absence. Over time, the mother's substance abuse may become chronic, and the members of the triangle may become fused. They lose a sense of identity, seeing each other as equal victims of the mother's behavior. In this case, they may respond as a group when any one of the individuals is threatened. They may respond angrily to the mother as a group even in instances where substance abuse is not involved. This is likely to result in increased separation and substance abuse. Even in sobriety, the mother will have difficulty developing one-on-one relationships with the members of the triangle.

Triangulation and fusion may become long-term relationship dynamics. In that case, the family may break up under crisis. Perhaps the parents divorce or one family member is **cut off**. When a family member is cut off, there is little or no contact among them and other family members. This can happen in cases of parental divorce or when an adult child moves out of the family home without any ongoing contact with others. Note that cutoff can be a physical separation or it can be an emotional one, where a family member is cut off while living in the same home as other family members.

SELF-REFLECTION 11: THE FAMILY-OF-ORIGIN SCALE

Consider your family experiences as you grew up. Take the Family-of-Origin Scale on pages 336–338 to think about the way you perceive your family members to have gotten along. Compare your score to the average scores provided.

How do you think your score will impact your future work with families?

CRITICAL THINKING AND COLLABORATIVE LEARNING EXERCISES 11.2

1. Titleman (1998) suggests that the social workers who work best with families maintain relationships with their own family members. Think about times when you created an experience or event to get family members together for a shared experience. If you have not done so, make it happen with some kind of special outing, memorable dinner, or other event. Share your progress in a small group.

Hero Images/Getty Images

Too much sympathy for a client can result in professional missteps.

Section 11.3: The Social Work Role of Mediator

This section is about the social work role of **mediator**. We consider the role and the skills that allow us to carry it out.

The Social Work Role of Mediator

Often the crisis that brings family members to us shows up as conflict between members. In this case, the social worker needs to metaphorically step between the members in conflict and help each to express their thoughts and feelings. This mediation may be necessary as early as engagement in the planned change process, since many families are in so much conflict that they cannot let each person speak in introductions. Such skills begin with the nonverbal skills that are used in work with individuals. The worker shows an engaging smile, encourages with nods, uses a genuine voice, and shows warmth with appropriate eye contact. It is important for the worker to share these nonverbal communications with each family member in turn.

Next, the social worker playing the role of mediator needs to demonstrate a number of skills. These skills are used by the worker in addressing each family member, usually one at a time. In addition, the skills are used by the worker to model the functional behaviors. That is, the worker uses the skills as part of teaching those skills to the family members. These skills are verbal, and they are used by anyone who wants to resolve conflicts between others or even in their own lives. Those skills include the following:

- Using "I" messages
- Being brief and specific
- Checking on others' thoughts and feelings

Using "I" Messages

Using "I" messages is important in family communication because it works against the tendency we all have to blame others for our problems. For example, a family member may accuse another by saying this: "You always make us late!" Inevitably the response will be one of anger: "I do not! It's your fault!" or "Shut up! Who cares?!" These types of interactions, where anger turns to blaming and blaming leads to more anger, are common in families facing conflict. A more productive conversation will happen if the troubled person says this: "I get so nervous when we're late. Can we work together on this?" Rather than say "You never listen to me!" a family member can say "I feel disappointed that I haven't had a chance to talk about the way I feel." Notice that the "I" statement always begins with *I*, then is followed by a feeling statement. The speaker's main point comes last.

The worker can teach this skill by modeling. If you are working with a family and someone speaks angrily to another family member, you can say that you get anxious when they raise their voice like that. Follow this with your skill of labeling feelings: "Seems like you are getting really frustrated. Let's talk about that."

WHAT IF . . . FOCUS ON DIVERSITY

Sahara asked Missy some focused questions during the meeting with every intention of changing the outlook of the staff members there. What characteristics of Sahara would help to make that work? Which would be barriers?

Being Brief and Specific

One way of avoiding painful or uncomfortable issues is for one person to talk and talk until everyone else is so exhausted they just agree with anything to get rest from the conversation. In this case, the worker can respond successfully if they are ready with a useful comment like this: "I think what you are saying is . . . I'd like to hear from others," or encourage **being brief and specific**.

Checking on Others' Thoughts, Feelings, and Understanding

This is another skill that the worker can model and then have family members practice. Just like in active listening, the worker asks these questions: "How do you feel about that?" and "This is what I hear you say," or **checking on others' thoughts, feelings, and understanding**. Another component to actively listening in work with families is to have family members ask each other these questions. The worker may say "Tom, can you tell Susan what you heard her say?" or "Janet, can you check how Bill feels when he hears you say that?"

Creating Safe Space

Finally, an important skill in family mediation is to help family members express their feelings, especially feelings of anger, without blaming, shaming, or threatening violence. If voices are raised, a worker can interrupt with this: "Sounds like you're angry; let's help everyone understand your feelings."

Skills for Family Mediation

Skill	Description	Example	Required Worker Characteristic(s)
Using "I" messages	Beginning a sentence with "I," such as "I feel . . . ," "I think . . . ," "I wonder . . ."	"I feel really angry when you say that . . ."	Self-reflection
Being brief and specific	Stating feelings and thoughts succinctly	I think we are discussing three themes . . ."	Focus
Checking on others' thoughts, feelings, and understanding	Active listening among family members	"John, I think I hear you say . . . is that right? Karey, is that what you've heard him say?"	Patience Focus
Creating safe space	Modeling use of feeling words without shouting, or verbal and nonverbal threatening behavior	"Steve, I see you clenching your fists when you are speaking. Could you talk about your feelings without doing that?"	Confidence Assertiveness

Sample Interview in the Family Mediation Example

Sam: I don't want to talk to her! I call her every day, and she never calls me. If she doesn't answer the phone, I don't get to talk to her. I have to stay off the phone at night so I call her in the morning, and she doesn't always answer and doesn't call me back. She . . .

Missy: Shut up, Sam! You always talk too much!

Worker: (*gently*) Sam, I think you mean to say that you felt angry when Missy doesn't call back. Is that right? *(modeling "I" messages and being brief and specific; labeling feelings.)*

Sam: Yes! (*clenching fists*)

Worker: Sam, it's okay to be angry, but when I see you clenching your fists like that it makes me a little scared. Could you say "I feel angry when Missy doesn't call me back" without shouting or clenching your fists? (*expressing feelings safely*)

Sam: (*more calmly*) I feel angry when Missy doesn't call me back.

Worker: Could you say that to Missy now?

Sam: Missy, I feel angry when you don't call me back.

Worker: Missy, what did you hear Sam say?

Missy: I should call him back.

Worker: Sam, did she hear you correctly?

Sam: Yes, she did.

Worker: Missy, how do you feel about this? *(modeling checking on others' feelings)*

Missy: I am sad. I am sorry.

Worker: Missy, you're doing a good job talking about your feelings. *(affirmation)* Can you tell Sam how you feel?

Missy: Sam, I am sorry.

Section 11.4: The Social Work Role of Family Facilitator

This section discusses another role in generalist social work with families: that of the **family facilitator**. We consider the role and the skills that allow us to carry it out.

The Social Work Role of Family Facilitator

Social workers often work with families whose members have difficulty communicating with each other. There may not be conflict that requires mediation, but there may be a lot of mixed and missed messages.

This role is significant in work throughout the entire planned change process, since families can have ineffective means of communication that have lasted for decades and even through past generations. In cases like this, it is common for the family to be labeled *dysfunctional*. Instead, it is best to use the strength-based language we've discussed before. As stated previously, this situation could be described as a family with long-standing ineffective means of communication. Like the role of mediator, social work skills begin with the nonverbal skills that are used in work with individuals. The worker shows an engaging smile, encourages with nods, uses a genuine voice, and shows warmth with appropriate eye contact. It is important for the worker to share these nonverbal communications with each family member in turn.

Next, the social worker playing the role of facilitator needs to demonstrate a number of other skills in addition to the basics like those we've discussed before: affirmation and open-ended questions, for example. Even though the worker is likely to speak to one individual at a time, these skills should be used by the worker in addressing each family member as needed. As in the role of mediator, the social worker in the role of facilitator often uses skills to model the functional behaviors. That is, the worker uses the skills as part of teaching those skills to the family members. In the session, family members get to practice increasingly effective ways to communicate. These skills include the following:

- Confidentiality assurance
- Reflective listening
- Behavior rehearsal
- Role play
- Reframing

Confidentiality Assurances

As we've hinted at in a prior discussion on ethical decision-making, **confidentiality assurances** can be challenging for the worker. Of course, confidentiality assurances are important in all settings. People always need to know that the worker does not discuss them or their situations outside of the session. People also have a right to know up front that there are exceptions to that rule. A worker may have to disclose what has gone on in a session if they have witnessed child or elder abuse, if the family members are in danger of harming themselves or others, if the worker is compelled to do so by a court, or if the worker needs to seek supervision. The worker should make sure that everyone in the client system knows that information will be given out in a "need to know" manner. In short, the client needs to know that there will be no gossiping about them. They may not want anyone to know that they are working with a social worker. The worker has to be sensitive about this fear and try to anticipate it. For example, you should talk to a client about what you will do if you run into the client out in the community. Will you greet them? What if people around you know that you're a social worker? If these topics are discussed early in the work, they are not likely to be problems later.

Confidentiality assurances in families have an added dimension to individual work. After a family session, it is often the case that one of the family members will be in touch and ask to share private information that they don't want to share in the group: One of the adults is having a romantic relationship outside of the marriage or partnership, one of the adolescents wants to know about birth control, and there has been some kind of violence in the home. Sometimes, especially when working with a couple, it is simplest to say that you will only talk with one person if the other is present. You can use this approach with larger families as well: "Please know that in order for us to work to enhance your family I'll need to always talk with all of you at once." On the other hand, there are situations where we want to know what we'll find out only from one person privately. Parents may want to discuss adult-only information without young children present, for example, or a child may want to disclose abuse. If you suspect this is the case, you can work in part with individuals or small groups of family members. You will plan this approach with the whole family together and allow everyone to have individual time with you for part of your meeting time over a period of weeks. You will almost always be working with the client or small group to be ready and able to share the information with the whole family as long as it is age-appropriate. This approach can also be stated up front such as "We've talked about confidentiality and how things said in here stay in here with just a couple of exceptions. I also want to talk about confidentiality among yourselves . . . "

Reflective Listening

Reflective listening is the verbal form of the embodied mirroring we've discussed early in the book. The point is to show that you are paying attention by doing the same thing someone else is doing—in this case, what they are saying. So you just repeat exactly what the person is saying. The beauty of this is that family members experience you doing this in a respectful way. Some phrases you might use include "I think I heard you say" or "I'm not sure I understood you . . . did you say . . . ?"

Behavioral Rehearsal

This skill is literally about rehearsal and can be particularly important with families. It's a way for clients to practice what they'd like to do and say outside of the session. Trust is necessary as well as the expectation that all family members will listen with respect. A good example for a **behavioral rehearsal** is the reflective listening we've just been thinking about. Once you have said "I think I heard you say" and have gotten a positive response, you can ask another family member to repeat your question back to the original speaker. It might look like this: "Kathy, would you please tell Bill what you've heard him say?" This way, Kathy rehearses a useful way to speak to Bill in the future. Behavior rehearsal is well studied and has recently been shown to help veterans learn social skills (Beidel, Stout, Neer, Frueh, & Lejuez, 2017).

Role Play

Similar to behavior rehearsal, **role play** involves actual practice of a behavior. Sometimes it helps to put two chairs facing each other. It may also be helpful to state that every person will have to do a behavior rehearsal. If need be, you can serve as the other side of the conversation. Behavior rehearsal can include two family members or someone from another system. "You all agreed to do role plays, and everyone will have a chance. Tommy, I'm going to pretend to be your mom trying to get you up in the morning. You play yourself. Let's see how this plays out in real life and how it could play out differently." While role play can be an important part of helping, a use of humor is not misplaced here!

Reframing

Reframing is a way of altering the family's interpretation of an event. Often, families with difficulty communicating come to see anything that affects the family as being negative. The negativity is shared and becomes an expectation. For example, a school-aged family member may say "I wanted to be in the play, and I practiced a lot, but I was sixth on the list and they only needed five people." A worker might reply with "You told me 60 people were trying out. You practiced, and you were fantastic. Not only that, you now know how to practice drama. You are in a great place for next semester's audition!" This kind of reframe can be difficult to do on the fly, so it helps to have a particular method. One way to go about reframing is to ask a series of questions that get at the following:

1. Does the event truly affect you?
2. Does the event threaten your view of yourself?
3. If so, who truly gets the credit or blame? Is it actually something that was out of your control?
4. What will happen in the future? (Cookston et al., 2015)

In the example that was just given, the play audition certainly impacted the child, and as we've seen, it likely impacted the family system as well. In the same way, the rejection impacts the way the child sees himself (active in the play) and the family (a family that has a student who is so successful as to be in the play). Here no one needs to take blame, the child practiced. The worker affirms the practice as well as the very good performance and sets up the child for success in the future. It's a different way of thinking about the experience—one that offers a lesson for the future and hope.

Skills for Family Facilitation

Skill	Description	Example	Required Worker Characteristic(s)
Confidentiality assurances	Helping clients understand the fact that their situations will not be discussed outside of the session unless certain conditions are in place	"If I see you in the grocery store, I'm going to act like I don't see you unless you say hi first . . ."	Integrity Ability to seek supervision
Reflective listening	Repeating the exact words a client said	"Did you say . . .?"	Focus
Behavioral rehearsal	Asking a client to practice words and actions they want to repeat outside the session	"Go ahead and say what you'd like to say to the teacher. Where are you? What will you say?"	Patience Focusing the interview
Role play	Having practice between family members where they engage in a conversation that they'd like to have outside the session; the worker may play one of the "characters" if sufficient empathy is present	"Let's practice this. I'll be the probation officer and you be yourself . . ."	Use of humor Empathy
Reframing	Restating an idea to highlight its positive aspects	"I'm sorry you didn't get the promotion, but you got to know the boss much better in the interview. That'll give you a better shot at the next opportunity."	Positive outlook Focus

Family Facilitation Example

Worker: Thanks for being here. It was Sam's idea to have his mom at one of the meetings between him and Missy.

Mom: *(defensive expression)* Okay. I have to spend a lot of time in these meetings.

Worker: It's really great that you and Sam have a close enough relationship for you to join us. *(affirmation; reframing)*

Worker: Sam and Missy have said that it's okay to talk about their previous meetings with me right now—although maybe not in the future. Do you have any questions about the other confidentiality stuff I mentioned? *(checking on others' thoughts; confidentiality assurances)*

Mom: No problem.

Worker: Sounds like you're not feeling happy about this meeting. Can you tell us more about that? *(labeling feelings; allowing safe expression of feelings)*

Mom: I've been to meetings with Sam in the past. Nothing comes out of them.

Worker: You feel like nothing comes out of them. *(reflective listening)*

Mom: Right.

Worker: Well, as you know, Transitions is an agency that serves to help adults with different abilities to live successfully in the community. As I said, my name is Sahara. I know it's unusual and easy to forget. It's my job to help Missy meet her goals toward having a good life. Today the only thing on my agenda is for us to talk about Sam and Missy and how much they miss seeing each other now that Missy has moved. We agreed to end in a half hour, so that's what we'll do. *(opening statement)*

Mom: Okay.

Worker: Sam, did you understand that we are talking about you and Missy spending more time together and that we only have a half hour? Do you have any questions? *(checking on others' thoughts and feelings; being brief and specific)*

Sam: I get it.

Worker: Missy, do you understand? *(addressing every member of the group; checking on others' thoughts and feelings)*

Missy: I do. *(begins to laugh)* Just like at a wedding. Ha ha!

Worker: Missy, you are really good at making people laugh sometimes, but we don't have much time here so let's move on. *(focusing the interview)* I think we can all agree that we're here to talk about Missy and Sam getting together more.

All: *(nodding)*

Missy: Sam, I think the problem is that you can't walk to see Missy and you have no other way to see her since she moved. *(being brief and specific; checking on others' thoughts and feelings)*

Sam and Missy:	Yes!
Worker:	Sam, I think you had something to say to your mom about this. *(empowerment)*
Sam to Mom:	You take me. *(Mom rolls eyes)*
Worker:	Can we practice what we talked about before? Do you want to ask, "Please can you sometimes take me to see Missy?" Don't look at the ground, look at me when you say it. *(behavioral rehearsal)*
Sam:	*(looking at worker)* Please, can my mom take me?
Worker:	You're getting close. *(encouragement)* Now say it to me as if I were your mom, and don't forget to look at me. *(role play)*
Sam:	Can you please take me to see Missy?
Worker:	Great job. *(encouragement)* Now can you say that to your mom?

Section 11.5: Financial Capacity Building With Families

In addition to the basic roles workers play with families, there are some specific issues that are important. This section discusses ways social workers can help families become financially empowered.

Financial Capacity Building With Families

Most of the families that find themselves in front of social workers have some kind of financial challenges. In fact, it may shock you to learn that nearly half of American families are financially insecure and that financial capability for all has been identified by the American Academy of Social Work and Social Welfare (AASWSW; 2017) as a "grand challenge" for social work. To start this discussion, we should consider what it means to be poor. The U.S. government has determined that it measures poverty based on an **absolute poverty** measure. In other words, the federal government has determined an estimate of what it costs to feed, clothe, and shelter a family. This amount becomes the poverty level. It is used to measure poverty and track the effectiveness of the social welfare programs and economic policies that attempt to reduce poverty (Schiller, 2008).

There are several things wrong with the poverty measure. First, it is not a **relative poverty** measure. In other words, it does not take into account what income and wealth others around you have accumulated. Even if you have enough income to buy food, you may feel poor if you cannot afford a cell phone since everyone else seems to have one, and they seem to have some safety benefits, especially for kids. If you are school-aged and you can't get to the library to borrow a computer, you're at a distinct disadvantage because your teachers expect you to access and hand in assignments online. Second, the poverty rate is not adjusted by geography. With a couple of exceptions, the official poverty level does not differentiate among the states. For example, the poverty level is the same in New York City, where the cost of living is relatively high, as it is in Detroit, one of America's poorest cities, with a relatively low cost of living. What that means is that when the U.S. government counts how many Americans live in poverty, it will miss many of the poor people of places like New York. For these reasons, the real U.S. poverty rate is probably much higher that the official estimate. Still, the U.S. Census Bureau reports that 13.5% of Americans lived in poverty in 2015. That's more than 1 in every 10 people. Look around your classroom. If you have 20 people in your class and you were a representative sample of Americans, 3 of your classmates would not be able to provide for themselves and certainly would not be able to provide for a family. Now you might say "Of course, we're poor. We're students." In some cases, you would be right. Some of you are working at low wage jobs to support yourself while you go to school. You may be trying to pay rent on an off-campus apartment and perhaps support a child. You'll have to pay student loans later, which will severely lower your buying power. Given those student loans, if you quit school before you graduate you will be in serious risk of being poor. Many of you, though, have your needs taken care of. Even though you may have little spending money, or **disposable income**, you still have food, clothing, and shelter available to you at school. When you graduate, you'll be much less likely to be poor than someone with a high school education or just a few college courses. Again, we're using the poverty level designated by the U.S. government. If you have just enough income to be above the poverty level, you may be what is called **near poor**, or experiencing an inability to provide basic necessities to yourself and your dependents even if your income is technically above the poverty level.

You should know that someone who works a minimum wage job, or even one with a slightly higher wage, cannot get their income above the poverty level. So you can see that if many of our clients are technically poor, many more of them are likely near poor in terms of an objective measure of their income. It is safe to say that most of the rest of our clients are relatively poor. In other words, they may not have things like cell phones that are now considered to be necessities. For this reason, nearly all of our clients are either poor or seriously financially challenged. Both groups need to manage their money carefully. Even if you can get a family living in poverty to have their needs met through social welfare programs like income assistance, housing assistance, or food support, you are likely to find that they still feel as though they can't get by. What all of these clients need is **financial empowerment.**

The World Bank (2017) calls financial empowerment the development of financial knowledge, or **financial literacy**, plus the ability to put that knowledge into practice. This means the ability to make conscious, planned spending and saving decisions along with the ability to know how to use **financial services**. Financial services, such as those offered by banks, include checking and savings accounts as well as opportunities to borrow money. While social workers are not qualified to give financial advice like what retirement plan to choose or what stocks make good investments, we are responsible to help our clients achieve financial empowerment. For this reason, we need to know basic financial information and have the ability to share it. See Figure 11.2.

Money as a Taboo Topic

As you know, taboo topics are those that are not usually discussed in everyday conversations. As social workers, we are sometimes called on to discuss taboo topics, and one of those topics is money. We need to constantly be looking out for ways to work money into our assessment and planning with families. One way is to address the topic head-on during assessment. Very often assessment includes a number of fact-finding, close-ended questions like "What is your address?" For that reason, it is possible to simply ask this: "What is your income?" This question is easily followed by an open-ended question like "Do you feel like you have enough money to meet your needs?" Later opportunities to bring money into the social work interview include when a client is applying for financial assistance, when a client gets or loses a job,

FIGURE 11.2 ● Elements of Financial Empowerment

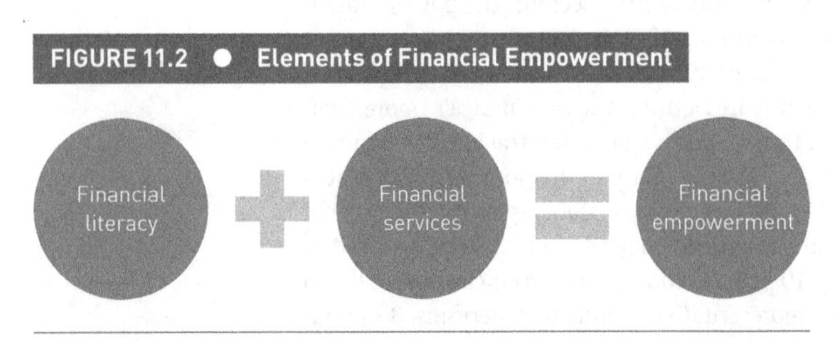

or when an unexpected expense comes up. You may ask who makes money decisions in the family or how people have experienced family money issues in the past. There will be many opportunities to discuss money; the social worker just has to get past the social norm that says someone else's money is not our business. Keep in mind the need for self-reflection. If you are not comfortable financially yourself, or if you don't have or stick to a budget, you will have a difficult time working with others on the topic of money. You'll need to take care of that problem right away by becoming financially empowered yourself.

Some basics about budgeting are supplied by the Consumer Financial Protection Bureau (2017). They include knowledge about the main elements of a budget as well as day-to-day tips and guidelines. A budget should begin with thoughts about financial goals—maybe a person has a goal to build up savings or get a new car. Then, the budget typically includes the following:

- Income (after taxes)
- Expenses
    - Home (rent or mortgage, utilities, phone)
    - Food
    - Personal (clothes, hair care, toiletries)
    - Transportation
    - Health care (insurance, deductibles, prescriptions)
    - Entertainment
    - Outstanding credit (credit cards, car loan)
    - Education (tuition, books, student loans)
    - Savings (ideally at least two months of expenses plus expected expenses like car repairs)

Some basic budgeting tips include the following:

- Pay monthly bills to avoid late fees, repossession, or eviction.
- Set aside money for weekly and day-to-day expenses like groceries and bus fare—a cash system might be best.
- Put money into savings to accumulate that 2 months of expenses as well as large goals.
- Either write down all of your expenditures for a month or review bank and credit card statements to see where your money is going.
- Before buying, consider the following:
    - Do I really need it?
    - Do I need it today? What will happen if I don't get it today?
    - Can I meet this need less expensively? (Wells Fargo, 2017)

Finally, there are widely accepted guidelines for expenditures:

- Housing: 20% to 30%
- Utilities (gas, electric, telephone): 4% to 7%
- Food (eating in and out): 15% to 30%

- Personal expenses: 2% to 4%
- Health care: 2% to 8%
- Clothing: 3% to 10%
- Transportation: 6% to 30%
- Entertainment: 2% to 6%
- Savings: 10%

There are many ways to learn about budgeting. The Consumer Financial Protection Bureau has a site online. There you can get help from a workbook they publish for people to learn how to help others with financial decision-making. It's a kind of train-the-trainer approach (Consumer Protection Bureau, 2017). You may dial 211 and learn about a local budget and credit counseling agency from this Essential Community Services number sponsored by the Federal Communications Commission. You may talk to a professional at a bank. As a social worker, you are in a unique position. You need to learn for yourself, and you need to learn how to help others. Whatever source you use, make sure you get knowledgeable and comfortable with your own financial situation so that you are in a good position to help others.

CRITICAL THINKING AND COLLABORATIVE LEARNING EXERCISES 11.3

1. Locate the federal Consumer Financial Protection Bureau's tool kit at https://s3.amazonaws.com/files.consumerfinance.gov/f/documents/201701_cfpb_YMYG-Toolkit.pdf.
2. Learn how to develop a personal budget. Draft one, and discuss the challenges you faced with a partner.

Section 11.6: Crisis Intervention With Families

This section discusses the appropriate social work responses when clients are in crisis.

Crisis Intervention With Families

Families don't often go to social workers for the personal development of members. Sometimes, they go to social workers because a chronic problem becomes too much. Most often, though, families come to social workers because they are in crisis.

What is a Crisis?

A **crisis** is an event that keeps people from coping the way they normally might. It is a temporary state of psychological disorganization (Langer & Lietz, 2015). There is an old saying based on a Chinese character that says crisis consists of danger and opportunity. According to this legend, there is no character for crisis other than the character that is a melding of the representation of danger and the representation of opportunity. Many times, a crisis is like that: It shakes up the system and forces change to happen. An easy slide back into the former homeostasis is not often possible.

In a crisis, the entire family system is likely to be affected. It can be an external event such as a flood or an internal event such as a serious illness in a family member. Kanel (2015) has identified four parts of a crisis that occur one after the other:

1. There is a triggering event.
2. The person sees the event as damaging.
3. The idea that the event is damaging leads to emotional distress.
4. There is a failure to implement usual coping methods.

When people cannot cope as they usually do, the emotional stress increases and the consequences spiral into fewer and fewer successful coping mechanisms. People may be physically injured. They may develop mental illness, behavior problems, and physical illnesses. As one family member is affected, others will follow. The ability of the family to act functionally as a group becomes less and less.

What a Social Worker Can Do

In a crisis, the worker begins the way they always begin a social work process—only faster. Their self-reflections serve to calm them down. This way, they don't add to the family's problems by conveying a sense of crisis themselves. Next, a quick engagement is carried out with a sentence or two followed immediately by an opening statement. It might be something like "Our agency is here to help survivors of the hurricane. My job is to get you the resources you need. We'll take 15 minutes to identify your priorities." Assessment follows in a very abbreviated way. The focus of the assessment is directly about the crisis. In cases like this, one quick implementation can make a difference. It's been shown that one-time implementations can be based on a single contact, and brief strategic family therapy, an evidenced-based practice, can be successful (Szapocznik, Muir, Duff, Schwartz, & Brown, 2015). In this way, a single encounter with a social worker can turn danger into opportunity.

After the brief assessment, the social worker quickly helps the client make a plan. Maybe the family develops a goal to find shelter and a way to contact relatives. An objective may be traveling to a shelter and waiting in line. Another might be traveling to a location where cell phones are available for survivors' use. Keep in mind that the family is likely to be unable to function as they did in the past. Recently, they may have been perfectly capable of finding the shelter, waiting in line, and completing the necessary forms. However, right now they are in crisis and aren't capable of either. Your implementation is based on the level of need. You may need to give them the address of the shelter and move to the next family. Or, you may need to walk them to the transportation line that is carrying people to shelters. It depends on what they need.

Remember that crisis can also be opportunity. The family may be one that had a chronic problem, but they did not seek help. The crisis throws them into the arms of a social worker who may be able to help them improve their functioning. For example, a social worker may observe that every family member seems to be yelling at a 10-year-old brother. They are responding to crisis by allying against one sibling and blaming that child for their problems. This may even be a long-term problem in which the relationships between other family members are fused, and they consistently blame that child in the face of any stress or crisis. In that case, you may say "I see everyone seems to be angry with Tom. Do you want to try to change that dynamic?" The family is in shock, and they blankly agree. You say "Tom, you look like a smart kid. I'm going to give you this pass to give to the bus driver. It's on a lanyard so you won't lose it." In this particular situation, Tom cannot be the scapegoat. Instead, he is a responsible member of the family. This one experience can help to alter the family dynamic in the future.

Suicidal Ideation

Thoughts about suicide, or **suicidal ideation**, are a special type of crisis. The World Health Organization (WHO) calls suicide a public health priority, since over 800,000 people complete suicide every year. Many more make unsuccessful attempts, and it's estimated that 20 times more experience suicidal ideation (WHO, 2017). Situations that seem to occur at the same time people are considering ending their lives include unemployment, illness, several crises, and a release from hospitalization (Kanel, 2015). Disaster, violence, and abuse are other factors, especially among vulnerable groups like refugees; lesbian, gay, bisexual, transgender, and intersex (LGBTI) people; and prisoners. The most important risk factor is one or more previous attempts at suicide (WHO, 2017).

Workers also need to be on the lookout for some of the following signs articulated by Aguilera (1990) as cited in Kanel (2015, p. 85):

- Giving things away
- Putting things in order
- Writing a will
- Withdrawing from usual activities
- Being preoccupied with death
- Mourning a friend or relative's recent death
- Feeling hopeless, helpless, or worthless
- Increasing drug and alcohol use
- Displaying psychotic behavior (irrational behavior disconnected from objective reality)
- Giving verbal hints such as "I'm of no use to anyone anymore"
- Showing agitated depression
- Living alone and being isolated

Seeing signs like this demands a suicide assessment. One of the first questions to ask is whether the person intends to do themselves harm. Kanel (2015) suggests that **completes suicide** is preferred over commit suicide, since that seems to imply that a sin or a crime is being committed. Here we face one of the greatest taboos we address as social workers. In our society, people do not talk about hurting themselves or completing suicide. Few people are able to ask someone if they are experiencing suicidal ideation—partly because it seems like the mention of it may put the idea into the client's head or push them to carry out their ideas. The opposite is true. Assessing suicide risk at its most basic level is finding out whether people *want* to hurt themselves, have a *plan* to hurt themselves, and have the *means* to do so. The only way to get this information is to ask.

Sommers-Flanagan and Shaw (2017) outlined some methods for asking these difficult questions:

1. *Normalizing*

   Instead of just asking whether a person has been thinking of harming themselves, it might be best to try to let them know that others sometimes feel the same way. You might say "Sometimes when people have experiences like yours they think about suicide. Do you think you might be heading there?"

2. *Gentle assumption*

   In this method, you assume that what you are worried about has already occurred for the client. Here you might ask how many times the person has thought of suicide.

3. *Mood ratings with a suicide floor*

   You may have heard a physician ask someone how bad their pain is on a scale of 1 to 10. Rating a mood is similar, but when you are concerned about a client's suicidal thoughts, you might ask how they feel with 10 being great and 1 being suicidal, or **mood ratings with a suicide floor**.

   Above all, it is important to remember that asking someone about suicide will not put the idea into their head or cause them to carry it out (Jobes, Eyman, & Yufit, 1995). It's frightening for you to ask the question, but it's not harmful for the client.

Having considered these risk factors and asked some of these questions, you may feel that your client is truly thinking of harming themselves. In that case, especially if the person has the means and a plan, it is likely that they need inpatient care in order to remain safe. It's best if you can help them to accept that need and voluntarily go to a hospital. If they refuse and you believe them to be in danger, you will have to call a local crisis intervention team or the police to have them **involuntarily hospitalized** (Kanel, 2015). Your client's well-being is your first concern, but keep in mind that suicide is likely to be illegal in your state, and that requires you to make the report in the same way you would make that kind of report if your client had the want, the means, and a plan to hurt someone else. If the client reports that they are not in immediate danger, you may enlist family and friends to conduct a **suicide watch** to be sure the client is safe (Kanel, 2015). In addition, you may create a safety plan or a **no-suicide contract** with a client. In this case, you have the client promise in writing not to harm themselves before your next meeting and to contact you if the urge becomes too strong. In this type of case where you can be confident that the client will be safe until the next time you see them, fall back onto what you know: the planned change process. Carry out your self-reflection, continue to engage the client, assess all of the systems, and help the client to make a plan that addresses their concerns and gets them thinking of the future. See Figure 11.3.

FIGURE 11.3 • Crisis and Crisis Intervention Process

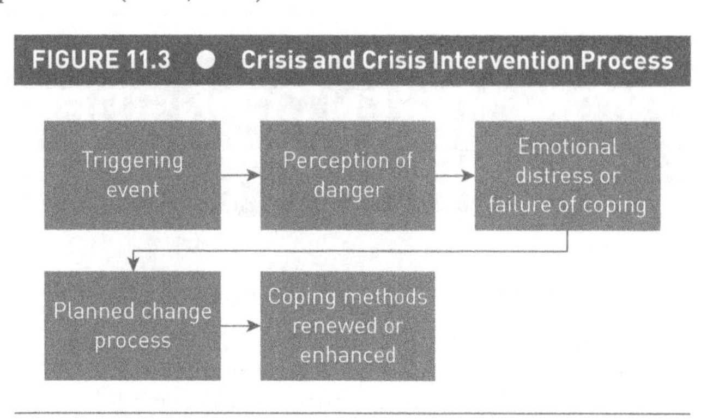

The Sympathetic Worker: Reflective Responses

©iStock.com/FangXiaNuo

It is important to maintain positive connections with colleagues.

Sahara identified closely with Missy. She remembered the old days when her parents limited her contact with one boyfriend or another, and she believed that Missy was being cheated. Her strong feelings could have clouded her thinking and caused her to form an alliance with Missy as if they were family members. This kind of alliance would not include the other professionals on the team. Sahara's supervisor knew that an alliance of that kind would keep the professionals from cooperating and would create dissention between Sahara and the team. In the long run, that would be detrimental to the services Missy was receiving. Sahara's supervisor guided her toward self-reflection. As a result, Sahara identified that she was feeling angry toward her colleagues because she believed they were purposefully keeping Missy and Sam apart. In fact, it was more likely that they were oblivious to the family relationship between Missy and Sam. As Sahara's anger dissipated, she was able to develop empathy for her teammates. She could best advocate for Missy by developing cooperative relationships with her colleagues. When she was no longer angry, she worked to create balance between the systems of the other professionals and Missy. Information was exchanged, and the professionals began to relate to Missy and Sam as a family.

CRITICAL THINKING AND COLLABORATIVE LEARNING EXERCISES 11.4

1. Find out a social worker's legal responsibilities related to suicidal ideation in your state. Have group partners find out those requirements in your neighboring states.
2. Role-play responses to statements about suicidal ideation.

Section 11.7: Review and Apply

CONCURRENT CONSIDERATIONS IN GENERALIST PRACTICE

Ethical Decision-Making Challenge

Where in the *NASW Code of Ethics* (NASW, 2018) does it suggest that clients and family members ought to be invited to be full participating members in an interdisciplinary meeting?

Human Rights

Is Missy being deprived of any fundamental human rights such as freedom, safety, privacy, an adequate standard of living, health care, and education? Reference the UN Universal Declaration of Human Rights.

Evidence-Based Practice

See whether there is any evidence about how to support intimate relationships among intellectually challenged clients.

Policies Impacting Practice

What happens to a client in your state if they have been involuntarily hospitalized for suicidal ideation? How long can they be hospitalized without their consent?

Managing Diversity

Imagine Sam was not intellectually challenged. How might his relationship with Missy play out?

Multilevel Practice

Identify examples of Sahara's work on all levels.

Micro: ______________________________

Mezzo: ______________________________

Macro: ______________________________

Dynamic and Interactive Planned Change Stages

Identify aspects of Sahara's work where she worked in the following stages:

Self-Reflection: ______________________________

Engagement: ______________________________

Assessment: ______________________________

Planning: ______________________________

Implementation: ______________________________

Evaluation: ______________________________

Termination and Follow-Up: ______________________________

Chapter Summary

Section 11.1: The Family-in-Environment Perspective

The FIE perspective is foundational to MSP. One of the main principles of FIE is that families can be empowered to define themselves; individuals can freely identify family members. Elements such as a shared history, emotional bonding, mutual support, and a family identity develop families rather than exclusively genetic or legal ties.

Section 11.2: Interactions Within Families

The family may be viewed as a social system. Individual members are interdependent and carry out individual, interrelated tasks. Families have boundaries that are more or less permeable, depending on the level of family identity and the degree to which individuals are allowed into the family. Members play particular roles including provider and caregiver. Other, less functional family roles include scapegoat, mascot, dependent and codependent members, and the hero child.

Section 11.3: The Social Work Role of Mediator

Generalist social workers can play the role of mediator in work with families. Mediators work to resolve conflicts among family members. To do so, they model conflict resolution skills like using "I" messages, being brief and specific, and checking on others' thoughts and feelings.

Section 11.4: The Social Work Role of Family Facilitator

The generalist social worker may play the role of family facilitator in work with families. The family facilitator helps family members to communicate. In this role, social workers use skills like providing confidentiality assurances and carrying out reflective listening, behavior rehearsal, role play, and reframing.

Section 11.5: Financial Capacity Building With Families

Many of the families social workers see have financial challenges. For that reason, it is important to help financially empower families through financial capacity building. This includes both the development of financial knowledge and the ability to carry it out. To financially empower families, social workers must know the basics of family budgeting.

Section 11.6: Crisis Intervention With Families

A crisis keeps people from coping the way they normally would. Crisis triggers include an event that a person sees as damaging. That perspective results in emotional distress. During a crisis, there is an opportunity to develop new coping methods as social workers move quickly through the planned change process. A particular type of crisis is suicidal ideation. Social workers need to look for signs of suicidal ideation and conduct suicide assessments to see whether a person wants to harm themselves and whether they have a plan and the means to do so. Some skills used to conduct suicide assessments include normalizing feelings of hopelessness; making the gentle assumption that someone in a particular situation may feel suicidal; and asking people to rate their moods with a suicide floor, or a low rating that includes the desire to complete an act of suicide. The term *complete suicide* is preferable to saying commit suicide, because it does not imply an illegal or immoral act.

SELF-REFLECTION 11: FAMILY-OF-ORIGIN SCALE

PURPOSE: To measure self-perceived levels of health in one's family of origin.

AUTHORS: Alan J. Hovestadt, William T. Anderson, Fred P. Piercy, Samuel W. Cochran, and Marshall Fine

DESCRIPTION: The Family-of-Origin Scale is a 40-item instrument designed to measure one's perception of the "health" of one's family of origin. The scale focuses on autonomy and intimacy as two key concepts in the life of a healthy family. In this model, the healthy family develops autonomy by emphasizing clarity of expression (CE: positive items 23 and 34, negative items 9 and 16), responsibility (R: positive items 11 and 38, negative items 5 and 18), respect for others (RO: positive items 15 and 19, negative items 4 and 28), openness to others (O: positive items 6 and 14, negative items 23 and 37), and acceptance of separation and loss (A: positive items 10 and 36, negative items 20 and 25). The healthy family is viewed as developing intimacy by encouraging expression of a range of feelings (RF: positive items 1 and 12, negative items 32 and 39), creating a warm atmosphere in the home referred to as mood and tone (MT: positive items 29 and 40, negative items 2 and 22), dealing with conflict resolution without undue stress (C: positive items 27 and 31, negative items 7 and 13), promoting sensitivity or empathy (E: positive items 21 and 35, negative items 17 and 30), and developing trust in humans as basically good (T: positive items 3 and 8, negative items 26 and 33).

NORMS: The Family-of-Origin Scale was studied with 278 college students in Texas. Means for each construct were as follows:

CC: 3.52

R: 3.43

RO: 3.5

O: 3.41

A: 3.44

RE: 1.37

MT: 4.06

C: 3.42

E: 3.51

T: 3.78

SCORING: For each item, the most healthy response (noted above as positive items) receives a score of "5" while the least healthy (negative items) receives a score of "1." Higher scores indicate perception of better family health.

RELIABILITY: The scale has fair to good internal consistency with an alpha of .75. Test–retest showed excellent stability.

VALIDITY: The scale discriminates between men in alcohol-distressed and nonalcohol-distressed marriages and between perceptions of current marriage and rationality of marriage partners. It was significantly correlated with perceived levels of health in respondents' current families.

PRIMARY REFERENCE:

Hovestadt, A. J., Anderson, W. T., Piercy, F. P., Cochan, S. W., and Fine, M. (1985). A Family-of-Origin Scale. In K. Corcoran & J. Fischer (Eds.), *Measures for clinical practice and research* (5th ed.). New York, NY: Oxford University Press.

FAMILY-OF-ORIGIN SCALE

The family of origin is the family with which you spent most or all of your childhood years. This scale is designed to help you recall how your family of origin functioned.

Each family is unique and has its own ways of doing things. Thus, there are *no right or wrong choices* in this scale. What is important is that you respond as *honestly* as you can.

In reading the following statements, apply them to your family of origin, *as you remember it*. Using the following scale, circle the appropriate number. Please respond to each statement.

5 = Strongly agree that it describes my family of origin

4 = Agree that it describes my family of origin

3 = Neutral

2 = Disagree that it describes my family of origin

1 = Strongly disagree that it describes my family of origin

1.	In my family, it was normal to show both positive and negative feelings.	5	4	3	2	1
2.	The atmosphere in my family usually was unpleasant.	5	4	3	2	1
3.	In my family, we encouraged one another to develop new friendships.	5	4	3	2	1
4.	Differences of opinion in my family were discouraged.	5	4	3	2	1
5.	People in my family often made excuses for their mistakes.	5	4	3	2	1
6.	My parents encouraged family members to listen to one another.	5	4	3	2	1
7.	Conflicts in my family never got resolved.	5	4	3	2	1
8.	My family taught me that people were basically good.	5	4	3	2	1
9.	I found it difficult to understand what other family members said and how they felt.	5	4	3	2	1
10.	We talked about our sadness when a relative or family friend died.	5	4	3	2	1
11.	My parents openly admitted it when they were wrong.	5	4	3	2	1
12.	In my family, I expressed just about any feeling I had.	5	4	3	2	1
13.	Resolving conflicts in my family was a very stressful experience.	5	4	3	2	1
14.	My family was receptive to the different ways various family members viewed life.	5	4	3	2	1
15.	My parents encouraged me to express my views openly.	5	4	3	2	1
16.	I often had to guess at what other family members thought or how they felt.	5	4	3	2	1
17.	My attitudes and my feelings frequently were ignored or criticized in my family.	5	4	3	2	1
18.	My family members rarely expressed responsibility for their actions.	5	4	3	2	1
19.	In my family, I felt free to express my own opinions.	5	4	3	2	1
20.	We never talked about our grief when a relative or family friend died.	5	4	3	2	1
21.	Sometimes in my family, I did not have to say anything, but I felt understood.	5	4	3	2	1
22.	The atmosphere in my family was cold and negative.	5	4	3	2	1
23.	The members of my family were not very receptive to one another's views.	5	4	3	2	1
24.	I found it easy to understand what other family members said and how they felt.	5	4	3	2	1
25.	If a family friend moved away, we never discussed our feelings of sadness.	5	4	3	2	1
26.	In my family, I learned to be suspicious of others.	5	4	3	2	1

(Continued)

(Continued)

27.	In my family, I felt that I could talk things out and settle conflicts.	5	4	3	2	1
28.	I found it difficult to express my own opinions in my family.	5	4	3	2	1
29.	Mealtimes in my home usually were friendly and pleasant.	5	4	3	2	1
30.	In my family, no one cared about the feelings of other family members.	5	4	3	2	1
31.	We usually were able to work out conflicts in my family.	5	4	3	2	1
32.	In my family, certain feelings were not allowed to be expressed.	5	4	3	2	1
33.	My family believed that people usually took advantage of you.	5	4	3	2	1
34.	I found it easy in my family to express what I thought and how I felt.	5	4	3	2	1
35.	My family members usually were sensitive to one another's feelings.	5	4	3	2	1
36.	When someone important to us moved away, our family discussed our feelings of loss.	5	4	3	2	1
37.	My parents discussed our feelings of loss.	5	4	3	2	1
38.	In my family, people took responsibility for what they did.	5	4	3	2	1
39.	My family had an unwritten rule: Don't express your feelings.	5	4	3	2	1
40.	I remember my family as being warm and supportive.	5	4	3	2	1

Recommended Websites

"Your Money, Your Goals: A Financial Empowerment Toolkit" from the Consumer Financial Protection Bureau: https://s3.amazonaws.com/files.consumerfinance.gov/f/documents/201701_cfpb_YMYG-Toolkit.pdf

Critical Terms for Roles and Skills in Work With Families

nuclear family 310
cash assistance 311
relational family 312
family system 312
natural supports 313
family tasks 315
family roles 315
family boundary 315
role flexibility 315
provider 316
caregiver 317
role strain 317
role enhancement 317
alliance 318
fusion 319
triangulation 319
cut off 320
mediator 320
using "I" messages 321
being brief and specific 321
checking on others' thoughts, feelings, and understanding 321
family facilitator 323

confidentiality assurances 323
reflective listening 324
behavioral rehearsal 324
role play 324
reframing 325
absolute poverty 327
relative poverty 327
disposable income 328
near poor 328
financial empowerment 328
financial literacy 328
financial services 328
crisis 330
suicidal ideation 332
completes suicide 332
mood ratings with a suicide floor 333
involuntarily hospitalized 333
suicide watch 333
no-suicide contract 333

Generalist Practice Curriculum Matrix With 2015 Educational Policy and Accreditation Standards

Chapter 11

Competency	Course	Course Content	Dimensions
Competency 1: Demonstrate Ethical and Professional Behavior		Feature 3: Self-Reflection Feature 4: Concurrent Considerations in Generalist Practice	Cognitive–affective processes Skills Cognitive–affective processes
Competency 2: Engage Diversity and Difference in Practice		Feature 1: Focus on Diversity Feature 4: Concurrent Considerations in Generalist Practice 11.1. Learn about work with families from the family-in-environment (FIE) perspective. 11.2. Explore the characteristics of interactions with families.	Skills Cognitive–affective processes Skills Cognitive–affective processes Knowledge Knowledge
Competency 3: Advance Human Rights and Social, Economic, and Environmental Justice		Feature 4: Concurrent Considerations in Generalist Practice	Skill Cognitive–affective processes
Competency 4: Engage in Practice-Informed Research and Research-Informed Practice		Feature 4: Concurrent Considerations in Generalist Practice	Skills Cognitive–affective processes
Competency 5: Engage in Policy Practice		Feature 4: Concurrent Considerations in Generalist Practice	Skills Cognitive–affective processes
Competency 6: Engage With Individuals, Families, Groups, Organizations, and Communities		Feature 4: Concurrent Considerations in Generalist Practice	Skills Cognitive–affective processes

(Continued)

(Continued)

Competency	Course	Course Content	Dimensions
Competency 7: Assess Individuals, Families, Groups, Organizations, and Communities		Feature 4: Concurrent Considerations in Generalist Practice	Skills Cognitive-affective processes
Competency 8: Intervene With Individuals, Families, Groups, Organizations, and Communities		11.3. Articulate the social work role of family mediator and related skills.	Knowledge Skills
		11.4. Articulate the social work role of family facilitator and related skills.	Knowledge Skills
		11.5. Consider financial capacity building with families.	Knowledge Skills
		11.6. Describe crisis intervention, including suicidal ideation, with families.	Knowledge Skills
		Feature 4: Concurrent Considerations in Generalist Practice	Cognitive-affective processes
Competency 9: Evaluate Practice With Individuals, Families, Groups, Organizations, and Communities		Feature 4: Concurrent Considerations in Generalist Practice	Skills Cognitive-affective processes

References

Aguilera, D. C. (1990). *Crisis intervention: Theory and methodology*. St. Louis, MO: Mosby.

American Academy of Social Work and Social Welfare. Grand challenges for social work: Build financial capability for all. Retrieved from http://aaswsw.org/grand-challenges-initiative/12-challenges/build-financial-capability-for-all

Beidel, D. C., Stout, J. W., Neer, S. M., Frueh, C., & Lejuez, C. (2017). An intensive outpatient treatment program for combat-related PTSD: Trauma management therapy. *Bulletin of the Menninger Clinic, 81*(2), 107–122.

Briar-Lawson, K., Lawson, H. A., & Hennon, C. B. (2001). The meaning and significance of families and threats to their well-being. In K. Briar-Lawson, H. A. Lawson, C. B. Hennon, & A. R. Jones (Eds.), *Family-centered policies and practices*. New York, NY: Columbia University Press.

Butterfield, A., Rocha, C., & Butterfield, W. (2009). *The dynamics of family policy*. Chicago, IL: Lyceum.

Consumer Financial Protection Bureau. (2017). Your money, your goals: A financial empowerment toolkit. Retrieved from https://s3.amazonaws.com/files.consumerfinance.gov/f/documents/201701_cfpb_YMYG-Toolkit.pdf

Cookston, J. T., Olide, A., Parke, R. D., Fabricius, W. V., Saenz, D. S., & Braver, S. L. (2015). He said what? Guided cognitive reframing about the co-resident father/stepfather-adolescent relationship. *Journal of Research on Adolescence, 22*(2), 263–278.

Devaney, C., & Dolan, P. (2017). Voice and meaning: the wisdom of family support veterans. *Child and Family Social Work, 22*, 10–20. doi:10.1111/cfs.1220

Gasker, J., & Vafeas, J. (2010). The family-in-environment: A new perspective on generalist social work practice. *The International Journal of Interdisciplinary Social Sciences, 5*(2), 291–303.

Gottfredson, M. R., & Hirschi, T. (1990). *A general theory of crime*. Stanford, CA: Stanford University Press.

Hart, A., & Luckock, B. (2006). Core principles and therapeutic objectives for therapy with adoptive and permanent foster families. *Adoption & Fostering, 30*(2), 29–42.

Hovestadt, A. J., Anderson, W. T., Piercy, F. P., Cochan, S. W., & Fine, M. (1985). A Family-of-Origin Scale. In K. Corcoran & J. Fischer (Eds.), *Measures for clinical practice and research* (5th ed.). New York, NY: Oxford University Press.

Jobes, D. A., Eyman, J. R., & Yufit, R. I. (1995). How clinicians assess suicide risk in adolescents and adults. *Crisis Intervention and Time-Limited Treatment, 2*, 1–12.

Kanel, K. (2015). *A guide to crisis implementation* (5th ed.). Stamford, CT: Cengage.

Langer, C. L., & Lietz, C. A. (2015). *Applying theory to generalist social work practice: A case study approach.* Hoboken, NJ: Wiley.

Lee, S., Lee, J., & Chang, Y. (2014). Is dual income costly for married couples? An analysis of household expenditures. *Journal of Family Economic Issues, 35*, 161–177. doi:10.1007/s10834-013-9364-1

Mahabee-Gittens, M., Khoury, J. C., Huang, B., Dorn, L. D., & Ammerman, R. T. (2011). The protective influence of family bonding on smoking initiation in adolescents by racial/ethnic and age subgroups. *Journal of Child & Adolescent Substance Abuse, 20*, 270–287. doi:10.1080/1067828X.2011

National Association of Social Workers. (2018). *NASW code of ethics*. Washington, DC: NASW Press.

Richmond, M. (2012). *Social diagnosis*. Retrieved from www.forgottenbooks.org (Original work published 1917)

Schiller, B. R. (2008). *The economics of poverty and discrimination* (10th ed.). Upper Saddle River, NJ: Pearson.

Sommers-Flanagan, J., & Shaw, S. L. (2017). Suicide risk assessment: What psychologists should know. *Professional Psychology: Research and Practice, 48*(2), 98–106.

Szapocznik, J., Muir, J. A., Duff, J. H., Schwartz, S. J., & Brown, C. H. (2015). Brief strategic family therapy: Implementing evidence-based models in community settings. *Psychotherapy Research, 25*(1), 121–133. doi:10.1080.10503307.2013.856044

Titleman, P. (1998). *Clinical applications of Bowen family systems theory*. New York, NY: Haworth.

Tsai, J., Desai, R. A., & Rosenheck, R. A. (2012). Social integration of people with severe mental illness: Relationships between symptom severity, professional assistance, and natural supports. *Journal of Behavioral Health Services & Research, 39*(2), 144–157. doi:10.1007/s11414-0110926-7

U.S. Census Bureau. (2015). Poverty in the US. Retrieved from https://www.census.gov/topics/income-poverty/poverty.html

Veriano, D. L., Peterson, G. W., & Hicks, M. W. (1990). Toward an empirical confirmation of the Wegscheider role theory. *Psychological Reports, 66*(3), 723–730.

Wells Fargo. (2017). Hands on banking: Money skills you need for life. Retrieved from https://handsonbanking.org.

White, J. M. (1999). Work-family stage and satisfaction with work-family balance. *Journal of Comparative Family Studies, 30*, 163–175.

White, J. M., & Klein, D. M. (2002). *Family theories* (2nd ed.). Thousand Oaks, CA: Sage.

Winkel, D. E., & Clayton, R. W. (2010). Transitioning between work and family roles as a function of boundary flexibility and role salience. *Journal of Vocational Behavior, 7*(2), 336–343. doi:10.1016/j.jvb.2009.10.011

Witkin, S. (2014). *Narrating social work through autoethnography*. New York, NY: Columbia University Press.

World Bank. (2017). Empower the consumer to choose and use financial services. Retrieved from https://s3.amazonaws.com/files.consumerfinance.gov/f/documents/201701_cfpb_YMYG-Toolkit.pdf

World Health Organization. (2017). *Suicide*. Retrieved from http://www.who.int/mediacentre/factsheets/fs398/en

Recommended Readings

Kanel, K. (2015). *A guide to crisis implementation* (5th ed.). Stamford, CT: Cengage Learning.

Roles and Skills in Work With Groups

This chapter continues the series of chapters on practice across systems. It introduces groups using an experience students are familiar with: the classroom work group. The chapter covers the benefits of group work and explores the function of various types of groups in the planned change process. Characteristics of group interaction are discussed as well as social work roles and skills used in work with groups.

Learning Objectives

12.1 Learn about the benefits of social work groups.

12.2 Identify a variety of group types.

12.3 Summarize the roles group members play.

12.4 Explore group process and characteristics of interactions within groups.

12.5 Articulate the skills associated with the social work role of group mediator.

12.6 Articulate the skills associated with the social work role of group facilitator.

Case Study: Classroom Work Group

I wish the professor would just be quiet. Lauren leaned over to Sophia and said, "I wish she would just let us get on with this week's project." Lauren was a little tense. At the beginning of the semester, the professor had facilitated all of the small groups of students. But later in the semester, she helped each group identify a leader to play the role of the professional social worker leading a group of peers. The setup was not unlike the way peer supervision might work in an agency. In this group, Lauren was identified as leader just last week. She muttered something about being 10 minutes into class already, but at that point the professor finally said, "Okay, get to it." Lauren, Sophia, Jessica, Johanna, and Kelly quickly turned their desks together and looked at the small group assignment. There was a moment of silence where no

Klaus Vedfelt/Getty Images

Social work students can practice their groupwork skills in classroom-based small groups.

one seemed to know what to do. Then Lauren grabbed the assignment, held it out at arm's length, and cleared her throat. "Ahem." Everyone giggled, and a bit of tension left the group. Lauren read the assignment out loud and asked, "How do you want to do it . . . Jess, do you want to do the library work again?" Jess answered with a nod and Sophia jumped in: "I'll do the proofreading again if that's okay." Everyone nodded and grinned. Sophia was working toward a second career. She used to be a paralegal and was a master at proofreading. Everyone knew she really wanted an A in the course. "Then it's just down to the writing," Lauren continued. "Johanna and Kelly, do you want to do that with me?" Johanna and Kelly looked down at their desks but nodded. Kelly quickly turned her phone backside up. Then Johanna suddenly looked up and said, "Okay, but we're supposed to pick a topic. Anybody have any ideas?" *Let me be quiet a minute*, Lauren thought. *I'm too quick to do the work for all of us.* Sophia jumped in. "I think we should use the same topic as last time, only elaborate. That way we won't get stuck on finding an idea, and we can move on quickly. How does everyone feel about that?" Lauren smiled. *My idea, too. Professor Weller said we could do it that way if we wanted.* At that moment, Professor Weller approached the circle of desks and asked how it was going. There was a moment of silence where all of the group members looked at Lauren. *This is on me, I guess.* She said brightly, "We already have a topic and tasks assigned." Professor Weller said that it sounded like they were ahead of schedule and mentioned that they needed to stick with the process of thinking through the assignment before they went any further. Sophia nodded and asked, "What do we already know about this topic?" Kelly turned her phone over and quickly glanced at a text. "You're right, Sophia," said Lauren. "We already do know a lot. Kelly? Do you want to write down the ideas as we say them?"

Section 12.1: Social Work With Groups

This section introduces the benefits of social work groups.

Every social worker should run a group sometime in their early career. This is true for three reasons: (1) groups have unique benefits for their participants; (2) groups are efficient; and, therefore, (3) groups are cost-effective. For these reasons, they're becoming more and more popular in a variety of settings, including mental health, substance abuse, hospital, and residential care. We're using a classroom group as a case study with what we'll call an **intrinsic leader**, or a member of the group that takes on leadership roles, because you're very familiar with classroom groups. We'll discuss a more traditional group when we talk about organizing people in the next chapters.

The third reason every social worker should run a group sometime early in their career is that facilitating a social work group can be a bit anxiety-producing. Whatever its purpose, a social work group usually involves from 6 to 15 people seated in a circle or rows. The worker calls the meeting to order. It takes a moment or two for everyone to settle down, and then somehow everyone knows the group has begun. People are suddenly still. All of the group members lean forward. Every person is making eye contact with the facilitator. There is an instant of complete silence where it seems as if no one is breathing. Everyone is waiting . . . for the social worker to speak. This is the case in most group meetings, even among rambunctious children and reluctant teens. There is the briefest split second of time that is yours alone. You might call this a pregnant pause, but it is much more than that. What you do and say in that instant will begin engagement with every person in the group and set the tone for the whole session. You might call this a group work **pause of promise**. That one instant may be the most important in the session, and it's on you to get it right. Needless to say, this can be scary.

You know the skills you need in that moment. They begin with all of the skills you use with individuals, only you spread them around the group: your genuine smile, your warm tone of voice, your open body language. You'll also fall back on your usual opening statement, stating the mission of the agency; your role; the length of time set for the meeting; and, most importantly, the meeting's purpose. After you manage that, the rest will be easy—kind of.

Why Group Work?

Despite any anxiety you may have, it's worth it to take on a group work assignment inside or outside the classroom. Group work presents the worker with unique challenges, but those challenges are due to a group's great potential. Here are a few things that groups can provide:

- Normalization and socialization
- Compounded empathy
- Multifaceted feedback and help

Normalization and Socialization

The moment a participant steps into the group work room, they'll see that there are others who share their situation. They may have felt very alone with a life challenge or a thorny organizational problem. As group members join them, there is more and more evidence that many people are struggling with the same issue or facing the same challenging situation. **Normalization** is a skill that social workers usually provide when they help clients find comfort in the fact that others share their experiences and emotions. In the case of groups, normalization is automatic and intensified (Rasool & Ross, 2017). Some group members will be able to reach out to others immediately and introduce themselves as they begin to take advantage of the opportunity to socialize with others who are sharing experiences like theirs.

SELF-REFLECTION 12: GROUP ENGAGEMENT

Engagement in groups can be tricky. We're not only engaging worker and clients but we're engaging clients among themselves. Often, an icebreaker activity is used. Carry out the icebreaker on page 365. Introduce it to a class or another group. Get together and talk with classmates, and discuss how it felt to have someone ask you to participate in an icebreaker.

Compounded Empathy

Empathy works the same way normalization does. Once a worker has established empathy between themselves and group members as well as among the group members themselves, it's like money in the bank. The social worker will use self-reflection to provide empathy (that's the money), but all of the group members provide it over and over again to each other (that's the compound interest). This is a case of synergy, where energy is exchanged in a balanced way and more energy is created. As group members interact, they see each other feel and express emotions. Seeing someone have emotions causes chemical changes in the body that make the person share the feelings they are witnessing (Gibbons, 2011). This way, experiences are truly shared, and the group members can feel empathy for each other. To a degree, everyone can relate to everyone else. In some ways, they understand each other in ways no one else can. As each group member expresses feelings, they can experience empathy from all the other group members.

Multifaceted Feedback and Help

Like normalization and empathy, groups can provide feedback and help from many perspectives (Toseland & Rivas, 2012). Because members understand each other to some degree, they can recognize familiar behaviors. Something they once did that didn't work out well is being considered by someone else. That person could benefit from hearing about their experience. The second person can identify unrealistic negative thoughts in someone else even though they believe in their own negative ideas. Someone may ask the group a question, and they will find a multitude of perspectives on the challenge. People will be at different stages of resolving their issues, and for that reason, they may exchange and intensify feelings of hope.

CRITICAL THINKING AND COLLABORATIVE LEARNING EXERCISES 12.1

1. Have someone in the class explain the meaning of compound interest (in financial terms) for the benefit of the rest of the group. Discuss how empathy, normalization, and feedback can be like compound interest in groups.
2. Work with a small group and identify groups you may have been part of throughout your life. Choose one, and consider the benefits you received. Next, consider how the group experience might have been different if a social worker had run the group.

Section 12.2: Different Types of Groups

This section identifies a variety of situations where social workers may be responsible for facilitating different kinds of groups.

Types of Groups

Like all social work, groups represent multisystem practice (MSP). In other words, groups are mezzo practice, but they might target other systems. There may be groups that target individual client systems or family systems. Other groups target organizational systems, and still, others may target entire communities. Let's take them one by one.

"Micro" Groups

The term **micro group** may not immediately make sense. A group is, after all, mezzo level practice. In micro groups, individuals who share a need for support, education, or life skill training come together. An Alcoholics Anonymous meeting is this type of group, as is a group of adolescents with learning disabilities. In this common type of group, the individual is the target for change. It is the group that provides the vehicle for change through the planned change process.

Family Groups

In these groups, whole **family groups** come together to manage similar life challenges. For example, a group of couples may come together to improve their relationships, or the families of runaway adolescents may meet for mutual support.

Organizational Groups

Organizational groups are made of up of individuals that are part of the same organization. These groups may be ongoing, such as a staff peer consultation group. Other organizational groups exist for a short, designated period of time. **Ad hoc committees**, or committees within committees that are charged with a specific task, are usually temporary groups. There can be ad hoc committees, for example, that consider specific policies that affect staff and clients.

Community Groups

Finally, groups may occur in the community among helping professionals or citizens. These groups may be developed and facilitated by a professional, or they may be grassroots groups that develop in response to a specific situation. There will be much more on these community groups in Chapter 14.

Caiaimage/Rafal Rodzoch/Getty Images

Social workers lead groups with a variety of purposes.

Purposes of Groups

Groups are also organized by identifying their purpose. This is an important part of group work since it helps workers focus their efforts. You need to know the purpose of your group to make a clear opening statement about the purpose of each and every meeting.

Task Groups

These are usually ad hoc groups organized to complete some specific task. They may be micro groups such as a group of adolescents developing their individual social skills by creating a mural. On the other hand, tasks may be organizational, such as a group developed to plan an agency event.

Mutual Aid Groups

These are micro groups that are brought together to serve a group of individual clients that have similar interests or challenges. They may meet only one time, or they may go on indefinitely, with members coming and going as they work through their problems. For example, there might also be an ongoing group for people who are caregivers to aging parents or one for people questioning their gender orientation.

Educational Groups

Often referred to as psychoeducational groups, **educational groups** are micro groups that bring people who need the same information together. They gain information but also talk about how they can use that information in their everyday lives. For example, there may be a group on medication side effects in an outpatient behavioral health agency.

Case-to-Cause Groups

The **case-to-cause group** is formulated to respond to a specific problem. Social workers often find that a number of their individual clients are facing the same problem. In those situations, the worker translates their concerns about individual clients to a concern for a community cause (Abramovitz & Sherraden, 2015). We'll talk about this in great detail in Chapter 14.

CRITICAL THINKING AND COLLABORATIVE LEARNING EXERCISES 12.2

Think about what the social worker might be called upon to do in each of the different types of groups. If you had the opportunity to facilitate a group, which type would you choose? Why? Share your answers with the class. What is it about the social worker's role that appeals to you? Do any cause you anxiety? See whether others feel the same.

Section 12.3: Individual Roles in Groups

This section is about all the roles people play in the various types of groups. Social workers carrying out the role of group facilitator or mediator need to be familiar with these roles so they can help group members to carry them out.

The seminal, or beginning, group work theory comes from Benne and Sheats (1948), who recognized that people played roles in groups and that the group leader was an important position to consider. They outlined four categories of groups and a whole lot of roles that fell under these four types. Ever since then, people have been thinking and writing about these roles (Kirst-Ashman & Hull, 2017). They're commonly used in practice too. In broad categories, the group members' roles are as follows:

- Leader
- Individual roles
- Task roles
- Maintenance roles

Since there are so many roles under most of these categories, we'll condense them and take one category at a time.

Leader

We'll discuss the group leader first. We do this because the leader is a category and a role at the same time and in part because you, the social worker, will function as leader in many if not most of the groups you experience. A group leader is part of a group yet not exactly a member. If a social worker is running a group, they stand a bit apart but still participate in every aspect of the group. The leader's job is to call the group to order. Then the leader guides the group through the planned change process. Having done a self-reflection, they begin engagement, often with an icebreaker like the one you've just practiced. While the engagement is occurring, they'll assess the group and its members while making some observations about the social environment including the agency policies that focus their work. Planning begins in the very first group meeting. Implementation is the most exciting part of groups. The worker gets to direct a dynamic process where group members collaborate and synergy is formed. After the implementation, or when the group's timeline expires, the worker helps group members evaluate the effectiveness of the group, and carries out termination. Follow-up will hopefully happen later. In some groups where membership changes each week, these steps may all take place in one session. Please note that Lauren is not a perfect example of a leader as she is a peer within the group. She is an intrinsic leader, or one who has been identified by the group members as having leadership qualities. Be sure to remember that term. It will become very important when we talk about work in and with communities.

ETHICAL PERSPECTIVES

How does Standard 1 of the NASW Code of Ethics *(National Association of Social Workers [NASW], 2018) apply to work with groups?*

As always, the most complex of the planned change stages is implementation. What does the worker do to help the group reach its goals?

The leader has one main job: to stand back and help the group members effectively play their roles. The group leader pays attention to people and the roles they need to play to make the group effective. This involves three tasks carried out by the worker:

1. The worker **identifies the roles** that are needed in the specific situation. Lauren knew from her experience with the group that they needed a role where one of the students kept records of the group meeting. She needed people to ask questions and people to contribute answers and productivity. She needed someone to set a high standard, and she needed someone to get the group to discuss feelings. She also knew the group was small and the project was big so she couldn't afford to have people sitting around.

2. The worker **allocates the roles** to group members. Many times this will happen on its own, like when Johanna stepped up and tried to get information from the group. But sometimes the leader needs to make the role allocation happen, like when Lauren immediately asked Jess to do the library work, or identified Kelly as the person best suited to keep records of their conversation, or called for work from Kelly and Johanna.

3. The worker **guides the group** by helping the members to stay or step into their roles and monitor role development. Guiding the group involves checking in about whether goals are being met and being mindful of time limits within each session and for the group experience overall.

The roles we're dealing with here are similar to those we discussed in the family chapter. Roles are sets of expectations that get condensed into a set of expected behaviors. The important thing to know about roles is that they are best if they are flexible. For example, Lauren needed to be sure that someone else could take notes if Kelly was sick one day.

The roles that Benne and Sheats (1948) identified are condensed next. As we've said previously, apart from the leader, they fall into three categories overall: (1) individual roles, (2) task roles, and (3) maintenance roles. We'll take them group by group, and we'll handle the individual roles first.

Individual Roles

Individual group roles are self-centered and even negative. People who go in and out of these roles are feeling left out of the group. They are focused exclusively on themselves for some reason or another, and they disrupt the flow of the group's process. Often you can identify someone in one of these roles as the person whose chair sits slightly outside of the group. Some of these individual roles are active and some are passive. Active roles include the **aggressor, blocker,** and **clown,** who verbally attack group members, continually shout out ideas that are not related to the topic, or play around in a disruptive way. Other active roles are the **recognition seeker, dominator,** or a **special interest advocate.** The first tries to get everyone to know that they themselves are informed and intelligent, the other talks so much no one else can get a word in edgewise, and the last has a small idea that they want to be sure to keep in the conversation. In a more passive way, the **help seeker** quietly speaks or projects "I can't contribute because I don't know." Another potentially, but not necessarily detrimental, role is that of the **group follower** who sits silently through the whole meeting.

As a leader, it is important for you to be familiar with these individual roles so that you can steer your members away from them. For example, you'll probably have to focus the interview when the dominator runs on. You'll probably briefly identify strengths when the recognition seeker continues to try to get your notice. You may out-and-out ask the clown in front of the group whether they want to participate or not. And you might try to **probe** for information from the group follower so they can make a valuable contribution. While doing so, they may recognize that their role as audience for the group may actually be a valuable one. Don't forget that roles are flexible. One person may be a clown one day and a valued contributor the following week.

Task Roles

The final group of roles, **task roles**, deals with the jobs that need to be done. These **roles** are important to the leader because without them a group can spiral down into a gripe session or float away into a nonproductive, feel-good group. Both ventilation of the gripes and good feelings are probably what you want sometimes, but you still have a group with a purpose, and that purpose needs your attention. Task roles include those related to facts: the **information seeker** and the **information giver**. Others could be related to thoughts or feelings: the **opinion seeker** and the **opinion giver**. You need people to help the group stay within its own guidelines as they were developed early on. This person is the **procedural technician**. Also, you usually need someone to take notes, the **recorder.** Finally, and most importantly, you need **group contributors** to initiate conversations and to carry out tasks. Again, keep in mind that roles are flexible. One person may carry out several roles, and roles will shift among people.

Maintenance Roles

Maintenance roles have to do with the group process. To keep the group moving, you'll need people to play roles that deal with the interactions between group members. You'll need a **standard setter** to help keep people on task. Then you need a **harmonizer** to smooth over disagreements and a **compromiser** to move the disagreements forward with negotiation. You'll need an **expeditor** to keep discussions focused and a **commentator** to provide summaries of the group's progress. Finally, you need an **encourager** to cheerlead, and you may need a group follower as a witness for the rest of the group. As leader, you want to identify the need for these roles and help the right people to play them. Then, you guide the discussion toward the group's goals.

Group Roles

Task Roles	Maintenance Roles	Individual Roles
Information seeker	Standard setter	Aggressor
Information giver	Harmonizer	Blocker
Opinion seeker	Compromiser	Clown
Opinion giver	Expeditor	Recognition seeker
Procedural technician	Commentator	Dominator
Recorder	Encourager	Special interest advocate
Group contributors	Group follower	

CRITICAL THINKING AND COLLABORATIVE LEARNING EXERCISES 12.3

Everyone in class should write down the name of the role they think they've been playing in the course. Exchange papers with a partner, and discuss whether your partner agrees with your description of yourself.

Is there anything you would like to change about the role(s) you're playing this semester? Remember that group follower may be a detrimental role.

Section 12.4: Group Process

This section deals with the group process stages that social work group leaders can expect as they travel through the planned change process.

Group Process

There is a typical way that groups play out that has been identified a long time ago (Tuckman, 1965, cited in Breshears & Volker, 2013). This process is unique to groups, but is in keeping with the planned change process. The process goes like this:

- Forming
- Storming
- Norming
- Performing
- Adjourning

Forming

In the **forming** stage, the worker begins with self-reflection and careful planning about who the group members might be. It is not unusual for a group leader to "advertise" a new group, because potential group members do not necessarily recognize their need for a group and because other workers need to know about the group so that they can refer appropriate clients to participate. Another good reason for announcing a group ahead of time is that some clients who would benefit from a group are participating in individual work and may need to set goals to prepare them for meaningful group participation.

Once the group is formed, individuals are dependent on the worker to make it begin. The worker engages in self-reflection and prepares a plan to *engage* members with each other as well as with the worker. It is significant that the worker understands and states the purpose of the group. Once engaged, the worker will *conduct multilevel assessment.* They will consider how to set the climate and provide structure to the group. Setting roles and expectations are important at this time. Clients are likely to be feeling ambivalent about participating and experiencing all of the hope and anxiety of beginnings, and the worker begins to assess their potential for group roles. Having clear expectations and norms within the group will help the hope to prevail. At this stage, the worker often facilitates a set of rules. They help the group to establish its goals and limits. These **group rules** can include items like respectful listening, confidentiality, and commitment to the group's purpose. Often group rules are put into writing, perhaps on a whiteboard or a poster board that is present at each session.

Storming

Shortly after beginning, groups experience a **storming** stage. People have started to get to know each other, and they start to trust each other enough to argue. There will be control issues about who will be the most visible members. Cohesion and harmony as well as deeper trust among members can come out of this stage along with a clearer sense of the group's goals. The leader is important here so that the group does not stay in this conflict mode. Clients wonder if they are being heard, and their trust in others is tenuous. The worker needs to validate the feelings of all sides of conflicts and invite input from all members. At this time, the worker will be thinking about who they can draw on to fill the roles of harmonizer, opinion seeker, and encourager. Ultimately, the storming can provide energy to *planning.*

Norming

In the **norming** stage, social norms are developed within the group. Conflicts have been ironed out, and some roles have become established—at least for the present. Members begin to have expectations of others, and trust is developed. Information begins to be shared productively. They are comforted by sharing and are making commitments to see the group through. In this stage, a sense of teamwork emerges and the work begins. The leader begins the planned change *implementation* stage here and needs to provide support to people as they carry out their roles. The leader keeps meetings focused and moving forward. They also work to identify intrinsic leaders, or those group members who have leadership potential and may take over some of the leader characteristics. In this way, the group begins to have an identity of its own rather than one imposed by the worker.

WHAT IF . . . FOCUS ON DIVERSITY

How might a group made up of a range of income levels experience the group process differently than what is described here? How might forming and norming be different in that type of group?

Performing

The **performing** stage is part of the middle of the group process. As you will recall, that means it may be very productive or it may fall into the doldrums. To encourage productivity as the planned change process is **implemented**, the worker reminds the group of why they are there in the first place. When productivity begins, this is the stage where the real work gets done.

Group members become dependent on each other. An absent member is really missed. Collaboration and commitment mark the group's progress, and goals begin to be reached. Ideally, members are comfortable in their roles and comfortable sliding in and out of them. The worker focuses the group on tasks, supports members in their roles, and affirms goal completion.

Adjourning

The **adjourning** stage is consistent with the social work planned change stages of evaluation, termination, and follow-up. As in all endings, clients and workers will feel ambivalent. There may be a great sense of satisfaction or achievement, but it is likely to be paired with feelings of loss. The worker helps the clients to label feelings and ventilate those feelings. They will provide validation and normalization. At that time, they help clients to formally or informally evaluate the group's process and outcomes. Then, the group ends. Clients either terminate their relationship with the agency or get referred elsewhere. It is often the case, though, that groups have particular power. Many times a group will find a way to continue. They may ask the worker to advocate for them through the agency, or they may advocate for themselves. If they are successful, follow-up will be simple because they'll be around to survey.

Group Process in Special Group Formats

As we've said, it is important for us to note that all of these stages can occur in one meeting. The group facilitator has to move things along quickly in two cases: (1) groups that are meant to meet only once, such as a psychoeducational group, or (2) groups that go on indefinitely, such as **mutual aid groups**. The facilitator will get through the process with some shortcuts since every meeting may include different participants. They may begin each session with an established set of rules, for example, or they may have a quick adjourning method in place for each time the group is held.

Group Process: Planned Change, Leader Behaviors, and Member Feelings

Group Process Stage	Description	Planned Change Stage	Member Feelings	Worker Tasks
Forming	Group is formed, members meet, group is dependent on leader, trust-building begins	Self-reflection Engagement Assessment	Hope, anxiety, ambivalence	Facilitate engagement, define goals, provide structure, clarify goals
Storming	Conflict, control issues, goals begin to emerge	Planning	Trust is tenuous, people wonder if they are heard, some relationships get stronger	Validate feelings, invite input, help clarify goals
Norming	Teamwork; productive discussion; work begins	Implementation	Expectations of others, trust-building, deepening relationships	Identify, allocate roles, support members in their roles, seek out leadership potential, use of the present, facilitate decision-making
Performing	Real work is carried out, collaboration	Implementation	Trusting, committed	Focus on tasks, use of the present, facilitate decision-making
Adjourning	Group is ended	Evaluation Termination Follow-up	Ambivalence	Evaluation, ventilation, validations, normalization

Section 12.5: The Social Work Role of Mediator

This section is about the social work role of **group mediator**. We consider the role and the skills that allow us to carry it out.

The Social Work Role of Group Mediator

Occasionally—or in some groups often—a conflict breaks out between two or more group members. Just as in family work, the worker needs to metaphorically step between the members in conflict and help each to express their thoughts and feelings. Again, these skills begin with nonverbals. The worker maintains an open body position (no crossed arms!) and shows warmth with as much eye contact as possible with the members in conflict and with all other members of the group. The idea is for the worker to show both group members that they hear their concerns equally and to let other members know that they will keep the argument from getting out of hand. They might interrupt the conflict by saying "Let me see if I understand this disagreement."

Next, the group worker playing the role of mediator needs to demonstrate conflict resolution skills. Just as in work with a family, the idea is to use the skills while modeling them for others. Many times, group members should be addressed one at a time. These skills are adaptable to anyone at any time a conflict erupts. Keep in mind that there is an aspect of group process (storming) where conflict has to be expected. The social worker should welcome conflict at that stage, since it indicates that the group work is progressing. Group mediation skills include the following:

- Teaching "I" messages in groups
- Being brief and specific
- Checking on others' thoughts, feelings, and understanding
- Expressing feelings safely
- Group eye contact

Teaching "I" Messages

Teaching "I" messages in groups is important because it keeps group members from verbally attacking other members, a behavior that will affect every other group member. Just as positive aspects of groups like empathy can be compounded, the tension that results from verbal attacks can be compounded too. For example, a group member may say "Shut up! You are talking all the time," and everyone will tense up. Often, the angry person is speaking for the group in response to a participant who really *is* talking all the time. As is the case we've discussed in families, anger turns to blaming, and blaming leads to more anger. It's time for the worker to step in. Anger within groups affects the worker too. You may feel intimidated by the level of anger, the number of participants, and the peaceful observers who are looking at you to solve the problem. If you develop empathy, you may discover that group members are likely to have relationships full of anger and blame outside the group. They have not learned a better way to deal with conflict or even discomfort in any other way. A more productive conversation will happen if the angry group member says this: "When I don't get a chance to talk, I just feel like I could burst." The worker can model that "I" statement to help group members learn the skill. Notice that the "I" statement always begins with *I*, then is followed by a feeling statement. The speaker's main point comes last. See Figure 12.1.

FIGURE 12.1 ● Components of the "I" Statement

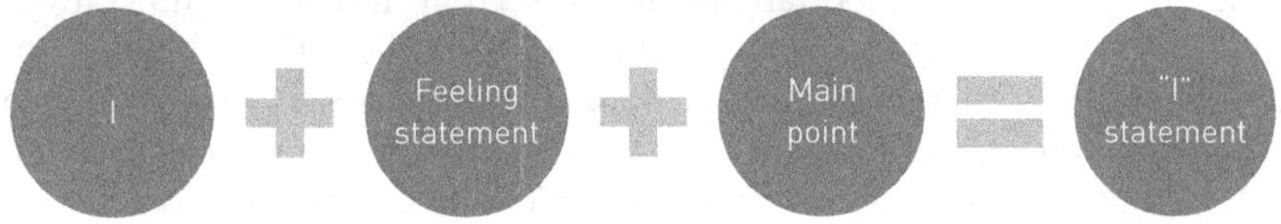

I + Feeling statement + Main point = "I" statement

The worker can also teach this skill by modeling other calm statements. "Sounds like you feel you have something important to say. Let's go back to our group rules for a moment. I remember we had something about not interrupting, but we also had something about sharing group time. Right now I feel like we should stop and reset. Bill, would you please start a sentence with *I* and say how you feel when you don't have a chance to speak?" Notice that the worker incorporated an "I" statement into what they said when they told the group: "I feel like we should stop and reset."

Being Brief and Specific

Something to be aware of is that the group member who talked and talked may have been avoiding painful or uncomfortable issues. They may not know it, but they are possibly speaking for part of the group that doesn't feel ready to discuss whatever topic is on the table. A worker can summarize for the group: "Seems like you are saying . . . Let's stop and see what others think." In this way, the worker models brief, succinct statements while adding another skill: that of stopping mid-conflict and seeing what others think and feel. What makes this skill a bit difficult is that it is not usually acceptable in everyday conversation to interrupt someone when they are talking. In a group, the taboo is strong because you are bringing up a taboo topic in front of others, not just family members. You need to display your self-confidence by taking on this taboo topic before that dominant person takes over the group. The group looks to you to keep the process moving forward, so your leadership is especially important when someone is acting in the role of dominator.

Checking on Others' Thoughts, Feelings, and Understanding

This is another skill that the worker can model. A benefit of the group is that group members will have many opportunities to practice this skill if you repeat it over and over. As in the individual skill of active listening, the worker asks "Joe, how do you feel about that?" and "Jim, this is what I hear you say." In work with groups, it is important to use first names. Every group member wants to feel that you are addressing them personally. Another component to actively listening in group work is to set up practice scenarios where you ask members to practice the skill of checking on others' thoughts, feelings, and understanding. Have group members ask each other these questions. The worker may say "Janet, can you tell Max what you heard him say?" or "Joe, can you check how Mary feels when she hears you say that?" You can use this opportunity to encourage member-to-member communication and make sure that everyone in the group gets to speak. An interesting method for teaching group members to check on each other's thoughts and feelings is to teach group members to use this phrase: "I make up that you . . ." When a group member says "I make up that you are feeling angry," the person is suggesting that they are making up a story about their peer and they are cautiously mentioning it so their peer has a wide open door to contradict the story. "I make up that even though you're seeing someone else you are still mourning the loss of your old boyfriend" is an example of a way to check on a group member's thoughts and feelings.

Group Eye Contact

Even in micro groups it is important to help the group feel like a unit rather than a group of individuals, especially when there is a conflict. The facilitator glances around to be sure that everyone is involved: **group eye contact**. If someone doesn't return their eye contact, they come back to that person again and may check on their thoughts, feelings, and understanding of the conflict that is taking place.

Expressing Feelings Safely

Finally, an important skill in group mediation is **expressing feelings safely**. You must help group members express their feelings—especially feelings of anger, without blaming, shaming, or threatening violence. It is a good idea for you to encourage the group to include a statement like this in the group rules they put together at the beginning of the work. If voices are raised, a worker can interrupt with "I'm thinking you're angry. Let's help everyone understand what's making that feeling happen." A reminder of group rules may be helpful too. "Remember that we said there will be no raised voices in this group?"

Skills for Group Mediation

Skill	Description	Example	Required Worker Characteristic(s)
Using "I" messages	Beginning a sentence with "I," such as "I feel . . . ," "I think . . . ," "I wonder . . . ," and following with the main point	(when interrupting a conflict) "John, from what you say I get the idea that you are feeling overwhelmed. Will you share your feelings with the group?"	Self-confidence
Being brief and specific	Stating feelings and thoughts succinctly	[Interrupting] " . . . Bill, hold on a second. Am I right in thinking that what you are trying to say is . . . ?"	Focus Ability to bring up taboo topics
Checking on others' thoughts, feelings, and understanding	Using active listening and helping group members practice active listening	"Jennifer, I'd like to find out how others are hearing what you say."	Patience Focus
Expressing feelings safely	Including feelings into group rules, modeling	"We all need to express our feelings safely here. None of us should judge others' feelings. How can we get this idea into our group rules?"	Confidence
Group eye contact	Making brief eye contact around the circle to make sure everyone is involved	"Bill, I can't get a look at you, and I wonder what you're thinking right now."	Confidence Ability to bring up taboo topics

Group Mediation Example

Lauren: Okay everyone, let's report on our work since last class. *(call for work)*

Jess: Sophia and I are making headway on the library research and have some abstracts to share with everyone.

Sophia: I decided to help Jess since there wasn't any proofreading to do yet.

Lauren: Great! *(affirmation)* Johanna and Kelly, do you have a draft of the introduction yet? I thought we'd be working on it already. Did you bring it today? *(call for work)*

Johanna: *(in an angry voice, glaring at Kelly)* No, we do not have it.

Lauren: Johanna, it sounds like you're angry. *(checking on others' thoughts, feelings, and understanding)* Do you want to tell us about it? *(encouraging her to express feelings safely)*

Johanna: I don't want to narc on anyone.

Lauren: *(Lauren looks around at all group members to be sure everyone was part of the conversation—it was not a private argument between Johanna and Kelly [group eye contact].)*

Kelly: *(banging her phone on the desk)* Everyone knows she's talking about me. Is anyone going to ask about my feelings? No!

Lauren: We decided at the beginning that there is no shame or blame about feelings. *(expressing feelings safely)* Let's have Johanna first, then Kelly.

Johanna: I'm pretty ticked off. She agreed to get some of the work done. I texted her three times, and she never got back to me.

Lauren: So, Johanna's mad about missing homework. *(being brief and succinct)* Kelly?

Kelly: *(beginning to tear up)* I'm mad too. She didn't care to find out why I didn't have the work done.

Lauren: Kelly, that sounds more like hurt feelings than mad. Am I right about that? *(checking on others' thoughts, feelings, and understanding)*

Kelly: Yes, you're right.

Lauren: Can you give us a summary of what went wrong for you? *(being brief and specific)*

CRITICAL THINKING AND COLLABORATIVE LEARNING EXERCISES 12.4

1. Break up into pairs and discuss classes where you have had the experience of completing assignments in small groups. What was it like? How would it have been if an advanced social worker had been the intrinsic leader in the group?
2. What type of group is the one in the case study? Can you identify various group roles that are being played by the members?

Section 12.6: The Social Work Role of Group Facilitator

This section is about the social work role of **group facilitator**. We consider the role and the skills that allow us to carry it out.

The Social Work Role of Group Facilitator

As we've said, the social work role of group facilitator consists of activities that carry a group through the planned change process. Most skills are common to work with individuals and families, such as confidentiality, reflective listening, behavior rehearsal, role play, and reframing. Two will be discussed here for the first time: (1) the use of the present and (2) **facilitating decision-making**.

Confidentiality in Groups

As with any social worker–client system interaction, one of the first discussion items is confidentiality and the limits to confidentiality (NASW, 2018). As we've said before, the worker explains that what is said in the meeting is private, but there are times when confidentiality must be broken and the worker must share information on a need-to-know basis. Mainly, times when confidentiality must be broken include potential harm to the client or others and required court testimony. Seeking supervision is also a time when client information is shared. In addition, there may be agency-specific situations that don't allow confidentiality, such as the need to inform a probation officer of a client's behavior. These categories need to be explained to clients in the group so that they are offering informed consent to participate in the social work process. With groups, confidentiality becomes more complicated. Not only do group members have to trust the social worker but they also have to come to trust each other. Confidentiality goes at the top of any set of rules developed by groups during their first interactions. Similar to work in families, the worker needs to facilitate a rule that states that the worker only interacts with group members as part of the group. No one should come individually to the worker with stories about other group participants.

Reflective Listening

We've talked about **reflective listening** earlier as well (Kadushin & Kadushin, 1997). It is where you verbally show that you are paying attention by saying the same thing someone else is saying. In other words, you just repeat in the same words what the person has just said. Some phrases you might use to include "I think I heard you say" or "I'm not sure I understood you . . . did you say . . . ?" This skill is magical in a group because you carry out the skill for one client and everyone benefits. You set in place an interaction with one client where they trust that you are listening carefully and you care about what they are saying. All group members watch that exchange and begin to believe that your careful listening and genuine caring may be there for them, too. Finally, you model this kind of speech to all of the people in the group. Eventually, they will speak to each other that way as well.

Behavior Rehearsal

Behavior rehearsal in a group is another group advantage (Murphy & Dillon, 2015). The benefit of one person's practice is magnified as all group members watch the interaction. You can help someone practice something they want to say and do outside the session (e.g., "Exactly what would you like to say to Bill? Take a shot at it here to get some practice."). In this case, the group provides benefit of the **multifaceted feedback** we mentioned earlier as a group advantage. Don't try using this skill until the group has met a couple of times. Trust is a prerequisite for people to make themselves vulnerable in front of the group by trying a skill they are just learning.

Role Play

Like behavior rehearsal, role play is a group experience that requires trust and will benefit from a very carefully applied use of humor (Murphy & Dillon, 2015). In this skill, clients practice speaking to another person. For example, one person may play a job applicant and the other may play a potential employer. It may help for you to request that other members do some type of role play so that those who need it at the moment will feel less self-conscious. In order to get multi-faceted feedback, it is tempting to put two chairs in the middle of the circle, but that requires a whole lot of self-confidence on the part of the people doing the role play, so it might be best to have the two participants in the role play sit next to each other in the group circle and just turn their chairs so that they can talk to each other. Another way to do it is for you to play the second role in the role play and just place your chair in the middle of the circle facing the client participating in the role play.

Reframing

As we've said before, reframing is a way of altering a person's or several persons' interpretation of an event and taking on a new perspective (Murphy & Dillon, 2015). Here is another skill where clients have benefits in the group setting. When speaking to an individual, you might say something like "I hear you say that your meal didn't turn out great when you cooked for your date. I understand that you're disappointed by that, but it sounds like you picked the perfect movie, don't you think?" Notice that there is a reflective listening statement followed by a validation of feelings before an attempt to reframe. This is significant. Reframing won't happen effectively unless the person is able to have their feelings acknowledged first. Group members quickly pick up on the benefit of this skill and will try to use it with each other right away. *One caution is this: You may repeatedly remind participants that validation of feelings should come before reframing, or you may soon have a lot of inappropriate advice being given among group members about the way they should feel rather than reframing the way they think, or evaluate, a situation.* For example, when the group member says "I wrecked the dinner I made for my date," it will be natural for a group member to say "You shouldn't be upset about that when you picked a great movie." In that case, you have to come right out and say something like "Joanne feels disappointed, and that is okay, so let's assure her of that first. Then, I think you are right to point out that she could really think about her date in a different way since she picked a good movie." This is a great skill for group members to learn because it will magnify the **compounded empathy** natural in groups as members take turns supporting each other.

Caiaimage/Tom Merton/Getty Images

Role play can be an effective activity in groups.

Use of the Present

Like all of the skills we are discussing here, the use of the present is a skill that works well with all system levels, but it is a great thing in groups. To practice **use of the present**, you do exactly what it says. You use what's going on right now to support planned change. That means you experience the moment as it is happening. It is similar to the mindfulness exercises you do to engage in self-reflection. Remember when you experienced the meditation where you think carefully about the chair you're sitting in and how it feels to sit in it right this moment? It's that kind of experience. Let's use a micro level example first. If you are talking to an individual about a routine thing like getting intake information and their eyes well up with tears, you might hand a box of tissues, give a genuinely caring look, and ask them this: "Do you want to talk about what the tears are about?" You can see immediately that this is another taboo topic. If that person were talking to a loan officer and filling out routine forms, their tears would go unmentioned. Of course, they wouldn't get any help with their emotional issue, but they wouldn't be expecting that from the loan officer. If you fill out the forms the way any loan officer would, in a matter-of-fact way, then your client will have the same experience: no emotional help. But you are a social worker, so you ask about the tears. This gives the person a feeling of license to express their feelings with you. To summarize, you weren't staring at the computer screen, you weren't worried about the next question you had to ask, and you weren't considering what to say next and how to say it. Instead, you were paying attention to the client and you were able to respond to what was going on right at that moment. If you hadn't looked up from your computer screen or paper form, the person may have hidden the tears by the time you looked up. And you would have missed the opportunity to let that person know they can express their feelings and that they can expect to get help from your agency.

In a group, use of the present is much more complicated and will require a lot of practice. When you are facilitating a group, you have a lot of balls in the air. You're listening to the speaker's message, and you're thinking about the best way to respond if dead air happens after their comment. On the other hand, you're imagining what other group members may say in response to the current message. A lot is going on. To use the present, you do one more thing. You pay attention to the feeling in the room. You watch the body language of every participant. You observe whether anyone is not listening and whether anyone is being strongly affected by what is being said in that moment. You try to guess what they may say next, and you plan ways to validate their feelings. It's complicated for sure. But if there is dead air following that speaker's message, it is your opportunity to look around you and see what's going on. Let's say you see Louise reaching for a tissue. You might say something like "Louise, what Tim just said seemed to really hit home for you. Would you mind sharing what you're thinking and feeling?" It's true that you've sort of called her out. She has the option to stay quiet though. More likely, she'll make a comment. Chances are, she'll be speaking for the group without knowing it. You may have hit on something really important to them. If you had been focused on the discussion questions you prepared in advance, you would have missed the opportunity. Use of the present can be a great boost to your work.

Facilitating Decision-Making

As a group worker, you will often be faced with the group's need to make a decision or clarify an issue among members. There are several methods of decision-making (Kirst-Ashman & Hull, 2017). It will be best if you are familiar with them so that you can give group members a choice in the type of decision-making they will use.

Consensus-Building

Consensus is a popular form of decision-making because it allows every group member to have a voice. And everyone gets something that they want. Consensus is also a difficult design for decision-making because it takes a long, long time, and very often nearly everyone has to compromise and accept a partial success. If you have a relatively small group of people who are invested in allowing everyone to have a voice and are willing to cooperate, consensus may be your method. This is assuming you also have a lot of time. Fortunately, there is help for reducing the time element of consensus decision-making. Hartnett (2011) presented a model that takes a part of two sessions only. Here's how it works:

Session 1

- Facilitator frames the topic (What are we making a decision about?)
- Group discusses the topic and identifies underlying concerns; no judgment of people's ideas; all ideas have equal value; discussion is free-flowing; notes are taken

Between Sessions

- Facilitator or selected group member(s) develops proposals based on the group discussion

Session 2

- Facilitator or assigned members present the proposals to the group
- Discussion leads to efficient decision-making

Decision-Making by an Individual

Many times groups would like to make decisions by consensus, but they find themselves unable to make a decision after a long debate. In that situation, **decision-making by an individual** may happen without any plan; it may seem to be the only logical choice (Kirst-Ashman & Hull, 2017). In this instance, someone who is either very persuasive or very knowledgeable might make a case for a particular decision. The rest of the group, tired of trying to come to consensus, may just go along with that person's choice. In the case of our student group, Laura knew that the group would look to her for the decision. She chose not to simply decide for the group because she wanted everyone to participate equally in the preparation and the presentation. In a larger group, it may be a small number of people who persuade the entire group.

Decision by Majority

If the group does not want to be swayed by an individual or small number of people, it may be logical to "let the **majority rule**." In this case, it is the facilitator's job to frame the question clearly so that the vote will be beyond dispute. This method works best in a larger group with a topic that has clear options. It is very often best to have a vote where voters cannot be identified, especially if the voters have not established a high level of trust. You want people to express their opinions honestly.

Nominal Decision-Making

Nominal decision-making is an evidence-based procedure to making group decisions in a variety of fields (Roeden, Maaskant, & Curfs, 2012). To carry out this method, you begin with a question or a choice. People come up with a list of responses, and the facilitator has them present their ideas in a round-robin (each person around the circle speaks one at a time). The facilitator writes down the ideas. Naturally, some of the ideas will overlap. The facilitator makes a check mark next to each idea that is repeated, and the ideas can be in rank order based on how many check marks each has. The benefit of this type of decision-making is that it is certain that every person will contribute, and everyone will have a chance to share a number of ideas. A drawback is that there is not a lot of discussion around the underlying concerns that people may have about the ideas of others.

Parliamentary Procedure

This is the type of formal decision-making where you hear things like "Can I have a motion?" and "All those in favor, say aye." This is a complex set of procedures for official decision-making based on a book called *Robert's Rules of Order* (Robert, Honemann, Balch, Seabold, & Gerber, 2011). It is often used at official meetings like boards of directors meetings or town councils. It's important for you to have a basic idea of these procedures, but the best way to get them is by watching and learning. You'll see shortly that simply being a **group participant** is an important role for social workers.

Skills for Group Facilitation

Skill	Description	Example	Required Worker Characteristic(s)
Confidentiality assurances	Group members developing rules related to when discussions that occur in group may occur elsewhere	"Let's have a rule about privacy. How does everyone feel about the things we discuss here and who should know about them?"	Focus Willingness to provide advice when needed Integrity Ability to seek supervision
Reflective listening	Repeating the exact words a client said or asking another group member to do so.	"Ralph, could you say what Bill said back to him? I'm interested to know if I heard him the same way you did."	Focus
Behavior rehearsal	Asking group members to practice words and actions they want to repeat outside the group	"Do you want to try that out on us? Practice it the way you'd like to do it, and we'll give you our feedback."	Patience Focus
Role play	Group members engaging in a conversation they'd like to have with others outside the group	"How about if you two go to the middle of our circle and practice? Bill, you be the boss, and Ralph, you be the employee. Then we can all give you feedback."	Use of humor Empathy Patience
Reframing	Teaching group members to restate an idea to highlight its positive aspects	"I see that you're disappointed. I'm sorry you didn't get the promotion, but you got to know the boss much better in the interview. That'll give you a better shot at the next opportunity."	Positive outlook Focus
Use of the present	Responding to behaviors in the moment	"John, you look a little confused. What is it you're thinking right now?"	Focus Ability to handle taboo topic
Facilitating decision-making	Allowing group members informed choice in decision-making and carrying out their choice	"We seemed to have agreed to use consensus to make our decision. Does anyone want to state the choice we're facing?"	Focus Patience

Group Facilitation Example: Decision-Making

Here is an example of consensus decision-making. Let's say Lauren, Sophia, Johanna, and Kelly are in class with 15 other students who are broken up into three other small groups. Early in the semester they learned that there would be presentations around midterm. By a random selection, Lauren's group gets to have first choice in the order of their presentation. They have to decide if they want to present before or after their peers. Will they be the first group to present? The last? The question was clear, and there were clear options. Lauren thought at first that she might point the group toward nominal decision-making. They could have gone around the group and asked each person for their top choice. Lauren knew there were underlying concerns though, so as intrinsic leader she suggested that the group use consensus making as their decision-making process. That way, everyone could be part of the decision-making and the issues that made this simple task complicated would emerge.

The first time they discussed the topic, several concerns were raised. These included Kelly's concern that going first means there is less time to prepare. Johanna's concern was that going second, third, or last risks ending up after a hard act to follow. They discussed this for some time. Sophia, the master proofreader, took notes, so it was a natural choice that she should be asked to develop proposals. Sophia agreed, and the next week she presented her proposals: (1) We go first even though we have to be prepared early and keeping in mind that Laura was going to be away for one week in early October. (2) We go last so that we can see everyone else first. We get the most time to plan, but we'll probably be too nervous to enjoy the other presentations. (3) We go second or third and give up the advantages of being first or last. Given the clear proposals, the group quickly decided to choose the second slot. They wanted to get the presentation over with but couldn't do it well without Laura. Those who were strong proponents of first or last had to accept the compromise, but everyone had a voice, and they were set to move forward.

The Overachieving Worker: Reflective Responses

Lauren was invested in school and her grades. She was paying her own way, and she was determined to get everything should could for her money. If she got anything less than an A in an assignment, she believed she was failing herself. The good part of this was that Lauren was committed to studying and every kind of class preparation. The downside appeared when she had to work in groups. Lauren's tendency was to take on every assignment herself. That way, she would be sure the group would get an A. But she knew she had to behave differently when she was identified as the intrinsic leader in the class group. She'd have to let others play their part. At first Lauren struggled. Some of her group members did not complete tasks on time; others did not complete them at all. Lauren went to talk to her professor, who was serving as her supervisor. She engaged in the critical thinking exercise "What do I feel/believe/know/do?" It became clear to her that she believed her entire grade depended on the group work exercise and that the other group members would tarnish her spotless transcript. She tested her assumption by checking it with her professor. At that point, the professor reminded her that there were individual grades in the course as well. Even if her group did not do well, Lauren could still get an A. Once she understood that, Lauren was able to step back and let group members share in the planning and implementation of their goals. As a result, group members were empowered. The whole group felt a sense of accomplishment when they completed their final presentation.

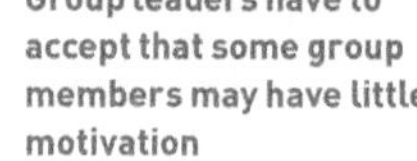

Group leaders have to accept that some group members may have little motivation

CRITICAL THINKING AND COLLABORATIVE LEARNING EXERCISES 12.5

The next time you and a group of friends or fellow club members are together, you may need to make what seems to be a simple decision: Where to go tonight? What toppings on the pizza? Before the discussion starts, suggest that the group consciously choose a decision-making method. What method did they choose? How did it work out? Share with the class.

Section 12.7: Review and Apply

CONCURRENT CONSIDERATIONS IN GENERALIST PRACTICE

Ethical Decision-Making Challenge

As a social work student and intrinsic leader, does Laura have any ethical responsibilities to her peers? If so, what are they? Consider Standard 2.

Human Rights

Do human rights matter in a simple classroom situation like the five girls were experiencing? Which might?

Evidence-Based Practice

Find out some of the fields in which nominal group decision-making has been tested.

Policies Impacting Practice

Look up the federal Family Educational Rights and Privacy Act (FERPA), and discuss how it would affect the students in this case.

Managing Diversity

What types of student diversity would make Laura's tasks as intrinsic leader more difficult or easier?

Multilevel Practice

Identify examples of Laura's work on all levels.

Micro: ____________________

Mezzo: ____________________

Macro: ____________________

Dynamic and Interactive Planned Change Stages

Identify aspects of Laura's work where she worked in the following stages:

Self-Reflection: ____________________

Engagement: ____________________

Assessment: ____________________

Planning: ____________________

Implementation: ____________________

Evaluation: ____________________

Termination and Follow-Up: ____________________

Chapter Summary

Section 12.1: Social Work With Groups

Although groups can be anxiety producing for the social worker, they have unique benefits. They all require normalization and socialization to happen immediately. People recognize that others share their concerns and have an opportunity to talk with them. Empathy is compounded as it is shared between and among group members. Finally, feedback and help are multifaceted due to the variety of perspectives available in the group.

Section 12.2: Different Types of Groups

Groups can target systems of all sizes. Micro groups are the most common, as they target all of the individuals in the group. Other groups consist of entire families. Groups can also target organizations and communities. Groups can have a variety of purposes, such as task groups, mutual aid, educational, and case-to-cause groups.

Section 12.3: Individual Roles in Groups

People play a variety of roles in groups. The leader identifies and allocates roles as they guide the group. In addition, there are three types of roles. Individual roles are self-centered and destructive. These include the aggressor, the blocker, and the clown. Maintenance roles keep the group process going. Maintenance roles include the harmonizer, the encourager, the commentator, and the expeditor. Task roles get the work done. They include the information and opinion givers and seekers as well as recorder; procedural technician; and, most importantly, the group contributors. Roles are flexible. People may occupy different roles, and they may carry out more than one role.

Section 12.4: Group Process

Groups often follow a predictable process. In the forming stage, the facilitator plans for the group and accepts participants. They carry out self-reflection; work to engage members with themselves and each other; and conduct assessment, especially related to potential roles group members may play. The next stage, storming, is marked by a period of conflict when planning is sorted out. Next is norming, where people settle into roles and develop trust and expectations for each other. Implementation begins. Later, the group begins the performing stage, where the work is carried out. The final stage is adjourning, which coincides with evaluation and termination.

Section 12.5: The Social Work Role of Mediator

Social workers may play the role of mediator as they work with groups. In this role, they help the group to manage conflict and to learn conflict resolution skills. Skills used by the worker include using "I" messages, being brief and specific, checking on others' thoughts and feelings, expressing feelings safely, and making group eye contact.

Section 12.6: The Social Work Role of Group Facilitator

Social workers may play the role of facilitator in groups. In this role, they help the group to accomplish its purpose. Skills used by the worker include **confidentiality in groups**, reflective listening, behavior rehearsal, role play, reframing, use of the present, and facilitating decision-making. Facilitating decision-making may take one of several forms, including consensus building, decision-making by an individual, decision-making by a majority, nominal decision-making, and parliamentary procedure.

SELF-REFLECTION 12: GROUP ENGAGEMENT ICEBREAKER

PURPOSE: Experience engagement exercise as facilitator and as group member.

DESCRIPTION:

1. Hand a small piece of paper to everyone in the room. (It's best to have people sitting in a circle.) Ask everyone to write down—neatly—something that others can't tell about them by looking at them. They should not put their name on the paper. Place papers in a hat or bowl. Each person around the room picks a paper. If the paper is their own, they put it back. Each person then reads what the paper says, and the group tries to guess the writer.
2. Use large pieces of heavy paper (card stock). Have more than you need in a variety of colors and designs if possible, along with a set of markers. Spread them on a table so each person has a chance to choose their own. Each person folds the card lengthwise, writes their name on them, draws some image that helps identify who he or she is, and places the nameplate in front of them. Each person introduces themselves in round-robin fashion. The facilitator goes around randomly asking each person why they chose their symbol, why they think they chose the colors they did, etc.

PRIMARY REFERENCE:

Breshears, E. M., & Volker, R. D. (2013). *Facilitative leadership in social work*. New York, NY: Springer.

Critical Terms for Roles and Skills in Work With Groups

intrinsic leader 344
pause of promise 344
normalization 345
micro group 346
family groups 346
organizational groups 347
ad hoc committees 347
educational groups 347
case-to-cause group 347
identifies the roles 349
allocates the roles 349
guides the group 349
individual group roles 350
aggressor 350
blocker 350
clown 350
recognition seeker 350
dominator 350
special interest advocate 350
help seeker 350
group follower 350
probe 350
task roles 350
roles 350
information seeker 350
information giver 350
opinion seeker 350
opinion giver 350
procedural technician 350
recorder 350
group contributors 350
maintenance roles 350
standard setter 350
harmonizer 350
compromiser 350
expeditor 350
commentator 350
encourager 350
forming 351
group rules 352
storming 352
norming 352
performing 352
implemented 352
adjourning 353
mutual aid groups 353
group mediator 354
teaching "I" messages in groups 354
group eye contact 356
expressing feelings safely 356
group facilitator 358
facilitating decision-making 358
reflective listening 358
multifaceted feedback 358
compounded empathy 359
use of the present 359
consensus 360
decision-making by an individual 361
majority rule 361
nominal decision-making 361
group participant 361
confidentiality in groups 365

Generalist Practice Curriculum Matrix With 2015 Educational Policy and Accreditation Standards

Chapter 12

Competency	Course	Course Content	Dimensions
Competency 1: Demonstrate Ethical and Professional Behavior		Feature 3: Self-Reflection	Cognitive-affective processes
		Feature 4: Concurrent Considerations in Generalist Practice	Skills Cognitive-affective processes
Competency 2: Engage Diversity and Difference in Practice		Feature 1: Focus on Diversity	Skills Cognitive-affective processes
		Feature 4: Concurrent Considerations in Generalist Practice	Skills Cognitive-affective processes

Competency	Course	Course Content	Dimensions
Competency 3: Advance Human Rights and Social, Economic, and Environmental Justice		Feature 4: Concurrent Considerations in Generalist Practice	Skills Cognitive–affective processes
Competency 4: Engage in Practice-Informed Research and Research-Informed Practice		Feature 4: Concurrent Considerations in Generalist Practice	Skills Cognitive–affective processes
Competency 5: Engage in Policy Practice		Feature 4: Concurrent Considerations in Generalist Practice	Skills Cognitive–affective processes
Competency 6: Engage With Individuals, Families, Groups, Organizations, and Communities		Feature 4: Concurrent Considerations in Generalist Practice	Skills Cognitive–affective processes
Competency 7: Assess Individuals, Families, Groups, Organizations, and Communities		Feature 4: Concurrent Considerations in Generalist Practice	Skills Cognitive–affective processes
Competency 8: Intervene With Individuals, Families, Groups, Organizations, and Communities		12.1. Learn about the benefits of social work groups.	Knowledge
		12.2. Identify a variety of group types.	Knowledge
		12.3. Summarize the roles group members play.	Knowledge
		12.4. Explore group process and characteristics of interactions within groups.	Knowledge Skills
		12.5. Articulate the skills associated with the social work role of group mediator.	Knowledge Skills
		12.6. Articulate the skills associated with the social work role of group facilitator.	Knowledge Skills
		Feature 4: Concurrent Considerations in Generalist Practice	Cognitive–affective processes
Competency 9: Evaluate Practice With Individuals, Families, Groups, Organizations, and Communities		Feature 4: Concurrent Considerations in Generalist Practice	Skills Cognitive–affective processes

References

Abramovitz, M., & Sherraden, M. (2015). Case to cause. In M. Santiago & Work Group 2 (Eds.), *Frameworks for practice: Report of the special commission to advance macro practice in social work* (pp. 4–12). Alexandria, VA: Council on Social Work Education.

Benne, K. D., & Sheats, P. (1948). Functional roles of group members. *Journal of Social Issues, 4*(2), 41–49.

Breshears, E. M., & Volker, R. D. (2013). *Facilitative leadership in social work*. New York, NY: Springer.

Gibbons, S. (2011). Understanding empathy as a complex construct: A review of the literature. *Clinical Social Work Journal, 39*, 243–252. doi:10.1007/s10615-010-0305-2

Hartnett, T. (2011). *Consensus-oriented decision-making: The COMD Model for facilitating groups to widespread agreement*. New York, NY: New Society.

Kadushin, A., & Kadushin, G. (1997). *The social work interview; A guide for human service professionals* (4th ed.). New York, NY: Columbia University Press.

Kirst-Ashman, K. K., & Hull, G. (2017). *Understanding generalist practice* (8th ed.). Stamford, CT: Cengage.

Murphy, B. C., & Dillon, C. (2015). *Interviewing in action in a multicultural world* (5th ed.). Stamford, CT: Cengage.

National Association of Social Workers. (2018). *NASW code of ethics*. Washington, DC: NASW Press.

Roeden, J. M., Maaskant, M. A., & Curfs, L. M. G. (2012). The nominal group technique as an evaluation tool for solution-focused coaching. *Journal of Applied Research in Intellectual Disabilities, 25*, 588–593.

Rasool, S., & Ross, E. (2017). The power and promise of group work: Consumer evaluation of group work services in Gauteng, South Africa. *Research on Social Work Practice, 27*(2), 206–214.

Robert, H. M., III, Honemann, D. H., Balch, T. J., Seabold, D. E. (contributor), & Gerber, S. (contributor). (2011). *Robert's rules of order newly revised* (11th ed.). Philadelphia, PA: De Capo Press.

Toseland, R., & Rivas, R. (2012). *An introduction to group work practice* (7th ed.). Boston, MA: Pearson Education.

Tuckman, B. (1965). Developmental sequence in small groups. *Psychological Bulletin, 63*(6), 384–399. doi:10.1037/h0022100

Recommended Readings

Belmont, J. (2016). *150 more group therapy activities and tips*. Eau Claire, WI: PESI Publishing & Media.

Roles and Skills in Work With Organizations

This chapter continues the series of chapters about social work on various levels of practice. It explores planned change in organizations with particular attention to the worker's own employer as the target for change.

Learning Objectives

13.1 Learn about the nature of human service organizations.

13.2 Discuss organizational vision and mission, organizational structure, and organizational culture

13.3 Translate the planned change process to work in organizations.

13.4 Describe the social work role of organization change agent and related skills.

13.5 Examine the social work role of supervisor and related skills.

Case Study: New Program Development

©iStock.com/AVAVA

Workers often engage in planned change within their own organizations.

Robin grabbed her padfolio on her way to supervision. She had some information to share with her supervisor that she hoped would lead to a new program in her agency. Supervision began with the usual review of her activities. Robin worked for a town–gown organization called MUnited, which was a part of the university. The mission of the agency was to begin and maintain positive relationships between the students of Marksfield University and the town of Marksfield. That meant Robin had two sets of clients: (1) the town's citizens and (2) the university's students. Robin's current tasks included coordinating several student and citizen collaborative activities. She was in charge of planning an annual street festival for the students and the townspeople to share. She also managed the volunteers who carried out a regular neighborhood watch and student-run snow removal for aging citizens. There was an ongoing litter removal project carried out by volunteers as well. Robin was also working with the local churches and the school dining services to develop a food bank for needy townspeople as well as needy students, and a project was underway for a collaborative childcare provider to work with students to help meet the needs of townspeople as well as university students and staff. There was something new she wanted to try though. She kept relationships with client representatives on campus including members of student government and the dean of students. From them, she learned that one problem facing students and townspeople was the constant ill will between the landlords and the students who rented apartments privately in town. She wanted her agency to develop a new program to address the needs of the student renters and landlords, and she had come to supervision with some information. "I think I have identified a problem we haven't dealt with before," she said to her supervisor. "I already have relationships with some client representatives and I wonder if it would be okay for me to do some assessment." Robin's supervisor was interested. She asked Robin to share what she already knew, and Robin reached for her padfolio. She had numbers about how many students rented off campus and how many landlords were members of the chamber of commerce. That conversation with her supervisor was just the beginning.

Section 13.1: The Nature of Organizations

This section discusses the nature of organizations with a focus on social work agencies.

Organizations

An organization is a group of people who come together for a particular reason (Hasenfeld, 2010). There are all kinds of organizations, such as sports teams, church choirs, and parent–teacher organizations. Usually, those types of organizations are part of one or more larger, overarching organizations. For example, a sports team is probably part of a sports league. The church choir is part of a church. The parent–teacher organization works within a school, and the school operates within a school district. It is important to think about organizations and how they fit into larger systems.

Consider businesses and social work agencies. These, too, can be part of larger systems. A business can be a regional operation of a national corporation. A social work agency can also be part of a larger corporation. In some ways, both businesses and social work agencies are the same. Both provide goods or services that people need, and both get paid in some way for providing the service. The provision of those goods and services are also similar in social work and business organizations. The *Social Work Dictionary* (Barker, 2003) defines a social work organization as one that delivers social services through human service personnel "including professional social workers, members of other professions, paraprofessionals, clerical personnel, and sometimes indigenous workers" (p. 202). Social service agencies work for and with vulnerable groups.

In other ways, social work organizations are unique. One reason social service organizations are unique is that their missions are altruistic. They are in business to improve the human condition. A business may produce goods and services that happen to make people's lives better. Think sticky notes. Where would we be without them? But the businesses that manufacture those little sticky pieces of paper are not in business to improve customers' quality of life. They have found a product that people want, and they produce it to make a profit. Social work organizations are fundamentally different. The "product" they produce usually consists of services. These services have to do with people and their situations, not with gadgets (Cohen & Hyde, 2013). The sole purpose of any social work agency is to improve the human condition.

An important thing that organizations all have in common is that they need money to operate. In the case of human service organizations—often called agencies—money is needed for salaries for social workers, wages for support staff like secretaries and fundraisers, computers, Internet service, facilities, supervisors, licensing fees, budget audits, legal services, insurance, and more. Different types of human service agencies have different ways of getting financial resources, but they all have budgets of one kind or another to document, manage, and plan for their expenses. We'll say more about nonprofit budgets below.

Types of Human Service Agencies

If you are going to be a generalist social worker, you're going to work in a social service organization of some kind. You might work in a multiservice agency or you might work in a social work program that exists within a host agency.

Social Work in a Host Organization

For example, you might work in a mental health program as part of a comprehensive wellness service or you might work in the social work department of a hospital. The hospital's business is people's physical health, but administrators recognize that to carry out their mission they need to make sure that their patients have access to social work services. They may have an entire program, such as an inpatient behavioral health department, that is dominated by social work services of some kind. In these cases, the hospital is the host agency. On the other hand, you may work in a program within a for-profit business. A corporation may have recognized a need for an employee assistance program (EAP) and may have a social work department to provide counseling for employees.

Social Work in the Context of a Social Service Provider

On the other hand, you may work for an agency that does nothing but provide social work services. It is important to recognize that these agencies work within environments like any other systems. As we said previously, a regional agency can be part of a larger, national agency. A smaller agency will be close to the neighborhood it serves and will be highly influenced by that neighborhood. Even if you become qualified to hang out a shingle that announces your private social work practice, you will still be working for an organization that is a system existing in a social environment.

From the private practitioner to the worker in a health care system employing many thousands of people, social workers work in organizations. These organizations fall into four broad categories:

1. Nonprofit
2. Public
3. For-profit
4. Faith-based

Nonprofit Agencies

A **nonprofit agency** does not struggle to make a profit to pay dividends to shareholders as a public corporation would. Nor does it struggle to make a profit to benefit the owners as a private corporation would. Instead, the nonprofit agency struggles to gain the money needed to provide services to the population it is trying to help. Nonprofit agencies can be corporations, associations, foundations, or individual enterprises. They are exempt from paying taxes on their income (Cornell Law School Legal Information Institute, 2017). Money comes from several sources. For example, since a nonprofit agency is usually tax exempt, it can offer tax benefits to those individual donors who make contributions. In addition to **individual donors**, the nonprofit agency gets money through **grants**. Sometimes those grants are private sources, such as when individuals and groups donate to the United Way, and the United Way distributes those funds to various agencies. Grants may also come from public sources. Public sources are those that come directly from government and its taxes. Another way nonprofits get funds is through **fee-for-service**. For example, an agency may be qualified to bill private insurance companies (think Aetna or Highmark) for the services it provides to individual clients or they may bill public insurance such as **Medicare** (the insurance for people who are receiving Social Security benefits). In addition, individual clients may pay for their own services. It seems like the nonprofit agency has many financial advantages: It does not need to make a profit, and it has several ways to get money. Unfortunately, there never seems to be enough money to serve the many people who need help. For this reason, a lot of nonprofits hold fund-raisers regularly to meet expenses. Traditionally, the government has supported private donations through fund-raising for nonprofit agencies with tax incentives for charitable giving. If a nonprofit agency makes profits, they are used to improve or expand services. Even though a nonprofit agency is private (i.e., not created and administered by government), it is guided by laws and guidelines created by government to serve the client group. For example, if a private, nonprofit agency provides services to aging people in the community, it has to abide by policies created by federal, state, and local government related to elder abuse. Robin's agency, MUnited, had to abide by policies on those levels as well as university and town policies that regulated how she could provide service.

Public Agencies

The aging community is one of many that are also served by **public agencies**. These agencies are created by government as a safety net to meet the needs of specific populations like children, people who are addicted to substances, people with behavioral health concerns, or people with developmental disabilities (Segal, 2016). The money for these agencies also comes directly from taxes that are allocated to public agencies for specific purposes. For example, the federal government mandates that every state have child abuse treatment and prevention services. Money flows from the federal government to the state and from the state to local governments, often counties, to provide these services. In addition to child abuse services, other public agencies include Social Security, federal food assistance programs like the Supplemental Nutrition Assistance Program (SNAP), Area Agencies on Aging, and **Medicaid** (health insurance for the poor). These agencies are often very large, and workers work directly for the part of the government that is funding them. For example, people who work in the Social Security office work for the federal government, and those who evaluate Medicaid applications work for the state. See Figure 13.1.

FIGURE 13.1 ● Types of Human Service Agencies

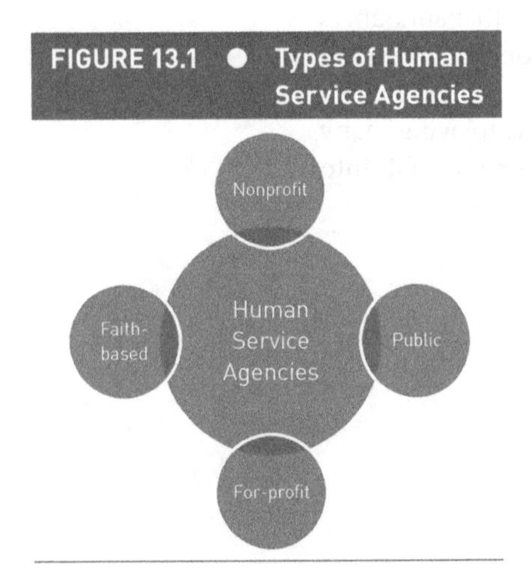

Profit-Making Agencies

Profit-making agencies are corporations that are created to serve people or make goods while creating a profit for shareholders and owners. They get money by charging for goods or services, by billing private insurance companies, or by billing public insurance like Medicare and Medicaid. Profit-making human services often receive government contracts that use public money to pay for the services they offer, or they get payment directly from private insurance and individuals. Although a profit-making human service company doesn't sound very altruistic, it has a mission statement similar to nonprofit and public agencies, and it has many benefits. For example, it is likely to have a stable budget that doesn't rely on unpredictable fund-raising. For that reason, it may be able to pay its employees more. There are serious concerns about profit-making human service providers though. For example, there isn't a lot of research that says they are better or cheaper than nonprofit or public agencies (Sanger, 2001). It may be difficult to regulate their services, so it is possible that service recipients may suffer from low-quality service to enable the company to make a profit. Another concern is that the profit-making agency is free to close if they don't make money. This means that they may serve a population in an area so completely that the public agencies are driven out. Then, when they close their doors because they weren't making enough profit, the people are left without services and become vulnerable (Sanger, 2001). Qualified social workers who start or are affiliated with private social work practices for such services as mental health counseling, substance abuse treatment, long-term residential care, and lobbying for political action committees should be aware of the ethical responsibilities they share with workers who work in the public or nonprofit arena.

Faith-Based Organizations

Faith-based organizations started attracting the attention of social workers when federal policy began to allow these agencies to apply for government grants (Gibelman & Furman, 2008). A faith-based organization follows the same policies as nonprofit agencies but under the guidelines of their religious affiliations. For example, Catholic Social Services will provide referrals to alternative service providers but will not provide abortion counseling (Cohen & Hyde, 2013). Even though a faith-based provider exists within a church, it needs resources just like any other organization. Resources for these and all social work organizations are organized into budgets.

Nonprofit Organization Budgets

As we've said, every organization has a budget to help guide spending and strategize future growth. There are several types of budgets, but the basic agency budget is the **operating budget**. This is a financial plan that the agency creates every year to show how much money is expected to come in and go out of the agency. **Revenues** (income) and **expenses** in the operating budget support all of the agency's programs. Another type of budget commonly used by social work agencies is the **grant or contract budget**. This type of budget may be required by an organization that offers the agency funds to carry out a specific task. For example, an agency may receive a grant to provide substance abuse prevention services to a high school. The grant budget shows only the income and expenditures that are specifically related to the grant (Corporation for National and Community Service, 2018). Overall, the budget is a picture of how the agency goes about carrying out its mission and goals.

SAMPLE OPERATING BUDGET

Revenues (Income)	Amounts ($)
Contributions	165,652
Special events	88,929
Grants	61,525
Rental income	20,300
Auxiliary activities	10,500
Investment income	2,000
Miscellaneous income	20,000
Total revenues	368,906
Expenses	
Salaries	232,000
Fringe benefits	46,400
Payroll taxes	34,800
Supplies	10,000
Communication	6,004
Professional fees	16,000
Publications	1,200
Conferences	3,200
Grants and awards	6,000
Rentals	1,500
Insurance	6,000
Travel and lodging	4,200
Total expenses	367,304
Excess (deficit) on operations	1,602

Source: Adapted from Corporation for National and Community Service (2018).

CRITICAL THINKING AND COLLABORATIVE LEARNING EXERCISES 13.1

Revisit the personal budget you created during the chapter on families (see Chapter 11). Have you tried to implement it? Discuss your process with a partner.

Section 13.2: Aspects of Organizations

A budget reveals how organizations carry out their mission and goals. Vision, mission, goals, and objectives are fundamental aspects of organizations. Other important characteristics of organizations discussed in this section include organizational structure and **organizational culture** as well as a particular organizational culture: **empowerment-oriented organizational culture.**

Vision, Mission, and Goals

Another way to think about organizations is to consider their vision, mission, goals, and objectives. The **vision** of an organization is its view of the big picture. It's the global statement that reflects the almost-impossible situation that the agency would like to see happen. It reflects the agency's values and gives it an identity. Robin's agency vision was "for Marksfield University and the town of Marksfield to enhance the lives of students and citizens through allied activities that celebrate each other's achievements and meet each other's challenges." See Figure 13.2.

The agency **mission** is a bit more specific than the vision. It is the statement based on agency values that reflects the day-to-day efforts that are carried out to meet the vision. The mission statement is brief; it explains which clients are going to be served and gives a general idea of how the goals are going to be met. In short, the mission says why the organization is in existence (Kirst-Ashman & Hull, 2017). The agency's mission is what a worker uses in their opening statement. It is important that the mission statement be in simple enough language for it to be understood by administration, staff, and clients (Proehl, 2001). The mission is a direct message to the worker about the purpose of their job. This is why the agency mission is part of the worker's opening statement. The opening statement helps remind both the client and the worker of the purpose of the agency. The mission statement narrows down the vision and makes it easy to see specific goals that might be used to reach for the vision. MUnited's mission was for "MU students and Marksfield citizens to maintain positive relationships through shared activities and problem-solving efforts."

The **organizational goals** of the agency reflect how the mission will be carried out. These are focused statements that help people recognize when the agency is operating within its mission and working toward its fulfillment (Nurcahyo, Wibowo, & Putra, 2015). Goals reflect the agency mission. They have three purposes: (1) they let people know what kinds of things the agency does, (2) they help make the agency legitimate, and (3) they

FIGURE 13.2 • Elements of an Agency's Identity

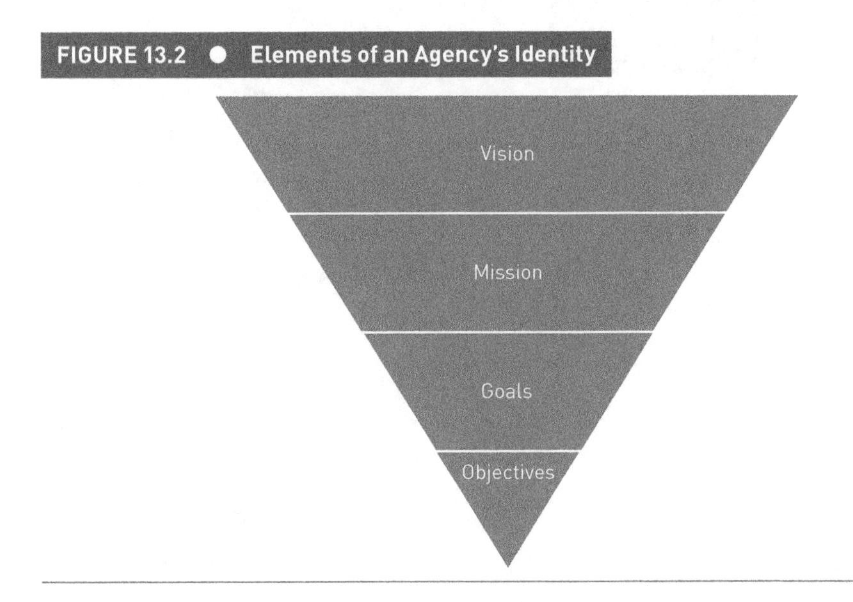

let people recognize that the agency is meeting its mission (Kirst-Ashman & Hull, 2017). MUnited had three goals: (1) to facilitate town–gown activities, (2) to resolve town–gown conflicts, and (3) to provide community enhancement projects.

Organizational objectives within an agency are those specific activities that the organization uses to meet its goals. You can measure an objective. For that reason, they allow the agency to know whether its goals are being met. MUnited had several objectives:

Goal 1: Facilitate town–gown activities.	Goal 2: Resolve town–gown conflicts.	Goal 3: Provide community enhancement projects.
Maintain the MUnited Spring Fest.		Develop and maintain litter removal.
		Develop and maintain a neighborhood watch.
		Pilot test a food bank program.
		Develop a child care program.

To pull it all together, MUnited's vision, mission, goals, and objectives looked like this (see Figure 13.3).

In summary, the vision of an agency informs its mission, and its mission is used to develop goals. Objectives are activities that are used to meet the goals. When people carry

FIGURE 13.3 ● Connecting Vision, Mission, Goals, and Objectives

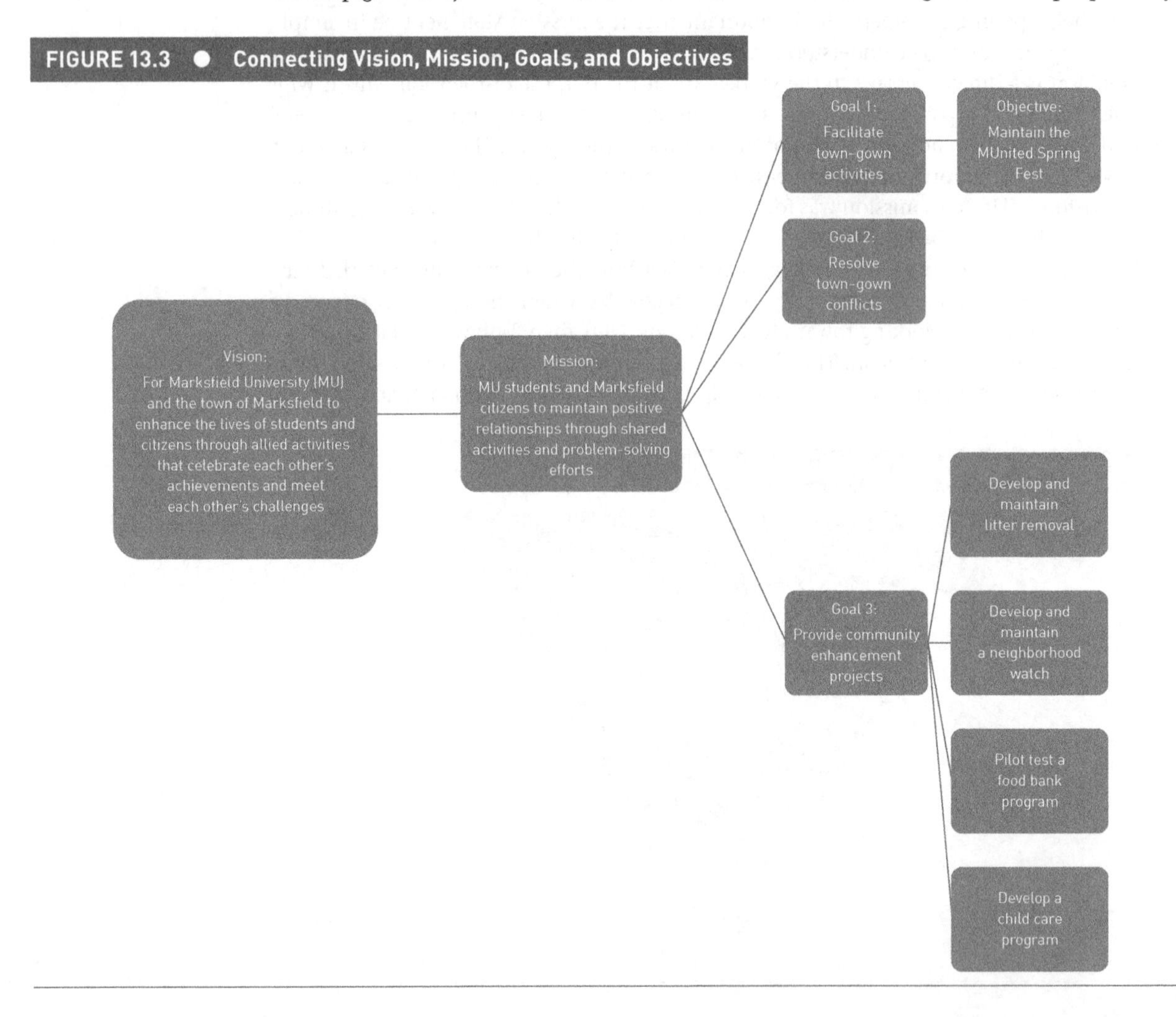

out the objectives, they can measure their success or failure. If they are successful, the goals are being met. And if goals are being met, the agency is achieving its mission.

Organizational Structure

Another important aspect of an organization is its **organizational structure**. The organizational structure is a formal description of the way the roles people play relate to each other. In the business world, the organizational structure may be called the authority structure (Flynn, 2015). You can think of it this way: The organizational structure lets you know who your boss is. Robin's agency was a small one, but it was part of the university. The dean of students was in charge of the agency, but it also had a **board of directors** like any other agency. The board was a group of volunteers that was in charge of overseeing all of the agency operations, including hiring, firing, and supervising the executive director. The executive director was responsible for all of the agency activities, including everything that Robin and her supervisor did. Like most agencies, the agency had a formal organizational chart. You should pay attention to the fact that the organizational structure is a set of roles that people play. Individuals may come and go, but the organizational chart stays the same until the board of directors changes it. This reminds us that no one is irreplaceable. In addition, the idea of the organizational chart being made up of roles, not individuals, can help explain why people do what they do when you interact with them at work. They may not be talking to you with their personal voice but their professional voice, and you can see where they're coming from with the organizational chart. Their job is to carry out a role. The organizational chart in Figure 13.4 shows what MUnited looked like:

FIGURE 13.4 • Example of an Organizational Chart

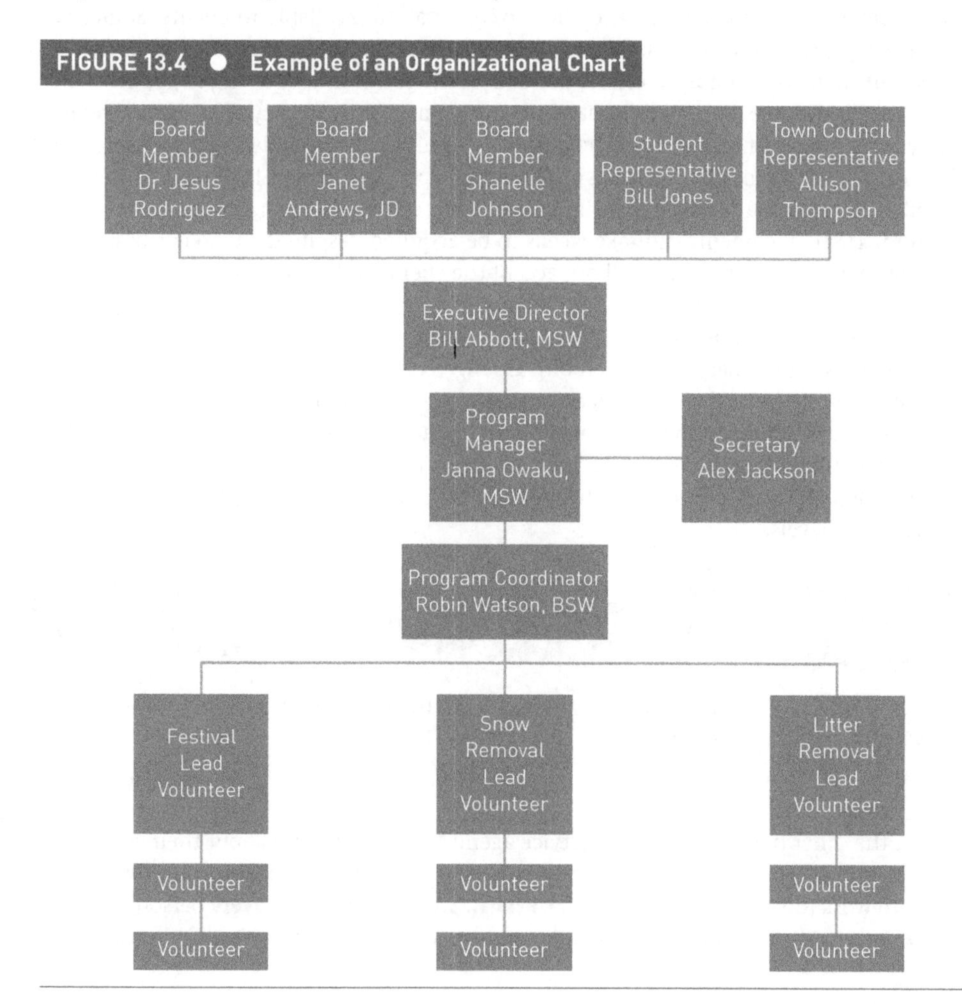

Empowerment Culture

While the organizational structure is a formal statement of how people in an organization relate to each other, an informal, unstated way they relate to each other is called the **organizational culture**. The organizational culture is shared values, beliefs, and norms that allow the organization to have an identity. It's how organizational members (professional staff, nonprofessional staff, and administrators) think and do things. They pass on this way of being to new members through orientation and socialization as they come on board (Cohen & Hyde, 2013; Proehl, 2001). Many times the organizational culture in human service agencies is an uncomfortable one. "Chaotic, uncertain, frustrated, and stressed are examples many leaders use to describe the current state of their 'organizational health'" (Stone, 2015, p. 33). This may happen in part because human service agencies often model their organizations on for-profit corporations in the business world, and the two are not necessarily compatible (Pyles, 2009). Whatever the reason, an organizational culture filled with stress has a lot of negative outcomes. People will be stressed, their work with client systems will suffer, they'll leave and have to be replaced with new people that have to be trained, etc. We've discussed burnout in terms of the way it is experienced by workers and what can be done about it, but it is important to note that burnout may be viewed from a person-in-environment (PIE) perspective. Think of the worker-in-environment, with the environment being the agency and the services that are available to clients. Sometimes, excessive paperwork can cause burnout. Other times, agency policies about clients can cause burnout. For example, consider a situation where a worker is trying to get their client admitted to the substance abuse treatment program in their agency. The agency requires some form of identification for the client to be admitted because identification is required for insurance billing. The client has no identification. The worker tries to help the client get identification, but a Social Security card or birth certificate is required to get the identification. These documents can take weeks to be acquired despite the worker's best efforts. During that time, the program will not accept the client, and the client may lose a precious window of opportunity to accept help. If this situation happens over and over again and the worker is continually turning clients away without help because of this agency policy, the worker is sure to become burned out. Change is often necessary for the benefit of the staff and the clients of human service agencies as they respond to environmental demands like insurance requirements, decreasing funds, and increasing calls for accountability. In systems terms, organizations are moved out of their natural states of homeostasis by environmental forces, particularly those of the economy and social welfare policies on all government levels.

Empowerment-oriented organizations partner with service recipients.

ETHICAL PERSPECTIVES

See Section 2.01(c) of the NASW Code of Ethics *(National Association of Social Workers [NASW], 2018) to consider why working toward empowerment in organizations is important.*

On the other hand, many social service agencies are purposeful about their agency culture, trying to influence it in ways that will benefit both workers and staff. One goal is often to work toward a **horizontal leadership** structure in which every person is to some degree a boss (Pyles, 2009). For example, many social service agencies work toward being

empowerment-focused organizations. In this way, they work to address core social work values that are part of the *NASW Code of Ethics* (NASW, 2018). For empowerment organizations, social justice, the dignity and worth of the person, and the importance of human relationships are paramount. Not only are these values paramount but they are applied to workers, not just clients. This type of organizational culture is a goal to work toward. In its most basic sense, it is an organizational culture that is inclusive and receptive to change. If workers face the same challenges over and over but they have a voice in creating agency change, their frustration will lessen. Agencies focused on empowerment work to empower a number of systems in their environment, including clients, staff, administrators, and sometimes even neighbors that share their community. Hardina (2005) has identified 10 characteristics of organizations with empowerment-focused missions. You'll see that these organizations are focused on inclusion for staff, clients, administration, and communities. The characteristics of empowerment focused agencies are as follows:

- Formal structures allow client participation in decision-making.
- Collaborative evaluation incorporates constituents.
- Policies bridge cultural barriers.
- Power differentials are minimized.
- Staff teamwork enables decision-making.
- Strategies increase staff psychological empowerment.
- Top administration commit to empowerment.
- Strategies increase job satisfaction.
- Staff is encouraged to advocate.
- Political power is sought for agency and client systems.

1. *Formal structures allow client participation in decision-making* (Hardina, 2005). This means that there are specific agency rules that create ways for clients to help make agency decisions. Clients may be advisers to programs, become part of task groups related to new programs, and become members of the board of directors. It is easy for agencies to feel like controlling bodies to clients—the place where they tell you what is okay to do and what is not okay to do. In response, the empowerment-oriented agency has rules that make sure clients have some control. Caution: It's important to note that clients can be token members of these organizational structures. It's possible to find boards of directors that meet when their client members are not available, or meetings in which client members are given no opportunities to speak. The best method seems to be to develop a sustainable, real system for feedback from people inside the organization and people who have some relationship to it. This process can begin with a very clearly worded mission statement that is easily understood (Proehl, 2001). The system should be one that has opportunities to change regularly (Galambos, Dulmus, & Wodarski, 2005).

2. *Collaborative evaluation incorporates constituents* (Hardina, 2005). "Empowerment evaluation" enables clients and community members to find a way to be part of an organization's evaluation of itself. It means programs are likely to respond better to community needs and the organization is likely to become more culturally responsive. This method of self-evaluation can be better than evaluation by experts who are tied to predictable ways of being in the organization. Allowing agency partners a voice in evaluation methods means

the outcomes that are measured are important to constituents. Clear and relevant outcome measures can enhance change efforts (Proehl, 2001).

3. *Policies bridge cultural barriers* (Hardina, 2005). Empowerment organizations provide services to specific ethnic groups and hire staff from those ethnic groups to provide both services to clients and input into organization policies. Agency values clearly point to continuous improvement (Proehl, 2001). The point is to keep the organization prepared for change (Galambos et al., 2005). The organization tries to ask the experts—the clients—how to be culturally sensitive by reaching out to the clients it serves.

4. *Power differentials are minimized* (Hardina, 2005). Power in an organization can consist of information, knowledge, rewards, and access to services. In the empowerment-oriented organization, there is increased sharing of power among staff, clients, and administrators. You might think of this as flattening the organizational chart so that information and decision-making is done by all members of the organization. It is important to keep information flowing so that everyone hears about changes and the way they are being implemented (Galambos et al., 2005).

5. *Staff teamwork enables decision-making* (Hardina, 2005). Employees need to be able to make some decisions on their own, but that can create problems where efforts are being duplicated or clients aren't getting the full range of the services they could. One answer seems to be to have staff work in teams to make decisions. If carried out with structured agendas, goals, and evaluation, staff teams can give staff effective decision-making power. Teams allow change to be holistic, so that solving a problem in one department will not cause a problem in another department (Proehl, 2001). Staff should also be encouraged to develop systems where good performance can be rewarded (Galambos et al., 2005).

6. *Strategies increase staff psychological empowerment* (Hardina, 2005). It's best if employees can feel like they are competent and full members of the organization. Teamwork can help but so can supervisors who are clear about their roles and able to pass some decision-making power along to staff. A constant flow of information and communication is essential (Cohen & Hyde, 2013).

7. *Top administration commit to empowerment* (Hardina, 2005). Executives who are committed to empowerment allow staff access to training they are interested in and develop tasks that can be shared by supervisors and staff. Staff morale is a priority.

8. *Strategies increase job satisfaction* (Hardina, 2005). Organizations should pay well so that staff members feel they are appreciated. When that is not possible, some low-cost employee benefits, such as flexible time off, can be helpful. Job satisfaction is also improved when work involves a greater variety of tasks and more chances to learn new tasks. Employers in empowerment-oriented organizations get continuous feedback from staff and reward good performance in creative ways.

9. *Staff is encouraged to advocate* (Hardina, 2005). An open mind from supervisors can help organizations be open to advocacy efforts. If staff members are encouraged to bring their ideas about improvements in service and they see some change take place as a result of their advocacy, they will feel empowered.

10. *Political power is sought for agency and client systems* (Hardina, 2005). The organization can find ways to help the people they serve to be more politically active. In that way, clients will feel more empowered and less marginalized from main stream society. In some cases, the organization can help connect service recipients and areas of government that can be responsive to change efforts.

CRITICAL THINKING AND COLLABORATIVE LEARNING EXERCISES 13.2

1. In a large group, write a vision, mission statement, goals, and objectives for your class.
2. In a small group, consider MUnited. From what you know, do you think the organization is empowerment-focused? What information do you need to make a decision?
3. In a large group, consider what questions you would have to ask to determine whether your class instructor is working for an empowerment-oriented organization.

Section 13.3: Planned Change in Organizations

This section continues the discussion on human service organizations with a focus on the challenge of applying the planned change process to macro level practice.

Planned Change in Organizations

As you saw, the empowerment focus is all about constantly monitoring the agency and its environment in search of changes in programs and policies that will improve service. Unfortunately, not every agency welcomes change. Remember that systems seek homeostasis, and organizations are no different (Gilley, Godek, & Gilley, 2009). However, change in organizations is part of the macro level of practice in multisystem practice (MSP). Organizational change is possible. Just like any other professional change efforts, organizational level change happens through the planned change process. While there are many theories of organizational change, multisystem generalist practice provides a basic foundation with the planned change process as its method. On the other hand, it is not simple to translate the planned change process into macro level change. In fact, many students have trouble making this translation, and that's one reason macro level practice is easily lost in generalist social work. Let's take the steps one by one.

Self-Reflection

At first glance, it may not seem that a worker would need self-reflection to work toward organizational change. After all, an organization is not a person who can push your emotional buttons. This is true, but an organization impacts your life and your clients' lives or you wouldn't be looking to change it. For example, it's likely that you feel strongly about fairness. When an agency doesn't seem to be fair to you or the people you serve, you are likely to feel anger based on the value you place on fairness. As we've seen, those strong feelings will create and feed off of beliefs that may not be rational. As part of self-reflection, you've got to think critically about your feelings related to the organization you'd like to change. For Robin at MUnited, the issue was one of courage. Robin valued courage highly, and it was one of the reasons she wanted to work on the macro level of social work practice. She believed that it took a lot of courage to advocate for change in organizations and communities, and she was happy and fulfilled to take on that challenge. When she looked at the agency's programs (snow and litter removal, town festival), she felt like the agency was frightened of taking on real challenges. She felt that there were larger issues at work that prevented a genuinely positive relationship between the town and the university. When she practiced mindfulness exercises and took a look at her feelings, she realized she needed to do some critical thinking. The agency was in fact making some progress working toward mutual change. The new food bank and child care programs addressed real problems, and that was a good start. It made her calm and resolved about the landlord–student renter program she was proposing. In this way, she could be objective and persuasive.

Engagement

In work with organizations, you never know who your client system representative may be. It may be a colleague in a different program or a different agency. It may be your supervisor, a client, or a member of your board of directors. It could even be some person that lives or works in the area served by the organization that is your target system. As is the case with work on the micro and mezzo levels of practice, your individual skills of engagement will be critical. To review, some of the basic skills that are especially important in work with organizations are the genuine smile, the firm handshake, professional dress, appropriate eye contact, embodied mirroring, and reflective statements. It's always appropriate to display warmth, empathy, and genuineness (WEG). The preparatory empathy process we discussed in Chapter 5 is important as well. Remember to network (more on this skill later) with all of your contacts inside and outside your agency. Don't leave home without your business card! Robin got her program change idea from talking with the student government representative who was on the agency board of directors. She got data that she needed from a worker at the office of the dean of students. She asked her supervisor to introduce her to a contact on the town chamber of commerce, and that person became another important source of information. She needed her engagement skills for all of these interactions.

Assessment

Assessing an organization has the same components as assessing individuals. One additional consideration you will have in the assessment of an organization is that before beginning you wonder about whether the vision, mission, goals, and objectives are clear and appropriate (Kaufman & Guerra-Lopez, 2013). Hopefully, you will see at least the mission statement on a website, and goals and objectives can often be found in program review materials or even marketing materials. Occasionally an organization will not be able to immediately produce a mission statement, goals, and objectives. You will probably find the information somewhere—maybe in the staff program handbook or the original organizational bylaws. Once you've located the mission, goals, and objectives, you can compare them to the agency as you see it. If they don't match, that is a place to stop and begin discussions with a supervisor. Probably they will recognize an opportunity for planned change. Vision, mission, goals, and objectives are critical. If they are not present, clear, and relevant, no other work can be done.

Assuming you find the mission, goals, and objectives and they are clear and relevant, picture the organization in an ecomap (see Figure 13.5) and consider the strengths and the challenges of each of the systems. You will be particularly interested in the economy as it relates to private donors, in the federal laws and policies as they influence funding, and in government on all levels as it relates to the social policies and procedures that govern the way people practice in the agency. When you come to the systems of "Individuals, families, and groups," you will think about your client system representatives and all of the individuals you know well within the organization. As with any assessment, map the lines of connection and tension so you can identify which systems to target for change. It is likely that you will be using the planned change process within the agency itself, so consider the motivation and the capacity of the organization for change (Lusthaus, 2002). When Robin assessed her organization, she discovered right away that the vision, mission, and goals were clear and on the mark. They matched what the agency was doing. There were other strengths as well. University policies supported the work she was doing, and the agency had a positive relationship with the town leadership. There weren't any problems with the justice system, but Robin realized that the agency did not have a relationship with the chief of police. She was pleased to realize the agency was strong in the education area: The person holding her job had to have a bachelor of social work (BSW) degree, and that degree was offered at the university. Staffing was strong: Both the director and her supervisor were happy with their part time hours and committed to their work. Robin was also surprised to discover that she really had no problems recruiting volunteers from the university or the town. Religion wasn't discussed much since the university was a public one, but the office secretary usually decorated for every possible holiday to be inclusive. Another major strength was that the university provided health care benefits even though all of the employees were part-time.

The agency faced challenges as well. The university funded the program, so no one thought about private fund-raising. She wondered if that were possible under the university umbrella.

FIGURE 13.5 • Ecomap for the MUnited Agency

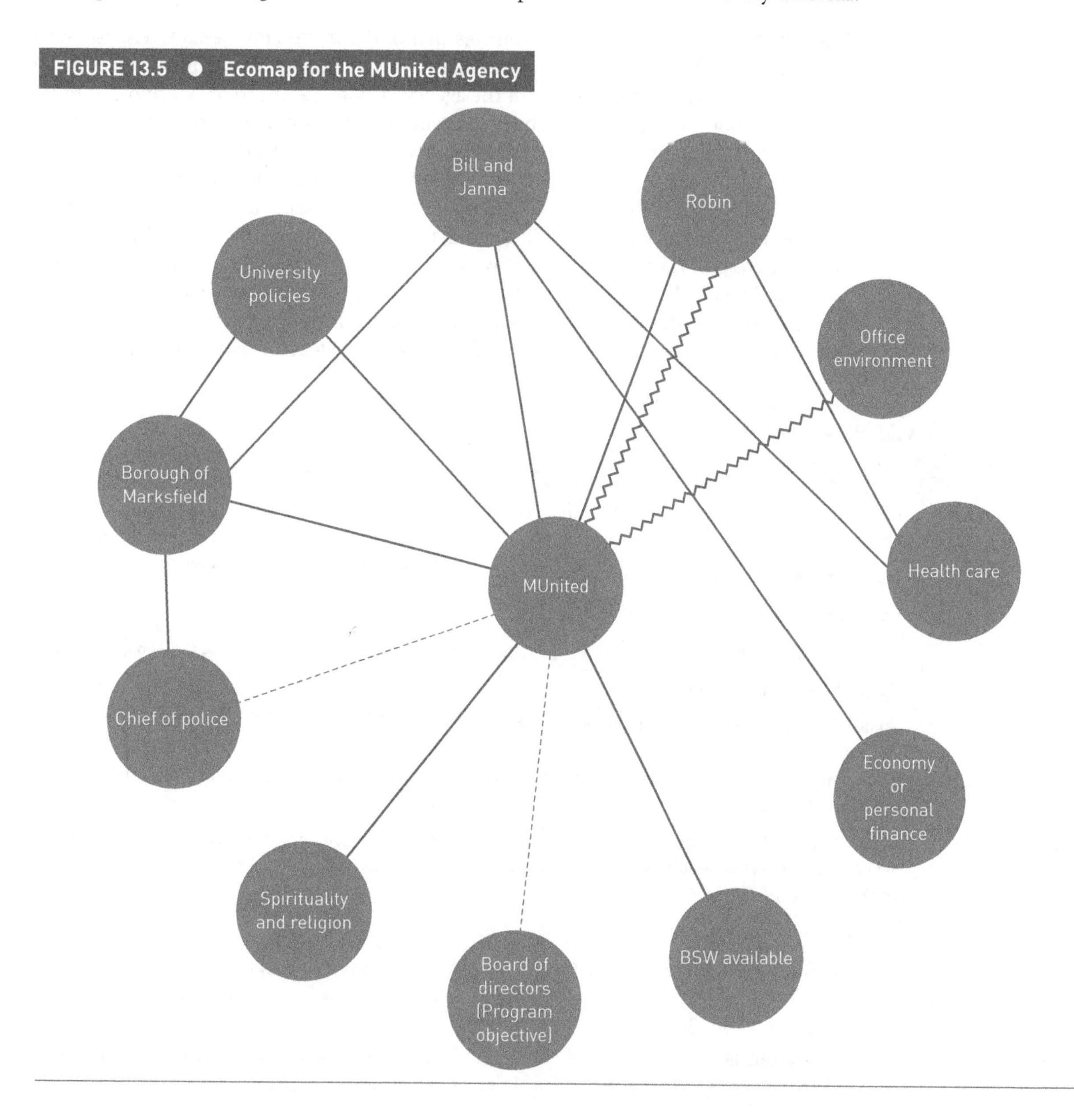

She recognized a mostly positive relationship between herself and the agency, but she was part-time, and she would have liked to be allocated more hours to complete her current tasks. She also noted that the physical environment of the office could be improved. They were located off campus in a downtown office building that was not well kept. There were weeds in the parking lot, the walls were dirty, and the carpeting was ancient. Most importantly, it seemed to Robin that the agency objectives could be improved. She didn't see an objective that related to the second of the agency's goals: to resolve conflict between the town and the university and students. As she continued the assessment, she discovered that the agency may not be capable of the change she had in mind. The new objective she was considering would require her to expand her part-time hours, and she didn't know if additional funding provided by the university would be available. On the other hand, she was pretty sure the agency would be motivated for change because her supervisor was already serving as a client system representative.

Planning

Planned change on the macro level mirrors that of the micro and mezzo levels. You work with the appropriate client system representative to make a plan for change that reflects the strengths, resources, and challenges of the agency. A note specific to organizations is to use the organizational chart to be sure you understand the organizational hierarchy. For example, Robin would not attempt an organizational assessment without going to Janna, the program manager, first. If she approached Bill, the executive director, before approaching Janna, her attempt at change is sure to fail. Bill will undoubtedly lose some respect for Robin and will send her back to Janna. Janna will find out that Robin "went over her head." Not only may Janna lose respect for Robin but she may be hurt and angry as well. In this case, Janna was serving as Robin's client system representative, so Robin continued to work directly with her. When Robin met with Janna, she brought along the Multisystem Practice: Assessment form below. She had already completed most of it, and Janna helped her with the rest.

Multisystem Practice: Assessment

Systems	Strengths and Diversity	Challenges
Social worker	Has conducted self-reflection; carried out "I feel, I believe, I know, I do" process with open mind Values courage and is determined Good educational foundation	The social worker must not allow strong value of courage to create feelings that are so strong they impact the work in a negative way.
Agency	Highly committed staff Cooperative program manager Cooperative chamber of commerce chairperson	Robin is not allotted enough hours to do her work. The board of directors doesn't recognize that current program objectives don't address every goal.
Client system representative: Janna	Biological, psychological, cultural aspects: Power, privilege, identity Committed, has family support, believes strongly in social justice, educational background in social work	Biological, psychological, cultural aspects: Discriminations Has experienced oppression based on gender; at risk of becoming too emotionally involved where fairness is concerned
Health care	Health insurance is provided by the university.	
Economy or personal finance	Executive director has training in budgeting.	Additional financing may not be available; changes in budget need to be approved at the university level.
Physical environment	The office is adequate.	Office maintenance or location could be improved. The landlord could be approached for change.

Systems	Strengths and Diversity	Challenges
Education	Both Robin and Janna are trained social workers; Bill is trained as a manager; the university offers a social work program.	
National and international policies	University can offer education and other services as a nonprofit entity and gain tax benefits.	
Spirituality and religion	The office is inclusive in holiday decorations.	
Justice		Need to become familiar with borough laws regulating landlords and tenants Need networking with chief of police
Individual, family, community, and peers	The chamber of commerce will be an ally. There is an existing positive relationship with student government leaders.	
Government		Need to learn about borough council's role in landlord–renter relationships
Social welfare policies	The university's policy is to support students who live off campus and allow MUnited to provide services.	

Creating Goals: Identifying System Interactions

Using the ecomap and the multisystem assessment made the areas for implementation easy to see. Robin looked for positive connections as well as systems in tension and systems with tenuous connections.

Systems Interacting

System Group	System 1	System 2
1	MUnited	Board of directors
2	MUnited	Justice system
3	MUnited	Robin
4	MUnited	Physical environment

Overall, most systems related to MUnited were experiencing positive relationships. On the other hand, there were four system groups that were out of balance. MUnited, as Robin assessed it, was off balance with its board of directors in that one organizational objective wasn't being addressed. MUnited was out of balance with the justice system because no staff member had knowledge of laws related to landlords and renters, and there was no connection with the town's chief of police. The organization was out of balance with Robin because she needed approval to work more hours in order to get her tasks done. Finally, the organization was out of balance with the physical environment in that the office building and its parking lot were not kept in good condition.

Creating Goals: Recognizing Strengths and Challenges

Because Robin's client system representative was Janna, she worked with her to develop goals for planned change.

To begin to establish goals, Robin and Janna considered the types of interactions and relevant resources and challenges. Robin used open-ended questions, reflective statements, and summarization to help both her and Janna to recognize the strengths in MUnited's situation. They found there were strengths and challenges within each system group.

As a result of their meeting, Robin and Janna created the following table:

System Group	System	Strength	Challenge
1	MUnited, Board of directors	Board members are experienced and positive about the organization.	Need to revisit agency goals and objectives
2	MUnited, Justice system	Positive contacts exist between staff and community leaders.	Need to learn about laws related to landlords and renters Need to develop a relationship with the chief of police
3	MUnited, Robin	Robin feels very positive about the organization and her work.	Need to evaluate whether extra hours should be approved
4	MUnited, Physical environment	Office space has a long-term lease.	Need to have building and grounds maintenance

Creating Goals: Building on Strengths

Taken together, the strengths of the system interactions could be used to respond to the challenges. Janna and Robin created the following responses to the challenges that were facing the family:

Goals. First, remember that it is necessary to identify concrete goals. As we've said before, goals are specific statements that describe ideal circumstances. They represent the intentions of the client and the worker and guide implementation efforts. Goals can be measured. Ultimately, a goal is a statement about how the worker and client will know whether the implementation has been successful.

Developing goals is a mutual process that includes collaboration and empowerment. Normally, the worker strives to empower the client and allow them to identify and create goals. Even though Janna is Robin's supervisor, in this case Robin is facilitating the planned change process. For that reason, she is the one encouraging Janna's participation in this particular meeting. In this way, goals are **organization-driven goals**. On the other hand, Robin may have goals of her own. Her desire to be allowed to work more hours is a **change agent–driven goal.** Again, even though Janna is Robin's supervisor, Robin is facilitating the planned change process here: She is the change agent.

Using the table they created, Robin and Janna created the following goals:

1. Get the board of directors to approve an MUnited program to facilitate positive relationships between landlords and student renters.
2. Have all staff members get familiar with landlord–renter laws and borough policies through the chief of police.
3. Get more hours for Robin.
4. Get the weeds removed from the parking lot.

WHAT IF . . . FOCUS ON DIVERSITY

Robin was a newly minted BSW. Did you picture her as being a young woman? Why, do you think? If Robin had been a mature student working on a second career, do you think her organizational change attempts might be more or less easy to implement?

Objectives. Once goals are established, **objectives** can be developed. As we've said, objectives are tasks that need to be carried out to accomplish a goal. Robin and Janna identified the following tasks that were necessary to carry out the four goals.

Goal	Objectives
Get the board of directors to approve an MUnited program for landlords and student renters.	Have Bill encourage the board of directors to reevaluate agency goals and objectives and point out the objective that is not being met. If he approves, have Bill recommend the board consider some kind of landlord–renter program.
Have all staff members get familiar with landlord–renter laws and borough policies.	Get information about laws and borough policies from the chief of police. Arrange for staff training.
Get more hours for Robin.	Gather data to establish need for more hours. Present data to Bill. If he approves, have Bill present data and make a request of the board to approve more hours.
Get the weeds removed from the parking lot.	Request that the landlord maintain the property. If necessary, point out borough policies about property maintenance.

Note that Robin and Janna used the ecomap to identify strengths and potential resources. The positive relationships among staff and between the agency director and the board of directors were major assets. Next, Robin and Janna specified expectations. As you know, in this stage of planned change it is important to identify "who will do what by when."

Goal	Objectives	Who	What	When
Get the board of directors to approve an MUnited program for landlords and student renters.	Have Bill encourage the board of directors to reevaluate agency goals and objectives and point out the objective that is not being met. Have Bill recommend a landlord–renter program to the board.	Janna	Meet with Bill, and ask him to speak to the board of directors about the agency goal review and recommended landlord–renter program.	In 6 weeks
Have all staff members get familiar with landlord–renter laws and borough policies.	Get information about laws and borough policies. Arrange for staff training.	Robin	Use the police chief contact to get information. Share information however Janna thinks appropriate.	In 4 weeks
Get more hours for Robin.	Gather data to establish the need for more hours. Present the data to Bill. Ask Bill to present data, and make a request of the board to approve more hours.	Robin, Janna	Robin will write down all of her activities and the length of time needed for 1 week. Janna will present information to Bill and request that he approach the board to request more hours for Robin.	Robin will complete the journal in 2 weeks; Janna will approach Bill within 6 weeks.
Get the weeds removed from the parking lot.	Request that the landlord maintain the property. If necessary, point out borough policies about property maintenance.	Janna	Janna will gain Bill's approval and will approach the landlord with the request.	In 6 weeks

Morsa Images/Getty Images

The planned change process can be carried out by social workers in all kinds of organizations.

Implementation

Robin and Janna will begin implementation with their first objective: to request a meeting with Bill. Continuing the planned change effort, Robin will check in with Janna during supervisory sessions to compare notes about task completion. As change agent, Robin will initiate these conversations. She'll use an opening statement to draw a boundary around work on the change project and her other work tasks. It might sound like this:

Robin: I think we've covered all of our supervision agenda items, right?

Janna: I think we have, unless you have any questions.

Robin: Well, I was hoping that we could spend 15 minutes talking about our organizational change project. Since I started the whole thing, I guess I'm responsible for it, so I thought I'd bring it up today. We both had some responsibilities, so could we check in?

Task Assessment

Next, Robin will make a task assessment. She'll talk about whether she completed her tasks, and she'll ask if Janna has completed hers. She may learn any of the following:

- Yes, they have carried out their tasks successfully.
- Yes, they've carried out part of their tasks.
- No, they didn't feel like it (or didn't have time, or forgot, or almost any other reason).
- No, they tried but it didn't work.
- No, there was a very real reason that was out of their control.

If Janna says yes, Robin will respond one of two ways: If the task has only been partially completed, she and Janna will identify their strengths and challenges on the way to trying again. A "yes, the task is entirely completed" from Janna calls for a reassessment—Robin will look to the contract for the next task or planning for the maintenance of change.

"Yes, a little" *Identify strengths and challenges.*

"Yes, it's done!" *Check for other tasks; plan to maintain change.*

If Janna's report is any kind of no, Robin will explore further. If Janna explains the incomplete task in a way that sounds like she's putting it off, Robin will have to find out whether the goals still apply. Is Janna still committed to the project? On the other hand, the no may be for a legitimate reason that was out of Janna's control. For example, Bill may not have been available. In that case, Robin and Janna need to reassess to be sure that the task is possible. Bill might be very hard to reach, or he may be only temporarily unavailable.

The implementation phase will continue. Robin with conduct task assessment with Janna until the tasks are complete or they decide to abandon the project.

Evaluation, Termination, and Follow-Up

At the end point that was identified, in this case a year, Robin will request a meeting to evaluate the success of their efforts. She and Janna will work together to conduct summative outcome evaluation by reviewing their original goals and objectives. If the program has taken off, they'll involve several landlords and some students in the evaluation process. They'll consider whether the objectives they set out in their plan were met. Maybe they should have been changed. If the program has been put into place, which objectives are still relevant and need ongoing evaluation?

In addition to outcome evaluation, they will conduct process evaluation to determine the success of the process of planned change. They will determine which of their efforts were useful and which were not. They'll talk about how they would carry out the planned change process in the future.

While relationships won't be terminated, Robin will formally end this planned change process and her role as organizational change agent during a meeting with Janna and Bill, and the three can discuss their thoughts and feelings about the project. It will be best if Robin puts a note on her calendar for one year from the termination so that they can follow up by revisiting the project. If it was successful, they will look at how it is being evaluated and whether the program or the evaluation has changed. If none was ever developed, they can revisit the strategies they used and consider how they might change them in the current environment. At that point, they may consider starting the change process again.

CRITICAL THINKING AND COLLABORATIVE LEARNING EXERCISES 13.3

Work in a large group, and consider this scenario: Your student government wants to expand the Student Union Building that they own. Using MSP methods, figure out how they would assess the resources and the challenges of your university. What information will they need? Where might they get it?

Section 13.4: The Social Work Role of Organizational Change Agent

This section is about the social work role of organizational change agent. We consider the role and the skills that allow us to carry it out.

The Social Work Role of Organizational Change Agent

While a social worker can be an outside consultant, chances are good that a social worker who is trying to change an agency is working within their own employing organization (Kirst-Ashman & Hull, 2017). In the role of **organizational change agent**, the worker takes on the task of instituting a planned change process within the agency. In this role, the employee takes the role of worker and looks to find a client system representative within the agency to facilitate the planned change process. Social workers in many roles, including supervisor, administrator, fund-raiser, and practitioner, can become organizational change agents. The goal of the organizational change agent is to develop **social innovations**, or to create new responses to social problems (Berzin & Pitt-Catsouphes, 2015). In addition, an organizational change agent's goal may be to improve service by improving the working conditions of staff (Hoefer, 2006).

Few people have "organizational change agent" in their job descriptions. However, since social workers follow a social work code of ethics, this role is implied, even required (Germak & Singh, 2010). In the *NASW Code of Ethics* (NASW, 2018), social workers have a commitment to agency change. We are required to "work to improve employing agencies' policies and procedures and the efficiency and effectiveness of their services" (NASW, 2018, 3.09(b), p. 21). For that reason, every social worker is a potential agent of change in their own agency. There are times when organizational policies become barriers to client services. Not only do workers need to address those barriers on behalf of clients; they also need to recognize that burnout can occur for systematic reasons as well as client-to-worker interactions. So workers may be helping each other as well as clients when they seek this type of change. Let's revisit our example where a client needs a photo identification to get services. The client has had difficulties in reaching out for services, the worker has finally gotten them to where they will accept services, and they find out that the client has no photo identification. The intrepid worker attempts to help the client get identification only to find that the client needs a Social Security number or birth certificate to get identification. To get a Social Security number or birth certificate is a long process that—you guessed it—requires proof of identification. In the meantime, the client is no longer interested in services. If that scenario occurs a few times a week, the worker is undoubtedly going to be burned out, and large numbers of clients will go without services. It is time to seek organizational change.

Organizational Change Agent Responsibilities

Organizational change agents have several responsibilities. As we have seen, one responsibility is to work toward improving the agency's effectiveness on behalf of clients. The other responsibility is to the agency itself. Since agencies have to respond quickly to environmental changes, it can be easy for them to lose or "blur" their identities (Schmid, 2013). The idea is to help the agency adapt to changes in the environment and client needs. It is not to harm the agency in any way or allow it to lose its identity. For that reason, it is critical that the organizational change agent keep the agency's mission in mind at all times. As we've seen, change agents like Robin may work to change the agency's goals and objectives or even its mission, but that should happen as a planned change process in concert with a client system representative. Major organizational change requires the organizational change agent to ally with many individuals and systems within the agency (Kirst-Ashman & Hull, 2017). Major organizational change can include fund-raising, in which the agency's programming is maintained or expanded by a staff member who gets more resources. Like other organizational change agents, a social worker who engages in fund-raising must keep the agency mission at the forefront of their efforts. Fund-raising efforts tell the community about your agency and its effectiveness (Pagnoni, 2014).

Skills for Organizational Change Agents

Since the organizational change agent is a role that addresses the needs of clients, of the staff, and of the agency, it requires a number of skills:

- Persuasion
- Networking
- Fund-raising
- Professional writing

As we've noted previously, keep in mind that organizational practice, a macro level of social work, has individual social work skills at its foundation.

Persuasion

Persuasion is a method of organizational change where one person gets what they want and the other person has been convinced that they want it too. Since everyone ends up happy, this is an effective means of implementation in organizational change. Here's where it fits into the planned change process: Once you've done self-reflection, engagement, assessment, and planning, it's time for implementation. If you remember, that's when the worker helps the client make changes. Part of that process is asking whether tasks have been completed. In organizational change, things may not happen because the system is in homeostasis or because an individual or group is blocking the way. Just like in work with individuals, you may help your client representative be persuasive, or you may get permission to be persuasive yourself.

SELF-REFLECTION 13: THE AUTHORITY BEHAVIOR INVENTORY

The acceptance of authority is necessary to maintain social order. For instance, if you accept authority, you are likely to obey laws. We've seen that supervision works well when people accept their own authority and that of others. On the other hand, the organizational change agent may need to question authority.

Take the Authority Behavior Inventory on pages 401–403 to find out how much you accept authority. Will you be a natural organizational change agent?

To back up to the beginning of the planned change process, you should know that self-reflection is extremely important when you are attempting to persuade someone. You will not make a convincing argument if you are emotionally tied to the outcome (Hoefer, 2006). Of course you will care about the outcome, but it's best if you do the "What do I feel/believe/know/do?" exercise so that you can look at your emotions using critical thinking. One way to sound objective is to use data. Having numbers to bolster your argument will help you to sound and feel like you know what you're talking about without being emotional.

To make persuasion work, Hoefer (2006) suggests four elements, including the context, message, sender, and receiver:

1. *Context*—Context refers to what is going on in the organization and how people are thinking about it and reacting to it. Once you understand how people are thinking about an issue, you can go about reframing it. This is the same skill you use in work with individuals where you help a person think about something in a way that benefits them. Here are some examples of reframing in an organizational context:

Nonpersuasive Argument	Persuasive Argument
It won't work.	It can be done in other ways.
It costs too much.	Long-term benefits outweigh costs.
It isn't fair.	It will help our clients.

Source: Adapted from Hoefer (2006, pp. 98–102).

2. *The message*—Hoefer (2006) refers to the characteristics of the message:

   Intent—Don't announce that you're trying to persuade a person unless they already expect it.

   Organization—Have key points of your message clear in your mind.

   Sidedness—Explain your side; then explain the opposite side and discredit it.

   Repetition—Make your point several times in the same way, but then practice other ways of saying the same thing.

3. *The sender*—This is you. You have to be an expert on your topic to convince people of your views. Here is where data can help. If you have some statistics from a reliable source to back up your opinion, you will show your expertise. You also need to carry out engagement before persuasion so that you are trusted. The way you speak—speed, tone of voice, and volume—should be appropriate to the setting. Your appearance is important too. You may dress formally to show authority or you may want to dress so that you are seen as one of the crowd. Whichever way you go, it's best if you make a conscious decision about your appearance.

4. *The receiver*—This is the person you are persuading. You will carry out preparatory empathy before you begin persuasion, so fall back on that to make an educated guess about what the person wants. Do they want to impress the board of directors? Do they want to look good to their peers? Whatever it is, make sure your idea will get them there.

The Skill of Networking

As we've mentioned before, in macro practice you never know who will be important to your cause. Networks have come to mean electronic relationships, but a network is still two or more people who are linked by communication (Rogers & Kincaid, 1981). That means you shouldn't forget the value of networking—meeting someone, shaking hands, or exchanging business cards. You should follow up in a day or two with a "nice to have met you" e-mail. Also, keep in mind that most people still have telephones on their desks. Phone calls can be nerve-racking for the caller, but if you have something complicated to convey or if you need a complicated answer, a phone call is much better than an e-mail. Of course, you'll often use some kind of electronic communication. Just be ready with your micro skills for any encounter. Think of every interaction you have at work as a social work interview: a conversation with a purpose done in the context of your agency's mission and your role.

The Skill of Fund-Raising

As we've said before, organizations need resources to provide and expand services. While many large agencies have professional fund-raisers, sometimes called development directors, smaller agencies may have to rely on the board of directors, the administration, and the staff to find money. This is where the generalist social worker comes in. In the role of organizational change agent, the worker may identify program developments and be charged with finding ways to fund them. A generalist worker may be asked to plan an event, solicit donations, manage volunteers, or occasionally to write grant applications. Using the planned change process, you'll begin with self-reflection. This stage is important in the skill of fund-raising because asking for money is taboo in our society, and someone carrying out the skill of fund-raising needs to be comfortable asking for money. Planning an event requires work with client system representatives to assess and plan carefully to account for the many details that will come up. The social worker who is planning an event will identify and evaluate successful past practices early in the planned change process. Directly soliciting donations requires an implementation stage where workers let people know how much money is needed, why it is needed, and how the prospective donor can help (Pagnoni, 2014). You also may know about some methods of soliciting funds electronically. You may do this via social media and ask donors to contribute using the agency's website (Castillo, Petrie, & Wardell, 2014). Organizational change agents may directly solicit donations electronically through social media. That method of soliciting donations has been demonstrated to increase giving both online and offline (Mano, 2014). When called upon to manage volunteers, the worker will study the best practices in supervision that we've discussed before, but they'll focus on the importance of saying thank you to volunteers in effective ways. Finally, a worker in the role of organizational change agent may be asked to write the description and expected outcomes of a new program in response to some organization's request for proposals (RFPs) for grants. In this case, professional writing is imperative.

Professional Writing

Since networking is done electronically as well as in person, **professional writing** is more important than ever. You'll be sending e-mails, text messages, and other communications, but you'll also be writing hard copy reports, letters, and memos. In any case, your writing must be professional. To be professional, you need to use the terms that are common at your agency and you need to use the strength-based language we've discussed. If there is a particular format, such as an intake report or case note, follow it meticulously. Because there are often specific formats for hard copy documents, you use them and then focus on grammar and style. We'll talk about electronic communication more in Chapter 15, but in the meantime know that where electronic communication is concerned, you should try to watch for the agency culture. Supervisors may text staff with a word or two and without punctuation. In that case, you do likewise. In other words, try to let someone else communicate first so you can figure out what is common practice. If you are the first to communicate, use full sentences and punctuation. You don't know what that person considers to be professional. With anything written at all—even a phone message scrawled on a piece of paper—be absolutely perfect with spelling and grammar. Read, proofread, and maybe get someone else to proofread. If you are still unsure, ask your supervisor to see samples of good writing at your agency. Your words represent you, and you are a professional. This is particularly important when you are acting as a change agent. You will not be persuasive with sloppy written work. In addition, high-quality professional writing is especially important when social workers work with professionals from other disciplines. In those cases, your work doesn't only represent you; it represents the social work profession.

Skills for Organizational Change Agents

Skill	Description	Example	Required Worker Characteristic(s)
Persuasion	One party getting what they want, and the other party becoming convinced that they want the same thing	"I know others think differently, but I think there is another way to do that."	Expertise Assertiveness
Networking	Connecting with colleagues in or out of a worker's agency	"I'm glad we got to cross paths. Do you have a business card?"	Assertiveness Focus
Fund-raising	Getting resources to maintain or expand the agency's programs	"We have an art therapy program that has been shown to be effective in helping troubled kids succeed in school. Right now, we need a kiln for the pottery projects. We need $1,000. Could you make a contribution?"	Assertiveness Professional presentation
Professional writing	Communicating with professionals in writing, either electronically or using paper in a way that is consistent with organizational culture	Supervisor's text: meet@2? Worker's response: Sure thx	Focus

Sample Organizational Change Agent Dialogue

Janna: Bill, I'm glad the three of us were able to get together today. I appreciate you being willing to take the time. *(affirmation)*

Bill: No problem. I'm happy to help you two with the good work you're doing in the community.

Robin: I'm sure you already know that we're here to get something out of you. *(use of humor)*

Bill: (*laughing*) I'm sure you are.

Robin: (*careful with the speed of her words knowing that she tends to speed up when she's anxious*) Janna and I have been talking about the idea of addressing our agency goal to help resolve town–gown conflict. We don't have any programs that do that. *(remains calm, objective)*

Janna: I was speaking to Mandy, the chamber of commerce chair, and she brought up the fact that she's been hearing a lot of complaints about student renters again. *(networking; use of data)* Robin and I were thinking we might want to meet the agency objective about conflict resolution with a program for landlords and renters. *(guessing that Bill—the receiver of the persuasion effort—wants to address agency objectives to look competent in front of the board of directors)*

Bill: Hmm. What do you have in mind?

Robin: Well, there are 67 landlords and 587 student renters in town. *(objective data demonstrates her expertise)* We know the chamber of commerce hears complaints from the renters, and the secretary at the office of the dean of students regularly gets complaints too. *(networking, use of data)* What we're thinking is that we could explore the idea of a meeting for landlords and a meeting for renters to begin to figure out what the resources and challenges are. *(assessment plan)*

Bill: It sounds great, but it would cost money. Robin, I know you're overworked as it is. You would need additional hours just to look at this. I don't know if the board will want to approach the university to ask for a change in our budget.

Robin: I know it will cost money, but I think the long-term benefits will outweigh the costs. The landlords are powerful people in the community, and we're just getting the child care and food bank programs off the ground. I bet there's some way they'll be able to help us in the future. If the board approves the program, I'm sure other ways of getting funding can be identified. *(reframing)*

Bill: All right. I'm sold. Let's talk about how I can convince the board.

CRITICAL THINKING AND COLLABORATIVE LEARNING EXERCISES 13.4

Work in pairs consisting of at least one person who is or has been employed. Your employer wants to cut your hours. How will you persuade them not to? Use the skills related to the role of organizational change agent to support your answer.

Section 13.5: The Social Work Role of Supervisor

This section is about the social work role of **supervisor**. We consider the role, its relationship to organizational change, and the skills that allow us to carry it out.

The Social Work Role of Supervisor

A supervisor is an organizational change agent by default. What they say in supervision and how they relate to their supervisees can go a long way toward creating an empowerment-oriented agency culture. They can create this culture even if the agency does not have formal structures that encourage empowerment. For example, sometimes supervisors have some decision-making powers. If a few of them invite their supervisees to share their thoughts, they are creating an open culture that respects individuals' ideas. Supervisors can also use group supervision for team-building activities that can work toward increasing job satisfaction.

Purposes of Supervision

Social work supervision is not the same as supervision in a corporate setting. Instead of just one purpose—monitoring productivity—social work supervision has three purposes. The three purposes of supervision are (1) administration, (2) education, and (3) support (Kadushin & Harkness, 2014). These purposes overlap in one supervisor–worker relationship. Each of the three is necessary to the competence of the worker. And they are necessary regardless of how many years the person has been a social worker.

Administration

The most commonly used purpose of supervision is the social work supervisor's responsibility to the administration of the agency. Specifically, the *NASW Code of Ethics* (NASW, 2018) reminds the supervisor that they are responsible to carry out the policies of their agencies. Much like in the corporate world, the supervisor carries out that purpose by monitoring the worker's performance. The supervisor needs to know whether the worker has put in enough hours meeting with clients. They need to know if the worker is creating and keeping relationships with their clients, client systems, and client system representatives. They need to know if the worker is documenting their work consistently and in keeping with the agency's policies. The supervisor needs to know whether the worker is getting along with their coworkers. For these reasons, the supervisor will ask pointed questions: How are your case recordings going? Are your client files complete? Are you able to meet with your clients as you've planned? Have you completed the tasks we talked about? The worker has to be ready to be compliant. They need to remember that their supervisor is, in fact, their boss. As always, a social work interaction begins with self-reflection and engagement. These steps facilitate the administrative function of supervision, which is similar to the assessment phase of planned change. The worker and the supervisor are collaborating to find out about the worker's ability to carry out the most basic parts of the job. Unfortunately, supervision often ends here even though other purposes of supervision are just as important (Chapman, Oppenheim, Shibusawa, & Jackson, 2003.

Education

Unlike other supervisory relationships where the administrative part of supervision is all there is, in social work supervision education takes place as well. If the worker has trouble engaging a client, for example, a supervisor may share some evidence-based practice. On the other hand, the supervisor may know from experience the best way to work with this particular type of client in this particular setting. In this way, the supervisor is educating the worker based on their own experience, or practice wisdom (Council on Social Work Education [CSWE], 2015). A supervisor may also provide education in helping a worker discover things that they need to learn and pointing out workshops, conferences, or other ways that the worker can get the needed information. This is all part of the supervisory process. Because workers and their supervisors often set goals for the worker's learning, this practice is similar to the planning stage of planned change.

Support

In social work, it's commonly understood that workers face difficult and emotionally painful situations every day. For this reason, support is an important component of supervision. A good supervisor is ready to spend some supervisory time listening to your painful stories. This support is essential to the supervisory process: it is known to facilitate workers' ability to stay on the job (Kapoulitsas & Corcoran, 2015). In the face of a very troubling situation, the supervisor may ask the worker what life experiences may be important to their current feelings. In other words, the supervisor is trying to help the worker identify why a particular case is especially troubling. If a connection is obvious—the worker has had a long but successful struggle with punctuality but their client is oblivious to their own perpetual lateness—the supervisor can help the worker see the connection. In this case, the supervisor could help the worker understand why they begin each session struggling with their feelings of anger toward their client. This knowledge alone may help the feelings dissipate. Sometimes, though, the connection is not so simple. There may be some barrier between the worker and the client that is accidently caused by the worker. The supervisor can help to get to the bottom of the cause. This gets tricky, though. The supervisor may need some personal information from the worker to help identify the barrier. The punctuality problem, for example, may stem in part from the worker's response to their partner's controlling behavior. They are in the habit of being late and their partner always gives them a hard time about it, so when they're on time at work and the client's is often late, it really annoys them. At that point, they're not able to provide the best social work services. As we've introduced in Chapter 4, the worker may have to self-disclose information to their supervisor to figure out their feelings related to a case. This becomes a problem if the worker or the supervisor forget the purpose of the self-disclosure and create a boundary violation. A detailed discussion about how boundaries develop in supervision and what we can do about them is in Chapter 4 since it relates to self-reflection. In short, the employee should share personal information only as it specifically relates to their job.

Skills for Supervisors

Staff Evaluation

Every agency has a method for evaluating the performance of employees. The supervisor is expected to consider how the workers are completing their tasks and whether they are keeping up agency policies. The best process for evaluations is a collaborative one: The supervisor and supervisee should each complete a **staff evaluation**. Then they get together and discuss the differences between the two. Finally, the supervisor completes the evaluation. A supervisor's ability to accept the power in their role is important for effective supervision (Kadushin & Harkness, 2014). Potential barriers to an appropriate supervisor–worker relationship are discussed in detail in Chapter 4. Most of the barriers are related to an inability for a supervisor to accept their own authority and an inability for an employee to accept their supervisor's direction.

Note-Taking

We'll be discussing **note-taking** and related ethical considerations in Chapter 15. For now, know that a supervisor is responsible for taking notes on interactions with supervisees. These notes are important since they support the administrative functions of supervision, evaluations, and disciplinary actions. For their own supervision, supervisors need to have a record of when they asked supervisees about their job performance and what the answers were. Their supervisors will want to know if the work is being done and if the agency's policies are being upheld. Also, when a supervisor hears of outstanding work, they can make a note in the employee's file for later reference. When they need to write an employee's evaluation, the information will be there. On the other hand, they may need to keep notes about unacceptable performance. They may want to reference these notes as they relate to disciplinary actions (Kadushin & Harkness, 2014).

Taking Disciplinary Actions

Legally, a supervisor is responsible (**liable**) for what their supervisees do and don't do. Legal precedent is clear that a supervisor can be legally charged with **malpractice**, or a deviation from a duty of care, based on what their supervisees do (Reamer, 2005). For that reason, a supervisor's use of administrative supervision is very serious. Supervisors' responsibility to verify that services are provided as they should be, that clients and colleagues are treated respectfully, and that agency policies are being followed is very serious. Supervisors must be consistent in applying rules and keeping records of their interactions with supervisees. Where service is not being provided as it should or rules are being broken, **disciplinary actions** may include a private, verbal reprimand or the formal documentation of repeated violations that may end up in the worker's employee file (Kadushin & Harkness, 2014). Ultimately, the employee can lose their job following a series of disciplinary actions. To carry out this process, supervisors need to be consistently assertive and comfortable in their roles. It's also important that they have good supervision themselves.

Skills for Supervisors

Skill	Description	Example	Required Worker Characteristic(s)
Staff evaluation	Compiling a description of an employee's strengths and challenges	"Susan, let's discuss your self-evaluation and compare it to my draft evaluation."	Comfort in role
Note-taking	Taking notes on supervision activities similar to case notes	The supervisor records each time they review their employees' work.	Focus, good time in management, accepting the role of supervisor
Taking disciplinary actions	Responding to worker noncompliance with agency policy	"Bill, you've been late three times this week. Can you help me understand that?"	Assertiveness, comfort in role

Sample Supervisory Dialogue

Janna: Before we end supervision, there's something I've been wanting to say to you.

Robin: What's that?

Janna: I don't know if you are aware of it, but every pay period I have to go into the computer and approve your hours. I'm supposed to do it by the end of the day every other Monday.

Robin: I knew that, yes. Is it a problem?

Janna: Well, it is when you haven't logged your hours. There's nothing there for me to approve.

Robin: Oh. I have been trying to get them logged, but I never seem to have time at the end of the day.

Janna: Robin, I've seen you here at the end of the day finishing up your case notes, and I've never seen you late with those. Do you think something else is behind it?

Robin: It's just that I don't have as many hours to log as I'd like because I still haven't been approved to work 30 instead of 20 hours a week. I get so annoyed every time I go to log my hours that I just avoid it.

Janna: Do you think you can resolve this? We're a small bureaucracy inside a big bureaucracy, and it's important that we follow the rules.

Robin: Sorry. I didn't know it was that important. It won't happen again.

Janna: Thanks.

The Overcommitted Worker: Reflective Responses

Robin was the kind of young woman that people called a go-getter. She was able to work fast and get things done. So she managed to be a part-time employee for MUnited, a part-time employee for another agency, a caretaker to an aging grandmother, president of her church youth group, and a volunteer Girl Scout leader. MUnited was a success due in great part to her commitment and energy. For that reason, Janna was surprised when Robin asked during supervision to have her hours extended. Robin wanted to be paid for the hours she was putting in and was advocating on her own behalf. It was especially important since Robin was proposing the new student landlord–renter relations program. When Robin brought the idea of the new program to Janna, Janna asked Robin to think carefully about taking on another task. Robin said she knew she could do it if she got more hours approved. She could quit her other job and devote her time to MUnited. Then Janna asked an important question: What would Robin do if the board approved the new program but didn't approve more paid hours for her? Robin engaged in some critical thinking. She *felt* passionate about the new program. She *believed* she could develop and implement it in addition to her other tasks. Then Janna asked her to think critically about her beliefs. She encouraged Robin to write down all of her weekly commitments in and out of work. She asked her to estimate the time each one took. Robin realized that she spent a lot of time working on some project or another all day, every day, including during lunch and even dinner. She also realized that she had cut down on time for socializing with

Self-reflection can help workers realize that they can't work all day and all night.

friends. After that reflection, Robin *knew* she was overcommitted. She needed to look at her commitments outside of work to see where she could delegate some responsibilities or even step out of leadership positions. Taking on another project at work without being paid for additional hours just didn't make sense.

CRITICAL THINKING AND COLLABORATIVE LEARNING EXERCISES 13.5

Go online to the NASW website, and learn what you can about malpractice insurance. Find out the price of student membership and the price of malpractice insurance that is specifically for students.

Section 13.6: Review and Apply

CONCURRENT CONSIDERATIONS IN GENERALIST PRACTICE

Ethical Decision-Making Challenge

Is there anything in the *NASW Code of Ethics* (NASW, 2018) that suggests it might be unethical for Robin not to record her hours in a timely way as her agency's policy requires? See Section 3.04.

Human Rights

Is it possible that the student renters might be denied human rights? Under what circumstances might that be true?

Evidence-Based Practice

Find out if there is any research available that deals with organizations designed to improve community or university relationships. What are some of their activities?

Policies Impacting Practice

Find out your college or university's policy on how students are expected to behave in the community.

Managing Diversity

How can Robin learn about landlords so she can develop preparatory empathy?

Multilevel Practice

Identify examples of Robin's work on all levels.

Micro: ____________________

Mezzo: ____________________

Macro: ____________________

Dynamic and Interactive Planned Change Stages

Identify aspects of Robin's work where she worked in the following stages:

Self-Reflection: ____________________

Engagement: ____________________

Assessment: ____________________

Planning: ____________________

Implementation: ____________________

Evaluation: ____________________

Termination and Follow-Up: ____________________

Chapter Summary

Section 13.1: The Nature of Organizations

An organization is a group of people together for a reason, but human service organizations are unique. Human service organizations work from altruistic motives, and the "products" they produce have to do with people. There are four types of human service organizations: nonprofit, for profit, public, and faith-based.

Section 13.2: Aspects of Organizations

Organizational budgets enable organizations to carry out their vision, mission, goals, and objectives. The process of carrying them out is reflected in the organizational structure, or the relationships among roles within the organization. Another impact on the process of carrying out the vision, mission, goals, and objectives is the culture of the organization itself. Some organizations have cultures that are empowerment-oriented. They empower their staff and clients to work together and play a role in agency decision-making by creating formal agency structures to do so.

Section 13.3: Planned Change in Organizations

Organizational change is part of macro practice in MSP. For that reason, organizational change is conducted using the same planned change process as change on any other system level. Workers typically carry out the process working alongside a client system representative. Engagement is carried out with the client system representative, and assessment makes use of the ecomap. Planning and implementation use the same task-centered approach used in micro and mezzo practice, while evaluation can be either process or outcome oriented.

Section 13.4: The Social Work Role of Organizational Change Agent

Social workers can serve as organizational change agents within their own agencies. Usually the goal of this activity is to ultimately improve the service to clients. Social workers use micro level skills as well as persuasion, networking, and professional writing.

Section 13.5: The Social Work Role of Supervisor

Social workers can serve as supervisors within agencies. Supervisors have opportunities to conduct organizational change as part of their everyday jobs. They can help create an empowerment-oriented organization within their own area of responsibility by encouraging their staff to use teamwork and engage in decision-making. In addition to micro and mezzo skills, supervisors use skills of evaluation, note-taking, and, when necessary, disciplinary actions.

SELF-REFLECTION 13: AUTHORITY BEHAVIOR INVENTORY

PURPOSE: To measure acceptance of authority

AUTHOR: Ken Rigby

DESCRIPTION: This 24-item instrument measures the acceptance of authority in the form of a behavioral inventory. A respondent with high acceptance of authority is generally considered pro-authority, is likely to follow rules, and tends

(Continued)

(Continued)

to obey social demands that include the legal obligation to conform. This could encompass such activities as obeying traffic regulations and refraining from illegal drug and alcohol use.

NORMS: The ABI has norms on a sample of social work students (n = 100) and nonstudents in the general public (n = 100) form Australia. The mean scores were 68.64 for the students and 75.78 for nonstudents. A separate sample of nonstudents had a similar mean, 74.85. The mean ABI scores were not different between women and men.

SCORING: Scores are the total of each item. Items 2, 5, 8, 9, 12, 14, 15, 17, 18, 19, 21, and 24 are reverse scored. Scores range from 24 to 200, with higher scores indicating more positive orientation toward acceptance of authority.

RELIABILITY: All items were significantly correlated with total scores, with arrange from .12 to .67. The ABI has good internal consistency, with an alpha of .84.

VALIDITY: Validity was estimated by correlating scores on the ABI items with a corresponding item when a rater independently evaluated the respondent. Respondents' scores were significantly correlated with the rater's evaluation. Similarly, a separate study of 150 respondents found correlations between ABI scores and ratings of perceived authority by a rater who knew the person. Respondents perceived as more pro-authority had significantly higher ABI scores that subjects perceived as less pro-authority.

PRIMARY REFERENCE:

Rigby, K. (2013). An authority behavior inventory. In K. Corcoran & J. Fischer (Eds.), *Measures for clinical practice and research: A sourcebook* (5th ed., pp. 86–87). New York, NY: Oxford University Press.

AUTHORITY BEHAVIOR INVENTORY

This questionnaire is intended to assess the frequency with which you *behave* in certain ways. Answer each question as carefully as you can by placing a number on the space by each one as follows:

1 = never

2 = rarely

3 = occasionally

4 = frequently

5 = very frequently

_____ 1. Do you listen attentively to what older people say about how you should behave?

_____ 2. Do you question the judgment of umpires or referees when you think they have made an incorrect decision?

_____ 3. When a person in authority whom you trust tells you to do something, do you do it, even though you can't see the reason for it?

_____ 4. Do you criticize people who are rude to their superiors?

_____ 5. Do you encourage young people to do what they want to do, even when it is against the wishes of their parents?

_____ 6. When you go to work, do you dress so as to be acceptable to the people who run the place?

_____ 7. Do you treat experts with respect even when you don't think much of them personally?

_____ 8. Do you support left-wing, radical policies?

_____ 9. Do you take part in demonstrations to show your opposition to policies you do not like?

_____ 10. Do you express approval for the work of schoolteachers?

_____ 11. Do you go to church?

_____ 12. Do you make fun of the police?

_____ 13. When things are bad, do you look for guidance from someone wiser than yourself?

_____ 14. Do you sympathize with rebels?

_____ 15. When you are in a hurry, do you break the speed limit or encourage your driver to do so, if it seems reasonably safe?

_____ 16. Do you follow doctor's orders?

_____ 17. Do you question what you hear on the news?

_____ 18. Do you cross the road against the pedestrian traffic lights?

_____ 19. Do you ask for a second opinion when you feel uncertain about a doctor's advice?

_____ 20. Do you stand when they play the national anthem in public?

_____ 21. Do you express contempt for politicians?

_____ 22. Do you get annoyed when people sneer at those in authority?

_____ 23. Do you show special respect for the people in high positions?

_____ 24. Do you speak up against your boss or person in charge when he or she acts unfairly?

Recommended Websites

Social work organizations: www.socialworkers.org/LinkClick.aspx?fileticket=WXklF7uD-Nk%3d&portalid=0

"Avoiding Malpractice Tips" from NASW Assurance Services: www.naswassurance.org/malpractice/malpractice-tips

Critical Terms for Roles and Skills in Work With Organizations

nonprofit agency 371
individual donors 372
grants 372
fee-for-service 372
Medicare 372
public agencies 372
Medicaid 372
profit-making agencies 373
faith-based organizations 373
operating budget 373
revenues 373
expenses 373
grant or contract budget 373
organizational culture 375
empowerment-oriented organizational culture 375
vision 375
mission 375
organizational goals 375
organizational objectives 376
organizational structure 377
board of directors 377
organizational culture 378
horizontal leadership 378
empowerment-focused organizations 379
organization-driven goals 386
change agent–driven goal 386
objectives 387
organizational change agent 390
social innovations 390
persuasion 391
professional writing 393
supervisor 396
staff evaluation 397
note-taking 398
liable 398
malpractice 398
disciplinary actions 398

Generalist Practice Curriculum Matrix With 2015 Educational Policy and Accreditation Standards

Chapter 13

Competency	Course	Course Content	Dimensions
Competency 1: Demonstrate Ethical and Professional Behavior		Feature 3: Self-Reflection	Cognitive–affective processes
		Feature 4: Concurrent Considerations in Generalist Practice	Skills Cognitive–affective processes
Competency 2: Engage Diversity and Difference in Practice		Feature 1: Focus on Diversity	Skills Cognitive–affective processes
		Feature 4: Concurrent Considerations in Generalist Practice	Skills Cognitive–affective processes
Competency 3: Advance Human Rights and Social, Economic, and Environmental Justice		Feature 4: Concurrent Considerations in Generalist Practice	Skills Cognitive–affective processes
		13.1. Learn about the nature of human service organizations.	Knowledge
Competency 4: Engage in Practice-Informed Research and Research-Informed Practice		Feature 4: Concurrent Considerations in Generalist Practice	Skills Cognitive–affective processes
		13.3. Translate the planned change process to work in organizations.	Knowledge
Competency 5: Engage in Policy Practice		Feature 4: Concurrent Considerations in Generalist Practice	Skills Cognitive–affective processes
		13.3. Translate the planned change process to work in organizations.	Knowledge
Competency 6: Engage With Individuals, Families, Groups, Organizations, and Communities		Feature 4: Concurrent Considerations in Generalist Practice	Skills Cognitive–affective processes
Competency 7: Assess Individuals, Families, Groups, Organizations, and Communities		Feature 4: Concurrent Considerations in Generalist Practice	Skills Cognitive–affective processes
		13.3. Translate the planned change process to work in organizations.	Knowledge
Competency 8: Intervene With Individuals, Families, Groups, Organizations, and Communities		13.2. Discuss organizational vision and mission, organizational structure, and organizational culture.	Knowledge
		13.3. Translate the planned change process to work in organizations.	Knowledge
		13.4. Describe the social work role of organization change agent and related skills.	Knowledge
		13.5. Examine the social work role of supervisor and related skills.	Knowledge Skills
		Feature 4: Concurrent Considerations in Generalist Practice	Cognitive–affective processes

Competency	Course	Course Content	Dimensions
Competency 9: Evaluate Practice With Individuals, Families, Groups, Organizations, and Communities		Feature 4: Concurrent Considerations in Generalist Practice	Skills Cognitive-affective processes
		13.3. Translate the planned change process to work in organizations.	Knowledge

References

Barker, R. L. (2003). *The social work dictionary* (5th ed.). Washington, DC: NASW Press.

Berzin, S., & Pitt-Catsouphes, M. (2015). Social innovation from the inside: Considering the "intrapreneurial" path. *Social Work, 60*(4), 360–362.

Castillo, M., Petrie, R., & Wardell, C. (2014). Fundraising through online social networks. *Journal of Public Economics, 114*, 29–35.

Chapman, M. V., Oppenheim, S., Shibusawa, T., & Jackson, H. M. (2003). What we bring to practice: Teaching students about professional use of self. *Journal of Teaching in Social Work, 23*(3/4), 3–14.

Cohen, M. B., & Hyde, C. A. (2013). *Empowering workers and clients for organizational change*. Chicago, IL: Lyceum.

Cornell Law School Legal Information Institute. (2017). Non-profit organizations. Retrieved from https://www.law.cornell.edu/wex/non-profit_organizations

Corporation for National and Community Service. (2018). *National service knowledge network: Preparing budgets*. Retrieved from https://www.nationalservice.gov/sites/default/files/olc/moodle/fm_reparing_the_grant_budget_forc_ac/view764b.html?id=3202&chapterid=2054

Council on Social Work Education. (2015). *Educational policy and accreditation standards*. Alexandria, VA: Author. Retrieved from http://www.cswe.org/File.aspx?id=81660

Flynn, S. (2015). Organizational environment. *Research Starters: Sociology*. Retrieved from http://eds.b.ebscohost.com/eds/detail/detail?vid=3&sid=fb926f08-e721-4242-a8d3-2085036b268e%40sessionmgr104&bdata=JnNpdGU9ZWRzLWxpdmUmc2NvcGU9c2l0ZQ%3d%3d#AN=89185615&db=ers

Galambos, C., Dulmus, C. N., & Wodarski, J. S. (2005). Principles for change in human service agencies. *Journal of Human Behavior in the Social Environment, 11*(1), 63–78.

Germak, A., & Singh, K. K. (2010). Social entrepreneurship: Changing the way social workers do business. *Administration in Social Work, 34*, 79–95.

Gibelman, M., & Furman, R. (2008). *Navigating human service organizations* (2nd ed.). Chicago, IL: Lyceum.

Gilley, A., Godek, M., & Gilley, J. W. (2009). Change, resistance, and the organizational immune system. *SAM Advanced Management Journal, 74*(4), 4–10.

Hardina, D. (2005). Ten characteristics of empowerment-oriented social service organizations. *Administration in Social Work, 29*(3), 23–42.

Hasenfeld, Y. (2010). The attributes of human service organizations. In Y. Hasenfeld (Ed.), *Human services as complex organizations* (2nd ed., pp. 9–31). Thousand Oaks, CA: Sage.

Hoefer, R. (2006). *Advocacy practice for social justice*. Chicago, IL: Lyceum.

Kadushin, A., & Harkness, D. (2014). *Supervision in social work*. New York, NY: Columbia University Press.

Kapoulitsas, M., & Corcoran, T. (2015). Compassion fatigue and resilience: A qualitative analysis of social work practice. *Qualitative Social Work, 14*(1), 86–101.

Kaufman, R., & Guerra-Lopez, I. (2013). *Needs assessment for organizational success.* Alexandria, VA: American Society for Training & Development.

Kirst-Ashman, K. K., & Hull, G. H. (2017). *Generalist practice with organizations and communities* (6th ed.). Belmont, CA: Brooks/Cole.

Lusthaus, C. (2002). *Organizational assessment: A framework for improving performance.* Ottawa, Canada: International Development Research Centre.

Mano, R. S. (2014). Social media, social causes, giving behavior and money contributions. *Computers in Human Behavior, 31*, 287–293.

National Association of Social Workers. (2018). *NASW code of ethics.* Washington, DC: NASW Press.

Nurcahyo, R., Wibowo, A. D., & Putra, R. F. E. (2015). Key performance indicators development for government agencies. *International Journal of Technology, 5*, 856–963. doi:10.14716/ijtech.v615.1840

Pagnoni, L. A. (2014). *The nonprofit fundraising solution: Powerful strategies to take you to the next level.* New York, NY: American Management Association.

Proehl, R. A. (2001). *Organizational change in the human services.* Thousand Oaks, CA: Sage.

Pyles, L. (2009). *Progressive community organizing: A critical approach for a globalizing world.* New York, NY: Routledge.

Reamer, F. G. (2005). Documentation in social work: Evolving ethical and risk management standards. *Social Work, 50*(4), 325–384.

Rigby, K. (2013). An authority behavior inventory. In K. Corcoran & J. Fischer (Eds.), *Measures for clinical practice and research: A sourcebook* (5th ed.). New York, NY: Oxford University Press.

Rogers, E. M., & Kincaid, D. L. (1981). *Communication networks: toward a new paradigm for research.* New York, NY: Free Press.

Sanger, M. (2001). When the private sector competes: Providing services to the poor in the wake of welfare reform. *The Brookings Institute.* Retrieved from https://www.brookings.edu/research/when-the-private-sector-competes-providing-services-to-the-poor-in-the-wake-of-welfare-reform

Schmid, H. (2013). Nonprofit human services: Between identity blurring and adaptation to changing environments. *Administration in Social Work, 37*, 242–256.

Segal, E. A. (2016). *Social welfare policies and programs: A values perspective.* Boston, MA: Cengage.

Stone, K. B. (2015). Burke-Litman organizational assessment survey: Reliability and validity. *Organizational Development Journal, 33*(2), 33–50.

Recommended Readings

Hardina, D. (2005). Ten characteristics of empowerment-oriented social service organizations. *Administration in Social Work, 29*(3), 23–42.

Hutton, S., & Phillips, F. N. (2016). *Nonprofit kit for dummies* (5th ed.). Hoboken, NJ: Wiley.

Roles and Skills in Work With Communities

This chapter concludes the series of chapters about social work on various levels of practice. It explores planned change in communities with particular attention to the feasibility of this type of practice for all generalist workers.

Learning Objectives

14.1 Learn about the nature of social work's commitment to communities.

14.2 Translate the planned change process to work in communities.

14.3 Consider the social work role of community change agent and related skills.

14.4 Examine the social work role of legislative advocate and its related skills

Case Study: Organizing Parents at School

"I'm so glad you could all make it here today!" Brianna said. She meant it too. She didn't expect it to be so easy to get 15 people to come to another planning meeting to save Eastwood Middle School's playground, especially since some of them had to take a long public transportation route to get to the school. It was easy for her to develop some empathy for the parents. For one thing, she knew what it was to have responsibilities at home. For another, she was absolutely sure she would not want her own child in a school without a playground. *They've all come back. I must be doing something right.* The school district planned to demolish the playground at the middle school to create a profit-making parking lot, and a lot of the parents were upset. Sure, middle schoolers didn't need a teeter-totter, really. And, yes, every day there was more litter just outside the fence, including broken glass, needles, and used condoms. On the other hand, the playground was a place that allowed the kids to let off steam, and teachers believed that ordinary things like swings and the teeter-totter helped with behavior problems. Brianna could attest to that; she felt

Luis Alvarez/Getty Images

Social workers often address small groups in community work.

confident in beginning this group because not only did she see the benefits of the playground for herself as school social worker but she'd spoken to every one of those teachers.

"We want to do what we can," said Sarah, a middle-aged Caucasian woman sitting just across from Brianna in the circle. Then there was silence. Everyone looked at Brianna, waiting for her to speak. Brianna took a breath. *I'd better say the right thing or I'm going to lose them. Wait! The opening statement. That's where I begin. Phew.*

"Okay, let's get started," Brianna said in a clear voice. "As you all know, I'm the social worker here at Eastwood, and the school district hired me to see that your kids do as well as possible in school. That includes families, so I get to work with you too. My supervisor and the principal have agreed that we should try to do something to save the playground. We have 2 hours to work with tonight. Maria, do you want to sum up what we did last week?"

"Sure," Maria said. "We decided we should try to save the parking lot. We have a goal of going to a school board meeting and stating our case. We made a plan to make sure that would happen. I'm in charge of asking to get on the school board agenda. I've already figured out who I need to talk to just like we planned."

"Excellent!" said Brianna. "Last time, when we were thinking about all of the things that are going on for the school board, we figured out what their arguments are probably going to be." At the last meeting, the group had recognized that the needles and condoms were on everyone's mind, and the school board members felt strongly that school kids shouldn't be playing near that litter. "The litter," said Josie. "We've got to do something about the litter."

"And we need to do it before the school board meeting," said Maria. Brianna looked around the room and saw that every head but Bob's was nodding. *Oh boy, this guy doesn't seem to agree with anything. But I can't let myself be annoyed with him. I know I'm at risk of being too emotionally involved, as if my whole reputation depends on this group. It doesn't. I'll stay calm.* "Bob," she said, putting a caring note into her voice. "You look like you're not sure."

"I don't think the litter is the problem at all. I think it's like we said last time when we talked about economics. I know from one of their meetings that the school board wants this place because they need the money when they sell it off to become a parking lot. They don't want to destroy the football team's practice field because people pay for football game tickets in the nice stadium on that side of town. So the team over at Westwood High gets two fields, and our kids get nothing. "

Brianna took a breath. All of the group members took a breath too. They looked at her in silence. She had a moment of real fear. They were all looking at her. *They are depending on me to know the answers. But I don't know the answers. Wait. I know how to do this. Step by step. I have to keep doing engagement all the time, and Bob is a good example of someone I didn't fully engage yet. And I can do that. I know about listening skills and group roles.* "Bob, sounds like you feel strongly about this," she said, making brief eye contact then looking all around the room. He nodded. *Okay. I'm doing this. Reflective listening and labeling feelings. I know he's in the role of blocker, but I want to see if I can turn him into an opinion sharer and information giver.* "You bring us a valuable opinion. I'm convinced we're going to need that opinion and information related to it very soon. I also believe it will be best if you keep bringing us different opinions. We're going to rely on you for that. But I think in order of priorities, the group feels like we should tackle the litter first."

"We do," said Maria decisively, and the rest of the group nodded, looking at Bob. Bob looked at Brianna. "Okay for now?" Brianna asked him, and he nodded. "So we're going to tackle the litter." Every head nodded. Brianna took a deep breath. *Thank goodness.* "In that case," she said, "we need a more detailed plan."

Section 14.1: Social Work in Communities

This section discusses communities and social work's commitment to work with and on behalf of them.

Social Work in Communities

We've already said that working with groups can give anyone anxiety. When the group is part of a community effort, it's easy to get even more anxious. When Brianna heard teachers talking about the playground's destruction, they all seemed resigned to it. They were concerned about the litter, but they never talked about it. This was partly because they didn't want to think about the potentially dangerous neighborhood they had to commute to every day from the suburbs. Everyone was overwhelmed thinking about the neighborhood. There had been gang-related shootings right in front of the school, and last year a kid had gotten stabbed on the bus. Teachers were afraid, and it was a situation they felt they could do nothing about. The principal's view was "we do what we can for them here, because goodness knows we can't do anything about where they live."

As a social worker, Brianna knew she needed to think differently. Social justice is a core social work value (National Association of Social Workers [NASW], 2018). The *NASW Code of Ethics* (NASW, 2018) is specific about Social Workers' Ethical Responsibilities to the Broader Society:

6.01 Social Welfare

> Social workers should promote the general welfare of society, from local to global levels, and the development of people, their communities, and their environments. Social workers should advocate for living conditions conducive to the fulfillment of basic human needs and should promote social, economic, political, and cultural values and institutions that are compatible with the realization of social justice. (p. 29)

WHAT IF . . . FOCUS ON DIVERSITY

Name the areas of diversity that existed between Brianna and the parent group she was serving. Consider the Aspects of Diversity section of Chapter 3. What might be some challenges she faced because of those differences? How might she capitalize on the strengths that existed in the differences?

Social Justice

Let's take a moment and look at the term **social justice**. We have seen that the search for social justice is one of the defining features of social work. While social justice can mean different things to different people, it is often related to making sure that everyone in a society has their human rights met (Gasker & Fischer, 2014). As we've said, human rights can be civil, political, environmental, economic, social, and cultural (CSWE, 2015). Let's take these one by one.

Civil Rights

The Universal Declaration of Human Rights was developed by the United Nations in 1948. The United States has committed to abide by the declaration. It is considered to be the basic resource for discussions of human rights. First, the document states that considerations of human rights should be made for every person regardless of who they are or where they live. It says that "All human beings are born free and equal in dignity and rights. They are endowed with reason and conscience and should act towards one another in a spirit of brotherhood" (p. 1). Some of the civil human rights that are mentioned specifically include the right to do the following:

- Have the law recognize them as a person
- Be legally considered to be equal to all other people and entitled to equal legal protections and fair, public hearings in cases of criminal charges in which they are presumed innocent until proven guilty and provided with necessary defense
- Be protected by the courts from discrimination and arbitrary arrest, detention, or exile
- Be protected by the courts from arbitrary interference with their privacy, family, home or correspondence, or to attacks on their reputation
- Have freedom of movement and residence in their own country
- Leave any country and return to their own
- Seek asylum from persecution
- Have a nationality and the right to change it

ETHICAL PERSPECTIVES

Are political rights specifically mentioned in the NASW Code of Ethics *(NASW, 2018)?*

Political Rights

The Universal Declaration of Human Rights (United Nations, 1948) also recognizes specific rights related to government. Most important is the right to take part in government, either directly or through freely chosen representatives that have been selected by secret vote where every adult has a vote. People have the right to join a group and to have meetings, and they should not be forced to join any group.

Environmental Rights

The declaration says that people are entitled to shelter, and it can be assumed that safe shelter is expected. In addition, the declaration requires safe working conditions. Since the declaration was written, though, people have become aware of the importance of the physical environment to well-being. The Council on Social Work Education (CSWE; 2015) suggests that environmental rights means when all people equally experience environmental protection and the decision-making process related to it. Most importantly, environmental justice suggests that no one should be "affected by a disproportionate impact from environmental hazards," and all should be free from ecological destruction. Finally, people should responsibly use ecological resources, including the land, water, air, and food (p. 20).

Economic Rights

Achieving social justice cannot happen where access to resources is not equitable. The declaration states that people have rights to be free from "want" (CSWE, 2015, p. 1). Economic rights include the right to a standard of living adequate for health and well-being, including food, clothing, housing, medical care, and necessary social services. They have rights specific to work, such as the right to do the following:

- Work and have free choice of employment
- Have fair and favorable working conditions with equal pay for equal work
- Have protection against unemployment and security when facing sickness, disability, widowhood, old age, or other inability to work
- Have fair wages that allow for human dignity
- Have social protection when wages do not allow for human dignity
- Form and join trade unions
- Own property
- Have rest and leisure time through limits to hours worked and periodic, paid holidays

Social Rights

According to the declaration, everyone has the right to freedom of opinion and expression. People should be allowed to think and form opinions. They should be able to share ideas with anyone anywhere. Everyone has a right to freedom of religion and its observance. Specific rights are set aside for family and marriage. People have a right to marry and to found a family, to have equal rights as a couple, and to have the right to divorce. Marriage should happen only when both spouses give full consent. The family is considered to be a fundamental group in society. It is entitled to protection. Slavery and the slave trade should be forbidden.

Cultural Rights

People have a right to participate in the culture of their communities. Everyone has the right to free (required) education in elementary stages. Technical and professional education should be available, and higher education should be accessible to all, based on merit. People should be taught to have respect for human rights and to value tolerance and friendship among nations and racial and religious groups. Education should teach people to work for peace. On the other hand, parents have the right to choose the kind of education their children receive. Finally, everyone has the right to participate freely in the cultural life of the community, to enjoy the arts, and to share in scientific advancement and its benefits.

Finally, the declaration says that people should pay attention to the duties they should carry out to maintain their own rights in their communities. If you think in terms of systems, you may wonder why civil rights are all stated about individuals. People exercise or are denied civil rights as they are part of families, groups, organizations, and communities. In fact, everyone finds their civil rights in their communities.

For Brianna, it was easy to value these human rights, but it was clear that the people living in the neighborhood of the school were being deprived of their human rights. It truly was overwhelming. What could a social worker do about poverty, unemployment, unsafe housing, gang violence, mass incarceration, and substance abuse? How could a social worker work toward social justice in people's communities? Just like the situation many social workers face, it would have been easy for Brianna to walk away. She could easily adopt the attitude of all of the other professionals in the school: Nothing can be done about the community.

Place and Nonplace Communities

One way to keep from feeling overwhelmed is partialize, or think of the community in manageable bits. On one hand, community work might be called the ultimate challenge in social work. It is a culmination of individual, group, and organizational skills (Hardina, 2013). However, we tend to think only of neighborhoods as communities. For these reasons, social workers often think communities are beyond their everyday, generalist social work abilities. Certainly there are social workers who specialize in community work, but the generalist practitioner can (and should) participate as well. To begin to consider how you might participate in community change, think about this: Communities aren't necessarily neighborhoods, towns, or cities. They aren't necessarily coalitions, or collaborating groups, of agencies and organizations. Instead, a community can be a "place or a non-place" (Hardcastle, 2011, p. 97). In **place communities**, we rely on location to define a group, such as the parents of children who all go to the same school, but in **nonplace communities**, we rely on a simpler definition: Nonplace communities can be groups of people who think alike in some way. They are connected by social bonds: identity, profession, religion, ideology, or common interests. A community is composed of people who feel a "we-ness" (Hardcastle, 2011, p. 97). For example, a church group can be a community even though members may not live near the church itself. A volleyball team can be a community. A cohort of students who do group work together and have classes in common can be a community. The generalist social work practitioner will identify communities that are important to their individual and group clients by getting to know those clients and looking for ways their systems intersect. The ecomap allows workers to consider these communities in assessment and planning through the circle marked "Individuals, families, and groups."

By considering the communities where our individual, family, group, and organizational clients belong, we may be able to see that many agencies are dealing with the same problems over and over again. In those situations, we are looking across the commonalities of all of our cases. In other words, we are finding the larger community issue that affects all of our cases. At that point, we can identify aspects of the larger systems that are not fair to our clients. We have a cause. One way to work toward social justice is to have a "case-to-cause" mentality (Abramovitz & Sherraden, 2013, p. 4). That means our focus may have begun on individuals or small groups, but when we recognize that they have challenges in common we begin to see the problem as a cause. For instance, a social worker who works with individual children may say this: "Preventing child abuse is my cause." Working with clients to further a cause is the best route. Community change should be carried out by community members (Stoeffler, 2018).

Caiaimage/Paul Bradbury/Getty Images

Community-based social work can be used to further social justice.

Social Justice and Society's Grand Challenges

Social work's commitment to social justice is embodied in the book *Grand Challenges for Social Work and Society* (Fong, Lubben, & Barth, 2018). The Grand Challenges initiative is a campaign developed by social work thinkers to move everyone toward thinking about our deepest problems and finding new solutions. The Grand Challenges initiative is designed to "promote scientific innovation in social work; engage the social work profession in strengthening the ties among social work organizations; foster transdisciplinary research; expand the student pipeline into the social work profession; and create greater acknowledgment of social work science within the discipline and by other, related, disciplines" (Fong et al., 2018, p. 1).

There are 12 Grand Challenges that confirm social work's commitment to social justice:

1. Ensure healthy development for all youth.
2. Close the health gap.
3. Stop family violence.
4. Advance long and productive lives.
5. Eradicate social isolation.
6. End homelessness.
7. Create social responses to a changing environment.
8. Harness technology for social good.
9. Promote smart decarceration.
10. Reduce extreme economic inequality.
11. Build financial capability for all.
12. Achieve equal opportunity and justice.

The elaboration of these 12 goals represents social work's commitment to justice. In addition, it reflects the importance of social work among disciplines in the common goal of working toward justice for all across the globe (Fong et al., 2018).

CRITICAL THINKING AND COLLABORATIVE LEARNING EXERCISES 14.1

1. In a small group, discuss ways that your human rights might be violated or threatened. If you assume they are not because you live in a democracy, look at each of the human rights and think again.
2. In a large group, think about the communities you all share. It's obvious that you share the class as a group, and some of you may belong to the same clubs. Look beyond those communities, and identify those in which you're a member and those that you share with classmates. What might be a common cause for all of you?
3. Work with a partner to come up with a definition of social justice in your own words. Be sure to include civil, political, environmental, economic, social, and cultural elements in your definition.

Section 14.2: Planned Change in Communities

This section continues the discussion on communities with a focus on the challenge of applying the planned change process to macro level practice.

Planned Change in Communities

Remember that systems seek homeostasis, and communities are no different (Carter, 2011). However, change in communities is part of the macro level of practice in multisystem practice (MSP). It is possible to change communities. You are very familiar with the method. It is the generalist social worker's planned change process. As in organizations, there are many theories and methods of community change. Multisystem generalist practice provides a basic foundation with the planned change process as its method. Community change has an additional challenge though. It is not simple to translate the planned change process into macro level change. As we've seen, macro practice has pulled away from micro and mezzo practices (Abramovitz & Sherraden, 2013). Many social workers find community practice to be a distinct type of social work. With the MSP method, macro practice, whether with organizations or communities, is just another part of generalist social work practice. When all levels of systems are assessed, any system can be a target for change. For that reason, all levels of practice are considered in every case.

Self-Reflection

Why think about your own feelings when you work with communities? Other than what may be your apprehension about community work in general, you should think about a community as capable of affecting your life and the lives of your clients in significant ways. That's why you are seeking change. For example, it's likely that you feel strongly about the dignity and worth of the person. As we've seen, those strong feelings will create and feed off of beliefs that may or may not be rational. As part of self-reflection you've got to think critically about your feelings related to the community you are targeting for change. For Brianna, the issue was one of dignity and worth for the students. She valued dignity and worth, and helping people to achieve dignity was part of her passion for community work. Brianna believed that people living in poverty lacked dignity due to their troubled neighborhood, and she was glad to be able to carry out that aspect of generalist social work. When she looked at the needles and condoms that littered the sides of the playground, she got really angry. It wasn't fair that the kids should be exposed to that. It didn't make sense that she should be angry with the parents, but somehow she was. Why didn't they do something? Her anger was also directed toward the other professionals in the school. In fact, she almost allowed her anger to affect her relationships with them. When she practiced mindfulness exercises and took a look at her feelings, she realized she needed to do some critical thinking. She recognized that she needed to get to know the parents. She had to allow them to be the experts about their own lives so she could understand them better. That way, she could begin to develop empathy and would be less likely to judge them. Likewise, the professionals were all caring people. She became objective and realized that the professionals felt helpless, but they really cared about the students. The sincere concern of the other professionals could be considered a strength of the school. She might be able to use that resource. Once she thought about it that way, she could move on with calm resolve.

Engagement

Caiaimage/Sam Edwards/Getty Images

Social workers use the planned change process on the macro level of practice.

When you work with communities, you have the same engagement experience as in work with organizations: You can find client system representatives everywhere. You never know who your client system representative may be. They may be an elected official or any community member. As always, you begin with your individual skills of engagement. Some of the basic skills that are especially important in work with communities are offering service, stating the obvious, and partializing challenges. Remember to display warmth, empathy, and genuineness (WEG), even when you have serious disagreements with client system representatives. Instead of jumping right in, use the preparatory empathy process we discussed in Chapter 5. Remember the importance of networking in organizational work. It is the same here. Always be prepared to develop relationships with others. You should not leave an interaction with a professional without exchanging business cards. It also makes sense to share your business card with interested people who are not human service professionals. Brianna was surrounded by people who were not human service professionals. Her relationships with them were important, and her relationship with her principal was particularly so.

Assessment

As with any level of practice, you need to carry out multisystem assessment work with a community. An important thing to think about in the assessment of a community is to be clear about who is included in the community and why. When you come to the systems called "Individuals, families, and groups," you will think about your client system representatives and all of the individuals you know well within the community as well as your agency. Think about what they have in common. This will allow you to clearly identify your cause. As always, use an ecomap that includes the lines of connection and tension so you can identify which systems to target for change. You may have to target individuals or groups to accomplish your community change, so make sure the ecomap is complete. In this case, the community consisted of the parents, the students, the staff of the school, the neighborhood location of the school, and the school board. When considering individuals and groups, Brianna began with a **focus group**, one method for assessing communities that allows participants to become involved in the change effort right away (Meenaghan, Gibbons, & McNutt, 2005). She thought about the parent organization and the roles the individuals were playing. Within the group that was assembled, Maria was easy to spot as the intrinsic leader.

Bob was acting in the role of blocker, but Brianna hoped to convert him to the roles of opinion seeker and information giver. He had already begun to help with the assessment by observing a school board meeting. This was the use of **expert presentation and testimony** for assessment (Ilvento, Garkovich, Hansen, Hustedde, & Maurer, n.d.). In the focus group that was rapidly becoming a task group, Josie was an encourager, and there were more than a few contributors, including Sarah, that could be relied on.

Another individual to be assessed was the principal. Brianna also planned this **key informant interview**, where individuals who have knowledge of situations are asked questions about the needs and challenges of the community (Ilvento et al., n.d.).

In addition, she used the key informant interview method of assessment by interviewing all of the teachers about the benefits of the playground. She learned from her client representative group that they interacted very little with the principal except for when their kids were in trouble. Brianna suspected that ethnic and cultural differences were part of the problem. She made a note of it and planned to interview the principal.

When Brianna considered the justice system, she realized that there were a lot of illegal activities affecting the school—substance abuse and gang violence to name just two. She was sure of this because she used the **secondary data** method of assessment, where sources like the census could be employed (Ilvento et al., n.d.). Brianna recognized that there wasn't a strong connection between the school and the police. She decided the potential to get the police involved was probably a strength she could use later.

There was also a weak link between the community and the school board. Community members knew little about the board and, except for Bob, had no experience attending meetings. The connection between the school and the school board was fraught with tension. Inadequate funding left the school short of staff and space. If there had been funds, janitorial staff could have expanded their hours to include cleaning up the playground.

The possible loss of the playground was a major problem for the school. Currently, though, there was tension between the physical environment and health care. The litter simply wasn't healthy. Brianna worked with the principal, as a key informant, and discovered that the health care plans for teachers had been cut. A conversation with Maria, her intrinsic leader, told her that many of the families were covered by Medicaid. Her client representative group, the parent organization, let her know that finding available health care was a problem. There wasn't a doctor anywhere in the neighborhood. Brianna filed that away to consider later.

Another area of tension was the institution of education. Federal taxes paid only a small portion of the school's budget. Much of the rest relied on local property taxes. With property values being so low in the neighborhood, the school board had few funds to meet the school's costs. Brianna wondered if any educators in her state were working to change that. She made a note to get that type of expert testimony. Immediately she thought of the statistics available through secondary data analysis that showed the United States falling behind other countries in student performance. That information could be useful later.

Social welfare policies were a support to the school, with families benefiting from income support, health care, and help with food expenses.

Spirituality was also a bonus. Most of the families attended the same Catholic Church that catered to Hispanic and financially challenged people of the neighborhood. See Figure 14.1.

Planning

The planned change process follows the same process in work with communities as it does on any other level. You work with one or more (probably more) client system representatives to make a doable plan that reflects the strengths, resources, and challenges of the community. In work with communities, you may have a **client representative group.**

Creating Goals: Identifying System Interactions

The ecomap and the MSP assessment clarified areas for planning and implementation. Brianna looked for positive connections as well as systems in tension and systems with tenuous connections.

FIGURE 14.1 • Community-Based Ecomap

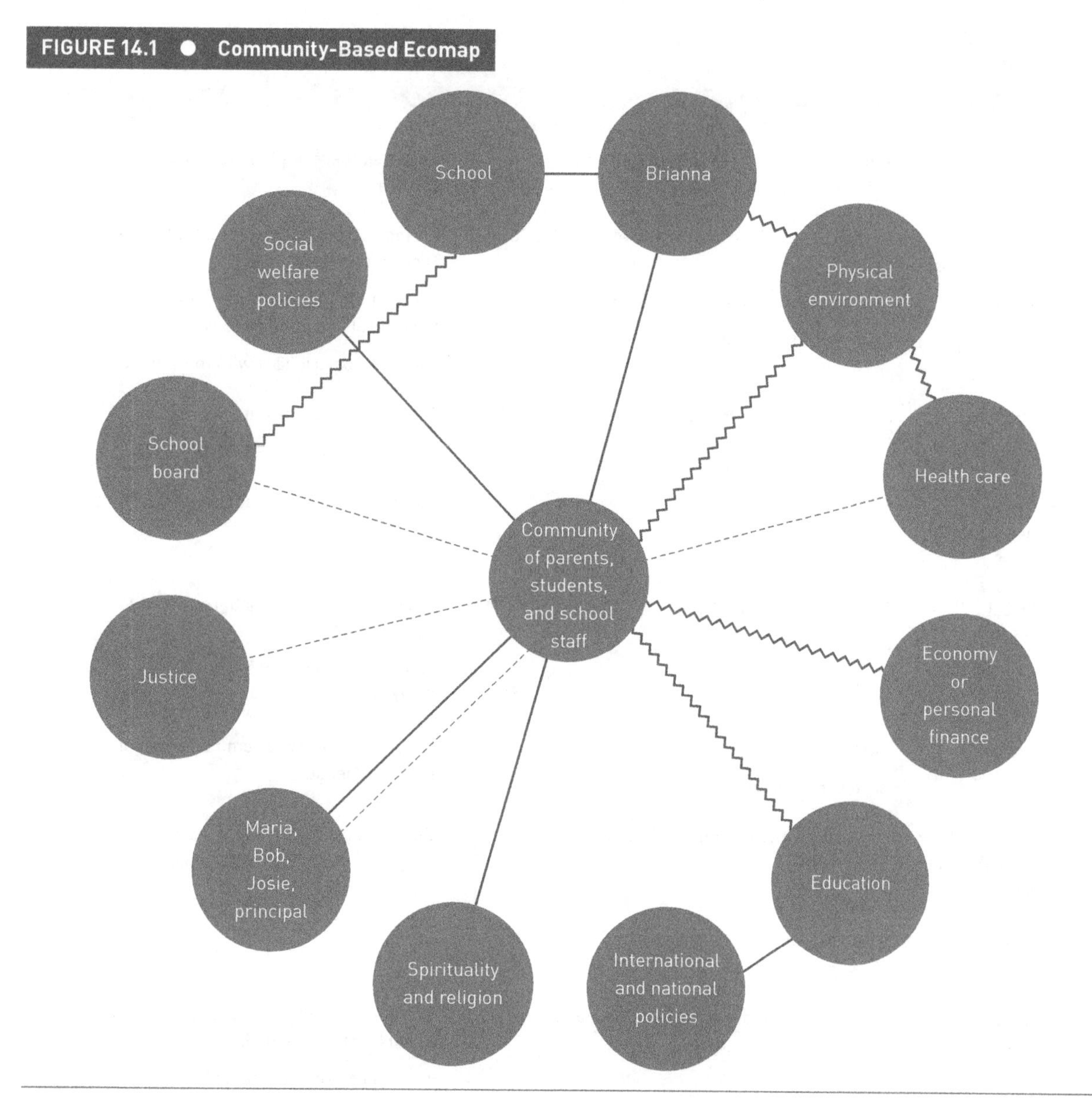

MULTISYSTEM PRACTICE: ASSESSMENT

Systems	Strengths and Diversity	Challenges
Social worker	Has conducted self-reflection; carried out "I feel, I believe, I know, I do" process with open mind Values dignity and worth of the person, especially for those who are financially challenged Recognizes that she feels the playground project represents her worth as a school social worker and works to minimize any negative impact of that	The social worker must not allow strong value of courage to create feelings that are so strong they affect the work in a negative way. The social worker must not be emotionally tied to the change outcome.

(Continued)

(Continued)

Systems	Strengths and Diversity	Challenges
Agency	School staff members are sincerely caring.	Staff members are hopeless about change.
Client system representative(s): Principal Parent group	Biological, psychological, cultural aspects: Power, privilege, identity Used to power; expects to have his way Committed to change	Biological, psychological, cultural aspects: Discriminations Has trouble relating to parents due in part to cultural and ethnic differences Negative experiences with the school
Health care	Medicaid available to most families	Teachers' coverage cut No local health care available
Economy or personal finance		Low property values leads to fewer local tax dollars.
Physical environment	Playground is currently in place and beneficial to students.	Playground litter is dangerous to students' health. The playground is scheduled to be destroyed.
Education	Public funding School is available and required.	Federal taxes pay too small a share of school expenses.
National and international policies	Provide positive examples of public education.	Comparisons reveal the United States lagging in student performance.
Spirituality and religion	Parents have church in common.	
Justice	Police are available in the neighborhood.	The police relationship with the school could be strengthened. The police presence could be improved.
Individual, family, community, and peers	Maria—leader; Josie—encourager; Close knit community of parents	Poverty, violence, drug dealing, etc.
Government: School board	The meetings are public.	Parents need to learn to attend board meetings productively. Funding is inadequate based on school board decisions.
Social welfare policies	Medicaid is available.	

Systems Interacting

System Group	System 1	System 2	System 3	System 4
1	Community	School		
2	School board	School		
3	Justice	School		
4	Physical environment	Health care	School	Brianna
5	Economy	School		
6	Health care	Community		
7	Principal	Community		

Overall, the physical environment was the most compelling. The goals would relate to that.

Creating Goals: Recognizing Strengths and Challenges

Brianna's client system representative group was the parent organization. She worked with them to develop goals for planned change.

To begin to establish goals, Brianna and the group considered the types of interactions and relevant resources and challenges. Brianna used the skills of group eye contact, reflective listening, and use of the present. She facilitated decision-making in a way we have discussed, through consensus building. She framed the topic one week, encouraged free-flowing discussion, and brought proposals the next. She and the group identified the strengths in the school. They found there were strengths and challenges within each system group:

Brianna and the group created this table:

System Group	Systems	Strength	Challenge
1	Physical environment, School, Brianna, Health care	Staff care about school; playground already exists and is a support for students; part of Brianna's job is to help parents; Brianna is passionate about change	Litter is unacceptable; health of students at risk Playground at risk

Creating Goals: Building on Strengths

Taken together, the strengths of the system interactions could be used to respond to the challenges. Brianna and the group created the following responses to the challenges facing the school:

Goals

First, remember that goals need to be concrete. They are specific statements, and they describe the situation that is ideal. Goals represent what the client and worker want to achieve. Implementation happens in the context of goals. You can measure a goal to see whether it has been met. A goal is a statement about how the worker and client will know whether the implementation has been successful.

The ideal is for the client system representative to identify and develop goals with the worker. In community work, this will result in **community-driven goals.** But the worker is controlling the change process and may recognize goals that they think should be addressed. These goals are **worker-driven goals.** In this case, the community-driven goal was to save the playground. Brianna's worker-driven goal was to clean up the litter.

Using the table they created, Brianna and the parents created the following goals:

1. Keep playground
2. Clean litter

Objectives

Each goal has at least one objective because objectives are the concrete, measurable tasks that need to be carried out to accomplish a goal. Brianna and the parent group identified the following tasks that were necessary to carry out the main community goal.

Goal	Objectives
Keep playground	Circulate petition Present petition at school board meeting
Clean litter	Organize Cleanup Day Create sustainable plan for the future

Next, Brianna and the group specified expectations. As you know, in this stage of planned change it is important to identify "who will do what by when."

Goal	Objectives	Who	What	When
Save Playground	Circulate a petition	Josie and Brianna	Create petition	In 1 week
	Identify school board meeting scheduler	Brianna and the administrative assistant at school	Circulate petition electronically and on paper to parents and tabulate results Talk to secretary at school district administration building	In 2 weeks
	Get on school board meeting agenda	Maria	Follow-up with Maria's contact and get permission to present at meeting	Immediately
	Organize staff members to join the parent group at Cleanup Day and at the school board meeting	Maria, Bob, and Brianna	Discuss with individuals; distribute handouts	Immediately
	Present to school board	Brianna, group, any willing staff members	Present support for playground, including petition and teachers' testimony Show photos of clean area	In 2 weeks In 2 months

Goal	Objectives	Who	What	When
Clean Litter	Organize Cleanup Day	Parent group	Select a day;	Immediately
		Josie	get bags, florescent orange vests, and rubber gloves from city public works	
		Parent group	advertise by word of mouth and electronically	In 3 weeks
	Carry out Cleanup Day	Parent group, interested staff, Brianna	Show up on time; take before and after photos	In 1 month
	Create a sustainable plan for ongoing cleanup	Parent group	Meet and discuss	In 3 months

Implementation

Brianna and Maria began implementation of the plan. Their first objective was to circulate a petition. Since last meeting, Josie and Brianna were going to create a petition. Maria was going to identify a person to contact about getting on the school board agenda, and she and Bob were going to get on the board schedule. In addition, they were going to choose a day for Cleanup Day, and Josie was going to get rubber gloves and trash bags. As organizational change agent, Brianna initiated the group conversation about what was happening with task completion. Brianna began each conversation with an opening statement that went something like this:

Brianna: Thanks for being here again, everyone. I see you made it all the way up the three flights of stairs. *(use of humor; engagement)* Seriously, is there any crisis going on that I'm not aware of? *(beginning implementation by determining whether there is a crisis)* You all know that I'm here because I'm the school social worker, and the school is here to help the kids learn. *(agency mission)* We know the playground is good for the kids, so I'm hoping to help you parents to achieve your goal of saving it. *(role)* We have an hour and a half today *(length of the meeting)*, and I think we need to start by seeing where we are with our tasks. *(task assessment)*

The opening statement helped the group to remember why they were there. Their long-term goal might otherwise be lost in the details of working out each objective. Brianna was also reminding them that she was the leader of the group and assuring them that it would be a focused meeting.

Task Assessment

As they compared notes about task completion and Brianna made a task assessment, it became clear that they had some success, but they were also facing challenges. Maria had already made a contact at the school administration office, but she and Bob had not been able to arrange an appointment since the board secretary was on vacation. That changed the "when" on the "Who Will Do What By When" chart. Josie and Brianna had created a petition, but it wasn't complete since the principal had to approve it. Again, the "when" would be changed. Josie did not get the rubber gloves and trash bags since she was busy with the petition. Finally, they needed to choose a day and time for cleanup.

Brianna: Josie, were you able to make arrangements for the gloves, bags, and vests?

Josie: No, I wasn't.

Brianna: I think I know why. You were working with me on the petition and didn't have time, right?

Josie: That's the story.

Brianna considered how to respond. She was thinking about the different kinds of yeses and nos that can appear in a task assessment:

- Yes, they have carried out their tasks successfully.
- Yes, they've carried out part of their tasks.
- No, they didn't feel like it (or didn't have time, or forgot, or almost any other reason).
- No, they tried but it didn't work.
- No, there was a very real reason that was out of their control.

Josie's answer fell in the "No, they tried but it didn't work" category.

A "No, they tried but it didn't work" from Josie calls for reassessment.

"No, they tried but it didn't work." *Identify strengths and challenges.*

Josie's challenge was time. On the other hand, she had proven to be very reliable. As leader, Brianna had to decide what to do next. She knew the petition might need revision, so Josie would again be pressed for time. She decided to get Josie some help on the trash bag task. She changed the task by asking another group member, Rhonda, to take it on. Rhonda had been a group follower, but Brianna hoped she would become a group facilitator.

Looking over the "Who Will Do What By When" chart, there was another objective that required immediate attention. "Okay," Brianna said, "We need to pick a day for Cleanup Day."

Decision-Making

Brianna had a small group that seemed to expect to share in decision-making, so she chose the consensus-building type of decision-making. To carry out the time-saving version of consensus building, she began by framing the topic and encouraging group discussion.

Brianna said, "Let's take the next 15 minutes to talk about the date of our Cleanup Day. We need to choose what day of the week, what time, and what day of the month. We'll discuss each of these by getting everyone's ideas on the table. Once we've had the discussion, I'll take your ideas and over the next week I'll come up with a proposal. You can vote on the proposal at the next meeting."

Eventually, the parents completed the consensus process and chose a date for Cleanup Day. On that day, other parents and school staff members, including teachers and the principal, came out in force. They were all happy to stop feeling hopeless and helpless. In addition, they responded enthusiastically to the petition. When the school board met, the meeting was an impressive display of parents talking about their children and their efforts to clean the playground and the teachers reporting that they felt the playground helped with behavior problems. The principal came out in support of all of them. In the end, every one of the group's objectives was met. The school board decided to keep the playground intact and sell another piece of school district property instead.

Evaluation, Termination, and Follow-Up

It was time for celebration. The group planned to meet again at the usual time and place. They decided to have a potluck meal to celebrate. Brianna asked if she could invite the school staff and parents who joined in Cleanup Day. In addition to the celebration, Brianna drew up a specific agenda for the meeting. It related to evaluation of the project. The agenda included reviewing their original goals and objectives. They involved the group in answering questions about whether the goals and objectives have been met. They also considered process evaluation. They wanted to know what worked well so they could do it in the future. They considered whether they would want to do things exactly the same way even though the effort was successful. Finally, and most specifically, they needed to discuss how they were going to make their litter control project ongoing, or sustainable.

The group decided to continue to meet as they had been doing before the playground project began. They made a new goal to keep Cleanup Day going. Brianna helped with objectives and encouraged Maria, Bob, and Josie to continue in their roles of leader, information seeker, and group contributor. They planned to recruit more members to their group and continue their planned change process. Brianna encouraged that idea since she knew that more members meant more potential leaders for the future (Pyles, 2009).

Brianna made a note in her mind to follow up with the group after a month to be sure all was going as planned. If she found that Cleanup Day was a regular part of the school week, she would know that the process had been a success.

CRITICAL THINKING AND COLLABORATIVE LEARNING EXERCISES 14.2

If you live with others, get together with those people. With the goal of "Clean the house/apartment," develop a "Who Will Do What By When" chart and try to carry it out. Conduct a task assessment, and bring the evaluation of your project to class. Discuss how you would do it differently if you had to do it over. Consider whether you and your roommates might want to continue achieving the goal in the same way in the future. Share with the class.

Section 14.3: The Social Work Role of Community Change Agent

This section is about the social work role of **community change agent**. We consider the role and the skills that allow us to carry it out.

The Social Work Role of Community Change Agent

As we've said, communities can be connections of place and nonplace. As you consider the ecomap of any case, you will come across communities that may become your target systems. In other words, since communities exist in the interaction of individuals and the environment, they are always of interest to the social worker. In systems terms, communities are their own systems. They exchange energy in balanced ways that result in synergy, or they become depleted and enter into the downward spiral of entropy. Given this, it's easy to see that communities have needs. These include the physical and mental health of community members, a functional economy, and effective policy-making (Homan, 2004).

Where communities exist in ongoing need, change is necessary. Community change can be thought of as developing different attitudes and better policies and practices, reducing problems, improving the way needs are met, and developing strengths within the community (Homan, 2004). Like most change, the best route is for members to be enabled to make their own changes. Enter the community change agent. The community change agent has three basic purposes: (1) to identify problems, (2) to organize people to solve the problems, and (3) to help focus and evaluate the change efforts. As in all social work, the worker is responsible to make sure the planned change process is carried out. Remember that the worker is not responsible for carrying out all of the tasks. Change has to be owned by clients and client system representatives. Community participation in activities like community organizing is by its nature empowering (Speer, Peterson, Zippay, & Christens, 2011).

Important note: Social workers have sanction to do their jobs because someone, perhaps representative government, is paying their agency to carry out its mission. Social workers do not engage in professional actions that are outside the agency's purpose. For that reason, any professional organizing you might do (with the exception of some changes within your own agency) must be done with your supervisor's knowledge and consent. Besides, you want to be paid for the professional actions you carry out. Of course you may serve as a community change agent on your own time as a private citizen. In those cases, you need to make sure that everyone involved understands that you are acting on your own, not as a representative of your agency.

Skills for Community Change Agents

Keep in mind that community practice builds on many of the skills used in generalist social work (Hardina, 2013). You will need the skills you use in work with individuals, groups, and organizations. The skills that are most specific to social work in communities are below.

Since the community change agent is a role that addresses the needs of large as well as small groups, it requires some specific skills:

- Assessing or researching community needs
- Organizing
- Coalition building
- Promoting programs
- Identifying intrinsic leaders

SELF-REFLECTION 14: THE ASSERTION SELF-STATEMENT TEST–REVISED

Macro level practice involves offering services and persuasion. This requires assertiveness, and for many people that means they have to display an absent attribute. As we've seen, developing the ability to display absent attributes includes self-reflection, particularly by engaging in critical thinking about workers' feelings related to assertiveness. Take the Assertion Self-Statement Test–Revised on pages 433–435, and figure out how you talk to yourself about your own assertiveness. Is there anything you have to change about the way you think in order to be an effective community change agent?

Community Needs Assessment or Research

As we've seen, there are a number of assessment methods that are specific to communities. These include running focus groups, analyzing secondary data sources like the census, interviewing key informants, and getting expert presentation and testimony. While community level assessment is important in every case, these specific methods are necessary when the focus for change is the community.

Organizing

Organizing requires imagination. Someone who will organize is the first to recognize that all is not well. It is the community change agent using their organizing skills who envisions different circumstances in the future. For this reason, the organizer often has to use their skills of persuasion to help community members to get out of their old patterns of thinking and doing. In a way, the organizer is reminding people that they are unhappy. A community can get used to unhappiness that grows over time as they slowly come to accept it. Community change requires a tension between how things are and an attraction to what they might become, so organizers may actually try to get people irritated (Fisher, 2001; Homan, 2004). You will go to members of the community, and you will share your vision. Point out that things are not as they could or should be. You'll need your individual skills. Begin with someone you recognize as an intrinsic leader, and recruit them to identify community members and to help with the organizing effort. Even in the beginning stages, you'll be modeling the skill of organizing so that the intrinsic leader will adopt those skills in the future. Then, your most important task will be to find a way for all of the community members to communicate with you and with each other (Fisher, 2001). You may have physical meetings that are held at an accessible location, or you may use telephone calls, conference calls, or texting, Listservs, and social networking sites (McKnight & Plummer, 2015).

Coalition Building

There may be times when you recognize that more than one community (place or nonplace) is facing the same challenges. For example, you work with homeless people in a city where there are many services addressing their needs. Everyone has a mission to help the homeless, but neither knows what the other is doing. Each food bank within walking distance may be trying to provide a range of foods when they might be better off becoming the go-to place for specific foods, like fruit or bread. Shelters across the city may have space for men and for women but no place for families. One shelter may offer case management services while the others do not. On top of it all, there is probably no one who knows what kind of services the people who are homeless feel will help them most. Part of the problem is that many of these agencies are forced into situations where they are competing against each other for funds. For that reason, they are not likely to interact. One individual, though, can pull them all together: the change agent using the skill of coalition building. This skill is similar to the skill of organizing, it is just done on the agency and community level. Target systems are not individuals but communities and organizations. Again, you need to be able to imagine a better system and you need to use your persuasion skills to convince system representatives that a better way is possible. You'll also use your networking skills, reaching out to people you know and seeking introductions to people you don't know. For example, if you contact the director of one shelter, they may know the name of a highly visible religious leader in the community. That person may direct you to someone who runs a food bank, and so on. As in organizing individuals, your goal is to get the groups communicating. Pagnoni (2014) has identified strategies for getting people involved and helping them to stay involved:

- Assess each potential partner to identify what might motivate them to participate. What will they get out of it? More comprehensive services for clients than they are currently equipped to provide? Potential partners in grant writing and other fund-raising?
- Consider the mission of each of the agencies. Will the collaboration help them to carry out their mission?
- Make sure all of the partners understand what success looks like. All of the groups should agree on what they'd like to see happen.
- Evaluate progress often using data you collect on a regular basis. Let participants know what is working and not working.
- Make opportunities to let others know about the good work the coalition is doing. Find ways to get the good news about the coalition to staff, volunteers, clients, other service providers, local businesses, and the members of the larger community. This will provide positive visibility for all of the coalition members.

Promoting Programs

Community change agents need to get the word out about their efforts. They need supporters, target communities, and the general public to know what is happening (Homan, 2004). In addition, community change often entails events of some kind. Whether it is a press conference, a professional conference, focus group, neighborhood block party, or a coalition meeting, the community change agent has to have skills in promotion. When carrying out the skill of promotion, the worker considers neighborhood groups and asks "What do I want from this group?" and "What do they need to know to respond?" Information can be carried through presentations (usually PowerPoint), brochures, meetings, newsletters, posters, and flyers. For these, you'll need expertise in software that has been designed to facilitate these types of communication. Don't be afraid to try them out—they're meant to be user-friendly. Another method of promotion is to use the media in all of its forms. There is a particular document—the press release—which you can use to get the media interested in covering your program. Keep in mind that word of mouth should always be a consideration. Electronic word of mouth works too. Depending on your target system, you might also use position papers and other serious reports (Homan, 2004). Like many macro level skills, promotion cannot be carried out by a person who acts shy. Notice that *acts* shy is different from *is* shy. You may have to display the absent attribute of assertiveness, but it can be done. Let your passion for your cause carry you through challenging situations.

Identifying Intrinsic Leaders

Two things are true about community change agents: (1) they want the successful community changes to last, and (2) they will not be a part of the community forever. For these reasons, it is critical to identify and cultivate leaders to gradually come to take over your tasks and eventually drive the efforts themselves. You will probably notice that there's a person who has a powerful voice in the group. Probably others already look to them for decision-making. That's one person you want to gradually allow to take over the leadership role. Remember that it is the leader who allocates roles to group members, so you may want to teach them about the roles people play and what you have done to assure that contributing members keep contributing. All of this leads us to think about identifying one person as potential leader, but that would be a mistake.

It is important to cultivate more than one leader, because you are looking for a long term plan to keep your changes in place (Homan, 2004). There are several reasons why your leader may not be able to continue in their role, including an inability to continue contributing so much energy to the project. You need some backups, and it is important to talk to the group about who will continue as leader and who might be recruited as a leader after that.

Skills for Community Change Agents

Skill	Description	Example	Required Worker Characteristic(s)
Community needs assessment or research	Uses methods like running secondary data analysis, running focus groups, interviewing key informants, and gaining expert presentation and testimony	Brianna created a focus group of interested parents and got them involved in the change process by asking them for assessment information.	Assertiveness Critical thinking
Organizing	Identifies problems and identifies and connects community members	Bill saw that people drove far above the speed limit in his clients' neighborhood, so he got the neighbors together to seek solutions.	Imagination Persistence Persuasion
Coalition building	Connects agencies and other groups with common interests	Jeff's clients were homeless and needed many services. He had a hard time identifying the most appropriate agency resources, so he began to connect the various agencies with the intention to create a resource directory.	Imagination Assertiveness Focus
Promoting programs	Gets the word out to constituents about an event	Would you please post this brochure about the upcoming meeting?	Assertiveness Ability to use graphic software
Identifying intrinsic leaders	Helps two or more participants to experience leadership so that changes will be sustainable	Maria, I see you are putting a lot of energy into this effort. Do you think you will be able to continue when I am gone?	Flexibility Patience

Sample Dialogue for Community Change Agents

Brianna: Mrs. Smith, I know as school secretary you are the guardian of the bulletin board. *(use of humor)*

Mrs. Smith: That's right. (*smiling*) Do I need to guard it from you?

Brianna: I think you do. I have a small poster here I'd like to get where everyone can see it. I have spoken to the staff and I've given handouts in the classroom, but I'd like to remind everyone that Cleanup Day is in 2 weeks.

Mrs. Smith: Oh! Cleanup Day. I was going to ask you when that was happening. Sure, I'll put it on the bulletin board.

CRITICAL THINKING AND COLLABORATIVE LEARNING EXERCISES 14.3

Practice the attribute of imagination. In a large group, discuss ways that students are empowered at your college or university. Try visioning an educational experience that empowers students more. Don't try to think about how you might go about achieving those conditions. First, engage in brainstorming. Remember that each person should be allowed to speak and that there will be no judgments on what is being said. Recruit someone to record your responses on a flip chart or blackboard. See whether any group members are interested in continuing the conversation.

Section 14.4: The Social Work Role of Advocate

This section closes the discussion of community practice with a social work role that is required on all levels of practice: the role of advocate.

The Social Work Role of Advocate

Advocacy is not optional for social workers. Our *NASW Code of Ethics* requires it of us. First, Section 1.01 of the code clearly states that "clients' interests are primary" (NASW, 2018, p. 7). In other words, our first responsibility is to clients. Sometimes our efforts at empowerment with individuals are not possible. A client may simply be unable to act on their own behalf. They might be disabled in some way, or they might just be too upset to manage one more thing. In those cases where the social worker has done their best to help the client help themselves, advocacy may be necessary. **Advocacy** is to represent and support a client system or a cause to others (Hardcastle, 2011). Advocating for a client system is known as **case advocacy**, and advocating related to a larger, systemic problem is called **cause advocacy**. When we are advocating, we are acting on behalf of others. We can advocate for an individual with another individual, group, or organization. For example, we might advocate with a landlord, a support group, or an employer. We can advocate for a group with an individual, organization, or community. In that case, advocacy might be with an agency administrator or a local decision-maker. We can advocate for an organization with another organization or with a community. Perhaps we want neighbors to accept a group home in their midst, for example. And we can advocate for a community with any other system. If we translate our case issues to cause issues, we may advocate with government on behalf of any other client system.

As we've mentioned previously, another portion of the *NASW Code of Ethics* (NASW, 2018) is more explicit about macro level advocacy. Standard 6 related to Social Workers' Ethical Responsibilities to the Broader Society presents us with broad areas of responsibility. We are to work on behalf of the general welfare of society, advocate for healthy living conditions, and we should promote "social, economic, political, and cultural values and institutions that are compatible with the realization of social justice" (NASW, 2018, p. 27). We're supposed to help others become advocates, and we're supposed to provide professional services in public emergencies. Finally, we're required to "engage in social and political action that seeks to ensure that all people have equal access to the resources, employment, services, and opportunities they require to meet their basic human needs and to develop fully" (p. 30). We're also required to study the way policies affect practice and to advocate changes where needed to promote social justice. We are required to work to expand choice and opportunity for all, especially disadvantaged groups, and we're responsible to promote respect for cultural and social diversity across the globe. We must promote policies that guard and provide equity and social justice for all people. Finally, we must act to "prevent and eliminate domination of, exploitation of, and discrimination against any group of people" (NASW, 2018, p. 27).

Skills for carrying out the role of advocate include all of the skills used in work with individuals. In addition, the following skills are particularly relevant:

- Direct advocacy
- Legislative advocacy

Skills for the Social Work Role of Advocate

Direct Advocacy

Sometimes people suffer because of circumstances that can be changed. It is the unique call of social workers to respond to these circumstances. People may have to pay high fees to cash checks because there is no bank in the community, they may live in housing that is exposed to environmental toxins, they may be denied services because of changes in eligibility (Hoefer, 2006). In situations like these, direct advocacy may be necessary. **Direct advocacy** is to speak and act on behalf of an individual, family, group, organization, or community. Direct advocacy is necessary when people cannot act or be taught to act on their own behalf. It may also be necessary when an intrinsic leader has not yet been cultivated in a group or when an organization or community needs a spokesperson. Keep in mind that direct advocacy on the part of a worker is done only as a last resort. It is preferable to empower client systems to advocate on their own behalf. First, try to teach the skills of advocacy. If your client system can still not act on their own, then try assisting them. Only when that fails should workers consider advocating for others. Workers need to be confident and to be able to address individuals and groups. A worker who carries out direct advocacy needs to draw on their skills of working with individuals and groups. Often it is necessary to locate a client system representative or group within the target system. In addition, it is always important to collaborate with your client system to plan your advocacy activities. You should not act on behalf of any client system when individuals are not aware you are going to do so. Speak on behalf of others only with their consent.

Legislative Advocacy

When government policies get in the way of clients having their physical and emotional needs met, legislative advocacy is likely to be necessary. Once assessment is complete and goals have been developed, it is important to carefully identify the legislative target system (Hoefer, 2006). Often local governments, like town and borough councils, have a surprising range of influence. Zoning laws that determine where residential facilities can be built, for example, come under the umbrella of a town council. As we've seen, many school-related decisions are made at the district level with the school board. While many social welfare policies are made at the federal level, spending priorities for social work services are most often made at the state level. More and more policy and funding decisions are moving from the federal to the state level, and there is a good chance you can have a powerful impact on decisions made at the state level (Homan, 2004). Once you've identified your target, it is critical that you understand how decisions are made at that level. There may be one individual who decides how a county will spend money on services for those who need substance abuse treatment. State and federal governments operate in similar ways, with a complex process for developing bills and creating laws, policies, and regulations. The best way to learn about these complexities is from your client system representatives. For example, if your state government turns out to be your target system, your local state representative will be your client system representative. That person, or more likely a member of their staff, will shepherd you through the process. Before you get that far, though, it is important to conduct research. Know where the problem you're addressing happens. Consider whether it is the law or policy that is the problem, or whether the problem lies in its implementation (Hardcastle, 2011). When you are knowledgeable about what you want to happen, spend time looking for allies. Conducting legislative advocacy is another potentially intimidating macro practice, but chances are good that you won't need to go it alone. Your client system is just one individual or group that is influenced by policies that affect many people. Look for people who are interested in your concerns. Some of those people may work for agencies that specialize in legislative advocacy for particular groups, and working with them will magnify your efforts. Use your ecomap to identify potential allies, and don't forget that your state NASW chapter will have a legislative agenda on the state level. Perhaps they are already focused on your issue, or they may be willing to consider helping your cause. In short, you need to talk to people to find out what level of government is in charge of decision-making related to your issue, you need to talk to more people to find out how the decision-making works, and you need to cast a broad net as you recruit others to help. Instead of beginning with a focus on who is against you, begin with a focus on who is with you. Legislative advocacy is only intimidating when you think about doing it alone.

Skills for the Social Work Role of Advocate

Skill	Description	Example	Required Worker Characteristic(s)
Direct advocacy	Speaking and acting on behalf of an individual, family, group, organization, or community when they are unable to do so themselves	Can you please tell me who can help me understand your eligibility policies?	Assertiveness Passion Patience
Legislative advocacy	Identifying a cause, learning about where and how decisions are made, recruiting allies to support the effort and provide direction	I wonder if Senator Schwank or someone from her office would be willing to talk to me about the current laws related to predatory lending.	Assertiveness Passion Patience

Sample Advocacy Dialogue

Worker: Mary, it seems like your problem is bigger than the two of us.

Mary: (*sighs*) I guess it is.

Worker: That doesn't mean we give up. I suspect others have the same problem, and I suspect they may already be working on a solution. I think we can find out who they are and what they're already doing. Let's start with getting a clear understanding of the situation. Would you be willing to work with me and make some phone calls?

The Shy Worker: Reflective Responses

When Brianna first thought about the plan to dismantle and sell the playground at the school where she worked, she was surprised and angry. She had to work not to be angry at the parents and the other staff members. After that, she had the energy to move forward with engaging others in a planned change process. She identified who had to be engaged and quickly moved to assessment. At this point, she nearly became stuck. It was easy for Brianna to do the analysis of secondary data related to the school population and crime in the school neighborhood. But she was terrified to even think about other methods of community assessment like developing a focus group, finding an expert to present information, or interviewing a key informant. At first, she casually interviewed the teachers. After that, she just put off the other assessment tasks. Finally, her supervisor called her on her hesitation by asking whether Brianna wanted to save the playground or not. Brianna *felt* scared. When she talked to her supervisor, she realized that she *believed* she just wasn't capable of the necessary tasks. Her supervisor helped her to think critically about her beliefs by asking her to identify occasions in the past where Brianna had overcome her shyness in her life outside of work. After she did so, Brianna recognized that she did have ways to cope with her shyness, and she began to *know* that she did have the capability. It still wasn't easy, but Brianna was able to take the coping skills she already had to get past her shyness, display self-confidence, and carry out the work.

Community level assessment can be intimidating.

CRITICAL THINKING AND COLLABORATIVE LEARNING EXERCISES 14.4

Call the local office of your state senator or representative. Ask to make an appointment with a legislative aid. Take a group of fellow students with you, and ask about the process of getting legislation developed or changed. You will find out there is more to it than you usually read about in books and that interactions with individuals who can help you are critical. Ask about a current project or concern of your legislator and, if you agree with the approach, find out how you can help in the effort. Talking to people and getting close to the decision-making process is the best way to learn it.

Section 14.5: Review and Apply

CONCURRENT CONSIDERATIONS IN GENERALIST PRACTICE

Ethical Decision-Making Challenge

Brianna was stirring up people to act against the wishes of the school board, a group of individuals elected by local voters to act on their behalf. Is there anything in the *NASW Code of Ethics* (NASW, 2018) that suggests it might be unethical to do that?

Human Rights

Is it possible that the students in this case were being denied human rights? Do you think they have the right to a playground? Use the Universal Declaration of Human Rights (United Nations, 1948) to support your answer.

Evidence-Based Practice

Find out if there is any evidence related to successful change efforts in schools.

Policies Impacting Practice

Find out where and when your school board meets. Attend a meeting.

Managing Diversity

Like most of the teachers in the building, Brianna was Caucasian. Do you think the mostly Hispanic parent group members might have trouble trusting her? What might she have to do to be culturally responsive?

Multilevel Practice

Identify examples of Brianna's work on all levels.

Micro: ____________________

Mezzo: ____________________

Macro: ____________________

Dynamic and Interactive Planned Change Stages

Identify aspects of Brianna's work where she worked in the following stages:

Self-Reflection: ____________________

Engagement: ____________________

Assessment: ____________________

Planning: ____________________

Implementation: ____________________

Evaluation: ____________________

Termination and Follow-Up: ____________________

Chapter Summary

Section 14.1: Social Work in Communities

Every social worker is committed to community level change, since the *NASW Code of Ethics* (NASW, 2018) requires attention to the welfare of the broader community. The social worker's concern is social justice, a concept that is often associated with human rights. According to the Universal Declaration of Human Rights as developed by the United Nations (1948) and ratified by the United States, human rights have many components, including civil, political, environmental, economic, social, and cultural rights.

Section 14.2: Planned Change in Communities

Because communities, like all systems, seek homeostasis, they are difficult to change. However, generalist practitioners who practice MSP are required to work with systems of all sizes. Work with communities is manageable when the generalist planned change method is used to guide practice.

Section 14.3: The Social Work Role of Community Change Agent

One social work role in work with communities is that of community change agent. A social worker in that role identifies problems, organizes people, and focuses and evaluates change efforts. Skills used by community change agents include those used in work with individuals and groups as well as organizing, coalition building, promoting programs, identifying intrinsic leaders, and fund-raising.

Section 14.4: The Social Work Role of Advocate

Another social work role required by the *NASW Code of Ethics* (NASW, 2018) is that of the advocate. In advocacy, we represent clients to others. We can carry out advocacy on all system levels, after we have seen that clients are unable to advocate on their own behalf. Skills used by advocates include direct and legislative advocacy. In all cases, it is important that workers collaborate with client systems in the advocacy process.

SELF-REFLECTION 14: ASSERTION SELF-STATEMENT TEST–REVISED

PURPOSE: To measure self-statements in relation to assertiveness.

AUTHORS: Richard G. Heimberg, Emil J. Chiauzzi, Robert E. Becker, and Rita Madrazo-Peterson

DESCRIPTION: The ASST-R is a 24-item instrument designed to assess the role of self-statements in assertive (or nonassertive) behaviors. Self-statements are assumed to have a crucial role in affecting assertiveness and unassertiveness. The ASST-R was devised to teach these self-statements and to assess the relationship to assertiveness. The ASST-R consists of 12 positive and 12 negative self-statements. The ASST-R is viewed as a useful measure for teaching cognitive changes in problems involving nonassertive behavior.

NORMS: The ASST-R was studied with three samples including 12 psychiatric patients of mixed diagnosis randomly selected from a mental health clinic in Albany, New York; 16 adults from the center's nonprofessional staff; and 20 college students.

The means for positive self-statements were as follows:

- Students = 44
- Staff = 39
- Psychiatric patients = 33

The means for negative self-statements were:

- Students = 27
- Staff = 23
- Psychiatric patients = 37

(Continued)

(Continued)

SCORING: Each item is rated for frequency on a 5-point scale, and the individual items are summed for scores on the positive and negative dimensions. Total scores are not used. Positive items = 3, 5, 6, 9, 13, 14–16, 19, 21–23. Negative items = 1, 2, 4, 7, 8, 10–12, 17, 18, 20, 24.

VALIDITY: The ASST-R significantly discriminates between patients and the other two groups for good known-group validity.

PRIMARY REFERENCE:

Heimberg, R. G., Chiauzzi, E. J., Becker, R. E., & Madrazo-Peterson, R. (2013). Cognitive mediation of assertive behavior: An analysis of the self-statement patterns of college students, psychiatric patients, and normal adults. In K. Corcoran & J. Fischer (Eds.), *Measures for clinical practice and research: A sourcebook* (5th ed.). New York, NY: Oxford University Press.

THE ASSERTION SELF-STATEMENT TEST–REVISED

It is obvious that people think a variety of things when they're responding in different situations. These thoughts, along with feelings, determine what kind of responses a person will make.

Below is a list of things that you may have thought to yourself at some time while responding in the assertive situations. Read each item, and decide how frequently you may have been thinking a similar thought during the assertive situations.

Circle a number from 1 to 5 for each item. The scale is interpreted as follows:

1 = *Hardly ever* had the thought

2 = *Rarely* had the thought

3 = *Sometimes* had the thought

4 = *Often* had the thought

5 = *Very often* had the thought

Please answer as honestly as possible.

1. I was thinking that I was too nervous to say what I felt. 1 2 3 4 5
2. I was thinking that the other person would suspect some ulterior motive if I said anything. 1 2 3 4 5
3. I was thinking that the other person should respect an honest expression of feelings. 1 2 3 4 5
4. I was thinking that many people fail to get involved or stand up for themselves in similar situations so there is nothing wrong with my keeping quiet. 1 2 3 4 5
5. I was thinking that I could benefit by expressing myself. 1 2 3 4 5
6. I was thinking that I should act in accord with what I think is right. 1 2 3 4 5
7. I was thinking that if I could avoid this situation I could somehow relieve my discomfort. 1 2 3 4 5
8. I was thinking that it would be selfish of me to let my own feelings be known. 1 2 3 4 5
9. I was thinking that I could express myself in a calm, relaxed way. 1 2 3 4 5
10. I was thinking that I would appear incompetent or inadequate if I tried to take a stand. 1 2 3 4 5

11.	I was thinking that something bad would happen to me if I tried to express myself.	1	2	3	4	5
12.	I was thinking that the other person wouldn't like me if I offered my opinion.	1	2	3	4	5
13.	I was thinking that my opinions and decisions should be respected if they are reasonable.	1	2	3	4	5
14.	I was thinking that since letting my feelings be known was an effective course of action in the past, I should do likewise now.	1	2	3	4	5
15.	I was thinking that I would only be hurting myself by not expressing myself.	1	2	3	4	5
16.	I was thinking that future interactions with the other person might be damaged if I didn't say what I felt now.	1	2	3	4	5
17.	I was thinking that since similar past experiences resulted in failure or ineffectiveness, I shouldn't bother to do anything now.	1	2	3	4	5
18.	I was thinking that I would probably feel guilty later if I refused to do the person a favor.	1	2	3	4	5
19.	I was thinking that there didn't seem to be a good reason why I shouldn't speak my mind.	1	2	3	4	5
20.	I was thinking that I would become embarrassed if I let my feelings be known.	1	2	3	4	5
21.	I was thinking that if I didn't state my opinion now, it might cause problems later on.	1	2	3	4	5
22.	I was thinking that my views are important.	1	2	3	4	5
23.	I was thinking that if I didn't speak up, it would interfere with my plans.	1	2	3	4	5
24.	I was thinking that a friendly person would not impose his/her views in this situation.	1	2	3	4	5

Recommended Websites

Universal Declaration of Human Rights (United Nations, 1948):
http://www.ohchr.org/EN/UDHR/Documents/UDHR_Translations/eng.pdf

Critical Terms for Roles and Skills in Work With Communities

social justice 409
place communities 412
nonplace communities 412
focus group 415
expert presentation and testimony 415
key informant interview 415
secondary data 416
client representative group 416
community-driven goals 420
worker-driven goals 420
community change agent 423
organizing 425
advocacy 428
case advocacy 428
cause advocacy 428
direct advocacy 429

Generalist Practice Curriculum Matrix With 2015 Educational Policy and Accreditation Standards

Chapter 14

Competency	Course	Course Content	Dimensions
Competency 1: Demonstrate Ethical and Professional Behavior		Feature 3: Self-Reflection	Cognitive–affective processes
		Feature 4: Concurrent Considerations in Generalist Practice	Skills Cognitive–affective processes
Competency 2: Engage Diversity and Difference in Practice		Feature 1: Focus on Diversity	Skills Cognitive–affective processes
		Feature 4: Concurrent Considerations in Generalist Practice	Skills Cognitive–affective processes
Competency 3: Advance Human Rights and Social, Economic, and Environmental Justice		Feature 4: Concurrent Considerations in Generalist Practice	Skills Cognitive–affective processes
		14.1. Learn about the nature of social work's commitment to communities. 14.2. Translate the planned change process to work in communities. 14.3. Consider the social work role of community change agent and related skills. 14.4. Examine the social work role of legislative advocate and its related skills.	Knowledge
Competency 4: Engage in Practice-Informed Research and Research-Informed Practice		Feature 4: Concurrent Considerations in Generalist Practice	Skills Cognitive–affective processes
			Knowledge
Competency 5: Engage in Policy Practice		Feature 4: Concurrent Considerations in Generalist Practice 14.1. Learn about the nature of social work's commitment to communities. 14.2. Translate the planned change process to work in communities. 14.3. Consider the social work role of community change agent and related skills. 14.4. Examine the social work role of legislative advocate and its related skills.	Skills Cognitive–affective processes
Competency 6: Engage With Individuals, Families, Groups, Organizations, and Communities		Feature 4: Concurrent Considerations in Generalist Practice	Skills Cognitive–affective processes
		14.2. Translate the planned change process to work in communities.	Knowledge

Competency	Course	Course Content	Dimensions
Competency 7: Assess Individuals, Families, Groups, Organizations, and Communities		Feature 4: Concurrent Considerations in Generalist Practice 14.2. Translate the planned change process to work in communities. 14.3. Consider the social work role of community change agent and related skills. 14.4. Examine the social work role of legislative advocate and its related skills.	Skills Cognitive–affective processes Knowledge
Competency 8: Intervene With Individuals, Families, Groups, Organizations, and Communities		14.2. Translate the planned change process to work in communities. 14.3. Consider the social work role of community change agent and related skills. 14.4. Examine the social work role of legislative advocate and its related skills. Feature 4: Concurrent Considerations in Generalist Practice	Knowledge Cognitive–affective processes
Competency 9: Evaluate Practice With Individuals, Families, Groups, Organizations, and Communities		Feature 4: Concurrent Considerations in Generalist Practice 14.2. Translate the planned change process to work in communities. 14.3. Consider the social work role of community change agent and related skills. 14.4. Examine the social work role of legislative advocate and its related skills.	Skills Cognitive–affective processes Knowledge

References

Abramovitz, M., & Sherraden, M. (2013). Case to cause. In Frameworks for practice: From learning to action for social justice. *Report of the special commission to advance macro practice in social work* (pp. 4–11). Alexandria, VA: Council on Social Work Education.

Carter, I. (2011). *Human behavior in the social environment: A social systems approach* (6th ed.). New Brunswick, NJ: TransAldine.

Council on Social Work Education. (2015). *Educational policy and accreditation standards*. Alexandria, VA: Author. Retrieved from http://www.cswe.org/File.aspx?id=81660

Fisher, R. (2001). Social action community organization: Proliferation, persistence roots, and prospects. In J. Rothman, J. L. Erlisch, & J. E. Tropman (Eds.)., *Strategies of community intervention* (5th ed., pp. 350–360). Itasca, IL: Peacock.

Fong, R., Lubben, J., & Barth, R. P. (Eds.). (2018). *Grand challenges for social work and society*. New York, NY: Oxford University Press.

Gasker, J. A., & Fischer, A. C. (2014). Toward a context specific definition of social justice for social work: In search of overlapping consensus. *Journal of Social Work Values and Ethics*, *11*(1), 42–53.

Hardcastle, D. A. (2011). *Community practice: Theories and skills for social workers* (3rd ed.). New York, NY: Oxford University Press.

Hardina, D. (2013). *Interpersonal social work skills for community practice*. New York, NY: Springer.

Heimberg, R. G., Chiauzzi, E. J., Becker, R. E., & Madrazo-Peterson, R. (2013). Cognitive mediation of assertive behavior: An analysis of the self-statement patterns of college students, psychiatric patients, and normal adults. In K. Corcoran & J. Fischer (Eds.), *Measures for clinical practice and research: A sourcebook* (5th ed.). New York, NY: Oxford University Press.

Hoefer, R. (2006). *Advocacy practice for social justice*. Chicago, IL: Lyceum.

Homan, M. S. (2004). *Promoting community change: Making it happen in the real world* (3rd ed.). Belmont, CA: Brooks/Cole.

Ilvento, T., Garkovich, L., Hansen, G., Hustedde, R., & Maurer, R. (n.d.). Alternative methods of community needs assessment. Retrieved from http://www.ca.uky.edu/snarl/CommunityPubs/AltMethodCommNeedsAssess.pdf

McKnight, J., & Plummer, J. M. (2015). *Strategies of community intervention*. Boston, MA: Pearson.

Meenaghan, T. M., Gibbons, W. E., & McNutt, J. C. (2005). *Generalist practice in larger settings: Knowledge and skill concepts* (2nd ed.). New York, NY: Oxford University Press.

National Association of Social Workers. (2018). *NASW code of ethics*. Washington, DC: NASW Press.

Pagnoni, L. A. (2014). *The non-profit fundraising solution*. New York, NY: AMACOM.

Pyles, L. (2009). *Progressive community organizing: A critical approach for a globalizing world*. New York, NY: Routledge.

Speer, P. W., Peterson, N. A., Zippay, A., & Christens. (2011). Participation in congregation-based organizing. In M. DeGennaro & S. J. Fogel (Eds.), *Using evidence to inform practice for community and organizational change* (pp. 200–217). Chicago, IL: Lyceum.

Stoeffler, S. W. (2018). Community empowerment. In R. A. Cnaan & C. Milofsky (Eds.), *Handbook of community movements and local organizations in the 21st century*. New York, NY: Springer International Publishing.

United Nations. (1948). *The universal declaration of human rights*. New York, NY: Author.

Recommended Readings

Hoefer, R. (2006). *Advocacy practice for social justice*. Chicago, IL: Lyceum.

PART IV

Complementary Competencies

Case Management, Technology, and Documentation

This chapter helps students understand case management as a social work role that is the culmination of the planned change process with micro, mezzo, and macro level client systems. A focus is on a nuanced look at the skill of brokering, interdisciplinary collaboration, and the ethical use of technology in social work. The chapter closes with some notes and examples on the various types of documentation that are central to generalist social work practice.

Learning Objectives

15.1 Consider a case management scenario with an ethical dilemma component.

15.2 Understand how case management intersects with a broad range of social work responsibilities.

15.3 Explore the social work role of broker and the skills associated with it.

15.4 Learn the skills involved in interprofessional collaboration.

15.5 Appraise the ethics of technology in social work.

15.6 Practice ethical documentation.

Case Study: Ethical Considerations in Hospital Case Management

Maria came to the emergency room with injuries she sustained when she was a passenger in a car accident. She was badly shaken, and it looked like her right arm might be broken where it hit the armrest on the car door. In addition to her injuries, she couldn't stop crying, so Jackie, the emergency room social worker, was asked to come in. Jackie stopped for just a moment of self-reflection. She was emotionally exhausted from the crises she had faced that day, and it was the end of her shift. Once she became conscious of her exhaustion, she knew she couldn't just run out of her office the way she normally did. Instead, she sat quietly and did a mindfulness exercise. It cleared her head and left her with a bit more energy. She considered what she knew about the case: Hispanic girl, 16 years old, car accident, crying uncontrollably. As Jackie moved to get out of her chair, it occurred to her that she had dealt with a similar young girl that day. She was the same age, Caucasian, and in with a broken arm. A gang of teenage Hispanic girls, sort of the sister gang to a boys' gang, attacked her, pulled out some hair, and twisted her arm until it broke. She, too, had been crying uncontrollably. When Jackie remembered that case, she knew that she had to pause again. She felt herself being angry at her new client just for being Hispanic and being a teenage girl. She realized that at that moment she believed all Hispanic girls are violent. She knew she needed to think critically about her feelings. Once she considered the Hispanic girls she knew, she realized that she had a great deal of evidence to the contrary. Jackie's son, James, went to a high school with a large Hispanic population. As a Caucasian, James had worked hard to fit in at school. Jackie remembered that two Hispanic girls were the first to invite him to eat lunch at their table. They had all been friends ever since. When she thought about Lissette and Olga, she remembered that some Hispanic people may have similarities, but they had many in-group differences. She recognized this as an important diversity consideration. She discovered that she couldn't make her anger go away, but she could display the absent attribute of empathy without much trouble.

Emergency department social work requires quick decision-making.

When Jackie entered the emergency room, she found Maria sitting on the side of a bed in a curtained area. She was wearing a sling and holding her arm and crying softly. Jackie began her work with engagement. She talked with Maria about the car accident, using a genuinely caring tone, and presented her usual opening statement carefully so that it didn't sound rehearsed. Maria looked up and wiped her face with her free hand. Jackie began her assessment. It had to be brief because Maria would probably be discharged shortly after her X-ray was complete. Jackie ran through the systems quickly in her mind. First, she found out that the police had been on the scene of the accident immediately and had charged the other driver with driving too fast for conditions. She learned that Maria was close to her parents and that they were in the waiting room. They had gotten citizenship when they first came to the United States years before, so they did not face any immigration problems. She learned that Maria's older sister was living at home with her 9-month-old son. She received support with her child care costs through the state Department of Human Services. In addition, once Maria's older sister filed for child support down at the court house, the baby's father had part of his wages sent to Maria's older sister for the baby's care. Overall, the family struggled financially but were sustaining themselves with both Maria's mom and dad working. The $200 insurance co-pay they would face for this emergency room visit would be a hardship. On the other hand, the hospital was situated in the inner city, making it easy for the family to get care. Both parents had high school diplomas. Maria's sister had finished high school too. She was working part-time and taking night classes under a grant for financially challenged adults to become certified nurses' aides. Maria was a solid performer in her high school classes. They lived in a two-bedroom apartment. It was cramped but okay. As a regular family activity, they all attended Catholic Mass on Sundays. As Jackie asked the questions, Maria's tears began to fall again.

Jackie knew she needed to continue with assessment before she did anything else.

Jackie: Can you tell me what the tears are about? *(displaying warmth in tone of voice, displaying genuineness by making eye contact, and displaying empathy about physical pain)*

Maria: No. *(suddenly beginning to cry harder)* Yes. I'm pregnant.

Jackie: Are you saying you are pregnant and you are sad about it? *(reflective listening, labeling feelings)*

Maria: *(Nodding, with her eyes looking at the ground)*

Jackie: Many times young women are sad when they find out. *(normalization)* When did you learn about it? *(assessment)*

Maria: I did one of those home tests. I think it is 6 weeks.

Jackie: Were you assaulted, or do you have a boyfriend? *(assessing for health and legal issues)*

Maria: I have a boyfriend at school. No, I *had* a boyfriend at school.

Jackie: *(Recognizing that where the "justice" circle on the ecomap would appear, she would make a note that as a 16-year-old, Maria was legally old enough to give consent to a sexual relationship.)* Would you like to talk for a minute about your ex-boyfriend?

Section 15.1: Ethics in Case Management

This section discusses some ethical considerations common to case management. It continues the case study above.

Determining Whether an Ethical Dilemma Exists

At that moment, the technician came to take Maria for her X-ray. Jackie knew that she had just a few moments to consider what might be aspects of a discharge plan for Maria. But first she needed to carry out an ethical decision-making process. Her first dilemma was about a pregnancy test. Her discharge plan would be very different if Maria was pregnant than if she wasn't, and Jackie didn't want to rely on a 16-year-old's home test kit. She had studied child development at college and knew that adolescents weren't always able to think clearly about the consequences of their actions. Jackie also knew her social work values, and she knew her ethical standards. Her first thought was that to ask a nurse to conduct a pregnancy test was breaking confidentiality with Maria. She went back to her office to look at her code. Yes, Standard 1.07 was Privacy and Confidentiality. Standard 1.07(a) says this: "Social workers should respect clients' right to privacy . . . Once private information is shared, standards of confidentiality apply (National Association of Social Workers [NASW], 2018). She nearly put the booklet down. Then she looked more carefully at 1.07. The next section, 1.07(b) said that "Social workers may disclose confidential information when appropriate with valid consent from a client . . ." Of course, she just had to get consent from Maria. She was over 16, and the hospital recognized the wishes of a 16-year-old. If Maria said yes, there really wasn't an ethical dilemma after all. She thought that if she could display empathy, Maria would consent to a pregnancy test. Jackie was right. As soon as she got back from getting her X-ray, Maria consented to a test, and Jackie was able to arrange it while they were waiting to have the X-ray read.

Ethical Time Management

While the pregnancy test was being conducted, Jackie quickly walked back to her office. She needed to get down some case notes related to her last patient. As she passed the patient rooms on the same floor as her office, she saw that family members of Mrs. Jackson had come to visit. She needed to grab them while she could. She stuck her head in the room and asked if they were going to be there a few more minutes. Then she went back to her paperwork mission. She wished she could focus on Maria's case, but she had a few minutes, and the reality was that if she didn't immediately tend to some of her patients' needs she wouldn't have time to do it. It was just that simple. The social work value of service included all of her clients. She opened her computer, quickly typed the outstanding case note, and answered the ringing phone. It was the portable oxygen company. They would be able to come to Mr. Schenk's room and get him set up with a home oxygen provider. She'd let him know on her way down to the Jackson family. All the while, Maria was on her mind. Before she made her way back to the emergency room, she stopped for a moment in her office, closed her eyes, and took five slow breaths. She knew she had to guard against compassion fatigue, and she had been keeping up a frantic pace all day. She was used to taking a few minutes to carry out a mindfulness exercise, so she was good at it. It took just five breaths for her to get a second wind. She realized at that point that she hadn't had a drink of water or a visit to the restroom in hours. She knew she had to stop and do both. She didn't feel like she had time, but she made time. She knew she had to take care of herself to be effective. And in about 2 minutes she was on the move again, headed down to the emergency room.

Ethical Decision-Making

Unfortunately for Maria, the pregnancy test was positive. She wasn't surprised to hear it, since she had been convinced she was pregnant from the start, but she was adamant that her parents not be told. At that point, Jackie had to face another potential ethical dilemma. She needed to decide whether or not to tell Maria's parents the news. She used the ethical decision-making process:

Write Down Social Work Values	Write Down Ethical Standards
a. service b. social justice c. dignity and worth of the person d. importance of human relationships e. integrity f. competence	a. clients b. colleagues c. in practice settings d. as professionals e. to the profession f. to the broader society
Assess the situation. Maria, 16, is pregnant. Her parents don't know. Identify relevant people: mom, dad, sister, boyfriend, etc.	Identify relevant social systems: health care (availability) Social welfare policy (abortion laws, adoption policy)
Identity values or standards in conflict. Does an ethical dilemma exist? Y/N Make a commitment to the client, including benefits of prenatal care.	Identify relevant ethical requirements from the *NASW Code of Ethics* (NASW, 2018): confidentiality, self-determination.
Identify a question ("Should I . . .") and at least two possible responses. Question: Tell Maria's parents? a. Tell Maria's parents, and facilitate a productive conversation before Maria is discharged.	b. Don't tell Maria's parents—just leave her with brochures from agencies who facilitate abortion and/or adoption.
List relevant systems, laws, agency policies, and specific ethical duties that support each option. Given what is known about adolescent psychological development, it is reasonable to assume that Maria may not be mature enough to exercise self-determination. Without help from her parents, she may convince herself the problem will go away. In the meantime, she will be neglecting prenatal care, putting the baby at risk.	Telling Maria's parents may limit her self-determination: She may want to terminate the pregnancy, and her practicing Catholic parents may not allow it.

(Continued)

(Continued)

Write Down Social Work Values	Write Down Ethical Standards
In addition, if she does want to terminate the pregnancy, state law determines that she has a limited amount of time to decide. Simply leaving her with brochures may be a way of letting the time run out. Maria may not be considering adoption as an option, and her parents may help her consider that with their priest's intervention. Once Maria's parents are over the shock, they may be willing to support a choice to keep the baby. This may be what Maria wants, and she may not realize it is an option if her parents don't know.	
Seek supervision. Seek information from the code's list of duties, from scientific literature, experts, and peers. Jackie phoned the supervisor on call. She explained the situation, and her supervisor, a self-proclaimed supporter of the pro-life movement, suggested immediately that she tell the parents. The *NASW Code of Ethics* (NASW, 2018) Standard 1.07 (c) says confidentiality can be broken under "compelling professional reasons."	The *NASW Code of Ethics* (NASW, 2018) Standard 1.07 (a) says this: "Once private information is shared, standards of confidentiality apply." The hospital policy supported the wishes of anyone 16 or over.
Determine a course of action. Consider pros and cons of various actions. Take action. Jackie considered whether Maria's father or another strong male figure in the family would disapprove enough to engage in corporal punishment. She wondered if she would be placing Maria at risk if she told her parents. If she told her parents, Maria's option of terminating the pregnancy might be gone.	Not telling Maria's parents could put her child at risk through lack of prenatal care. Was this a "compelling professional reason" to break confidentiality? She may decide she wants to terminate the pregnancy but lose the self-determination due to letting too much time pass. Maria seemed to Jackie to be mature enough to follow a referral for prenatal care. Jackie provided her with brochures about terminating pregnancy and the associated time limit as well as information about adoption and keeping the baby, including Catholic Social Services. She decided there was no "compelling professional reason" to break confidentiality. Jackie did not tell Maria's parents about her pregnancy.
Evaluate and share results. Jackie decided to share the scenario with her supervisor first, then at the next staff meeting to get input for future decisions. She was able to concisely say that she made her decision because she did not see a compelling professional reason to break confidentiality.	

Once the ethical decision-making process was over, Jackie decided not to tell Maria's parents without her permission. When she stripped away all of the emotional aspects of the situation, she thought that the central point was whether the potential lack of prenatal care was a "compelling professional reason" to break confidentiality. She decided it was not. Jackie upheld hospital policy and her interpretation of the *NASW Code of Ethics* (NASW, 2018) against her supervisor's suggestion; she would process that in supervision later.

Instead, she completed her obligations as a case manager: She provided Maria with options for prenatal treatment, for adoption, and for abortion. She carefully assessed Maria's ability to act on her own and decided that she was capable. She stopped short of strongly suggesting to Maria that she consider telling her parents. That was for Maria to decide.

CRITICAL THINKING AND COLLABORATIVE LEARNING EXERCISES 15.1

If you were in Jackie's place, what do you think you would do? How much of your own values and beliefs about terminating pregnancies would influence your decision?

WHAT IF . . . FOCUS ON DIVERSITY

The supervisor on call was perceived by Jackie to be "pro-life." How might Jackie's response to that perception affect her work? Suppose Jackie had 30 years of experience working as a hospital social worker. Do you think her response to the ethical dilemma would be different than if she were a new worker?

What does this tell you about the best way for a new worker to approach the dilemma?

Consider this: How might the situation be different for Jackie if Maria came from a very wealthy family?

Section 15.2: The Social Work Role of Case Manager

In this chapter's case study, Jackie's job title was case manager. This section is about the definition of the social work role of case manager.

Case Management

Case management is a term used to describe a way for social workers to be sure that their individual and family clients are getting the services they need. As a case manager, social workers carry out several tasks (Woodside & McClam, 2018). They do the following:

- *Provide a broad range of services*
- *Refer out*
- *Coordinate providers*
- *Evaluate services*

These complex tasks are required for a number of reasons, including changes in the way services are provided based on funding sources like insurance companies. In addition, groups of vulnerable people who need long-term services have expanded. Some of these groups include aging populations, people with physical and mental disabilities, and young children (Rothman & Sager, 1998). Let's take the case manager's tasks one by one.

Providing a Broad Range of Services

First, the case manager often provides services themselves. As we've seen, the social worker may serve in the roles of educator, counselor, supporter, advocate, family mediator, and family facilitator when they work with individuals and families. This is the practice of the generalist social worker. A case manager may work with a client individually to learn new life skills only to find that their individual progress in planned change requires change in their family system. There may be conflict in the family requiring family mediation. At any point in the planned change process, individual family members may need the social worker to act as counselor or supporter in order to carry out the tasks necessary to goal completion. The individual or family may also need an advocate at any time in the planned change process. As you now know, in multisystem practice (MSP) the worker is constantly assessing the systems in the client's environment to look for systems that are out of balance. The worker must be flexible enough to change roles as clients change needs. Particularly in rural settings where there are few social workers, the worker has to be prepared to respond to a broad range of client needs.

Refer Out

On the other hand, there are times when the worker can't be all things to all people. For example, their agency mission and the role they play within that agency's structure will put a boundary around the services they provide. While a social worker may play a variety of roles at one time or another with all of their cases, the boundaries of their agency's services may keep them focused on just a few. For example, a worker may find that they are allowed to work only 1 hour per week with an individual client and that they are expected to provide individual service during that hour. In that case, they need to **refer out**, or help the client find other needed services in the community. In other cases, funders will only pay for certain services. A mentoring program, for example, may be limited by their grant funding in such a way that they are not allowed to work with family members. Finally, the social worker may not be competent in a specific role with a specific client group. In that case, the *NASW Code of Ethics* requires that they should "accept responsibility or employment only on the basis of existing competence or the intention to acquire the necessary competence" (NASW, 2018). A simple example of this is where the worker assesses the client in their environment and discovers that there is a tension between the client and the health care system. The worker may come to suspect that the client has a need for medication to respond to their mental health concerns. In that case, the worker will have to search for psychiatric services in the community. Sometimes the worker may work for a large agency with a lot of different programs and may be able to find resources within their own agency, and other times they may have to find services in the community. You can easily see that the worker needs to be intimately familiar with the services that are available in different programs in their agencies as well as in their clients' neighborhoods to do a good job at referring out. It's not only that, but referring out requires the social worker to play the complex role of broker, which we'll be discussing in detail in a minute. Once the worker has involved other professionals, other aspects of case management come into play.

Coordinate Providers

In situations where clients are referred to other services, it is the case manager's responsibility to coordinate providers. This means the social worker keeps an eye on what services are being provided to make sure the client is connected to all of the providers they need and that no one is duplicating services. For example, a case manager may be carrying out planned change related to substance abuse and may find out that the client's family counselor is referring the client to an agency out of town that provides substance abuse treatment services. Naturally, this would confuse the client and probably undermine any other services they are receiving. A lot of times the worker manages the coordinating service task by scheduling meetings among providers so that everyone is on the same page in terms of services provided. This type of meeting also helps providers coordinate the goals they are working on with their clients so that one does not contradict another. For example, one worker may have collaborated with a client to develop the goal of getting a driver's license. At the same time, another worker may be helping the client to learn how to use public transportation. In the end, the client probably needs to address both goals, but it will be a much greater benefit if they focus on public transportation immediately and address the driver's license later. When a case manager schedules a meeting to pull together a number of service providers, it is the responsibility of that worker to provide an agenda and facilitate the meeting. How to make an agenda and use it to run an interprofessional (or interdisciplinary) meeting will be discussed below. For now, just know that it is the case manager's responsibility to make the meeting happen. Because coordinating services is such a central role to the case manager, agencies—especially those who provide health care services—often call the case manager a care coordinator rather than a case manager. In one way, this works well because no one can misinterpret the term *case management* for "managing" a client in a condescending way (Woodside & McClam, 2018). On the other hand, a job title like care coordinator is likely to tie the social worker's hands when they are competent to provide a service that is not available in the community and have to settle for coordinating available providers. In addition, care coordinator or care manager implies that a needy client is being cared for rather than seen as a collaborator in the planned change process. For these reasons, *case management* is probably a better term for the activities we're describing here.

Evaluate Services

Once the case manager puts necessary services in place, it is their responsibility to make sure they are working. After a referral is made, the case manager needs to check whether the client followed up with the referral. In addition, the case manager needs to figure out whether the service is beneficial to the client. If not, a different referral may be in order. In any case, the worker needs to know specific details of the services provided by agencies so they become better at linking clients to the provider that meets their needs best. One way the worker can evaluate services is to keep track of client goals using the goal attainment scaling (GAS) process we discussed in Chapter 9.

CRITICAL THINKING AND COLLABORATIVE LEARNING EXERCISES 15.2

Think about how a generalist social work practitioner who is a case manager might work on the macro level of social work practice. Discuss in a small group.

Section 15.3: The Social Work Role of Broker

This section discusses the social work role of broker and associated skills.

Terry Vine/Getty Images

Social workers help clients explore options.

The Social Work Role of Broker

Since the case manager cannot always provide all of the services clients need, the role of broker is at the center of case management. The case manager who plays the role of **broker** connects clients with community agencies (Kirst-Ashman & Hull, 2018). As we've said, the broker may also connect clients with different programs in a larger agency.

The broker needs skills related specifically to the services available. These skills include the following:

- Comprehensive knowledge of available services
- Understanding of up-to-date eligibility requirements
- Professional contacts
- Follow-up abilities

Comprehensive Knowledge of Available Services

The case manager needs to be able to identify all providers in the area. In other words, they have a comprehensive knowledge of all of the services within reach of their clients. They also know about service locations. Which services are available by walking or public transportation for any given client? Which agencies can only be accessed by a car? This basic knowledge can come through a community resource list or from coworkers who refer out to the same agencies.

Understanding of Up-to-Date Eligibility Requirements

A more in-depth level of community resource knowledge comes with experience. Case managers who follow up on their referrals and evaluate whether they have met the needs of their clients constantly build their knowledge base about the resources available to their clients. In this way, they know more than the contact information and location of various agencies. They learn about current eligibility requirements for each agency so they don't refer clients to places where they cannot receive services.

Professional Contacts

Most importantly, case managers use networking skills to develop contacts at different agencies. Remember the networking skills of getting the names and business cards of people you meet. Those contacts may make it easier for you to advocate for your clients one day. Perhaps there is only one bed available in a residential facility. The case manager's contact may hold the bed briefly to meet the needs of the case manager's clients just because they have a close professional relationship with the admissions director of the facility.

Follow-Up Abilities

Finally, the case manager playing the role of broker needs to be able to assess their client's abilities to follow up on referrals. Specifically, the understanding of client abilities to follow up undergirds the important broker's skill of **making referrals**.

Skills for the Social Work Role of Broker

Making Referrals

While the case manager playing the role of broker uses all of the skills important to work with clients and families, the most important one is that of stretching the capabilities of the clients. It is important to begin where we begin in any social work process. Carry out self-reflection, engage the client system, and assess environmental systems. Try to alleviate the client's natural anxiety by working with them to create a clear goal. Then go back to assessment. Assess how capable they are to reach the goal on their own. Similar to work in crisis intervention, use your assessment skills to determine what they have been able to accomplish in the past. This will allow you to figure out what level of help they will need to carry through the referral in the present. The levels of help you might offer are as follows:

- Independent follow-through
- Verbal assistance
- Direct assistance

Independent Follow-Through

Once you recognize the client's need and identify an agency where they qualify for services, you need to assess how much help they need to carry through on the referral. Some clients have not reached out for help from a community resource simply because they didn't know the resource existed. If you talk with them and you determine that they normally successfully reach out for services they need, you can proceed with very minimal assistance. They will have the capacity to follow through on referrals. For example, you find out that a mom has recently made an emergency dentist appointment for her daughter and has successfully gotten the girl to the appointment on time. In this case, you know that the family has the ability to follow through with receiving services in the community.

Where your client has the ability to follow through independently, you need to make a few considerations. First and foremost, revisit the goal. It will be very helpful if you have GAS to reference. Your immediate task is to make sure that the client really does want to proceed with the attainment of that goal. Note that your GAS is a type of research evaluation, and in research there is a phenomenon called "social desirability bias" (Engel & Schutt, 2017). When a social desirability bias is in play, people answer questions the way they think the interviewer wants them to answer. In other words, they say what you want to hear. If you have a client who is capable of independent follow-through but does not respond to a referral, chances are they are not truly invested in meeting that goal. There is a miscommunication between you and the client about what they want to accomplish.

Next, you will share the service provider's contact information with the client. You want to carefully consider how to do that. If you have just one resource, you discuss the services they provide and allow the client to choose whether to try them. You may talk with them about how to stop service if they are not happy with them. On the other hand, you may have a long list of providers of the same service. If you just hand that list to a client, they may become overwhelmed. In addition, they don't have enough information to make informed choices about the options. If you want to introduce your client to more than a few options, you will have to give some description of what makes one different from the other. You'll need to let the client know your experiences with each. In that case, you may have to be careful: It is likely that your agency has a policy that you cannot directly recommend specific providers. In that situation, you simply state the pros and the cons of the providers and comment on which seems to offer services that match the needs of the client. For example, you may work in a rehabilitation center and need to refer an aging client's family members to a long-term care facility. You have a list of 12 providers in the area. You give detailed information about each one and talk to the family members about what is important to them in a facility. Here you slip into the role of educator and let them tell you what they need to know. Take your time with this. Remember that being an educator does not mean dumping information into a person and expecting it to be understood. In the situation of the search for a long-term care facility, the priority may be a simple, concrete thing like distance from their homes. They want to visit frequently, and they need you to tell them which facility is closest and how it might be accessed. They may have other priorities, though. Maybe their family member is restless and likes to paddle around on a wheelchair. In that case, their biggest priority might be the size of the rooms or the width of the hallways. You'll help them to understand the character of each place. You can see that it is best for you to visit each one of these facilities early on so that you can give clients detailed information. You may suggest that they visit facilities to see which they like best. In short, you give people as much choice as possible. Be careful not to do things for them that they are capable of doing themselves. That is how we respond to our professional value of the dignity and worth of the person (NASW, 2018). We use information and education to empower people to make choices. At the same time, it may be appropriate for us to advocate for the independent client by being in touch with our contact at an agency so that the client's services begin smoothly. Keep in mind that independent clients may make a very sound decision to decline services entirely.

Verbal Assistance

Of course, not all of your clients will be independent. Chances are they are coming to you for services precisely because they cannot reach out to them on their own. This is particularly true for people who require long-term case management. Again, you begin by assuring that you are working on the right goal. Find out whether the client is really interested in finding a community service. It may be the case that you are working on a worker-initiated goal that the client has not fully accepted. If you intend to send them out to follow through on a referral without any assistance, it is not likely to happen. So you take the time to carefully figure out if your client cares about the goal. Then, assess to what degree they can follow through on their referral. Sometimes, people simply need **verbal assistance**. They need you to help them understand what to do. If they are just handed contact information and an agency name, they may be unable to follow through. Assess carefully. Find out the level of help they usually need to complete tasks. They may need clear directions on the steps that have to be taken. Or they may not have strong telephone skills, and they need to practice calls before they make them. Again, if you want to empower your client, you don't do any more than you have to.

Direct Assistance

Some clients require **direct assistance**, or physical help to follow through on the referral. Once again, make sure your client is interested in meeting the goal the referral is attempting to address and assess how much help they have needed to follow through in the past. They may be able to get to an appointment independently but only if you call and set it up. They may be able to set up an appointment but not be able to arrange transportation on their own. Or they may need to have someone make the appointment and transport them as well. Some clients will need you to literally follow through on the referral yourself. For example, you may need to attend an appointment with a psychiatrist along with the client to help them articulate their needs. In all of these situations, you have the opportunity to slip into the role of educator and help the client learn a new skill so that they are more empowered in the future.

Making Referrals in the Social Work Role of Broker

Skill	Description	Example	Required Worker Characteristic(s)
Making referrals	The ability to make a successful referral by assessing a client's ability to follow using the skills they already have or can learn	Independent follow-through: Monica, here is the number of the group counselor we talked about. Do you think you'll be able to call and get information about the group so we can discuss it next week? Verbal assistance: Mrs. Wilson, I know you've said you're not comfortable with making phone calls. How about if we role-play a phone call to the agency, and then you can call from here in my office? Direct assistance: Richard, let's make an appointment for you to see Dr. Rogers. We'll make it at a time when Linda will be able to take you. Is that okay with you?	Focus, patience

Sample Brokering Dialog

Worker: Julie, are you interested in addressing the goal you set to improve your parenting skills?

Julie: (*hesitating*) I think so. What would I have to do?

Worker: Well, I know of a parent training class that's being offered at the school just down the street from here. Do you think you might be interested in attending a class for parents?

Julie: I might be. What do you have to do?

Worker: People who join the program go to class once a week on Monday nights for 6 weeks. There is no cost for people who live in this school district. I will tell you that the instructor is a man, though. I know you aren't very comfortable around men, so I wanted you to know.

Julie: How many people go to the classes?

Worker: I know the instructor, Randy, and he's told me that about 12 people attend each week. When one 6-week session ends, the next begins. People are welcome to keep coming to get support in their parenting efforts.

Julie: I'd like to do it, but I hate to go places where I don't know anyone. I never know what to say.

Worker: Suppose I meet you there and just introduce you to Randy before the group starts?

Julie: I think I can meet you there. Yes, I can do that.

CRITICAL THINKING AND COLLABORATIVE LEARNING EXERCISES 15.3

Visit one of the nonacademic departments on campus. Find out what services they provide and who is eligible to receive them. Find out their hours of operation and anything you need to know to send someone there for help. You might go to alumni services, the career center, the counseling center, writing center, tutoring program, health care center, etc. Share your findings with the larger group.

Section 15.4: Interdisciplinary Practice

This section is about the case manager's task of working with a variety of professionals on an **interdisciplinary team**.

More often than not, social workers need to work with professionals in a variety of disciplines such as doctors, nurses, crisis management workers, marriage and family counselors, substance abuse workers, and so forth. This is especially true where social workers are housed in host agencies like hospitals where people in other professionals are constantly around.

Because social workers use MSP, we are aware of the importance of these other elements in each client's environment. For this reason, it often falls on us to coordinate the efforts of each professional in every client's case. For a case manager, this expectation is a given. In order to work effectively with other professionals such as health care professionals, attorneys, justice officers, and even other social workers on clients' behalf, there are several practices to follow. The Interprofessional Education Collaborative (IPEC; 2017) has been created to respond to the need for collaboration across 20 disciplines, with the Council on Social Work Education (CSWE) being a member along with the American Association of Colleges of Nursing, the American College of Academic Physical Therapy, and the Association of American Medical Colleges. IPEC has identified four competencies for working on interdisciplinary teams. They are competencies associated with the following:

- Interprofessional values and ethics
- Roles and responsibilities
- Interprofessional communication
- Teams and teamwork (IPEC, 2014)

ETHICAL PERSPECTIVES

Is it ethical behavior for a shy social worker to sit quietly throughout an interdisciplinary team meeting if they have some meaningful observation to make? See Section 2.01(c).

Interprofessional Values and Ethics

IPEC, in collaboration with organizations like CSWE, hopes to improve health and social justice in health care through interdisciplinary work. Several primary concerns of IPEC might have been pulled right out of the social work code of ethics. IPEC is focused on the dignity and worth of the person. An important concern is integrity while providing confidential services. Another important concern is the importance of embracing diversity among client groups in addition to provider groups. In this way, it becomes obvious that the social worker has to develop cultural sensitivity related to all of the colleagues around the table where mutual clients are discussed. In other words, it is the responsibility of the social worker to develop empathy for colleagues as well as clients.

Social workers on interdisciplinary teams soon find out that different disciplines do not follow the *NASW Code of Ethics* (NASW, 2018). They will offer different solutions to problems, and they may not place the same focus on such considerations as dignity and worth of the person as social workers do. However, it is important to remember that every profession is committed to its own code just as every profession has its own area of expertise. Ideally, every member of the team respects the contribution, ethical code, and expertise of all other team members. Each group has a desire to engage in effective helping relationships with clients.

Roles and Responsibilities

As social workers, we know the importance of the opening statement in which we explain our agency's mission and our role within the agency. It is also important to share that information when we work with others to serve families, community members, and other professionals. When a social worker shares their role with other professionals, it becomes clear that there are limits to their areas of capability. Professionals pool their knowledge and expertise on behalf of clients. The social work caseworker learns how to communicate with other professionals using language that everyone can understand. For example, that means that the caseworker who is employed by a hospital must learn medical terms, the school social worker learns the language spoken in the school, and the caseworker who works in probation and parole must learn legal jargon. Social workers need to constantly keep up on the language of the other professions they need to work alongside. On the other hand, it is not helpful to the group if the social worker uses jargon specific to social work. No one will know what you mean if you talk about the person-in-environment (PIE) perspective, strengths-based language, or even preparatory empathy. We need to speak in ways that others will understand while we learn the language of others. It's the way of social work. We're about meeting the needs of others.

Interprofessional Communication

In addition to using language that all of the team members use, case managers also need to use the communication aids that other professions use. It may be that videoconferencing pulls team members together. Maybe common charts (we call them case notes) are used to help members of different professions communicate with each other. Social workers know the value of communication, so it is our responsibility to facilitate it as best as possible. In addition, it is the responsibility of all team members to communicate their professional contributions in a timely way. In these team-based settings, social workers need to listen, consider ideas and opinions of others with an open mind, then express their own knowledge and opinions clearly and respectfully. Social workers also continually remind professionals of the importance of teamwork.

SELF-REFLECTION 15: FREQUENCY OF SELF-REINFORCEMENT QUESTIONNAIRE

Social work may not be highly valued on every interdisciplinary team. For this reason, it is important that the social worker be able to encourage, support, and value themselves. Take the Frequency of Self-Reinforcement Questionnaire (FSRQ) on pages 468–469 and find out whether you need to improve your ability to support yourself.

Teams and Teamwork

Teams need to come together and decide what is best for clients with client preferences at the center of the conversation. It is best if they reach agreement on which ethical principles are important as they work collaboratively to address client challenges and barriers to success. There will be disagreements, and those situations can be used to help the group of professionals understand and respect each other's points of view. In this way, professionals, clients, and communities share possibilities and accountability for prevention as well as intervention. Finally, teams reflect on their performance so that services can be improved in the future. In some cases, a team member's job may put that person at odds with the rest of the group. For example, an agency representative may push for the discharge of a rehabilitation patient whose Medicare is running out because they face the realities of billing and budgets. At the same time, a physical therapist may argue against the discharge of the same person. In these types of cases, it is often the job of the generalist social worker to serve as a mediator to help other professionals come to an agreement.

Interprofessional Language

Again, a generalist social work practitioner understands that each professional on the multidisciplinary team uses terms specific to their areas of expertise. Sometimes, it may seem like they speak different languages. Garthwait (2012) has put together some basic social work terms and their definitions. Many are used across fields of social work by various professionals. Some are specific to particular fields of practice, but all social workers should be familiar with those selected. Some of those terms are as follows:

Terms Used in Justice Settings

Adult Protective Services (APS)—**Adult Protective Services (APS)** is the system of services provided to adults vulnerable to abuse, exploitation, or neglect (Garthwait, 2012, p. 8). When Jody suspected that her aging client was being neglected, she knew she had to call APS.

Brawner Rule—The **Brawner Rule** is the legal standard that holds a person to be not guilty by reason of insanity. Andrea had to testify on behalf of her client in case the Brawner Rule applied to her situation.

Child Protective Services (CPS)—**Child Protective Services (CPS)** is the system of services provided to children and youth vulnerable to abuse, exploitation, or neglect (Garthwait, 2012, p. 11). Timothy wasn't sure, but he suspected his young client was being abused, so he called CPS.

Due process—**Due process** is the practice of ensuring rights, fair processes, and adherence to laws when an individual is accused of misconduct or a crime (Garthwait, 2012, p. 19). The hospital had procedures in place to assure that individuals were not involuntarily committed to the behavioral health unit without due process.

Durable power of attorney—**Durable power of attorney** is a legal document that allows an individual to give someone the legal power to make decisions on their behalf should they become incapacitated (Garthwait, 2012). When Michael's father was comatose, he had to make health care decisions since his father named him as responsible through a durable power of attorney.

Duty to warn: A **duty to warn** is the legal obligation to report a client's threats or danger to another person based on the *Tarasoff* ruling of 1976 (Garthwait, 2012, p. 19). When Thomas's client threatened to "cut" her boyfriend's new girlfriend, she said she had a knife and a plan for doing it. At that point, Thomas knew he had to call the police and try her best to notify the vulnerable girlfriend as well.

Guardian—A **guardian** is a person appointed by a court to assume responsibility for the custody and welfare of an individual who is a minor, incapacitated, or incompetent (Garthwait, 2012, p. 29). Suzanne had to get an informed consent form completed by Billy's guardian, his foster mother.

Guardian ad litem—A **guardian ad litem** is a person appointed by a judge to protect the interests of a vulnerable or incompetent individual who may be subject to some form of legal action, only for the time that the individual's case is under consideration (Garthwait, 2012, p. 29). The guardian ad litem of the children in foster care could not get to know all of the children, so the social worker did home visits to check on their welfare.

Parens patriae—***Parens patriae*** is a legal term describing the need of the state to ensure the welfare of others or to act as guardian for those in need of care (Garthwait, 2012, p. 41). The family court found that Allison's parents were unfit, so it took on the role of *parens patriae* and placed Allison in an emergency foster home.

Privileged communication—**Privileged communication** is the agreement, often supported by law and professional codes of ethics, that the communication between a social worker and a client is protected unless the client gives permission for it to be shared or when there exists a duty to warn someone that the client has threatened to harm (Garthwait, 2012, p. 45). Elizabeth learned that she had to either break the law or testify in court since her meetings with her client were not legally considered to be privileged communication.

Least restrictive environment—A **least restrictive environment** is a legal and best practice of placing an individual in an environment that places the fewest restrictions on that individual while simultaneously providing the level of support and services required to maintain that individual's social functioning (Garthwait, 2012, p. 35). Thaddeus advocated for his client to be moved from the group home to an independent living apartment because he felt it was the least restrictive environment appropriate for his client.

Malpractice—Negligent actions on the part of a professional that violates professional ethics, standards of care, and which causes harm is **malpractice** (Garthwait, 2012, p. 36). Bridget made sure she provided her client with a careful referral to new services when she moved to another job so that she would not be leaving her client without service, or committing malpractice.

Malpractice insurance—**Malpractice insurance** is obtained by a professional to protect themselves against financial losses based on an allegation of malpractice (Garthwait, 2012, p. 36). Michelle had malpractice insurance because she was responsible for the behavior of every social worker she supervised.

Vicarious liability—**Vicarious liability** is a legal premise that not only is a defendant liable for their actions, but that liability may also extend to that person's employer, supervisor, or instructor (Garthwait, 2012, p. 79). Michelle made sure that vicarious liability would be covered by her malpractice insurance.

Terms Used in Health and Mental Health Settings

Advance directives—**Advance directives** are written guidelines regarding end of life care developed by a client while competent. This term can include living wills and the designation of a health care representative to make medical decisions for the client if needed (Garthwait, 2012, p. 9). Edward took a copy of his advance directives to his doctor's office so that they would know he expected his nephew to make health care decisions for him if he became incapacitated.

Diagnosis—**Diagnosis** is the process of identifying a condition and assessing the causes and contributors to that condition, based on symptoms and course, and allowing for a plan of care (Garthwait, 2012, p. 18). Jeannine looked up her client's diagnosis to be sure she understood it prior to the interprofessional team meeting.

Diagnostic and Statistical Manual of Mental Disorders (DSM): The manual of the American Psychiatric Association describes and classifies mental disorders based on prescribed symptoms, severity, and length (Garthwait, 2012, p. 18). Jeannine used the ***Diagnostic and Statistical Manual of Mental Disorders (DSM)*** as a reference whenever the team discussed a client's mental health diagnosis.

Discharge planning—**Discharge planning** is the process of planning for the discharge and placement of an individual following hospitalization or residential care that allows for a smooth transition and whatever supports will be needed to maintain the client's level of functioning (Garthwait, 2012, p. 18). Alex began discharge planning the moment a patient entered the hospital.

Managed care—A company that facilitates, monitors, and evaluates services provided by an organization, often used with the purpose of maintaining quality and reducing costs, is **managed care**. In Alex's state, Medicaid was overseen by a managed care company. Alex's client had Medicaid, so he had to call the managed care provider to find out what services were eligible for reimbursement.

Mandated client: A **mandated client** is required to seek and utilize services (Garthwait, 2012, p. 36). After her son was truant for 2 months, the mother was mandated to participate in a parenting skills training program.

Terms Used Across Practice Settings

Activities of daily living—**Activities of daily living** are basic self-care activities that allow an individual to live independently, including bathing, eating, and toileting (Garthwait, 2012, p. 8). William had to assess his client's ability to carry out activities of daily living independently before she could be discharged from the rehabilitation facility.

Co-payment—A **co-payment** is the amount a client needs to pay for a service covered by insurance, sometimes a percentage of the total cost and sometimes a specified dollar amount (Garthwait, 2012, p. 14). Marcia's client had Medicare health insurance, so she had a co-payment of 20% of the services she received.

Deductible—A **deductible** is the amount an individual is required to pay for a health or other insurance claim before the insurer pays their share of the claim (Garthwait, 2012, p. 16). George had a high deductible insurance plan, so he had to pay $5,000 of health care costs before he could get reimbursed for additional costs by his insurance company.

Dual diagnosis—A **dual diagnosis** is two coexisting, overlapping, and mutually interacting conditions. Also referred to as coexisting disorders or comorbidity (Garthwait, 2012, p. 19). Daniel's agency got a grant to work with clients who were seen as dual diagnosis—in this case people with both behavioral health and substance abuse problems.

Fee for service—A **fee for service** is the charges to a client or client system for a unit of service provided (Garthwait, 2012, p. 23). The agency's grant was about to expire, so clients needed to pay for their services on a sliding scale.

Immigrant—An **immigrant** is an individual who has voluntarily moved to another country (Garthwait, 2012, p. 31). Joshua's job was to help immigrants get the necessary paperwork so that they could legally get jobs.

Refugee—A **refugee** is an individual who experiences persecution or danger on the basis of political beliefs, religion, or ethnicity and who seeks protection in another country (Garthwait, 2012, p. 46). Akos came to this country as a refugee who was escaping a communist dictatorship.

Third-party payment—A **third-party payment** is a monetary reimbursement to an agency by an insurance company or government agency for services provided to a client (Garthwait, 2012, p. 78). Once James had insurance, the agency could get a third-party payment and save him a lot of money.

CRITICAL THINKING AND COLLABORATIVE LEARNING EXERCISES 15.4

Join a small group. Each member should look up the code of ethics of a profession that might intersect with social work—law, pharmacy, physical therapy, psychiatry, psychology, etc. Compare how each profession addresses social justice in their code.

Section 15.5: Ethical Use of Technology in Social Work

This section discusses the ethical use of technology in social work.

Definition of Technology

One challenging aspect of case management relates to continual developments in technology (Woodside & McClam, 2018). As technology develops, social workers have more and more ways of interacting with their clients. Services can be provided through online and video counseling; counseling using avatars; self-guided web-based interactions; live, online chats; social networks; e-mail; and texts (Reamer, 2013). Let's start by considering one aid to communication that you may not even consider to be technology: the old-fashioned telephone. Even though most professional interactions take place via e-mail or in-person meetings, the desk telephone still has a role to play in social work.

While social work can be facilitated by advances in technology, there is still an important role for the telephone to play.

When to Call

Sometimes you will find yourself struggling to write a complicated e-mail and wondering how you will explain yourself without being misunderstood. Chances are, that is a time you should pick up the phone. If the message is complicated enough to make you struggle to write a message, you are better off explaining yourself verbally. You'll have chances to back up and review aspects of your statement that your listener doesn't understand. You can also gauge by tone of voice and the length of pauses in your conversation how your message is being received. Another time that a phone call is required is when you will be giving someone a lot of work to answer your question. You may have a simple question that can be asked in a line or two of e-mail. If you empathize with the recipient, though, you may discover that they would have to write a long response to answer you. In that case, it's best for you to ask your question over the phone. You may send an e-mail to find out a good time to call, but let the person know you are willing to talk if they're not willing to write. Here's an example of an e-mail that is unnecessarily burdensome to the recipient when a phone call would be much more convenient:

Dear Professor,

What did we do in class last Thursday?

How to Begin Calls

Like most of us, you are probably so used to e-mails that you have to stop and think before you make a call, especially to a colleague that you don't know well. You don't want there to be an awkward silence after the initial how-are-you-I'm-fine exchange. So make a plan about what you want to say. It is not unreasonable for you to make yourself a script. It's best if you build your script around an opening statement.

When to Answer a Call

There are times when you will want to drop everything to answer the phone during work hours. Make a conscious decision about when those times will be. You may want to commit to answering your phone if your supervisor is calling. Have a phrase ready for situations where you have to interrupt a conversation or another phone call to pick up that call. You might say "Excuse me, but my supervisor's calling. I'll get back to you in a second." If you are with a client or client system representative, you typically would not answer calls. On the other hand, if you've decided you will always take your supervisor's call, you may say something like "You always have my full attention during our meetings, but I see that this is my supervisor calling. Do you mind if I pick up?" Other occasions when you might interrupt a client meeting can be planned ahead and briefly explained: "As you know, I normally have my phone turned off when we meet, but my mother is in surgery right now, and I'd like to keep it on this one time if it's okay with you."

Personal Calls

In the situation just given, it is understood that you may need to take a personal call. Let people you're speaking with know in advance that you may have to interrupt your conversation if the expected call comes in. Other than rare situations like relatives in surgery or a family emergency, you should not take personal calls at work unless you are on a break. If an emergency should occur, you may have to end a personal or phone conversation quickly, even mid-sentence. You might find it helpful to have a phrase in mind for that purpose, like "Please excuse me, I'm receiving an emergency call. I'll get back to you as soon as I can."

Of course, conversations that are carried out using technology are not limited to the phone or e-mail. Since technology has evolved so quickly and has become such an important way of doing business, we now have specific standards for the wide variety of uses of technology in social work. These standards were developed in 2017 through collaboration between the NASW, the CSWE, the Association of Social Work Boards (ASWB), and the Clinical Social Work Association (NASW, 2017). This group has defined technology as "any electronic device or program that may be used to communicate, gather, store, analyze, or share information (for example, computers, mobile phones, tablets, facsimile machines, smart watches, monitors, Web sites, social networking applications, and computer software" (NASW, 2017, p. 57). Taking all of these into account, the groups worked together to create a series of standards specifically related to the use of technology in social work.

Standards for the Use of Technology in Social Work

The standards we've discussed previously include some that are most important to social work practitioners who hold advanced degrees. Others are important to all social workers, and we'll discuss those here. The standards are organized into four sections:

- Provision of Information to the Public
- Designing and Delivering Services
- Gathering, Managing, and Storing Information
- Social Work Education and Supervision

Provision of Information to the Public

Technology has changed social work for the better. We can help more people and can reach people in ways that meet their individual needs. One way technology helps us serve more people is by helping us let people know about the services we offer and to share information with current or prospective clients. What we have to remember is that we must always treat information that we share using technology the same way we treat other information: We use it in ways that are consistent with the *NASW Code of Ethics* (NASW, 2018). We should provide information only from sources we know to be reliable and should advertise only services that we know are provided by qualified workers (NASW, 2017). As always, websites we can rely on include but are not limited to .edu and .gov sites. To determine the quality of a source, look to see whether a legitimate, reputable organization sponsors the web content you want to share and whether the content is up to date (Charbonneau, 2015). Information provided by an individual alone should not be considered to be reliable.

Designing and Delivering Services

Creating and providing social work services that are offered through technology has benefits and risks. Benefits include the opportunity to communicate with clients efficiently, gather information effectively, provide information, and carry out interventions in new and efficient ways. Clients who cannot access services due to where they live or how they get around can find social work within their reach. Workers can monitor clients' status in real time and respond to their needs rapidly. Services can be cost-effective. Communities can be quickly engaged and empowered. Fund-raising can be facilitated. On the other hand, risks include technology failure at critical times and breaches of confidentiality as well as unauthorized use of the means of communication. Given the risks, the standards suggest that we should use technology to create and provide services only in the following situations (NASW, 2017):

- *When in-person services are not necessary*
    - Situations where in-person services are necessary may include risks of self-harm, cognitive impairment, or crisis situations.
- *When services can be confidential*
    - Access to electronic communication should only be accessible by those who need the information. Clients should be aware of who those people are, and your agency should have established policies related specifically to services provided through technology.
- *When professional boundaries can be maintained*
    - Services should not be compromised because the worker's private information has become available to the client via social media. Rest assured that any information you disclose about yourself on social media will be discovered by your clients, including professional websites and blogs.
- *When you can confirm your client's identity*
    - You need to find ways to be sure that you are communicating with your client and only your client. For example, you might start an online meeting with a phone call or you might have a different password for every client.
- *When you can be sure that technology is accessible and available*
    - The client needs to be comfortable and proficient with the technology, and it has to be reliably available. For example, the client needs access to the Internet, and you need access in emergencies.
- *When you are proficient and the technology is reliably available*
    - You need to be able to access the technology your client has become used to at any time to handle emergencies. It is a temptation for social workers to use their own cell phones to send text messages, for example. If you are texting, certain specific considerations apply. We'll consider them next.

Gathering, Managing, and Storing Information

As with the provision of services, gathering, managing, and storing information has benefits and risks. For example, information can be accessed easily, stored relatively safely, and used efficiently. Risks include someone hacking the system and gaining access to your clients' data; devices being stolen or misplaced; information accidentally being sent to the wrong person; and clients experiencing abuse or exploitation that find their information in the hands of family members or others that put the clients' safety in jeopardy. The standards suggest that clients should have the opportunity to consent to the way their information is gathered and stored. They need to know where workers are getting information, and their confidentiality needs to be maintained. The social worker is responsible to separate personal and professional data using separate devices and accounts. Keep in mind that a client has a right to see their own records. You need to be able to provide them without jeopardizing your own privacy. Agencies should have policies specific to

©iStock.com/Sitthiphong

Confidentiality is an important consideration when technology facilitates social work services.

the gathering, managing, and storing of client and program information (NASW, 2017).

Social Work Education and Supervision

Educators and supervisors should help students understand the benefits and risks of the use of technology in social work. In addition, they should take steps to assure that students' information is confidential and that their organization's policies take student rights into account. Field instructors and supervisors should help students understand their organizations' policies related to the use of technology (NASW, 2017).

E-Mail Communications

As you know, nearly everyone uses e-mail for business and personal communications. You should keep in mind that your business e-mails should be very different from your personal ones. Whether you are communicating with clients or colleagues, you will want your business emails to have certain characteristics (Tuffley, 2014):

- *Use a subject line that clearly summarizes the message (e.g., Next Week's Supervision).*
- *Use a formal greeting ("Good morning, Alfred" or "Greetings, Mr. Andrews").*
- *Use complete sentences ("I'm hoping we will be able to get together later, but in the meantime . . ." or "Please remember that you have an appointment on Wednesday").*
- *Use correct grammar.*
- *Use correct formatting: The greeting is on a line by itself, paragraphs are separated by spaces, and the closing is on a line by itself.*
- *Keep the message as short as possible, but provide enough context to be understood (e.g., not "that case we discussed," but "the case about Shawn, the adolescent with behavior problems and truancy we discussed").*
- *Use a formal closing ("Best Wishes," "Sincerely," "Regards," even "See you then" or "Thanks").*
- *Add your name on a line by itself.*

Finally, your e-mail should present you as a professional. Always use a "signature," or a standard description of your role at the agency and your contact information, like this:

Susan Phillips, BSW

Family Social Worker

Best Practices Agency for Children

450 Third Street

Evansville, ND 19188

467-564-1200, ext. 456

sphillips@bpa.org

Another important thing to remember about business e-mails is that professionals are often snowed under by e-mails at the same time they are struggling to get their jobs done. When you sit down to write an e-mail, ask yourself this: "Why should someone read this message?" (Matorin, 2012). Then, allow at least a couple of days before you expect a reply (Tuffley, 2014).

Text Messaging

Text messaging may soon become the most frequently used method of delivering social work services, and it has its own unique conditions. One common concern that is made even more challenging with text messaging is managing the client's confidentiality. While e-mail and other technologically mediated conversations can potentially be seen by others, the text message comes across a phone that may very well be shared by others. One password is likely to be shared among several people and, as you know, text messages pop right up without any encryption. You may want to send a text saying that you'd like your client to send you a password that only the two of you know before you send the actual text. Your exchange might look like this:

Worker: Johanna, it's Sandy. Is it you?

Client: Yes. The password is wellness.

Worker: Okay. I'm writing to remind you that you were going to bring your journal to tomorrow's appointment so we can discuss it.

Client: Will do.

Sometimes it is effective to be vague in your messages. For instance, it's not a good idea to use a computer-generated message that says this:

You have an appointment tomorrow at Safe House with Karen at 9am

To begin to resolve this problem, you might simply write a text that says:

See you tomorrow. Karen

This may facilitate client confidentiality while using the advantages of the quick turnaround of text messages. You may ask your client to respond, or you may have an automatic "read receipt" let you know that the text has been received. These methods are helpful, but you will never know if the client is sending you a reply or if it's coming from someone who is borrowing the phone. Still, you may decide that the quick, timely reminder of an appointment to a client who has difficulty remembering appointments is a benefit that outweighs the risk of having another person read it. In the end, only your client can decide.

Another challenge that is made more complex through text messaging is managing the worker's boundaries. For example, you may text a person at 3:00 p.m. reminding them of an appointment at 4:00 p.m. They may text you at 6:00 p.m., saying this:

Sry missed appt tom 9 am ok?

You are off at 5:00 p.m., and you don't begin work the next day until 9:00 a.m. But you see the text at 6:00 p.m. because you are using your private phone to conduct professional conversations. It is tempting to send a quick reply:

k.

There are two problems here. First, if you respond, the next time you may receive the text at 9:00 p.m., and it may be an emergency. You will probably experience compassion fatigue if you try to work 24 hours a day. If you begin answering texts at odd hours, you'll be setting a precedent that you are available all the time. Second, in this case it is hard for you to avoid seeing work texts because they are appearing on your personal phone. While it is recommended that agencies provide phones to workers, it isn't always the case (NASW, 2017). You can use a cloud-based number to avoid giving out your personal phone number, but you can't avoid knowing about the texts when they come in if you're using your own phone for professional communications. If you are fortunate enough to be provided with a work phone, you should make a commitment to yourself that the phone will be turned off when you are not working or on call. Let your supervisor know that you will be maintaining this boundary.

The best way to manage all of these issues is to develop agency policies that prevent at least some of the problems before they happen (Kimball & Kim, 2013). Perhaps you will engage in an organizational change effort to develop appropriate social media policies. If you do, you might consider making a policy that says every client has to fill out a form that explains your social media policies. (You'll see an example later in this chapter.)

The Experienced Social Worker: Reflective Responses

Jackie had worked at the hospital for 21 years. She knew the routines, the systems, and the referral sources like the back of her hand. She had positive relationships with the medical staff, the other social workers, and community agency contacts. Effective brokering was second nature. Her practice wisdom allowed her to enjoy her work more and more each year. Sure, it was a hectic job, but she knew what she was doing so well that each day's crisis could either be resolved or put off in a satisfactory way. New social workers often came to Jackie for mentoring, and it was fulfilling to watch their development. Jackie had been offered supervisory positions over the years but had turned them all down. She wanted to spend her time working with clients. Jackie's meetings with her supervisor had become conversations about the hospital. It was assumed that Jackie knew her job and would keep on doing it well. Everything was going fine until her supervisor retired.

It can be challenging to accept supervision.

The new supervisor, Jodi, had finished her master of social work (MSW) degree with two hospital internships under her belt. After graduation, she immediately got a job on the pediatric floor. After 2 years, she was seen as such an outstanding performer that she was offered a supervisory position. One of the staff members she would be responsible for was Jackie. Jodi was anxious about supervising such an experienced worker, so she was absolutely determined to do a good job. She studied management techniques and reviewed her notes on supervision in the planned change process. As a social worker, Jodi knew she had to carry out self-reflection to understand her anxiety before she could display the absent attribute of self-confidence. She did so and sought supervision herself. Finally, she felt ready to begin a process of engagement with Jackie, but Jackie suddenly found herself unavailable. Somehow there was always some emergency when she planned to meet with Jodi. The interactions they had were the fleeting "I'll catch up with you later" type. One day after a few weeks had passed, Jodi approached Jackie with slow but determined steps. Jodi put her hand on Jackie's forearm, effectively causing Jackie to cut off her fast-paced stride. When she stopped, Jodi made fleeting eye contact with Jackie and told her that it was absolutely necessary that they have a supervisory meeting.

Jackie could see that Jodi was struggling, and she remembered mentoring all of the new workers over the years. They had struggled too, at first. Jackie suddenly experienced empathy for Jodi. She looked at Jodi and saw her as a colleague—a new colleague, an inexperienced colleague, but a colleague the code required her to respect. "You know, Jodi," she said, "I think you're absolutely right. Let's make a time to meet."

CRITICAL THINKING AND COLLABORATIVE LEARNING EXERCISES 15.4

It's been suggested that people in professions like social work have to hold themselves to higher standards than others in their private use of social media (Strom-Gottfried, Thomas, & Anderson, 2014). Consider your use of social media. Is there any information on the Internet that is about you and that you wouldn't want a client to see? How can you take steps to keep it private? What's the best way for you to manage this in the future? Brainstorm in a large group to come up with methods to ensure your professional boundaries and privacy when it comes to your private use of social media.

Section 15.6: Ethical Documentation

This section provides clarification and examples of some of the documents that are regularly required by generalist social workers, particularly when they play the role of case manager on an interdisciplinary team.

Memos

A memorandum is a formal message among service providers and administrators. While it can be on paper or electronic, it carries more weight than an everyday e-mail. Its formality is expressed in its format. Note that there are many memorandum templates available. In a work atmosphere, don't go with pretty or fancy. Simple is best. Essential elements of a memo include the title "Memorandum." A sample format is below:

Memorandum

To: John Mitchell, MD; Sandra Owens, MSW; Jake Townsend, PT; Janet Sanders, Children and Youth Services

From: Jessica Barnes, BSW

Re: Catherine Matthews

Date: October 12, 2018

This is to remind everyone that Janet of Children and Youth Services has agreed to transport Catherine's mother to Renewal Rehabilitation to visit with Catherine. Janet will supervise the visit from 11 to 12 on Monday, October 20 and will return Mrs. Matthews to her home. Hopefully no medical procedure will be scheduled for Catherine during that time.

Meeting Agendas

As we've said, it is the social worker's responsibility to arrange and facilitate interdisciplinary team meetings. Meetings can easily lose focus, so workers usually provide formal meeting agendas to keep everyone on track and on time. It's best if meeting agendas are provided to participants a day or so in advance. This allows people to plan for their participation and serves as a reminder of the date and time of the meeting. Some people will print out their agendas and bring them to the meeting. Others will not, so the meeting facilitator should bring some extra copies.

Meeting Agenda

Case Planning: Donna Harwick

Monday, November 3, 2018

3:00–4:00 p.m.

Call to order: Jane Addams, BSW

Purpose of the meeting: Treatment Review

Old Business

1. Donna's current goals and contract
2. Progress since last meeting
3. Donna's input
4. Family member's feedback

New Business

1. New treatment plan development

Other Concerns

Meeting Minutes

During a professional meeting, minutes are taken to record the proceedings. Minutes can be taken by a clerical staff person, but it is likely that a member of the team will need to do so. The social worker who is facilitating the meeting should ask for a volunteer or take the minutes themselves. They should review and approve the minutes before submitting them to meeting participants. Everyone should receive a copy of the minutes so that they have time to review them before the next meeting. It is customary to review and approve the minutes of the previous meeting before beginning a new one. Again, some meeting participants will print out their copy of the minutes and bring it along. The facilitator should have copies for those who do not.

Meeting Minutes

Case Planning: Donna Harwick

Monday, November 3, 2018

3:00–4:00 p.m.

Present: Jane Addams, Donna Harwick, Mrs. Christine Harwick, Don Johnson, Melody Freeman
Absent: Dr. Mitchell
JA called the meeting to order at 3:00 p.m.
Review of last meeting's minutes. Minutes approved without changes.

JA stated the purpose of the meeting was to plan the transition of Donna from the group home to an independent living arrangement.

DH said she is eager to move. CH is supportive but concerned about transportation from the new apartment to home.

DJ reported DH practiced public transportation to and from the apartment and the Harwick home successfully. She needs assistance but will probably be independent soon.

MF is looking forward to her new role as residence manager for DH. She reports an initial meeting with DH at the group home and said they seemed to get along fine. DH concurred.

Plan: DJ will continue to work with DH on public transportation. MF will facilitate the move on November 30.

The group is to reconvene December 15 to check progress.

Use of Technology Consent

As stated previously, technology can be extremely beneficial in allowing workers and clients to communicate between meetings. Confidentiality concerns and boundary problems might be mediated with agency policy and a client consent form like this one:

Informed Communication Consent

Please let us know how you'd like to be reminded of appointments. Check all that apply:

- *Phone*
- *Voicemail*
- *E-mail*
- *Text*

Note: Your social worker will not use the agency name in any correspondence, but please remember that someone else who has access to your phone or computer may have access to your messages.

You may be in touch with your social worker via phone, e-mail, or text. Please use the following:

_________________________ office phone number

_________________________ agency e-mail

_________________________ cell phone number for texts

E-mails, texts, and phone calls made after working hours will not be read until the next workday. E-mails, texts, and phone calls will be answered as soon as possible, during regular office hours.

In cases of emergency, please call ___________________. If you let your worker know that you have done so, they will be in touch with you during regular office hours the next workday.

___________________________________ _______________

Client Date

Section 15.7: Review and Apply

CONCURRENT CONSIDERATIONS IN GENERALIST PRACTICE

Ethical Decision-Making Challenge

Do you think Jackie spent enough (or too much) time trying to convince Maria to talk to her parents about her pregnancy? What part of the Code of Ethics might inform your answer?

Human Rights

Is anyone in this case being deprived of any fundamental human rights such as freedom, safety, privacy, an adequate standard of living, health care, and education? When you think of "anyone in this case," do you consider the rights of the fetus? Explain why.

Evidence-Based Practice

Find out whether young women have long-term emotional problems after terminating a pregnancy.

Policies Impacting Practice

Look up the current law in your state that determines at what point a pregnancy can be legally terminated.

Managing Diversity

Imagine that Maria and her family had little sense of spirituality and no affiliation with a religion. Do you think Jackie's decision would or should have been different?

Multilevel Practice

Identify examples of Jackie's work on all levels.

Micro: ____________________

Mezzo: ____________________

Macro: ____________________

Dynamic and Interactive Planned Change Stages

Identify aspects of Jackie's work where she worked in the following stages:

Self-Reflection: ____________________

Engagement: ____________________

Assessment: ____________________

Planning: ____________________

Implementation: ____________________

Evaluation: ____________________

Termination and Follow-Up: ____________________

Chapter Summary

Section 15.1: Ethics in Case Management

Ethical dilemmas are common challenges in case management. It is important to question whether there are values or ethical duties that are in conflict before assuming a situation is truly a dilemma. However, in fast-paced settings, the use of time can be governed by the social work value of service. Where an ethical dilemma exists, the ethical problem-solving method should be employed. It is important to close that process with a concise statement of rationale for the worker's decision. That rationale should cite specific language from the *NASW Code of Ethics* (NASW, 2018).

Section 15.2: The Social Work Role of Case Manager

Case management is a broad range of social work services that workers use to be sure a wide variety of client needs can be addressed. Case managers provide a broad range of services to their clients, especially when other providers are available. When their agency or level of competency restricts the services they may supply, workers need to locate alternate services within their own agency or the community. They then refer their clients out to those services. Once clients are referred out, it is the case manager's responsibility to coordinate the providers and evaluate their services so that current and future client needs can be met.

Section 15.3: The Social Work Role of Broker

Because services need to be referred out at times, the social work role of broker is central to the case manager. The broker needs a comprehensive knowledge of available services and an understanding of up-to-date eligibility requirements. This understanding is often built on professional contacts. Referral is a complicated process in which social workers determine the level of the client's ability to follow through on referrals and provide only as much assistance as needed.

Section 15.4: Interdisciplinary Practice

The case manager's role of broker often places them on interdisciplinary teams. These teams face challenges in working together, so IPEC has developed a series of competencies. One competency relates to ethics and values, and it suggests that professionals recognize that all of their colleagues follow their own codes. Another competency requires that professionals be clear about their roles and responsibilities on the team. They should be able to articulate those boundaries and work within them. A third competency relates to interprofessional communication. For the social worker, this means learning the terms that other professionals on the team routinely use. It also means that the social worker should avoid jargon and speak in ways that can be understood by all members of the team. The final competency relates to teams and teamwork and suggests that teams collaborate with the interests and wishes of the client consistently at the center of the conversation.

Section 15.5: Ethical Use of Technology in Social Work

Technology is constantly changing the ways social workers provide services. In response, collaboration between the NASW, the CSWE, the ASWBb, and the Clinical Social Work Association resulted in a set of standards for social work practice related to technology. One standard is related to the provision of information to the public. Social workers should provide information from reputable sources and should be cautious about what information about them is available to others online. Another standard suggests that service design and delivery should follow the same ethical requirements as any other service. Services should be designed and delivered using technology only under the following conditions: when in-person services are not necessary, when services can be confidential, when boundaries can be maintained, when the worker can confirm the client's identity, and when technology is accessible and available to both worker and client. Another standard refers to gathering, managing, and storing information. It suggests social workers be aware that information can be lost or misrouted, that clients have the right to see their records, and that workers are responsible to keep their professional and personal records separate. Finally, supervisors and field instructors should be aware of their agency's policies related to technology.

Section 15.6: Ethical Documentation

Documentation is critical to social workers in general and case managers in particular. Important documents include memos, meeting agendas, meeting minutes, and use of technology consent forms.

SELF-REFLECTION 15: FREQUENCY OF SELF-REINFORCEMENT QUESTIONNAIRE

PURPOSE: To measure skill at self-reinforcement

AUTHOR: Elaine M. Heiby

DESCRIPTION: The Frequency of Self-Reinforcement Questionnaire (FSRQ) is a 30-item instrument designed to assess respondents' encouraging, supporting, and valuing themselves and their own efforts. Items on the FSRQ were initially selected from a pool of 100 items, based on judgments of content validity by 10 clinicians.

NORMS: The FSRQ has been studied with several samples of educated adults and undergraduate college students. Actual norms on the latest version of the FSRQ are not available.

SCORING: Reverse-score negatively worded items and sum the individual items to obtain an overall score. The range of scores is 1 to 90 with higher scores indicating greater frequency of self-reinforcement. Scores below 17 suggest deficits in self-reinforcement skills, dependence on others for approval, and possible vulnerability to depression.

RELIABILITY: The FSRQ has very good internal consistency, with split-half reliability of .87. The FSRQ has excellent stability, with an 8-week test–retest correlation of .92.

VALIDITY: The FSRQ has good concurrent validity as demonstrated by correlations between FSRQ scores and self-monitoring of self-reinforcement and experimenter ratings of respondents' tendency to engage in self-reinforcement. The FSRQ is not correlated with social desirability response set and is sensitive to change following training in self-reinforcement skills. The FSRQ is also reported as having good construct validity as demonstrated by negative correlations with self-punishment, the Beck Depression Inventory, and measures of cognitive distortion.

PRIMARY REFERENCE:

Heiby, E. M. (2013). Assessment of frequency of self-reinforcement. In K. Corcoran & J. Fischer (Eds.), *Measures for clinical practice and research: A sourcebook.* New York, NY: Oxford University Press.

FREQUENCY OF SELF-REINFORCEMENT QUESTIONNAIRE

Below are a number of statements about beliefs or attitudes people have. Indicate how descriptive the statements are for you by rating each item as indicated below. There are no right or wrong answers.

Rate each item for how much of the time it is descriptive for you. In the blank space before each item, rate the following:

0 = Never descriptive of me

1 = A little of the time descriptive of me

2 = Some of the time descriptive of me

3 = Most of the time descriptive of me

_____ 1. When I fail at something, I am still able to feel good about myself.

_____ 2. I can stick to a boring task that I need to finish without someone pushing me.

_____ 3. I have negative thoughts about myself.

_____ 4. When I do something right, I take time to enjoy the feeling.

_____ 5. I have such high standards for what I expect of myself that I have a hard time meeting my standards.

_____ 6. I seem to blame myself and be very critical of myself when things go wrong.

_____ 7. I can have a good time doing some things alone.

_____ 8. I get upset with myself when I make mistakes.

_____ 9. My feelings of self-confidence go up and down.

_____ 10. When I succeed at small things, it helps me to go on.

_____ 11. If I do not do something absolutely perfectly, I don't feel satisfied.

_____ 12. I get myself through hard things mostly by thinking I'll enjoy myself afterward.

_____ 13. When I make mistakes, I take time to criticize myself.

_____ 14. I encourage myself to improve at something by feeling good about myself.

_____ 15. I put myself down so that I will do things better in the future.

_____ 16. I think talking about what you've done right is bragging.

_____ 17. I find that I feel better when I silently praise myself.

_____ 18. I can keep working at something hard to do when I stop to think of what I've already done.

_____ 19. The way I keep up my self-confidence is by remembering any successes I have had.

_____ 20. The way I achieve my goals is by rewarding myself every step along the way.

_____ 21. Praising yourself is being selfish.

_____ 22. When someone criticizes me, I lose my self-confidence.

_____ 23. I criticize myself more often than others criticize me.

_____ 24. I feel I have a lot of good qualities.

_____ 25. I silently praise myself even when other people do not praise me.

_____ 26. Any activity can provide some pleasure no matter how it comes out.

_____ 27. If I don't do the best possible job, I don't feel good about myself.

_____ 28. I should be upset if I make a mistake.

_____ 29. My happiness depends more on myself than it depends on other people.

_____ 30. People who talk about their own better points are just bragging.

Recommended Websites

National Association of Case Management: https://yournacm.com

Critical Terms for Case Management, Technology, and Documentation

Generalist Practice Curriculum Matrix With 2015 Educational Policy and Accreditation Standards

Chapter 15

Competency	Course	Course Content	Dimensions
Competency 1: Demonstrate Ethical and Professional Behavior		Feature 3: Self-Reflection Feature 4: Concurrent Considerations in Generalist Practice	Cognitive–affective processes
		15.1. Consider a case management scenario with an ethical dilemma component. 15.5. Appraise the ethics of technology in social work. 15.6. Practice ethical documentation.	Skills Cognitive–affective processes
Competency 2: Engage Diversity and Difference in Practice		Feature 1: Focus on Diversity	Skills Cognitive–affective processes
		Feature 4: Concurrent Considerations in Generalist Practice	Skills Cognitive–affective processes
Competency 3: Advance Human Rights and Social, Economic, and Environmental Justice		Feature 4: Concurrent Considerations in Generalist Practice	Skills Cognitive–affective processes

Competency	Course	Course Content	Dimensions
Competency 4: Engage in Practice-Informed Research and Research-Informed Practice		Feature 4: Concurrent Considerations in Generalist Practice	Skills Cognitive–affective processes
		15.3. Explore the social work role of broker and the skills associated with it.	Knowledge
Competency 5: Engage in Policy Practice		Feature 4: Concurrent Considerations in Generalist Practice	Skills Cognitive–affective processes
		15.4. Learn the skills involved in interprofessional collaboration.	
Competency 6: Engage With Individuals, Families, Groups, Organizations, and Communities		Feature 4: Concurrent Considerations in Generalist Practice	Skills Cognitive–affective processes
		15.2. Understand how case management intersects with a broad range of social work responsibilities.	Knowledge
Competency 7: Assess Individuals, Families, Groups, Organizations, and Communities		Feature 4: Concurrent Considerations in Generalist Practice	Skills Cognitive–affective processes
		15.2. Understand how case management intersects with a broad range of social work responsibilities.	Knowledge
Competency 8: Intervene With Individuals, Families, Groups, Organizations, and Communities		15.2. Understand how case management intersects with a broad range of social work responsibilities.	Knowledge
		Feature 4: Concurrent Considerations in Generalist Practice	Cognitive–affective processes
Competency 9: Evaluate Practice With Individuals, Families, Groups, Organizations, and Communities		Feature 4: Concurrent Considerations in Generalist Practice	Skills Cognitive–affective processes
		15.2. Understand how case management intersects with a broad range of social work responsibilities.	Knowledge

References

Charbonneau, D. H. (2015). Health disclaimers and website credibility markers. *Reference & User Services Quarterly, 54*(3), 30–36.

Engel, R. J., & Schutt, R. K. (2017). *The practice of research in social work* (3rd ed.). Thousand Oaks, CA: Sage.

Garthwait, C. (2012). *Dictionary of social work*. Retrieved from http://health.umt.edu/socialwork/Master%20of%20Social%20Work/Curriculum/SocialWorkDictionary_booklet_updated_2012_Oct23.pdf

Heiby, E. M. (2013). Assessment of frequency of self-reinforcement. In K. Corcoran & J. Fischer (Eds.), *Measures for clinical practice and research: A sourcebook*. New York, NY: Oxford University Press.

Interprofessional Education Collaborative. (2014). Core competencies. In *What is interprofessional education?* Retrieved from https://nebula.wsimg.com/2f68a39520b03336b41038c370497473?AccessKeyId=DC06780E69ED19E2B3A5&disposition=0&alloworigin=1

Interprofessional Education Collaborative. (2017). Vision and mission. In *What is interprofessional education?* Retrieved from https://www.ipecollaborative.org/about-ipec.html

Kimball, E., & Kim, J. (2013). Virtual boundaries: Ethical considerations for use of social media in social work. *Social Work, 58*(2), 185–188.

Kirst-Ashman, K., & Hull, G. (2018). *Understanding generalist practice* (8th ed.) Stamford, CT: Cengage.

Matorin, S. (2012). Administrative writing. In B. L. Simon & W. Green (Eds.), *The Columbia guide to social work writing* (pp. 193–213). New York, NY: Columbia University Press.

National Association of Social Workers. (2017). *Technology in social work practice*. Washington, DC: Author.

National Association of Social Workers. (2018). *NASW code of ethics*. Washington, DC: NASW Press.

Reamer, F. G. (2013). Social work in a digital age: Ethical and risk management challenges. *Social Work, 58*(2), 163–173.

Rothman, J., & Sager, J. S. (1998). *Case management: Integrating individual and community practice* (2nd ed.). Needham Heights, MA: Allyn & Bacon.

Strom-Gottfried, K., Thomas, M. S., & Anderson, H. (2014). Social work and social media: Reconciling ethical standards and emerging technologies. *Journal of Social Work Values and Ethics, 11*(1), 54–65.

Tuffley, D. (2014). *Email etiquette: Netiquette for the information age* [Kindle edition]. Retrieved from https://www.amazon.com/Email-Etiquette-Netiquette-Information-Age-ebook/dp/B0057CTXGS

Woodside, M., & McClam, T. (2018). *Generalist case management: A method of human service delivery* (5th ed.). Boston, MA: Cengage.

Recommended Readings

National Association of Social Workers. (2017). *Technology in social work practice*. Washington, DC: Author.

• Appendix •

Social Work's Living, Breathing Code of Ethics

Allan Barsky, social worker and attorney, chaired the NASW Code of Ethics Review Task Force. He worked with colleagues Frederic Reamer, Kim Strom-Gottfried, David Barry, Luis Machuca, Bo Walker, Dawn Hobdy, and Andrea Murray (nonvoting member). The group created significant changes to the 2008 NASW Code of Ethics, which were approved by the Delegate Assembly of NASW in August of 2017. The code officially went into effect January 1, 2018. Barsky (2017) has published a summary of the changes to the code. That work, along with the old and new codes (National Association of Social Workers [NASW], 2018), are referenced here as is the comprehensive list of Standards for Technology in Social Work Practice (NASW, Association of Social Work Boards [ASWB], Council on Social Work Education [CSWE], & Clinical Social Work Association [CSWA], 2017).

2018 Changes to the 2008 *NASW Code of Ethics*

Topic	Relevant Sections of the Code	Implications for Practice
Disability to Ability	1.05(c, d), 1.06(g), 2.01, 4.02, and 6.04	Social workers should talk about (and think about) people's diverse abilities rather than disabilities. For example, use strengths-based language to describe physical abilities, emotional abilities, and intellectual abilities. Avoid the use of the term *disability*.
Technology	Preamble: Purpose of the *NASW Code of Ethics* (The last paragraph is new.)	The use of technology in social work is growing. Ethical standards apply whether social work is done in person or technology-assisted. Social workers are responsible to know about new technologies that may help client systems. Social workers are also responsible for applying all ethical standards to technology-assisted work. Specific standards related exclusively to technology are available (NASW, ASWB, CSWE, & CSWA, 2017). Among other things, they focus on providing information about social work to the public; designing and delivering services; and gathering, managing, and storing information. It also focuses on social work education and supervision.
Informed Consent	New sections: 1.03(e, f, g, h, i)	Workers must discuss practice policies related to technology. They must obtain client consent to use these technologies and when using technology must be sure of the client's identity and location. Consent must also be sought when conducting electronic searches unless workers need to do so to prevent serious harm to the client or others. Social workers have to assess all clients' abilities to use technology. When in doubt, alternate services must be available.

(Continued)

(Continued)

Topic	Relevant Sections of the Code	Implications for Practice
Competence	New sections: 1.04(d, e)	Social workers using technology in their practice must be competent in its use and must understand related challenges. Social workers are reminded that laws and social welfare policies like professional licensing laws may be different in their location from their clients' location and that they are responsible to comply with both.
Cultural Competence and Social Diversity to Cultural Awareness and Social Diversity	1.05	The heading of the section has changed to reflect new thinking about cultural competence. However, the change does not reflect newer concepts such as cultural awareness, cultural humility, or cultural responsiveness. Social workers should strive to be competent, not just aware, of the diversity of client systems.
Cultural Competence and Social Diversity: Technology	New section: 1.05(d)	Social workers should think about clients' areas of diversity when they are using technology to provide service. In some situations, technology can be used to make services more accessible, and in others, the use of technology may provide challenges. In other words, some people only have access to social work services, and others cannot access services if technology is used.
Conflict of Interest	New sections: 1.06(e, f, g, h)	It is tempting to use technology to communicate with clients, but those communications must not be personal. Workers have to be cautious about what personal information they post online since access to personal information can confuse boundaries. They should avoid being "friends" with clients over social media.
Privacy and Confidentiality	1.07(a)	The phrase "essential to providing services or conducting social work evaluation or research" was replaced with "compelling professional reasons" as a shorter way of explaining that social workers should only try to find information that is essential to a case (NASW, 2018, p. 11).
Privacy and Confidentiality	1.07(c)	The phrase "identifiable person" was changed to "others." This section of the code refers to instances when workers should break confidentiality, specifically when there is risk of harm. The basic rule of confidentiality does not apply if the worker is trying to prevent "serious, foreseeable, and imminent harm to a client or others" (NASW, 2018, pp. 11–12). This change is meant to remind workers that there may be danger to a group of people, such as students at a school, not necessarily just an "identifiable person."
Privacy and Confidentiality	1.07(f)	Agreements workers make with clients about confidentiality should include language about electronic communications.
Privacy and Confidentiality	1.07(i)	Workers should not share client information "electronically or in person" unless privacy can be assured (NASW, 2018, p. 12). The change is the new code's focus on electronic information in which it is difficult to assure privacy.
Privacy and Confidentiality	1.07(m)	Social workers are allowed to transmit identifying information electronically, but they should take steps to ensure confidentiality. (Previously, the code required social workers to avoid sharing any confidential information using any type of technology.)

Topic	Relevant Sections of the Code	Implications for Practice
Privacy and Confidentiality	New sections: 1.07(n, o)	Social workers should let clients know their policies about breaches of confidential information. If clients' information is breached, they should be informed immediately so they can take actions like protect themselves against identity theft.
Privacy and Confidentiality	New sections: 1.07(p, q)	Social workers should think carefully about seeking information electronically and should inform clients about their policy for doing so. There may be compelling professional reasons to seek information about clients, but social workers should obtain informed consent first.
Privacy and Confidentiality	New section: 107(r)	Social workers should avoid posting identifying or confidential information about clients on websites or social media unless consent is obtained. The client should realize that information is then available to others including prospective employers.
Privacy and Confidentiality	1.07(s)	"State statutes" was changed to "applicable laws" because social workers have to abide by the laws of their location as well as their clients' locations when they are offering services electronically (NASW, 2018, p. 14).
Sexual Relationships	1.09	The 2008 code prohibited sexual activities with clients and former clients, clients' relatives, and others close to clients. Now, social workers are warned against sexual contact through the use of technology as well. This includes photos and videos that are transmitted electronically.
Sexual Harassment	1.11	Sexual harassment can include "verbal, written, electronic, or physical contact" (NASW, 2018, p. 16).
Derogatory Language	1.12	Social workers should avoid derogatory language in person and electronically, including electronically transmitted photos and videos.
Interruption of Services	1.15	Social workers should be prepared to respond to technological failures.
Sexual Relationships	2.06(a) [was 2.07(a)]	Sexual relationships with supervisees, students, trainees, or colleagues where one person has authority over another are prohibited. Electronic contact of a sexual nature is also prohibited, including text messages, electronically transmitted videos, and photos.
Sexual Harassment	2.08 [was 2.07(a)]	Prohibited contact—sexual advances, sexual solicitation, requests for sexual favors—also includes electronic content.
Unethical Conduct of Colleagues	2.10(a) [was 2.11(a)]	Once a colleague with an impairment that threatens their competency has been consulted and no improvements have been made, a social worker is responsible to take measures to "discourage, prevent, expose, and correct" that colleague's unethical behavior, including electronic conduct (NASW, 2018, p. 20).
Supervision and Consultation	3.01(a,c)	Supervisors have the same standards whether they conduct their work in person or electronically. Supervisors and workers should know that they can have harmful dual relationships using social networking.

(Continued)

(Continued)

Topic	Relevant Sections of the Code	Implications for Practice
Education and Training	3.02(d)	Dual relationships between educators and students can also occur using social networking.
Client Records	3.04(a, d)	Social workers must be sure that any records are accurate, whether they are paper or electronic. Again, laws apply where workers and where clients are. Social workers must abide by them when storing client records.
Evaluation and Research	New section: 5.02(f)	When social workers use technology for evaluation and research, they must obtain informed consent as with any other kind of information gathering.

References

Barsky, A. (2017). Ethics alive! The 2017 NASW Code of Ethics: What's new? *The New Social Worker*. Retrieved from http://www.socialworker.com/feature-articles/ethics-articles/Ethics_Alive%21_The_NASW_Code_of_Ethics_and_Other_Social_Work_Obligations

National Association of Social Workers. (2018). *NASW code of ethics*. Washington, DC: NASW Press.

National Association of Social Workers, Association of Social Work Boards, Council on Social Work Education, & Clinical Social Work Association. (2017). *NASW, ASWB, CSWE, & CSWA standards for technology in social work practice*. Washington, DC: NASW Press.

• Index •